Friends Indeed?
The United Nations, Groups of Friends, and the Resolution of Conflict

Friends Indeed?

The United Nations, Groups of Friends, and the Resolution of Conflict

Teresa Whitfield

UNITED STATES INSTITUTE OF PEACE PRESS
Washington, D.C.

The views expressed in this book are those of the author alone. They do not necessarily reflect views of the United States Institute of Peace.

UNITED STATES INSTITUTE OF PEACE
1200 17th Street NW, Suite 200
Washington, DC 20036-3011

First published 2007

Printed in the United States of America

The paper used in this publication meets the minimum requirements of American National Standards for Information Science—Permanence of Paper for Printed Library Materials, ANSI Z39.48-1984.

Library of Congress Cataloging-in-Publication Data

Whitfield, Teresa.
    Friends indeed? : the United Nations, groups of friends, and the resolution of conflict / Teresa Whitfield.
      p. cm.
    Includes bibliographical references and index.
    ISBN-13: 978-1-60127-005-4 (pbk. : alk. paper)
    ISBN-10: 1-60127-005-4 (pbk. : alk. paper)
    ISBN-13: 978-1-60127-006-1 (hardcover : alk. paper)
    ISBN-10: 1-60127-006-2 (hardcover : alk. paper)
    1. United Nations. 2. Peacekeeping—International cooperation—Case studies. 3. Conflict management—International cooperation—Case studies. I. Title.
    JZ6368.W55 2007
    341.5'84—dc22

                                 2007029616

*For Jason,
Isabel, and Harry*

True happiness
Consists not in the multitude of friends,
But in the worth and choice.

—Ben Jonson, *Cynthia's Revels* (1600)

Contents

Foreword by *Chester A. Crocker*   ix

Acknowledgments   xiii

Introduction   1

1. At Cold War's End: Peacemaking   19
and the Emergence of Groups

2. The First Friends: Friends of the   51
Secretary-General for El Salvador

3. Friends and the "Ripening" of Peace in Guatemala   79

4. Principal Friend: The United States   105
and the Long Haul in Haiti

5. The Georgian-Abkhaz Conflict: Friends   135
and the Anomaly of Russia

6. Self-Determination and Realpolitik: 165
The Story of Western Sahara

7. East Timor and the Core Group: A Question of Timing   191

8. Groups and the Variable Geometry of UN Peacemaking   223

9. Conclusions   259

Appendix   285

The United Nations' Groups of Friends
and Other Mechanisms

Notes   297

Index   381

About the Author   429

Foreword

The subject of *Friends Indeed?* is a little-noted but newly emerging phenomenon in modern diplomacy—groups of states that attempt to manage or resolve violent conflicts. Specifically, these groups—or Friends—represent a particular manifestation of multiparty mediation in which diverse actors collaborate, compete, and coexist while conducting parallel or sequenced interventions in a given conflict arena. With this important study, Teresa Whitfield places these diplomatic coalitions of the willing in the widest analytic context, deriving significant conclusions for the UN secretary-general, his secretariat colleagues, national decision makers who participate in or may consider participating in such groups, and other relevant policy audiences. The book blends together six original, in-depth case studies, an overview of eight additional cases, and a masterful familiarity with post–Cold War conflict management and mediation efforts, particularly as relates to the United Nations. The result is an authoritative assessment of the accomplishments, the potential, and the limits of Friends as a mechanism for allowing third-party participation in peacemaking and peacebuilding.

In publishing this study, the United States Institute of Peace deepens its already strong reputation for publishing and promoting the latest research and scholarship on best practices in the mediation of violent international conflicts. In particular, *Friends Indeed?* reflects the Institute's continuing commitment to exploring, defining, and articulating practical lessons from hard-won experience in the field of peacemaking. Past Institute volumes include *Herding Cats: Multiparty Mediation in a Complex World* (1999), which contains analytic essays and a series of first-person practitioner case studies that explore complexity in mediation, *Taming Intractable Conflicts: Mediation in the Hardest Cases* (2004), which examines best practices in tackling the most stubborn of conflicts, and *Grasping the Nettle: Analyzing Cases of Intractable Conflict* (2005), which analyzes the defining characteristics and underlying dynamics of intractable conflicts. In fact, Whitfield was a contributor to *Grasping the Nettle*, joining forces with Cynthia Arnson to write a chapter on peacemaking in the Colombia conflict

Drilling down into some fourteen case histories—six of which represent unique, detailed accounts based largely on primary sources—Whitfield is here able to portray the full dimensions of the Friends phenomenon. We come to see how Friends groups began in the immediate post–Cold War period, how they have evolved from a mere handful of groups to more than thirty, why they have emerged more often in certain regions (Latin America, Europe, the former Soviet Union, and Africa) than in others, and when they are most likely—and least likely—to make a constructive addition to the modern diplomatic arsenal. Additionally, we learn what roles they have played and are continuing to play, and what types of conflicts are most propitious for this form of multiparty activity.

Groups of Friends, we learn here, are a unique diplomatic innovation sometimes built around a particular constellation of UN Security Council members that served together at a particular moment in time and "adopted" a conflict in order to sustain their own direct mediation role. This was the original basis of one variant, the Namibian Contact Group, which arose in 1978 and continued on into the mid-1980s. More recent Friends groups tend to be ad hoc and informal in origin, and may escape any form of official recognition in the resolutions of international or regional organizations. The groups typically have no address or headquarters, no letterhead, no written records (apart from member state archives), no formal charter, and few bylaws or agreed-upon operating principles. Some groups focus on supporting the UN secretary-general's peacemaking role (and especially that of his envoys), some adopt a country or conflict in order to lead or backstop a peacemaking or mediation process (whether or not there is a major UN role), and some take on the critically important role of coordinating international monitoring and implementation efforts during the post-settlement phase.

The groups operate in diverse ways depending on the specifics of each case, the nature of the surrounding regional environment, the internal composition and leadership chemistry of the members and their motives for participation, and the timing of the group's activity in relation to the conflict's life cycle. Whitfield singles out a number of significant contributions that Friends groups have the *potential* to make. They can (1) bring additional leverage to the lead mediator in relation to the parties, (2) create a more level playing field among the parties and surround them with a reassuring political context, (3) serve as a potential venue for post-settlement planning and rally interest and financial support for implementation, (4) provide a clearing house or gateway in order to coordinate external engagement and discourage rival, contradictory mediation initiatives, and (5) buffer a UN-led peace process from direct intervention by powerful individual states. Whitfield sharply distinguishes the operation of Friends groups during a peace process from their role during peace implementation.

A central argument in this volume is that the potential contribution of such groups can be maximized by learning the lessons of past groups and conflict case studies. A powerful core of the author's message is signaled by her title, *Friends Indeed?* This is nuanced wording indicating that the jury is still out on this new diplomatic mechanism, that much depends on the way the Friends operate in any given case, and that Friends can become part of the solution as well as part of the problem in conflict management and mediation. When Friends allow themselves to be used or deployed as tools of the government in an internal conflict, there is little likelihood of real progress on peacemaking. A similar outcome appears likely when Friends exercise their role primarily to protect or support one side or to advance solely their own national interest. Little can be expected from a group that is internally divided along the lines of the conflict itself, that cuts across the efforts and authority of the lead mediator, or that effectively shields the conflict parties from the necessity of taking tough decisions. A number of the cases that Whitfield presents—Haiti, Georgia-Abkhazia, and Western Sahara—illustrate these concerns, and the operation of Friends groups in these cases contrasts starkly with the more successful of the six cases on which she develops individual case histories (El Salvador, Guatemala, and East Timor). Whitfield also cautions that less can be expected when Friends groups succumb to the status anxiety and sensitivities of would-be participants and grow too large to be effective institutional adjuncts of the primary mediator.

The volume concludes with lessons about the conditions for success of Friends groups, lessons that will produce a smile of recognition from close students and practitioners familiar with these and similar cases of low-to-middle-profile conflicts typically mediated outside the klieg lights of big power politics. Regional context makes a decisive difference: this sort of peacemaking stands little hope when neighbors and regional hegemons are actively intervening to pursue their own interests in the conflict or to dominate possible outcomes. Whitfield argues that the composition of Friends groups is perhaps the most important single ingredient in their success or failure and offers readers a detailed typology of the kinds of states that *ought* to be included if one wishes to build an effective group. At the same time, she recognizes that no one is really in charge of the process of selecting or recruiting members: Friends select themselves and are attracted to cases for a wide range of motives.

Friends Indeed? offers many rewards to the reader interested in comparative diplomatic practice, in the role of the United Nations in conflict management and peacebuilding, and in mediation tradecraft more generally.

The six cases developed in the volume represent the fruits of important and original fieldwork cultivated by the judgment of a talented conflict researcher. Whitfield's depth and breadth of familiarity with the natural history of conflict since 1990—as well as with the proliferation of informal Friends mechanisms—makes this an especially worthy addition to the Institute's growing library of materials on best practices in mediation.

Chester A. Crocker
Washington, D.C.

Acknowledgments

I n the five years since I first embarked on *Friends Indeed?* I have incurred
many debts of gratitude.

Friends and former colleagues at the United Nations—notable among
them are my two former bosses, Alvaro de Soto, who had pioneered the
concept of Friends of the Secretary-General in El Salvador, and Kieran
Prendergast, who served as under-secretary-general for political affairs from
1997 to 2005—provided unstinting encouragement of the endeavor from
its earliest days. The Center on International Cooperation at New York
University was kind enough to give me a home as a visiting fellow from
2002 to 2005. While at the center, my research and writing was generously supported by the Fafo Institute for Applied International Studies
(Norway), the Ford Foundation, the Federal Department of the Foreign
Affairs of Switzerland, the United Kingdom's Department for International
Development, and the United States Institute of Peace. Since March 2005,
my colleagues at the Conflict Prevention and Peace Forum and Social
Science Research Council warmly encouraged my efforts to finish the book,
not without an understandable degree of self-interest that I be done with it.

The subject of *Friends Indeed?*—diplomatic mechanisms characterized
by their informality and discretion as much as by their engagement in political situations of extreme complexity—is one that has placed a particular
emphasis on interviews as a primary resource. Since 2002 I have conducted
more than two hundred interviews with UN officials, diplomats representing individual states or regional organizations, representatives of state and
nonstate conflict parties, academics, and other analysts of conflict. To
these individuals, some of whom I returned to time and time again, and
many of whom preferred, for obvious reasons, to remain anonymous, I express my deepest gratitude.

Notwithstanding the discretion requested by many who have contributed to this book, the list of those I wish to thank publicly is still a long
one. That it is so is perhaps an inevitable consequence of a comparative
exercise that involved attention to many different conflicts and peace processes, on all of which I have been privileged to draw on the much greater
expertise of others. The following individuals provided a welcome mix of
encouragement for this book as an idea, counsel along the way, and, in
some cases, wisdom in reviewing some portions of the manuscript: Sal-
man Ahmed, Jean Arnault, Neil Briscoe, Tatiana Carayannis, Simon

Chesterman, Jack Christofides, Jonathan Cohen, Chris Coleman, Elizabeth Cousens, Robert Dann, Jim Della-Giacoma, Martha Doggett, Michael Doyle, Jan Egeland, Shepard Forman, Michele Griffin, Humayun Hamidzada, Stephen Jackson, Bruce Jones, Jared Kotler, Nicole Lannegrace, Andrew Mack, David Malone, Ian Martin, Thant Myint-U, Bill O'Neill, Morten Pedersen, Kieran Prendergast, Barnett Rubin, Tamrat Samuel, Renata Segura, Alvaro de Soto, William Stanley, Stephen J. Stedman, Anna Theophilopoulou, Brian Urquhart, Francesc Vendrell, and Elisabeth J. Wood. While I remain, of course, solely responsible for any errors that may remain within its pages, without their various contributions this book would be the poorer.

Particular thanks are due to David Malone and Simon Chesterman, in whose edited volumes—*The U.N. Security Council: From the Cold War to the 21st Century* (Lynne Rienner Publications, 2004) and *Secretary or General? The UN Secretary-General in World Politics* (Cambridge University Press, 2007)—I was delighted to publish chapters that reflected work in progress; Teresa Cherfas for her good company and translation in Tbilisi and Sukhumi in July 2003; and Andrew Mack and Eric Nicholls of the Human Security Report Project for helping interject some kind of clarity into my understanding of my own data.

At the United States Institute of Peace, I was fortunate to count on the support of Taylor Seybolt in the Grant Program, and the sound judgment and editorial skill of Nigel Quinney, who rescued me from a slough of authorial despondency, and Kurt Volkan, who ably steered the manuscript through production. I am also indebted to the three anonymous reviewers for their perceptive and constructive comments.

Finally, this book would probably not have been begun without Rick Hooper, tragically killed in Baghdad on August 19, 2003, and missed to this day, who was the first person to push me to take the plunge. Nor would it have been completed without the love, support, and patience of my husband, Jason Rosenbaum, and children, Isabel and Harry, whose contribution is reflected in the dedication.

Introduction

A Photograph

On December 31, 1991, in the last few minutes of Javier Pérez de Cuéllar's term in office as UN secretary-general, a photograph was taken. The secretary-general sits at the end of a long conference table. Flanked by Alvaro de Soto, his personal representative for the Central American Peace Process, and representatives of the negotiating delegations of the government of El Salvador and the insurgents in the Farabundo Martí National Liberation Front (FMLN), he is signing the agreement that will pave the way for the peaceful resolution of the conflict in El Salvador. Its achievement is one of the signal successes of his tenure as secretary-general.

The photograph is included as the final illustration in Pérez de Cuéllar's memoir, *Pilgrimage for Peace*. Its protagonists are named in the text and said to be accompanying this "midnight signature of the El Salvador Peace Accord."[1] Not identified are the four men standing immediately behind the secretary-general. Hands neatly clasped, heads bowed toward the document on the table, they are, from left to right, the ambassadors to the United Nations of Spain, Mexico, Venezuela, and Colombia—countries that had come to be known as the "Friends of the Secretary-General for El Salvador."

Although some of these ambassadors would later grumble that Pérez de Cuéllar's memoir had paid their efforts on behalf of peace scant tribute (the chapter on Central America included only sparing reference to their countries' role), their anonymity was, in many respects, no less fitting than their inclusion in the picture in the first place. On the basis of a relationship of "solidarity, even complicity" with de Soto[2] and their support of the secretary-general, the Friends had played an important part in helping all gathered in this New York conference room reach the point at which the historic signature they were witnessing was possible. But they had done so as a wholly informal entity—they did not even meet as a group for more than half the period of the negotiations—largely unrecognized in the documents and statements of the United Nations. And exactly what they had done was difficult to quantify, as befits the quiet labor of the diplomacy that attends a complex mediation of an ongoing internal conflict.

Briefed by de Soto on the progress of negotiations throughout their two-year period, the Friends had used the relationships they each enjoyed

1

with both government officials and insurgents to encourage sometimes recalcitrant parties to move toward an agreement. By their involvement in the process, they had lent credibility to the United Nations and enhanced the secretary-general's leverage with the parties. That their association with the secretary-general had also gained legitimacy for their own role in El Salvador ensured that everyone was happy.

In the years that followed, the original four Friends were joined by the United States, and the group became known as the "Four plus One." During implementation of the agreements, the assistance provided by the Friends took many forms. It ranged from providing security to guerrilla leaders and diplomatic support to successive heads of the United Nations' mission in El Salvador, to funding peace-related programs and managing the issue of El Salvador in the Security Council and General Assembly. Quite properly, the contribution made by the Friends to the peace process in El Salvador was formally acknowledged by Secretary-General Kofi Annan as he closed the door on the United Nations' role in verifying the agreements in December 2002.[3]

What This Book Is About

Friends Indeed? has been written with clear, practical goals in mind. It seeks to further the understanding of how and in what circumstances the UN secretary-general and secretariat can work productively with groups of states to resolve conflict and to arrive at conclusions and recommendations that might be helpful to policymakers in both. A secondary goal is to broaden understanding of informal groups as a little-studied aspect of international conflict resolution in the post–Cold War era. *Friends Indeed?* argues that although such groups have had varying impacts on conflicts, they have developed as a critical element of an incipient system of post–Cold War global security governance.

A narrative, and at times anecdotal, approach to the cases examined within the book reflects both the widely varying roles played by Friends and source material that of necessity has drawn heavily on interviews. Documentation of the little-known phenomenon that Friends represent is complemented by comparative analysis of core factors or variables in each case. This has been complicated by three distinct problems: the self-selecting nature of groups of Friends, which derives from the central importance of individual state interest to the formation of such groups; an essential amorphousness that complicates groups' classification into neatly distinguished categories and, consequently, direct comparison between them; and the

Figure 1: Number of Groups of Friends and Other Mechanisms, 1946–2006*

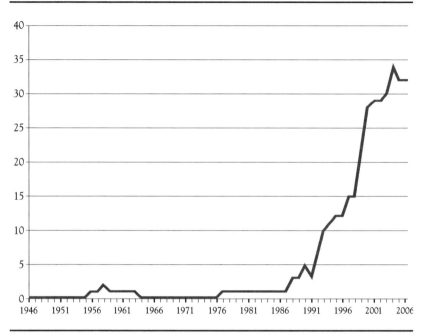

*Reflects data contained in Appendix: UN Groups of Friends and Other Mechanisms

difficulty of determining their impact on the outcomes of the peace processes. Brief discussions of each of these three issues present the necessary context to the description of case selection and the book's organization contained in this introduction.

With the evolving role of the United Nations as a background, the chapters that follow trace the evolution of groups of Friends from the cooperative climate for peacemaking that emerged at the end of the Cold War to the more complex environment for conflict resolution of recent years. From the mid-1990s, a natural shift away from peace processes in which the UN secretary-general had a clear lead limited the creation of groups of "Friends of the Secretary-General" as conceived in the early part of this decade. But, as figure 1—based on data derived from the list of groups contained in the appendix—demonstrates, between 1990 and 2006 groups of states created to support UN peacemaking and peace operations multiplied exponentially. With a growth from four to more than thirty such mechanisms, a larger than sevenfold increase developed in parallel to the surge in conflict prevention, conflict management, and post-conflict peacebuilding activities by the United Nations and others in the international community in this period. Many of these activities—like some of the groups of Friends—fell far short of the expectations held out for them individually. However, together they have been credited by the *Human Security Report 2005* as being the single best explanation for a decline of more than 40 percent in armed conflicts and 80 percent in civil wars in this period.[4]

Groups of Friends represent but one small component of the United Nations' increased involvement in conflict management. But it is one that in some circumstances brought clear and specific functional benefits. These were first identified by work conducted on Cambodia and El Salvador by Michael Doyle and others in the mid-1990s.[5] Among the benefits were leverage, information, and practical help to the secretary-general and his representatives, including through coordination of action in the Security Council; legitimacy and influence to the states in the groups; a level of equilibrium, as well as technical and other assistance, to parties to the conflict; and attention, resources, and strategic coordination to the peace process as a whole.

Such results, however, have been by no means guaranteed. Internal differences or other factors related to some of the groups' composition limited their utility in a process, creating a layer of interests to be managed and negotiated in addition to those of the parties to the conflict. Groups assumed an identity of their own that was at times at cross-purposes to the good offices of the secretary-general and complicated the delicate relationship between the United Nations and fractious parties to an internal conflict. Strong groups led members of the Security Council to fear that their authority might be undermined, while competing national interests caused Friends' sometimes fragile unity to crack and be exploited by the parties. Meanwhile, sensitivities regarding composition—reflecting a perennial balancing act between the efficiency of a small group and the legitimacy offered by a broad representation of states—led in some circumstances to the creation of large groups that did no harm but were not well placed to do the good that was intended.

This mixed experience can be traced in part to the fact that the varied groups that assembled over the years did so in an unstructured manner, in many cases belying the strategic intent that lay behind the earliest mechanisms. In 2002 a Security Council working group came up with "recommendations" on groups of Friends in the African context that bore no relationship to the development of the mechanism outside the region and had little effect within it.[6] Meanwhile, no systematic review of the use of groups took place within the secretariat, nor, despite significant work by the United States Institute of Peace on the perils of "multiparty mediation," was much attention paid to them in the academic literature.[7] Exceptions included the discussion of groups of Friends by Michael Doyle and his colleagues cited above, firsthand accounts by Alvaro de Soto and others directly involved in El Salvador and Haiti, Chester Crocker's analysis of his interaction with the Western Contact Group on Nambia—an important antecedent of the Friends—when peacemaking in the "rough neighborhood" of Southern Africa in the late 1980s, and the work of Jean Krasno and Jochen Prantl, writing separately and together.[8] Krasno's work derived from an early paper written for the Carnegie Commission on Preventing Deadly Conflict, and drew largely from the ample documentation available on the Friends of the Secretary-General for El Salvador, Haiti, and Namibia.[9] Prantl's work, on the other hand, focused on the implications of informal groups for the governance of the Security Council, notably in a book published in May 2006, *The UN Security Council and Informal Groups of States*, that represented the first full-length treatment of the subject.[10]

Through an analysis of three contrasting cases—the Western Contact Group on Namibia, the Friends of the Secretary-General for El Salvador, and the different mechanisms engaged in Kosovo—in which the respective groups had widely varying relationships to the UN Security Council, Prantl argued that informal groups "increasingly complement or even compete with" the Council. He saw their development as representing a "variant" of collective security comparable to those identified by Adam Roberts as evolving over the years in response to the Council's Cold War paralysis. These variants were the tendency to regional alliances and military action in a multilateral framework; the delegation of enforcement powers of the Security Council to coalitions of states or regional arrangements sanctioned to use force on behalf of the United Nations; and peacekeeping operations carried out under the authority of the United Nations.[11] However, while informal groups certainly evolved "as part and parcel of the development of UN crisis response," as Prantl puts it, they differed from the other three "variants" in a number of respects. Most obvious, they did not involve the operational deployment of forces. Indeed, the trajectory of Friends analyzed in *Friends Indeed?* suggests that a significant feature of informal groups is precisely that they have emerged alongside other developments in collective security, and that much of their potential utility lies in their flexibility.

Indeed, a single mechanism may support peacemaking activities that run the gamut from the quiet consultations preceding negotiations to mediation and implementation of a peace agreement, regardless of what combination of actors may be carrying out the intervention.

An apparent neglect of Friends as they relate to the diplomacy practiced by the UN secretary-general and his staff reflected both the poor capacity of the secretariat to learn from its own experience and the fact that the informal nature of the groups meant that very little documentation of their work was available in the public realm.[12] Expertise on the potential of and risks attendant on the use of Friends instead remained concentrated in those with firsthand experience of the mechanism. This led, on the one hand, to carefully modulated uses of Friends or similar mechanisms by some of the officials with experience of the practice in the past, and on the other, to a proliferation of groups created, inside the United Nations and out, with broader goals: as a positive avenue for marshaling attention on otherwise neglected conflicts or sharing information among the multiple external actors involved. Formal acknowledgment of the need for strategic coordination of international actors was seen in the final days of 2005 with the United Nations' creation of an intergovernmental Peacebuilding Commission, capable of meeting in country-specific configurations to encourage "a coordinated, coherent and integrated approach to post-conflict peacebuilding and reconciliation."[13] But this could not deny the continuing utility of smaller and more informal mechanisms to support complex processes of peacemaking and implementation.

Analysis developed in this study's six case chapters and extended into the varied cases more briefly examined in chapter 8 attempts to elucidate the mixed direction that Friends have taken. Consideration of five core factors or variables—the *regional environment* in which the conflict takes place; the *conflict parties'* demands, practices, and interaction with the secretariat and the Friends; a group's *composition* and the resources that this may bring with it; questions of *leadership* encompassing a group's relationship to the secretary-general and/or his representative; and *timing* or *phase of the process* with which the Friends are involved—underlines a series of questions pursued throughout the book: Do Friends work better in some regions or regional environments than others? To what extent does the nature of the conflict or conflict parties affect the role they may play? What do different kinds of states—members of the Security Council, regional actors, other "helpful fixers"—bring to a group of Friends? What relations between Friends and the secretary-general and Security Council have proved most effective? Are Friends better suited to a particular phase in a peace process than others? And are there circumstances in which it may be best not to assay a group of Friends at all?

Self-Selection and the Friends

A central methodological problem in analyzing groups of Friends is that the cases are to a certain extent self-selecting. "We should not imagine," as Stephen John Stedman has put it, "that all civil wars are equally likely to have Friends."[14] The sustained involvement of a group of Friends is a result of significant external interest in a peace process. But it also indicates the absence of an overriding interest in a conflict's outcome from the major powers, which are not likely to relinquish a driving role in conflicts at the top of the international agenda to an informal group of states working in support of a UN peacemaker. Policy toward the Balkans, the Middle East, and Iraq has been driven by direct diplomacy by the powers most immediately involved. Large groups of Friends may be formed for briefing purposes, but no one will be under any illusion that these will be able to influence the directions taken by the major states involved acting bilaterally, through mechanisms such as the Contact Group on the former Yugoslavia (France, Germany, Italy, Russia, the United Kingdom, and the United States) or, in the case of the Middle East, the Quartet of the European Union, Russia, the United States, and the United Nations. Consequently, conflicts in which Friends are found are neither those in which "high politics" are engaged nor the true orphan conflicts such as Burundi and Somalia, where the big powers have no security and other interests.[15] Rather, it is those conflicts that command a middle level of international attention that have left room for the development of a substantive role for the United Nations and its secretary-general.

Certain geographic tendencies can be discerned in the occurrence of Friends. This has, on one hand, been a consequence of the perceived success of the earliest mechanisms in Central America; on the other, it has to some extent reflected (as could be expected) the incidence of UN peace operations. Thus, there has been a predisposition toward Friends in Latin America; away from them in Europe, the Middle East, and Asia; and toward groups of some kind, although not necessarily Friends, in Africa.[16] However, geography alone has no more determined a group's formation than the type of conflict to be addressed. Friends have rarely been engaged in the "hottest" phase of a conflict's activity, nor have they played prominent roles in resolving many of the most deadly conflicts of the post–Cold War period (such as Rwanda, the Democratic Republic of the Congo [DRC], and the Balkans). But they have been present both in conflicts recognizably easier than others to settle, such as those in Central America, and in some of the most intractable (Georgia-Abkhazia, Colombia, and Cyprus), involving issues of territory as well as government and sustained by the presence of illicit resources and ideology.

It is as axiomatic that that there are no disinterested peacemakers as it is difficult to generalize about the interests themselves.[17] These may be determined by historical or ideological allegiances deriving from colonialism, the Cold War, or geography; security concerns related to direct threats, strategic location, the flow of arms and/or armed actors across borders, or the attractiveness of a failed state to criminal and terrorist networks; economic issues involving trade and investments and the presence of oil or other resources; and a variety of issues, ranging from the escalating costs of humanitarian assistance to concern about immigration, raised by large-scale flows of refugees. Since the end of the Cold War, other "softer" interests, including values such as human rights and democracy, have also emerged.[18] These reflect the "gradual normative shift against the use of violence in human relationships" that is described by the *Human Security Report*.[19] In policy terms, this has translated into what the veteran British diplomat Robert Cooper identifies as "the invention of peace as a foreign policy goal."[20]

A decision to become involved in a peace process, whether as a lead mediator or in the supporting role of a Friend, will be taken as a consequence of a choice. Indeed, Chester Crocker, Fen Osler Hampson, and Pamela Aall, in their study, *Taming Intractable Conflicts*, find that states and interstate groups decide to engage in mediation under the "guiding motive of obtaining a settlement" and on the basis of three distinctive and sometimes overlapping rationales—humanitarian, strategic, and regional security and governance—as well as a variety of political reasons.[21] These may be entirely consistent with the peaceful resolution of a particular conflict. However, this will not always be the case.

Participation in a group of Friends offers a significant opportunity to maintain a front-row seat in the diplomatic process without any hard undertaking to commit resources, troops, or diplomatic muscle to the effort. There is thus no basis to suggest that the mere fact of being a Friend will, in itself, alter patterns of allegiance or the pursuit of outcomes prioritized by national interests. In some cases these may actually subvert the cause of peace. In many others even a normative interest in the promotion of peace and security will not be without a degree of self-interest. States motivated by the most exemplary of motives—like the UN secretariat, or nongovernmental peacemakers—will always, for example, have an interest in raising their international standing through their successful participation in a peace process.[22] Pressure to be included as a Friend will therefore be high, and the potential for cooperation will be vulnerable to institutional and other rivalries as well as the capability of conflict parties to shop around among multiple actors vying to engage them.

Distinguishing the Friends

An attempt to introduce conceptual clarity to a classification of even those Friends, Core, Contact, and other groups that have been actively engaged in issues of peace and security within the orbit of the United Nations is a complex undertaking. With a broad brush, Friends' groups can be described as ad hoc, informal, issue-specific minicoalitions of states or intergovernmental organizations that become involved in and provide support for resolving conflicts and implementing peace agreements. Beyond this, however, there are many differences between them that their titles do little to explain. Indeed, groups discussed in this book differed in the circumstances of their creation, in the mix of states of which they were composed, and in their functions; they have led to different relationships between the secretary-general, his representatives, and involved member states; and they have had widely different impacts on the broad range of conflicts with which they have been engaged. Moreover, in several cases groups have varied considerably during the period of their engagement or have been complemented by supplementary mechanisms.

With these caveats in place, and with a nod to Ludwig Wittgenstein's suggestion that the instances of a concept will resemble each other only as family members do, sharing certain traits but not others,[23] it may be helpful to distinguish between the following categories of groups:

1. *Friends of the Secretary-General* are understood as informal groups of states formed to support the peacemaking of the secretary-general or his representatives. They tend to be small (four to six members) and will usually have the capacity to function in distinct locations, most commonly some combination of New York, the field, and capitals. This recognition of the Friends as a group distinguishes the mechanism from standard diplomatic practice, in which a senior UN official or other mediator will regularly consult with the representatives of the states most closely involved. A group of Friends may be engaged throughout a peace process, although the group will fulfill different functions during peacemaking and in helping to implement any subsequent agreement. Its interlocutors will be the secretary-general or,

more commonly, his representative or envoy; it is also likely to be in-volved in coordinating Security Council and/or General Assembly action on the conflict in question. Although not all the groups ana-lyzed in this study bear the moniker "of the Secretary-General," most of them fall in this category, as it is in these groups that the issues of the interplay between the secretariat and the United Nations' mem-ber states are most evident.

2. *Friends of a country* are usually somewhat removed from the secretary-general and his representatives and thus from the operational process. Like the Friends of the Secretary-General, they have been formed on the initiative of both the secretariat and the member states them-selves. However, they tend to be larger and concentrate their activity in New York. Their purposes have ranged from the sharing of infor-mation in situations at the top of the international agenda to briefing and attempts to mobilize attention and resources on conflicts further removed from "high politics." Although Friends of a number of Afri-can countries—Angola, the Central African Republic, and Guinea-Bissau, for example—have drawn attention to conflicts that were otherwise forgotten, their impact has nevertheless been less than was hoped of them. A related phenomenon in recent years has been the creation by the United Nations' Economic and Social Council (ECOSOC) of Ad Hoc Advisory Groups on countries emerging from conflict (Haiti, Burundi, and Guinea-Bissau).[24]

3. *Contact Groups*, like groups of Friends, have come in different forms, but generally reflect a more distant relationship to the United Nations. They have represented vehicles for the direct diplomacy of member states, centered on communication between capitals and unham-pered by "friendship" of the secretary-general. A Contact Group made its first appearance in Namibia, where the Western Contact Group worked outside the Security Council—while keeping the secretary-general informed of its efforts—to craft the plan that became the basis for the Namibian settlement. The Contact Group on the former Yugo-slavia was created in 1994, in part to circumvent the United Nations, and since then has allowed for differences between the states with the most obvious interests in regional stability to be hammered out away from the glare of Security Council attention. Different again are the Contact Groups that have come and gone in Africa. These larger, more irregularly convened groups have generally included the United Nations—meaning a representative of the secretariat—as a member. They have combined regional actors, representatives of the

five permanent members (the P-5) of the Security Council (China, France, Russia, the United Kingdom, and the United States), and donor states for the purposes of information exchange, coordination, and occasionally, fundraising.

4. *Implementation and monitoring groups* have increasingly been established in peace agreements whose implementation is to be monitored by UN peacekeeping operations. They can be distinguished conceptually from the previous categories of groups by a mandate establishing their responsibilities in a foundational agreement, but they vary greatly in the extent to which they are directly engaged in monitoring activities. In most circumstances, these mechanisms have followed a model established in Namibia, where the Joint Monitoring Commission was chaired by the special representative of the secretary-general and included representatives of the parties to the conflict as well as key external actors. However, in some instances, such as the International Commission to Accompany the Transition (CIAT) in the DRC, the mechanism has not included the parties and bears a closer resemblance to a group of Friends.

Further complicating the picture are the many other kinds of groups that meet at the United Nations. These range from the regional groups of member states through which much day-to-day business is conducted[25] to thematic groups of Friends ("of rapid reaction," "of conflict prevention," "of the rule of law," "of the High Level Panel") formed to promote consensus for a somewhat random selection of individual issues.[26] Countries that contribute troops to particular peacekeeping operations meet for regular briefings by the secretariat in the format of "troop-contributing countries," while the establishment of the Peacebuilding Commission provided for large and formal country-specific meetings held at the invitation of its Organizational Committee.[27] These groups manifest as a logical expression of the need for the organization's almost two hundred disparate members to caucus and consult outside the structures established by the General Assembly and Security Council. But they are distinct from the hands-on interaction with conflict parties and the diplomacy of peacemaking that has characterized groups of Friends engaged more directly with conflict resolution.

Friends and Outcomes

Success in the mediation of a peace agreement and its subsequent implementation is determined by many different factors. Quantifying the precise contribution made by a mechanism such as a group of Friends—which is structurally limited to playing an auxiliary role, takes different forms and functions in different circumstances, and is rarely established by any agreed mandate—is harder still and probably impossible. This is not least because of the difficulty of analyzing the counterfactual (the impact of the secretariat's efforts, Mexican diplomacy in Central America, or Russia's policy toward Georgia in the absence a group of Friends, let alone, say, what peacemaking in the DRC might have looked like if the key external actors had been able to work together from an early stage in a unified group of Friends). That individual Friend states are likely to see the success of the collective effort in terms of its utility to their own national interests complicates analysis even further, and lies behind the question in this book's title—*Friends Indeed?*

Rather than attempt a quantitative approach, the book seeks to establish under what circumstances Friends stand the best chance of contributing to the success of peace processes in which the United Nations is centrally involved. Analysis in the six case chapters and in the varied cases more briefly discussed in chapter 8 is rooted in consideration of core factors or variables relating both to the internal aspects of the groups themselves and to the conflicts with which they are engaged. These bear some relation to the framework for evaluating peace implementation developed by George Downs and Stephen John Stedman for *Ending Civil Wars: The Implementation of Peace Agreements*, the first comprehensive work on this subject.[28]

Downs and Stedman accept relatively modest standards for success: stopping large-scale violence in the short term and ending the war on a self-sustaining basis. With a universe of cases in which, between 1990 and 1997, warring parties reached an agreement in which international actors were expected to play a major role in implementation, their evaluation is derived from two sets of variables, one related to conflict environment and the other to international involvement. They find, unsurprisingly, that the greater the difficulty of the conflict environment, the higher the likelihood that implementation of a peace agreement will fail, and the greater the degree of international involvement, in terms of both resources and coercive capacity, required to overcome a conflict's inherent difficulty. The three most significant environmental obstacles to successful implementation emerge as the presence of spoilers (understood as factions or individuals who oppose a peace agreement and use violence to undermine it), neighboring states (or networks operating within or from them) opposed to the peace agreement, and the presence of disposable natural resources, such as gems, minerals, or timber. Meanwhile, international involvement varies with a "willingness" to provide resources and troops that is itself a function of whether a major or regional power sees its own security and other interests at stake.[29]

Although not a subject of Downs and Stedman's analysis, the presence of a group of Friends might be considered a relevant indicator of "willingness." However, Friends' amorphous nature and the varied factors involved in both a group's formation and its performance—not least the preferences, commitment, and abilities of the individuals concerned—suggest the risks involved in treating the fact of their engagement as a measurable variable. Such considerations also inform any consideration of what relationship Friends may have to an outcome of a peace process. It is as easy to dismiss the role of Friends in a successful process as negligible, given a benign set of underlying conditions, as it is to lower expectations of what Friends might be expected to contribute in more adverse circumstances. That said, it is a central argument of this book that lessons from the past can be applied to the use of such mechanisms in the future in order to maximize their potential to contribute to a given peace process. For this reason the variables briefly introduced below—and running through the case studies—help ground *Friends Indeed?*'s attempt to further understand what configuration of Friends has worked best where and why.

The importance of *regional environment* to the successful implementation of a peace agreement identified by Downs and Stedman is of direct salience to groups of Friends. Indeed, conflicts at the heart of what Barnett Rubin and others have dubbed "regional conflict formations," such as Afghanistan and the DRC—like those that take place under the shadow of the pronounced interests of a larger and more powerful neighbor, such as Somalia or Sri Lanka—have generally been Friend-less.[30] (The "six plus two" group of neighboring states, plus Russia and the United States, on Afghanistan was very far from a group of Friends, as it was composed of states actively arming and supporting the warring factions in Afghanistan.) Where the regional environment is more propitious to the conflict's settlement, Friends, on the other hand, have been found to be highly effective vehicles for engaging regional actors, as the role played by Mexico in the Central American cases, or by Australia and other regional actors in that of East Timor, demonstrate. Indeed, the provision of a vehicle for the central involvement of regional actors not consistently present on the Security Council emerges from the case studies as one of the principal benefits of the mechanism.

In considering the conditions for the successful involvement of Friends, more important than the conflict's typology is the nature of the *conflict parties*. Interaction with Friends has varied to reflect both the relative importance of the states in conflict to the interests of the Friends and the characteristics of the nonstate armed actors. Individual Friends are representatives of governments with bilateral relations with the governments involved, often with clearly held positions on the issues at stake. In most cases, they are likely to encounter problems in engaging directly with nonstate armed actors.[31] As composite bodies with ill-defined roles in the process, these have been even more marked in the case of groups of states than those met by the UN secretariat or individual state mediators, both of which regularly run into government reluctance to accept parity at the negotiating table with rebel or secessionist forces they hold as illegitimate, subversive, and perhaps terrorist as well. However, critical factors for the constructive engagement of Friends emerge from the case studies. These include the nonstate actors' demands (ideological, decolonialist, or secessionist), practices (more or less abusive of human rights or identified as "terrorist"), and the degree of international engagement they have pursued in the conflict and efforts to end it (bringing with it the potential for leverage).

The *composition* of a group of Friends will be all-important. Like its formation in the first place, it will also be directly related to the interests of its members. In an attempt to establish how these relate to a state's contribution as a Friend, the case studies dedicate considerable attention to each group's inception, the strategic purposes pursued by its architects, and the distinct contributions made within each process by different Friends and kinds of Friends. In most cases the question of size has been perceived to be key to a group's efficacy. Groups have involved some mixture of Security Council members (including the five permanent members), interested regional actors, and midsized donor states or helpful fixers with experience of the conflict. Such a membership brings the promise of different combinations of resources to the table: diplomatic leverage with one or more of the conflict parties, financial assistance for relief and reconstruction, and the possible commitment of troops in a UN peace operation or alongside it.

Issues of *leadership* go to the heart of what or who Friends are created for, as well as the delicate relationship between the secretary-general as a peacemaker acting with the implied consent or overt support of the Security Council and the United Nations' member states. Groups have interacted in distinct manners with the secretary-general or, more common, the senior official representing him in a peace process. In some circumstances they have (as was one of their purposes in El Salvador) helped to bridge the gap between the fragile independence of the secretary-general and the power politics of the Security Council. Sustained support of the secretary-general has involved a commitment to work behind a clearly identified UN lead and brought recognizable benefits to the coherence of the international effort. But in other processes this has not proved possible, and states' conflicting interests at times have complicated the relationship with the secretary-general, his representatives, and other members of groups of Friends.

The *timing* of a group's formation has had a central bearing on both its functions and incidence in a given process, as distinct operational needs have led to varied relationships with the actors involved. The emphasis of *Friends Indeed?* is on peacemaking. However, cases in which this has contributed to a settlement and its implementation—such as in El Salvador, Guatemala, Haiti, and East Timor—as well as in those instances discussed in chapter 8 in which a Friends or related mechanism has been created at an early stage provide opportunities to assess the viability of Friends' mechanisms at *different phases of the process*. Most obvious, the relationship between the UN secretariat and a group of Friends that has been involved in peacemaking will change upon the signing of an agreement and establishment of a peace operation mandated by the Security Council. Meanwhile, a separate set of challenges may be faced by Friends' involvement in processes that become stalled.

Case Selection and Organization

The self-selecting nature of Friends is openly acknowledged in the structure of this book. Chapter 1 places the emergence and evolution of groups of Friends in the context of peacemaking in the post–Cold War era. In so doing, it provides a framework in which the core case studies addressed in the chapters that follow can be assessed. These cases—El Salvador, Guatemala, Haiti, Georgia, Western Sahara, and East Timor—were selected to illustrate the utility and limitations of groups of Friends where they were centrally involved. All six groups were formed to support processes in which the secretary-general had a leading role; at least some of their members considered themselves as Friends of the Secretary-General even in the cases in which the mechanism did not carry that name (Guatemala, Western Sahara, and East Timor).

Together, these six case studies offer rich material for comparison of what a Friends' group, once constituted, may offer in widely different circumstances. They document (1) a variety of conflicts: ideological conflict fanned by the Cold War in Central America, civil conflict rooted in centuries of repression in Haiti, secessionist conflict following the collapse of the Soviet Union in Georgia, and self-determination after mangled decolonization in Western Sahara and East Timor; (2) a variety of regions: Latin America and the Caribbean, the former Soviet Union, and North Africa and Southeast Asia; and (3) a variety of outcomes: negotiation and implementation of comprehensive peace agreements, international intervention and failed transition in Haiti, a stalemate in Georgia and Western Sahara, and a newly independent state in East Timor. They also provide clear contrasts with respect to the capacities and performance of the individuals involved, and the constraints imposed on peace efforts by the extraneous interests of the states engaged as Friends.

In El Salvador and Guatemala, groups of Friends supported the negotiation and implementation, under UN auspices, of far-reaching peace agreements between the respective governments of each country and insurgent forces. In Haiti, Friends dominated by the United States were centrally located in a fifteen-year saga centered on the polarizing figure of Jean-Bertrand Aristide. This period saw elections, a coup, sanctions, international intervention, and peacebuilding before a return to internal unrest, Aristide's second departure from the presidency, and a new round of UN peacekeeping from 2004, supported by a variety of group mechanisms. In Georgia, a group of Friends formed by member states was hampered from the beginning by the clear alignment of its members with the parties to the conflict. Although the group was gradually transformed into a mechanism more directly affiliated with the United Nations, even as "Friends of the Secretary-General" it remained circumscribed by the extensive interests of Russia in the outcome of the conflict. In Western Sahara, a group of Friends was formed to preserve the interests of the key external actors in the region, the United States, France, and Spain. These were clearly distinct from the goal pursued by the United Nations: the implementation of a referendum in fulfillment of the population of Western Sahara's right to self-determination. The group controlled action in the Security Council but differences among its members prevented it from providing active support to the United Nations in its attempt to break the stalemate in the political process. The Core Group on East Timor, in contrast, was formed by the secretariat only when it became clear that the interests of key states would align with the United Nations' long-drawn-out effort to secure the self-determination of the people of East Timor.

A more crowded field for conflict resolution placed new demands on the United Nations as a peacemaker, principally with respect to its readiness to play distinct roles within different peace processes, reflecting the different configurations of actors involved.[32] Friends as conceived in the past gave way to more diverse structures, some of which are assessed in chapter 8. Secretariat officials engaged with groups established for a variety of purposes. In some instances they did so from a position of leadership—Myanmar, Afghanistan, Angola, and Cyprus—but were thwarted in their efforts by obstacles created by the regional environment and the essential unwillingness of the conflict parties. In others they interacted with processes in which a leading role for the United Nations was either not desirable or possible, or was clearly proscribed (Colombia and across Africa), yet group mechanisms emerged nonetheless. The chapter builds on the findings of the case studies to underline the importance of a disciplined yet "variable" approach to the use of groups and coalitions. Despite the wide variety of the cases considered, its conclusions are surprisingly consistent with those that emerged from the individual case chapters, with the variables of regional environment, the conflict parties, a group's composition, leadership, and timing determining the extent to which it might be well placed to play a constructive role.

The concluding chapter summarizes findings related to the five core factors identified in this introduction as they are manifested in the six case studies and the more varied UN peacemaking discussed in chapter 8. These lead into recommendations regarding circumstances in which a group of Friends may or may not be formed or other more informal coalitions pursued. The chapter argues that the collective approach to peacemaking epitomized by the emergence of groups has been a significant characteristic of post–Cold War peacemaking. It has been encouraged by recognition that national interest can be affected by distant conflict and turmoil and of the benefits of a multilateral approach. But it has also been complicated by the competing interests that individual states will bring to the table. Although an increasing number of nongovernmental peacemakers, states, and multilateral organizations recognize the virtue of coordination and complementarity, in many situations it remains an elusive goal. The formation of a group analogous to a group of Friends will, like mediation itself, not be a panacea. But when the circumstances are right Friends may represent the best available option to harness the considerable resources that concerned representatives of the international community can bring to bear on the complexities of conflicts.

1

At Cold War's End
Peacemaking and the Emergence of Groups

T he end of the Cold War transformed the United Nations and facilitated the resolution of many conflicts. It did so in three fundamental ways: by staunching the flow of resources from the United
States and the Soviet Union to parties in "proxy" wars across the developing world; by largely removing, or at least undermining, the ideological
causes of such conflicts; and by liberating the Security Council from the
shackles imposed on it by the politics of the Cold War and thereby allowing it to play the role its founders had intended. This chapter traces the
emergence of collaborative peacemaking, as expressed through the formation of a variety of groups of states, both within the United Nations and
outside it, as a central element of this process. The chapter emphasizes the
evolving relationship between the secretary-general and the organization's
member states.

Cooperation between the Soviet Union and the United States allowed
the five permanent members of the Security Council to act on the basis of
consensus and underpinned the United Nations' capacity to help bring an
end to conflicts in southern Africa, Southeast Asia, and Central America.
But the demise of the Cold War also removed barriers to the cooperation
of other configurations of states, evident in the proliferation of Friends and
other groups. This was not a straightforward process. The moment of
post–Cold War euphoria—of which the negotiations on El Salvador and
creation of the first Friends of the Secretary-General had formed a part—
was short-lived, and the capacity of the United Nations and its membership to respond to the new challenges in peace and security with which
they were faced was rapidly outstripped by their number and complexity. A
tendency to form groups of some kind did not diminish, but many of them
differed markedly from the earlier mechanisms. This was not least because
of the erosion of the primacy of the secretary-general's role as peacemaker
and the United Nations' gradual accommodation to an arena for conflict
resolution increasingly crowded by other actors. Groups working both

within and outside the orbit of the United Nations had a variety of impacts on the conflicts they sought to address. Their mixed record could be attributed to both the widely differing circumstances in which they were engaged and the complex motives of their members. These are analyzed in the case study chapters that follow.

The Secretary-General's Good Offices

The job of secretary-general of the United Nations has always been unlike any other. It is a precarious balancing act between three distinct roles: chief administrative officer of an unwieldy multilateral organization; political instrument of the Security Council, bound to implement the sometimes imperfect mandates it hands down; and a more ill-defined moral authority, trusted to look beyond the narrow interests of individual states or groups of states (although constantly buffeted by them) and safeguard a wider interest rooted in the principles of the UN Charter.[1] The potential and limitations of this third role were caught by James Traub in his account of Secretary-General Kofi Annan's controversial negotiations with Saddam Hussein in February 1998:

> Whatever moral romance is associated with Annan's job stems from its essential powerlessness. The secretary-general steps into a situation bristling with menace, armed only with his mandate and his moral authority. He has something of the Pope's spiritual status, but of course he has no church—no army of believers. He is a small, solitary figure, situated against an enormous backdrop.[2]

Mandate and moral authority alike are entwined in article 99 of the charter, which provides for the secretary-general to bring to the attention of the Security Council "any matter which in his opinion may threaten the maintenance of international peace and security." Article 99 has rarely been directly invoked.[3] However, its existence and implied responsibilities have given the secretary-general broad discretion with respect to the informal diplomatic activity (consultations of all kinds, fact-finding missions, and so forth) necessary to establish exactly what—in his opinion—might constitute a threat to international peace and security and why.

In practice, the development of an independent political role for the secretary-general was to prove a delicate task, circumscribed by the politics of the Cold War, although pursued to differing extents by every secretary-general since Trygve Lie.[4] Perhaps most famously, Dag Hammarskjöld developed a "Peking formula" by which, in early 1955, he undertook direct negotiations with China to secure the release of fifteen captured U.S. air-men. His efforts were initiated as a result of a request by the General Assembly. But he took pains to explain to the Chinese premier Chou En-Lai that he had come to Peking on the basis of his responsibilities under the charter, which were greater even than those given him by a majority of states in the General Assembly and were applicable to members and non-members (such as China at this point) alike of the United Nations.[5]

Much of a secretary-general's peacemaking fits under the capacious umbrella provided by the concept of "good offices." Not itself mentioned in the charter—although perhaps implied in article 33 (I), which lists "other peaceful means of their own choice" among measures available to states to achieve the peaceful settlement of disputes—good offices, as the phrase has come to be used in the United Nations, can very helpfully mean almost anything. Thus, although the 1899 and 1907 Hague Conventions for the Pacific Settlement of International Disputes treated good offices and mediation interchangeably, good offices as practiced by the secretary-general can mean much less than mediation, as well as more.[6] While the term is most generally employed with respect to peacemaking (in the Central American cases, a good offices mandate provided the secretary-general with a foot in the door to full-fledged mediation), the gamut of activities it covers extends from a well-timed telephone call to a reluctant president to the UN Good Offices Mission in Afghanistan and Pakistan, established in 1988 to help ensure the withdrawal of Soviet troops from Afghanistan.[7]

A secretary-general can undertake good offices with or without a specific mandate on the basis of the fragile independence and authority derived from the charter and the somewhat ephemeral legitimacy of the United Nations behind him. Impartiality is his essential attribute. In 1961 Hammarskjöld offered an impassioned defense of the idea of the inde-pendent and impartial international civil servant in a speech delivered at Oxford but directed toward the permanent members of the Security Coun-cil at loggerheads over the complex situation in the Congo.[8] He argued for an interpretation of neutrality that meant that such a man "must remain wholly uninfluenced by national or group interests or ideologies" but that he would unavoidably have to take action that might run counter to the views of at least some member states. Thirty-eight years later Kofi Annan, himself struggling to emerge from the controversy surrounding the posi-tions he had taken on Iraq, would offer a similarly robust defense of the par-ticular responsibilities that attend a secretary-general in this area: "Impar-tiality does not—and must not—mean neutrality in the face of evil. It means strict and unbiased adherence to the principles of the charter—nothing more, and nothing less."[9]

Consultations with state and nonstate actors engaged in conflict take place in a complex and circumscribed environment. But the difference between the public nature of positions taken in the Security Council and the confidentiality with which the secretary-general engages in peacemaking, informing the Council of his efforts at his discretion, is an essential feature of the organization's ability to contribute to the resolution of conflicts. It is also one easily misunderstood, exemplifying the thinness of the line between the secretary-general as chief executive officer of a multilateral organization and as an individual, able to act as an agent empowered by a broad consensus that peace should be pursued, but not bound to "clear" the policy or steps taken in pursuit of that end with individual states.[10] UN-led mediation represents a multilateral commitment to peace, but is not in itself multilateral mediation.

The public advocacy of a secretary-general may bring attention to neglected conflicts and crises, and his quiet diplomacy may breach differences between conflicting parties and build consensus between external actors on the way ahead. But while he—or, one day, she—may represent a powerful voice in the international community if able to act with the support of a united Security Council, he is otherwise left to work, as Annan put it on the same occasion, "only with tools of his own making."

Commanding none of the obvious sources of leverage represented by military force or ready access to financial resources, successive secretaries-general have instead relied on two principal sets of "tools," in addition to their own inherent abilities: senior officials designated to act as their envoys or representatives, and states motivated to provide encouragement to their efforts and, in theory at least, bound by article 100 (2) of the charter to respect their "exclusively international" character.[11] The advantages of the first are obvious: trusted officials acting on behalf of the secretary-general can be charged with tasks that vary from the conveying of a targeted message, to full-fledged negotiation or the management of a complex peace operation. They offer the possibility for the projection of the United Nations' diplomacy around the globe—increasingly necessary as, in the post–Cold War period, the demands on the organization grew exponentially—while simultaneously providing a degree of protection of the authority vested in the person and office of the secretary-general. But without the implicit or explicit support of the second tool, a secretary-general and those who act on his behalf will be able to achieve little.

In his speech at Oxford, Hammarskjöld distinguished different forms of interaction with states as being among the "varied means and resources" with which the secretary-general could implement controversial political decisions. First among these was what he referred to as "the institution of the permanent missions to the United Nations," a resource he cultivated assiduously. This was particularly true of a number of the representatives of middle powers, such as Canada, Norway, and Ireland, or other individuals—such as the permanent representative of Tunisia, Mongi Slim—with whom he felt most affinity. The second such resource, which he described as "a further development of the first," was the group of advisory committees of member states he established to support him in creating and managing peacekeeping operations. Such committees were put in place for the United Nations Emergency Force (UNEF), established in 1956 to help stabilize the situation in the wake of the Suez crisis, and the much larger and more complex United Nations Operation in the Congo (ONUC).[12] The committees represented a deliberate effort by Hammarskjöld to gather like-minded states around him to improve his leverage to steer controversial operations through the General Assembly, in the case of UNEF, and the Cold War rivalries in the Council over the Congo.[13]

Unlike at least the first generation of Friends groups in the 1990s, which were created to support the secretary-general's peacemaking, the origin of the advisory committees was the management of operations in the field. From this flowed a number of important differences: the formation of the committees for both UNEF and the Congo was formally discussed with the General Assembly and Security Council and, in the case of UNEF, mandated by a resolution;[14] their members were troop contributors to the operations[15] (seven countries in the case of UNEF: Brazil, Canada, Ceylon, Colombia, India, Norway, and Pakistan; a much more unwieldy eighteen countries in the case of the Congo), rather than states selected for their political or other leverage over a particular issue; and although the meetings were private, records of the meetings were kept and circulated and— perhaps inevitably—leaked to the parties concerned.

In February 1958 Hammarskjöld cited the work of the UNEF committee as an example of "the practical value in the United Nations of a formal instrument of private diplomacy in carrying forward action once the main policy lines have been laid down."[16] Later that year, in the summary study of UNEF that he wrote for the General Assembly, Hammarskjöld expanded on the idea of the UNEF advisory committee as something of a model. He praised the "free exchange of views in closed meetings where advice can be sought and given," the fact that "ultimate decisions rest with the secretary-general as the executive in charge of carrying out the operation," and that "dissenting views are not registered by votes, but are put on record in the proceedings." He suggested that it was useful for troop contributors to be represented on such a committee—but warned, accurately, as it turned out in the case of the Congo—that "if the contributing states are numerous, the size of the committee might become so large as to make it ineffective." He also reached the clear conclusion that parties to a conflict should not be members of such a committee and that—following the practice he had established by which permanent members of the Security Council did not contribute troops to a given operation—the permanent members should not "normally" be represented on an advisory committee either.[17]

Unlike field operations, the isolated peacemaking initiatives under-taken by successive secretaries-general during the Cold War did not involve the organized support of groups of member states. These initiatives ranged from proposals made by Trygve Lie on the Berlin Crisis in October 1948, to Hammarskjöld's quiet encouragement of Thailand and Cambodia to settle their border dispute in 1958, to his successor U Thant's involvement in the Cuban missile crisis in 1962, solitary and unhappy search for a solution to the Vietnam conflict in the mid-1960s, and more successful involvement in mediating a dispute over the future of Bahrain.[18] In many respects, the initiatives bore no comparison with the frenzied pace of events that would develop around the secretary-general and his senior staff in later years, when the pressures on the secretary-general's time and attention trans-formed the job comprehensively. However, the precedent they set would become evident as the United Nations entered the post–Cold War world. It was in this environment that the mechanism of Friends would be devel-oped, in the best of cases to complement and provide leverage to the unique, but necessarily limited, powers of influence and resources brought to the table by a UN mediator and to help make and manage peace on a consensual basis.

Untangling the Cold War

In mid-1996 Secretary-General Javier Pérez de Cuéllar could not identify a single conflict during the previous five years that had been resolved as a result of the United Nations' efforts.[19] Yet in 1987 he was able to write somewhat lyrically of change. It was "as if the sails of the small ship in which all the people of the earth are gathered, had caught again, in the midst of a perilous sea, a light but favorable wind."[20] An early indication of this shift came with the surprisingly cooperative manner with which the five permanent members of the Security Council agreed to a second term for the secretary-general himself. And it was as he began this second term in

January 1987 that Pérez de Cuéllar threw the political ball into the court of the permanent five, thereby initiating a process that, he would write, "began a new era in the United Nations' history."[21]

In response to a question posed by a reporter primed to ask whether the United Nations' silence on the long-standing war between Iran and Iraq was "an indication of a failure to do anything," Pérez de Cuéllar suggested that the members of the Security Council needed to reach a "meeting of the minds" to end the war. A journalist expressed doubts about the ability of the United States and the Soviet Union to work together, but Pérez de Cuéllar brushed them aside, insisting, in a somewhat headmasterly fashion, that the permanent members "had an obligation to try to reach agreement on the solution of problems related to peace and security."[22] This public démarche was complemented by a private invitation he extended to representatives of the five permanent members to join him for tea in his office. As the U.S. diplomat Cameron Hume—a participant and privileged observer in the process—tells it, the secretary-general "asked the ambassadors to reflect on his request that the Security Council find a common line for dealing with the war. The ambassadors might meet privately and informally, keeping their discussions off the Council's agenda until they had explored all possibilities for a meeting of minds."[23]

The process set in motion was to have far-reaching implications for Iran and Iraq, which agreed to a cease-fire in August 1988, for the way that diplomacy at the United Nations would be conducted in the future, and for the United Nations' capacity to help resolve a range of conflicts in southern Africa, Southeast Asia, and Central America. It would establish the "permanent five" (P-5) as the most powerful of groups in the United Nations and provide the basis for them to work together in response to Iraq's invasion of Kuwait in August 1990, eventually authorizing coalition forces to use "all necessary means" to reverse it (S/Res/678). "By 1990," Brian Urquhart would write, having retired from a long and distinguished career at the United Nations, "it seemed that the United Nations, and particularly the Security Council, were beginning to function more or less as the UN's founders had intended."[24]

The practices initiated in early 1987 heralded a period in which the dominance of Security Council action by veto-bearing permanent members was as marked as their determination of its inaction during the Cold War, when they were actually using their vetoes.[25] Consultations on Iran and Iraq soon fell into a pattern, where meetings between the permanent representatives, generally held in the residence of the British ambassador, would be interspersed with more freewheeling meetings of the counselors held at the U.S. mission. Gradually, the new cooperation evident in New York on Iran-Iraq extended to a broad range of subjects and became more directly articulated with the national foreign policy priorities of each permanent member.[26] Central to these would be the untangling of the conflicts of the Cold War, on which progress was evident as early as 1988. That year saw the signing of UN-mediated agreements on the withdrawal of Soviet troops from Afghanistan, but also forward movement in southern Africa, where the United Nations had long been engaged in efforts to achieve the self-determination of Namibia, and in Southeast Asia, where it had for a decade pursued the elusive goal of peace in Cambodia.

In both these cases, interaction between the United Nations and evolving groups of the most involved external actors assumed a central place in peace processes of intricate complexity. In Namibia, a Western Contact Group composed of Canada, France, the United Kingdom, the United States, and West Germany and dating back to the mid-1970s engaged with a frontline group of African states (Angola, Botswana, Mozambique, Tanzania, Zambia, and Zimbabwe); in Cambodia, the key actors were the P-5 of the Security Council, acting as a group, but also in partnership with interested regional actors. None of these structures approximated Friends of the Secretary-General as they developed in El Salvador, most obviously because of the subordinate role played by the secretary-general's own diplomacy. However, together, like the Core Group of states created to support the United Nations' efforts to implement the peace agreement in Mozambique, they fostered confidence in the validity of coalition involvement in peacemaking by which the United Nations might approach the uncharted territory of post–Cold War security.

Namibia

A former German colony, Namibia, or "South West Africa" as it was then known, had been under international supervision since the days of the League of Nations. It appeared regularly on the agenda of the General Assembly and Security Council, but little headway was made in persuading South Africa to grant it self-determination. Rather "the question of Namibia" became a battlefield for bitter debates between nonaligned states, whose accusations of Western complicity in colonialism and apartheid in South Africa were vigorously supported by the Soviet Union and the West, which, if not in open support of South Africa, was at a minimum reluctant to put any real pressure on it to let Namibia go.[27]

The Contact Group was initially quite separate from the secretary-general (who was perceived by the states in the group as being too tied by the General Assembly's resolutions on Namibia), as well as the Security Council. However, both were kept informed of its mediation. The group succeeded in putting forward a plan that became the framework for a Namibia settlement (contained in Security Council Resolution 435 of September 29, 1978), but progress stalled in the early 1980s. The interests of its members precluded the imposition of the tough measures (such as sanctions)[28] that would make the South Africans budge, and the regional process became subsumed into the insistence of the United States on linking the withdrawal of Cuban troops from Angola with progress in achieving independence in Namibia.

Negotiations of Byzantine complexity, led by U.S. Assistant Secretary of State Chester Crocker, would consume much of the 1980s, but only come to fruition as the tensions of the Cold War eased and it became possible to build consensus around the advantages offered to all exhausted parties by Crocker's formula.[29] Talks between Angola, Cuba, and South Africa, with the presence of the Soviet Union as an observer, began in 1998. These talks, known variously as the "tripartite" or "quadripartite" talks, led to the rapid conclusion of linked agreements on the withdrawal of Cuban troops from Angola and implementation of the UN settlement plan in Namibia in December 1988. In 1989 the United Nations fielded the United Nations Transition Assistance Group, the first of the multifunctional peacekeeping operations that would become a hallmark of this period.[30]

Cambodia

The Security Council had first considered Cambodia in 1979, following Vietnam's invasion of the previous year. Predictable differences among its permanent members—most obviously expressed by Soviet support for Vietnam and the Hun Sen regime established in Phnom Penh and by Chinese, U.S., and regional support for the coalition of factions (including the Khmer Rouge) led by Prince Sihanouk—had prevented it from taking any action. The good offices of the secretary-general were pursued by his special representative, Rafeeuddin Ahmed, parallel with regional and other efforts to promote dialogue. But as the 1980s wound down, the good offices began to be overtaken by evolving dynamics within the P-5, and the United Nations, although never in the lead in the peacemaking, became, in U.S. mediator Richard Solomon's words, a "screen behind which China, the Soviet Union, and Vietnam privately resolved their differences over the future of Indochina."[31]

The internal dialogue began to gather momentum after July 1988, when Indonesia hosted the first of two Jakarta Informal Meetings among the four Cambodian factions. Representatives of the P-5 attended the Paris Peace Conference convened by France and Indonesia in August 1989, and in January 1990 began a series of meetings that concluded in their agreement on a framework for a peace process in Cambodia that August.[32] As it was, another year of intense negotiations at the factional, regional, and great power levels would go by before the essential conditions—including China's normalization of its relations with Vietnam—were given for the Cambodians to accept in October 1991 a peace plan hammered out among the P-5, but largely drafted by UN officials who had worked on Cambodia for nearly a decade.[33]

During implementation, the leading role passed to the United Nations and the secretary-general's representative, Yasushi Akashi, at the head of the UN Transitional Authority in Cambodia (UNTAC). But the P-5 remained key players within informal mechanisms to support and finance UNTAC's operation. With the original five states "extended" outward to include others such as Australia, Indonesia, and Japan, which had been integrally involved in the negotiations, a group that became known as the "Core Group" or "Extended P-5" played a role analogous to that of a group of Friends—if distinguished from the Salvadoran Friends by the major powers at its center—both in Phnom Penh and in New York.[34] This group provided essential support to Akashi. It functioned as a forum through which UNTAC could convey what it needed to member states in the field, in New York, and through their capitals, but also as a sounding board for the exchange of information and ideas and an important source of financial support. Meanwhile some of its members also proved indispensable conduits for messages and requests to the Cambodian parties.[35]

Mozambique

The Core Group in Cambodia bore some relationship to a distinct Core Group established in Mozambique. This was created to support the efforts of the secretary-general's special representative, Aldo Ajello, and the UN operation in Mozambique he led to implement a peace agreement reached in October 1992. This had been greatly facilitated by the changing political dynamics across southern Africa and followed two years of negotiations largely conducted in Rome. The group was more informal than the advisory committees of the 1950s, but it reaffirmed the "practical value" identified by Dag Hammarskjöld of an instrument of "private diplomacy" carrying forward action once the tasks to be achieved had been outlined within a mandate of the Security Council.

Mediation between the government of Mozambique and the National Resistance of Mozambique had been led by a nongovernmental organiza-tion, the Roman Catholic Community of Sant'Egidio, and Italy, supported, particularly in the latter stages of negotiations, by four observer countries —France, Portugal, the United Kingdom, and the United States—and the United Nations.[36] Representatives of these five key states plus Germany (in several cases officials transferred by their governments from Rome to Maputo to maximize the continuity of their engagement) met frequently in Maputo with Ajello as the international members of a Supervision and Monitoring Commission established within the peace agreement. Ajello would recall them as "genuine actors in the process . . . invaluable allies."[37] To an extent that his superiors in New York were not at the time aware, he treated this Core Group as a virtual Security Council, solving problems through frank discussion with them and even sharing advance drafts of reports to the Council to ensure that they went forward to New York with their blessing. Highly effective as a means of reinforcing Ajello's authority, the Core Group reflected an international community in broad consensus in its efforts to help secure peace in Mozambique, ably deployed to support this end by Ajello's charismatic and confident leadership.

From Cold War to Different War

In January 1992, as he concluded the first-ever meeting of the UN Security Council held at the level of a head of government—an occurrence that itself reflected the changes afoot in the world—the British prime minister, John Major, speaking as president of the Security Council, invited the sec-retary-general to prepare his "analysis and recommendations" on ways to strengthen the capacity of the United Nations for preventive diplomacy, peacemaking, and peacekeeping.[38] This request would give the newly as-sumed secretary-general, Boutros Boutros-Ghali, the opportunity to craft and present *An Agenda for Peace*. In it he proposed an ambitious blueprint of how action by the United Nations—in the three areas identified by the Security Council, but also through what he termed "post-conflict peace-building"—could help secure peace in the new era that was unfolding before it.[39] No small influence in its analysis was the United Nations' mediation of negotiated agreements in El Salvador, signed in early 1992. *An Agenda for Peace* publicly acknowledged the contribution made by the group of Friends, which was heralded as a "unique arrangement."[40]

The United Nations' elation would last a little longer, but the rapidity of the expansion of its operations and the complexity of the international panorama in which they took place proved more than anyone had fore-seen. Between 1987 and 1994 the number of conflicts in which the United Nations was actively involved in peacemaking nearly trebled, the resolu-tions passed by the Security Council on an annual basis quadrupled, and peacekeeping operations jumped from five to seventeen. Troop deployment increased from fewer than 10,000 to more than 73,000, and the annual budget for peacekeeping rose from $230 million to $3.6 billion.[41] However, the United Nations' performance in the field could not keep pace with the demands made upon it. What Michael Doyle has described as a "temporary conjunction of power and will" led the international community to pursue a strategy of assertive multilateralism that charged the United Nations with responsibilities for peace enforcement, the management of humanitarian emergencies, reconstruction, and peacebuilding that it had neither the resources nor the experience to handle.[42] Early successes in the post–Cold War period bred overconfidence and led to mistakes on the part of mem-ber states and secretariat alike: "The level of risk and the prospects of suc-cess were not thoroughly analyzed," Marrack Goulding, under-secretary-general for peacekeeping operations until 1993, would write; "Mandates were not clearly defined; the necessary resources were not provided; and there was too much reliance on things being all right on the night."[43]

Although a small element within this period of momentous transition, the path of groups of Friends, a number of which were formed in the wake of the positive experience in El Salvador, would be no different. Between 1992 and 1995, as the demand on the United Nations rose, Friends of the Secretary-General and the process itself were established to support the organization's efforts to reach and sustain peace in a number of situations, including Georgia, Guatemala, Haiti, Tajikistan, and Western Sahara.[44] Less auspicious circumstances for peacemaking than those presented in El Salvador contributed to the mixed performance of some of these groups, but were not the only factor.

The powerful group on Haiti was dominated—and at times divided—by positions taken by the United States, even as the Haitian process as a whole failed to sow the seeds of lasting peace. Groups on Guatemala and Tajikistan formed by the parties and the secretariat, respectively, were largely positive in their contributions to the process. Other groups formed on the initiative of the Friends themselves prioritized the interests of the states concerned over the resolution of the conflict before them. Stale-mates in efforts to overcome the stasis on the ground in both Georgia and Western Sahara preserved the life of the Friends in each case. But else-where, from the mid-1990s, a move away from peace processes in which the secretary-general had a clear lead limited the creation of groups of Friends of the Secretary-General, particularly where the interests of powerful states were directly involved. Perhaps most notable, the United Nations' nominal lead of the political process in the Balkans was displaced by the Contact Group and then by the decisive intervention of the United States, most obviously in its emphatic negotiation of the Dayton peace agreements in 1995.[45]

Resolution of the Cold War conflicts had been helped by the strings these conflicts had left to be pulled by the powerful states on the Security Council. But in their wake had come a series of conflicts in weak, new states—principally in Africa, the Balkans, and the former Soviet Union—where freedom from the former colonial or metropolitan power unleashed a series of contending forces that the traditional tools of the United Nations were poorly suited to address. These conflicts were characterized by multiple nonstate armed actors, many of them undisciplined or criminal in nature;[46] a preponderance of civilian rather than combatant victims; massive movements of refugees and of the internally displaced; increasingly complex (though widely varying) conflict-sustaining economies; the presence of spoilers; and a ready access to weapons of all kinds and particularly small arms. Conflicts proliferated within states, but also across borders to create regional clusters of conflict, or vulnerability to conflict, such as the Balkans, the Great Lakes, the Horn of Africa, West Africa, Central Asia, and the Caucasus.

The extent to which these represented "new wars" or forms of conflict, quantifiably distinct from those that preceded them, or harked back to earlier forms of "criminal war" has been widely debated.[47] But they were certainly new to the United Nations. In the past, article 2 (7) of the charter had precluded UN intervention in "matters which are essentially within the domestic jurisdiction of any state" except when enforcement measures under chapter VII of the charter were adopted. This had kept the organization and its secretary-general at a safe distance from the messy business of internal conflicts. But with the demise of the clear lines of great power influence established by the Cold War and a more gradual erosion of the primacy of sovereignty, internal conflict and the humanitarian emergencies it created became legitimate areas for the engagement of the United Nations.[48] This shift allowed the United Nations to lead the way in the rapid expansion of a range of activities designed to prevent and end conflict and keep and build the peace.

Problems came quickly. The optimism expressed in *An Agenda for Peace* in mid-1992 was already threatened by the quagmire of the wars in the former Yugoslavia by mid-1993. Tensions with the United States exploded over the deaths of eighteen U.S. Army Rangers in Somalia in October 1993 and were to be a defining feature of the remainder of Boutros-Ghali's five-year term. It was symptomatic of the times that the U.S. Rangers, although nominally part of the UN-led effort, were killed during an operation that had been ordered directly by the United States.[49] This not inconsequential fact was blurred in the public outcry against the United Nations that followed. The episode contributed to the development by the United States of Presidential Decision Directive 25 providing for tougher conditions for its support for UN peacekeeping, and dampened any enthusiasm there might have been for engaging in Rwanda in the spring of 1994.[50] The United Nations' failure to avert or stop the genocide that ensued—some 800,000 Rwandans were slaughtered within a four-month period—shamed all who were associated with it. But there again, as with the massacres in the supposed UN "safe area" of Srebrenica in Bosnia in 1995, much of the blame that lay with member states who had provided UN operations with inadequate or unimplementable mandates fell on "the United Nations" (meaning the secretariat) and its secretary-general. By the mid-1990s its engagement in peace and security had slowed dramatically.[51]

As the United Nations as a whole struggled to keep pace with a succession of crises, the opportunities presented to Boutros-Ghali in peacemaking were fewer than had been the case a few years earlier. His good offices were employed directly and through an ever-increasing number of envoys and special representatives—the latter generally heading peace operations—engaged in activities to facilitate negotiations between conflicting parties, sometimes in partnership with regional actors, to further the implementation of an agreement or mediate a boundary dispute. But the arena for peacemaking had become more populated. The circumstances in which the secretary-general was able to retain a clear leading role were generally limited to those cases in which the intractability of a particular conflict had kept it on the agenda of the United Nations for many years. Although success was seen in ending the conflict in Tajikistan, the subordination of what the United Nations was able to achieve to the regional needs of the Russian Federation deprived it of some of its luster. Even the most conspicuous of peacemaking achievements of this period, the moderation by the United Nations of agreements on Guatemala, was one achieved with minimal personal involvement of the secretary-general, who was otherwise engaged in crisis management and his own losing battle with the United States for reelection.[52]

Meanwhile, relations between secretariat officials and several of the Friends' groups had become far from straightforward. Frustrated with being "bossed about" by the United States on Haiti, and with Friends of Georgia whose bilateral positions undermined any hope of impartiality on the conflict in Abkhazia, officials in the UN secretariat began to wonder whether, in some instances, groups of Friends were not themselves part of the problem.[53] In the *Supplement to the Agenda for Peace* presented in 1995, with the United Nations' credibility battered by the events of the preceding years, the creation of Friends groups was no longer just a positive footnote to peacemaking in El Salvador. Described as a "new trend in recent years," Boutros-Ghali warned that in establishing such a group it was necessary to "maintain a clear understanding of who is responsible for what" and argued for arrangements more similar to the Salvador mechanism than those that had sprung up in its wake: "The secretary-general has the mandate from the relevant inter-governmental body and must remain in the lead. The members of the 'Friends' group have agreed to support the secretary-general at his request. If they take initiatives not requested by the secretary-general there is a risk of duplication or overlapping of efforts which can be exploited by recalcitrant parties."[54]

This somewhat imperious attempt to corral a horse that had long since bolted reflected a change in relations between the secretary-general and the Security Council as well as differences in the personalities of Pérez de Cuéllar and Boutros-Ghali, who was showing signs of increasing impatience with the United Nations' distortion by states' own interests.[55] Early in 1994, de Soto—now working as one of Boutros-Ghali's senior advisors —had suggested to some of his colleagues that it might be time to "phase out" the concept of Friends of the Secretary-General altogether, dropping any pretense that the secretary-general was "in charge" of a process, and with it that the states engaged in it were, in a reliable sense, friends. A less loaded title—such as liaison or Contact Group—might more accurately reflect the possible limits of the relationship between the Secretariat and states gathered as "Friends." Caution on the future of Friends would be echoed in a suggestion submitted by Goulding to the incoming secretary-general, Kofi Annan, in 1997. He recommended that a clear distinction be made between Friends selected by the secretary-general and self-appointed Contact Groups.[56] The suggestion was not acted on, but the extraordinary proliferation of peace efforts in the years that followed relegated Friends as conceived in the early part of a decade to a much more occasional occurrence, even as they contributed to the creation of new groups of all kinds.

Enter Annan

Kofi Annan arrived in office in January 1997 with an extensive mandate for reform and the paradoxical advantage of an almost uniquely discredited and embattled organization to run. Although personally involved in many of the most high-profile failures of the recent past—he had served as under-secretary-general for peacekeeping operations from 1993 to 1996— he commissioned a hard-hitting report on Rwanda (S/1999/1257) and issued a highly critical one on Srebrenica himself (A/54/549) that enabled him to acknowledge the organization's failings with some dignity and move on from them. Early in his tenure he recommitted his office to efforts to reach solutions in four conflicts in which the secretary-general's good offices had long been engaged—Cyprus, East Timor, Georgia, and Western Sahara—and over time he developed a capacity to "walk the international tightrope," as the *New York Times* in 1999 described the balancing act required for his job, with skill.[57]

An intuitive political actor rather than an intellectual player, Annan's personality was perhaps his greatest asset, not least in the contrast it offered to the brittle arrogance of his predecessor. With an underlying commitment to human dignity and individual rights, he presided over the reexpansion of the United Nations' activities that followed the Kosovo crisis of 1999, including the development of a new generation of complex missions charged with broad responsibilities for transitional arrangements in Kosovo, East Timor, and Afghanistan; the reengagement of the United Nations in the Middle East, following a long period in which the dominance of the United States had effectively denied the United Nations a political role in the region; a substantial reform of peace operations spurred by the report of a panel under the leadership of the veteran Algerian diplomat Lakhdar Brahimi he had commissioned in 2000;[58] and a sustained effort to follow in the footsteps of his predecessor in helping focus international attention on the myriad challenges of Africa. This underpinned the creation of large peacekeeping operations in the Democratic Republic of the Congo, Ethiopia-Eritrea, Sierra Leone, Liberia, and elsewhere as well as smaller political presences engaged in good offices and peacebuilding across the continent. It also, as is discussed below, included an open encouragement of the formation of groups as vehicles for international engagement.

With the exception of East Timor, which emerged as the newly independent state of Timor-Leste in 2002,[59] and the UN role in facilitating the transition in Afghanistan initiated by the Bonn agreement of December

2001, major peacemaking successes of the United Nations were not a hallmark of this period. This did not represent a failure of UN peacemaking so much as a shift away from the patterns of the past and the scarcity of opportunities to distinguish a "UN role" from broader efforts of which the United Nations formed a part. However, the reinvigoration of the secretary-general's efforts in Cyprus came tantalizingly close to a solution that would have allowed a united Cyprus to enter the European Union, while in Western Sahara too, the sustained engagement of former U.S. Secretary of State James Baker as Annan's personal envoy offered the best opportunity yet for a settlement and, in late 2005, it was as Annan's special envoy that Martti Ahtisaari, the former president of Finland, assumed the lead of the effort to determine the future status of Kosovo. The secretary-general's good offices helped facilitate discussions with Libya regarding its responsibilities for the Lockerbie bombings, addressed territorial disputes between Nigeria and Cameroon, Equatorial Guinea and Gabon, and Guyana and Venezuela, and supported efforts toward peace in Nepal. Meanwhile, his envoys undertook a variety of peacemaking assignments elsewhere. In some instances, as in Myanmar, this led the United Nations to assume the fragile lead of processes that other international actors could or would not touch; in many more, and notably in Africa, the United Nations worked from below to facilitate complex processes of peacemaking led by others. Different again was the UN role in Colombia, where advisers to Annan struggled to engage effectively despite an ill-defined mandate and ambivalence on the part of Colombian actors.

What the United Nations did not do in the field of peacemaking was readily identifiable. Like his predecessors, Annan did not have an active role in a number of conflicts in which the paramount interest of the powerful state or states concerned was that the United Nations should keep out. This, of course, had been amply demonstrated during the Cold War. Yet, even in the activist years since its end, the strongly held views of Russia, India, and China ensured that the United Nations had no role in the conflicts in Chechnya, in peacemaking in the dispute over the Kashmir between India and Pakistan, or in Tibet. Meanwhile, the margins for an independent role for the secretary-general were much narrower on issues such as the Balkans, the Middle East, or Iraq, in which the direct interests of the major powers were engaged and in some degree of tension with one another. This was clearly illustrated in the late 1990s, when in the months that preceded the explosion of the situation in Kosovo, Kofi Annan twice raised with the Security Council his concern that the situation was rapidly deteriorating beyond the capacity of the major Western powers to control it. He was told, "not very politely," as Kieran Prendergast, under-secretary-general for political affairs at the time, recalled, "to mind his own business."[60]

Moreover, there were a number of other situations in which sensitivity to the United Nations for a variety of reasons precluded a peacemaking role for the secretary-general. This sensitivity derived from a perception that the United Nations was too beholden to powerful members of the Security Council—particularly the United States—or simply too biased toward governments and thus unsuited to mediate within a civil war context; a loss of credibility as a result of recent failure in the region (the legacy of Rwanda, Angola, and the Balkans); a visible gap between expectations held out by Security Council resolutions and the failure to implement them (particularly in the Middle East); or the suspicion that intervention by the United Nations would bring with it unacceptable intrusion on sensitive issues such as human rights. For these reasons a mediation role for the secretariat did not develop in conflicts as diverse as those in Algeria, Rwanda, and Sudan, as well as in Aceh (Indonesia) and Sri Lanka.

Like each of his predecessors, Annan ran into trouble in his relations with the major powers, most notably the United States. The "indispensable nation" for the United Nations, as it was referred to by President Bill Clinton's secretary of state, Madeleine Albright, or "permanent one" as its demonstration of power and authority under President George W. Bush led it to be perceived, the United States had a weight and influence in the United Nations greater as the sole remaining superpower than it had had during the Cold War.[61] Positions taken by the United States had underpinned the activism of the United Nations in the early 1990s, as well as the retrenchment that followed; Boutros-Ghali's acrimonious departure as well as the appointment of Annan as his successor; the marginalization of the United Nations represented by NATO's bombing of Kosovo as well as the renewed engagement in peacekeeping of the early 2000s; and the charged political and security environment within which the United Nations found itself working in the wake of the United States' declaration of a war on terrorism after the attacks of September 2001.

Iraq and Beyond

Annan's trouble built slowly—for many years his standing in Washington and elsewhere ran high—and would be epitomized by a contentious relationship over Iraq.[62] Indeed, his second term in office became inextricably bound up with the profound crisis provoked by the decision of the United

States to invade Iraq in March 2003 without explicit authorization from the Security Council and by the far-reaching process of reform he initiated in its aftermath. The invasion itself, and the doctrine of preemptive action it embodied, flouted fundamental provisions of the UN Charter and provoked deep divisions within the international community.[63] But in the interests of retaining a working relationship with the United States, Annan was relatively muted on this issue. In the weeks running up to the military action, he presented himself as the servant of the Council and appealed for consensus; in the face of imminent war, he lamented the "sad day" for the United Nations and the international community.[64]

The Security Council was subsequently able to adopt Resolution 1483 of May 22, 2003, and in it to request that Annan appoint a special representative for Iraq to work in "coordination with the Authority" (as the occupying powers were described). This in many ways compounded Annan's difficulties. The mandate the office was given was inadequate; its very existence raised concerns that it was providing retroactive legitimacy to the invasion and subsequent occupation of Iraq and, to top it all, on August 19, 2003, the office became the target of the most brutal attack on UN staff in the organization's history. Twenty-two staff members, including Annan's special representative Sergio Vieira de Mello, were killed. Commentators across the political spectrum attributed the attack to the fact the United Nations was seen to be furthering U.S. interests in Iraq.[65] In 2004 Annan would be goaded away from the diplomatic assessment that the invasion of Iraq was "not in conformity with the UN Charter" to state that it was "illegal."[66] The fury that this unleashed from Washington confirmed that Annan had ended up in the worst of positions: he was held by many member states to be overly compliant in his dealings with the United States, yet bitterly resented by the U.S. administration as well.

The reform effort on which Annan then embarked was impelled by two drivers: the work of a high-level panel he commissioned to assess the new threats and challenges the United Nations faced in the aftermath of the invasion; and a damaging series of scandals, including accusations of fraud and mismanagement in the oil-for-food program the United Nations administered for Iraq, sexual misconduct by UN peacekeepers, and serious irregularities in peacekeeping procurement. Progress in implementing both substantive and administrative reforms was clouded by a climate increasingly poisoned by the polarization of international politics around positions taken by the United States and the emergence of clearly marked differences between the North and South with respect to the priorities and purposes of the United Nations. These obstacles were so pronounced that in early 2006 Brian Urquhart would lament that they had "succeeded the forty-year East-West deadlock as a brake on international policy and action."[67]

It was a paradoxical feature of the final period of Annan's time as secretary-general that the multiple crises from which the organization suffered did nothing to lessen the demands upon it. In Iraq, the United States continued to need both the limited engagement of UN officials (and the cover they could bring it) and the legitimacy that the Security Council could bestow if it was to begin to try to assemble a new government and restore sovereignty.[68] But elsewhere, too, action with and through the United Nations had never been more necessary. In mid-2004, the United States joined forces with France (its most vocal critic on Iraq) to act through the Security Council to address the unstable situation that was developing in Lebanon as its government struggled to shake itself free from Syrian control. Meanwhile, UN peacekeeping mushroomed to record levels as new operations were launched in Burundi, Côte d'Ivoire, Haiti, Sudan, and East Timor and, from mid-2006 on, efforts were increased to wrest agreement from Sudanese authorities in Khartoum on a UN peacekeeping operation in Darfur. By late 2006, the United Nations had nearly 100,000 personnel (80,000 of them uniformed) serving in eighteen peace operations and an annual peacekeeping budget of approximately $4.75 billion.[69]

These new developments put extraordinary pressure on Annan's diplomatic resources even as he struggled to move forward with his reform agenda. This culminated in a lengthy "Outcome Document" agreed to by states gathered for a summit meeting of the General Assembly in September 2005. Although the document was a generally disappointing product of an acrimonious process, the UN membership did agree upon the formation of the Peacebuilding Commission and, perhaps more surprisingly, endorsed the responsibility of each individual state to protect its civilians from genocide, war crimes, ethnic cleansing, and crimes against humanity.[70] This significant innovation in international affairs would be recognized by Annan in his final press conference as secretary-general—along with broader progress on human rights—as first among the achievements of the United Nations under his stewardship.[71]

Events in the latter part of 2006 demonstrated both the limits and potential of UN peacemaking. In the Middle East, Annan and his envoys had been intensely engaged—individually and through collaborative mechanism such as the Quartet and a Core Group on Lebanon created by the United States in 2005[72]—as Palestinian elections in January brought Hamas to power and, in the summer months, war between Hezbollah and

Israel erupted. An independent stance of the secretary-general on the election results was subordinated to Quartet politics. These determined a hardline position that all but curtailed donor assistance to the Hamas government and influenced a subsequent decision by Annan that his own envoy should not have contacts with its representatives.[73] However, international efforts to bring the conflict between Hezbollah and Israel to an end illustrated the continued utility of the United Nations in the absence of other avenues for the parties involved. In the process they cast Annan—who appealed for a cease-fire from the conflict's early days—against the United States, which sustained the illusion of an Israeli victory. When this failed to materialize, action through the Security Council took center stage. Agreement was finally reached on August 11 on a resolution (SCR 1701) that established a robust peacekeeping operation and gave broad responsibilities to the secretary-general to negotiate a long-term solution between Israel and Lebanon.

At the other end of the spectrum of international attention, Nepal emerged as a new theater for UN engagement in support of a national process. Annan had first offered his good offices to help achieve a peaceful solution to the country's internal conflict in 2002.[74] The offer was never explicitly rejected or accepted, although it was viewed with some concern by the increasingly authoritarian king and Nepal's powerful neighbor India. From 2003 onward, Tamrat Samuel, a very able official in the Department of Political Affairs, had undertaken frequent visits to the country in order to establish contacts and build trust. The UN profile within the country was raised by the opening of an office of the high commissioner for human rights in mid-2005, and the prospect of the United Nations' playing some kind of third-party role was openly discussed by all parties.[75]

In April 2006, weeks of strikes and protests against King Gyanendra forced dramatic changes: the king backed down, brought his direct rule to an end, and restored parliament. Nepal's Maoists called a cease-fire, and political parties moved from opposition to government and undertook to reach agreement with the Maoists on plans for elections to a constituent assembly to decide the country's future.[76] The political process dragged out, but on August 9 Annan received separate but identical letters from the government and the Maoists requesting UN involvement in the electoral process, in arms management, and in the monitoring of the cease-fire and human rights. With India's active involvement behind the scenes, a peace agreement was finally reached in late November. A small UN team led by Annan's personal representative, Ian Martin, began preparing to field a mission to monitor the cantonment of combatants and also stepped up support for preparations for elections to the constituent assembly. Although largely overlooked by most of the world, Nepal appeared to represent a good example of a case in which a small amount of personal attention by the secretary-general—and able diplomacy by those acting on his behalf—could harvest direct benefits for the cause of peace.[77]

A Crowded Field

From the mid-1990s on, after a steady rise for more than four decades, there was a sharp decline in the numbers of wars, genocides, and international crises and a notable growth in the number of conflicts that ended in negotiated peace agreements rather than in victory.[78] But although more civil wars ended between 1990 and 2005 through negotiation than in the preceding two centuries, mediation led to settlement in only about 25 percent of these cases, and approximately half of these "successful" cases slid back into conflict within a decade.[79] This confluence of circumstances not only underpinned the increased demand for peacekeeping and reconstruction but also encouraged further attempts at mediation of even the most intractable conflicts.

The United Nations remained the preeminent international actor in the pursuit of peace, but its efforts were part of an extraordinary growth in conflict prevention, mediation, peacekeeping, and peacebuilding undertaken by other multilateral institutions, regional and subregional organizations, individual states, nongovernmental organizations (NGOs), and private peacemakers. This significant development in the means by which the international community addressed peace and security reflected a global context in which the culture, distribution, and use of power and influence were, perhaps paradoxically, both dominated by the assertion of the might of the United States and defused by the emergence of new actors and forces on the international scene. A direct result of the varied configurations of actors involved in each process was the proliferation of groups and other ad hoc coalitions around the different issues the United Nations and others faced.

Outside the United Nations, regional and subregional organizations gradually developed their own capacities to respond to internal conflicts. The Organization for Security and Cooperation in Europe's (OSCE's) High Commissioner for National Minorities emerged as an effective actor in conflict prevention, while the OSCE itself assumed a prominent part in efforts to address conflicts in the Balkans and the Caucasus. Meanwhile, the European Union came to assume a major role in regional security and increasingly ventured into engagement in conflicts beyond its borders (including through the appointment of special representatives or envoys to the Great Lakes and West Africa, the Caucasus, Afghanistan, and the Middle East). Within its own region, the Organization of American States (OAS) gradually expanded its capacity to address conflicts, with high-profile, if somewhat unrewarding, interventions in internal political conflict in Venezuela and Haiti, as well as the establishment of a controversial mission to monitor agreements reached between the Colombian government and paramilitaries.

Regional attempts to fill the vacuum left by the United Nations in Africa after 1993 were constrained by political considerations deriving from the respect for state sovereignty enshrined within the Organisation of African Unity (OAU). A slow realization that concerns about sovereignty were trumped by the obstacle to Africa's development represented by the persistence of conflict led to a rise in peacemaking. The OAU's successor, the African Union (AU), began its existence in 2002 determined to dedicate substantial resources and effort to conflict management, including through the creation of a Peace and Security Council, and significantly increased its engagement in peacemaking in situations as diverse as Darfur and Côte d'Ivoire in the years that followed.[80] Subregional organizations such as the Economic Community of West Africa (ECOWAS), the Southern African Development Community (SADC), and the Intergovernmental Authority on Development (IGAD) and regional powers such as Algeria, Nigeria, and South Africa became increasingly active in conflict mediation and resolution as well.[81] But it was not easy. Broad support from inside Africa and beyond of the mantra of "African solutions for African problems" was challenged by problems of capacity and resources. Meanwhile, the regional aspects of most conflicts in Africa took their toll as, for example, SADC's members engaged directly in the conflict in Zaire/DRC, and fundamental differences within IGAD impeded efforts to resolve conflicts in Sudan and Somalia.

Individual states have long been prominent peacemakers. In some cases these states were powers of global reach and projection, such as the United States, while in others regional actors were motivated by more immediate interests to get involved.[82] While both types of states remained active, new actors in conflict mediation in the post–Cold War period included states whose avowed disinterest in the outcome of the conflicts with which they were engaged represented one of their principal advantages, as well as an increasing number of nongovernmental or private mediators.

Norway's involvement in this field stems from the Oslo process in the Middle East in the early 1990s. Since that time its experience included facilitating talks between the government of Sri Lanka and guerrillas in the Liberation Tigers of Tamil Eelam, and between the government of the Philippines and the communist National Democratic Front. In these cases, as in Guatemala and Sudan, where Norwegian officials worked closely with other actors, Norway brought to the table a potent combination of factors. It had the resources and vision necessary to make a sustained commitment to peacemaking and the impartiality to present itself as an "honest broker" in a peace process. The skill of some of its senior diplomats was ably complemented by a readiness to draw on the expertise to be found in NGOs. Meanwhile, the low profile and discretion that rendered Norway's presence and implied recognition of nonstate actors acceptable to governments was helpfully paired with a significant degree of credibility with the big powers, including the United States, by whom Norway had long been considered a staunch NATO ally.[83] The prominence of Norway as a middle-power peacemaker and the plaudits it gained even when its efforts were not successful encouraged other states. Perhaps most notable among them was Switzerland, which had its historical neutrality and proven commitment to humanitarian issues as an asset and declared conflict resolution a foreign policy priority. [84] Others such as Canada, the Netherlands, and Sweden tried to follow suit.

Nongovernmental or private entities, such as the Community of Sant'-Egidio and the Centre for Humanitarian Dialogue in Geneva, are "weak mediators," even in the anomalous case of the Carter Center, which is headed by a former U.S. president. Unlike state actors they have no political power or economic resources and thus bring neither leverage to a negotiation nor the promise of resources to peacebuilding. However, in some circumstances—particularly the early stages of a peace process—this weakness has been seen to work to their advantage.[85] A lack of strategic or economic interest can be attractive to conflict parties cautious of intervention by state or intergovernmental actors (not least because it brings with it the comfortable prospect of incurring only negligible political costs for bad faith, or worse, behavior). The "private" capacity in which the mediation is conducted also preempts the delicate issue of recognition of the nonstate armed actors involved. These factors contributed to make nongovernmental actors the mediators of choice in some circumstances, such as the early days of the Mozambique process, or in Aceh (Indonesia)—for which between 2002 and 2003 the Centre for Humanitarian Dialogue facilitated the negotiation of a short-lived peace agreement—in which state involvement would not be welcome. However, as both these processes (and indeed the successful effort on Aceh launched in 2005 by Martti Ahtisaari in a private capacity) demonstrated, progress would be predicated on what the Community of Sant'Egidio has described as a "synergy of efforts at all levels," with state actors gradually lending their weight to negotiations led by NGOs.[86]

The consequence of the engagement of these many and varied actors was peacemaking of unparalleled complexity, involving interventions by single and multiple mediators acting in representation of a state, multilateral, or nongovernmental organization, as well as other formally or informally constituted composites. These actors were engaged simultaneously or in sequence within structures that sought to bolster coordination or to make it more diffuse. The results were not always optimal, as the desire for a role in a peace process could lead to discreet but nonetheless unseemly competition that did neither the peacemakers nor the cause of peace much favor.[87] The phenomenon was recognized by the United States Institute of Peace as "multiparty mediation"; its resistance to control is suggested by the title—*Herding Cats*—of the edited volume of practitioner accounts dedicated to its elucidation. Perhaps unsurprisingly, a principal conclusion reached by the volume's editors was that there was "almost an inverse relationship between the number of participants and issues in a multiparty mediation and the likelihood of developing and sustaining a coordinated intervention strategy."[88]

The Proliferation of Groups

The rise of groups was itself a direct manifestation of this abundance of would-be peacemakers. It went far beyond the mechanisms established at the United Nations and reflected three distinct factors: the enormous challenge represented by the resolution of the "harder" conflicts with which the international community was now grappling, many of which were of longer duration than those in the immediate aftermath of the Cold War and had been sustained by issues, resources, and dynamics distinct from those that had caused the conflict in the first place;[89] a fundamental ambivalence regarding the effort and resources that such conflicts, which rarely presented a direct threat to the national interests of the major powers, merited; and countervailing pressures related to an increasing realization of the implications for both regional and collective security of distant conflict and chaos and a general preference for a peaceful global environment. These factors led external actors to seek to engage more directly with regional efforts to end conflict, but also to do so in partnerships that would promote a united international community to provide essential leverage on the parties in conflict and share the considerable diplomatic and financial burdens.

Outside the United Nations, groups ranging from the Group of Eight (G-8) industrialized countries to shifting configurations of states took leading roles in conflict resolution. This was even as groups —including a short-lived Core Group on the 2004 tsunami—were created for a variety of other purposes as well.[90] The Contact Group on the former Yugoslavia, originally created as a Franco-German initiative in February 1994, had a long and varied history as a central actor in efforts to address the Balkan wars, and was perhaps the closest equivalent to the great power "Concert" of the past.[91] Its six members (France, Germany, Italy, Russia, the United Kingdom, and the United States) divested themselves of Russia to address the Kosovo crisis in 1999 as the "Quint," but regrouped in the mid-2000s as efforts to move Kosovo toward talks on its final status quickened.[92]

States worked together in the Minsk Group on the Nagorno-Karabakh and the Friends of Albania to support peacemaking conducted by the OSCE. The four Guarantor States established within the 1942 Rio de Janeiro Protocol between Ecuador and Peru successfully oversaw the resolution of the two countries' border dispute more than half a century later.[93] And a group of "Friends of Venezuela" was formed in early 2003 after a brief flurry of consultations at the United Nations. The group lost profile quickly, but then reappeared as a group of Friends of the OAS Secretary-General César Gaviria that worked to support his search for a solution to the internal crisis provoked by attempts to force President Hugo Chávez from power.[94] Meanwhile, even nongovernmental peacemakers derived expertise and leverage from the use of groups, as both a group of "Wise Men" and a heavyweight "Tokyo Group" of donors came to support the efforts of the Centre for Humanitarian Dialogue in Aceh.[95]

In the United Nations an extraordinary number of groups were established as a result of initiatives taken by secretariat officials, member states, and even the parties to a conflict themselves. Friends were formed to address conflicts as diverse as Angola, Kosovo, Guinea-Bissau, and Iraq. They were joined by Core Groups, Contact Groups, Troikas, and the Quartet on the Middle East, as well as a slew of monitoring mechanisms established within peace agreements as a means of engaging key external actors in their implementation. Collectively the groups highlighted both the operational limitations of the structures, most prominently the Security Council, charged with maintaining international peace and security, and also their surprising resilience in the face of a world—and a landscape of conflict—quite transformed since the end of the Second World War. The workload of the Security Council was so heavy, and the composition established by the UN Charter more than fifty years before so obviously unrepresentative, that the creation of groups in some cases brought welcome expertise and flexibility.[96] In other instances groups maintained, or were kept at, a greater distance from the decision-making process, while nevertheless providing a forum for engaging interested states from the region and elsewhere.

From inside the Council, it was generally acknowledged that the groups most closely engaged in its activities had a lot to offer. Their marrying of substantive and procedural benefits by the introduction of well-grounded drafts of resolutions and other texts undoubtedly facilitated its work. But the increasing prominence of Friends was not universally welcomed, as grumbling regarding the tight control maintained by the Friends of Georgia, Western Sahara, and other cases illustrated. This reflected the extent to which the rise in relevance of the Security Council to global peace and security was accompanied by ongoing resistance to the domination of the Council by the P-5 (four of which were represented on the Friends of both Georgia and Western Sahara), exacerbated by the tendency for most of the Council's decisions to be taken privately in "informal consultations." Pressure for greater transparency resulted in a higher proportion of meetings being held in public, but the extent to which this affected the backroom nature of decision making was doubtful. "Everyone knows that the more you make public the more the real decision making will get moved elsewhere," was the comment of a representative of one Western state who served on the Council in 2001–02. "[I]t is not always even in 'informals' anymore. Somebody has to make the decisions and in many cases it's the Friends."[97]

Those who criticized the work of the groups were generally elected members of the Council, such as Bangladesh, Colombia, Ireland, Jamaica, New Zealand, and Singapore, concerned with the usurpation of their authority as Council members by elite ownership of specific issues.[98] They objected that the groups were opaque, included few developing countries, and perpetuated the sense of "us" and "them" already present in the Council's two-tiered structure. In early 1999 frustration with the control exercised over a number of the processes under the Council's authority—in particular, the tight hold on Cyprus maintained by the P-5, the monopolization of Georgia by its Friends, and the behavior of the Contact Group on the former Yugoslavia, which at the time was considered by many to be in the first instance an effective tool to prevent Security Council engagement—led to the issuance of a Note by the President of the Council (Canada) on February 17, 1999. The note pointed out that "contributions by members of groups of friends and other similar arrangements" are welcome, but emphasized that "the drafting of resolutions and statements by the President of the Council should be carried out in a manner that will allow adequate participation of all members of the Council" (S/1999/165).

The groups that were active outside the Council—a number of which are discussed in chapter 8—could be divided into two broad categories: the ad hoc mechanisms created or encouraged by officials involved in peacemaking outside Africa, largely as a result of the diplomatic predilections of the individuals involved, and the multiple groups formed to address conflicts in Africa. The first category of groups included low-key and informal structures on Myanmar and Afghanistan, Colombia and Cyprus, directly informed by the secretariat's experience with earlier groups in Central America, Haiti, and elsewhere as well as by the complexities presented by situations of deep intractability with which they were now faced. The second category, in contrast, reflected an emerging approach to African peace and security broadly shared in the international community as its representatives struggled to find in their interventions an appropriate balance between African ownership and international partnership. In this context, Annan offered his public encouragement—most notably in a recommendation endorsed by the Africa Action Plan adopted in July 2002 by the G-8 —of the creation of groups to marry the influence and resources of international actors to the legitimacy and expertise available in the continent.[99]

The use of groups in Africa was not itself a new idea. They had, after all, been engaged in peacemaking within the UN orbit since the Contact Group on Namibia was formed in the 1970s. A strong troika of interested states—Portugal, Russia, and the United States—led efforts to negotiate an end to conflict in Angola in 1991 and had its role in the process formally established in the Lusaka Protocol of 1994. Meanwhile, Aldo Ajello had successfully used his more informal Core Group to support peace implementation in Mozambique. In Burundi in the mid-1990s, the secretary-general's representative, Ahmedou Ould-Abdallah, had tried a short-lived experiment with a group of NGOs as his Friends.[100] However, from the late 1990s on, initiatives variously taken by the secretariat and, more often, member states, had led to groups' appearance in Angola, the Central African Republic, Guinea-Bissau, and Ethiopia-Eritrea. In most cases they prioritized the involvement of African states.

These groups, like those that would follow them—the International Contact Group on Liberia cochaired by the European Union and

ECOWAS, the informal Troika that emerged to support the regionally led negotiations on southern Sudan, the Core Group supporting efforts to bring peace to Northern Uganda, the International Working Group and smaller Mediation Group created by the African Union for Côte d'Ivoire in late 2005, or the new International Contact Group on Guinea-Bissau created in 2006 —differed in many respects from Friends groups elsewhere. One, the Friends of UNMEE (the UN Mission in Ethiopia and Eritrea), espoused formal "friendship" of a peacekeeping operation. This reflected not only the objections of Ethiopia and Eritrea to a group more tightly aligned to the political process, but also the priorities of the Netherlands, which established the Friends to safeguard its own interests in an operation to which it was contributing troops.[101] Others, such as the groups on Guinea-Bissau, had a broader interest in promoting international support for peacebuilding and development,[102] whether working from New York or more specifically anchored in the field, as was the case of the Commission to Accompany the Transition in the DRC (CIAT) or the Burundi Partners Forum proposed by the secretary-general in September 2005.[103] The groups were rarely directly responsible for drafting Security Council resolutions. Instead, their relationship to the efforts of the secretary-general and his representatives reflected the diffuse and fluid nature of the United Nations' own role in Africa and the interplay of interests among members of the Security Council and African actors.

This profusion of groups had led states that were included as Friends of one process or another, and those that were not, to begin to consider their use with more attention. Within the Security Council, the subject of groups was taken up by an Ad Hoc Working Group on Conflict Prevention and Resolution in Africa that had been formed in February 2002 under the leadership of Mauritius. The working group held several discussions on establishing groups of Friends and even arrived at a set of recommendations on their composition and attributions.[104] These recommendations were that (1) the groups could provide a useful and informal framework for in-depth discussion of issues of which the Security Council was seized; (2) groups would work best if "relatively small (about twelve to fifteen members), but would remain open to all members" and include neighboring states as appropriate; (3) it would be desirable if groups had a lead nation; and (4) they should have "clarity of objectives," and would work best if they focused on implementing agreements by the parties to a conflict.[105] As a first attempt by the Security Council to codify the composition and practice of the mechanism, the recommendations outlined a model that prioritized the interests of African states to combine into groups, rather than echoed the preference of the big powers for smaller, more flexible mechanisms. Perhaps for this reason they were widely ignored. However, the existence of the recommendations reflected an emerging consensus that groups represented a positive framework for the international community to approach the challenge of Africa's conflicts.

Conclusions

During the extraordinary period of change that dates from the waning years of the Cold War, the United Nations acquired a new relevance and legitimacy in conflict resolution. In the process it learned how difficult making and sustaining peace might be. The optimism of 1992, founded not only on the transformations across Eastern Europe but also on the part played by the United Nations in helping the old Cold War adversaries extricate themselves from conflicts elsewhere, was dashed by the reversals that followed in Somalia, Rwanda, and the Balkans. Although demand for UN involvement in conflicts across the world accelerated from the late 1990s on, the tasks with which it was faced did not grow easier. Different kinds of conflicts—predominantly internal—brought new challenges. Tools developed to respond to the more limited and predictable circumstances of the United Nations' Cold War operations proved inadequate to the new demands. Meanwhile, although the many actors involved brought both resources and energy to their efforts, their management was a significant challenge in itself.

Friends of the Secretary-General, as first conceived in El Salvador, bore a direct relation to the more cooperative environment for peacemaking that developed at the end of the Cold War. However, this group could be clearly distinguished from the efforts in Namibia and Cambodia that had preceded it for the specific support it gave to the secretary-general and his representatives in negotiating an end to an internal conflict—a first for the United Nations—and the welcome counterweight it represented to politics of the Security Council still dominated by the legacies of the Cold War. But the conceptual clarity that had been a hallmark of the Salvadoran process was difficult to maintain. The rapidly expanding field of conflict resolution of the 1990s soon overwhelmed the somewhat rarefied environment in which the United Nations had sought to conduct its diplomacy in earlier years, and improvisation came to characterize much of the United Nations' involvement.

Friends and the related mechanisms that succeeded them were no exception. They were created to address a range of conflicts with diverse possibilities to engage external actors successfully. Despite a somewhat un-even history, they would continue to represent an attractive means by which to try to bring interested states to the peace table, and by the mid-2000s, groups of some kind were an accepted if little-analyzed feature of conflict management.

2

The First Friends
Friends of the Secretary-General for El Salvador

For the United Nations, the hegemony exercised by the United States over a region considered "the most important place in the world for the United States today"[1] ensured that the conflicts in Central America were firmly off limits. For much of the 1980s, the secretary-general stayed quietly in the shadows while regional states pursued democratization and dialogue to bring the conflicts to an end. However, when Javier Pérez de Cuéllar, the first Latin American secretary-general, engaged directly, he was able to have a remarkable effect. During the 1990s the United Nations attained some notable and groundbreaking achievements. These included monitoring elections in Nicaragua, mediating internal conflicts in both El Salvador and Guatemala, and fielding complex field operations to verify far-reaching peace agreements signed in January 1992 and December 1996. The outcomes of these efforts were broadly successful in attaining self-sustaining peace in both countries. This is the case despite the fact that the peace remains flawed by the daily reality of poverty, insecurity, and inequity, and—perhaps inevitably and most obviously in Guatemala—less than the promise held out by the peace agreements.[2]

El Salvador was the first instance in which a group of Friends of the Secretary-General was used, and it is still among the most successful. This chapter argues that this was the case for a number of reasons. The conflict in El Salvador was devastating to its victims and to the development of an overpopulated country the size of Massachusetts. But in hindsight its resolution appears relatively straightforward, particularly when compared with other conflicts the United Nations addressed in later years. The conflict had pitted strong and politically able guerrillas, thinking strategically about external actors, against a state whose legitimacy was undermined by a history of human rights abuses and weak and abusive institutions. Forces of these two, largely cohesive, actors fought themselves to a stalemate from which negotiation of core grievances provided a way out. Moreover, solution

of the conflict was facilitated both by the broader international environment of the end of the Cold War and by favorable regional conditions.
The Friends were united in their support of a negotiated settlement and
were well orchestrated by strong leadership from the United Nations to
support the secretary-general and help out in the Security Council when
necessary. Although not directly affiliated with the donor process, the
Friends remained involved in both San Salvador and New York during implementation of the agreements. In doing so, they represented the ongoing
engagement of the international community.

The Conflict in El Salvador

During the 1980s, Central America was convulsed by the victory of the
Sandinista Front for National Liberation over the Somoza dynasty in
Nicaragua in 1979, the outbreak of an armed conflict that would rage for
more than a decade in neighboring El Salvador, and the persistence of a
dark, dirty war in Guatemala. The countries shared a common history and
geographic proximity. The conflicts within them arose from a potent mix
of social and economic inequalities and authoritarianism, exclusion, and
repression. Revolutionary movements contesting these conditions were, in
turn, fired by the example of Cuba and the changes within the Catholic
Church. The conflicts were exacerbated by international factors, including the supply of arms and training to state and nonstate actors and the
provision of sanctuary to guerrillas in regional states, and cannot be understood in isolation of their regional dynamics. However, the relative weight
of internal, transnational, and external aspects in each was such that their
resolution required a favorable international environment and regional
framework, but also separate national processes.[3]

By the time the Sandinistas swept to power in Nicaragua in July 1979,
El Salvador was nearing the end of a tumultuous decade, characterized by
the closing of political space to any opposition to the military government.
Small political-military organizations formed in the early 1970s won support from popular movements made up of unionists, Christian leaders
mobilized by the teachings of liberation theology, university students, and
others.[4] The activities of individuals and organized bodies were repressed
through torture, assassination, and disappearance conducted by "death
squads" originating in the country's security forces; the ranks of the revolutionary organizations grew.

A final effort to prevent the country's descent into the abyss of war
came with a coup conducted by a group of progressive young officers in

October 1979. But the new government could not hold and, in the following year, the fabric of the country crumbled. That year, 1980, saw more than 10,000 people assassinated. The victims included Archbishop Oscar Romero, the leaders of the social-democratic Democratic Revolutionary Front (FDR),[5] the president of the National University, and, in December, four U.S. churchwomen, who were pulled from a minibus near the airport by members of the National Guard, raped, and left in a shallow grave. The FDR allied itself with rebels now gathered in the broadly Marxist Farabundo Martí Liberation Front (FMLN) soon afterwards. Open armed conflict began in January 1981, with a misnamed "final offensive."[6]

Between January 1981 and January 1992, when the peace agreements that brought El Salvador's civil war to an end were signed, an estimated 75,000 Salvadorans were killed and well more than a million more internally displaced or driven to leave the country as refugees. Buffeted by the consequences of natural disasters, including droughts and a major earthquake, El Salvador's economy was plunged into crisis, but then began a process of structural adjustment that would have far-reaching consequences for the post-conflict period.[7] An army that had begun the war with some 10,000 men in its ranks was expanded and transformed by more than $1.1 billion in U.S. military assistance to a more professional fighting force of 60,000. Meanwhile, the somewhat ragtag collection of revolutionary combatants of the early 1980s underwent a no less profound transformation into a disciplined guerrilla army. At war's end, 12,300 combatants were demobilized under the terms of the UN-brokered agreements.[8] That this relatively small number was able to force the country's elites to accept the significant institutional reforms the agreements contained was due not only to its ability to impose a military stalemate on the battlefield but also to its support from what Elisabeth Jean Wood has termed "political mobilization from below."[9] While the guerrilla struggle was sustained by military assistance from Cuba, Nicaragua, and, to a lesser extent, countries of the Soviet bloc, essential financial support also came from an extensive international solidarity movement.

The Regional Context:
From Contadora to Esquipulas

The Cold War left little room for multilateral initiatives to seek peace in Central America. The Organization of American States (OAS), dominated since its creation in 1949 by the United States, was viewed as partisan by the Sandinista government in Nicaragua, and for this reason, played an insignificant role in the region through much of the 1980s.[10] The United Nations, for its part, was hindered by multiple factors: stasis in the Security Council, compounded by U.S. policy interests in the region, as well as the suspicion of the U.S. allies (El Salvador, Guatemala, and Honduras) about the implications for their sovereignty of any involvement by a body of which the Soviet Union was a permanent member.

Into this void stepped the ad hoc mechanism of Contadora, born out of a meeting of the foreign ministers of Colombia, Mexico, Panama, and Venezuela on Panama's Contadora Island in 1983. The meeting had been initiated by Mexico to discuss the threats to the region's peace and security posed by the conflicts in Central America and particularly their tendency to spill over into neighboring countries, complicating relations between them. It concluded in a declaration that appealed to the countries of Central America to engage in dialogue and negotiation, marking a fundamental difference with the positions assumed by the United States. The four countries also indicated that they considered the region's conflicts to be caused by its socioeconomic injustices and not by the ideological differences of the Cold War.[11]

From 1983 to 1987 the Contadora group put forward a series of proposals that reemphasized the value of dialogue and negotiation and called for demilitarization and a reduction of foreign interference. For the countries involved, the process represented an unprecedented investment in political and institutional resources and a public commitment to the future of Central America. After 1995 this regional effort was extended outward by the creation of a Support Group composed of Argentina, Brazil, Peru, and Uruguay. However, the pertinence of Contadora's proposals for achieving concrete progress was limited by the purely intergovernmental approach they represented and a failure to acknowledge that a solution to the conflicts would have to involve the insurgent forces. Moreover, the group's initiatives were consistently thwarted by the United States, whose own policy toward Central America in this period opposed negotiations on the basis of an unswerving determination to remove the Sandinistas from power in Nicaragua.

A formal Contadora Act was finally signed in 1996, but by this time the group's efforts were flagging. A peacemaking role for the United Nations in Central America appeared still out of the question, but Alvaro de Soto, then executive assistant to Secretary-General Pérez de Cuéllar, devised what he would later term "a scheme for the United Nations to insinuate itself into a diplomatic role."[12] This built on the minimal part afforded the secretary-general since 1983 as the "conveyer" of Contadora's reports to the Security Council,[13] as well as the political opening created by the breaking of the Iran-Contra scandal in late 1996, which constituted a serious blow to the credibility of the United States in the region. The idea, which de Soto developed in partnership with his deputy Francesc Vendrell, was to have the secretary-general break the deadlock on both UN and OAS action by initiating a joint démarche.[14] Accordingly, in November 1986 Pérez de Cúellar invited João Baena Soares, his counterpart at the OAS, to New York. The two summoned the ambassadors of the Central American countries and then those of the Contadora and Support Group countries in order to present them with a "menu" outlining the services—including good offices—that the organizations could, jointly or separately, provide.

This initiative was followed by invitations to the two secretaries-general to join the Contadora and Support Group countries in a tour of the region in early 1997. In August they attended the summit at which the Esquipulas agreement establishing "Procedures for the Establishment for the Firm and Lasting Peace in Central America" was signed. The agreement, which was reached as a result of an initiative by Oscar Arias, the president of Costa Rica, passed the baton to the Central American presidents. They undertook to initiate processes of democratization and national dialogue in their countries, to bring about cease-fires, and to promote free and fair elections. It also assigned both the United Nations and the OAS a role in international verification of its undertakings. However, an emphasis on the cessation of hostilities within the existing legal and constitutional frameworks ensured its rejection by rebel movements. Meanwhile, its failure to address the question of external assistance to the contending parties in the region's conflicts—at this stage a central feature within its complex political landscape—limited the extent to which it represented a realistic basis for regional peace.

The verification mechanism proposed proved too unwieldy to be effective,[15] but in February 1989 the five Central American presidents asked the United Nations to fulfill a more direct verification role. This would materialize at the end of the year, when the Security Council authorized the UN Observer Group in Central America (ONUCA) to verify compliance by the Central American governments with the security aspects of the Esquipulas agreement.[16] Before then, Resolution 637 of July 27 had given the Council's full endorsement of the secretary-general's good offices in support of efforts to achieve the goals of Esquipulas—the entry to peacemaking for which secretary-general had been waiting.

Ripe for Resolution

Events within El Salvador had been moving precipitately. In March 1989, Alfredo Cristiani, a conservative businessman, won presidential elections at the head of the Nationalist Republican Alliance (ARENA). This was a party that had its origins in the death squads, but had since taken pragmatic strides toward modernization in the service of the economic elites it represented. At his inauguration in June, Cristiani called for "dialogue" with the FMLN, initiating a process that would see two meetings between government and FMLN representatives, in September and October, facilitated by the Salvadoran Catholic Church. The latter meeting was attended by representatives of the United Nations and the OAS as observers.[17]

The meetings in the fall of 1989 achieved little, but reflected profound changes within El Salvador and beyond its borders. With the electoral triumph of ARENA and the failure of the Salvadoran state to defeat the FMLN, the country had, for the first time, the real centers of its power lined up in opposition to each other—something that was not the case during the years of Christian Democratic rule between 1994 and 1989. The end of the Reagan era and the rise of *perestroika* were, on the international scene, evident in the cooperation between the superpowers on arms treaties and in East Asia, and in the withdrawal of Soviet troops from Afghanistan and Cuban forces from Angola. Within El Salvador they were having an effect too, most notably in the evolution of thinking within the FMLN. A long period of internal reflection in which the FMLN had been encouraged by its international supporters to move toward a political solution had culminated in a twin-pronged strategy that pursued political initiatives while undertaking military preparations for the largest offensive of the war.[18]

This offensive was launched on November 11, 1989, and was to prove a turning point. The FMLN overran San Salvador, demonstrating a military strength that took both the Salvadoran government and the United States by surprise. Reprisals ranged from the bombing of zones of the city occupied by the guerrillas to the cold-blooded murder of six Jesuit priests by the Salvadoran military on the misguided basis that they represented the "intellectual leaders" of the revolution. When the dust settled, it was clear that the popular insurrection that some members of the FMLN had hoped to trigger had failed to materialize and that no clear military victory could be expected by either side. Meanwhile, international condemnation of both the guerrilla offensive and the murder of the Jesuit priests increased pressure for a political solution. In a classic example of the "mutually hurting stalemate" that William Zartman has argued is indicative of a "ripe moment" for the resolution of a conflict, the two sides turned to the United Nations.[19]

The Origins of the Friends of the Secretary-General

As they did so, a key consideration was what might be the role of other states strategically engaged in the conflict or otherwise involved in efforts to pursue peace. The issue was discussed at length during a discreet meeting held between de Soto and representatives of the FMLN in Montreal on December 8, 1989.

Over the years, the FMLN had placed a great deal of emphasis on what Joaquín Villalobos, one of its most prominent leaders, would later describe as the "moral advantage in the use of force."[20] While its own performance was by no means perfect in this area, this involved attention to respect for human rights and humanitarian law in the conduct of the war with an eye to the legitimacy it could gain among the Salvadoran population and in terms of international support. At the official level, the joint FMLN-FDR Political-Diplomatic Commission, which was based in Mexico but well represented across the United States and in Europe, as well as within the Soviet bloc, played a critical role. The high caliber and diligence of some of the commission's international representatives ensured that they were frequent visitors to foreign ministries of countries sympathetic to the plight of the Salvadoran population and in broad opposition to U.S. policy in Central America.

Diplomatic contacts and attention to the machinery of the United Nations had helped secure the FMLN recognition in the United Nations as a "representative political force," as established in the Franco-Mexican Declaration agreed to in 1981.[21] But the FMLN remained wary of the secretary-general's capacity to act independently of the Security Council, which it perceived to be increasingly dominated by the United States. This caution had been exacerbated both by the FMLN's disagreement with "the entire Central American peace process," including the recently established ONUCA, and by actions of the United Nations elsewhere.[22] Particularly disturbing had been events in Namibia where, in April 1989, the secretary-general had taken the difficult decision—mistakenly attributed by the FMLN to pressure from the United States—to unleash the South African Defense Forces (SADF) from their bases in Namibia to counter South West Africa People's Organization (SWAPO) incursions committed in violation of the peace settlement.[23]

More pressing than these concerns, however, were the consequences for the FMLN of shifting international relations at the end of the Cold War. The foreign policy of the Soviet Union now not only supported a political settlement in Central America, but did so as a function of bilateral relations with the United States. Soviet funding of the FMLN had been drastically reduced in recent years and none was expected for 1990.[24] Sticky relations with the Soviets had not been improved by an episode that occurred in early October 1989. Schafik Handal, the leader of the Salvadoran Communist Party and a senior figure in the FMLN's general command, had been incensed to find that letters he had written to Mikhail Gorbachev, critical of those addressed by Gorbachev to communist parties across the world on the subject of *perestroika*, were being shared with the United States. Accordingly, when Foreign Minister Eduard Shevardnadze visited Managua in October 1989 and asked to see the General Command, the FMLN said no. The request was repeated, but the FMLN said no again. Relations between the two did not recover, and the FMLN would subsequently inform de Soto that efforts to exert leverage over them through the Soviets would not prosper.[25]

In Montreal, de Soto probed the representatives of the FMLN regarding their readiness to negotiate, including by asking whether, after the November offensive and against the backdrop of the changes in the Soviet bloc, they were in a position to do so from strength. The FMLN's representatives assured him that this was the case and raised the question of the involvement of states that might provide them with a counterbalance to the Security Council. Their idea was to create two concentric circles of states with differing levels of engagement in the conflict. In the first circle—the "support group"—should be countries knowledgeable and concerned about the Salvadoran conflict, but with no strategic interest in its outcome. An outer circle of the United States, the Soviet Union, and Cuba would form a different group of "guarantor states."[26]

De Soto saw that the FMLN wanted to ensure the impartiality of the secretary-general, but was uncomfortable with instituting a formal system of tiered groups. In 1996, he recalled his reaction to their suggestion:

> It occurred to me that the secretary-general might borrow on a device that is frequently used in inter-governmental bodies, which is the notion of "friends of the chairman" or "friends of the president." Very frequently, you have a stand-off, a deadlock on some issue in, say, the General Assembly or a committee of the General Assembly, where it is clear that

you need to miniaturize the negotiating forum in order to achieve results. . . . So one practice that has developed over the years is that sometimes the president, or the chairman of the committee, will simply gather a group of friends. It is noncommittal on anybody. But he will choose them properly so that he will have inside the room, rather than outside, all those who he feels need to be a party to any deal that must be struck. He retains a certain degree of deniability to the extent that he can always say, "I was just meeting with a group of friends," hence, the expression "a group of friends."[27]

After ascertaining the seriousness of the FMLN, de Soto called New York to give the go-ahead for identical letters, already signed by the secretary-general, to be dispatched to the five Central American presidents, who were due to meet on December 11 and 12 in Costa Rica. The letter offered the assistance of the secretary-general in bringing guerrilla groups into efforts to solve the region's conflicts and in securing the commitment to this process of interested powers outside the region. Its central points were reflected in the statement adopted by the presidents at the end of their summit meeting. The statement asked the secretary-general to take steps to ensure the resumption of dialogue between the government and FMLN and also to establish "the necessary connections to involve states with interests in the region more directly in the peace effort."[28]

The secretariat followed up on this request with alacrity and on December 14 presented a "nonpaper"—an accepted diplomatic device by which an unofficial proposal is presented to counterparts, on paper but anonymously—to Cuba, Russia, and the United States, soliciting views on the possible form that a mechanism to involve them should take. While the nonpaper stressed that the "secretary-general does not have a pre-conceived scheme over how this should be designed," it also suggested several possible models—all of them quite distinct from that of the regional framework in Central America—that could be drawn upon: "the [United Nations Emergency Force] UNEF I Advisory Committee, the Jakarta Informal Meetings on Cambodia, and the Quadripartite talks on Angola." In the end, and largely as a result of positions held by the United States—which preferred to handle relations with the USSR bilaterally and was reluctant to enter into a relationship of this nature with Cuba while the latter had neither committed itself to the Esquipulas process or ceased its assistance to the FMLN—efforts to formalize a mechanism were put aside.[29]

During the early months of 1990, de Soto downplayed discussion of any kind of group. He had a clear sense of the states he would draw on for the secretary-general's "friends" and initiated separate contacts with the ambassadors in New York of Colombia, Mexico, Spain, and Venezuela. However, he was from the beginning wary of the consequences for the United Nations' lead of a still fragile process of a group that might develop an identity of its own, and somewhat haunted by recollection of the diplomatic travails of Contadora.[30] As a result, the terms of the Geneva agreement of April 1990—which committed the parties to the fourfold goal of termination of the armed conflict, democratization, guarantee of human rights, and national reconciliation—also included the open formulation that the secretary-general "may maintain confidential contacts with governments, states, members of the United Nations or groups of such governments which may contribute to the success of the process through their advice and support."[31]

The agreement represented a significant step forward by the Salvadoran government. President Cristiani had been wary of the involvement of the United Nations. However, the FMLN offensive and the pressure on him at the meeting of the Central American presidents in December 1989 had left him little choice. Cristiani himself had traveled to New York in January 1990 to ask the secretary-general for help in bringing the parties together, but his view of the UN role fell far short of the active mediation being sought by the FMLN. His concern was rooted in the implications for Salvadoran sovereignty for what was, in 1990, an unprecedented role for the United Nations in an internal conflict. Above all, it was difficult to accept the idea of the United Nations' impartiality between "parties" at the negotiating table when one party was a member state of the United Nations and the other, in the eyes of the government, an illegal insurgent force.

Cristiani recalled in an interview that he had seen two out of the four Friends (Spain and Venezuela) as part of the "political support of the FMLN," and a third, Mexico, simply as "where they lived—their home." But he had gradually come to accept that it was important for the secretary-general to have Friends in a position to exert influence over the FMLN.[32] Over time, however, the Friends came to serve a purpose for the government too. This was described by David Escobar Galindo, a government negotiator and confidant of Cristiani, as that of a kind of "cushion" that created a greater level of confidence in the process than if "we had been left alone with *them*—the United Nations."[33] That the Friends were themselves governments, with actively involved heads of state who were personally supportive of Cristiani, brought with it certain guarantees. The bottom line, as Cristiani put it, was that "no government was going to recommend to another government that it accept something that it would not itself accept."

The Friends: How They Got in the Picture

De Soto would describe the Salvadoran negotiations as taking place "almost in laboratory conditions."[34] The formulation reflected the fortunate confluence of internal and external factors that brought two strong and unified parties—the government and the FMLN—to the table, with their readiness to negotiate reinforced by the positions of the great powers behind them. The Salvadoran military, which had the most to lose from negotiations in which emphasis was placed on the constitutional revision of Salvadoran national security as well as public security structures, represented a potential spoiler. But it was kept under constant pressure by the credible threats of cuts in military assistance emanating from a U.S. Congress energized by the ongoing investigation into the military's role in the Jesuit murders and its cover-up.[35]

The role of the UN secretary-general evolved naturally from that of good offices to mediator, and in that capacity de Soto shuttled between the parties, prepared texts for their consideration, and maintained a constant dialogue with actors outside the negotiations themselves, all broadly supportive of a negotiated solution to the conflict. These outside actors included a range of Salvadorans from political parties, the business sector, the Church and other areas of civil society; representatives of the United States, Cuba, and, to a lesser extent, the USSR; the emerging group of Friends; and others, such as the Nordic countries and particularly Sweden, in a position to provide material or other support of the United Nations' efforts.[36] As a compatriot and protégé of the secretary-general—de Soto had joined the United Nations from the Peruvian diplomatic service to work with Pérez de Cuéllar—de Soto also enjoyed a privileged relationship with the secretary-general, who followed the process closely and was available to it when his personal authority was required.

In retrospect, the "laboratory conditions" can also be seen to have extended to the Friends. The choice of states derived from the history of engagement represented by the regional process, in the case of the three Latin Americans, and from Spain's ties to the continent and active support of regional efforts for peace since the early 1980s. But the four countries also brought with them other benefits that would come into play as the negotiations progressed and the role of the Friends evolved within them. These related both to the nature of the Friends' governments at the time (Venezuela and Spain both had left-leaning governments that were members of Socialist International and thus were able to communicate with the FMLN-FDR with comfort), and to the fact that they were relatively unchallenged internally, allowing for a freedom of action with respect to El Salvador that extended to the direct involvement of their presidents. Moreover, their cultural and linguistic homogeneity allowed a relationship of great trust to develop among the countries' four ambassadors in New York; at a certain point they agreed that in the absence of one member of this "four-engined vehicle," the other three could make decisions on its behalf.[37]

Mexico was a natural choice. Its proximity to Central America, regional standing, and development of a pragmatic and independent foreign policy had given it leadership in the Contadora process. However, this leadership had strained the delicate balance of relations with the United States and led to bruising battles with the Reagan administration. Its position was not helped by its coauthorship of the Franco-Mexican Declaration in 1981, the strong stance it had taken in the UN Human Rights Commission on abuses committed in El Salvador and Guatemala, and the fact that it had allowed both the FMLN-FDR and the guerrillas of the Guatemalan National Revolutionary Unity to run their political and diplomatic offices from Mexico City, while maintaining open and generally positive relations with both Cuba and the USSR throughout the period of the Cold War.

These connections reflected a degree of empathy with the positions espoused by the guerrillas and especially their Social Democrat partners in the FDR, but also a level of self-interest. There were national security risks inherent to Mexico's shared border with Guatemala, and the established relationship with both guerrilla movements allowed for closely monitored rules of the game to be enforced. (Mexican officials and guerrilla commanders alike believe these were largely, if not entirely, respected.[38]) These determined that the guerrillas' activities were limited to the political sphere and were to involve no military operations, arms trafficking, kidnapping, or other illegal activities. In sum, the presence of the guerrillas' representatives and their frequent contacts with officials from the foreign and interior ministries gave Mexican officials unequaled influence and leverage over them. This was something that President Carlos Salinas de Gortari did not hesitate to employ—even assuring Cristiani at one point that Mexico would, if so requested, close down the FMLN's offices in Mexico City.[39]

In late 1988, as Salinas assumed the presidency, Mexican officials had come to realize that the best chance of resolution of the conflicts lay with the United Nations. With George H.W. Bush in the White House and an English-speaking technocrat in the Mexican presidency, there was, moreover, an opportunity for Mexico to play a constructive role while also restoring relations with the United States. Jorge Montaño, who would become Salinas's ambassador to the United Nations, accompanied Salinas to a meeting with George H.W. Bush when both were presidents-elect. Salinas had presented a somewhat surprised Bush with the idea that the United Nations might take a leading role in Central America. As Montaño recalled: "Salinas saw that Central America was a thorn in the side of Bush, and therefore turned it into a priority. Central America suited both our internal and external agendas, which explains how active we were. We helped out, but we were also passing the bill to the United States, on NAFTA and other issues."[40]

Venezuela's engagement reflected not so much its foreign policy, but the commitment, energy, and wealth of contacts in the region of President Carlos Andrés Pérez. Pérez had begun his second presidency in 1989 and immediately sought to take up the engaged and populist style of diplomatic intervention that had characterized his earlier term, notably in his efforts to encourage Somoza to voluntarily leave power in Nicaragua.[41] His personal commitment to the Salvadoran process—evident in a somewhat hyperactive barrage of ideas and telephone calls to all parties at all hours of the day or night—was never in doubt, but required a considerable amount of steering by de Soto, who went to painstaking ends to try to keep his frequent interventions with all sides "on message."

The activist position taken by the Venezuelan president reflected an unspoken rivalry with Mexico for influence over the secretariat in the process. Montaño described this as "healthy for the process—but perhaps not for de Soto, who had Diego [Arria, the Venezuelan ambassador in New York] and me repeatedly pulling him by the sleeve in different directions" —but it was something of which the FMLN, in particular, became increasingly suspect. They were critical of Pérez's desire for personal protagonism—something they did not see reflected in President Salinas's interventions—and came to distrust some of Venezuela's positions. Although they were grateful for Pérez's availability and generosity toward them, they were perturbed by what one FMLN negotiator described as "indecent flirtations with the United States," and generally considered him and his behavior as "altogether too Caribbean."[42]

The role played by Spain, represented by Ambassador Juan Antonio Yañéz-Barnuevo but with Prime Minister Felipe González behind him, was, in contrast, exemplary in its professionalism and somewhat aloof from the undercurrents evident in the relationship between Mexico and Venezuela.[43] Although González had debts to Socialist International (of which both he and Carlos Andrés Pérez had been vice president), and perceived the differences between Pérez and Salinas very clearly, Spain's own contribution remained untainted by them. Rather, engagement in the Central American effort proved an effective channel through which to realize a number of benefits: the reestablishment of ties between Spain and Latin America in ways that reflected not the colonial links of the past but the potential utility of Spain as a bridge to the European Union (EU); an enhanced standing within the EU as a result of Spain's demonstrated importance to Latin America; and domestic support for a policy that was clearly distinct from that of the United States (important for Spain's left), yet publicly recognized as contributing to peacemaking.[44] This engagement took many forms: it had already been evident in the contribution of troops and resources to ONUCA; Spanish personnel would hold key positions in the United Nations' Observer Mission in El Salvador (ONUSAL), established in July 1991; and Spain would play a leading role in the reform of the public security sector in the years ahead.

Although never less than supportive of the process (indeed, as a member of the Security Council in 1989, Colombia had been a cosponsor of Resolution 637), and a full participant within the Friends through its ambassador in New York, Fernando Cepeda, Colombia carried less weight than the other Friends, in part because of preoccupation with its own internal conflict. Indeed, Cepeda recalled that he had acted almost entirely without instructions or communication with Bogotá regarding the role he played as a Friend, and had at times felt uncomfortable to be influencing a process about which he knew little.[45] An exception to the distance from the process maintained by his foreign ministry was an explicit instruction not to support the approval of FMLN reintegration with the army—a position showing the extent to which Colombia viewed the negotiations from the perspective of its own conflict. Meanwhile, as agreements were reached on an unprecedented role for the United Nations in the verification of human rights, sweeping changes in El Salvador's constitution to allow for the restructuring of the armed forces, a new national civil police force (on which former members of the FMLN would have the right to serve), and the establishment of both a truth commission to look into past abuses and an ad hoc commission to purge the military, Colombia became a little uneasy. Indeed, the first lesson that Cepeda recalled extracting from his experience on El Salvador was "let's hope this never happens in Colombia." A second lesson was that a country engaged in a conflict of its own, such as Colombia, whose primary interest was "not to become involved in negotiations that might cause problems in Colombia," should not be a member of a group of Friends.

An "Authoritarian Conductor":
Relations with the United Nations

Salvador Samayoa, who had been at the meeting with de Soto in Montreal and became one of the FMLN's lead negotiators, would remember the group of Friends as "a phantasmagorical work of art of de Soto's—it existed, but didn't exist, like a nonpaper."[46] Indeed de Soto's conception and management of the group—which he would later liken to "a quintet with a very authoritarian conductor"[47]—is difficult to quantify. In a deliberate attempt to cultivate individual relations, he invested many hours in separate meetings with the four ambassadors in New York, only beginning to meet with them as a group on a regular basis from April 1991 on. In their individual meetings they generally preferred to see him unattended, and often abstained from taking notes, encouraging the aura of confidentiality that surrounded the conversations. These meetings were supplemented for de Soto by contacts with Friends' ambassadors in El Salvador, foreign ministries, presidential staffs, and embassies as the occasion required. In all of them, the ground rules were clear: the Friends were not engaged in the negotiations, but would be informed, on a somewhat discretionary basis, of their progress; they were there to support the secretary-general's efforts and would undertake specific tasks at his or his representative's request.

The Friends were not, of course, oblivious to what was going on, and soon developed the habit of comparing impressions among themselves. These were not all complimentary, as de Soto's personality and presentation contain elements of haughtiness derived as much from his aura of intellectual superiority as from characteristics that other Latin Americans attributed to his being a scion of the Peruvian elite. But more substantively, and to the point of the Salvadoran process, the four ambassadors came to admire his "enormous discretion" in his handling of them, even as they felt at times that what he was doing to them was precisely that. "He was immensely disciplined," Montaño recalled. "It was clear that he said exactly what he wanted to each of us and nothing more. At times we were left comparing notes afterwards—why did he say that to you and not to me?"

The Friends themselves would date their involvement in the Salvadoran process as a group to October 1990, following explicit requests for assistance from the secretary-general in meetings with the presidents of Spain and Mexico and Venezuela (the latter together).[48] At this point the negotiations had slowed, most fundamentally over FMLN demands for the dissolution of the Salvadoran army, and the secretariat was under pressure from the United States to assume a more assertive stance than either de Soto or the secretary-general believed appropriate for an impartial intermediary. The FMLN was already in regular contact with members of the Friends, but the Salvadoran government remained reluctant to accept the formation of a recognizable "group." However, in his meetings with the presidents, Pérez de Cuéllar asked for their help in several areas. He urged them to try to persuade President Cristiani to form a multiparty delegation for negotiations with the FMLN and to encourage the United States to establish direct contacts both with the FMLN itself and with Cuba. The negotiations were to some degree unblocked by the parties' acceptance of a more active role for de Soto as a mediator, but their development was complicated by the FMLN's launching of a new offensive in November. This prompted the secretary-general to meet for the first time with the ambassadors of the four Friends in New York; he appealed for their help in influencing the FMLN to bring the offensive to an end.[49]

Unwilling to second-guess the secretary-general, the Friends were disposed to offer assistance of all kinds. Over time this came to include providing practical support through the hosting by Mexico and Venezuela of numerous rounds of negotiations; facilitating the travel of FMLN field commanders by Friends ambassadors in El Salvador to talks outside the country; providing airplanes to bring Cristiani to New York; and providing additional funds to the FMLN to ensure that they could pay their hotel bills once they got there. As the process advanced, it also extended to substantive diplomatic support of the UN effort through pressure on the parties, first evident during the tense weeks of the negotiations on constitutional reform in Mexico City in April 1991. Later, the ambassadors in San Salvador developed a close working relationship with Iqbal Riza, an experienced official from Pakistan who arrived from Nicaragua to head ONUSAL in July 1991, while negotiations were still ongoing. The presence of ONUSAL helped build confidence that the visible engagement of the international community would translate into guarantees that agreements reached through negotiation would be implemented.

Minor differences of opinion within the Friends and between the Friends and de Soto regarding the course taken by the negotiations were an inevitable—and probably healthy—part of the fabric of a complex process. But there was only one occasion when the disciplined support of the secretary-general's lead in the negotiations broke down.[50] This constituted an attempt by Carlos Andrés Pérez to persuade the two parties to sign an agreement—the "Miraflores declaration," presented as a "proposal of the Friends of the good officer"—behind the back of the United Nations.

This occurred on July 7, 1991, at a moment at which the negotiations had run aground as they entered substantive discussion of the future of the armed forces. Pérez had summoned government and FMLN negotiators to Caracas, having given no clear indication to the latter as to what their visit entailed. Only over lunch did the FMLN discover that the government delegation was meeting with the president as they spoke, and that they would be expected to sign the document they had just been presented with that afternoon. Somewhat alarmed, they refused to meet with President Pérez and instead called Pedro Nikken, the Venezuelan jurist who was the principal drafter in de Soto's negotiating team, for assistance.[51]

The FMLN's rapid inquiries with Colombia and Mexico assured them that neither had been consulted; both reiterated their support of the UN-led process.[52] Declassified U.S. documents and Venezuelan sources suggest that Pérez's initiative was conducted at the request of President Cristiani and with the support of the United States for this effort to drive a wedge between the secretary-general and his Friends.[53] That Pérez responded to the distress of President Cristiani, rather than to the rules of the game established for a Friend of the Secretary-General, suggested a fundamental allegiance between governments that ran contrary to the delicate architecture of the process.

Perhaps fortuitously, the "hijacking" episode had taken place just ten days before the first Iberoamerican Summit was held in Guadalajara. The assembled heads of states allowed for an apparently chastened Pérez to be reined in and the identity of the Friends to be formalized and strengthened by a meeting of the four presidents with the secretary-general. Yañéz-Barnuevo recalled that the Friends "ganged up" at Guadalajara, with the presidents collectively pressing the secretary-general to become more directly involved.[54] A public statement issued at the meeting's end established the Friends as central actors in the process.

Plus One: The Role of the United States

During implementation of the Salvadoran agreements, the United States became appended to the original four Friends as "plus one." But the U.S. role in the peace process as a whole was far from that of an appendage: its efforts and resources would be essential to the successful conclusion of the negotiations and the viability of peace in El Salvador.

The United States had expressed its support of negotiations in El Salvador in the midst of the FMLN's 1989 offensive.[55] But its relationship with the secretariat was, until the latter stages of the process, patchy at best, with de Soto, in particular, a frequent target of its criticism. This had its origins in an insistence by the United States—contrary to agreements between the parties—on the a priori desirability of a cease-fire; an effort to push de Soto and then Marrack Goulding, who was responsible for negotiating cease-fire agreements, to impose deadlines they considered arbitrary and counterproductive; and a basic perception that de Soto was biased in favor of the FMLN and "less than energetic pursuing the peace process" and thus somehow complicit in its delaying tactics.[56]

Underlying these concerns were problems related to both the dynamics and structure of the negotiations. It was in the nature of negotiations between an established government and an insurgency that the insurgents put forward proposals and made demands of the government rooted in their analysis of what was wrong with the existing institutional arrangements. That UN officials, like many others in the international community, could agree with much of the denunciation (for example, regarding human rights) contained in the guerrillas' position (if not what they had done or proposed to do about it) contributed to a perception of bias. Moreover, neither the United States nor President Cristiani spoke to the FMLN, while de Soto did so all the time. As mediator, he was therefore in the position of conveying the guerrillas' positions and viewpoints to Cristiani and his interlocutors from the United States on a regular basis.[57]

In September 1990 these issues became entwined with a separate question: the relative authority of the Security Council and secretary-general in the process. At a moment when, as described above, the United States was pushing the secretariat hard to accelerate the process, it gave open support to an initiative of the Salvadoran government to alter the negotiation framework established in the Geneva agreement by preparing and then circulating a draft Security Council resolution urging a cease-fire.[58] The draft did not prosper, as Soviet and Cuban diplomats (the former president of the Security Council at the time) asked de Soto whether the resolution had the support of the secretary-general and would be helpful to his efforts. De Soto answered no to both questions, and there the initiative died, although not without criticism by the U.S. assistant secretary of state, Bernard Aronson, of the secretariat's "active intervention."[59] In this instance, however, the secretariat had no difficulty maintaining its position that leadership of the process needed to rest on the impartiality that only the secretary-general was in a position to offer.

A perceptible change in the U.S. position was first evident during the April 1991 negotiations on constitutional reform. Although doubts about de Soto continued—and indeed would be raised at a meeting between

President Bush and Pérez de Cuéllar in May[60]—the successful conclusion of these negotiations was to prove a turning point. U.S. efforts, culminating in pressure on the ARENA-dominated legislative assembly to reverse a decision to reject two of the provisions agreed to in the negotiations in Mexico, were essential. That they were echoed and reinforced by the Friends, including through the direct engagement of the Friends' presidents, was indicative of a symbiotic relationship that was to develop between the four Friends and the United States during the latter part of 1991.[61]

The basis for this relationship was simple: it was evident to all that the United States would remain the key external actor in the Salvadoran process, both with respect to the leverage that only it could bring to bear on the Salvadoran government and armed forces and as a guarantor of the implementation of the peace agreements (which the United Nations at this stage assumed would also be paid for by the United States, almost in their entirety). But the Friends had both access to and the confidence of the FMLN, some members of which they known for many years, as well as a distinct set of relationships with the UN secretary-general and his staff. Consequently, their function as "cushion" identified by Escobar Galindo (or "shock absorber" as Samayoa put it) grew into one almost as useful between the United States and the FMLN (and indeed the United States and the United Nations) as it was for the two parties to the negotiations and the United Nations itself.

Confidence in the process as a whole was enhanced by the Security Council's authorization of the deployment ONUSAL in July 1991 to verify the provisions of the human rights agreement agreed to the previous year. But the negotiations stalled soon afterward. It had become clear that the FMLN would not lay down its arms before reaching agreement on conditions and guarantees for its combatants' reintegration. A public push to the process, implicitly critical of de Soto and the United Nations, came in August when the United States joined with the Soviet Union in addressing a letter to the secretary-general urging him to take "personal leadership" of the process to move it forward and offering the "full cooperation" of the two powers with the Friends of the Secretary-General to this end.[62] Pérez de Cuéllar responded in a twofold manner. He assured the United States and the Soviet Union that he was indeed providing personal leadership to the process through his personal representative, and that he could only contemplate leading negotiations himself if the principals on both sides were at the table. He also made a play to overcome the impasse by inviting all the parties, including President Cristiani, to New York in September.[63]

The intensity of the negotiations required to break the deadlock lifted the engagement of both the Friends and the United States to a new level. During September, and again in December when New York negotiations resumed, the Friends became a ubiquitous part of the process. They met separately with the parties and members of the UN team and consistently pushed for the process to move forward, citing the end of Pérez de Cuéllar's term of office on December 31, 1991, and the possibility that his successor would have little interest in El Salvador, as a very real deadline. Although the Friends never participated directly in negotiations, they were at times engaged with their substance, their very informality increasing their utility as a go-between. Spain was particularly influential with respect to both the presence of former FMLN combatants in a new civilian police force (a formulation pushed by de Soto's Spanish police adviser) and the creation of an institutional mechanism to involve the FMLN in the agreements' implementation, an idea put forward by Felipe González himself.[64] Meanwhile, before the December round of negotiations, de Soto enlisted the help of the Friends in interceding with Cristiani directly, encouraging him to return to New York and advance his plans for a reduction of the armed forces and the appointment of a coordinator for the new police force.[65]

The efforts of the Friends were reinforced by the active role taken by Ambassador Thomas Pickering, a former U.S. ambassador to El Salvador and consummate diplomat in whom the Friends found "a ready ear,"[66] and other officials from the U.S. mission in New York. (A channel of communication also developed between Mexico's Jorge Montaño, who had assumed an informal leadership within the group, and Bernard Aronson, who was charged with overseeing the process from Washington.) Increasing harmony between the positions held by the United States and those of the Friends helped create the confidence that allowed Montaño to facilitate confidential meetings between the United States and the FMLN. At the first of these meetings—held in the Mexican mission in September without the presence of UN officials—the Friends were profoundly impressed by the courtesy with which Pickering addressed the assembled *comandantes*, as well as the substance of what he had to say: he could understand the reasons for which the FMLN had seen his country as the enemy in the past, but the task facing them today was the construction of El Salvador's future, and in this they would have the United States' full support.[67]

The final round of negotiations took place in New York at an extraordinary historic moment, brought home to the Friends when, during a meeting with Pérez de Cuéllar on Christmas Eve, the news arrived that the Soviet Union had officially ceased to exist. With separate "tables" of negotiations—one on the cease-fire issues, headed by Goulding, the other on the political issues, led by de Soto—running simultaneously, the Salvadoran delegations housed in offices on different floors of the secretariat, and the Friends and an increasingly high-level U.S. delegation circulating between them, the atmosphere was charged. Tensions were increased by fears among some of the Friends—chronicled by Diego Arria in his account of the process—that de Soto was pushing the government too hard and might forfeit an opportunity to reach an acceptable agreement to a desire to hold out for a better one.[68]

Differing accounts of these final days reveal differing interpretations of the tactics necessarily involved in a negotiation of this complexity rapidly approaching the wire. These came to a head on the evening of December 31. With the clock ticking down toward midnight, the Friends and the United States demanded to see the secretary-general. They met him with representatives of the two parties. The light was fading, and the secretary-general announced that he had decided to suspend the negotiations. His wife was waiting in the office next door; his bags were packed for the Bahamas. And there was a private airplane waiting for him on the runway. Montaño made an impassioned request for him to stay, but appeared not to sway him.[69] An hour and a half later, the "four plus one" went to the parties with a final appeal that had been stage-managed with the United Nations' connivance. Montaño threatened to call a press conference suspending the negotiations: "We'll say that the parties in conflict have decided that peace in El Salvador is not a priority, and we will spell out the very minimal differences that still remain between you"—and he read out a list prepared for him by de Soto. There was more than an element of theater in the whole performance, but it helped. And the Friends had earned their place in the photograph taken of the signing of the New York agreement later that night.

Implementation and the Friends

In the final months of the negotiations, the FMLN had placed great store in the potential they saw in the Friends as a mechanism that might assume a role of informal guarantor for implementation of the peace agreements, complementary to the oversight that would be provided by the Security Council.

The agreements themselves did not contemplate "security guarantees" in the classical sense but rather an interrelated set of actions to be carried out by internal actors and verified by the United Nations.[70] A phased demobilization foreseen in the military agreements negotiated by Gould-ing would give the FMLN some leverage in this period, but after that the support of the international community would be key. A separate set of concerns related to the individual security of commanders and others who would be reentering public life, in some cases for the first time in twenty years, in a political culture in which the practice of targeted assassination was all too commonplace. In the end the Friends undertook to provide personal security for individual commanders (the Mexican ambassador had three of the five members of the FMLN's general command stay in his house after their return to El Salvador; the ambassadors of Spain and Venezuela hosted the other two). They also committed themselves to sup-port the United Nations in verifying the agreements and to seek inter-national funds for their implementation.[71] Visible demonstration of their commitment was given by the presence of the four Friends' presidents and the vice president of the United States at the formal signing of the Salvadoran peace agreement at Chapultepec Castle in Mexico City on January 16, 1992.

The United Nations played a major role in assisting Salvadorans in implementing the provisions of their peace accords.[72] It faced delays and obstacles attributable to predictable exploitation of loopholes in the agree-ments by both parties and foot-dragging on the part of the government authorities—on whom the greater part of the burden of implementation fell—as well as overly optimistic timetables and other flaws in the accords themselves. A lack of experience in the international community in sup-porting post-conflict peacebuilding—most evident in the poor coordina-tion between the macroeconomic policy imposed by international finan-cial institutions and the demands of the peace process[73]—and the sheer difficulty of the kind of institutional and societal transformation foreseen in an ambitious transition from war to peace also took their toll. However, the bulk of these problems were overcome in a process of implementation that, while imperfect, achieved many of the goals articulated by the peace accords.[74]

The year following the signing of the peace accords saw repeated delays in the demobilization of the FMLN. A complex land transfer pro-gram and other measures for reintegrating former combatants also proved unwieldy and contentious. The process later weathered crises caused by government reluctance to purge the army and the explosion of secret arms caches kept by the FMLN in Nicaragua. But the political will that under-lay the negotiations and the dynamics established within them both per-sisted: successive ARENA governments held the presidency, and the

FMLN, despite internal problems, established its place as the country's second political force and upheld its role as "party" to the peace agreements. The United Nations was able to use the strength of the two parties as leverage to support steady forward progress in implementing the agreements. Ongoing mediation between the parties by ONUSAL—sometimes requiring direct meetings at the highest level—was reinforced by visits from New York by both de Soto and Goulding, who brought additional authority to the United Nations' efforts.

The status of the Friends changed with the signing of the final agreements. Their role in implementation was specifically addressed by the new secretary-general, Boutros Boutros-Ghali, in the report he submitted to the Security Council outlining the requirements for ONUSAL's expansion. He noted the support given to his predecessor by the Friends and indicated his intention to rely on them for the backing they could offer his good offices and reconstruction. This continuing involvement was subsequently reflected in the Security Council resolution on ONUSAL's enlargement.[75] However, this formal acknowledgment of the Friends belied reluctance on the part of the government to grant continued recognition to a mechanism that implicitly conferred status on the former guerrilla forces. Indeed, while the FMLN continued to perceive the group as part of their "mechanisms of guarantee," Cristiani and his foreign minister, Oscar Santamaria, both recalled that the "Friends ended with the negotiations" and that what came next was "accompaniment."[76]

In New York the original group of Friends, plus the "one" of the United States, remained the primary interlocutors of the secretariat. The group played a useful and—given the broad support afforded the United Nations in Central America by this stage—uncontroversial role in shaping action taken by the Security Council. It was briefed regularly by UN officials on progress—or the lack of it—in El Salvador and would also be lobbied by both parties. Friends serving on the Council—Venezuela from 1992 to 1993 and Spain from 1993 to 1994, in addition to the United States—helped inform the positions it took by drawing attention to delays in implementation and violations of the agreement, but did not usurp the Council's primary responsibility to oversee the process.[77] At moments of tension, the weight they threw behind positions taken by the United Nations significantly strengthened the secretariat's hand, championing its arguments before the broader UN membership, which respected their expertise on the minutiae of the process.[78]

The Friends in El Salvador fulfilled a number of different roles: in addition to practical assistance in matters such as security, individual ambassadors helped smooth relations with the government; they also provided political leverage at moments of difficulty and functioned as a forum for the informal exchange of information and ideas.[79] They not only bolstered the credibility of ONUSAL in its representation of a unified international community, but facilitated the delicate role of the secretary-general's special representatives in a still very polarized country. But the distinction between the original four Friends and the United States, whose influence in the country and sustained support of the government put it in a quite distinct structural position to that of the other Friends, was marked.[80] The ties that developed between some of the Friends and the FMLN contributed to their assumption of positions that were, as Iqbal Riza put it, "objective but not impartial." However, he appreciated the opportunity they gave him to receive multiple perspectives on the pressing issues of the moment and their ability to deliver pointed messages to the parties at the United Nations' request.[81]

Riza's practice of convening regular meetings of the Friends at ONUSAL's headquarters was one continued by his successors, Augusto Ramírez Ocampo and Enrique ter Horst. But over the years the relevance of the Friends in El Salvador gradually diminished as the ambassadors who had been most personally vested in the negotiations moved elsewhere and were replaced by those to whom serving as a "Friend" of the secretary-general was just another aspect of their job. The waning influence of the group also reflected the eclipse of the Latin Americans by donor states—the United States and Spain, among the Friends—whose participation in the process was determined by bilateral funding priorities. Ter Horst recalled "cultivating" the Friends as a group but also in separate meetings.[82] He met most regularly with the U.S. ambassador, in deference to the United Nations' complex, but essential, relationship with the United States. This was characterized by the United Nations' dependence on U.S. support for many of the toughest areas of the peace agreements, including the new police force and the program to transfer land to demobilized combatants of the FMLN, but also the reluctance of the United States to accept any "coordination" by the United Nations in its provision of technical assistance, particularly in the area of public security.[83]

The growing influence of donor states, rather than the original Friends, became more evident as the process advanced. As pressure for ONUSAL's departure increased, the United Nations found reinforcement from the Nordic states of Denmark, Norway, and Sweden, as well as the Netherlands. The coincidence of the priorities of these states with those of the United Nations was illustrated not only by their support of institutions and structures that had emerged from the peace agreements, such as the human rights ombudsman, but also by their funding through voluntary contributions of a trust fund that helped finance the small political missions that succeeded ONUSAL in 1996 and 1997.[84] Secretariat officials meeting with the Friends in New York in this period routinely included these states, conscious that their knowledge and commitment to the institutional development of peace in El Salvador would continue, through collaboration with the United Nations Development Programme (UNDP) and other agencies, long after the departure of the United Nations' political presence.

Conclusions

The group of Friends of the Secretary-General on El Salvador was conceived as a counterweight to the Security Council at a moment and on an issue in which the secretariat's own relationship to the Council was clouded by the legacy of the Cold War. But it turned out to be much more than that, exceeding expectations held out for it at the moment of its creation and setting an example for the successful involvement of an informal group of states in a UN-led peace process that would be frequently attempted in the future.

The group enhanced the room for independent action of the secretary-general and his representatives, brought leverage to bear on both parties to the negotiations, and bolstered the equilibrium between them. A strange feature of the mechanism, as one FMLN negotiator recalled, was that it was the Friend closest to each party—the United States to the government and Mexico to the FMLN—that put most pressure upon them.[85] Implicit and explicit agreement that acceptance of the secretary-general's invitation to be a "Friend" precluded unilateral initiatives ensured that would-be rival mediators were harnessed to the United Nations' effort but did not insulate the secretariat from occasional pressure from the Friends as well. The group acted as a "cushion" or "shock absorber" between the many actors involved in the negotiations. It greatly enhanced the influence and diplomatic standing of its members, particularly Mexico and Spain, and provided an effective vehicle through which to bring the United States in from a role as "party" to the government's war of counterinsurgency to a multilateral effort to make and support peace. It remained an important champion and informal guarantor of the peace agreements and the UN role in their implementation.

The case study highlights the extent to which the five variables outlined in the introduction—regional environment, the conflict parties, a group's composition, leadership, and the phase of the process with which it was involved—intertwined to support the successful development of the process in undeniably favorable conditions. Involvement by the United Nations took place in an international environment determined by the support of the superpowers for a negotiated settlement. It was preceded by regional efforts that helped succor the idea of a negotiated peace, even if they had not been effective. The long engagement of regional states helped foster a deep understanding of the issues at stake in El Salvador, build relationships with key representatives of both parties, and ensure a shared vision that a negotiated solution offered the best way forward for El Salvador and the region as a whole. All these factors greatly contributed to the productive role that Colombia, Mexico, and Venezuela were able to play as Friends.

El Salvador's civil war had been exacerbated by the politics and resources of the Cold War. It was fought to a stalemate by two strong and relatively unified parties, prepared to make historic concessions that foresaw the reintegration of the rebel forces into society in exchange for a substantial reform of the structures of the state. Both of these parties—the government with more reluctance than the FMLN—revealed themselves to be open to the engagement of the Friends and indeed came to rely on their involvement in a number of different respects. The creation of the group of Friends in the first place owed a considerable debt to the sophistication of the strategy with which political representatives of the FMLN approached the United Nations. This in itself was a product of the remarkably effective diplomacy pursued by the FMLN-FDR's Political and Diplomatic Commission throughout the years of the conflict. However, as the negotiations developed, the government no less than the FMLN was able to reap the benefits of the Friends' sustained engagement. The involvement of the Friends' presidents, in particular, reassured President Cristiani that his interests would be protected from over-encroachment by secretariat officials he never ceased to see as more favorable to the demands of the FMLN than to his own position. That the government was less inclined to view the Friends as an asset during the period of implementation is not surprising: the group's representatives remained ambassadors accredited to a sovereign government and were, to the extent possible, treated as such.

But favorable underlying conditions do not necessarily determine a favorable outcome. The leadership demonstrated by the United Nations during the negotiations—not least in de Soto's composition and handling of the Friends—was an important aspect of their success, as was the individual commitment and capacity of many of the Friends' representatives.

The Friends were, in the first instance, chosen with an eye to what they might bring to the table. They were also introduced only gingerly into the process: de Soto's caution regarding the creation of an autonomous mechanism led him to begin meeting with them regularly as a group only in April 1991. The Friends differed from earlier groups in the close relationships that developed between the protagonists in New York and in the direct engagement of their presidents. A harmonious relationship with the Security Council during implementation, despite the fact that the Friends took shape as a mechanism outside the Council, was secured by the uncontroversial nature of the Salvadoran process by this stage, as well as by the sustained involvement of diplomats in New York and their counterparts in the field.

In many respects the composition of the Salvadoran Friends represented a narrow focus. The small size of the group and the trust that developed among its members facilitated flexibility, discretion, and, for the most part, coherence in the support provided to the secretariat. Their selection reflected not just their history in the regional process, but also knowledge of the FMLN and in some instances, established relationships with the guerrillas' political leadership—a key factor in the group's emerging utility. Linguistic and cultural affinities brought the Friends together, as did allegiance to the first Latin American secretary-general. Meanwhile, the domestic political circumstances of most of the Friends' governments gave them latitude for their involvement and ensured attention at the highest level. Although the Friends on occasion grumbled about the conspiratorial fashion in which they were, for much of the process, "managed" by de Soto, they were also aware that it was the clear leadership of the secretary-general that stood the best chance of producing a sustainable peace. For Mexico and Spain, in particular, participation in the Friends reflected a central focus of their foreign policy. The multiple benefits it brought would inform both countries' relations to the region and to the United Nations in the years to come.

Despite the continuing role played by the Friends during implementation, the group was unashamedly a mechanism of support for the United Nations' peacemaking, its slow emergence well timed to evolve in parallel to the development of substantive negotiations. During this process too little thought, as has been widely recognized, was given to the role of the international community in implementing the agreements reached. Moreover, the composition of the Friends limited the weight that the group could carry among bilateral donors or with the international financial institutions. Consequently, the prominent role they played in the latter months of negotiations and first few months after the signing of the peace agreements receded quite naturally as implementation advanced and the tensions that were evident throughout 1992 and into mid-1993 gradually diminished.[86] In this relatively short time frame, the continuity of most of the ambassadors in New York and San Salvador proved an important aspect of the Friends' utility. Many of these individuals were fully caught up in the mystique of the Salvadoran process and the optimism surrounding the United Nations in this period. For good reason they look back on their participation as Friends of the Secretary-General for El Salvador as one of the high points of their diplomatic careers.

3

Friends and the "Ripening" of Peace in Guatemala

Guatemala bore a superficial resemblance to its neighbor El Salvador in the nature of its civil war, the favorable external conditions in which the negotiations to end it took place, and its resolution on the basis of peace agreements mediated and verified by the United Nations. But the slow maturing of the peace process in Guatemala also offered an obvious contrast to the conditions within which the negotiations on El Salvador were conducted. The weak military capacity of the Guatemalan guerrillas and the fragility of the Guatemalan state contributed to less solid grounds for a role for the United Nations, more gradually developing negotiations, and agreements that were both broader and less deeply rooted than those seen in El Salvador. In contrast to the Salvadoran peace process, the powerful Guatemalan economic elite was adamantly opposed to any negotiation with the guerrillas. The accompaniment of the international community, most visibly present in a group of states that emerged as the Friends of the Guatemalan Peace Process, was centrally important, but quite distinct from the role played by the Friends for El Salvador. Moreover, the timing and location of the Guatemalan peace process meant that it was something of a sideshow. Negotiations moderated by the United Nations took place between 1994 and 1996, a period in which international attention was fixed on events in the Balkans, Somalia, and Rwanda. Far from the optimism surrounding the United Nations at the time of the Salvadoran peace agreements, the standing of the organization was at a low ebb.

The path taken by the Guatemalan Friends was one that demonstrated both the potential and limitations of international leverage within a peace process. Diplomats of the Friends and members of the Guatemalan National Revolutionary Unity (URNG) were able to overcome the group's original formulation as Friends of the Guatemalan President, and, in time, a group that included Norway and the United States as well as the original four Friends from El Salvador (Colombia, Mexico, Spain, and

Venezuela) fell behind an established UN lead. The Friends filled a variety of roles: they brought credibility to the process both within Guatemala and outside it and helped level the playing field between two unequal parties. They also provided essential leverage to the United Nations and assured that attention was paid to an issue that, without their engagement, risked suffering from international neglect. During a protracted period of implementation the Friends continued to meet in both Guatemala and New York. However, in Guatemala in particular they were overtaken by a donor-driven process—and eventually a donor-led Dialogue Group (see appendix for a list of members)—that struggled to reconcile the ambitious agenda for change represented by the agreements with the uncertain political will to implement them evident within Guatemala. Tensions between these two remained as the United Nations' political presence closed its doors at the end of 2004 amid public recognition of a broadly successful engagement.[1]

The Guatemalan Conflict

The civil war in Guatemala shared characteristics with that of its neighbor El Salvador, among them the broad-brush outline of its historical origins in impunity, injustice, and poverty; the ideological orientation of its rurally based revolutionary movement; and its relationship to the wider politics of the Cold War. But it was also very different, taking place in a country whose ethnic composition—some 60 percent of the country's population is indigenous—distinguishes it from its Central American neighbors. A history of exclusion, abandonment, and repression of Mayan, Xinca, and Garifuna populations denied the country's multiethnic and multilingual identity and perpetuated profound divisions between the country's urbanized elites and its rural communities that would not be easily overcome.

Guatemala's conflict, surpassed in length on the continent only by Colombia, derived from the violent overthrow in 1954 of a progressive regime headed by Jacobo Arbenz in a military coup backed by the United States. Initiated by a small armed insurgency in 1960, the conflict went through phases of varying intensity. Mobilization escalated during the 1970s as economic growth followed by economic crisis fostered radical change in Guatemala's countryside. Communication between indigenous populations and Spanish-speaking *ladinos* (including those heading the revolutionary movement) was improved, but contributed to a reinforced defense of Mayan cultural identity and the mobilization of resistance to an increasingly repressive state.[2] The guerrilla offensive reached a peak in the early 1980s, but was met with a crushing response as the military unleashed "scorched-earth" tactics of unprecedented brutality, the intensity of which was fueled by a fear of a repetition of the revolutionary victory in Nicaragua or the lapse into prolonged civil war evident in El Salvador.[3] In its thirty-six-year duration, the conflict claimed some 200,000 victims among the dead or disappeared, almost all of them civilians. As would be evident in Guatemala's post-conflict period, the legacy of such profound political violence and the racism that it reflected was long lasting.

The guerrilla movement, which had united in the URNG in 1982, never recovered from the assault. Although almost 3,000 members of its four constituent parts would be demobilized under the peace agreements, secretariat officials involved in the negotiations had estimated combatants to number no more than 1,000.[4] Far from a military stalemate, the URNG —which had never enjoyed either the levels of nongovernmental organization (NGO) support or the external assistance afforded the Salvadoran guerrillas[5]—had suffered a strategic military defeat that left it in control of only small pockets of the country. This led many in the military and the private sector to dismiss the need for negotiations out of hand. Meanwhile, the state itself, which had returned to civilian authority only in 1986, was weak and circumscribed by the counterinsurgency machinery that had been developed to conduct the war. In the countryside this included paramilitary "civilian self-defense patrols" (PACs) that at one point were estimated to involve one million peasants, a quarter of the adult population.[6]

Taken as a whole, the conditions for peacemaking did not appear auspicious. Pressure for negotiations, initiated by the Catholic Church, mounted from within civil society, but outside "interference" in the affairs of Guatemala was resisted and the ability of even the United States to wield influence over either the civilian or military authorities was limited. Guatemala had rejected U.S. military assistance following criticism of its human rights record during the Carter presidency. Although assistance was restored in 1985, in late 1990 renewed concerns about human rights, especially the army's attempt to cover up its murder of a U.S. citizen, provoked the suspension of U.S. military assistance and left a lingering shadow over relations between the two countries.

Guatemala's Slow Train to Peace

The six-year process that led to the signing of comprehensive peace agreements in December 1996 followed a very different course than the intense twenty months of the Salvadoran negotiations. In El Salvador the two parties, locked in a military stalemate, had been powerful enough to all but exclude other social sectors from the negotiating table.[7] Credibility and legitimacy had been given to the process by the presence of the United Nations, represented by a trusted aide to the secretary-general who was himself closely involved in the process and supported by a disciplined group of Friends.

In contrast to the strong and unitary actors in El Salvador, in Guatemala negotiations were to stretch through four governments. One of these, that of Jorge Serrano, self-destructed in an *autogolpe* or "self-imposed coup," while the one that followed, the caretaker government of Ramiro León de Carpio, lacked the legitimacy to take some of the hard decisions that the peace process demanded. Although the business-minded National Vanguard Party (PAN) of his successor, Alvaro Arzú, signed the final accords, the party's narrow majority in the legislative assembly and poor internal discipline left the peace agenda vulnerable during implementation.[8] Meanwhile, the URNG was in the strange position of being militarily weak but politically strong, by virtue of the power of its denunciation of what was wrong with Guatemala and the broad coalition it could count on, inside and outside the country, to support it. The role of the UN secretariat grew from "observer" to "moderator" (and mediator in function) but never represented the kind of authority it had held in the negotiations in El Salvador.

Consequently, as the UN moderator, Jean Arnault, observed, the credibility required of the process had to be acquired by other means.[9] These included an Assembly of Civil Society, which was created under the leadership of the Catholic Church to ensure that the positions of a wide spectrum of national actors were heard in the negotiations, and the influence of interested states in the group of Friends of the Guatemalan Peace Process. The direct engagement of these two composite actors in support of the United Nations reinforced the pressure for change and contributed to a process of "substitution" for the URNG that enhanced the weight it could carry in negotiations. However, progress would not have been achieved without the negotiations themselves exacerbating divisions within Guatemala's powerful armed forces. These pitted reformers who understood that a controlled peace process might be in the armed forces' best interests against traditionalists who resisted all moves toward change. That the reformists won through was a key factor in Guatemala's ability to reach a negotiated settlement of its conflict.

The combination of these circumstances allowed the negotiating teams of the government of Arzú and the URNG to achieve in December 1996 a remarkable feat—agreement to a package of reforms with far-ranging implications for Guatemala's economic, social, and institutional life—broader in their scope, if less precise in their details, than the agreements reached in El Salvador.[10] But the history of their implementation—including the defeat in a referendum of the constitutional reforms derived from the peace process—questioned whether the agreements constituted a realistic framework for the national agenda for a state with Guatemala's deep divisions, or an extraordinary aspiration, pulled off as a result of fortuitous circumstances ably exploited by men and women, Guatemalans and foreigners, who recognized in Guatemala's initially unpromising circumstances a unique opportunity for a chance at reform, but underestimated the strength of forces that would oppose it.

Early Days

Guatemala's peace process developed slowly, in parallel to the gradual opening toward democracy initiated by the election in November 1985 of the country's first civilian president since Arbenz, the Christian Democrat Vinicio Cerezo.[11] Cerezo had presided over the signature of the Esquipulas II agreements in Guatemala City and took steps to ensure that their provisions had impact in Guatemala. These included the creation of the National Reconciliation Commission (CNR) under the chairmanship of Bishop Rodolfo Quezada Toruño and, from 1989 on, the promotion of a national dialogue within Guatemalan civil society.[12] Direct talks had been initiated in 1987 with the URNG and remained at a stalemate until 1990 when, conscious of domestic and international pressure to move forward, Cerezo appointed Monsignor Quezada as "conciliator" and agreed to secret talks in Oslo between the CNR and URNG under the auspices of the Norwegian government and the Lutheran World Federation.

The Oslo Accord committed the parties to a "search for peace by political means" and provided for a series of consultations between the URNG and Guatemalan political parties and popular, religious, and business sectors. The UN secretary-general was formally asked to observe these meetings and to act as "guarantor of compliance" with the terms of the agreement.[13] The meetings that ensued represented only consultations—not "dialogue" and still less "negotiation"—but they did help breach barriers between the URNG and some sectors of civil society, demonstrating that an agenda for reform could find common ground in some areas.

The first round of direct talks between the URNG and the Peace Commission of the new government of Jorge Serrano Elías was held in Mexico in April 1991 in the presence of the UN observer, Francesc Vendrell. The talks led to agreements on a procedure for negotiations on a broad range of issues, but the process moved slowly. Persistent stumbling blocks were government attempts to force the URNG to agree to a cease-fire before negotiating the substantive items on the agenda and doubts about UN verification of an eventual accord.[14]

Skepticism about a UN role in Guatemala grew with the signing of the peace agreements in El Salvador. Consultations between the two government militaries reinforced Guatemalan fears of a bias in the secretariat toward the guerrillas, while the presence of UN peacekeepers in neighboring El Salvador only confirmed the view of many Guatemalans that agreements of such an intrusive nature should never be accepted in Guatemala.[15] Vendrell's position as observer—a role he described as "initially very modest" but that was soon extended by his energetic approach to diplomacy—was an early casualty. His active facilitation of discussions of a future human rights agreement antagonized both the government and the conciliator; the final straw came when he was found to be assisting in the arrangement of a meeting between Serrano and the URNG in the offices of the Lutheran World Federation in Geneva. An embarrassed government asked for him to be relieved for having exceeded his mandate. His place was taken by Jean Arnault, an official junior enough to be considered a "real" observer.[16]

The appointment of Arnault reflected uncertainty about the future of UN engagement in Guatemala from within the secretariat. Boutros Boutros-Ghali paid little attention to what he perceived as an unimportant relic of the Cold War and was, in any case, otherwise engaged in more pressing concerns in the Balkans and in Africa. Other senior officials—most notably de Soto, who had become a senior adviser to Boutros-Ghali—openly expressed reservations that conditions were given for the process in Guatemala to prosper. Consequently Arnault, while ably supervised by Marrack Goulding, now the under-secretary-general for political affairs, labored in the shadow of persistent doubts that peace in Guatemala and a UN role within it were possible.

Serrano and His Friends

A new and somewhat surprising actor in the Guatemalan context was Norway. The leading role it assumed as a "helpful fixer" in the peace process from its earliest days was one that was developed, like a number of Norway's "soft power" engagements in peacemaking, outside the Ministry of Foreign Affairs.[17] In this instance, Norway owed its status in the process to individuals from church groups, and particularly Peter Skauen of

Norwegian Church Aid, who participated in the relief effort after Guatemala's earthquake of 1976. Skauen involved the Lutheran World Federation, which under the leadership of Secretary-General Gunnar Stälsett brought Guatemala to the Foreign Ministry and took the initiative for the meeting in Oslo in 1990.[18] Norway financed the participation of the URNG throughout much of the negotiation process. Its officials also discreetly nurtured contacts across the political spectrum, with particular attention to the armed forces—a reflection of Norway's perception that without military acquiescence peace would never be possible.[19]

The Lutheran World Federation maintained an active presence in the process, arranging "ecumenical consultations" outside the country for informal exchanges of opinion among national and international NGOs and even facilitating contacts between the URNG and the U.S. State Department. Stälsett would periodically assure the secretariat that the Lutheran World Federation was not itself seeking a role in the peace process. It wanted nothing more than to support the UN lead that Stälsett himself believed was imperative to the success of any negotiations. However, Norway, through the Lutheran World Federation, was so embedded in the process that officials at the United Nations were never quite sure that they knew the whole story.[20]

A shift in the engagement of international actors was precipitated by Serrano's presentation in January 1993 of a proposal that offered acceptance of immediate international verification of a human rights agreement in exchange for the URNG's agreement to a cease-fire within 90 days.[21] Soon afterward, at a meeting in Caracas of the presidents of Colombia, Mexico, and Venezuela, the ever-active Carlos Andrés Pérez, still flush with success from El Salvador, suggested to Serrano that Guatemala could benefit from a group of Friends. Serrano reportedly "seized the idea mid-air" and urged the presidents to serve as Friends of himself and his peace initiative. Privately he also asked them to take on a more direct mediating role. The presidents agreed to support Serrano's efforts and constitute themselves as his Friends.[22]

Hoping to replicate the arrangement in El Salvador (but having forgotten its origins and relationship to the secretary-general), the presidents called their ambassadors in New York and instructed them to travel to Guatemala to meet with President Serrano. The diplomats, who were joined by Rosario Green, Mexico's deputy minister of foreign affairs, were somewhat alarmed by their presidents' readiness to serve as Serrano's Friends and tried to suggest that as such they would have no credibility with the guerrillas. They left Guatemala for a meeting in Mexico with a somewhat startled URNG, intent on reassuring the *comandantes* that they wanted to be Friends not just of Serrano, but also of the peace process.[23]

The URNG responded cautiously, if not negatively, to this rather clumsy initiative, and the status, functions, and composition of the group became part of the negotiating agenda. While the URNG had separately considered the question of Friends and had agreed that they could be useful, it was concerned that the wholesale transfer of the Salvadoran group was not adequate to the situation in Guatemala. The URNG had good bilateral relationships with Mexico and Spain. A relationship with Venezuela, or rather Carlos Andrés Pérez, developed as a result of the Friends' initiative.[24] But the URNG saw little point in including Colombia, which was increasingly preoccupied with its own internal conflict and hardly sympathetic toward long-standing rural insurgencies elsewhere. However, rather than risk offense, the URNG pushed for the group to be expanded through the addition of Norway—an obvious candidate for the URNG, but one viewed more warily by the government—and after much internal debate, the United States (which had already been approached separately by Serrano), a development viewed cautiously by Mexico.[25]

Mexico had more direct interests in resolving Guatemala's conflict than in the case of El Salvador, which distinguished it from the other Friends. Guatemala was an immediate neighbor and important trading partner; its northern border areas had seen some of the heaviest fighting of the conflict, prompting the flight of almost 46,000 Guatemalans into refugee camps in southern Mexico. Mexico had played an exemplary role as a host government and in facilitating these refugees' return,[26] but the presence of the refugee camps closely aligned, in some instances, with the guerrillas represented a problem for Mexico's internal security. Concern was heightened during 1993 when some in the Mexican government began to get a sense that "something was brewing" in Chiapas (the Zapatista rebellion that would burst upon Mexico in January 1994). Fears of "contamination" across the border from Guatemala led to pressure from President Salinas and Rosario Green for a speedy resolution of Guatemala's conflict.[27]

The preeminence of Mexico within the Friends in this period also reflected structural factors. The group's meetings and activities were concentrated around negotiations between the parties, which generally took place in Mexico City. Mexico convened meetings of the Friends with one or another of the parties or with the conciliator, Monsignor Quezada; these were generally, but not exclusively, held in the Mexican foreign ministry. As disagreements over President Serrano's peace proposal persisted, the

efforts of the group begin to appear, under Mexico's lead, more like mediation. But the process stood little chance of making substantive gains. The
talks broke down shortly before Serrano's *autogolpe* of May 25. Both a more
sharply defined role for the United Nations and the support of the international community were required to overcome Guatemala's entrenched
internal resistance.

The aftermath of Serrano's *autogolpe* strengthened this argument. Guatemalans had reason to be grateful to the firm position taken by the United
States and other governments that had threatened to withhold both trade
and aid unless the constitutional order was immediately restored. Meanwhile, the initial efforts of the government of de León Carpio to abandon
many of the gains made in the process so far were roundly rejected. Rumors
of an increased role for the United Nations or Organization of American
States (OAS) (a course of action encouraged by the United States)
abounded.[28] Jan Egeland, state secretary of Norway at the time, recalled a
determined strategy by Norway to persuade both sides that the United
Nations was the only way to go.[29] In October the secretary-general was
asked to employ his good offices to resume negotiations, and in the latter
part of 1993 the United Nations was able to facilitate the resumption of
direct contacts between the two parties after a lapse of seven months. The
two sides had come to realize that the prestige, impartiality, and resources
of the United Nations brought important advantages. Key for the URNG
was a visit to New York in late 1993 in which Goulding took a rather
didactic line in explaining the possible range of UN involvement in a
peace process. Shortly afterward, negotiations resumed with the signing on
January 10, 1994, of a framework agreement that would provide for a UN
moderator to "make proposals to facilitate the signing of a firm and lasting
peace agreement."[30]

Back in the Box: UN Moderation

The framework agreement gave formal roles in the process both to organized civil society in the Assembly of Civil Society (ASC) and to the
Friends, now identified as Friends of the Guatemalan Peace Process. The
ASC would be established in May 1994 with Monsignor Quezada at the
head of a wide range of grassroots organizations, political parties, universi-
ties, and small- and medium-sized business associations (but not the powerful private sector). In addition to submitting consensus proposals on
issues to be discussed in the negotiations, the ASC was given the capacity
to discuss agreements reached by the parties and endorse them as "national

commitments." While the Guatemalan Friends were not "Friends of the Secretary-General" in name, their primary function—"to support the representative of the Secretary-General of the United Nations in order to facilitate the negotiating process"—derived directly from El Salvador. In addition, as witnesses to agreements reached, the Friends were charged with giving "greater certainty and firmness" to the commitments they contained. For the United Nations, these terms represented an effort to put the Friends "back in the box" behind a clearly identified UN lead.

As the negotiations developed, Arnault came to see them as sustained by structures of support arranged in concentric circles. At the center were the two parties, the UN moderator and the experts he brought in from the UN system and Bretton Woods institutions, each of which helped the parties toward accepted "best practices" on issues such as indigenous rights and fiscal reform. The ASC and the Friends formed a first circle, each with their role specified in the framework agreement. A second, outer circle was formed by donor countries, which met as a group from 1994 on in a concrete demonstration of the "carrots" that interested countries might contribute to a successful peace process, and the international consultations organized by the Norwegians at regular intervals.[31]

Within this structure the Friends themselves fulfilled various roles. The most obvious one was to exert leverage on both parties (the Friends would "whisper in the ears of the parties at the UN's request," as one participant in the process observed).[32] But beyond this, their involvement greatly enhanced the credibility of the process with sectors in Guatemala opposed to a negotiated settlement—on the basis that if countries of the status of the United States, Spain, and Mexico supported it, it could not all be bad. It also helped create what Arnault described as "a framework of parity, in which both parties feel they can negotiate without losing status."[33] In the absence of the military pressure seen in El Salvador, it would otherwise have been very difficult for the Guatemalan government to explain, even internally, why it was discussing fundamental issues for the country's future with a group of aging, defeated Marxists. These somewhat intangible benefits were underlined by the appearance of representatives of the Friends at the signing ceremonies of the eleven consecutive agreements reached between January 1994 and December 1996.

For the UN secretariat, the most surprising feature of the newly constituted group was the presence of the United States. It was a major addition and one that provided Arnault with grounds for quiet optimism when, as he put it, "everybody else was skeptical."[34] The United States' decision to participate in the group responded to lessons learned from El Salvador.

Discussions with the FMLN in 1992 had led State Department officials to realize that a policy that had not included direct contacts with the guerrillas during the negotiations, and instead had relied on third-party intermediaries, had been a mistake.[35] Direct contacts were initiated with the URNG that year and contributed to the decision to participate in the Friends.[36] Officials of the Clinton administration, principally Richard Nuccio, a senior adviser with the State Department, and John Hamilton, Central America Office director and then deputy assistant secretary of state (and from 2002 U.S. ambassador to Guatemala), as well as successive ambassadors in Guatemala, proved themselves, in Arnault's words, "ideal friends—responsive and low profile." They surprised other Friends by not assuming a dominant role, even as they complemented activity in the group with their bilateral relationship with the government and other actors in Guatemala. That the United States was careful to keep the two distinct—engagement as Friend in the negotiations was run from Washington—allowed it to reap the benefit of direct involvement in the UN process while also maintaining pressure on Guatemala's elites. This remained the case even when U.S. policy of the past came under a barrage of criticism amid revelations of Central Intelligence Agency involvement in Guatemala's dirty war.[37]

As the negotiations advanced, the Friends—and particularly the four key states among them, Mexico, Norway, Spain, and the United States—became a permanent part of their landscape. Arnault met with them in Mexico, sometimes before and after each meeting with the parties, and consulted with them in between. The Friends also met separately with the URNG and the government delegation, while individual representatives of "friend" states in Guatemala City cultivated relationships not only with the parties, but also with the many other actors (in the military, the private sector, and civil society) whose confidence in the process was required for it to move ahead. One Spanish diplomat closely involved in both processes would describe the role of the Friends in Guatemala as being, in contrast to El Salvador, "that of individuals, not states."[38] The many different levels on which the Friends worked derived from the long engagement that some of them had in the process, but did not translate into detailed engagement on the substance of the negotiations. As a group they could deliver messages at the United Nations' request. But they could not micromanage the process. The reason was that, as Arnault recalled, the "most difficult issues—the role of the state in the socioeconomic agreement, the multiplicity of 'peoples' in the indigenous agreement, the mandate of the army —would have divided them."[39]

The Friends in New York were regularly briefed by colleagues in Mexico and Guatemala as well as at meetings with Arnault and Goulding. However, the somewhat conspiratorial relationship that had developed between de Soto and the permanent representatives of the Salvadoran Friends in New York was absent. This reflected a difference in style and status between the two UN officials. While de Soto was Latin American, a career ambassador, close to Pérez de Cuéllar, and well known within the UN community, Arnault was something of an oddball. Still relatively junior in the hierarchical structure of the secretariat, he had entered the United Nations as a translator and had come to fill the functions he performed as a result of his somewhat maverick brilliance alone. Greatly admired by those who worked with him on the negotiations, he remained, nevertheless, somewhat distant from the diplomatic game as it was played in New York.

That Arnault and the United Nations relied on heavy lifting by the Friends at key moments was demonstrated by the negotiation of the agreement on the "historical clarification commission" in June 1994. Military resistance to the formation of a commission to address the country's violent past had been intense. The publication of the report of El Salvador's truth commission in March 1993 had not helped. The report had attributed blame for 85 percent of the cases it investigated to forces aligned to the Salvadoran state, and in cases where it had incontrovertible proof of responsibility, it had named names.[40] The terms of Guatemala's commission were eventually negotiated in Oslo. Norwegian officials took a central role in pressuring both sides to accept a commission considerably weaker than that seen in El Salvador, with no reference to "truth" in its title and no commitment to name names or issue binding recommendations. Together with the United States and Sweden, which had joined the Friends in Oslo, they prevented the army from deserting the talks altogether and impressed upon the URNG that the government could be pushed no further.[41]

The URNG, the United Nations, and the Friends all came under intense criticism for an agreement widely perceived as betraying core demands for accountability and transitional justice.[42] In the following months negotiations on indigenous rights bogged down as the government delayed implementing commitments under the human rights agreement and the URNG stalled as a consequence of internal differences. The United Nations, too, held back and did not deploy a mission to verify the terms of the human rights agreement reached earlier in the year until November 1994.[43] Some representatives of the Friends and other donor states began to worry whether they were not more committed to the peace process than the Guatemalans themselves.

Curiously, the greatest difference between the Friends and the United Nations came not over the substance of the negotiations but with secretariat officials in New York over the question of authorization of the UN mission. Meeting with the Friends in July 1994, Goulding had counseled that, as in the case of El Salvador, a human rights mission, fielded in advance of a larger multidisciplinary operation, should be established by the Security Council.[44] This would ensure that it enjoyed the status and close political supervision that the Council was able to provide as well as the Council's more agile budget procedures. This position was strongly opposed by Mexico, which with Colombian and Venezuelan support argued for authorization by the General Assembly. The argument was cast in terms of the possible undermining of the General Assembly by the Council's authorization of a human rights mission, but reflected the Latin Americans' protection of their own influence in the General Assembly as well as Guatemalan concerns that it not follow in the footsteps of El Salvador. That the United States also insisted on the General Assembly route, largely for budgetary reasons, clinched the deal.[45] In the face of unified opposition from the Latin American Friends and the United States, Goulding had no option other than to advise the secretary-general to go to the General Assembly.[46]

A Conspiracy of Peace

Discussion of the socioeconomic agreement would last more than a year, from April 1995 until May 1996. The issues it contemplated were complex and, for the first time in the negotiations, touched the interests of conservative sectors of the business community. Signature of the agreement and its acceptance as the central pillar of the economic and social policy of the incoming government of President Alvaro Arzú represented a turning point. It also reflected the apparent evolution of a national consensus, reinforced by international support among the Friends, donors, UN agencies, and international financial institutions, regarding minimal reforms needed in Guatemala for the viability of any peace process.

El Salvador cast a long shadow. During the negotiations the ARENA government had made it clear that its macroeconomic policy was not subject to discussion; the FMLN had to accept that economic policy was the prerogative of the ruling political party and be content with extensive reforms that would allow its members to compete for power. If they won power , they would then be able to effect change. Consequently they had left discussion of socioeconomic issues to the end of the negotiations and then limited them to matters relating to reintegration. The URNG, many of the groups represented in the ASC, and reformers within government circles saw this deficiency in the Salvadoran process as unacceptable in Guatemala, where the underlying economic situation of the country was much weaker and many sectors had assumed the negotiations as the banner for basic, but long overdue, reform of the Guatemalan state.

External actors were also anxious to do better in Guatemala. Many of them were simultaneously grappling with problems encountered in El Salvador as a result of tensions between the economic policies pursued by international financial institutions and the political demands of the peace process. That these had been openly exploited by the Salvadoran government, which used prior commitments to the International Monetary Fund (IMF) as an excuse to soft-pedal on reintegration issues, only made things worse.[47] On Guatemala the IMF, the Inter-American Development Bank (IDB), and especially the World Bank all worked closely with Arnault to shape the agreements. Attempts to coordinate with bilateral donors had also begun early, with an informal donor meeting convened by the World Bank in June 1994. A further meeting was held in June 1995 as discussion of the socioeconomic agreement was beginning. Its message was clear. At 7.7 percent of GDP the fiscal burden in Guatemala was the lowest in Latin America: tax reform was a necessity and external assistance could only supplement the mobilization of domestic resources for peace and social development.[48]

Events leading up to Arzú's election in late 1995 had helped build confidence in the peace process. These included the commitment by all political parties to respect agreements already reached, a substantial showing in legislative elections by a center-left front of popular and indigenous organizations aligned with the URNG, and the successful deployment of the United Nations' Verification Mission, MINUGUA. Consequently, Arzú arrived in power determined to finish with the negotiations during his first year in office and appointed officials well qualified to help him do so. Even before reaching office he had held secret meetings with the URNG, sponsored by the Rome-based Community of Sant'Egidio (a development the United Nations viewed warily, leading Arnault to warn both parties that maintenance of this parallel channel was inconsistent with a continued UN role). On the advice of his new minister of defense, General Julio Balconi, Arzú selected as the head of his negotiating team Gustavo Porras, who had once been a URNG militant. Balconi himself had served as military representative to the talks since April 1991 and had formed a friendship with Rodrigo Asturias, one of the URNG's four senior commanders, which had led to a series of secret meetings between the URNG's leadership and senior military officers. Once in power, Arzú took steps to further military reform that offered reassurance to both the URNG and the army, winning the confidence of the latter by limiting the extent to which they would be forced to make concessions to the former at the negotiating table.[49]

Arzú's foreign minister, Eduardo Stein, saw in the Friends a mechanism that had the capacity to accelerate the pace of the negotiations, put pressure on the URNG to move things along more quickly, and finish up what still remained to be negotiated.[50] As the year progressed agreements were negotiated with a remarkable and—for secretariat officials aware of problems created by last-minute deals in El Salvador—somewhat alarming speed.[51] The attention of the Friends turned to their roles in the "post-peace" period and to planning for a "signing tour" that contemplated formal signing ceremonies for agreements on a definitive cease-fire in Oslo, on constitutional reforms and the electoral regime in Stockholm, and on reintegration of the URNG in Madrid, all in anticipation of the signing of agreements on a timetable and the "firm and lasting peace" in Mexico City on December 29.

The tour was designed to generate interest in Guatemala's needs as well as acknowledge the support given Guatemala's peace process by its Friends. But its preparations highlighted the extent to which the negotiations had become directly entwined with considerations of the funding bonanza that would follow them. The government perceived access to funds from the international community as part of its negotiating strategy, while potential donors were jockeying to protect their own agendas. At the request of the two parties, Arnault developed guidance for a coordinated position that stressed the centrality to implementation of a formal Consultative Group meeting planned for January 1997.[52]

Preparations for the signing tour indicated the extent to which all involved had, by mid-1996, taken peace in Guatemala for granted. The shock to the process was therefore profound on October 19 when it emerged that the July kidnapping of a ninety-year-old grandmother from one of Guatemala's most prominent families had been carried out by the faction of the URNG led by Asturias. Negotiations were suspended and confidence plummeted to the floor. With the country in the midst of a crime wave and peace apparently around the corner, the fact that the URNG should be so brazenly involved in kidnapping was a serious setback. Only intense activity on the part of Arnault and the Friends prevented the process from breaking down altogether. Years of investment in relationships with the parties paid dividends in the Friends' capacity to meet with the URNG as a group and then, in the case of the United States and at Arnault's request, individually with Asturias to impress upon all the necessity of complying with the government's demand for his withdrawal from the negotiating table.[53]

Negotiations resumed on November 9, but their legitimacy was badly damaged. The URNG lost much of its leverage in the discussion of the outstanding agreements, and implementation began in January 1997 with the entire peace process still tainted by the kidnapping and its fallout.[54] One casualty was the Friends. Seeking coherence with the framework agreement of 1994, the URNG had wanted mention of a continuing role for the group in the final agreement. But the government, with an eye to the URNG's vulnerability after the kidnapping episode, resisted it, and so the agreement restricted itself to expressing the parties' appreciation of the support the Friends had provided to the negotiations.[55]

Implementation

Implementation of the Guatemalan peace agreements was a long process. In early 1997 MINUGUA's mandate, which from the beginning had paid more explicit attention to institution building than had been the case in El Salvador, was extended to encompass verification of all aspects of the agreements, as well as good offices and public information. The mission remained in place until December 2004, with a gradual reduction in its size reflecting at times painfully slow progress in furthering the broad agenda for change represented in the peace agreements.[56] As the United Nations prepared for its departure, Kofi Annan welcomed the important strides taken by Guatemala in the eight years since the accords had been signed, but acknowledged that "the deeper structural reforms envisaged in the peace accords have lagged far behind the advances in the political realm." This dichotomy had left "a sense of frustration that progress always seeks to fall short of the goal." The accords, he suggested, should be seen as a program of work that would remain valid for years to come.[57]

The speed with which the Friends were displaced as a central actor in the political process was quite distinct from the experience of the group in El Salvador. Although the Friends would continue to meet in Guatemala for briefings from the mission, they quickly lost the political purchase that their commitment to the common enterprise of the negotiations had brought them. Moreover, by the early 2000s, a new group of donors, the Dialogue Group, had eclipsed the Friends quite comprehensively. This group worked in close cooperation with the United Nations to assume the voice of the international community in Guatemala through the protection of the central place of the peace agenda in successive Consultative Group meetings. In New York, things were a little different. The original group of Friends remained the primary interlocutors of the secretariat, and worked under the leadership of Mexico to ensure MINUGUA's support within the General Assembly. But the sustained involvement of the Friends could not compensate for the diffuse and unwieldy nature of the Assembly itself or substitute for the oversight provided by the Security Council to the peacekeeping operations it establishes.[58]

Implementation of the military aspects of the accords proceeded in an exemplary manner.[59] However, in many other areas forward progress was impeded by the weakness of the parties that had signed the agreements, and the unexpected fragility of the consensus in support of peace that the negotiations had been thought to nurture. Both the PAN and the URNG were less representative and less disciplined political forces than the ruling ARENA party in El Salvador and the FMLN. Moreover, those who had negotiated on the PAN's behalf were not truly representative even of the party itself, and had little to do with the most entrenched sectors of Guatemalan power.[60] Consequently, on controversial issues Arzú could neither stand up to the interests of the powerful private sector nor deliver the PAN's slim majority in the legislative assembly. He also faced a political challenge from a right-wing party, the Guatemalan Republican Front (FRG), which had long assumed a stance in opposition to the peace accords and would indeed win the presidency in late 1999. Although the new president, Alfonso Portillo, pledged to implement the peace accords, his years in office were plagued by open conflict with diverse sectors of Guatemalan society, high levels of incompetence and corruption, and targeted political violence attributable to "hidden" or "parallel" powers in Guatemalan society. Together, these factors seriously impeded advances in the peace agreements.[61] For its part, the URNG, which had historically been less anchored in a base of popular organizations than the FMLN, neglected its role as "party" to the peace agreement in favor of a rapid transition to a political party, and then, failing to gather much support in this capacity, soon fragmented.

The United Nations' ability to exert leverage on the process was inhibited not only by its counterparts and absence of the Security Council, but also by the nature of the agreements themselves, which emerged as hugely ambitious in the context of the underlying characteristics of Guatemalan society. A decision to appoint Arnault as MINUGUA's head ensured continuity with the process of negotiations. His efforts would be supplemented by periodic visits by senior officials from New York, but the obstacles on the ground were considerable.[62] The United Nations had hoped to sustain the mobilization of proagreement social forces through their participation in a series of sectoral commissions that were charged with transforming the general principles of the agreements into more precise proposals for legislation. However, this drawn-out process contributed not so much to a consolidation of support around the agreements but to the mobilization of both pro- and anti-reform constituencies that favored further polarization. It also underlined the price paid for the exclusion of the private sector from a more direct involvement in the negotiations. The gradual erosion of support, particularly elite opposition to both fiscal reform and indigenous rights, was painfully evident when, in a referendum held in May 1999, Guatemalan voters roundly rejected fifty constitutional reforms of central importance to the peace agreements.[63] This exposed what Arnault would later describe as a "problem of political will that [came] from the difference between the center of gravity of the political agreement and the center of gravity of the political system."[64]

Friends, Donors, and the Dialogue Group

The rapid disappearance of the Friends in Guatemala can be attributed to three factors. The first was the government's desire, noted above, not to give the Friends a formal status in the peace agreements.[65] The second was differences between the most powerful Friends, and between some of the Friends and the United Nations. Arnault recalled that "the first sign that the group was not going to work anymore was when I found out that one ambassador had described in great detail to his counterpart in the Guatemala government a meeting that I had with the Friends and the recommendations I had made there, which he obviously disagreed with and made sure that the government would disagree with too."[66] The third factor was the emergence of successive Consultative Group meetings as the focal point for international engagement in Guatemala. This imposed a direct correlation between influence and a capacity to pay that led to the rapid exclusion of the Latin American Friends—and most important, Mexico—from a prominent role.[67] In these circumstances the common interests of the six Friends in the peace agreements signed under the United Nations' auspices did not prove strong enough to withstand the rivalries between them.

A particularly delicate issue was the behavior of Spain. Although hitherto an exemplary Friend, and in many respects an active promoter of the peace agenda (an early example being its training of ex-URNG combatants as bodyguards), Spain pursued a bilateral policy on public security that undercut the United Nations–led effort. Even before the "Agreement for the Strengthening of Civilian Authority and the Role of the Armed Forces in a Democratic Society" had been signed, Spain negotiated an exclusive relationship between the new national civilian police and its militarized rural police force, the Civil Guard (*Guardia Civil*). Both governments were motivated by the experience of El Salvador, where cantonment of the two armed forces and delays in establishing the new police force had contributed to a post-conflict crime wave, and international assistance had been hampered by competition between donors pursuing differing models of policing.[68] Guatemala's focus on rapidity of recruitment, training, and deployment paid an initial dividend, but it did so at the expense of quality, and the path taken by Guatemala's new police force was to be a sorry one. Indeed, the damage done by the Civil Guard "remedy" to the problems identified in El Salvador was to prove much greater than the problems themselves. Nor was donor competition avoided.[69] Meanwhile, a separate factor that contributed to the gradual distancing of Spain from the UN process was political change within Spain itself. As officials appointed by Felipe González's Socialist party were replaced by appointments made by his successor, the conservative President José María Aznar, the commitment to a peace process viewed as a Socialist party priority began to falter.[70]

The Consultative Group meeting held in Brussels in January 1997 was the product of efforts by the United Nations to involve bilateral and multilateral donors throughout the peace process, thereby overcoming the mismatch between "peace priorities" and "donor priorities" that had been seen in El Salvador and was already evident as a risk in Guatemala.[71] Previous meetings had created conditions under which donors were prepared not only to give generously to Guatemala's reconstruction ($1.9 billion was committed for 1997–2000)[72] but also to introduce conditionality for their assistance, linking disbursement of funds to the increase in Guatemala's tax revenue (from less than 8 percent to 12 percent) contained in the peace agreements.[73] However, even this structured effort to encourage coordination was unable to corral donors' individual interests in the assistance frenzy that followed the signing of the final accords. As Ricardo Stein, Arzú's peace secretary, recalled: "Contrary to what we had hoped, each one of the diplomats had his own independent idea of what peace was and how he should contribute to it. There was no coincidence either with the peace agreements or with national priorities."[74] Meanwhile, the Arzú government fell victim to its own internal divisions and what Susanne Jonas termed "peace opportunism": "being more than happy to accept international praise for the easier advances in compliance, but without being willing to fight for (or to pay any domestic political price for) the truly difficult advances."[75]

Under these circumstances, it was unsurprising that Arnault and his successors—Gerd Merrem took over the leadership of MINUGUA in 2000 and Tom Koenigs in 2002—dealt primarily with individual states, while also endeavoring to sustain the support of the World Bank, the IMF, and the IDB (itself vulnerable, like that of the Friends, to the commitment of individual officials).[76] Without the consistent backing of the United States, maintenance of the fragile architecture of the peace process would simply not have been possible. But other countries, notably but not exclusively Norway and Sweden, also maintained a steadfast commitment to the peace agenda that reflected a long investment in the process and dedication to its outcome. This was evident in the generosity and consistency of the financial support provided, often through civil society organizations, but also in the high caliber of diplomats the Nordic states continued to send to Guatemala and the leading role that these diplomats took in the efforts to galvanize the international community to support the peace agenda.

Swedish diplomats were behind the creation of the Dialogue Group of donor states, initially as one of several parallel groups established in 1999 to coordinate the international response to the damage done to Central America by Hurricane Mitch the previous year.[77] In Guatemala the hurricane's effects had been relatively minor, but the group, which consisted of the largest bilateral and multilateral donors in the country, developed an unexpected utility with respect to Guatemala's peace agenda in the years that followed.[78] "We are the engine," was how the Swedish ambassador, Maria Leissner, would describe the role of the group in December 2002, the assertion tinged with a steely realism that, even in this capacity, there were limits to what the international community could hope to achieve.[79] Paradoxically, both the need and the space for such an activist role by the donors were created by the poor performance of the Portillo government and the mounting opposition to it voiced within Guatemala as well as by its international partners, including the United States.[80]

MINUGUA, like the United Nations Development Programme (UNDP), was formally an "observer" and not a full member of the Dialogue Group (Merrem tried to maintain what he described as a "tricky balance" between the old group of Friends—which had never been formally disbanded—and the Dialogue Group),[81] but both were centrally involved in its work. UNDP functioned as the Dialogue Group's secretariat, while MINUGUA's verification and analysis consistently informed the group's interaction with officials from the Guatemalan government. It also prepared hard-hitting reports that set the agenda of the Consultative Group meetings organized by the IDB in 2002 and 2003.[82] However, although the Dialogue Group proved itself, in Tom Koenigs's words, "a very important instrument to coordinate bilateral support" in favor of the peace accords, it had its limits. These included actual donor coordination, but extended to an ability to exert pressure on the banks.[83]

The absence of the Latin American Friends and particularly Mexico from the Dialogue Group contributed to an uneasiness, shared by Spain (which, though a member, distanced itself from the Dialogue Group to some extent), with its unprecedented level of intervention in Guatemala's affairs. It also highlighted the distinction between the political role played by the Friends during peacemaking and the financially driven leverage exerted by donors on implementation. Mexico did retain its leadership of the Friends in New York. However, the role of the New York group was for periods largely constrained, as Guatemala's influential UN ambassador, Gert Rosenthal, would put it, "to keeping MINUGUA alive."[84] Moreover, during the Portillo years it took its orientation either from positions worked out within the Dialogue Group in Guatemala or from Rosenthal himself, whose high personal standing in New York ensured considerably more support than the Portillo government could muster elsewhere. From late 2003, however, a slightly expanded group of Friends and donors provided effective support to the secretariat in discussions of plans to establish an Office of the High Commissioner of Human Rights in Guatemala and, more controversial, a commission to investigate the murky world of Guatemala's "parallel" powers (the Commission of Investigation of Illegal Groups and Clandestine Security Forces, CICIACS).[85]

The extension of MINUGUA's mandate through the end of 2004 allowed the mission to take steps to secure its legacy under the government of President Oscar Berger, a former member of the PAN who ran on the ticket of the Grand National Alliance coalition. Berger's inauguration had brought, in the secretary-general's words, "a sense of relief and renewed optimism" after the four years of rule by Portillo's FRG. The new government recommitted itself to the peace agenda and took several steps to promote it—including, most dramatically, introducing cuts in the size of the army that far exceeded the requirements of the peace accords. But the path ahead was not going to be easy.

Consequently, as MINUGUA prepared for its departure, it dedicated considerable effort to a transition program that offered training to Guatemalans from all regions of the country as well as resources to strengthen the human rights ombudsman and civil society organizations working in areas relating to the peace accords.[86] It did so in full knowledge that, while the United Nations' long engagement in the country had brought notable benefits, the persistence of inequalities and insecurity cast a troubling shadow over Guatemala's future. And indeed, despite the valiant effort of Guatemalans and their partners in the international community, many of the divisions in the society that contributed to the outbreak of the conflict remained all too much in evidence.

Despite underlying resistance from those sectors of Guatemalan society that had had their fill of intervention from outside, the United Nations was finally able to establish its human rights office in September 2005. But it did not try to force through agreement on CICIACS; by this late stage in the process it had realized that taking a forceful stand would probably prove counterproductive.[87] Instead, it was able to secure agreement with the government in December 2006 on a new International Commission Against Impunity in Guatemala (CICIG) with an initial mandate of two years, pending approval by Guatemala's Congress.[88]

Conclusions

There has been a tendency to equate the Guatemalan Friends with the Salvadoran group for the inspiration owed the latter by the former, and similarities with respect to their composition and functional benefits they delivered.[89] Certainly the Guatemalan Friends, as their Salvadoran predecessors, provided vital support to the UN mediator, introduced a degree of equilibrium between the governments and the insurgents they confronted at the negotiating table, and largely kept rival negotiating initiatives at bay. But as this chapter has demonstrated, there were also significant differences between the two groups, as well as in the conflicts.

The conflict in Guatemala presented obstacles to its resolution not seen in El Salvador. The long civil war both sprung from and exacerbated the marginalization of the country's indigenous population; it left weak civilian institutions in a state dominated by powerful military and counterinsurgency structures. The role of the United Nations was uncertain, with the suspicion with which it was held demonstrated by the government's dismissal of the first UN observer. In the early 1990s the peace process was also complicated by a plethora of potential mediators with their own ties to and channels of communication with the parties. Over time, however, the patient diplomacy of the United Nations and its partners was able to nurture and sustain a slowly ripening peace process. The engagement of the Friends helped compensate for the structural disadvantage of the URNG and brought essential continuity and legitimacy to negotiations moderated by the United Nations that the organization would not have been able to carry on its own. It also rewarded the group's members with influence in the process and international recognition for the contribution they made to it.

By the mid-1990s the backing of the former superpowers for the resolution of what was perceived as minor unfinished business of the Cold War was assured. The Friends' inclusion of Colombia, Mexico, and Venezuela represented an effort coherent with the regional processes of the past. But the relatively low profile maintained by Colombia and Venezuela relegated the mechanism's ties to regional diplomacy to a secondary feature. Much more significant was the shadow cast by El Salvador. Guatemala's observation of developments in the neighboring country encouraged openness in both parties to the involvement of a group of Friends. Periodic consultations with Salvadoran counterparts also informed positions taken in the negotiations. This translated into clear limits on the extent of military reform that Guatemala's authorities would countenance and demands from the URNG and civil society for more specific attention to the country's economic and social injustices at the peace table than the Salvadorans had been able to achieve.

The engagement of the Friends was contingent on the receptivity to them demonstrated by the parties to the conflict. Indeed, both parties actively pursued the creation of a group of Friends of some kind. That they did so with a sharp eye as to what might benefit their own positions most is not surprising. But that they wanted their involvement opened the door for the Friends' resources and influence to play a positive role in moving both parties forward to accept the broad agenda for change that the agreements represented. A basic trust in the good intentions of the Friends allowed them, and perhaps most obviously Norway, to push the parties hard on issues such as the historical clarification commission or Asturias's withdrawal from the negotiating team after the kidnapping debacle, but also to help broaden the horizon of the possible, notably in the development of thinking in Guatemala's military. In this respect the Friends were not so much a "cushion" between the parties and the United Nations as a force multiplier of the secretariat's efforts that brought important credibility to a process conducted far from the international limelight.

That the parties fragmented soon after the agreements' signing was to prove a significant obstacle to their implementation, not least because it limited the extent to which the United Nations and the Friends could engage with coherent counterparts.

The composition of the Friends was a product of negotiation between the parties themselves and not a construct of the United Nations. The addition of both Norway and the United States to the four Salvadoran Friends fundamentally changed the dynamics determining the group's actions in several respects. At one level, a broader mix of states imposed a natural limit on the camaraderie that had developed between Spain and the three Latin American states engaged on El Salvador.[90] At another, the involvement, interests, and connections of the four principal Friends contributed to their assumption of complementary roles once they were constituted as Friends of the Guatemalan Peace Process. Thus, Mexico retained a role as host to the negotiations and convener of the Friends, while Norway's adroit and generously resourced diplomacy represented a significant example of what could be achieved by a determined and patient "helpful fixer." Spain brought its experience in El Salvador and long engagement in Guatemala and functioned—as it had in El Salvador—as an effective bridge to the EU. More surprising, perhaps, was the low-key yet effective contribution made by the United States. This was in good part a determination to learn from the lessons of El Salvador, facilitated by the United States' more distant relationship to the Guatemalan government and the freedom given to the officials involved to pursue a collegial role as a Friend without placing fundamental bilateral interests in jeopardy.[91]

The relationship of the Friends to the United Nations was a curious one, not least because of the anomalous position of Arnault, who benefited from low expectations of the Guatemalan process within the secretariat and a consequent lack of interest by his superiors (with the notable exception of Goulding). Paradoxically, it was only by providing the Friends with a formal role in the framework agreement that it was possible to assert the leadership of the secretariat and recapture the supportive relationship that had been present in El Salvador. Overall, the Friends successfully reinforced Arnault's efforts, whose standing among them grew as he honed a quiet choreography of the many different Guatemalan and international actors involved. But a greater degree of autonomy from the United Nations than had been evident in the Salvadoran Friends directly allied with the secretary-general was demonstrated by the stand taken in favor of MINUGUA's authorization by the General Assembly. Insistence on the General Assembly may have strengthened the influence of the Friends in the short term, but it also deprived the process of the oversight by the international community provided by regular consideration by the Security Council.

Nearly fifteen years separated the Oslo meeting in March 1990 that first gave the United Nations a role as observer in Guatemala's peace process from MINUGUA's departure at the end of 2004. Overall, the Friends remained a surprisingly durable mechanism, but one whose intrinsic value as a partner to the United Nations varied extensively throughout its lifetime. Effective as individual actors in nurturing a fragile process of dialogue toward negotiations, the Friends functioned best as a collective entity between 1994 and 1996, in support of negotiations whose forward movement assured them clearly assigned tasks. The United Nations' capacity to exert its leadership over the multiple actors involved in Guatemala diminished markedly once the final agreements were signed and the stark reality that leverage over implementation is closely related to resources took hold. Donor priorities in some instances trumped a stated commitment to the peace agenda or shifted with domestic political change, even as other actors remained steadfastly loyal to the priorities outlined by the United Nations. Meanwhile, internal conditions in Guatemala allowed for unusually heavy-handed intervention by the Dialogue Group. While unquestionably more effective than its component states would have been individually, the group too had its limitations, exposed by a greater susceptibility to the government's positions in the international financial institutions than in many of its bilateral members.

The value of agreements reached through negotiation and the solidity of the social forces behind them only become evident during implementation. Problems encountered during implementation of the Guatemalan agreements highlight the importance of planning for partnerships in implementation during the peacemaking stage. However, the path taken by the Friends and then the Dialogue Group suggests that the partners may not always be the same. It also demonstrates that the substitution of international pressure for national political will and capacity has its limits. That the broad international consensus around the agreements reached at the negotiating table was not adequately reflected in national constituencies was exposed during implementation as the central flaw of the Guatemalan peace process. It represents a humbling conclusion, for the United Nations as well as for the Friends, as it demonstrates that years of meticulous diplomacy, ably practiced by dedicated individuals with deep ties to a country, can achieve a great deal, but guarantees neither comprehension of the complex internal dynamics of a society emerging from years of internal conflict nor an ability to overcome them.

4

Principal Friend
The United States and the Long Haul in Haiti

The United Nations became involved in Haiti in the early 1990s at a moment of optimism regarding its capacities in the post–Cold War era. Critical to this involvement was a powerful group of Friends of the Secretary-General, comprising the United States—always the essential external actor on Haiti—but also Canada, France, and Venezuela. The Friends played a central role in persuading Security Council members reluctant to support interference in the internal affairs of a state to engage in Haiti and in formulating policy designed to restore Haiti's exiled president, Jean-Bertrand Aristide, to power. This included imposing punitive sanctions on an already desperately poor country and, in mid-1993, negotiation, of a sort, of the Governors Island Agreement, which fell apart soon afterward. The United States benefited directly from the possibility of addressing Haiti multilaterally as a member of the Friends, but its status as first among equals was never in doubt. Indeed, the military intervention to restore Aristide to Haiti in October 1994 was authorized only after a deal cut between the United States and Russia balancing Haiti against Georgia ensured that neither would oppose operations proposed for the other's backyard.[1] And when the United Nations took over the lead of the peacekeeping effort in early 1995, it did so within conditions that were circumscribed as much by the political requirements of the United States as by Haiti's traditional ambivalence, rooted in its long and conflictive history, toward outside interference.

Over a fifteen-year period the polarizing figure of Aristide, a charismatic former priest who had caught the popular imagination but failed to deliver anything approximating the democratic process that had been hoped of him, dominated developments in Haiti. Always a controversial figure in the United States, to the other three Friends he had represented an attractive option to Haiti's military authorities. His appeal was only increased by the persecution he had suffered and his vilification by some on the right of the U.S. political spectrum. From 1995 on, a succession of

UN peace operations, as well as a human rights mission launched in partnership with the Organization of American States (OAS), struggled to
establish security, train a new police force, and encourage elections. But
both the nation building conceived by the United States and the extent to
which Haitian authorities—with Aristide behind them—would accept
the tutelage it represented had limits that the international community,
led by the Friends, failed to address. Disillusion set in and in 2001, as Aristide returned to the presidency, the United Nations abandoned its peacebuilding effort and left the country. Corruption, violence, and drug trafficking flourished as Haiti descended into mob rule. In 2004 Aristide was
forced into exile again and the United Nations returned in circumstances
more daunting than those encountered a decade earlier. The "old Friends"
drove decisions in the Security Council, but were in the company of
broader and more diffuse mechanisms for international support than in the
past. Their prospects for success were no more certain.

Civil Conflict in Haiti

Haiti won independence in 1804, and in doing so became the first independent republic in Latin America and the only nation ever born of a slave
revolt. Surrounded by slave colonies and the slave-owning United States,
it had few friends.[2] A gradual recognition of its independence by outside
powers did little to offset the domination of the majority of the population
by a small *mulatto* elite and a history marred by instability, repression, and
exclusion. Long the poorest country in the Western hemisphere, Haiti has
progressively declined in the rankings of human development maintained
by the United Nations Development Programme (UNDP), and in 2005
ranked 153 out of 177 countries. These factors combine with Haiti's location to dictate that its strategic importance has been limited to its proximity to the United States, only 600 miles away, and the extent to which this
has facilitated unwanted migration and drug trafficking.

    Under French rule from 1697, Haiti had been more lucrative for France
in the eighteenth century than all the Spanish colonies in the Americas
combined.[3] The brutality of the colonial administration both triggered
Haiti's war for independence and left behind it a legacy of violence and
poverty, exacerbated by the massive reparations demanded by France for
assets seized during the war for independence. In a political culture that
favored strong presidential rule, removal of the president proved the only
avenue for change; Haiti saw twenty-two of them come and go between
1843 and 1915.[4] At this point the United States stepped in and occupied

the country until 1934. Order was imposed by the creation of a new gendarmerie, the *Garde*—later to become the Haitian army—to counter popular resistance, but the bases for genuine stability were not established. The militarization of society facilitated the rise of strongmen François "Papa Doc" Duvalier and his son Jean-Claude "Baby Doc," who held sway over Haiti between 1957 and 1986 in a period infamous for the brutality exercised by paramilitary units such as the feared *tontons macoutes*.

"Baby Doc" Duvalier succeeded his father in 1971. International donors had welcomed his commitment to economic and political modernization, but soon became disillusioned. Unrest among Haiti's urban and rural poor, the opposition of the Catholic Church, and discontent within the army fueled a mounting campaign that eventually forced him to leave Haiti in early 1986. His departure was followed by a period of direct military rule, but it also triggered an explosion of popular energy at the grassroots level as the majority of Haiti's population, some of them represented by nongovernmental organizations (NGOs) of all kinds, demanded justice, an end to the terror perpetrated by the *tontons macoutes*, and decentralization of the state.[5] Popular mobilization and international pressure eventually led to the installation of a provisional civilian government that oversaw a process that would culminate in elections on December 16, 1990. In an unprecedented development, Haiti's authorities approached the OAS and the United Nations with a request that they observe them.[6]

The elections swept into the presidency a former priest called Jean-Bertrand Aristide, at the head of a movement, *Lavalas* ("the flood"), which had captured popular imagination for its commitment to the poor, its outspoken opposition to government repression, and the possibility of change that it represented. Aristide took office in February 1991 and began his reforms by announcing at his inauguration a purge of the army high command. Initial suspicion from the military grew into outright hostility.[7] During the night of September 29, 1991, shortly after returning from a visit to the UN General Assembly, Aristide was deposed in a coup, escaping with his life only because of the timely intervention of French, American, and Venezuelan diplomats.

Haiti was plunged into violence and uncertainty by a sustained assault on Aristide's supporters. Human rights groups estimated that as many as 1,000 people were killed in the two weeks following the coup and more than 3,000 before the return of Aristide in October 1994; thousands more suffered arbitrary arrest, beatings, and torture.[8] Freedom of expression was stifled and Haitians took to the sea. Between 1991 and 1994, 68,500 asylum seekers were interdicted by the U.S. Coast Guard and Navy and returned to Haiti in compliance with a U.S. policy that treated them as economic migrants, not political refugees.[9] Human rights and refugee organizations decried the policy as a clear breach of international law.

The United Nations' efforts to restore Aristide to power involved an ultimately fruitless attempt to pursue dialogue between the exiled president and the de facto military rulers, the imposition of sanctions, and then the authorization of military intervention. Aristide's return was successfully achieved, but in its very success it sowed the seeds of continued instability, reinforcing Haiti's "winner-take-all" approach to political power and distracting attention from the roots of Haiti's conflict. Despite a substantial commitment from the international community, it did not take long for the problems that led to the coup in 1990 to reappear and for the country to lurch back into crisis. What was assumed to be a final UN mission came to a close in March 2001 as donors, frustrated by their inability to exert leverage on Haiti's recalcitrant political leaders and particularly by the marked deterioration in the Haitian National Police, a force in which they had invested heavily, suspended international assistance.[10]

The United States and Its Interests

The United States may have no compelling interest in tiny, impoverished Haiti, but its power and proximity render it the ultimate arbiter of what takes place there. In 1994 a series of weaker interests coalesced with domestic political circumstances and the somewhat amorphous humanitarianism of the Clinton administration to prompt sustained engagement at the highest levels of government, culminating in military intervention.[11]

The United States' interests in Haiti are largely determined by geography (as one former U.S. ambassador to Haiti bluntly put it, the United States' "fundamental interest" in Haiti is "to defend Miami Beach").[12] They derive neither from national security concerns nor commercial relations (total Haitian imports before the embargo was introduced in 1992 amounted to about $400 million, or less than one-tenth of 1 percent of U.S. exports). Instead, they reflect the broader interest that the United States has avowed since the time of the Monroe Doctrine in furthering political stability and economic progress in the Americas. In themselves desirable goals, in the context of a small island state such as Haiti, they become most pertinent in their absence, as a lack of stability and economic progress will create conditions that allow illegal migration and drug trafficking to flourish.[13] Since the mid-1990s, drug trafficking has been of increasing concern. Indeed, in 2000 it was estimated that approximately 9 percent of the cocaine destined for the United States transited Haiti and the Dominican Republic.[14]

Response to Haiti's coup, however, was conditioned by something else: a specific commitment to the promotion of democracy in the Western hemisphere, crystallized in the Santiago Declaration adopted by the OAS in June 1991, just three months before Aristide's removal from power. This committed the nations of the hemisphere to respond to any threat to a member state's democracy collectively and through the organization; Haiti was its first test.[15] James A. Baker III was secretary of state at the time. He would describe in his autobiography how the Republican administration did not much like Aristide—"reputedly to be anti-American," he was "a leader with a mixed reputation and record"—but had supported and funded the elections that brought him to power and would stand by the results of this process. Moreover, Baker had been conscious that "would-be coup makers were watching our response." Accordingly, he spoke strongly in the OAS just two days after Aristide's ouster, and encouraged the organization to adopt a trade embargo against Haiti and its de facto rulers: "Until President Aristide's government is restored, this junta will be treated as a pariah throughout this hemisphere—without assistance, without friends, and without a future."[16]

The George H.W. Bush administration saw a national interest in restoring democracy to Haiti, but not one "sufficiently vital" to use military force. During the Clinton administration the waters were to become much muddier. Clinton raised and then dashed hopes that he would reverse the Republican policy of interdiction of asylum seekers, reneging on a campaign promise within days of assuming the presidency. But as the refugee crisis escalated in early 1994 he was forced to adopt a radical shift in policy in response to pressure from domestic lobbies skillfully mobilized by Aristide and his supporters. This led to effective U.S. leadership of the very military intervention that the Republican administration had deemed not in American interest, justified on the basis that it was the right thing to do on humanitarian grounds. "The need is great; the cause is just; the ability to make a difference is real," Ambassador Madeleine Albright told the Security Council on July 31, 1994.[17] However, Republican victories in congressional elections soon afterward prompted protracted battles over aid to Haiti and accelerated the pace at which Democrats sought to extricate the United States from Haiti as soon as they could.

Ten years later, in early 2004, as Haiti once more descended into chaos on the Republicans' watch, there was, as Secretary of State Colin Powell put it, "no enthusiasm" for sending peacekeepers to the country until after

Aristide himself had left.[18] Haiti had long been a highly partisan issue and in the preceding years old antipathies to Aristide had resurfaced. To the chagrin of some of Aristide's Democratic supporters, they had also been vindicated in many respects by Aristide's erratic, abusive, and authoritarian performance. With the return to public office of many of the individuals who had so opposed Aristide in the early 1990s, U.S. policy shifted away from the direct engagement and dialogue maintained by the Clinton administration to one of estrangement. Official aid was never high on a per capita basis (U.S. assistance was a tenth of that distributed in Kosovo and fell rapidly after the departure of U.S. peacekeepers in 1996)[19] and was frozen in the fall of 2000 following disputed municipal and legislative elections that May. The administration maintained support of the diplomatic efforts of the OAS and assistance to NGOs and the private sector as a way out of dealing with Haiti's authorities directly. Meanwhile, unofficial actors—some with close ties to the Bush administration and Congress—channeled funding and support to Haiti's opposition forces, undermining the credibility of those pursuing a political solution.[20] Only after Aristide had resigned, with what the *New York Times* would describe as "a shove from the United States," did the Marines go in, with any commitment to the constitutional process in tatters as the United States reluctantly embarked on another round of nation building in Haiti.[21]

Haiti's Four Friends and the United Nations

Cooperation between the four states that would form the Friends of the Secretary-General for Haiti dates back to a meeting in Caracas in October 1989 between President François Mitterand of France and President Carlos Andrés Pérez of Venezuela. Pérez had suggested that, because of their respective histories—during Simon Bolívar's campaign for Venezuelan independence, Haiti had twice given Bolivar sanctuary[22]—the two countries had a special responsibility to help Haiti develop a democratic system. The presidents agreed that any effective action on Haiti required the involvement of both the United States and Canada, which had become one of Haiti's largest donors and hosted a significant Haitian diaspora population. Accordingly, in early 1990, Pérez asked first Mitterand and then Prime Minister Brian Mulroney of Canada to raise the idea with President George H. W. Bush. Prompted by Mulroney, Bush called Pérez and agreed to collaborate in support of the democratic process in Haiti.[23]

Secretary-General Javier Pérez de Cuéllar had visited Haiti in 1986 after the younger Duvalier's ouster, and even discussed the possibility of providing UN technical assistance for elections.[24] But until 1990 conditions did not exist for the United Nations to respond positively to a request for help. At that point, prompted by the knowledge that the influential states of Canada, France, Venezuela, and the United States were anxious for the United Nations to become engaged, Pérez de Cuéllar sent a trusted Haitian aide, Jean-Claude Aimé, to Haiti to assess developments on the ground.[25] A formal request to the United Nations and to the OAS to assist in holding elections through technical assistance, electoral observation, and the provision of "specialized observers" to keep the Haitian army in check soon followed.[26]

In retrospect, as Diego Arria, Venezuela's ambassador to the United Nations, lamented, "The international community seems to have considered a day at the polls sufficient for launching Haiti's democratic process."[27] No residual presence remained in Haiti to accompany the fragile government led by President Aristide, and international attention moved on to other things. Consequently the coup that ousted Aristide in late September 1991 came as something of a shock. Aristide flew to Caracas on an airplane sent by Pérez, who lost no time in persuading him to mobilize international support at the OAS and United Nations. All four "future Friend" ambassadors to Haiti saw Aristide off into exile at the airport in Port-au-Prince; all four ambassadors to Venezuela were there to welcome him in Caracas, where he would stay for three months before moving to Washington. This direct involvement in these dramatic events would cement the determination of many of the diplomats involved to secure Aristide's return.

On October 8, 1991, the OAS adopted a resolution urging its members to impose a trade embargo and cut all international aid except humanitarian assistance. The embargo was porous and inconsistent.[28] As efforts to restore Aristide flagged in mid-1992, Canada, France, the United States, and Venezuela constituted themselves first as a "quadripartite" group and then, in response to an overture made by Boutros-Ghali to the prime minister of Canada, as the secretary-general's Friends.[29]

Boutros-Ghali had a long-standing interest in Haiti for the resemblance he saw in it to parts of Africa, as well as a desire to pursue collaborations between regional organizations and the United Nations. When he met Aristide for the first time in September, Aristide had pressed for engagement by the Security Council, where the Group of Latin American and Caribbean States (GRULAC) was strongly resistant. Boutros-Ghali had advised him to try to gain greater support among UN member states, which he did, in part through an electrifying performance before the

General Assembly in late September.[30] On November 24 the General Assembly gave Boutros-Ghali the opening for a more active role by asking him, in cooperation with the OAS, to assist in resolving the crisis in Haiti.[31] He moved promptly to appoint Dante Caputo, a former foreign minister of Argentina, as his special envoy (Caputo also became representative of the OAS soon afterward).

Officials advising Boutros-Ghali on Haiti, among them Francesc Vendrell, had encouraged his overture to the Friends for a number of reasons. He was going to need all the leverage he could muster to persuade a reluctant Security Council to take action on this issue. Moreover, the group's "other" members had the potential to act as a significant counterweight to the essential presence of the United States. France was a permanent member of the Council, with both lasting influence in Haiti and links to Europe; it rapidly assumed a leading role in the group's actions at the United Nations. Canada, meanwhile, had credibility on Haiti gained from its long-term commitment to the development of the country, a desire to make a success of its new (1990) membership in the OAS, and a strong record of cooperation in UN peacekeeping in Central America.[32] Venezuela brought the proactive Pérez as well as a Latin American seat on the Security Council, which it occupied from 1992 to 1993.[33] Together, the four would be described by Ambassador Hervé Ladsous of France as states with "specific if different interests in trying to achieve something for Haiti itself."[34]

Canada, France, and Venezuela were aware that no action in the United Nations was possible without the United States, but also welcomed an opportunity to work with the United States in a small and informal group in which they would state their own positions, and might even influence the its actions.[35] For the United States, meanwhile, the group of Friends was to prove what Ambassador Edward Walker would describe as "a helpful vehicle to project U.S. policy in a multilateral form," both in overcoming suspicion of the United States in the United Nations and in providing multilateral support to a policy that faced a good deal of domestic criticism.[36] In this respect the mechanism was viewed as an experiment to see whether the United Nations "could not be effective in pursuing U.S. policy," as Walker put it. Collaboration with the United Nations and the Friends was praised as "a good example of the emerging era of multilateral diplomacy."[37] The Friends would at times work at cross-purposes (often against the United States), but U.S. representatives were never in any doubt as to which country was taking the decisions.

These origins were to determine the role—or roles—that the Friends would play in the future. The creation of the group reflected the secretary-general's capture of a natural body of states motivated by interests that were, as Ladsous had put it, "specific if different." But the kind of fealty to the secretary-general that lay behind the Friends in El Salvador was not present. The Friends would be managed more or less closely by the secretariat and UN officials in Haiti, depending on the political moment and the personalities involved. Yet there was, from the beginning, an independence of action that ensured the Friends a driving role in the United Nations' long-drawn-out engagement.

Friends and the Political Process

During the twenty-two months in which Caputo served as the secretary-general's special envoy, he worked closely with the Friends. The four states were most commonly represented in New York by Canadian Ambassador Louise Fréchette or her deputy, David Malone; Hervé Ladsous, the deputy permanent representative of France; Edward Walker, the deputy permanent representative of the United States, who sometimes acted in support of Ambassador Madeleine Albright; and—until Pérez's departure from the presidency in mid-1993 provoked a reversal of Venezuelan policy on Haiti and a new ambassador—Diego Arria for Venezuela. Caputo, at times accompanied by other senior UN officials, met with them as a group with a regularity that varied with the intensity of the process; he also consulted with them separately in between meetings, with their ambassadors in Port-au-Prince and with officials from their foreign ministers in their capitals.

To an extent that distinguished the Friends from the groups in Central America, the group was intimately involved in discussing and shaping policy. It fully supported Caputo's efforts to secure agreement to the deployment of a joint UN-OAS human rights mission (the International Civilian Mission, MICIVIH) in early 1993[38] and worked hard to overcome reluctance to intervene in Haiti within the Security Council. It was closely involved in the decision to impose sanctions on Haiti and in the political process that concluded in the signing of the Governors Island Agreement in July 1993. But as this fell apart in the months that followed, so did the cohesion among the Friends deteriorate, with the positions assumed by Canada, France, and Venezuela increasingly irrelevant to the evolution of the U.S. policy toward Haiti, the "principal Friend," as one UN official described it. In contrast to the other three, which openly supported Aristide at this point, the United States was more complex, not to say contradictory, in its stance on Haiti: publicly claimed political support of Aristide was not only ambivalent, but was constantly undermined by military and intelligence communities with close ties to Haiti's military authorities. The latter made sure their influence was exerted by contracting Washington lobbyists to fuel their denigration of Aristide.

Caputo's efforts to find a political settlement of the crisis were reinforced by the appointment in March 1993 by President Clinton of Lawrence Pezzullo as his special adviser for Haiti and Clinton's public commitment to "step up dramatically the pace of negotiations to restore President Aristide."[39] While Caputo retained separate channels of communication with the other Friends (he found particular support from France, which benefited from connections Ladsous had made serving as chargé of the French embassy in Haiti after the coup against Aristide), his relationship with the United States was necessarily of a different order. The United States was consulted more directly than other Friends; Caputo traveled to Haiti with Pezzullo and included the U.S. official in some of his meetings with the Haitian parties. Some within the secretariat and among the Friends took a pragmatic approach to the reality of U.S. weight on Haiti. Others found it increasingly uncomfortable and came to resent the subservient role into which they believed they had been cast.[40]

Draft agreements were presented to the military in late March. Like the Washington agreement reached under OAS auspices in February 1992, the documents outlined a future coalition government, "pacification" and amnesty, the return of President Aristide, and international assistance. New proposals envisaged the removal of the army high command and the replacement of the chief of police.[41] Efforts to force agreement included first, the "stick" represented by the threat of sanctions, and second, the "carrot" of a military and police assistance mission that would give General Raul Cédras and other coup leaders the security guarantees they demanded. Neither was possible without the Security Council. Conscious that securing its support would be difficult, the Friends encouraged Aristide to have Haiti's UN ambassador, Fritz Longchamp, write to the Council on June 7, 1993.[42] They then embarked on an intensive period of lobbying. Latin American and Caribbean states that supported the sanctions were pressed into service, while assurances were obtained from those that did not at least not to lobby against them. Resolution 841, adopted on June 16, 1993, threatened to cut off the sale of fuel and arms to Haiti and established a committee to monitor the implementation of the sanctions.

The threat of sanctions brought both Cédras and Aristide to New York to participate in talks with Caputo at Governors Island. Boutros-Ghali would credit the "invaluable support" of the Friends as "crucial" to their successful completion.[43] The Governors Island negotiations—which were conducted in shuttle form, because of the refusal of the protagonists to meet with each other—were indeed a notable example of multilateral diplomacy, albeit of a somewhat coercive nature. Caputo led the effort, with reinforcement from Marrack Goulding and Pezzullo, particularly with Cédras. The other Friends were present on the island, although Canada, France, and Venezuela had a clearly subordinate role to the United States.[44] Cédras agreed to the text first, and then left the island, placing pressure on Aristide, who would be told by everyone ranging from his own team of advisers to Boutros-Ghali, U.S. Secretary of State Warren Christopher, and the Friends that he faced no other option than to sign.[45] The resulting agreement, signed on July 3, provided for the return of Aristide following a political dialogue, a new civilian government, the lifting of sanctions, assistance from UN personnel to modernize the army and create a new police force, an amnesty, and the retirement of Cédras.[46]

The Governors Island Agreement was met with mixed feelings in the secretariat. It had not mentioned human rights, but represented UN endorsement of a blanket amnesty and indeed triggered an almost immediate spike in human rights violations in Haiti.[47] Moreover, by some oversight, reference to a government of "national concord"—an idea that had been central to previous discussions of a resolution of Haiti's crisis—had been omitted. These doubts were quickly confirmed in the following months as mounting violence in Haiti dispelled any hope that the agreements reached at Governors Island might be implemented. The turning point came on October 11, 1993, when in a spectacular reversal of international efforts in Haiti, armed thugs and demonstrators took advantage of the uproar caused by the killing of eighteen U.S. Army Rangers in Somalia a few days earlier to stage a noisy protest (complete with signs marked "Remember Mogadishu") against the landing of the U.S.S. *Harlan County*, which had the first substantial deployment of U.S. military troops and Canadian police on board. With its foreign policy caught between expectations for humanitarian action and demands that it should not assume a role as the world's policeman, the Clinton administration ordered the *Harlan County* to turn around and come home. It was humiliation of the first order. But as senior White House aide George Stephanopoulos recalled, "So soon after Somalia, no one had the stomach for another fight."[48]

Dante Caputo, in Port-au-Prince at the time, was not even informed of the United States' decision. Boutros-Ghali addressed a confidential letter of protest to Ambassador Albright on October 13, but the damage was done. As the Friends met in New York that day, the Canadian ambassador warned that it would be difficult to persuade Ottawa not to withdraw all the Canadian police who had arrived in Haiti forthwith. A few days later the United States withdrew all its military personnel, and on October 16 the United Nations evacuated MICIVIH. The Friends would continue to refer publicly to the Governors Island Agreement as "the only viable framework" with which to address the crisis in Haiti for some time to come, but wondered, when they met again on October 21, how to tell the Security Council about its "complete failure."[49]

After *Harlan County*: On the Sidelines

In the wake of the *Harlan County* debacle, the Security Council declared Haiti a threat to peace and security, reintroduced sanctions, and introduced a naval blockade.[50] But the political process had broken down. The inconsistencies of U.S. policy—heightened by renewed assaults on Aristide's character in late 1993—were evident, and Caputo and the Friends were soon sidelined by the emerging struggle between the Clinton administration and Aristide.

In early November Caputo had tried to organize a meeting in Haiti between the government of Prime Minister Robert Malval, who had been appointed in accordance with the Governors Island Agreement, and the army in Port-au-Prince, but Cédras and other military leaders failed to show up. Caputo left Haiti and never returned. The Friends took up the baton and at France's urging, held a high-level meeting in Paris that was attended by both Caputo and Malval. The meeting concluded with a public statement, circulated as a document of the Security Council, that endorsed a middle way between Aristide and the de facto authorities.[51] But the Friends, too, were rebuffed when, after a tricky meeting with Aristide in Washington (which they attended without Caputo), Cédras refused to meet with the military delegation they sent to Haiti. Caputo and the Friends continued to meet regularly throughout the winter and spring of 1994, but their utility was undermined by deepening differences among them. Only Canada and France held to the view that the military had to go, while paralysis had overcome a U.S. administration that was undermined by the contradictory messages it was projecting. Officials at the United Nations were assured that "private American advisers," some of them former civilian officials, were telling the Haitian military not to negotiate because sooner or later the United Nations and the United States would lift sanctions on humanitarian grounds.[52]

That sanctions had not worked had been evident for some time: they were inflicting real economic hardship on the vast majority of the Haitian population that was poor, while actually enriching the de facto authorities they targeted as well as prominent families who had backed the coup.[53] But there did not appear to be other alternatives. Support from the Friends for strengthening the sanctions and introducing monitoring of the border with the Dominican Republic was mixed, with France and Canada in favor of positions assumed by Aristide while the United States, backed by Venezuela (which since the departure of President Pérez had radically altered its stance on Haiti), was reluctant, fearing that new sanctions would lead to a greater exodus of refugees without delivering any political benefit. MICIVIH began returning its observers in early 1994, but found the situation worse than at any time during its presence in 1993. Indeed, MICIVIH would be forced out of the country in July, this time by Haiti's authorities.

With the UN-led process in disarray, relief came only when domestic pressures on Clinton, fueled by sustained pressure from refugee and human rights organizations and Aristide himself, forced a radical rethinking of U.S. policy. Protests were led by the Congressional Black Caucus, a political constituency that Clinton could not ignore in a year of congressional elections. They came to a head in April when six congressmen chained themselves to the White House, and Randall Robinson, the prominent leader of the advocacy organization TransAfrica Forum, embarked on a hunger strike. Aristide stood at his side and denounced U.S. policy toward his country as racist and a "cynical joke." Clinton caved in. The United States reaffirmed its support of Aristide, pushed for the introduction of extensive new sanctions through the Security Council, and reversed its policy on refugees by promising to determine their status before returning them to Haiti.[54] Pezzullo was asked for his resignation and was replaced as Clinton's special adviser by William Gray, a former leader of the Congressional Black Caucus.

At the United Nations, the first whisper of the full implication of the change in the U.S. position came from a phone call to the desk officer in the Department of Peacekeeping Operations (DPKO) on May 11. The UN official was casually asked whether the United Nations "was inclined to rule out unilateral intervention in Haiti followed by a UN peace operation?"[55] Boutros-Ghali held out against U.S. pressure for the United Nations to undertake the intervention in favor of a U.S.-led multinational force, rightly considering—in light of lessons painfully learned in Bosnia, Rwanda, and Somalia—that the United Nations could not secure Aristide's return. Notes from a meeting between Boutros-Ghali and his senior advisers in early June, leaked to the *Wall Street Journal*, revealed that officials were wary that even a multinational intervention followed by a UN peace operation might leave the United Nations "holding the baby."[56]

Efforts to secure Security Council approval of the resolution that would authorize a multinational force "to use all necessary means to facilitate the departure from Haiti of the military leadership" were initiated by the United States. The Friends tried to find support from Latin American and Caribbean states. But weakened by their own divisions and pressure from members of the Council complaining that they were micromanaging the process, they could not overcome opposition to U.S.-led military action in the region.[57] While Argentina, which had joined the group in early 1994 as it assumed a seat on the Security Council, hewed closely to the U.S. position, Venezuela was openly against the prospect of U.S.-led intervention in the Caribbean. Canada and France, along with Argentina, cosponsored the resolution (Security Council Resolution [SCR] 940) approved on July 31 (even as the other Latin American state on the Council, Brazil, abstained). But they did not take part in the multinational force launched in September 1994. For the moment, with U.S. policy ascendant, the Friends, like the UN special envoy who had long opposed military intervention and resigned in September, were out of the picture.[58]

From Peacekeeping to Nation Building

Between March 1995 and March 2001, three successive UN peacekeeping operations, a police assistance mission, and a peacebuilding mission were established in the wake of the U.S.-led multinational force, "Operation Uphold Democracy," that on October 15, 1994, returned Aristide to power. The first of these missions, the United Nations Mission in Haiti (UNMIH), was mandated to help sustain the "secure and stable environment" created under the multinational force, professionalize the armed forces—a task overtaken by Aristide's decision to disband the army in 1995 without consulting with the United Nations or codifying the action in the constitution—create a new police force, and help establish conditions for free and fair elections.[59] It was succeeded by smaller missions with similar, but diminishing, mandates.[60] These continued to work closely with MICIVIH, which had extensive responsibilities both for human rights monitoring and institution building. Yet it is telling that, in a two-volume RAND Corporation study of nation building, Haiti is classified as a U.S.-led, not UN-led, endeavor. This distinction was judged "entirely correct" by Lakhdar Brahimi, who took over from the U.S.-led force in March 1995 as the secretary-general's special representative and head of the first UN peacekeeping operation.[61]

The terms for the United Nations' operations in Haiti were set by the goals of the Clinton administration. In a highly partisan Washington, where the idea of "nation building" had been irrevocably tainted by the U.S. experience in Somalia, these goals fell short of the stated commitment to the restoration of democracy. Indeed, the RAND study, led by James Dobbins, who had served as Clinton's special envoy to Haiti, found that the restoration of democracy "became defined as the return of President Aristide and then the renewal, through three elections, of all Haitian electoral offices: local, legislative, and executive."[62] In the long run, the equation of democracy with the return of Aristide—who had, in Brahimi's words, "maneuvered beautifully to get the international community to give him total victory"—was to prove a fundamental mistake. The international intervention had followed the collapse of a negotiated settlement and not an agreed blueprint for reform contained in a peace agreement. It promoted the concentration of power in the hands of the president (Aristide would remain the power behind René Préval while the latter held the presidency from 1996 to 2001) and the exclusion of opposition forces aligned with former military authorities, who, though hardly palatable, remained an important factor in the governance of Haiti.

Domestic politics within the United States continued to cast a long shadow. Ambivalence about Aristide was expressed in U.S. insistence that he serve out only the five-year term to which he had been elected and relinquish power at the end of 1995 (by this logic the years of his exile counted toward his presidency), a decision he evidently resented.[63] Meanwhile, Republican opposition to the Clinton administration's policy and actions in Haiti was fierce, particularly after the advent in January 1995 of a Republican-controlled Congress bent on curtailing assistance to Haiti. An obvious vulnerability to criticism contributed to Democrats' presentation of a consistently rosy picture of the limited successes achieved in order to ensure the rapid departure of U.S. forces. Democrats also were reluctant to distance themselves from Aristide and his behavior lest it be construed that they were wrong to have returned him to Haiti in the first place.

The representatives of the Friends in Port-au-Prince had long been engaged with UN officials in the field. They had liased closely with Dante Caputo during his visits to Haiti and would provide material and moral support to the fragile mission of MICIVIH throughout its eight-year presence in Haiti. Relationships between the Friends and successive representatives of the secretary-general—Lakhdar Brahimi, Enrique ter Horst,

Julian Harston, and Alfredo Lopes Cabral[64]—varied in accordance with the personalities involved and the demands of the political moment. But this period of UN peacekeeping in Haiti was one of broad consensus among the international actors involved. The Friends, both in Port-au-Prince and New York, offered support to UN officials while also representing a forum within which their individual positions could be discussed and if necessary, resolved.

At the practical level, the Friends assumed leading roles in the UN missions and in providing assistance to Haiti. Canada took over the military command of UNMIH from the United States in early 1996,[65] relinquishing it to withdraw its troops and cut back on police assistance in late 1997 in view of deteriorating relations with the Haitian authorities. France had a lower military profile and in general, lost the driving interest it had maintained in Haiti during Aristide's period of exile. However, like Canada, it contributed substantively to police assistance, particularly during the period of the United Nations Civilian Police Mission in Haiti (MIPONUH, 1997–2000). This unusual operation was reinforced by Argentina's provision of a rapid reaction force to provide protection to others' unarmed police, a significant contribution on its part.[66]

The transition of authority from the United States to the United Nations had a somewhat difficult start, while the United States became accustomed to the fact that its force commander answered to Brahimi and not the U.S. ambassador. But relations between the two otherwise developed well. Brahimi instituted weekly meetings with the Friends at his residence, in addition to frequent contacts with individual members. Regular meetings would continue to be held by his successors, on occasion extending to combined meetings with President Préval. These meetings of the Friends and other donor states helped contribute to the presentation of the international community as a united entity. However, it was one that was limited in its ability to stick to the clear benchmarks it put to the Haitian authorities, particularly in the areas of justice and public security.[67] Meetings with the president would occur less frequently after August 1997. The United Nations' decision to withdraw technical assistance from the electoral council to protest irregularities in the electoral process precipitated deterioration in relations with Préval. As efforts to appoint a prime minister and a functioning government faltered in a dispute between the two main factions of the ruling *Lavalas* movement, Haiti's political process slid into a crisis.[68]

UN officials who served in Haiti generally concur with the view held by MICIVIH's executive director Colin Granderson that "the United

States, at the level of the Friends, played the game in Haiti." Coordination was helped by the comportment of the U.S. ambassadors, perhaps particularly William Swing, a genial Southerner stationed in Port-au-Prince from 1993 to 1998. The bottom line was that the UN presence in Haiti had been specifically designed to serve the requirements of the United States, which therefore had every interest in a credible group of Friends.[69] Differences, as Enrique ter Horst would recall, tended to be subordinated to the enormity of the challenge faced by the international community in Haiti. When differences did occur—most notably after the 1997 elections, which the Clinton administration, needing to demonstrate progress in Haiti, reluctantly accepted—they reflected underlying disagreements on the timing and pace required for profound institutional transformation. The United States had its internal constituencies to answer to, and both Congress and the Pentagon were pressing hard to achieve a rapid exit from Haiti that was inconsistent with the time, investment, and disposition of the Haitian authorities necessary to secure lasting change.[70]

Donor coordination was a direct beneficiary of planning and communication among the Friends for the obvious reason that the United States, France, and Canada were the principal funders of the Haitian National Police and efforts to reform the justice sector.[71] However, over time extensive efforts to coordinate were undermined by a lack of Haitian follow-through, and differences over policing and the judiciary began to emerge. Pressure to meet timetables set in Washington or New York left donors complaining about the poor absorptive capacity of the Haitian government while trying to implement programs on which Haitian partners had not been adequately consulted. Such pressure failed to take into account the structural conditions of poverty and institutional decay in which they were attempting to operate or the obstruction from Haitian authorities.[72] In the meantime, the conditions for international involvement gradually deteriorated. The dismissal of the Haitian armed forces without adequate provision for pensions (UN help on this sensitive issue was rejected by Aristide) or reintegration, a climate of increasing polarization, and Haiti's emergence as an important transit point for drug trafficking all contributed to rising crime and a return of what one Haitian observer would describe as "old patterns of corruption, nepotism, and incompetence . . . at all governmental levels."[73] A police force undermined by the failings of the justice system and the arbitrary promotion of Aristide loyalists, including the paramilitary groups known as the *chimères*, was overwhelmed. Some of its members lapsed into the brutality of the past; others left as armed groups outside established structures flourished.[74]

Friends and the Long Term

During the five years of UN peacekeeping operations in Haiti that began in 1995, the Friends actively sought to maintain the support of the Security Council for the United Nations' efforts. Joined by Chile when it took a seat on the Council in 1996, from February of that year on they countered criticisms from Russia and China that the tasks appropriate to the United Nations had already been completed and that, in the absence of a credible threat to international peace and security, the UN presence should end. These arguments precipitated complicated mandate renewals, for which requests from the Haitian authorities, extracted at times with difficulty by the special representative of the secretary-general (SRSG) and Friends in Port-au-Prince, were essential. In 2004 the United Nations' Department of Peacekeeping Operations would conclude that the short and finite mandates of successive operations in Haiti both impeded forward planning and wasted time and energy on repeated "drawing-down."[75]

Over the years, discussions on Haiti in the Council provided a vivid illustration both of the extent to which the United States, reinforced by the other Friends, was able to muster support for its preferred policy and of the unsuitability of the Security Council as a forum for the long-term requirements of peacebuilding. However, by 1999 it was evident that the end of the road had been reached. The United States led an effort to pass responsibility for a future role in Haiti to the Economic and Social Council (ECOSOC).[76] Secretariat officials were skeptical, given ECOSOC's lack of operational capability, and concerned that the idea had been developed without consultation with the Haitian authorities, who were increasingly opposed to a continued international presence in Haiti. An effort to improve the confidence of the Haitians in the international effort was an invitation from the secretariat to Jamaica—which enjoyed good relations with Aristide and became a member of the Security Council in January 2000—to join the Friends. But Jamaica, unusually, declined the invitation, arguing that it was "too close" to Haiti to be a Friend.[77] In the end, although an Ad Hoc Advisory Group on Haiti was established within ECOSOC and it even conducted an assessment mission to Haiti, the initiative was deflected by differences within the Friends (while the United States pushed the ECOSOC route, the Canadians lobbied the secretariat against it). The secretariat and the Friends decided instead to pursue authorization of a mission of technical assistance through the General Assembly, to be financed in part by the Friends' own voluntary contributions.[78]

The establishment of the International Civilian Support Mission in Haiti (MICAH) was almost entirely driven by the Friends, with Canada in particular exerting itself to see some kind of continuity in the United Nations' work in Haiti. (In a highly unusual development, a needs assessment mission sent to Haiti in October 1999 by the secretariat included national representatives of Canada, France, and the United States.[79]) The mission had a mandate that encompassed technical assistance to the police and justice sectors, human rights monitoring, and good offices. But within the secretariat, some "Haiti fatigue" had set in. Senior officials had long since stopped paying attention to the travails of Haiti. Their creativity was sapped by the poor state of relations between the United Nations and Haitian authorities and a passive acceptance of the leading role taken by the Friends in decision making. Saying "no" to a new mission was not an option, but some officials feared that, as a Friends-driven and financed operation, MICAH risked putting the United Nations in the position of a private contractor responding to client demand.[80]

In the end, the concerns proved somewhat self-fulfilling. Funding problems, largely attributable to the difficulties encountered in extracting funds from the U.S. Congress, hampered the establishment of the mission, while the Haitian authorities were reluctant to use the assistance that MICAH offered to its full extent. The representative of the secretary-general, Alfredo Lopes Cabral, was a former ambassador of Guinea-Bissau with no experience of Haiti or the region before his appointment in October 1999 (itself an indication of the disregard paid to Haiti at the highest levels of the secretariat).[81] He failed to gain the confidence of some of his colleagues in the United Nations as well as of important Friends (the United States and Canada in particular) and did not successfully develop the political role that was envisaged for him. As the international community struggled to respond to the situation that developed in Haiti following the May elections, in which vote counts in key Senate races were manipulated to favor the ruling *Fanmi Lavalas*, the United Nations was increasingly irrelevant. During September 2000, Madeleine Albright chaired a meeting of the Friends of the Secretary-General at the ministerial level to which the United Nations was, inexplicably, not invited (the United States apologized to the United Nations for the oversight).[82]

It was only in its later stages that MICAH became fully operational, but neither the secretariat nor the Friends sought an extension of MICAH's mandate, in part because of the disappointing performance of its leadership. As a group the Friends were, in any case, in some disarray. In Haiti they had been joined by the key donor states of Germany and Spain and exhibited increasing signs of division between the Europeans (led by France), the Latin Americans, and the United States and Canada.[83] Although France argued for the retention of a political role for the United Nations (and Lopes Cabral), the secretariat did not want it. The OAS had embarked on an effort to broker a settlement between Aristide's *Fanmi Lavalas* and the coalition of opposition parties. After the closure of MICAH in March 2001, it assumed formal leadership of the process as Aristide returned to the presidency. Canada helped steer the Friends toward reincarnation and enlargement as a group of Friends of the Secretary-General of the Organization of American States.[84] From 2002 this group, which met irregularly at the OAS in Washington and in Port-au-Prince, would support the efforts of a small OAS Special Mission in Haiti, engaged in police and judicial assistance, human rights monitoring, and other rule-of-law activities.

The United Nations Returns

Juan Gabriel Valdés was appointed the UN SRSG for Haiti in July 2004. A former academic with extensive political and diplomatic experience behind him, he would recall in an interview a few months later that he "did not remember a single mention of Haiti all the time that he was in New York."[85] The admission was a poignant one. Valdés served as Chile's ambassador to the United Nations from 2000 to mid-2003, after a brief stint as his country's foreign minister. Chile had been a member of the Friends for years and was on the Security Council again from 2003 to 2004. Valdés did not stay to serve out this term only because the steadfast opposition Chile maintained to the U.S.-led invasion of Iraq led the United States to "run him out of town," as one U.S. official put it.[86] But he would have heard little about Haiti until early 2004 if he had. Since MICAH's departure in March 2001, Haiti had been off the UN map.

In retrospect, giving up on Haiti was a costly mistake—as well as questionable on ethical grounds. The political impasse that followed the disputed elections of May 2000 developed into a bitter standoff between Aristide and opposition forces, many of which had once been part of *Lavalas*. Efforts of the OAS and the Caribbean Community (CARICOM) to broker a solution initially appeared hopeful but foundered in September 2003. As in the past, mixed messages coming out of Washington were a complicating factor, with an official commitment to work with Aristide as the country's democratically elected leader consistently undermined by the messages transmitted by other channels, such as the International Republican Institute.[87] A new coalition between the political opposition and the private sector came together to call for Aristide's resignation, but promotion of a peaceful transition was overtaken by mounting repression and what the OAS described as the degeneration of Haiti into "mob rule."[88] Prodded by the United States, CARICOM tried again to force direct talks leading to a settlement; these yielded a prior action plan and an implementation plan worked out by a Group of Six (Bahamas for the CARICOM, Canada, the European Union, France, the OAS, and the United States). Although Aristide accepted both, the opposition refused to contemplate any arrangement that provided for him to serve out his term as president.[89]

In February 2004 armed conflict broke out in the north of the country between insurgents calling for the departure of Aristide—many of them former members of the army and paramilitary groups disbanded after Aristide's return to the country in 1994—and Aristide's supporters. In a meeting of the Security Council held on February 26, representatives of CARICOM and Haiti appealed directly and unambiguously for immediate intervention by the United Nations to help restore peace and security to the country and save Aristide. But they were met with the UN equivalent of stony silence. In a direct rebuttal of CARICOM's efforts, the Security Council issued a presidential statement to the effect that it was "deeply concerned" and would "consider urgently options for international engagement."[90] Meanwhile, outside the Council, pressure on Aristide was mounting. On the day before the Council met, the foreign minister of France effectively called for him to go. Aristide "bears heavy responsibility for the current situation," he said. "It is up to him to accept the consequences." The United States had not yet been so forthcoming, but was not at all displeased to see France out ahead on this issue, and soon began to make its own views felt.[91]

On February 29 Aristide resigned under controversial circumstances and was whisked out of Haiti on a U.S. airplane to the Central African Republic. Supreme Court President Boniface Alexandre assumed the presidency, in accordance with Haiti's constitution. Hours later, the new authorities in Haiti asked the Security Council for help. France and the United States—working in lockstep to an extent that amazed colleagues who had grown used to the post-Iraq antipathy between them—sprung into action to push through a resolution (SCR 1529) later that day. This authorized the immediate deployment of a multinational force that would be replaced within three months by a UN peacekeeping operation.[92]

This unusual and somewhat unseemly haste owed not a small debt to the reactivation of the group of Friends. This had been done on the basis of a mid-February request by U.S. Ambassador John Negroponte that staff in the U.S. mission to the United Nations "watch Haiti." After consultations at the working level, U.S. and French officials decided that the composition of the Friends of Haiti "was and is the United States, France, Canada, and the Latin Americans on the Security Council," in this instance Brazil and Chile. Whether the actions of the group could be described as friendly to Haiti was highly questionable, particularly given the strong hand played by the United States and France in ensuring that the Security Council did nothing while Aristide remained in office. But in the final few days of February it met on a near-constant basis. This allowed its members, once the departure of Aristide had been confirmed, to present the Council with a draft resolution, on which the most powerful international actors all agreed, providing for the immediate deployment of a multinational force.[93] The Friends would continue to meet in the months to come. They found a working-level presence of the secretariat to be helpful, but there was no illusion that this was anything other than a group formed to drive Security Council action in accordance with the priorities of its members.

The secretariat itself responded slowly both to the rapidly deteriorating situation in Haiti and to the diplomatic mess that accompanied it. After 2001 the United Nations had no political presence in Haiti (although it remained engaged through UNDP). Like other actors it had been content to let the OAS take the lead in efforts to broker an agreement between the Haitians and had watched from the sidelines as things took a turn for the worse. Only on February 26, as Haiti, CARICOM, and the OAS all appealed for help, did the secretary-general appoint John Reginald Dumas his special adviser on Haiti.[94] Expectations that he should fulfill a role in furthering the political process were overtaken by Aristide's departure three days later and the precipitation of the secretariat into mission-planning mode.

"Not Again"

"Not again," was how Kofi Annan, writing in the *Wall Street Journal* two weeks later, characterized the reaction in the United Nations and national governments to the prospect of a return to Haiti. "We had been there, and done that, ten years before."[95] But this time around the challenges were much greater.

In the decade between the two interventions, a more complex set of conditions for international engagement had developed. The legitimacy of the transitional government established by a Council of Wise Men

(*Conseil de Sages*) was unclear; there were a greater number of armed actors involved; weapons had proliferated; impunity was widespread; and such progress as had been made in building the institutions of the Haitian state had all been lost. Haiti's economic situation had deteriorated steadily to the point where 55 percent of its population lived on less than $1 a day and 42 percent of children under the age of five were malnourished.[96] Existing problems had been exacerbated by the destruction of infrastructure and would be damaged further by devastating floods in May and September 2004. The dashed expectations of the last ten years meant that there was less popular support for and little confidence in an international presence. Meanwhile, the task of that international presence would be complicated by the lack of clarity regarding its relationship to any political process. The United Nations began work during a transition in which interim mechanisms, timetables, and an endgame were all in play. Delays in appointing an SRSG, a slow troop deployment, and the less-than-assertive comportment of those troops would contribute to a failure to stabilize Haiti in the early months of international involvement, complicating the way ahead.[97]

At the international level the difference was no less striking. International actors had produced an improvised and divisive response to the quickly developing crisis. CARICOM accused the United States of failing to respect the Inter-American Democratic Charter, which calls on member states to oppose coups and unconstitutional regime change, and withheld recognition of the transitional government in Haiti. The Friends in New York at times conferred with Caribbean representatives. But they spent little effort pretending that their views would influence decisions by the Security Council; moreover, such contacts could do little to paper over the serious differences now evident between Haiti's immediate neighbors and the wider region.

How to reflect the complexity of international involvement in Haiti in the mission it was planning became an issue of some contention within the secretariat. An OAS proposal for a joint UN-OAS mission, similar in concept to MICIVIH, was brushed aside, in part by perceptions (unfairly) held by some UN staff that the current morass could be attributed to a "failure" of OAS and CARICOM negotiators.[98] In the end, the recommendation presented to the Security Council in April to establish the United Nations Stabilization Mission in Haiti (MINUSTAH) foresaw a more conventional multidimensional operation, well endowed with "coordination and liaison mechanisms" to enhance interaction with others. These included, most notably, a Core Group to be composed of the SRSG and his deputies, "representatives of regional and subregional organizations, international financial institutions, and other major stakeholders." The Core Group "of a consultative nature" was envisaged as meeting regularly in Port-au-Prince and also as needed in New York or Washington.[99]

The Core Group had been conceived by secretariat officials as a more inclusive alternative to a group of Friends.[100] They had hoped to ensure that its composition in New York mirrored that in Port-au Prince. However, control over the new group's membership was limited by its gradual evolution, at least in Port-au-Prince, from the Friends of the Secretary-General of the Organization of American States. Consequently, when the Core Group first met as such in September, its composition was a broad one: Argentina, Brazil, Canada, Chile, France, Germany, Mexico, Spain, and the United States, accompanied by representatives of the World Bank and the Inter-American Development Bank, CARICOM, and the OAS. Differences in political priorities within this group ranged from the strong opposition to Aristide and his former followers expressed by France (especially) and the United States to more openly sympathetic views held by Mexico and other Latin Americans and CARICOM. The picture was further complicated by the reemergence—originally resisted by France and the United States—of a separate Ad Hoc Advisory Group on Haiti within ECOSOC, now with Canada as chair, to further economic and social development in Haiti in the long term.[101]

Moreover, this time around it was not the United States, France, and Canada that were the troop contributors—an absence that reflected the low priority they now accorded Haiti's fate—but Latin Americans such as Chile, Argentina, Uruguay, Peru, and Ecuador, operating under Brazil's lead. The United States itself, while calling for a more robust military engagement, contributed just four officers to MINUSTAH's military contingent.[102] For their part the Latin American states had sent troops to Haiti as a result of what Juan Gabriel Tokatlian described as "a hurried decision, taken without planning or regional coordination and based on a series of pre-conceptions rather than realistic analysis."[103] An uneasy mixture of desire for enhanced prestige—in Brazil's case closely linked to its quest for a permanent seat on the UN Security Council—a sense of international obligation, hemispheric solidarity, and a need to rebuild relations with the United States fractured by the battles over Iraq offered poor preparation for the situation in Haiti. As this proved more difficult, and dangerous, than the various countries had suspected at the outset, each faced hard questions from domestic constituencies.[104] Differences with the "old Friends" were most obviously expressed in repeated criticisms by the United States and others of the timid manner in which the Brazilians undertook their responsibilities and of persistent doubts among the Latin Americans regarding the extent to which they could, or should, pursue an interventionist role.

Valdés had arrived in Port-au-Prince in August to find the Core Group already in place, although he presided over its first formal meeting in Port-au-Prince in September and a parallel meeting in New York in late November. He saw the group as a necessary means to ensure the regular exchange of information and the coordination of resources and actions.[105] But it was not a forum either small or like-minded enough to be operationally engaged in shaping the United Nations' efforts. There was little enthusiasm for regular meetings of the mechanism in New York; in Haiti its size determined a level of formality that ensured that most productive consultations took place elsewhere.[106] Meanwhile, the enormity of the challenges facing the United Nations was clear. Violence had surged and the political climate remained tense; disarmament was delayed and the transitional government was increasingly fragile and resistant to the recommendations of MINUSTAH; disbursement of donor funds was slow, and the government's ability to spend them was constrained by both capacity and a macroeconomic orthodoxy such that even the International Monetary Fund questioned the limited boost to economic activity provided for in its budget. Against this backdrop hope for an inclusive political process that might provide the basis for sustainable peace and security seemed distant.[107]

During 2005 political efforts were concentrated on preparations for elections scheduled for the latter part of the year. These proved fraught with practical and political difficulties and in the end would be postponed four times to February 2006 amid an increasingly acrimonious climate. Tensions rose as the elections approached and it became evident that the likely winner would be the one-time protégé of Aristide, former president René Préval, an outcome very far from the hopes and expectations of Haiti's still powerful elites. "They thought they could get rid of one government and have the country to themselves and their friends," as one UN official put it. "But Préval has come and ruined the party."[108] Amid a worsening security situation characterized by dramatically high levels of kidnappings (241 individuals were reported kidnapped in the month of December 2005 alone),[109] MINUSTAH came under criticism from all sides. It was accused of doing too little to address the violence spawned by pro-Aristide gangs when it held back, and of answering to the bidding of the very elites the international community was seen to have installed in power in 2004 when it did undertake offensive operations. The possibility of its peacekeepers coming under direct attack and/or inflicting civilian casualties remained a constant risk.[110]

Under such circumstances the support MINUSTAH received from international partners ably choreographed by Valdés was critical. Over time he developed close working relationships both with individual ambassadors—the ambassadors of Brazil and the United States in particular —and in many cases the troop contributors' foreign ministers as well.[111] Formal meetings of the Core Group became opportunities for the delivery of messages finely crafted in advance. This was perhaps most noticeable in September 2005, when Prime Minister Gérard Latortue met with the sec-retary-general at a ministerial-level meeting of the Core Group in New York; and in January 2006, when a high-level delegation of members of the Core Group visited Haiti for meetings with the presidential candidates. Valdés as *chef d'orchestre* was able to draw on the different countries repre-sented as "a bass to treble range that he could play as he chose," as one of his colleagues described it.[112] Meanwhile, his high-wire act in Haiti re-ceived reinforcement from the Friends in New York. With the influence of the Latin Americans in the ascendant, the diplomacy of the "ABC" countries of Argentina (which joined the Council, and the Friends, in 2005), Brazil, and Chile, working effectively alongside Canada, France and the United States, came to be appreciated by the secretariat as "invaluable," particularly to the financing of MINUSTAH's increasingly robust security requirements.

In the end, national elections that had threatened to tip the country back into crisis did not. A high turnout produced a clear plurality for Pré-val, but one just short of the 50 percent of the vote required to avoid a runoff. Amid swirling allegations of voter fraud and other irregularities, Préval's supporters erupted in protest. An accommodation was reached, and Préval—quite sensibly under the circumstances—was declared presi-dent and inaugurated at the head of a multiparty government in mid-May. His evident popular support and immediate commitment to reconcilia-tion, dialogue, and an ambitious policy agenda offered Haiti what Kofi Annan would describe to the Security Council as "a unique opportunity to break the cycle of violence and poverty and move towards a future of stable and peaceful development."[113] But an absence of institutional or bureaucratic capacity, persistent challenges with respect to security, human rights, and the justice system, as well as the country's desperate economic and social situation, represented daunting obstacles ahead. Sixteen years after the United Nations and the OAS had observed the elections that first brought Aristide to the presidency, very little remained certain about the future of Haiti other than that international assistance would be needed for many years to come.

Conclusions

In many respects the long history and varied engagement in a complex period of history make it difficult to generalize about the Friends in Haiti. The Friends changed in almost every way—in composition, relationship to the secretariat, influence with Haitian actors, the role played by dominant individuals and states—as the situation evolved. But while the original Friends of the Secretary-General assumed an independence of the secretariat, segued into the Friends of the Secretary-General of the Organization of American States, and reemerged as the Friends of Haiti to drive action (and inaction) in the Security Council in 2004 and to serve as the backbone of the Core Group, two constants remained: the Friends retained a central place in the formulation of policy toward Haiti, and the bottom line remained what the United States was, or was not, prepared to countenance. Overall the Friends' path represents a stark example of a mechanism that enjoyed formal success as an instrument of process (and was welcomed as such by its members), yet was centrally placed within an international effort that failed either to achieve political stability in the country or to lift Haitians out of the worst poverty in the Western Hemisphere. Responsibility cannot, of course, be directly attributed to the international engagement alone, and still less to actions taken or not taken by the Friends. But neither can it and they be absolved of their part in the process.

The political settlement represented by the Governors Island Agreement collapsed soon after its signing and was never revisited. The United Nations sanctioned a multinational effort led by the United States to restore Aristide to the presidency under circumstances that did little to ensure anything beyond success in the very short term. In the interests of a "quick win," the absence of an inclusive process that might have helped safeguard a democratic transition was not adequately considered. U.S. requirements for a foreign policy success, timed for the benefit of an election cycle, blunted the extent to which the United Nations and the Friends addressed the limitations of the peacebuilding on which they then embarked. A loss of leverage with the Haitians and disappointment with the opportunities and assistance squandered contributed to the United Nations' withdrawal from Haiti in 2001. When it reengaged in 2004 it did so under circumstances determined by key states that reactivated the Friends as an effective vehicle through which to project their policy. That they insisted on Aristide's departure in many respects complicated the environment into which the United Nations then deployed. An irony of the process is that, two years later, hope rested on the prospect of a president elected by the broad majority of Haitian people, who have, since 1990, been solidly behind the promise for the poor held out—if often abused— by Aristide.

The political and humanitarian crisis that developed in Haiti in the early 1990s had little to do with the dynamics of the Cold War. Yet the challenge that Haiti represented—how to foster a democratic process in a weak or failing state—was to be emblematic of the tasks before the United Nations in the post–Cold War period. Haiti could not be ignored within a region that openly championed the spread and maintenance of democracy. Together and separately, the Friends played a critical role in persuading the broader region of the value of UN engagement in Haiti—something that the United States alone would not have been able to do. Although Venezuela fell by the wayside as a result of domestic political change, its place as a Latin American Friend was taken by others. A gradual move toward regional engagement would become evident as the OAS assumed responsibility for Haiti in the early 2000s. Despite the critical stance taken by CARICOM, Latin American states took the lead in the operation launched in 2004 and gradually adapted to conditions in Haiti considerably more challenging than they had been prepared for.

The Friends' relationship to the Haitian actors differed from that seen in Central America, where the groups were poised between conflict parties struggling to negotiate a settlement. Aristide had been elected president through elections sanctioned by the international community and was then deposed by a coup. Despite doubts about him in Washington, neither the desirability of his restoration to the presidency nor the central part to be played in the effort by the Friends was ever in doubt. After 1994 the structural position of the Friends shifted. Their assistance was essential to forward progress in peacebuilding, but it did not come without pressure for Haiti to comply with priorities that appeared donor driven. That this provoked resistance from Haitian authorities highly sensitive to external intervention and bent on the pursuit of power by means of what Robert Fatton Jr. has termed "predatory democracy"[114] was not surprising. In 2004 in particular, when the Friends actively facilitated the departure of President Aristide, the extent to which many in Haiti and the region would consider them to be acting as actual "friends" of Haiti was debatable, even as the Friends themselves believed they did so in accordance with the long-term interests of the country.

The composition of the first group of Friends derived from the "quad-ripartite" group first established outside the United Nations. It proved a balanced mix of permanent members of the Security Council and regional actors with genuine concern for the future of Haitian democracy. Over time, it was to become a flexible diplomatic instrument, with a capacity to oper-ate in New York, in the field, or elsewhere as required. It provided effective support to SRSGs heading peace operations and consistently drove action in the Security Council—in the mid-1990s successfully beating back objec-tions to continuing UN involvement in Haiti. For the United States, the utility of the Friends was evident. The group helped ensure that its policy on Haiti was undertaken within a multilateral framework and with the legiti-macy that only the United Nations could supply. It also allowed other states interested in effecting change in Haiti a place at the "top table" of decision making, an achievement of particular importance to Canada, which from outside the Security Council (except for 1999–2000) retained a primary role. And it provided both the secretariat and those other states with an informal forum in which differences, including with the United States, could be assayed outside the Security Council.

But there were evident downsides too. The power of the Friends effec-tively precluded others—including Security Council members—from what was a small circle of decision makers. Moreover, the Friends represented a mixed blessing for the secretariat. In his memoirs, Boutros Boutros-Ghali praised the United Nations' relationship to the United States on Haiti as both "a constructive division of labor" and an example of "near excellent diplomatic and military cooperation."[115] The praise reflected the value to the United Nations of proving its utility to the United States. But the rela-tionship was one that left little room for leadership or independent ini-tiatives by secretaries-general fully absorbed in crises elsewhere. Tacit acceptance of the power of the Friends, combined with resignation to con-tentious relations with Haitian interlocutors, bred an understandable but nonetheless culpable degree of passivity that at times effectively devolved decisions to the Friends. At key moments in the process the United States simply went its own way, setting the course for military intervention in September 1994, the terms of the UN operations that would take over from early 1995, and in 2004, together with France, the terms that would determine the reengagement of the Security Council after Aristide's resig-nation. Overall, in a long engagement that institutionalized the policy-set-ting role assumed by the Friends, the group revealed itself to be a more effective mechanism for influencing the United Nations secretariat than authorities in either Washington or Port-au-Prince.

The resilience of the Friends saw the mechanism centrally placed through many different phases of engagement in Haiti. In this process, the degree of informality and intensity that characterized the workings of the group in its earlier phases was distinct from the more routine backstopping of field operations it carried out from 1994 on. The center of gravity turned, quite naturally, to Port-au-Prince, where the Friends formed a gradually expanding nucleus of the international community that struggled to support an essentially flawed Haitian process. The circumstances of the United Nations' withdrawal from Haiti, its neglect in the following years, and its mangled reengagement in 2004 established the basis for very different mechanisms for coordination. That the exclusive kind of group represented by the original four Friends of Haiti was no longer adequate to lead the response was evident. Less clear was how to align the distinct histories, interests, and capacities that the various international actors brought to the table for the benefit of Haiti's long-suffering people, who were at this point, and with good reason, more diffident and distrustful of international engagement than before. The Core Group itself was too large and unwieldy to assume this role, but it became one among a number of tools upon which the secretary-general's special representative could draw as Haiti moved towards the election of a new president in 2006 and beyond.

5

The Georgian-Abkhaz Conflict
Friends and the Anomaly of Russia

The United Nations' involvement in Georgia followed the outbreak of conflict in the former Soviet autonomous republic of Abkhazia in August 1992. From 1994 onward the United Nations Military Observer Mission in Georgia (UNOMIG) monitored a cease-fire between the secessionist forces of the Abkhaz and the Georgian military as Russian troops in a force of the Commonwealth of Independent States (CIS) took primary responsibility for peacekeeping. A peacemaking role for the secretary-general was present from the beginning alongside a formal role for Russia as "facilitator." But negotiations to find a political settlement of the conflict and bring about the return of Georgian refugees to Abkhazia made little progress. A group of Friends of Georgia was created in 1993 by states (France, Germany, the United Kingdom, and the United States, in addition to Russia) with clearly opposed positions on Abkhazia's conflict, as well as quite distinct levels of interest in its outcome. Secretariat officials would not have considered creating Friends in this instance. However, they invested considerable diplomatic effort in the mechanism's transformation into a means by which to engage with the various actors involved and maintain at least the appearance of momentum in an otherwise stalled process. The group was renamed the Friends of the Secretary-General for Georgia in 1997 and was more engaged from 1998 on than in the early years of its existence, meeting in New York, Tbilisi, Moscow, and at a high level, in Geneva, and dominating action in the Security Council.

The utility of the Friends to peacemaking on Abkhazia was hindered by several factors. The first is the strategic importance to Russia of Georgia and the significance of Abkhazia in the complex relations between the two countries. The second is a structural flaw: as a mediation effort between two parties, the UN process is inherently biased in that it takes place within the Security Council's clear and consistent endorsement of Georgia's territorial integrity. This bias was reinforced by an open "friendship" of Georgia by the Western members of the Friends that significantly undermined any confidence the Abkhaz authorities might have had in an international process. A related problem is that the UN process, and the emerging centrality of the Friends within it, encouraged a degree of passivity among internal actors comfortable (enough) with the status quo. By 2006, the Abkhaz authorities had in many respects been strengthened by their hold on a de facto state for more than a decade.[1] Their claim to independence had received an unexpected boost when Russian President Vladimir Putin explicitly linked Abkhazia to the precedent that would be set by the possible international recognition of Kosovo.[2] Meanwhile, the United Nations and the Friends had become part of a landscape of sustained political stalemate, preventing the deterioration of the situation into renewed hostilities but making very little headway in moving it toward resolution.

Ethnic Conflict in Abkhazia

Poised on an isthmus between the Black and Caspian seas, Georgia stands at a juncture between Europe and Asia and Orthodox Christianity and Islam, and has long been a conduit for goods—and more recently, energy—from the Caspian Sea and Central Asia. In the aftermath of September 11, 2001, its strategic importance increased dramatically as preoccupation about terrorism rose and the airspace over the South Caucasus became a crucial corridor for U.S. and allied overflights to Afghanistan and Central Asia.[3] Yet, in historical terms Georgia's strategic location—Eduard Shevardnadze would refer to it as "geopolitically crucified"[4]—has been as much a liability as an asset, playing a defining part in its long and complex relationship with its northern neighbor, Russia.

In the country's northwest, Abkhazia is a fertile land between the eastern shores of the Black Sea and the peaks of the Caucasus Mountains, highly valued as a destination for holidaying Georgians and Russians as well as for its cash crops of citrus fruits, nuts, tea, and tobacco. Abkhaz historians claim that it became independent of Georgia after the Russian revolution of 1917. It was briefly constituted, like Georgia, as a full Soviet Socialist Republic from 1921 until 1931, when it was downgraded to an autonomous republic within the Union Republic of Georgia. In the last Soviet census, taken in 1989, Abkhazia had a population of 540,000, of which the Abkhaz titular nation represented some 18 percent; other nationalities included Georgians (about 47 percent), Armenians (18 percent), and Russians (13 percent). The low percentage of ethnic Abkhaz—a people with close ties only to the other predominantly North Caucasian mountain peoples in their language group—reflected a mass exodus of

Abkhaz to Turkey after the territory was annexed by czarist Russia in 1864. Policies implemented by the Soviet regime, particularly from the 1930s to the 1950s, also saw considerable numbers of ethnic Georgians settle in Abkhazia from other parts of the Soviet Socialist Republic of Georgia.[5]

In the latter period of Soviet rule the Abkhaz launched numerous appeals to Moscow, asking for secession from Georgia and either Abkhazia's constitution as a Union Republic or its integration into Russia. Moscow responded by privileging the Abkhaz minority within local government structures. In a period of internal turmoil, in the midst of which Georgia declared itself independent of the Soviet Union in April 1991, the nationalist policies of President Zviad Gamsakhurdia exacerbated separatist tendencies in Abkhazia as well as in the region of South Ossetia.[6] Gamsakhurdia was ousted in a coup in late 1991 and replaced by a State Council that came to be headed by Eduard Shevardnadze, the former secretary of the Communist Party in Georgia as well as the Soviet foreign minister under Mikhail Gorbachev. Without consulting the autonomous republics, the Council reintroduced Georgia's pre-Soviet constitution of 1921, a document that referred to, but did not clearly endorse, Abkhazia's autonomous status. The Abkhaz leadership responded by introducing a draft constitution that had been prepared in 1925, but never adopted, declaring Abkhazia to be a sovereign state.

In August 1992, on the pretext of rescuing Georgian officials who had been kidnapped by Gamsakhurdia's forces, Georgian troops entered Abkhazia. Fighting broke out and would continue, despite the parties' agreement to three cease-fires brokered by the Russians, until late 1993. Abkhaz military units fought with the unofficial support of Russians stationed in the region and irregular forces from the North Caucasus, particularly Chechnya.[7] Russia's multifaceted role in the conflict was further complicated by the role it played in its endgame. In September 1993 the Abkhaz broke the third cease-fire to take over their capital, Sukhumi. Gamsakhurdia seized this moment of humiliating defeat for the Georgians to launch an attack on the Tbilisi regime that Shevardnadze was able to repel only with Russian assistance. To secure it, he had to overcome his earlier reluctance and take Georgia into the CIS. In February 1994 he signed a treaty that preserved the right for Russia to maintain four military bases on Georgian soil and established defense cooperation between the two states.[8]

By May 1994, when the Moscow Agreement on a Cease-fire and Separation of Forces was signed, the war had claimed up to 10,000 lives, and some 250,000 Georgians, many of whom had lived in the Gali region of Abkhazia, had been forcibly displaced into Georgia. Over the following decade there would be no war in Abkhazia, thanks in no small part to the presence of Russian peacekeepers and UN observers in UNOMIG, but no peace either. Negotiations on the central issue of Abkhazia's political status were further stalled by Abkhazia's declaration of independence in 1999, while other developments preserved an underlying distrust between the parties. These included provocations by Georgian partisans with close ties to elements in the Georgian government to which Abkhaz militia forces commonly overreacted; a complex web of criminal economic activities (representing one area in which ethnic Georgians, Abkhaz, Armenians, and Russian peacekeepers collaborated with some success) that developed to counteract the effect of an economic blockade introduced by the CIS, at Georgia's urging, in 1996; Georgian rhetoric threatening a military solution to the conflict; and the increasingly complex and sensitive dynamics of the bilateral relationship between Georgia and Russia.

Like other unresolved conflicts in the former Soviet Union that have led to de facto states (in South Ossetia, Nagorno-Karabakh, and Transdniestra), the conflict in Abkhazia has commonly been referred to as "frozen." But as Dov Lynch and others have pointed out, this is in many respects a misnomer, for a decade of failure to resolve the conflicts transformed the problem at hand comprehensively. As Charles King put it in 2001: "The territorial separatists of the early 1990s have become the state builders of the early 2000s, creating de facto countries whose ability to field armed forces, control their own territory, educate their children, and maintain local economies is about as well developed as that of the recognized states of which they are still notionally a part."[9] In the case of Abkhazia, this situation was facilitated by international intervention. Peacekeepers preserved the cease-fire, while the peace process conferred a degree of recognition on the Abkhaz, and humanitarian and rehabilitation assistance from the United Nations and other international actors helped sustain their livelihoods.[10] Sensitivities regarding the status of Abkhazia precluded direct support of central structures of the de facto state, but in the mid-2000s an enhanced presence of the European Union (EU) in particular brought substantial resources to infrastructure (such as the Enguri hydropower plant) and community development projects.[11] "With each passing year," Ghia Nodia wrote of Georgia's "alternative national projects" in 2005, "the prospect of reintegration becomes more and more problematic."[12]

Georgia had its weakness as a state exposed to the world by the ousting of President Shevardnadze in the "Rose Revolution" of November 2003. However, as it attempted to look to the future under the avowedly reform-minded leadership of President Mikheil Saakashvili, the persistence of statelike entities in Abkhazia and South Ossetia—which together account for some 17 percent of the national territory—represented a fundamental dilemma. In the absence of democratic consolidation there could be little that was appealing to the Abkhaz or Ossets in a formal link to Georgia, yet without resolution of the conflicts it was difficult to see how Georgia could advance in consolidating its democracy. Saakashvili committed himself to the reestablishment of Georgia's territorial integrity as a central goal of his presidency, intimately linked to a struggle to reassert Georgia's broader independence from Russia. But as time went by the prospect of somehow "attracting" the Abkhaz and Ossets appeared more and more of a fallacy: after more than a decade of de facto separation the Abkhaz and Ossets were no more capable of conceiving of Abkhazia or South Ossetia within Georgia than were the Georgians of contemplating Georgia without them.

Russia and Its Interests

Russia's interests in Georgia primarily reflect strategic concerns that stretch back to the Russian empire. Conquest of the Caucasus was pursued for a period of three centuries in the context of a triangular "great power" rivalry among Russia, Turkey, and Iran. Consolidation of Russian power in the Caucasus came in the early nineteenth century through management of the unruly peoples of the Caucasus by tactics of "divide and rule." This gave the Russian empire, and the Soviet Union after it, the ability to play the role of arbiter to which all sides in any internal conflict had to appeal.[13]

At the end of the Cold War, debate over the nature of Russia's interests in its "near abroad" divided Moscow's political elite between those ready to abandon the former Soviet republics as an expensive reminder of a discredited past and other, mainly military, forces who took advantage of chaotic internal situations within the new republics to secure personal interests when they could. Gradually, the prodemocratic and Western rhetoric that had characterized the first flush of disintegration of the Soviet Union came to be replaced by a harder and more pragmatic line. By late 1993, for example, Russian Foreign Minister Andrei Kozyrev spoke of Russia's "historic sphere of influence" and of Russian interests in the "immediate vicinity."[14] His successor, Yevgeny Primakov, took a still more assertive approach to the defense of Russia's "permanent interests," including through the use of both mediation and peacekeeping to maintain influence in the former Soviet space.[15]

Russia's most immediate interests in Abkhazia have related to the prospect of "losing" control and influence over the key buffer zone represented by Georgia, which borders on Turkey, a member of the North Atlantic Treaty Organization (NATO). These interests have reflected both a traditional Russian fear of the risks of an exposed southern flank in the Caucasus and the view that the peoples of the North Caucasus can only be kept in check when Russia, or those friendly to Russia, control the entire range of the Caucasus mountains. Moreover, the prospect of widespread conflict in Georgia opened up the possibility of severing transport links to Armenia, Russia's closest partner in the region. Consequently, in the early 1990s Russia had no desire to see the violent conflict that erupted in Georgia either spread or persist. Nor did it welcome the precedent that an independent Abkhazia might set for regions of the Russian Federation— Chechnya, most obviously, but also Ingushetia and Tatarstan—that might consider pursuing a similar path themselves. "We had to stop the war," President Yeltsin's envoy Boris Pastukhov would recall in an interview, "and that was what Russia did."[16]

But Russia's engagement was not limited to stopping the war. On the contrary, while diplomatic efforts were directed toward mediation, no attempts were made to prevent Russian military support of the Abkhaz forces—without which the Abkhaz would have faced certain defeat. This apparent contradiction reflected positions taken by the Russian armed forces toward both Abkhazia and Shevardnadze. Thus, while Russia remained formally committed to the territorial integrity of Georgia and Abkahzia's position in it, many in the Russian military elite saw their immediate interests in retaining control of Abkhazia, not least because of the strategic and commercial importance of access to the Black Sea. Also at stake was a sense of ownership of the land viewed, in Pastukhov's words, as "God's own country": many Russians lived in Abkhazia and were staunchly defended by nationalists in the Russian Duma; Abkhazia was the preferred destination for members of the Soviet nomenklatura who vacationed in their dachas on the coast; and hundreds of thousands more had routinely holidayed in its sanatoriums. Finally, retaining a presence and influence in Abkhazia provided a perfect opportunity to complicate the life of Shevardnadze, who was considered by the military to be guilty of the breakup of the Soviet Union and the demoralized state in which the army was left at its end.[17]

Georgia's eagerness to turn to the West was facilitated both by the "special relationship" that many Western leaders had developed with Shevardnadze and by the hope that was pinned upon his U.S.-educated successor,

Saakashvili. Perhaps unsurprisingly, it was viewed with increasing suspicion, and then hostility, by Russia. Georgia directly challenged Russia's control of Caspian oil both by agreeing with Azerbaijan to build the Baku-Supsa pipeline (as an alternative to the Baku-Novorossiisk pipeline through Russia), and in cooperating with Azerbaijan, Turkey, and the United States to build the Baku-Tbilisi-Ceyhan pipeline. Georgia also pressed Russia to withdraw its military bases in accordance with the agreement reached at the Organization for Security and Cooperation in Europe (OSCE) summit meeting of 1999, and reiterated its desire to join NATO. (In early 2005 Georgia created a "new" group of Friends, quite unrelated to the United Nations, to assist in its process of internal reform and help it pursue membership in both NATO and eventually, the Euripean Union.[18]) In 2002, as U.S. concerns regarding the strategic importance of Georgia as a safe haven for international terrorists as well as a crucial air corridor mounted, Georgia welcomed U.S. military trainers to improve the capacity of its armed forces.[19] The presence of U.S. forces on Georgian soil was greeted with outrage in some circles in Moscow and served to sharpen Russian concerns that its interests in Georgia be preserved.[20] During 2003 Russia's grip on Georgia's fragile economy was secured by its acquisition of Georgia's vital gas and electricity grids.

Tensions between Georgia and Russia increased from mid-2005 on. A brief visit paid to Tbilisi by President George W. Bush in May 2005 provided an opportunity to hail Saakashvili's Georgia as a "beacon of liberty" for the region and the world and pointedly warn Russia that Georgia's sovereignty "must be respected by all nations."[21] The visit marked a public relations success for Saakashvili—particularly at a moment when domestic opposition and even international criticism was for the first time mounting[22]—and vindicated policies that had sought to court the United States at every turn. But Russia's irritation was evident.[23] Relations with Georgia were not improved by Russian support of military activities in Abkhazia in August, Saakashvili's appeal to the United Nations to put an end to "the forcible annexation of Abkhazia" in September, and a resolution by the Georgian parliament in October that criticized the performance of Russian peacekeepers in Abkhazia and South Ossetia and threatened to withdraw consent for their presence in the course of 2006.[24] These actions, which were accompanied by a dramatic increase in Georgia's spending on defense and an aggressive pursuit of closer ties to NATO, contributed to Georgia's emergence as what one U.S. commentator would describe as "an arch-nemesis of the Kremlin's geopolitical interests."[25]

Georgia's Friends

The group of Friends of Georgia was formed in 1993 on the initiative of France. More specifically, it was "cooked up" between the recently appointed special envoy of the secretary-general, Edouard Brunner, who was also Switzerland's ambassador to France, and the French ambassador in Tbilisi at that time, Bernard Fassier, at a moment at which international involvement in the management of the conflict was being pursued by all engaged in it.[26]

The Security Council had first discussed the conflict in Abkhazia in September 1992.[27] Prompted also by persistent appeals from Shevardnadze, who warned in late 1992 that an escalation of the conflict in Abkhazia could destabilize the entire Caucasus region, Secretary-General Boutros-Ghali sent two missions to Georgia during the latter part of 1992 and opened a small UN office in Tbilisi at the end of the year.[28] Brunner was appointed in May 1993, and in August an advance team of military observers—subsequently authorized by the Security Council as the United Nations Observer Mission in Georgia (UNOMIG)—was dispatched to Abkhazia to help verify compliance with what would turn out to be a very short-lived cease-fire. As the battle for Sukhumi raged, in mid-September 1993 the foreign ministers of Georgia and Russia wrote jointly to the UN secretary-general to ask for "the speediest possible deployment to Abkhazia of a full contingent of United Nations Observers," as well as negotiations on a comprehensive settlement of the conflict.[29] The negotiations began in Geneva on November 30, two months after the fall of Sukhumi, under UN auspices but with Russian facilitation.

The group of Friends was composed of France, Germany, Russia, the United Kingdom, and the United States, states considered to have a "direct concern" in Georgia. With the exception of the United Kingdom, all of them were represented by embassies in Tbilisi (a British embassy would open in 1995). Although initial soundings with Under-Secretary-General Marrack Goulding had been conducted in October 1993, the group quickly established an identity of its own. During December it met for the first time in Geneva, in the margins of Brunner's negotiations with the Georgian and Abkhaz parties; in New York, both with Goulding and independently of the secretariat; and then in Moscow. Meanwhile, Ambassador Jean-Bernard Mérimée, who had assumed the French role as coordinator with alacrity, had met on several occasions with the Georgian ambassador to the United Nations.[30]

The group was ready to meet regularly with Goulding and other secretariat officials, but resisted suggestions that it establish itself as Friends of the Secretary-General for Georgia. The secretariat had favored this formulation for a number of reasons: it would anchor these powerful states to the secretary-general's efforts and bring clarity to a somewhat uneasy division of labor that had been agreed for the Southern Caucasus with the Conference on Security and Cooperation in Europe (CSCE) (the latter had taken the lead on the conflicts in South Ossetia and Nagorno-Karabakh, while offering support to the United Nations on Abkhazia).[31] But it would also help avoid the problems raised by a Friends' group supposedly created to support a process of negotiations between two parties, yet formally designated "Friends" of one of them. The Friends, however, preferred to retain their affiliation with "Georgia." Reminded by the secretariat of the CSCE's experience on Nagorno-Karabakh, for which a large and unwieldy "Minsk Group" had been established,[32] the Friends discussed the possibility of including Denmark, Sweden, and Italy, but in the end limited their membership to the original five.

The interests of the Western states engaged in the group of Friends were somewhat contradictory. They wanted stability on the outer reaches of Europe and in the important Transcaucasian corridor, and they hoped to see Georgia evolve into a democratic state in which a free market could prosper; to these ends they favored the development of its independence with respect to Russia. These goals, and the great esteem in which Shevardnadze was held, particularly in the United States and Germany, for his role in ending the Cold War ("Western countries feel somehow obligated to him," the de facto foreign minister of Abkhazia would complain in July 2003, "as if he tore the Berlin Wall down with his own hands"),[33] ensured sustained interest in developments in Georgia and relatively high levels of aid. But engagement was subordinated to the regional priority of the West as a whole—the emergence of a stable, secure, and prosperous Russian Federation—as well as differing priorities in the various states' bilateral relations with Russia. Consequently, the Western states approached the issue of Georgia, and the conflict in Abkhazia in particular, with caution.[34]

The prospect of access to Caspian oil and the terrorist attacks of September 11, 2001, increased the level of attention paid by Western states and institutions to the Southern Caucasus. But they did not overcome a challenge to the involvement of the West posed by its lack of cohesion as a region, on the one hand, and the sustained importance of Russia to it on the other. This ambiguity would remain evident even as NATO, the

European Union, and individual states—the United States, the United Kingdom, and Germany in addition to Russia—in the early 2000s appointed a succession of special envoys to the Southern Caucasus and its conflicts. This bevy of envoys, many of whom would become leading actors in the Friends, vividly demonstrated increased interest from beyond the Southern Caucasus in addressing the region's insecurity. But it also led to efforts in which the possibility of playing these distinct external actors off against each other mounted.[35]

Caution within the Western members of the Friends did not belie a clear stance on the issues at stake. The United Nations' respect for the right of self-determination is one guided by rules for its application, which is limited to processes of decolonization. In other circumstances, the United Nations, as a body of sovereign states, decries "any attempt aimed at the partial or total disruption of the national unity and the territorial integrity of a country."[36] From its earliest statement on the conflict in Abkhazia, the Security Council emphasized both its support of a negotiated settlement to the conflict and the inadmissibility of any encroachment on Georgia's territorial integrity and internationally recognized borders.[37] To these principles were added the need for refugee return, which would be sanctioned in an agreement reached in April 1994 but impeded by the central demographic challenge of the conflict—the fact that the Abkhaz were a minority in the land they claimed as their own.[38]

A stance on the outcome of negotiations so clearly staked out by the Security Council reflected a peace process founded on a bias that complicated the life of its mediators.[39] As a member state, Georgia had access to the United Nations and a platform at its meetings that the Abkhaz did not. Moreover, unlike other rebel or resistance groups considered within this study, the Abkhaz retained no "diplomatic" representation in New York and visited it only infrequently. Secretariat officials sought to maintain a level of impartiality between the parties to negotiations, a position that was helped by the fact that the United Nations, unlike the OSCE, had not formally designated the Abkhaz action against the Georgian population of Gali as "ethnic cleansing."[40] But as states themselves and genuine friends of Georgia, the Western members of the Friends were not able to adopt a similar stance. Indeed, for some years the Friends saw no reason why they should even meet with representatives of what one described as a "repellent secessionist regime."[41] Secretariat officials recall that their relationship with the Abkhaz leader, the de facto President Vladislav Ardzinba, was seriously complicated by the readiness of the Western Friends in Tbilisi to heed the Georgian government on this point. The ambassadors "saw the Abkhaz as representing an illegal effort to secede and themselves as ambassadors to the government," one official involved in the talks in the mid-1990s recalled. "We tried to persuade them that they were ambassadors to the whole country, but it didn't get through. . . . Ardzinba, correctly, understood the Friends of Georgia to be on the side of Shevardnadze."[42]

Russia: Peacekeeper, Facilitator, and Sometime Friend

During 1994 the Western members of the Friends—also powerful members of the Security Council—were thrown into something of a dilemma by the prospect of authorizing a peacekeeping force for Abkhazia. The United Nations was overstretched elsewhere, the situation in Abkhazia was unstable, and the political process was unpromising. Moreover, the Security Council was reluctant to assume a peacekeeping role in a regional conflict. The solution—a "Liberia model" that foresaw the deployment of a small observer mission alongside a peacekeeping force of the CIS—was far from ideal.[43] As in Liberia, UN observers demonstrated international support, but also tried to ensure that international norms were observed and to counter the dominant presence of the regional power. The CIS was neither truly regional nor much of an organization, but rather an instrument of Russian foreign policy whose engagement in peacekeeping, in Georgia as in Tajikistan, was used to further Russian interests in the former Soviet space.[44] The "welcome" given to such an arrangement by Security Council Resolution 937 (July 21, 1994) thus conferred legitimacy both on the emerging role of Russia in its "near abroad" and on the CIS itself. It also assured Russia's role as the guarantor of security along the cease-fire line, something the Georgians had come to view as akin to putting the fox in charge of the chicken coop.

Concern as to precedent set by attributing peacekeeping roles to countries with "direct political interests" in the conflict was raised by several Council members.[45] No objections were raised by members of the group of Friends, who had cosponsored the resolution after confidential discussions described by U.S. Ambassador Madeleine Albright as "a little diplomatic poker" cleared the way for action on Georgia, in the backyard of Russia, to be traded off against action on Haiti, in the backyard of the United States.[46] "Having taken its lumps trying to be a world police force," was the comment of the *New York Times* editorial, "the UN has now fallen into the unhealthy habit of licensing great-power spheres of influence."[47]

The presence of Russian peacekeepers on Georgian soil represents a complicating factor in the resolution of the conflict in Abkhazia. But in the years since deployment of the CIS force, no Western state has responded positively to Georgia's periodic call for their withdrawal, or still less, replacement by a UN mission acting under chapter VII of the charter. Russian peacekeepers were criticized both for the heavy-handedness with which they fulfilled their mandate and for their passivity—particularly during the events of May 1998, when intrusion into Gali by Georgian partisans prompted a violent reaction by the Abkhaz militia that included the looting and burning of up to 90 percent of the houses in some villages and the expulsion of some 30,000 Georgians.[48] However, they kept a peace that would not have survived their departure and in the process suffered levels of casualties unacceptable to an international force.[49]

The United Nations' relationship with Russia as facilitator of the peace process was always uneasy. The Russian role as peacemaker preceded that of the United Nations and then proceeded parallel to it. Negotiations were led by Brunner and took place in the presence of Russia and a representative of the CSCE (which became the OSCE in 1995). But they were complicated by the "games" that Russia played outside this format, calling separate and joint meetings with the parties, of which the United Nations was only intermittently informed, and by the complex web of interests and relationships that tied Russian officials to both parties in ways that the UN secretariat had little hope of penetrating. Shevardnadze himself was part of the problem: publicly committed to turn Georgia toward the West, his relations with Russia were founded on personal ties built up during his long Soviet past that ensured a certain ambiguity in his actions.[50] Meanwhile, UN officials would recall their frustration at having discussion of the central question of the political status undermined by the dealings between the Russians and the Abkhaz. They would go to Moscow and get Russian agreement on a particular point, and then get a "no" from Sukhumi, only to find out that the "no" was under Russian instructions. While they never knew quite how to read him, Ardzinba—a man with deep ties in the Russian Duma and in the army, a former pupil of Primakov, and a one-time deputy to the USSR Supreme Soviet—would tell them he could find an answer "if it wasn't for the Russians."[51]

The Friends would develop into a significant tool of leverage on Russia, yet during Brunner's time as special envoy they were not actively engaged in the negotiations. They represented a forum for discussion and their more informed knowledge of the process helped explain to others why the United Nations' efforts to resolve the conflict were getting nowhere.

But they frequently met without Russia, and when Russian officials did attend they did so more to be informed of what the others were saying than to contribute to a forum they did not, at this stage, acknowledge as a "player." Interviewed in 2003, senior Russian officials engaged in the peace process in mid-1990s professed no recollection of the Friends' presence at all. "They were not there, thank God," was Pastukhov's response, with a guffaw, "Brunner was enough."[52]

Russia's gradual encroachment on the United Nations' nominal lead of the process—a development facilitated by the fact that Brunner did not live in the region and visited it rather reluctantly—was acknowledged in a meeting held in early 1995 between Boutros-Ghali and Russian Foreign Minister Kozyrev.[53] It was agreed that the United Nations had made little progress on the core issues of the conflict, in part because of Russian influence over the parties. Since Russia had sticks and carrots to wield, Boutros-Ghali suggested that it should be given an opportunity to do so, while keeping the UN secretariat and the Friends informed of its efforts. These would culminate in the promotion by Foreign Minister Primakov of a draft protocol based on the idea of a "common state." In August 1997 President Yeltsin invited both Shevardnadze and Ardzinba to meet with him in Moscow in an effort to encourage agreement on the Russian proposals, but they balked at the opportunity and instead met with Primakov in Tbilisi.[54]

A Note on Tajikistan

Travails in the UN process on Georgia were in notable contrast to the UN's involvement in negotiating the peace agreement on Tajikistan, which was signed in Moscow in June 1997.

The conflict that broke out in Tajikistan in 1992, like those in Georgia, derived directly from the collapse of the Soviet Union. However, that it was a conflict over the government and not one of secession radically altered the possibilities for outside actors to contribute to its resolution. Social and economic insecurity had intersected with regional competition in Tajikistan to fuel a proliferation of rival groups and factions competing for political dominance. Exacerbated by both foreign governments and nonstate armed movements from outside the country, the conflict quickly escalated, with 60,000–100,000 people killed and some 600,000 internally displaced before most fighting ended in February 1993.[55]

From the beginning UN involvement was closely affiliated with regional actors.[56] UN fact-finding teams dispatched by Boutros-Ghali to Tajikistan in the latter part of 1992 worked closely with an ongoing mediation effort led by representatives of Kazakhstan, Kyrgyzstan, Russia, and Uzbekistan. And when the United Nations, supported by the OSCE, assumed the lead of the political process in 1994, it did so aiming to help find a compromise acceptable to the external actors as well as the Tajik parties. A small UN observer mission (the United Nations Mission of Observers in Tajikistan, UNMOT) was deployed to monitor the situation and help coordinate the international humanitarian response. It also maintained communication with Russian border forces and a substantial peacekeeping operation of the CIS, largely composed of Russian troops, which had been established on the Tajik-Afghan border. In accordance with Russia's interests at the time, the efforts of these forces were specifically directed toward preservation of the (non-Islamic) status quo.

When the Inter-Tajik negotiations got under way in April 1994 under pressure from Russia and Uzbekistan, their progress reflected both the evolving interests of the key external actors and the direct leverage these actors wielded over the Tajik parties.[57] The UN team carefully calibrated the location of each round of talks with a view to which of the capitals of the eight states officially designated as observers to the talks (Afghanistan, Iran, Kazakhstan, Kyrgyzstan, Pakistan, Russia, Turkmenistan, and Uzbekistan) offered the best possibilities of achieving the goals of the moment.[58] The United Nations' senior envoys maintained regular consultations with the individual capitals, and with representatives of the observer states and international organizations (OSCE and the Organization of the Islamic Conference (OIC)) in New York. And in early 1995 secretariat officials decided to facilitate these contacts through the creation of an informal group of Friends of Tajikistan. Although too large—its membership of eleven countries and two international organizations included all ten observers, as well as Turkey, Saudi Arabia, and the United States—to be operational, the group proved a helpful means by which to keep these varied actors engaged, and on occasion to ask them to undertake specific tasks or carry coordinated messages at the secretariat's request.[59]

A breakthrough in the negotiations came only in 1996. Russia's engagement had been given new impetus by the appointment of Primakov as foreign minister and the store he appeared to set by settling conflicts in the Soviet periphery. Moreover, a desire to settle the Tajik conflict increasingly brought Russia's interests into line with those of Iran (the two had begun by backing opposing forces). These included providing a bulwark against the Taliban (supported by Pakistan and Saudi Arabia), which was rapidly gaining ground in Afghanistan, while limiting Western involvement in Central Asia, not least to retain access and control over the resources of the Caspian Sea.[60] After the 1997 agreement was signed, the eight observer states were reconstituted in Dushanbe as a Contact Group (the Friends, which had met as such only in New York, ceased to exist). They met frequently with the special representative of the secretary-general (SRSG) heading UNMOT and continued to play a constructive role in maintaining the country's fragile peace in the years to come.[61]

Friends of the Secretary-General: Into the Fray

Managing the Friends of Georgia was, in comparison with the group formed on Tajikistan, always a complex issue. "Within the secretariat we saw the creation of the Friends of Georgia with some concern," one official would recall. "We even wondered whether we could do something to stifle it. We couldn't, of course, so we did the UN thing and tried to work with it."[62] Secretariat officials, subjected to constant complaints by the Abkhaz regarding the partiality of the Friends, had long encouraged the group's renaming. As a result of a concerted effort to revive the flagging peace process and assert the United Nations' role within it, in 1997 the group was finally persuaded to reconstitute itself as the Friends of the Secretary-General for Georgia.

Liviu Bota was appointed SRSG in July 1997. Unlike Brunner, he lived in Georgia and divided his time, as would his successors, between UNOMIG's headquarters in Abkhazia and a political liaison office in Tbilisi. Bota initiated the Geneva process, which envisaged regular meetings between the parties within a complex set of mechanisms. These included high-level meetings between the two sides, but also a coordinating council that oversaw working groups on security issues, the refugees and internally displaced persons (IDPs), and economic and social problems. These groups met within an intricate international framework, spelled out by the secretary-general to the Security Council as "under the chairmanship of my Special Representative or his authorized representative, with the participation of the representatives of the Russian federation in its capacity as facilitator, representatives of OSCE, as well as with the group of Friends of the Secretary-General."[63] The status of the Friends was defined (rather unhelpfully in light of this study) as "analogous to the status of the other groups of Friends of the Secretary-General." They could participate in meetings—France, as coordinator, would generally speak on their behalf—and could make "statements and proposals" on the peace process, but they were not parties to the negotiations and therefore would not sign agreements reached with them.[64]

Meetings deriving from the Geneva process continued through 1998 despite the major reversal suffered as a result of the events in Gali that May. The United Nations also was able to organize two meetings on confidence-building measures, held in Athens and Istanbul in October 1998 and June 1999, respectively. But initial optimism that progress could be made without agreement on the central political questions underlying the conflict soon foundered. An example of this was an exploration of the possibility of employing economic assistance—an area in which the Western Friends and the European Union could expect to be deeply involved—to support the political effort, undertaken on the basis of a needs assessment mission to Abkhazia led by the United Nations Development Programme (UNDP). The Georgians, who had effectively closed down legal economic activity in Abkhazia through the CIS-imposed embargo, looked forward to the reintegration of an economically active Abkhazia into Georgia, while the Abkhaz sought assistance to bolster their viability as a separate entity.[65]

The Geneva process generated a lot of activity, but UN officials were frustrated by the extent to which the substance of the discussions that took place within it "danced around" the central political issue of status.[66] Consequently, the secretariat decided to begin preparatory work on the question of Abkhazia's political status, receiving firm endorsement of its initiative both from the Security Council, in Resolution 1255 of July 30, 1999, and from Shevardnadze, who met with Kofi Annan in the margins of the General Assembly that September. Progress was slowed by the lack of an SRSG during much of 1999, but when Dieter Boden took up the job in late November, he assumed the task as one of his priorities. In doing so, he was eagerly supported by the Western members of the Friends and Georgia—both had complained to the secretariat that the United Nations was being slow to advance on this initiative—but not by Russia or Abkhazia. Indeed the Abkhaz were clearly opposed to the process being headed in this direction and in October 1999 called a referendum on Abkhazia's independence that passed by a large majority.

Conscious of opposition, the United Nations decided that any paper on "the distribution of (constitutional) competencies," as it became known, had to be agreed upon by all of the secretary-general's Friends—obviously including Russia—before it was submitted to the two parties. That this was not going to be easy, even though the paper was envisaged only as a framework for further negotiations, drawn up on the basis of principles already articulated by the Security Council, became evident as soon as the first draft of the paper was presented to the Friends in May 2000. The Western Friends responded with constructive comments, but the reaction of Russia was ambiguous. Wanting a draft that would "equally hurt" both sides, Boden was asked to "water down" the text.

In the end, discussion of what became known as the "Boden paper" would be drawn out until mid-December 2001 against the backdrop of a deteriorating situation on the ground that included conflict in the Kodori Valley and the downing of a UN helicopter.[67] Agreement was achieved only after the focus of negotiations between the Friends had been moved from Tbilisi to New York in order to facilitate more sustained pressure on Russia by the others. Almost daily meetings at the expert level on a controversial "status" paragraph concluded by specifying that Abkhazia was a "sovereign entity" within the "State of Georgia." Reflecting the outcome of a deal between the Friends that gave Georgia its territorial integrity, Abkhazia broad autonomy (less than it wanted, of course), and Russia the role of "guarantor," a point that was spelled out in a transmittal letter to the parties, the document was presented as a starting point for negotiations. But by defining Abkhazia's status in the absence of the Abkhaz, the Boden paper was open to criticism that it represented an attempt to dictate an endgame to the process, and not its beginning.

Agreement on the Boden paper was welcomed by Annan as "a significant step forward."[68] However, any sense of triumph was undercut by the Abkhaz's steadfast refusal to receive the paper in the years ahead, despite the exhortations of the Security Council and the efforts of both Boden and his successor, Heidi Tagliavini. In the circumstances it was unsurprising that, more than three years after work on the paper began, a representative of the Abkhaz authorities would comment, "The authors of the Boden paper don't realize that without us they cannot resolve this conflict."[69]

The Friends at Work

The Boden paper brought the group of Friends into the foreground of the peace process, but also made explicit questions of influence that had long been latent within it. The paper was negotiated within the Friends because the UN secretariat and the group's Western members saw the extraction of a specific commitment from Russia to Georgian sovereignty as being more valuable in the framework represented by the Friends than in the broad terms of Security Council commitments, and thus key to Abkhaz intransigence on the issue.[70] Georgia maintained that Russia had "full and absolute control of the Abkhaz," as Malkhaz Kakabadze, the minister of special affairs responsible for the peace process under Shevardnadze, put it, "110 percent control." It welcomed the Boden process because of the direct engagement of the Western Friends, which were viewed as useful to the extent that they demonstrated "a level of readiness to take on Russia."[71] This expectation that the Friends would somehow do the heavy lifting required to move the process forward reflected a fundamental misunderstanding of Georgia's relatively low level of importance to relations between the West and Russia, frequent protestations of the geopolitical significance of the Southern Caucasus notwithstanding. It also helped perpetuate a degree of apathy among the Georgians, who notably failed to take initiative with respect to proposals that might advance the process or concrete steps to build the confidence of the Abkhaz.

Many of the Friends' representatives had assumed, like the Georgians —and despite Russian protestations that their ability to tell the Abkhaz what to do was much more limited than they believed—that agreement from Russia would force a change of heart upon the Abkhaz.[72] From January 2002 resolutions of the Security Council urged "those with influence over the parties," meaning Russia, to use it to ensure that the paper could at least be transmitted to them. The Western members of the Friends would be frustrated that Russia did not "try hard enough," but the Abkhaz, who had rejected the initiative from the outset, had no intention of receiving the Boden paper now. After their declaration of independence in 1999, a move in part precipitated by the initiation of the discussion on their political status, they believed they had nothing to talk about. "Our position is that the status of Abkhazia has been defined," Ardzinba's adviser, Astamur Tania, would explain, "and that status is independence."[73] "The Friends all believe Georgian propaganda that we are totally under the influence of Russia," the de facto Foreign Minister Sergei Shamba maintained. "They do not have the most elementary comprehension of what our interests are."[74]

The process of negotiation of the Boden paper and efforts to secure its transmittal to the parties highlighted some of the mechanism's peculiarities. Since assuming a formal role within the peace process, constituent groups of Friends had taken shape in Tbilisi, Moscow, and New York. In each a tendency for the Western members of the group to meet without the Russians had given rise to two distinct groupings, the "Western Friends," an entity that, in diplomatic terms, did not exist (rather like a nonpaper), and the Friends of the Secretary-General, a group that included Russia and sometimes, but not always, met under the chairmanship of a representative of the secretary-general. These groups were active at the level of ambassador in Tbilisi and at both expert and ambassador (or deputy) levels in New York and Moscow. The Tbilisi manifestation of the

Friends had begun meeting with the Abkhaz as a group in the framework of the Geneva process, but did not continue to do so beyond the Istanbul meeting held in June 1999. The Boden process served to undermine any confidence established in that period; gradually some of the Friends came to realize the structural problem that this created. "With the Boden paper on the table," one expert would comment in 2003, "we have lost access to the Abkhaz entirely."[75]

Although differences in position within the Western Friends were evident—determined by the extent to which support for Shevardnadze was tempered by his failings to lay the basis for a functioning state, as well as their level of willingness to at least try to understand the perspective of the Abkhaz[76]—they tended to be subordinated by their desire to present a unified position toward Russia. The three incarnations of the group were in constant communication with each other and their capitals, but their locations determined significant differences between them. The ambassadors to Georgia were appreciated, as Heidi Tagliavini put it, as "a very important tool in the peace process" that gave the United Nations direct access to the key states on the Security Council and firm support in its primary task of preventing the recurrence of conflict. Yet secretariat officials viewed the Western ambassadors in Tbilisi as hewing too closely to the line of the government to which they were accredited.[77] Meanwhile, the Friends in Moscow were challenged by the structural position Russia assumed as interlocutor between the Western Friends and the Abkhaz. Meetings of the Friends took the less-than-satisfactory form of the Western Friends "calling on" the Russians in the Foreign Ministry. Western ambassadors were constricted both by the diplomatic protocols attendant on the format of the meetings (Russian hosts down one side of the table; Western Friends down the other) and by the many higher priorities than Abkhazia that each was juggling in their bilateral relations with Russia at any time.[78]

It was in New York that the group was perceived to work best; distance from both Tbilisi and Moscow gave the Western Friends what they believed was greater leverage over Russia. The group's members maintained regular contact with each other, the secretariat, and through the group's coordinator (which remained France until mid-2003, when Germany took over the role), with both Boden and Tagliavini in Tbilisi. But the Friends continued to act with the autonomy that had characterized the group from the beginning. In late 1999, the Friends decided, for example, to add Ukraine, which was shortly to take a seat on the Security Council, to their number without prior consultation with the secretariat. After discussing the issue with Boden, who raised concerns about both the unwieldiness of an enlarged group and the extent to which opening the door to Ukraine might encourage other applicants, the Friends were persuaded to limit Ukraine to the New York group.[79] (A similar arrangement was adopted for Bulgaria and Slovakia, which joined the Friends in New York in 2002 and 2006 respectively as they began two-year terms on the Council.)

Meetings of the Friends were concentrated around the quarterly consideration of Georgia by the Security Council, and especially the mandate renewals of UNOMIG due in January and July. The group dominated Council consideration of the issue by its drafting of all resolutions and even presidential statements on Georgia. Although Western members of the Council were well briefed by the Friends, other elected members sometimes protested the extent to which they were asked to "rubber-stamp" their actions.[80] But the Friends themselves, including Russia, appreciated a forum in which differences could be resolved outside the Security Council and among countries with detailed knowledge of the issues. "It isn't democratic, but it is effective," one senior Russian official put it.[81]

Geneva Again

During the second half of 2002 the impasse that had developed on the Boden paper threatened to divide Russia from the other Friends and undermine the fragile architecture of the peace process. Boden's efforts to arrange a joint meeting between the Abkhaz leadership and the Tbilisi Friends had come to nothing, and planned meetings between the Friends and the Abkhaz authorities in Moscow did not take place when it became clear that the new SRSG, Heidi Tagliavini, was not to be included.[82] The mechanisms that had been created under the Geneva process had fallen into disrepair, a series of projects agreed to at a third confidence-building meeting held in Yalta in March 2001 had not materialized, and the security situation in the Kodori Valley and for refugees seeking to return to Gali remained precarious. Meeting in New York with representatives of the Friends, secretariat officials warned that the Boden paper had a limited life span and risked having its credibility undermined. The Friends, with France and Germany in the forefront of the discussion, emphasized that the credibility of the document was also that of the Security Council (which had "welcomed and supported" the document's finalization, but at Russia's insistence, neither endorsed nor published it) and it therefore needed to be maintained.[83]

By the fall of 2002 the extent to which progress in the peace process depended on the broader question of Georgian-Russian relations was

evident. Increased ties between Russia and Abkhazia included the exemp-
tion of the Abkhaz from a new visa regime introduced for Georgians; the
introduction in July 2002 of fast-track legislation that allowed thousands of
Abkhaz citizens to obtain Russian citizenship; a decision to privatize numerous Black Sea resorts and sanatoriums in order to attract an influx of
Russian capital; and the declaration of the previous year, following a vote
in the Georgian parliament to remove the CIS peacekeeping force, that
Abkhazia wished to apply for "associate status" with the Russian Federation. Georgians viewed these measures, as they would Russia's reopening of
railway and maritime links to Abkhazia in 2003, as "indirect annexation"
and a direct assault on their sovereignty.[84] The situation had been further
complicated by Russian allegations that Georgia was "harboring Chechen
terrorists" in the Pankisi Gorge and Georgia's counterclaims that Russia
had violated Georgian airspace to carry out bombing raids on its villages.[85]

Discussion between Tagliavini and the secretariat focused on how to
counter the growing mistrust on all sides: between the Georgians and the
Abkhaz, the Georgians and the Russians, and within the Friends, between
Russia and the West and particularly the United States. In this respect the
heightened U.S. interest in Georgia and the broader region since the
attacks of September 2001 was both an asset and a complicating factor.
Tensions over the presence of Chechens in the Pankisi Gorge diminished
after combined U.S. and Russian pressure encouraged Georgian forces to
clear out most of them. But the presence of U.S. military trainers, as with
other aspects of Georgia's westward tilt, contributed to the lack of trust
between the parties and with Russia.[86] This reflected a tendency on the part
of both Georgia and Russia to see their relations in terms of a zero-sum
game: Georgia was either with Russia or with the United States. From this
oversimplified perspective, enhanced U.S. interest in Georgia encouraged
both Georgia and Russia to be less compromising on Abkhazia by fueling
Georgian expectation of what the United States would be able to do for it,
while prompting Russia to extend its grip. The U.S. ambassador in Tbilisi,
Richard Miles, countered such expectations categorically: "As for the U.S.
putting real pressure on Russia on this issue," he said in an interview in July
2003, "it is not going to happen."[87] Meanwhile, as the Russian nationalist
Vladimir Zhirinovsky put it, expressing a view that security analyst Oksana
Antonenko would describe as not exceptional, "the closer Georgia comes
to NATO membership, the faster Abkhazia becomes a part of Russia."[88]

The secretary-general and his officials began to raise concern at the
impasse over Abkhazia at a higher level than the issue was usually addressed.
As they did so, they found a particularly receptive audience in Britain,

which had just appointed as special envoy Sir Brian Fall, a former ambassador to Moscow with pronounced doubts regarding what could be gained by "hammering away at the Boden paper."[89] Fall suggested a high-level meeting to bring together special envoys already named by Russia, Deputy Foreign Minister Valery Loshchinin, and by the United States, Rudolph Perina, as well as other senior representatives of the Friends. This meeting, it was decided, would be chaired by the United Nations' under-secretary-general for peacekeeping, Jean-Marie Guéhenno. It would take place in Geneva in order to introduce an element of separation from the existing three manifestations of the group of Friends and ensure Russian participation at the highest level.

The meeting held February 19–20, 2003, launched what would again become known as the Geneva process, giving new impetus to the negotiations by facilitating discussion of substantive issues without casting to one side—as Russia would have preferred—the question of political status entirely ("it is good to discuss the Boden document," one Russian official explained, "but impossible"[90]). Presented as a high-level "brainstorming" among the Friends, the Geneva meeting concluded by recommending the establishment of task forces to address economic issues, the return of IDPs and refugees, and political and security issues (which the Friends understood to include the status question as well as security guarantees). It closed with a statement that reiterated the support of the Friends for the SRSG and promised the convening by the United Nations of a further high-level meeting within a few months.[91]

Reaction from Russia came quickly. In early March President Putin, who had been "informed in detail" about Geneva,[92] called a hastily arranged meeting with Shevardnadze at Sochi, a Black Sea resort to the north of Abkhazia. Also in attendance was the de facto prime minister of Abkhazia, Gennady Gagulia. (Days earlier in Sukhumi at the first encounter between the group of Friends and the Abkhaz held in four years, he had rebuffed the Friends' presentation of the conclusions of the Geneva meeting.[93]) The two presidents agreed to establish bilateral working groups to address the return of refugees and IDPs to Gali, the reopening of the railway between Sochi and Tbilisi (understood to be tied to progress in refugee return), and energy projects. The statement issued at the meeting's end made no reference to the agreements entered into at Geneva or the group of Friends. It limited itself to "noting" the role of the United Nations and that the meeting's conclusions were reached "in compliance" with previous decisions and recommendations of the international community.[94]

The outrage of the Western Friends—"we have been painlessly neutralized," was the comment of one[95]—was compounded by reports of the meeting distributed to them by somewhat defensive Georgian officials. These described an unpleasant exchange between Georgia's deputy foreign minister, Merab Antadze, and Putin that had taken place while Shevardnadze stood quietly by in tacit support of the Russian position. Antadze had tried to stand up for Geneva and the UN process but his efforts had been brushed aside. "I do not understand what you want," Putin was reported to have said. "Break a stalemate and solve a specific problem or just talk and talk endlessly on the Geneva process, the group of Friends. What have they done for ten years? What could they do?"[96]

The agreements reached at Sochi, with their marked exclusion of political issues, came as a slap in the face to the United Nations, but they could not be ignored. Painstaking efforts on the part of Tagliavini and both Georgian and Russian officials involved in the Geneva process (Lochshinin, the United Nations' principal interlocutor, had not been at Sochi) were gradually able to bring the two initiatives together in order to maintain some kind of forward momentum on both. Further UN-chaired meetings of the Friends were held periodically, while Tagliavini also initiated meetings between the two sides, with participation of the Friends, on the issue of security guarantees. Representatives of both Georgia and Abkhazia participated in parts of a Geneva meeting held in July 2003, which was deemed a positive step forward in itself. However, by February 2004 the Abkhaz side declined to turn up for reasons attributed to uncertainties surrounding the policy of the new Saakashvili government as well as Abkhazia's concentration on the run-up to its "presidential" elections scheduled for October 2004.

The Geneva process had broken the deadlock created by the Boden paper, and in doing so, helped introduce new momentum to the process and to efforts to secure refugee return to Gali in particular. But officials involved at the senior level of the Friends had few illusions as to what Geneva might be able to achieve in the absence of a political settlement. Geneva gives the "impression of movement" Jean-Marie Guéhenno had explained at the end of June 2003. This was, in itself, a "modest benefit" in that in its absence the situation would only deteriorate.[97] But it was very far from constituting a breakthrough on the major issues underlying the conflict, something that most engaged in the process believed could only be expected in the context of Georgia's relations with Russia and, given the evolution of regional dynamics and interests, agreement at the very highest level between Russia and the United States.

From Standstill to Confrontation

Mikheil Sakaashvili had arrived in office determined to reestablish his country's territorial integrity. Exactly how he was going to do this, he did not spell out, and although his government projected an image of youthful, pro-Western vigor, publicly committed to uproot the corruption that was endemic to Georgian life, it was no less firmly anchored in Georgian nationalism than was its predecessor. A mix of diplomacy and the threat of force, backed up by somewhat ambivalent support from Russia, helped Saakashvili regain control of the province of Ajara. But success in that instance—Ajara's autonomy from Tbilisi neither followed a separatist conflict nor was based on ethnic difference—proved no harbinger of similar feats in either South Ossetia or Abkhazia.[98] Indeed, attempts to implement a similar strategy in South Ossetia backfired badly, leading to an increase of tensions in the secessionist state and in relations with Russia.[99] The latter were not improved when in late July 2004, Georgia fired on a foreign cargo ship in the Black Sea near Sukhumi and then threatened to sink any ships trying to enter Abkhazia without its permission, including those carrying Russian tourists. On the following day the Abkhaz authorities suspended their participation in the peace process, as well as in ceasefire monitoring and other security-related mechanisms in which they had participated.[100]

The Abkhaz remained outside the political process until early 2005, absorbed by the drama that developed in the wake of their October 2004 elections. Expectations that the favored candidate of Ardzinba and Moscow, Raul Khajimba, had his path to victory assured were upended by his apparent defeat by Sergei Bagapsh, a former prime minister supported by a wide range of the Abkhaz political establishment. Abkhazia's authorities, reinforced by Russian support, refused to accept this outcome and instead ruled that a new election be held in December. But Bagapsh supporters would not go quietly and took to the streets. Russia ratcheted up the pressure through visiting delegations from Moscow, and economic penalties including the closure of Abkhazia's northern border. Abkhazia teetered on the brink of conflict, divided between two candidates whose only common ground was the vehemence of their support for Abkhazia's independence. A last-minute deal paved the way for elections in January that, as expected, confirmed Bagapsh in the Abkhaz presidency.[101]

The Friends had met in Geneva in December 2004 "to remind each other that they existed," as one British official put it.[102] An intense period of diplomatic activity followed before they reconvened in April. This time representatives of both Georgia and Abkhazia attended. The meeting offered glimmers of possibility: both sides expressed their willingness to pursue practical discussions within the framework of the working groups on security issues, the return of refugees, and economic cooperation.[103] But on the fundamental issues dividing them the two remained far apart, with the Georgians unable to renounce the possibility of violence and the Abkhaz ready to develop only a peace plan that would guarantee "the peaceful coexistence of two states."[104] In the latter part of 2005 and early 2006, this gulf grew wider as Georgia's relations with Russia deteriorated. In January 2006 Saakashvili accused Moscow of intentionally blowing up the Russian gas pipeline that supplies Georgia, plunging the country into an energy crisis at the coldest point of the winter. Putin's appeal for "universal principles" to settle frozen conflicts came soon afterward. As he linked Abkhazia and South Ossetia to the future status of Kosovo, he introduced a fundamental shift in Russia's discourse on the conflicts that complicated relations among the Friends.[105]

Tensions within the Friends surfaced during discussions preceding the renewal of UNOMIG's mandate. In the past this had been a fairly routine affair, with agreement on the continuation of UNOMIG the least controversial aspect of any resolution on Georgia. But on January 20 Bagapsh had addressed a letter to the Security Council offering Abkhazia's readiness to conduct "civilized negotiations on all issues except the status of the Republic of Abkhazia," citing Abkhazia's close following of "the development of international practice in this field" and making an explicit reference to Kosovo.[106] A few days later Russia surprised the Western Friends by objecting to the inclusion in the proposed resolution of reference to the Boden paper or even the standard UN formula that reaffirmed the sovereignty and territorial integrity of Georgia and supported a political solution that included Abkhazia in the state of Georgia. Only a temporary compromise hammered out by the Friends outside the Council itself enabled it to adopt on January 31 a two-month technical rollover of UNOMIG's mandate.[107]

In the following weeks, the secretariat and the Friends struggled to get the UN process back on its familiar track. In doing so, they were conscious that the issue of the Kosovo precedent was one with immense repercussions for a number of other Council members, notably China and Greece, the latter of which had joined the Council in January 2005 and had its political antennae finely attuned to any situation that might have implications for the status of Cyprus. The sixth high-level Geneva meeting took place on February 2 and 3, chaired, as in the past, by Guéhenno. In the statement to the press after the meeting ended, the Friends underlined that "the basis of their efforts was the settlement of the conflict by peaceful means and in the framework of relevant Security Council resolutions."[108] This compromise position allowed for the renewal of the mandate of UNOMIG at the end of March. Language reaffirming the commitment of all member states to the sovereignty and territorial independence of Georgia was back in, as was reference to the Boden paper. But the Council also indicated its readiness to welcome "additional ideas that the sides would be willing to offer with a view to conducting creatively and constructively a political dialogue."[109]

In the Georgian-Abkhaz context, this represented a modest but not insignificant opening, and indeed the following months offered a brief glimpse of what concrete progress might look like. Saakashvili's newly appointed representative for the peace talks, Irakli Alasania, displayed a capacity to engage with the Abkhaz that distinguished him from any of his predecessors and quickly won their respect. The two sides met in May in the context of the Coordinating Council—a body that had not sat since January 2001—and exchanged proposals with concrete suggestions for the future. With the burden of the Boden paper finally lifted, they agreed to concentrate on informal consultations and the development of confidence-building measures, while continuing discussions they had begun the previous year on joint declarations on both the non-use of force and the return of IDPs, as well as preparations for a meeting of their highest authorities. These positive developments were encouraged in late May by an unprecedented visit of a high-level delegation of the group of Friends to both Tbilisi and Sukhumi.[110]

Unfortunately, however, the broader political context did not favor further progress. In July the Georgian parliament passed a resolution calling on the government to suspend the peacekeeping operations in Abkhazia and South Ossetia; days later the government launched a large-scale police and military operation to restore law and order in the Georgian-controlled sector of Abkhazia, the upper Kodori Valley. Russia supported the Abkhaz in denouncing the operation as a gross violation of the 1994 cease-fire agreement and alleged that it had been launched in preparation for a broader offensive against Abkhazia. Georgia did little to help dispel this impression: the chairman of the parliament's Defense and Security Committee stated publicly that the operation would establish control over "an extremely important political base . . . a place from which one can reach Sukhumi by air in just over five minutes."[111] Tensions were still high when, in September, Georgian authorities arrested four Russian military intelligence officers on espionage charges. Moscow responded aggressively, recalling its ambassador from Georgia, imposing punitive measures to disrupt trade, and forcibly repatriating ethnic Georgians from Russia. The crisis marked a low-point in the checkered history of Georgian-Russian relations since the end of the Cold War.

Difficulties among the Friends came to the surface as they tried to agree on a presidential statement of the Security Council. While Russia proposed to "condemn" Georgia's operation in the Kodori Valley, the United States insisted it should be "welcomed." After some hesitation the European Friends, led by the United Kingdom, suggested that the Council might express "concern." However, the gulf between Russia and the United States on the Kodori Valley action—as on Saakhashvili's Georgia more broadly, where the United States, as one UN official described it, had become "part of the decision-making structure"—was a deep one.[112] The effort to agree on a presidential statement was abandoned.

Several weeks later the Friends again returned to the drawing board, this time to craft a resolution extending the mandate of UNOMIG. Unusually, Russia—rather than Germany as the coordinator of the Friends—tabled the first draft of a text that, again, proposed to "condemn" the action in the Kodori Valley. The European Friends were able to bring the Russians around to a text that proposed that the Security Council "express its concern."[113] But the United States, which had argued, somewhat implausibly, against any mention of the Kodori Valley action if the Security Council refused to welcome it, resisted and for the first time did not cosponsor the resolution with the other members of the Friends. While hardly an earth-shattering development, the episode represented a "reality check" for Georgia in its aspirations to provoke greater engagement by the West in fighting its battles with Russia. The path back to the nuts and bolts of an evidently fragile political process looked difficult.

Conclusions

The Friends of Georgia came to fill a central role in a peace process in which the United Nations sought to end a separatist conflict with its origins in the collapse of the Soviet Union. These two characteristics of the conflict—its separatist nature and its complex relationship to the regional power—effectively limited the utility of the UN effort. In the context of this study, they also determined both the relationship of the Friends to the regional environment and to the conflict parties themselves. Russia's participation in the Friends was inevitable. But the role it played makes it hard to assess the regional environment as anything but a central obstacle to the conflict's resolution. Meanwhile, the replication of the conflict dynamics in the Friends determined the group's relationship to the parties. The open opposition of the other members of the Friends to the secession-ist aspirations of the Abkhaz was one that fed Abkhazia's alienation from the UN process; the Georgians, meanwhile, came to appreciate the United Nations and the Friends as an essential buffer between themselves and Russia. Neither of these positions was conducive to the development of meaningful negotiations.

The group's creation was somewhat accidental in that it responded to an initiative taken by member states that was not directly articulated within a strategy to address the conflict or with a particular demand by the con-flict parties. When constituted as "Friends of the Secretary-General" in the late 1990s, the group was supposed to play a role analogous to that of groups of Friends elsewhere—a proposition that clarified little. The shift represented an attempt to introduce a course correction to a group that had complicated the secretariat's efforts until that time. But even in its new incarnation, a group of states so fundamentally divided on the prob-lem at hand and distracted by the many other issues on which the Western members engaged with Russia was in many respects ill suited to help the United Nations. The prominence of the Friends was raised again in the Geneva process initiated in 2002 to prevent an open rift between Russia and the Western Friends. This injected new life into a diplomatic effort to move the two parties toward discussion of the fundamental political issues dividing them. But though creative in procedural terms, the effort could make little headway on the substance.

Secondary obstacles to the conflict's settlement can be identified as a fundamental mismatch between the model for conflict resolution pursued by the international community—based on a perception of a "frozen" con-flict whose outcome would be driven by parties disposed to hammer out agreements through negotiations—and a reality of a stalemate that brought the Abkhaz some benefits even as the international community dismissed out of hand their aspirations for independence. Despite their differences with the Western Friends, the Abkhaz gained time, implicit recognition as a counterpart to the Georgian state in a UN-sanctioned process, and, under cover of the presence of international peacekeepers, the security and even resources to build some of the structures and institutions of a state. But whether these gains would be sustainable over the long term was ques-tionable. Abkhaz authorities were not able to respond to the needs of their population. They faced persistent problems of emigration by their young as well as fears that the growing influence of Russia could lead to the loss of

Abkhaz identity. Meanwhile, although the stalemate in Abkhazia in itself represented both a source of regional insecurity and an obstacle to national consolidation, Georgia's own economic and institutional weakness led it to prioritize other issues, confident that international involvement in the conflict would provide the best available buffer against the predatory tendencies of Russia.

With a lack of traction on the conflict itself, the Friends evolved into a mechanism that was principally engaged in managing relations among its members. An absence of other regional actors—such as Turkey or except in a limited fashion, Ukraine—had several consequences. It emphasized the extent to which the composition of the group rendered it primarily a forum in which to address differences between Western states and Russia. It thus magnified the extent to which the Abkhaz conflict was vulnerable to geopolitical rivalries deriving in the first instance from the Cold War and then from the reaccommodation of interests in the region after September 2001 and in the context of Vladimir Putin's newly assertive Russia. The composition of the group of Friends also facilitated its development as a subgroup of the Security Council, usurping the Council's broader authority to a considerable extent. Members of the group themselves, however, would agree that its existence served their interests—confused and contradictory as they were—well. For the Western states the Friends brought access to Russia on an issue in which they otherwise would have had little say and a ringside seat in a political process in which the secretary-general and Russia had the leading roles (benefits particularly prized by Germany, the one Friend not a permanent member of the Security Council).[114] Although it chafed under the restraint imposed in late 2006, for the United States the group and the UN process for many years served as a means to downgrade Georgian expectations of the extent to which it was prepared to face down Russia on this issue.[115] And for Russia the Friends provided an international forum that was smaller and more discreet than the Security Council in which to address the preoccupations of the West.

For the UN secretariat the question of the group's utility is more complex. Its existence helped sustain interest in a situation that was for years of low priority for many international actors; it proved a flexible, if time-consuming, diplomatic instrument, and it helped bolster the position of successive SRSGs with authorities in Georgia as well as in Moscow. Secretariat officials did their best to exert the leadership required to make the Friends useful—despite their limited influence over Russia's actions—and over time the group became a permanent feature of the complex diplomatic landscape determining the United Nations' relationships to the parties. But how much it actually helped is a different matter. "Without the Friends we wouldn't get anywhere on Georgia," a secretariat official remarked rather defensively in mid-2003, "but then we don't get anywhere with them either."[116] The long-drawn-out process of the Boden paper made things demonstrably worse. That the Western Friends maintained the Boden paper as a central aspect of Security Council action complicated the task of UN negotiators. With Security Council resolutions until January 2006 repeatedly reiterating their "strong support" for the document, a pragmatic placing of the Boden paper on the shelf, to be dusted off as a useful contribution to any endgame discussion of status, became extremely difficult.

By the mid-2000s, the Friends were so fully institutionalized that few of those engaged in the Georgian-Abkhaz process could imagine them not being part of the picture. That in itself was a problem. Their constant presence encouraged a tendency for the Georgians to sit back and wait for the Western Friends to exert pressure on Russia and for the Abkhaz to sit out the process altogether, secure in the knowledge that UN officials would exert themselves to achieve the appearance of movement. The commodious nature of this situation for the parties was obvious. Ending the Friends had never been an option for the United Nations. Indeed, it was perhaps inevitable that the rising interest of external actors in the Southern Caucasus and in direct engagement in conflict resolution as an activity itself should have propelled them into a more central role. Preventing a recurrence of open conflict in a situation as volatile as Abkhazia is not a negligible achievement. However, the lack of tangible results in a peace process that, although stuck in an early phase of peacemaking, was arguably further from resolution some fourteen years after the United Nations first became involved constituted a serious challenge to all engaged in it.

6

Self-Determination and Realpolitik
The Story of Western Sahara

The United Nations' involvement in the conflict in Western Sahara, like that in East Timor that is addressed in the following chapter, long predates the end of the Cold War. A former Spanish colony, Western Sahara was placed on the United Nations' list of "non–self-governing territories" in the early 1960s. Its decolonization was aborted in the mid-1970s when it fell prey to the unfortunate combination of territorial ambition by Morocco and studied disinterest from states in the broader international community unwilling to jeopardize relations with a strategically located regional power. Spain ceded administration of the territory to Morocco and Mauritania in early 1976 in defiance of resolutions of the Security Council and an opinion of the International Court of Justice (ICJ). A protracted period of peacemaking led by the Organisation of African Unity (OAU) then ensued. UN Secretary-General Pérez de Cuéllar's good offices were engaged from 1985 onward and led to the establishment of the UN Mission for the Referendum in Western Sahara (MINURSO) in 1991. But a lack of clarity on who was to take part in this referendum was never resolved, and the possibility of it taking place perennially receded.

A group of Friends was formed in 1993 as a direct result of the efficacy that member states saw in other groups of this period. It helped retain attention on a neglected conflict and coordinate the work of the Security Council, but it remained at some distance from—and limited utility to—the secretary-general and his representatives, even as it became the focus of intense lobbying conducted by Morocco, representatives of the Popular Front for the Liberation of Saguia el Hamra and Rio de Oro (Polisario), and their Algerian supporters. Kofi Annan addressed the stalemate he found in Western Sahara in 1997 by appointing James A. Baker III, the former U.S. secretary of state, as his personal envoy to assess the feasibility of implementing the referendum or failing that, explore the possibility of resolving the conflict by means of enhanced autonomy for the territory.[1]

Baker did not work with the Friends as a group, but pushed them and the Security Council as a whole to confront the substantial obstacles to a settlement masked by stasis on the ground. In the process, long-standing differences between members of the Friends that had been papered over by the utility to them of the status quo surfaced to render the group dysfunctional. This chapter argues that the limitations of the Friends were attributable to an evident lack of coherence between the national interests of the powerful states that constituted the group's core members—France, Russia, Spain, the United Kingdom, and the United States—and between those interests and the goals of the United Nations. In these respects Western Sahara is an example of circumstances in which the utility of an informal group to the resolution of a conflict, as opposed to its management, is minimal.

The Conflict for Western Sahara

Western Sahara was described by Tony Hodges, author of the definitive study of the conflict's origins, as "one of the most inhospitable places on Earth."[2] Stretching across the sparsely populated western flank of the Sahara Desert between Morocco, Algeria, and Mauritania, it measures more than 260,000 square kilometers. A Spanish census conducted in 1974 documented its population as fewer than 74,000.[3]

Spain had begun trading along the northwest African seaboard in the mid-fifteenth century. Its interest in the region increased during the nineteenth century as its vast colonial territories in the Americas won independence, and in 1884 it claimed Spanish Sahara as a colony.[4] In the late 1940s the discovery of large deposits of phosphates in the territory increased General Francisco Franco's determination to hold on to it. A referendum in the Sahara was called for by the General Assembly from 1966 on, but Spain undertook no preparations.[5] Only as political unrest in the Sahara mounted—Polisario initiated guerrilla actions against Spain in 1973—and the authority of the ailing Franco began to deteriorate did Spain announce that a referendum for self-determination would be held in early 1975.

Claims over the territory made by Morocco and Mauritania interrupted its planning. These had first been put forward by Morocco's nationalist Istiqlal party in the context of demands for the return of a "Greater Morocco" that included not only Western Sahara but also Mauritania and parts of Algeria and Mali. King Hassan II took up the cause and developed the idea that it was central to Moroccan identity. His bid to reclaim the

"Saharan provinces" provided a convenient distraction from domestic dissent, serving to unite competing social, political, and military interests in Rabat at a moment of low popularity for the monarchy. These political benefits, however, had both economic and social costs. War and occupation would represent an extraordinary financial outlay by an impoverished Moroccan state that could ill afford it.

In December 1974 the UN General Assembly asked the ICJ for its advisory opinion on the matter. The ICJ reported in October 1975 that it found no evidence "of any legal tie of territorial sovereignty" between Western Sahara and Morocco, but "indication of a legal tie of allegiance between the [Moroccan] Sultan and some, although only some, of the tribes in the territory." The ICJ concluded that these ties did not affect the decolonization of Western Sahara or the principle of self-determination.[6] Hassan, however, chose to interpret its ruling as an affirmation of Morocco's claims. In November he launched the "Green March," in which 350,000 Moroccan civilians followed Moroccan troops into the desert to "reintegrate" the territory.

In the days before the Green March took place, Spain brought the situation in Western Sahara before the Security Council, which asked the secretary-general to undertake consultations with all concerned. These had no more noticeable effect than did a resolution passed by the Security Council after the march's conclusion that called for Morocco's immediate withdrawal from the territory.[7] Spain's domestic circumstances, Morocco's strategic importance to Western states, U.S. concerns about "another Angola" on the eastern flank of the Atlantic Ocean, as well as the carefully balanced relationship that Morocco—a founding member of the nonaligned movement—maintained with Moscow, all militated against any possibility of the Council's appeals being heeded.[8]

In Spain, Franco lay dying. The country had already entered into a fragile period of transition and was in no position to risk conflict with Morocco. Moreover, it had been offered a profitable fishing agreement and a stake in the exploitation of Western Sahara's phosphate deposits in return for its surrender of the territory.[9] On November 14, 1975, Spain, Morocco, and Mauritania concluded secret "Madrid Accords" in which Spain ceded administrative control over Western Sahara to Morocco and Mauritania. The day after Spain's withdrawal, Polisario declared Western Sahara an independent state, the Saharan Arab Democratic Republic (SADR), and turned the attentions of its guerrilla struggle on Morocco and Mauritania, with occasional sallies against Spanish fishermen who still ventured into Saharan waters.

In the early years of the war Polisario proved an effective guerrilla force, its military prowess forcing Mauritania to sue for peace in 1978. The Organisation of African Unity began to call for a referendum that would allow for self-determination, but the struggle with Morocco intensified. Polisario was fortified by the powerful champion it had in Algeria and, until 1983, military assistance from Libya. Algeria's sustained commitment included military, logistical, and diplomatic assistance as well as shelter to tens of thousands of refugees in camps around Tindouf. It was motivated by a variety of factors, none of them independent of a multilayered rivalry with Morocco.[10] Tensions between the two were fueled by unresolved disputes over stretches of the border between them that went back to the brief War of the Sands in 1963. But in the position it maintained on Western Sahara, Algeria also held fast to the principles of self-determination and *uti posseditis*—the idea that colonial boundaries are retained after independence—which it saw as egregiously violated by Morocco.[11] Moreover, a sense of pride in its own bloody struggle for national liberation would not let Algeria countenance defeat of a political movement it had chosen to support. At stake was the balance of power within the Maghreb, but also the two countries' permanent rivalry with respect to their relations with Sub-Saharan Africa, Europe, and the United States.

Both the United States and France provided substantial levels of military assistance and hardware to help turn the war in Morocco's favor.[12] Morocco, meanwhile, poured troops and resources into the territory as it began construction of an enormous sand wall (or "berm"), 1,600 kilometers long, to prevent Polisario's incursions into the 80 percent of Western Sahara it held. It also encouraged settlement and economic development in the major population centers that, like the lucrative phosphate deposits, now lay in its control.[13] Whether such expenditures could be sustained without inflicting crippling social and economic costs on the rest of the country would remain, as Toby Shelley would write in 2004, "a key determinant of the outcome of the conflict over Western Sahara."[14]

The United Nations: Questionable Beginnings

The United Nations' role in Western Sahara was inherited from the OAU and the resolution adopted at a summit meeting held in Nairobi in 1981. This had established broad guidelines for an internationally supervised cease-fire and referendum, foreseeing a "controlled referendum" that was somehow to respond to the OAU's objective of self-determination as well as Moroccan views on the legitimacy of its rights. Not clearly addressed, however, was the central issue of exactly who would be allowed to take part in it.[15] How to establish the electorate was complicated by a lack of agreement on who had been a Sahrawi at the time of Spain's withdrawal from the territory, or how to assess the competing claims of nomads, refugees, or others internally displaced by the hostilities or who had settled in the territory.

The lack of definition reflected profound differences between the parties that would be upheld over the coming years with remarkable consistency. Morocco assumed a position based on *ius sanguinis* ("right of blood"), considering that the right to take part in a referendum had to be extended to all Sahrawi tribes linked to or originating in the former Spanish Sahara. In Polisario's view, largely based on *ius soli* ("right of territory"), the potential electorate was much narrower and should be established on grounds similar to those used for the census conducted by Spain in 1974. That Morocco's envisioned electorate would most likely favor integration and Polisario's independence underlined the gulf between the idea of a referendum and its application, which under the circumstances could not provide anything other than a winner-take-all solution.[16]

King Hassan accepted the OAU's guidelines with some reservations but hindered efforts to resolve outstanding issues by refusing to talk to Polisario. Morocco's position was that the question of Western Sahara was a bilateral issue that it would address in the context of its relations with Algeria and not in direct talks with an entity it considered illegitimate. Algeria resented this stance and began lobbying for the recognition of the SADR as a state and its admission to the OAU. This strategy had considerable success. By 1983 the SADR had achieved recognition by fifty-four countries and the OAU itself had been plunged into crisis over the issue.[17] Morocco's "reintegration" of Western Sahara had, on the other hand, not been recognized by any external actor. In 1984 it resigned from the OAU after twenty-six of the organization's fifty-one members accepted the membership of the SADR.

A direct UN role derived from a decision taken by the OAU in 1983 that the referendum should be jointly conducted by the two organizations, as well as from the obvious impediment to OAU mediation created by the controversy surrounding the SADR. Pérez de Cuéllar visited the region at Morocco's invitation in 1985 and offered his good offices to arrange indirect talks between the parties in the following year. These took place with a representative of the chairman of the OAU in attendance, while Algeria and Mauritania were both kept informed of their proceedings. A somewhat secretive process, led by Pérez de Cuéllar and his adviser Issa Diallo, would culminate in August 1988. Both Morocco and Polisario accepted "in principle" settlement proposals that were to pave the way to a UN-administered referendum in which the people of Western Sahara would be asked to choose between independence and integration with Morocco. However, as Pérez de Cuéllar's own account of the process indicates—especially when supplemented by Marrack Goulding's somewhat anguished telling of the same tale—there were serious flaws in the basis on which agreement was reached and the UN mission established.[18]

Pérez de Cuéllar had, in the first instance, concealed from the Security Council the seriousness of comments and observations offered by both sides on the settlement proposals. These were, as Goulding would put it, so serious as to be "incompatible with the proposals they were accepting."[19] Meanwhile, contacts with Hassan had reinforced the impression the king had given at the Nairobi summit that he could contemplate only a "confirmative" referendum in Morocco's favor, something that Pérez de Cuéllar appears to have accepted with equanimity.[20] The implementation plan accompanying the proposals provided a timetable for voter identification, a phased reduction of Moroccan troops, and the exchange of prisoners of war and the repatriation of refugees, but details remained sketchy and open to manipulation by both parties.[21]

The timetable had foreseen a referendum nine months after the UN mission's inception. But implementation got off to an unprepossessing start. MINURSO arrived in Western Sahara in September 1991 and faced a hostile environment, cease-fire violations, and an impasse on the all-important question of voter registration. Pérez de Cuéllar's departing report to the Security Council in December 1991 downplayed the importance of Morocco's intention to move a population two and half times that documented by the 1974 census into the territory to vote. The report also introduced new criteria for voter eligibility that clearly favored Morocco.[22] Outraged accusations of bias in favor of Morocco from Polisario and its supporters were understandable. The United States, too, felt that the report was "simply unacceptable."[23] But with the clock running on the secretary-general's term in office, and energies at the United Nations focused on the negotiations in El Salvador, the Security Council tepidly "welcomed" the secretary-general's report and passed the problem on to his successor, Boutros Boutros-Ghali.[24]

Boutros-Ghali had a long history on Western Sahara. The issue had been his responsibility as Egypt's foreign minister and before that as minister of state for foreign affairs for more than a decade. He had actively opposed the entrance of the SADR to the OAU in 1984, and had a heated exchange on the subject with the Saharan "foreign minister," Omar Mansur, that Polisario had not forgotten.[25] In the early months of his term of office he did nothing to reverse the course set by Pérez de Cuéllar. Rather, he antagonized Polisario further by appointing as his special representative Sahabzada Yaqub-Khan, a former foreign minister of Pakistan and close personal friend of King Hassan.[26] The appointment would perpetuate the perception of bias on the part of UN officials, a problem that MINURSO itself, whose operations were tightly controlled by the Moroccan authorities, would struggle to overcome.

Friends of Western Sahara

Polisario's rejection of Pérez de Cuéllar's identification criteria stalled the process throughout 1992. It was in early 1993, as the UN tried to hammer out a compromise proposal, that the United States took the initiative to form the Friends of Western Sahara.

The moment was one in which the optimism of the immediate post–Cold War period still prevailed. Cooperation among the five permanent members of the Security Council was good; officials in the Clinton administration saw a synchronicity of interests between the United States and the United Nations and on this basis, were upbeat about the United Nations' capacity to resolve regional conflicts, if concerned about the lack of progress in Western Sahara. Moreover, experience with the group of Friends on Haiti disposed them to think that a similar mechanism might usefully be employed to further their interests in the conflict over Western Sahara. These were summarized by Edward Walker, the prime mover of the group's formation, as "trying to preserve our relationship with Morocco and improve our relations with Algeria, while preventing Western Sahara from triggering a renewed war."[27] Noticeably absent from this list was implementation of the United Nations' settlement plan.

U.S. officials were conscious that the creation of the Friends represented something of a balancing act, both with respect to their own policy in the region and in the involvement of France and Spain, countries with long histories and strong interests at stake. The positions of all three on Western Sahara were determined by bilateral relations with Morocco and Algeria. They also reflected an unspoken rivalry for influence across the region, between France and the United States on the one hand, and France and Spain, in the context of European Union–Mediterranean trade and policy, on the other.[28]

The United States avowed neutrality on the conflict and wanted to magnify its influence and protect its relations with all parties—both Morocco and Polisario had vocal constituencies in Washington —without getting too far out in front on the issue itself. But a clear limit to its positions was determined by extensive ties to Morocco and its monarchy and tacit acceptance of Morocco's unwavering stand that independence for Western Sahara would threaten the country's internal stability. Morocco had long been recognized as a stable and a constructive force in the region whose openness to modernization and secular forces contrasted to its advantage with Algeria. Since 1950, it had received more U.S. aid than any other Arab or African country except Egypt. Morocco had sent troops to fight in the U.S.-led coalition to liberate Kuwait in 1990, cooperated with the United States in Africa in supporting pro-Western regimes and destabilizing others, and with a reputation as Israel's closest friend in the Arab world, played a positive role in the Middle East peace process.[29]

Work on a U.S.–Morocco free trade agreement began in 1995 and would conclude in 2004. Trade talks were accelerated under the administration of President George W. Bush, and in the context of the "war on terrorism" prosecuted by the United States after 2001, the importance of stability and cooperation across the Mahgreb only grew. The United States supported the program of economic and political reforms developed by King Mohammed VI after he came to power in late 1999, and in 2004 rewarded Morocco with recognition as a "major non-NATO ally." Meanwhile, relations with Algeria also improved markedly, a product of the domestic process of liberalization, the country's emerging role as a regional peacemaker (Algerian officials worked closely with the United States on Ethiopia and Eritrea, for example), and not least, the cooperation it offered on counterterrorism. Under these circumstances, the question of Western Sahara was relegated to a secondary level, even as the presence of James Baker as the secretary-general's personal envoy from 1997 to 2004 encouraged U.S. officials to retreat behind the United Nations on this issue.

France had a close historical link and enormous commercial and other interests in Algeria, but it had long been Morocco's primary economic and political partner and a staunch defender of its claim to Western Sahara. Like the United States, France had given Morocco extensive military assistance during the years of open conflict and during the 1990s, motivated in no small part by fears of the spread of Islamic fundamentalism, continued to deliver substantial quantities of weaponry.[30] Almost all French multinationals were active in Morocco; indeed, in 2001 TotalFinaElf, the French oil giant, together with the U.S. company Kerr-McGee, signed controversial contracts to explore the waters off Western Sahara.[31] Meanwhile, many within the French elite retained financial—and emotional—ties to the country and its monarchy. Most prominent of Morocco's French supporters was President Jacques Chirac. He chose Rabat for his first official visit abroad in July 1995 and returned to the country frequently in both public and private capacities, developing a close friendship with both Hassan II and his son Mohammed VI. Moroccan officials were particularly delighted when, during a visit to Morocco in late 2001, Chirac referred to Western Sahara as the "provinces of Southern Morocco" in a statement that was seized on as public endorsement of Morocco's sovereignty over the territory.[32]

This complex but comprehensive basket of interests guaranteed a level of support of Morocco's positions on Western Sahara that Morocco's ambassador to the United Nations would describe in 2004 as "absolute."[33] As one representative of a different Friend put it, "With France there, you have Morocco sitting in the chair."[34]

In contrast to France, Spain's history and geographic proximity to Morocco left its policy on Western Sahara precariously suspended. A guilty conscience over the circumstances of Spain's departure from the territory contributed to enormous popular support for the Sahrawi cause.[35] But at the diplomatic level, the Spanish government had to balance a commitment to self-determination for the Sahrawi people and the maintenance of good relations with Algeria with a highly complex bilateral relationship with Morocco. Vulnerable to the influx of illegal immigrants, drugs, and terrorism, Spain's strategic interest was to contribute to Morocco's economic development and with it stability in North Africa, while not undermining its own agricultural and fishing concerns. Spain and Morocco signed a Treaty of Friendship, Good Neighborliness, and Cooperation in 1991 and in the following years Spain became, after France, Morocco's most important trading partner. Yet ongoing territorial disputes over Ceuta and Melilla, cities on the North African coast that Spain has held since the fifteenth century, as well as rocky islets off the Moroccan coast, had the potential to flare up unexpectedly, as Morocco's occupation of the island of Perejil in July 2002 demonstrated.[36]

The two countries worked closely together in curbing the passage of both illegal immigrants and drugs across the Strait of Gibraltar and, especially after the terrorist attacks in Rabat in 2003 and Madrid in 2004, on counterterrorism. Spanish relations with Morocco reached a low point during the conservative government of José María Aznar and improved markedly during the period in office of his Socialist Party successor, José

Luis Rodríguez Zapatero, yet they could never be straightforward. That Western Sahara was one of the most delicate issues between the two coun-tries ensured Spain's wholehearted support of the UN process, behind which Spanish officials hid with some relief, generally avowing a policy of "con-structive neutrality."[37] This did not belie, however, the gradual erosion of a principled stand on Western Sahara, as was clearly demonstrated by the fisheries agreement between Morocco and the European Union adopted in May 2006. With obvious benefits to the Spanish fishing industry, this gave the European Union access to Western Sahara's territorial waters—which are among the richest in the world—in disregard of provisions of the Law of the Sea and other instruments regulating sovereignty over natural re-sources in the case of non–self-governing territories, as well as an opinion of the UN Legal Counsel.[38]

In the group's initial incarnation, the Friends developed as an informal working group of the Security Council, combining the "permanent three" (P-3) of the United States, France, and the United Kingdom with Cape Verde and Venezuela, both elected members of the Council and states that had recognized the SADR. Within a few months the group was expanded to include Spain, which was an elected member of the Council for 1993–1994 and remained on the group thereafter. Unlike the other two perma-nent members, the United Kingdom had few obvious interests in North Africa, which in itself gave it a utility in a group so obviously determined by the interests of the others. Over the years it would be pragmatic in the manner in which it addressed Western Sahara and perceived by secretariat officials as the most helpful of the Friends. But while British officials ex-pressed a level of sympathy for Polisario, which lobbied hard and to great effect in the British parliament, this did not conceal a bottom line that placed the United Kingdom firmly alongside France and the United States in not wanting to do anything that might threaten stability in Morocco.

During the mid-1990s the group's membership would shift as Cape Verde and Venezuela left the Council, other elected African and Latin American states took their place, and Russia, which had been complicat-ing the life of the Friends from outside, assumed a permanent place in it.[39] Maintaining "normal" relations with Morocco and Algeria, Russia pro-claimed neutrality in the conflict, but in practice its ties to Algeria from the past and a commitment to the principle of self-determination in the context of decolonization assured that it was a steadfast advocate of Polisario within the Friends.[40] A halt was called to the rotation of states through the group by the P-3, who tired of the polemics of some elected representatives and especially the polarization that the African states brought to the issue.

(Morocco openly pushed for the membership of Gabon in 1998, and the following year Namibia tried to get on the group too, advocating a no less subtle position as a mouthpiece for Polisario.) However, the presence of the elected members had brought a helpful diversity and a degree of regional representation to a group in which, as one former UN official would describe it, "the P-3 were biased in varying degrees" toward Morocco.[41]

The United States had believed that the group would carry more weight if it could be established as "Friends of the Secretary-General," and indeed suggested such a thing to Boutros-Ghali. But the secretary-general was, as Walker would put it, "too smart for us," and said no.[42] Members of the group would reflect that they "considered themselves" to be Friends of the Secretary-General, and in this capacity worked to ensure that the recommendations of the secretary-general and his envoys were acted on by the Council. However, they were never conceived as such by the secretariat and had little direct interaction with the special representatives of the secretary-general (SRSGs) heading MINURSO except when the latter visited New York. This was in part because MINURSO's isolated location in Laayoune determined that diplomatic contacts had to be made elsewhere—in Rabat, Algiers, and on occasion, Nouakchott.[43] Successive SRSGs—Yaqub-Khan was followed by Erik Jensen of Malaysia, who served as acting SRSG from August 1995 until February 1998—would regularly meet with diplomats of key states, especially the United States and France, when they traveled, but such encounters were on the basis of their accreditation to the states concerned and not as "Friends." By the end of Jensen's tenure, the parties made their preference known for SRSGs from the United States, as only a U.S. national, in Polisario's view, could prevail on Washington to lean directly on Morocco when so required.[44]

Friends and the Status Quo

That Western Sahara was not the subject of dramatic developments, for good or ill, precluded the hands-on attention of busy senior representatives of the powerful states that made up the Friends in New York.[45] Ambassadors saw no glory to be gained from attention to Western Sahara and instead let their "expert" junior officers master the intricacies of the voter registration process, negotiate draft resolutions for consideration by the Council as a whole, and deflect from them, whenever possible, the active lobbying of Morocco, Algeria, and Polisario, for whom Western Sahara was the central issue at the United Nations. Although the majority of the group's meetings were held without the participation of the secretariat, at the working level contacts with secretariat officials—particularly Louise Laheurte and Anna Theofilopoulou, both of whom followed the issue for many years—were frequent.

An exception to the level at which Western Sahara was generally considered was evident in 1995, which saw a series of meetings with Under-Secretary-General Goulding and even a Security Council mission to Western Sahara, in which several members of the Friends (Argentina, France, and the United States) participated.[46] The shift reflected an increasing involvement of members of the Security Council in the identification process, galvanized in part by the open sympathy to Polisario expressed by the representatives of Argentina and Germany, both elected members of the Council for 1995 and 1996, and their disposition to raise technical questions fed them by Polisario's representative. As Argentina and France tussled with each other in informal consultations held in September 1995 over amendments each was introducing on behalf of Polisario and Morocco, respectively, the U.S. ambassador warned members of the Council that the conflict parties were making them parties to the dispute itself.[47]

In the latter half of the 1990s the low profile adopted by the group could not disguise the hold that it maintained on the work of the Security Council. This was—somewhat paradoxically—increased by the tenuous basis of the consensus on which it operated. The Friends could agree that "Polisario had justice on their side and Morocco *realpolitik.*"[48] But beyond this there were strong differences as to what their respective governments were prepared to do about it. This situation had both procedural and substantive consequences. Painstaking negotiations between Friends with divergent positions on some of the core issues meant that agreed drafts were handed to the Council with the plea, "Please, don't even think of changing a comma."[49] They also encouraged a preference for "technical" and not "political" resolutions, even under circumstances in which states recognized the behavior of the parties to be quite egregious. A combination of these two factors meant that all votes on MINURSO taken by the Security Council until late 1999 were unanimous. This "balanced approach" would be lamented by officials within the secretariat as "completely wishy-washy."[50]

Stasis in the Council mirrored that in the conflict itself. The settlement plan foresaw a winner-take-all outcome to the referendum; with such high stakes to play for, endless foot-dragging in the UN process was a more attractive option for Morocco, Algeria, and Polisario and their respective supporters than any of its alternatives. There were, in James Baker's words, "no action-forcing events."[51] This was a stalemate that hurt nobody enough, except the long-suffering Sahrawis in their desert refugee camps, to impel forward movement. The lack of resolution undermined economic development across the region, and specifically the construction of the Arab Maghreb Union that had been formally established in 1989 to further economic integration among its members. But against this potential carrot for Morocco—whose poverty and underdevelopment carried a constant risk of domestic unrest—were considerations that Morocco had won the war, was in possession of the contested territory (indeed, the United Nations referred repeatedly in its reports to Morocco as the "administrative power," to the profound displeasure of Polisario and Algeria),[52] and could only benefit from prolonging the status quo. Meanwhile Algeria—whose oil wealth had long ensured a greater degree of economic independence than enjoyed by other states in the region—retained Western Sahara as a burr under Morocco's saddle that it appeared in no hurry to remove.

MINURSO's Identification Commission was established in May 1993 and took more than a year to begin identifying voters. But as identification progressed on a stop-start basis throughout the 1990s (from August 1994 to late 1995, from December 1997 to September 1998, and from June to December 1999), it was plagued by difficulties. The parties maintained the fundamental differences in their concept of the electorate that had divided them from the outset. Morocco's demand for vastly increased voter lists was based on vague ethnic and tribal referents that were at odds with Polisario's more legalistic and territorial approach. Meanwhile, an alleged lack of transparency in the work of the Identification Commission was compounded by the unprecedented degree of control that Morocco continued to exert over MINURSO.[53] At the more technical level, problems were evident in the extent to which the expert witness system established in the settlement plan—by which two tribal *shaykhs* appointed by Morocco and Polisario were to vouch for the identity of applicants from each of eighty-eight tribal subfactions and groupings—was subject to political pressure from the parties, as well as ongoing difficulties in identifying voters from three "contested tribal groupings." This issue proved so thorny that it stopped the process for two one-year periods, in 1996, when the impasse led Boutros-Ghali to recommend to the Security Council that the work of the Identification Commission be suspended and the size of the mission drastically reduced, and again from 1998 to 1999.[54]

Over the years the Friends encouraged forward movement in this tortuous process and expressed concern for the release of more than 2,000 prisoners of war held by Polisario (one of its few bargaining chips), the conditions of the estimated 160,000 Saharan refugees in Algeria, and occasional flare-ups in tension between the parties. But in the absence of a likely return to armed conflict, management rather than resolution of the conflict suited every external actor except the United Nations, whose credibility was gradually sapped by the endless delays. "No one would jeopardize anything else for Western Sahara," was the comment of one former U.S. official, "so the big states on the Council were content to just let it putter on, costing millions of dollars a month, getting nowhere."[55] The competing interests of the group's members worked against the creation of a mechanism more directly engaged in implementation of the settlement plan. But they also gave the parties no incentive to compromise, and instead brought reassurance that core positions—the sovereignty of Morocco and the right to self-determination for the people of Western Sahara in an indeterminate future—would not be abandoned.

The existence of the Friends remained unknown outside the narrow UN community. But at several points during the 1990s more operational mechanisms to encourage implementation of the settlement plan were proposed. Among these was a Joint Monitoring Committee advocated from 1993 on by Jarat Chopra and others, originally as a recommendation emanating from a visit to the region by a bipartisan U.S. delegation. This was conceived as a "peace-maintenance" mechanism, loosely modeled on the Joint Monitoring Commission established in Namibia, which would have been composed of the parties, Algeria and Mauritania, as well as interested other states, such as the United States, France, and Spain.[56] Norwegian diplomats, fresh from the perceived success of the Oslo process in the Middle East, agreed to explore the possibility of such an initiative, and it was publicly pursued by Polisario through a call for an international conference of its likely members. But this was early 1994, and the idea soon got lost in the shuffle of other priorities, notably the escalating international engagement in the Balkans.[57]

Baker Moves In

As Kofi Annan assumed the office of secretary-general in 1997, the situation in Western Sahara was stalled. Boutros-Ghali's report to the Council the previous November had described the positions of Morocco and Polisario on further identification as "irreconcilable" and warned of intensification of military activity on both sides aimed at "ensuring combat readiness."[58] An internal review led to a decision to appoint a senior U.S. statesman as Annan's envoy, tough enough to stand up to the considerable obstacles presented by the parties. Both Jimmy Carter and Cyrus Vance were dismissed as "too nice" before the secretary-general settled on James A. Baker III, a former secretary of state as widely admired for his negotiating skills as for his robust integrity. In February 1997 Annan sent Marrack Goulding to Houston to persuade Baker to accept an appointment as his personal envoy. Baker would recall that Western Sahara was presented to him as "ripe for settlement by way of an autonomy approach"; he was intrigued by the challenge it presented, as well as the echoes he saw in it of the conflict in the Middle East, and took it on.[59]

The pursuit of a "third way" to resolve the conflict in Western Sahara had long lurked beneath the surface of the United Nations' engagement. Pérez de Cuéllar reported a conversation with King Hassan in 1991 in which he had welcomed the king's commitment to grant autonomy to Western Sahara "once the Sahrawis had opted for integration to Morocco."[60] Goulding suspected that mediation of a political deal based on enhanced autonomy lay behind some of Pérez de Cuéllar's actions in the early days of MINURSO. And in December 1995 Boutros-Ghali shocked members of the Council—and even some of his own staff—by stating during informal consultations that he had never believed that a referendum would actually happen, and that he hoped that Western Sahara could be resolved through direct negotiations.[61] Such views were fraught with complication, as they could be perceived as a betrayal of the right to self-determination of the population of Western Sahara recognized by the General Assembly, the Security Council, and the ICJ and codified in the settlement plan that the United Nations had negotiated and was bound to implement. But by early 1997, MINURSO had been in the field six years and it was time to confront some hard—and pragmatic—questions. Accordingly, Annan reported to the Council that he would be considering whether the settlement plan could be implemented, and if not, whether there were "other ways by which the international community could help the parties resolve their conflict."[62]

In his initial meeting with King Hassan, Baker was somewhat surprised to be reassured of Morocco's commitment to the settlement plan. Over the following months, he convened four rounds of talks to assess its feasibility (with the exception of a secret encounter in Geneva organized in July 1996, these were the first direct talks since 1993). These concluded with agreement on outstanding issues in the identification process in the Houston Accords of September 1997. When the identification process was resumed in December 1997, it went well. But differences over the contested tribal groupings returned to halt it again amid bitter complaints from

Morocco regarding the conduct of the United Nations. The United Nations proposed a package of measures to overcome the outstanding difficulties in October 1998, and the process of identification and appeals began again in mid-1999.[63]

The conclusion of the identification process prompted officials in the secretariat to confront what one would call "the myth, all these years, that if we kept on going the parties would see the light and negotiate."[64] It had taken almost nine years and nearly $440 million to establish a voter list of 86,000 individuals, only 12,000 more than the Spanish census of 1974. But Morocco submitted 131,000 appeals while questioning whether any voter list would be fair. A sustained period of unrest across the territory involving not only local Sahrawis but also Moroccan settlers had led the authorities in Rabat to assess that, as Toby Shelley put it, "they could not ensure a sufficiently high proportion of the electorate to vote the way [they] wanted."[65] Morocco, even under King Mohammed VI, was no more willing than before to contemplate a referendum that was likely to result in the independence of Western Sahara. Algeria's position was difficult to discern, given the enigmatic and sometimes contradictory pronouncements of President Abdelaziz Bouteflika. However, officials at the United Nations assumed a strategic understanding between Morocco and Algeria that encouraged a lack of movement. "The bluff of Algeria has been called," as one Western member of the Council put, "and they are not prepared to go to war over this. Morocco is therefore prepared to hold out."[66]

From late 1999, reports of the secretary-general to the Security Council began to assume a very different tone. The numbers of appeals and the differences between the parties on how they should be handled suggested that any referendum could not be held until 2002 or even later. Recent experience in East Timor had brought home the risks in attempting to impose the results of a referendum without the political will to implement its outcome or an enforcement mechanism. Suggestions from Polisario that the two cases were directly comparable that looked toward an intervention sanctioned by the Security Council if things went wrong were actively discouraged: throughout 2000 the secretary-general and his officials repeated that no regional power would be prepared to intervene between Morocco and Algeria, there was no "Australia" in North Africa.[67]

In early 2000 Annan signaled his intent to reengage the efforts of his personal envoy to explore with the parties how "to achieve an early, durable, and agreed resolution of their dispute."[68] This new tack served only to highlight the differences between the parties and forced the states within the Friends to begin to confront for the first time the essential

structure of the conflict: a zero-sum game on which they had clearly opposing views. Both the United States and France were determined to press for
a "third way," while Polisario's supporters continued to express enthusiasm
for the settlement plan and the right to self-determination.

Baker's work was facilitated by the fact that the United States had
retained the coordination of the Friends from the beginning and, in part
out of deference to his personal stature, subordinated any bilateral position
on Western Sahara to his efforts.[69] (Baker would recall that he had worked
"extraordinarily closely" with both the Clinton and Bush administrations,
but also admitted that he had provided the United States, as the other
states involved, with a useful shield behind which to go about its bilateral
business.[70]) But otherwise he operated at some distance from the Friends
—he never met with them as a group—not least out of fear that information on his activities would be willfully or otherwise leaked to the parties.
Confidentiality assumed added importance during 2001. Early in the year
Morocco had approached Baker with ideas for the autonomy of Western
Sahara. Finding these inadequate, over the following months Baker developed instead a draft "Framework Agreement on the Status of Western
Sahara" that to a considerable extent drew on an autonomy plan developed by the secretariat for East Timor during the summer of 1998. This he
presented to Algeria and Polisario on May 5, 2001, confident "that the
Kingdom of Morocco would support [it]."[71] While UN officials would
assert that the draft did not preclude the idea of self-determination in
that it called for holding a referendum after five years, the terms of the
referendum—specifically, whether independence would be a choice—
were not spelled out. This, like the provision that the referendum would be
open to all residents in Western Sahara during the preceding year, was
immediately deemed unacceptable by both Polisario and Algeria. Polisario's leader Mohamed Abdelaziz refused even to keep a copy of the draft.[72]

The draft framework agreement reflected preferences from the United
States and France for a "third way," a position the United Kingdom could
also support, but left Spain and Russia aligned with Polisario and Algeria.
However, Annan's suggestion of a program of action for the months ahead
—in his report he had urged Polisario, Morocco, Algeria, and Mauritania
to meet under Baker's auspices to discuss "with specificity" the proposed
elements of the framework agreement—allowed the Friends to thrash out
the terms of a draft resolution. Polisario's backers among the elected members felt pushed around by the Friends and accepted the Friends' draft
somewhat grudgingly. It gave Baker the green light to initiate negotiations
on the framework agreement, while allowing for the ongoing validity of

the settlement plan, conveniently deferring until another day the incompatibility of the two approaches.[73]

Friends and the Security Council: Seeking Endgame

Negotiations in the fall of 2001 failed to overcome the impasse. In early 2002, an openly "disappointed" Baker dropped what one member of the Friends would describe as a "bombshell" on the Council. Defying a conventional deference to differences in the Security Council adopted by the secretariat—some members of which had cautioned Baker against "embarrassing" the Council—Baker presented a report of the secretary-general on February 27 that offered four options for future action on Western Sahara and asked the Security Council to choose between them. None of the options—to implement the settlement plan, revise the draft framework agreement, explore a possible division of the territory, or withdraw MINURSO—stood any chance of being accepted by both parties.[74] However, in presenting them to the Council, Baker argued that the international community had reached a critical point in its eleven-year engagement in the conflict. A solution to Western Sahara would not be found unless the United Nations required one or both of the parties to do something they did not want to do. He accused the Council members of being "enablers" to the disputants and challenged them to decide whether it actually wanted to solve the conflict or preferred to extend the status quo.[75]

The gauntlet Baker threw down before the Security Council was to split the Friends, exposing divisions between them long concealed by the fog of the United Nations' attempt to implement the settlement plan. Members of the group had been caught off guard by the bluntness of Baker's briefing as well as the demand that he and the secretary-general made of them for decisive action. It was, quite simply, not what they were used to. Their struggle to provide a response was laced with criticism of an approach that they believed reflected a lack of understanding of "the home truths" of the Security Council.[76] Discussion focused on the second and third options presented by Baker—the draft framework plan, evidently Morocco's preference, and partition, a proposition that had originated with President Bouteflika of Algeria and was anathema to Morocco. A resolution was due before the Council before the end of April, but a succession of meetings among the Friends failed to result in a consensus. The United States prepared a draft, backed by France and the United Kingdom, which offered the parties a way forward on the basis of the draft framework agreement. It was not acceptable to either Spain or Russia, but the United States took it to the Council anyway, intimating that, if it were not adopted, Baker might resign.[77] By the end of April all that the Council could achieve was the decision to extend MINURSO's mandate until the end of July.

The process exposed fissures not just among Friends but between the Friends and some of the elected members of the Council. Some of them—for example, Ireland and Mexico—had long supported the Sahrawi right to self-determination and were not about to see the Security Council impose a solution that, in their view, violated it. Others, including Singapore, saw the abrogation of the settlement plan in normative terms, and feared its implications for small states, such as themselves. As the parties lobbied hard, Ireland led a campaign to prevent a majority from emerging that would ask Baker to move ahead with the framework agreement.[78] Six months after the four options were put before it, the Council was finally able to reach agreement on a resolution that fell far short of the decisive action Baker had hoped to provoke. Baker recalled a telephone call from Sir Jeremy Greenstock, the British ambassador and president of the Council for the month of July, asking whether he would agree to "soldier on" toward an agreed solution, even if the Council were not able to agree on one of his four options. Baker responded that he would not, unless the resolution specified that the political solution be one that provided for self-determination; "that has to be in there or I am out of here." Resolution 1429 (2002) duly sent him back to the drawing board, asking him to continue his efforts to find a political solution to the conflict while expressing its "readiness to consider any approach which provides for self-determination."[79]

The divisions exposed by the developments of 2002 remained evident when in 2003, the Friends and the Council were once again called upon to respond to a proposal put forward by Baker. This time, the "Peace Plan for Self-Determination for the People of Western Sahara"—quickly dubbed the "Baker plan"—was conceived as a proposal that "no reasonable person would turn down." A more detailed (five-page) proposal than the draft framework agreement, it included elements from it, but also aspects of the settlement plan. It provided for a four- to five-year period before a referendum for self-determination (a choice between integration and independence, with a third option of self-government or autonomy added to mollify the Moroccans in early July 2003) and included in the electoral list those persons with continuous residence in the territory since 1999. Baker introduced the plan to the Council members at an informal lunch held in early May. The secretary-general commended the plan to the Security Council as the "optimum political solution" for Western Sahara and asked it to recommend that the parties accept the plan "as proposed."[80]

To the surprise of many observers—including Baker himself, who had thought that the expansion of the electorate would work in Morocco's favor—Morocco rejected the plan, reversing its qualified acceptance of the draft framework agreement. Its principal objection appeared to be that the referendum would contemplate independence—as had the referendum under the settlement plan that, so long ago, Morocco had purported to accept. Polisario initially rejected the plan too. However, in early July 2003, under heavy pressure from Algeria and Spain, Polisario changed position and accepted the plan, albeit expressing concern that it be considered in light of previous agreements.[81] In so doing it pulled off a considerable diplomatic coup (although of course Algeria, with nothing to lose, was the real winner). Morocco was wrong-footed, left to defy the United States and the great majority of states on the Security Council. That its only ally, France, was at loggerheads with the United States over Iraq rendered its position all the more uncomfortable. Polisario, meanwhile, could argue that it had taken the plunge to support the Baker plan in the interests of the peace process as a whole. "The plan represents a risk," as Ahmed Boukhari, Polisario's representative to the United Nations, put it in an interview, "but it also allows us the possibility of success."[82]

Discussion within the Security Council soon hit an impasse. A key issue for many delegations was a reluctance to "impose" a solution on the parties, despite the request of the secretary-general for the plan to be endorsed as "proposed." This position was most actively (and somewhat hypocritically, given the position it had assumed on the Boden paper on Georgia) championed by France, which began the month by indicating that it would not support the Baker plan. Lobbying from—and of—all sides intensified. While the Moroccan press erupted in criticism of Baker and the United Nations, Annan spoke directly to the king as well as to several Council foreign ministers. President Chirac himself worked the telephones in Morocco's support, but once Russia decided to back the plan—a move that brought with it other Polisario supporters such as Mexico and Pakistan—France was left on its own. In a year that had seen such deep divisions over Iraq, such a prospect was not tenable. In the end France caved in, although not without extracting as a price the watering down of language that had proposed to have the Council "endorse" the Baker plan. Resolution 1495, adopted unanimously on July 31, instead expressed "support" for the peace plan as "an optimum political solution on the basis of agreement between the two parties" and called on the parties to work with the United Nations and each other "toward acceptance and implementation of the plan."

The United Nations would wait for Morocco's final response to the Baker plan until April 2004. As the months passed, it became clear that although the resolution had appeared to line up the world's powers against Morocco, its achievement represented the high point of international pressure upon it. France was prepared to ask Morocco to "seriously consider" the Baker plan, but not push it any further than that.[83] The United States was in the midst of trade negotiations and unwilling to jeopardize the prospect of an agreement with an important partner in the Arab world for an uncertain future in Western Sahara. In this calculation concerns about terrorism, highlighted by the bombings in Rabat in May 2003 and Madrid in March 2004, were pronounced. As one British official put it, "We can deliver tough messages on Western Sahara, but they know we are not serious."[84] Morocco calculated—correctly—that it could hold out.

Morocco's reply, when it eventually came, was a devastating rejection not just of the Baker plan but of the entire basis of the UN effort—the right to self-determination of the people of Western Sahara—supposedly agreed upon in the settlement proposals sixteen long years before. In a letter dated April 9, 2004, and addressed to Baker, Morocco ruled out the possibility of independence being submitted as an option in a referendum or any negotiations over the "sovereignty and territorial integrity" of Morocco.[85] The letter was forwarded to the Security Council by the secretary-general in a report that presented a stark choice between terminating MINURSO and returning the issue of Western Sahara to the General Assembly—in its essence an admission of defeat—and trying, once again, to move the parties toward acceptance and implementation of the peace plan. The Security Council responded with a resolution that marked a distinct step backward from the position it had taken in July, offering reaffirmation of support for the Baker plan in one paragraph and of "strong support" for the efforts of the secretary-general and his personal envoy to achieve a mutually acceptable political solution (that the Baker plan was evidently not) in another.[86]

Baker resigned soon afterward, addressing a letter to Annan that was pointed in its criticism of the positions taken by the parties, particularly Morocco's insistence on "a proposal to negotiate autonomy, but only after the other party acknowledges Moroccan sovereignty. The issue of sovereignty is, of course, the fundamental issue that has divided the parties since 1976."[87] Morocco, let off the hook by the Security Council, held up

Baker's resignation as a trophy, with its foreign minister, Mohamed Ben-aissa, expressing Morocco's regret at Baker's resignation while also claiming that it was the "outcome of tenacity of Moroccan diplomacy."[88]

Beyond Baker

If Morocco saw Baker's departure as something of a victory, Polisario understandably received it as a deep blow. Baker's presentation of the draft framework agreement in 2002 had represented a low point in its relationship with him, but Polisario's representatives had come to respect his impartiality more than that of any of the secretaries-general they had dealt with (they rightly suspected that Annan himself had proven susceptible to direct pressure from Morocco and France on the issue).[89] In Baker's absence they would continue to hold fast to the Security Council's somewhat ambiguous support of the Baker plan, and derived some comfort from South Africa's surprise recognition of the SADR in mid-2004. But their prospects did not look good.

The United Nations' response to the newly assertive position claimed by Morocco was weak. The Security Council's April resolution did not refer to it. Nor did the letter by which the secretary-general informed the Council of Baker's resignation. Baker's departure was attributed only to the fact that "the parties have not been able to reach an agreement" and his belief that "he has done all he can do on this issue."[90] An impression that the secretariat would treat Morocco's stance as business as usual was cemented by the letter's announcement that Alvaro de Soto, who had been serving as the SRSG in Laayoune (while also overseeing the United Nations' effort to resolve the conflict over Cyprus), would assume the peacemaking functions so recently relinquished by Baker. This was a development that Polisario and then Algeria greeted with some dismay, citing concerns that de Soto was in some way tainted by his past association with Pérez de Cuéllar (not that he had had any involvement in Western Sahara in that period, as they well knew); that as a Peruvian—or more explicitly a non-American—he would lack the access to Washington they saw as a central requirement for the job; and that he would be "used by Morocco and France to undermine the Baker plan."[91]

Doubts about de Soto reflected not on his professional capacities but on the United Nations' broader acquiescence to Morocco and the geopolitical realities that sustained it in sliding the goalpost away from the referendum outlined in the settlement plan. This slide would be described by a French official in October 2004 as "an emerging consensus"—shared by the United States and France, and with which the United Kingdom was deemed likely to concur—that "a reasonable solution" was taking shape, if not yet in sight. Such a solution would provide for Western Sahara to remain within Morocco with the highest degree of autonomy that neither prejudiced Morocco's sovereignty nor allowed for "a mechanism [such as a referendum] that in a few years' time might put the whole thing in question again." The prospects of such a consensus eventually developing had been boosted both by Baker's departure—his stature and ties to the Bush administration commanded "due respect" even from those who did not agree with him—and by the changes evident in the Spanish government elected into power after the terrorist attacks of March 2004.[92] Although the Spanish position remained complex, an increased disposition to sacrifice Western Sahara to long-term relations with Morocco made eventual support of France and the United States more likely than it had appeared at any time in the past.[93]

With Russia "still far away" from such a position and Algeria maintaining its insistence on the right to self-determination, there was little expectation that anything would change soon.[94] MINURSO was in place; the Sahrawi refugees remained stuck in the Algerian desert, as they had been for the last thirty years. But in the United Nations neither their fate nor the principle of self-determination was of sufficient importance to the Security Council for states to expend any political chips on them. And the capacity of the secretary-general and his representatives to exert an independent role without the political engagement of the powerful states among the Friends was minimal.

In May 2005 de Soto accepted an appointment as the United Nations' special coordinator for the Middle East peace process. An Italian diplomat, Francesco Bastagli, was appointed to head MINURSO, while the political dossier passed to Peter van Walsum, a former ambassador of the Netherlands to the United Nations, whom Annan appointed his personal envoy in September. Both faced dauntingly difficult tasks. A series of demonstrations in the two major Western Saharan towns, Laayoune and Smara, calling for secession, and the violence with which they were put down came as a reminder of the gravity of what was at stake. The United States exerted its influence to help secure the release of the final 404 Moroccan prisoners-of-war by Polisario as a means to build confidence and fan a small spark of hope in the benefits that diplomacy might bring.[95] But the release had little effect on the inhospitality of the conflict's underlying political dynamics or the serious questions raised by the social, economic, and human rights conditions of the Sahrawi people and the scant ability of the United

Nations to respond to them. Frustration with the limitations imposed on MINURSO in these areas contributed to Bastagli's decision to submit his resignation in July 2006.[96]

After his first visit to the region to meet with the parties, van Walsum had characterized their positions as "almost irreconcilable."[97] In a blunt assessment of the state of affairs he gave to the Security Council in early 2006 he recognized Morocco's rejection of a referendum that included the option of independence, as well as the impossibility of the United Nations' endorsement of anything that excluded it so long as it claimed to provide for the self-determination of the people of Western Sahara. He therefore encouraged direct and unconditional negotiations between the parties as the only possible alternative to "indefinite prolongation of the current deadlock." Such negotiations should aim to achieve what no plan could, he argued: a compromise between "international legality" with respect to Western Sahara and "political reality." Movement in this direction was impeded by a long delay in the submission of a promised proposal of autonomy from Morocco and Polisario's resistance to any departure from their bottom line. Meanwhile, obstacles to negotiations developing in good faith extended far beyond the parties themselves. As van Walsum had put it to the Council in early 2006, the impasse had been sustained in large part because it was what best suited "forces outside the region."[98] Implicitly if not explicitly included as such were the countries within the group of Friends.

Conclusions

The group of Friends of Western Sahara was by the early 2000s an evidently flawed mechanism. Indeed, it is difficult not to conclude that Boutros-Ghali had been correct in his assessment that on the "question of Western Sahara" the secretary-general was better off without Friends. The group as it emerged in the mid-1990s had indeed included the key external actors on the issue. But their interests were not only at odds with each other but in each case outweighed a concern to support the stated goal of the United Nations, the self-determination of the people of Western Sahara.

In obvious contrast to Abkhazia, the terms of the UN relationship to the conflict was not the problem. Like that in East Timor, the conflict for Western Sahara had a history in a process of decolonization that, although belatedly initiated by a Western colonial power, had the full support of the United Nations. In both cases, this was abruptly interrupted by the intervention of larger neighbors, newly independent themselves and bent on exerting their territorial control.[99] That this was tolerated was attributable both to the relative weakness of the colonial powers at the time and to the studied disinterest and even complicity of the big powers on the Security Council. The United Nations recognized the right to self-determination, but its capacity to act to see it exercised was limited, even in circumstances in which the population claiming self-determination could count on broad sympathy from the international community. In the stark juxtaposition of international law and political realism that Western Sahara represents—and East Timor represented until 1999—realism won out, with the interests pursued by the Friends a central driver in a process that was not able to move beyond the zero-sum options pursued by the parties.

The formation of the group of Friends responded to the desire of its members to protect their own interests in a conflict arena that was already deeply polarized. This had been dramatized by the challenge posed by the Polisario's establishment of the SADR. Recognition—or not—of this entity forced states into open declaration of their allegiance to one side of the conflict for Western Sahara or the other and divided the OAU. To a certain extent the Friends held out some hope for an alternative solution in this essentially inhospitable regional environment. It was therefore perhaps unsurprising that the group gradually came to exclude regional actors. This was understandable from a pragmatic perspective, particularly given the tendency of the parties to cultivate the Friends as their proxies and the willingness of some of the Friends to go along with this. However, the decision would deprive the Friends of any legitimacy within a regional context and contribute to the criticism of elected members of the Council that they were routinely excluded from a process controlled by the permanent members on the Friends.

In contrast to other groups considered in this study, the Friends of Western Sahara remained limited to the workings of the Security Council. However, a peculiar feature of the process was that this did not preclude contact with the parties. On the contrary, representatives of Morocco, Polisario, and Algeria maintained close contact with the Friends at the working level and appreciated the access the mechanism gave them to the Council's decision making. But the utility of the group to the Council's proceedings was maintained only so long as the issues at hand were technical and did not address the central political problem: that Morocco would not countenance a referendum that included independence as a possible outcome, while the entire international process was predicated on the demands of the Sahrawis for the right to make that choice. As there was little substantive interaction between representatives of the secretary-general and the Friends as a group, and certainly nothing that could be described as "leadership" by the secretary-general of their efforts, what benefits the Friends' existence did bring were largely procedural. These included the maintenance of good channels of communication between working-level officials in the secretariat and Friend "experts," which helped the Friends' understanding of developments in the field.

By 2007, when direct talks resumed, thirty-two years had passed since Spain relinquished control of Western Sahara and sixteen years since MINURSO had first been deployed to oversee a referendum on the territory's future. Control of the territory by Morocco had given it an advantage reflected in the gradual sliding of political goalposts toward its position. The Sahrawi refugees in the desert retained the sympathy of many in the international community, who were nevertheless prepared to accept their continued suffering as an unfortunate, but not deeply troubling, corollary of their own good relations with Morocco. Meanwhile, a group of Friends created to address a process that was already at a standstill in 1993 had long since become institutionalized as a means by which this particular bit of UN business—an unpalatable mix of the deeply divisive and a low strategic priority—should be managed, even if this meant little more than sustaining the stalemate.

How this situation had come to pass reflects problems that extend far beyond the existence, or not, of an informal group of Friends. Shadowing the entire process are the serious questions that have been asked of the terms under which the United Nations engaged in the first place. Secretary-General Pérez de Cuéllar's fudging of the grounds on which MINURSO was established concealed the fact that the political will of Morocco to enter into a referendum for independence and respect its outcome was never there. Morocco's supporters, including some of the Friends, knew this all along. This did not matter so long as it appeared likely that Moroccan manipulation of the electorate would ensure a "confirmative" result of the referendum. However, once it was obvious that this was not the case, efforts to broker a "third way" foundered on Morocco's intransigence and its knowledge that, given the support it received from its Friends, there would be no price to pay.

7

East Timor and the Core Group

A Question of Timing

I n September 2002 Xanana Gusmão, the first president of the Democratic Republic of Timor-Leste[1] and a charismatic hero of more than two decades of guerrilla struggle, addressed the UN General Assembly on the occasion of the new state's formal admission to the organization. As he did so, he paid tribute to the "remarkable amount of history" his people shared with their Sahrawi brothers.[2] Like Western Sahara, East Timor, a former colony of Portugal, had been on the United Nations' list of non–self-governing territories since the 1960s. Decolonization had been interrupted by Indonesia's violent annexation of the territory in late 1975, an act of blatant aggression facilitated by the silence and even complicity of powerful states in the region and beyond. During the long and painful struggle that followed, more than 100,000 people lost their lives.[3] The Security Council had condemned Indonesia's action when it occurred and then studiously ignored East Timor in the following years. But the "shame of East Timor," as a former British ambassador to the United Nations would call it, could not easily be erased.[4] Change when it came was precipitated by dramatic changes in Indonesia in 1998 and 1999. It was facilitated by years of painstaking dedication by the secretary-general and his staff to a peace process that appeared to be going nowhere, and the timely formation of a "Core Group" of states, as the endgame began to unfold, to assist them in the extraordinary effort that was then required of the United Nations to conclude the process.

The role played by the Core Group offers clear lessons on the timing and circumstances in which an informal group of states may helpfully be enlisted to increase the efficacy of UN action. Like the Friends of Western Sahara, the Core Group on East Timor was originally composed of the key external actors on the issue: Australia, Japan, New Zealand, the United Kingdom, and the United States. However, any parallels ended there. The group responded to a carefully articulated strategy implemented by secretariat officials who had resisted earlier suggestions to form a group of Friends. It brought together a mixture of permanent members of the Security Council and interested regional actors well suited to furnish UN officials with all sorts of diplomatic and practical assistance as they struggled to carry out a popular consultation on East Timor's future in August 1999 under unpropitious circumstances. Although the Core Group, like the secretariat, would be unprepared for the violence that followed the consultation, its members' engagement reinforced the active role assumed by the secretary-general and greatly facilitated the Security Council's prompt response to the postballot crisis. In the years ahead the Core Group assumed a leading role in guiding Security Council action on East Timor, even as it gradually moved away from the close alignment with the secretariat that had characterized its early days. Like others in the international community, it received a sharp reminder of the long-term challenges of nation building in 2006, when an outbreak of violence with origins deep in the Timorese past imperiled the new state and led it to turn to again to the international community for assistance.

Decolonization Deferred

The crocodile-shaped island of Timor lies at the eastern end of the Indonesian archipelago, some 420 kilometers north of Australia. Its western end was colonized by the Dutch and, as part of the Netherlands East Indies, joined Indonesia at independence. The eastern part of the island, some 14,500 square kilometers, was settled by Portuguese friars in the sixteenth century.[5] During World War II Portugal's professed neutrality did nothing to prevent Australia from landing a preemptive force on the island. This, in turn, provoked invasion by Japan. Timor became a battleground and, after Australian troops withdrew in 1943, succumbed to a brutal period of Japanese occupation.[6]

In April 1974 a leftist military revolt, impelled by the disintegration of Portugal's colonies in Africa, overturned the country's authoritarian regime. Portugal's new leaders conceded the right of its colonies to self-determination and independence, but the rapid development of events in distant East Timor interrupted any orderly progression toward this end. Three rival political parties quickly emerged, and in 1975 the situation deteriorated into civil war. The Revolutionary Front for an Independent East Timor (Fretilin) achieved control of the territory and declared independence as the "Democratic Republic of East Timor"; days later, on December 7, 1975, Indonesia invaded with a startling level of force.

In December 1975 and April 1976 the Security Council called on Indonesia to withdraw from East Timor, urging all states to respect its territorial integrity and its people's right to self-determination.[7] But nothing happened. The key external actors, the United States and Australia, took a "pragmatic rather than a principled stand" to Indonesia's invasion and looked the other way.[8] They had both seen it coming. Indeed, just hours before he ordered the troops in, President Suharto of Indonesia had met with U.S. President Gerald Ford and Secretary of State Henry Kissinger. He had asked for and received the American president's "understanding" for the "rapid and drastic action" he might need to take in East Timor.[9] Indonesia was the fourth most populous country in the world. It had extensive commercial ties to the West and was strategically placed at the entrance to the Indian Ocean. In that turbulent period in Southeast Asia it was also impeccably anticommunist: Suharto had come to power in 1966 after cracking down on an alleged coup attempt with an anticommunist witch-hunt that killed at least half a million Indonesians. He derived his power base from the armed forces, which were given authority in political affairs as well as security matters, and imposed control over other political forces with a repressive regime he dubbed "New Order." During 1976 Indonesia established a "Popular Assembly" in areas of East Timor controlled by its forces, engineered its petition for "integration," and on this basis proceeded to annex the territory as its twenty-seventh province.

Inside East Timor, the Indonesian army met with determined opposition from Fretilin's armed wing, the Armed Forces for the National Liberation of East Timor (Falintil). However, it was gradually able to push the liberation forces back into the mountains, restricting combatants' access to both the civilian population and the means for their survival. By the early 1980s the resistance had ceased to offer a serious military threat and was in internal disarray.[10]

Xanana Gusmão had been elected both commander-in-chief of Falintil and national political commissar of Fretilin's Central Committee, but his advocacy of resistance based on national unity rather than Fretilin partisanship precipitated lasting tensions between his own military base and Fretilin's political leadership, largely in exile in either Portugal or Mozambique. A split between the two first appeared in 1984 as senior Falintil officers, who were also members of Fretilin's Central Committee, attempted a coup against him.[11] In 1987 Gusmão severed Falintil's connections with Fretilin by resigning from its Central Committee to establish a new National Council of Maubere Resistance (CNRM); Falintil was its armed wing, and Fretilin and other nationalist parties constituent members.

The consequences of this Fretilin-Falintil divide would be long-lasting. Indeed, rivalries between Fretilin's political leadership, and particularly a group based in Maputo led by Mari Alkatiri (years later the country's first prime minister) and Gusmão and Falintil would critically impact upon the post-independence period.[12]

Indonesia, meanwhile, invested in East Timor's long-neglected infrastructure and encouraged the movement of Indonesian settlers into the territory.[13] Extensive human rights violations were perpetrated against proindependence activists and those suspected of supporting them. However, only in 1991, when international journalists witnessed Indonesian security forces open fire on proindependence mourners at the Santa Cruz cemetery, killing an estimated two hundred people, did the outside world begin to take note. In the years that followed, the determined efforts of NGOs and parliamentarians, as well as the energetic diplomacy pursued by leaders of the Timorese resistance gradually gained attention.[14] East Timor's cause was helped by the firm legal principles on which it rested as well as the clear-cut moral and human rights issues it presented. In 1996 the Nobel Peace Prize was awarded to two of its most prominent champions, Bishop Carlos Filipe Ximenes Belo and José Ramos Horta. But the prospect of independence remained a distant dream.

At the United Nations

Until 1999 Indonesia would maintain that the Popular Assembly it had engineered in 1976 represented the exercise by the East Timorese of their right to self-determination. This position was not accepted by the United Nations, which continued to recognize Portugal as the administering power of the territory and to pass annual resolutions of the General Assembly reaffirming the inalienable right of the East Timorese to self-determination. However, the margin with which these resolutions were passed gradually dwindled, reflecting the implicit acceptance by many states of the annexation of East Timor as an unfortunate aspect of what it took to maintain "business as usual" with Suharto's Indonesia. In 1982 the General Assembly passed the buck to the secretary-general, asking him to "initiate consultations with all parties directly concerned."[15] Discussions between Indonesia and Portugal, chaired by the secretary-general, began in 1983. These tripartite talks would continue in a somewhat desultory manner for the next fifteen years, their utility seriously hindered by Indonesia's refusal to countenance any attention to the positions of proindependence East Timorese. This position was rooted in the idea that, as one UN official put it, "solution would come from a piece of paper signed by Portugal."[16]

During this period members of the Timorese resistance would look with envy at the plight of the Sahrawis. "They had far more than us," José Luis Guterres, Timor's ambassador to the United Nations until 2006 would recall of Polisario's struggle for independence. "We thought they almost had it."[17] Unlike Fretilin, which Guterres had represented internationally since 1974, Polisario had a government in exile; had a powerful champion in a neighboring state, Algeria; and had even achieved membership of the regional organization, an occurrence unthinkable to the Timorese, who saw the steadfast support of Indonesia offered by the Association of Southeast Asian Nations (ASEAN). The East Timorese, instead, had Portugal. Portugal had a commitment to promote the right to self-determination and independence of East Timor written into its constitution, but little capability to protect that right. A low point came in 1986, when Portugal, with UN encouragement, agreed that East Timorese participation in the Indonesian elections scheduled for 1987 would, when duly certified by UN observers, be treated as an act of self-determination by the population of the territory. Fortunately for the Timorese and the credibility of the United Nations on the issue, a change in government in Portugal led to a rapid reevaluation of the country's position.[18]

Both the United States and Australia shifted their positions in the United Nations from voting in East Timor's favor to voting against it.[19] The change reflected recognition of Indonesian sovereignty over East Timor, although not the means by which it had been brought about. In the case of Australia, explicit de jure recognition was granted in 1978 in the context of opening negotiations with Jakarta on the seabed boundary between East Timor and Australia.[20] These would conclude in 1989 with a controversial treaty that governed the exploitation of the oil and gas resources in the undemarcated part of the Timor Sea between East Timor and Australia known as the Timor Gap. This temporary arrangement was widely seen to have granted favorable terms to Australia in reward for its recognition of Indonesian sovereignty over East Timor.[21]

During the 1990s a gradual increase in international attention to East Timor reinforced Portugal's commitment to a valid act of self-determination, but did nothing to alter the Indonesian position that East Timor's integration was final. As these positions remained far apart, the United Nations gradually assumed a more active role.

In the wake of the Santa Cruz massacre a political officer, Tamrat Samuel, was assigned to the Timor dossier (his Eritrean nationality a cause of delight to the Timorese resistance). From 1994 his efforts would support those of Francesc Vendrell, now director of the East Asia and Pacific Division in the Department of Political Affairs. Vendrell's familiarity with the issue of East Timor and friendship with individual Timorese stretched back to the 1970s when he had written reports on East Timor for the General Assembly's Decolonization Committee. Both officials were motivated by the need to uphold international legality but also by their personal affront at the injustices heaped upon the Timorese, as well as a determination to avoid anything reminiscent of the United Nations' administration of the deeply flawed "Act of Free Choice" that had facilitated the takeover of West Papua by Indonesia in 1969.[22] But contrary to the views held by some Indonesian officials and proindependence East Timorese, the secretariat was agnostic on the issue of independence versus some form of association with Indonesia.

The secretariat worked to ensure that space for consideration of Timorese viewpoints was gradually introduced into the process. In September 1993, with Indonesia continuing to reject any form of East Timorese participation in the negotiations, a statement issued at the end of a round of meetings between the foreign ministers of Indonesia and Portugal, chaired by Secretary-General Boutros-Ghali, pointedly referred to the secretary-general's "intention to carry out contacts, as he deems useful"—meaning the Timorese.[23] In 1994 Vendrell prevailed on the Indonesians to let him meet with the recently imprisoned Xanana Gusmão for a first time, opening an effective channel of communication between the United Nations and this authoritative figure. And in the same year Portugal and the secretariat secured Indonesian acceptance for Timorese leaders to meet in the format of an All-Inclusive Intra-East Timorese Dialogue (AIETD). At Indonesia's insistence, the AIETD could not discuss East Timor's political status or future, but it gained value as a forum in which prointegration and proindependence Timorese sat together in unstated acknowledgment that each had to be part of any solution, however distant that solution still seemed.

East Timor 1999: A Window Opens

The morning meeting of the senior staff of the United Nations' Department of Political Affairs is a businesslike occasion. Officials deliver brief updates on breaking developments under their purview; the under-secretary-general asks questions and may raise issues that have come up in his meetings of the previous day. Administrative "housekeeping" is quickly dispatched.

At the meeting on the morning of January 27, 1999, Francesc Vendrell was visibly agitated. Clutching wire stories datelined Jakarta, he reported a most unexpected development: President B. J. Habibie of Indonesia had announced that if the East Timorese did not accept the offer for autonomy that was under discussion within the UN-led process, he was prepared to grant them their independence. Unable to check the veracity of these reports before the morning meeting began, Vendrell left in a hurry, fully aware that, if true, Habibie's surprising move would change everything.

The tripartite talks had shifted to a new level of UN engagement with the decision by Kofi Annan, a little more than a month after taking office, to appoint Jamsheed Marker, a former ambassador of Pakistan, his personal representative for East Timor. Marker, who would be supported throughout by Vendrell and Tamrat Samuel, took up the challenge represented by the Timorese process in February 1997. He began what was to be a peripatetic few years with visits to Lisbon, Indonesia, and East Timor the following month, and chaired a first round of negotiations between Indonesia in Portugal that June.[24] Over the following year little progress would be made. The talks were taking place against a backdrop of mounting economic and then political crisis in Indonesia, precipitated by the bursting of the bubble of the Asian economic miracle upon which Suharto had ridden so high. Contemplating the situation in April 1998, when the formally stable rupiah had shot through the roof and riots and unrest were spreading across Indonesia's dispersed and complex territory, Marker remarked to Annan that working on East Timor resembled polishing the silver on the *Titanic*. The secretary-general responded with a chuckle: "Well then, let's go on doing it."[25]

The fall of Suharto after thirty-two years in the presidency brought great instability to Indonesia; the state was revealed as beholden to the armed forces and quite unprepared to address the secessionist forces driving events in Aceh and Irian Jaya (as West Papua then was known) or the sectarian and ethnic violence elsewhere. But surprisingly, it offered a brief window of opportunity for East Timor. The incoming President Habibie was neither a politician nor a diplomat. He made decisions quickly and without much thought for their consequence. On this basis he announced in June, just three weeks into his presidency, that he was prepared to give East Timor the "special status" of a wide-reaching autonomy. Although officials within the Indonesian Foreign Ministry had long entertained the possibility of some kind of autonomy for East Timor, the offer represented what two close observers of Indonesia would describe as "the biggest shift in Indonesian policy toward East Timor since the invasion."[26]

The promise of autonomy had far-reaching effects. The United Nations moved forward with an effort to develop a proposal for a broad autonomy that left the question of final status open for future consideration. But developments in East Timor were not promising.[27] The proindependence movement, gathered since April 1998 under the umbrella of an even more inclusive body than the CNRM, the National Council of Timorese Resistance (CNRT), had emerged into the open to conduct an increasingly assertive campaign. This was countered by the Indonesians on a number of levels: through the regular armed forces (TNI); with special forces; and through the organization, by the army, of anti-independence militia and other groups to act on their behalf.[28]

Meanwhile, outside East Timor, Australia was reevaluating its long-held position on East Timor. Australia retained a clear preference for East Timor to remain part of Indonesia, but in December Prime Minister John Howard wrote to President Habibie to suggest that Indonesia consider addressing the desire of the East Timorese for an act of self-determination, albeit "in a manner which avoids an early and final decision on the future status of the province."[29] The letter was met with impatience by Habibie; the prospect of a delayed process of self-determination left East Timor hanging like a millstone around Indonesia's neck. His reaction, scrawled on the original version of Howard's letter when it reached him in mid-January, was that it would be "reasonable and wise," should the Timorese not feel able to be "united with the Indonesian people," to let East Timor go.[30] Days later, apparently convinced that it would not be in Indonesia's interest to embark on a drawn-out period of transition, he publicly offered the East Timorese an opportunity to "part ways" with Indonesia if they rejected the offer of autonomy.

Habibie's decision prompted an immediate escalation of prointegration militia activity in East Timor, with evident—if repeatedly denied—support from the TNI, as well as a flurry of activity at the United Nations. After much uncertainty about the seriousness of Habibie's offer and how the East Timorese would be consulted, this activity culminated in the signing of tripartite agreements among Indonesia, Portugal, and the United Nations on May 5, 1999. The agreements included a request to the secretary-general to conduct a "popular consultation" that would ask the East Timorese whether they would accept or reject an autonomy plan, on the understanding that a vote against autonomy would be one for independence; modalities for the popular consultation's arrangement; and an agreement on security that, at Indonesian insistence, left Indonesia alone responsible for security in East Timor during the consultation and until its Peoples' Consultative Assembly (MPR) endorsed the outcome of the vote.[31] The CNRT responded to the security agreement with dismay. Mounting violence in East Timor had included the killing of more than forty-five civilians seeking refuge at a church compound in Liquica, the worst single massacre since 1991.

UN and Portuguese officials, who had pushed for more specific security proposals, were acutely conscious of the agreement's inadequacies and their risks.[32] However, the secretariat had been encouraged by Australia and the United States to accept Indonesia's position—put forward by its articulate foreign minister, Ali Alatas, who the talks made clear could not budge on this issue even if he had wanted to—that this was a deal breaker.[33] The secretary-general sought a different route through which to minimize the damage and on April 30 addressed a letter to Habibie specifying the nature of security measures the United Nations expected from the Indonesians, including "as an urgent first step the bringing of armed civilian groups under strict control and discipline." The letter was returned "not received," an unusual diplomatic insult. Although Australia and the United States were both warning Marker that the United Nations should not "push Habibie over the edge," the contents of the letter were reworked into a memorandum handed to Alatas and his Portuguese counterpart Jaime Gama by Marker, on the secretary-general's behalf, on May 4.[34]

The agreements reached on May 5 called for the secretary-general to set up a UN mission to oversee the popular consultation upon their signing and specified that the consultation itself was to take place on August 8, 1999. The timing was dauntingly tight, but all involved in the process understood that this might be their only opportunity. Habibie's decision had defied clear, if muted, opposition from his military and had led to criticism in Jakarta, including from his rival for the presidency, Megawati Sukarnoputri. Elections were to be held in June and the MPR was expected to convene before the end of August to elect a new president and take action on the results of the popular consultation. Any delay by the MPR was likely to imperil the self-determination the East Timorese had waited for so long. As officials contemplated the diplomatic complexity, short time frame, and straightforward expense of the course that lay ahead of them, an informal group of states, some of which had been actively involved in the run-up to the May 5 agreements, became increasingly engaged in their efforts. The secretariat, rather than continuing to consult these states separately, decided the time had come to maximize their contribution through their collective diplomatic, political, and financial support.

The Core Group

Francesc Vendrell would recall that the idea of forming a group of Friends to support the secretary-general's good offices on East Timor was something that had been suggested to him for some time. He had always cast it aside, conscious that any configuration of interested states would have been, before 1999, just "a pressure group on Portugal."[35] But in early 1999 the situation was quite different.

Both Marker and Vendrell had, in the course of the years of the tripartite talks, developed a roster of diplomatic contacts and allies in New York, Lisbon, Jakarta, London, Washington, and elsewhere. During the latter part of 1998 diplomats in New York were, as the United Kingdom's deputy permanent representative, Stewart Eldon, put it, "nagged" by Vendrell "to start thinking about East Timor and do more." The nagging was to good effect. Delegations swapped notes on their meetings with officials from the Department of Political Affairs and began to familiarize themselves with the painful history of East Timor. By the time a suggestion came to form a group, the states concerned were so attuned to these consultations that the group's composition appeared to emerge quite naturally, belying a careful crafting by the secretariat.[36]

In early 1999 bilateral action on East Timor was driven by the Foreign Ministry of Australia, which, after Habibie's surprise decision in late January, swung into high gear, determined not to find itself behind Indonesia on East Timor. While the UN secretariat warmly welcomed the shift in Australia's policy toward East Timor, it did not in turn want to find itself behind Australia. Consequently the news in mid-February that Downer was visiting Indonesia and Portugal with the intention of establishing a Contact or Friends group prompted Vendrell to raise the issue of a group with Marker and Under-Secretary-General Kieran Prendergast, who then took the proposal to the secretary-general. What he recommended, and Annan readily accepted, was a two-tier structure of a large Support Group (twenty-two members were originally suggested), designed to be as inclusive as possible, within which a smaller steering committee or Core Group would be established. The latter was conceptually analogous to the groups of Friends of the Secretary-General of the early 1990s and met more frequently and informally with the secretariat than the former. While the existence of the Support Group—which met for the first time in early March, shortly before a round of the tripartite talks—was not publicly announced, neither was it kept secret. The Core Group, however, remained confidential, although Indonesia, Portugal, and the Timorese were briefed on its formation.

The composition of the Core Group—Australia, Japan, New Zealand, the United Kingdom, and the United States—was carefully balanced. It responded to a variety of needs, all of which would be facilitated by its small size. These included the coordination of international efforts behind a UN lead; information sharing as the political process advanced; political leverage, particularly over Indonesia; and logistical and financial support through a trust fund established for this purpose, as officials struggled to field the UN Mission in East Timor (UNAMET) to oversee the conduct of the popular consultation in record time.[37] One UN official would describe the group as an "ideal mixture of very vested and very benevolent forces."[38]

A group without Australia was clearly inconceivable: its close ties to Indonesia, long history on East Timor, geographic position, and ample resources to support a UN operation placed it in a unique position. Moreover, it had much at stake in a positive outcome. East Timor had been the most contentious aspect of Australia's foreign policy since Vietnam, and the UN process offered the possibility of resolving the situation with the legitimacy of the United Nations behind it. The secretariat was in regular contact with Australia's permanent representative, Ambassador Penny Wensley. Although officials would come to view Australia as playing "a Jekyll and Hyde role" with respect to its relations with Indonesia (Prendergast would recall "an over-understanding of Indonesia to a degree that was distasteful"), they knew that Australia's close cooperation would be essential to any success. Australia's leading role on the issue was one readily recognized by the other states involved and was reflected in the tendency for Australia to speak first in most Core Group meetings.[39]

The United States was also an inevitable (but nonetheless welcome) choice. During the 1990s U.S. relations with Indonesia had gradually cooled as concerns for human rights and democracy became more prominent in U.S. foreign policy.[40] However, while an active NGO movement had lobbied Congress to introduce restrictions on the weapons and training provided to the Indonesian armed forces, there was no change in policy toward East Timor.[41] Assistant Secretary of State Stanley Roth was deeply knowledgeable about the region and a strong supporter of the secretary-general's good offices on East Timor. He maintained frequent contact with Marker, at times conveying messages to both the Indonesian and Timorese leadership at the latter's suggestion. But U.S. policy had held that an independent East Timor was not an economically viable prospect. Officials had been as surprised by Habibie's January announcement as other observers and were initially concerned that it might so anger the military as to provoke a confrontation.[42] However, as the process advanced during 1999 the

United States became increasingly involved in supporting the UN effort, with Ambassador Nancy Soderberg most frequently engaged in meetings with the secretariat, Australia, and Portugal and then in the Core Group.

Japan was an important, although usually fairly silent, member of the group. It was the largest donor to Indonesia and, despite economic troubles of its own, had been deeply involved in efforts to help Indonesia through its financial crisis. In a meeting with the secretariat in February 1999, Japan's Ambassador Yukio Takasu had expressed his country's great interest in East Timor and disposition to offer its wholehearted support of the UN process there.[43] Although Japan's constitution included strict provisions preventing its military from participating in peacekeeping operations, Japan was eager for enhanced engagement with the United Nations in peace and security and promised substantial financial support of any UN operation in East Timor. Its interest in joining the Core Group stemmed in part from its positive experience as a member of the Core Group in Cambodia in the early 1990s. Over time, its engagement in East Timor would facilitate the amendment of its peacekeeping legislation and include the contribution of civilian police and engineers to the United Nations' peace operations. Morever, in 2004, a Japanese national, Sukehiro Hasegawa, was appointed special representative of the secretary-general.[44] To begin with, however, Japan's reticence in Core Group meetings was attributable to its concern with not being seen by Jakarta as anticipating independence for East Timor. This position was clearly understood by the secretariat, which counted on Japan's presence to offer reassurance to Indonesia and its supporters on the Security Council and to bring some balance to an otherwise overwhelmingly anglophone membership.

The inclusion of New Zealand and the United Kingdom responded to perceptions of personal capacity and engagement, as well as of strategic utility. The secretariat—and Vendrell in particular—had a high opinion of both New Zealand's ambassador to the United Nations, Michael Powles, and the British officials directly engaged with East Timor. New Zealand brought regional expertise, coupled with deep sympathy for the Timorese cause, that the secretariat believed could provide a useful foil to its larger and more powerful neighbor, Australia. It would contribute significant resources to the United Nations' efforts in East Timor, including a military commitment that involved a third of its army over a significant period of time.[45] The membership of the United Kingdom, in contrast to that of New Zealand, was questioned at first as a somewhat surprising choice. Although its representation of the European Union was helpful, and it had taken a growing interest in East Timor in the 1990s, the United Kingdom had no obvious interest in East Timor and had not sought an active role on the file in the United Nations. However, looking ahead, Vendrell thought that the United Kingdom would be well placed to pilot consideration of East Timor through the Security Council, not least because its remove from East Timor might endow it with a greater degree of impartiality.[46] Meanwhile, the British ambassador to Indonesia, Robin Christopher, worked closely with the United Nations during the heady months of the summer of 1999, coordinating parallel meetings of the Core Group in Jakarta at key moments and providing hospitality to Xanana Gusmão after the latter's release from prison.

In its early days the Core Group met several times without a UN presence, but it quickly fell into a pattern whereby its meetings would be chaired by and either convened or requested through secretariat officials. In the difficult months between the May 5 agreements and the popular consultation itself, the group became increasingly involved in supporting the secretariat on a variety of levels: practically, in facilitating the financing and other requirements of UNAMET, and diplomatically, in ensuring that the broader international community was informed of and behind the UN effort (the monthly meetings of the bigger Support Group played a helpful part in this) and in the much more delicate task of reinforcing the secretary-general and his staff in their dealings with Indonesia. In this respect, the group's central contribution was to not leave the secretariat alone in its attempt to implement solemn commitments that Indonesia had signed but showed little disposition to abide by, instead accusing the United Nations of "taking sides."[47]

Consultation

On May 7, 1999, the Security Council unanimously adopted Resolution 1236, its first on East Timor since 1976. The resolution welcomed the May 5 agreements, looked forward to the secretary-general's submission of detailed plans for UNAMET, and, echoing the agreements themselves, requested him to inform the Council on whether "the necessary security situation exists for the peaceful implementation of the consultation process." Its consideration by the Council had followed discussion in the Core Group of the "deficiencies" of the May 5 agreements but also reflected a consensual position that more robust (and intrusive) security arrangements would "almost certainly have led to the collapse of the peace process."[48]

Over the following months a variety of steps were taken to pressure Indonesia on security and prepare for a ballot that would necessarily be conducted in circumstances that were far from ideal. These included direct appeals from the secretary-general and his staff to the Indonesian authorities, reinforced by repeated expressions of bilateral concern by the Core Group members, use of the Security Council itself, and, too late in the day, measures to strengthen the UN presence in East Timor for the post-ballot period.

Although in many respects the coordination of these activities between the secretariat, the Core Group, and the Security Council was most effective, it is nevertheless hard to conclude that everything possible was done. Australia and the United States had solid intelligence linking the militias to the Indonesian military, yet they, like other states on the Core Group, were wary of the consequences for the stability of Indonesia of pushing too hard on the issue of East Timor.[49] Australia, which a former U.S. official would characterize as "more hard core than we were on not destabilizing Indonesia," withheld key intelligence on the extent of TNI involvement in the militias from the United States out of concern that it would lead to greater pressure on this point.[50] The Australian defense minister had even told secretariat officials that they would be "astonished" by results of the ballot and that East Timor would vote for integration. Meanwhile, the United States itself was somewhat inconsistent in the messages it passed to the Indonesian military, with the line adopted by the State Department undermined by contradictory messages from the Pentagon.[51] Against this background, the capacity of both the secretariat and the Core Group to engage the Security Council was limited by Indonesia's insistence that it was fully complying with the May 5 agreements, the echoing of that insistence by its nonaligned supporters on the Council, especially Malaysia and Bahrain, and diplomatic conventions regulating the extent to which the secretary-general can openly contradict the assertions of an influential member state.[52]

Energetic diplomacy in New York was reinforced by the efforts of Core Group members in their capitals and through their embassies in Jakarta. Australia led efforts to ensure that UNAMET was established quickly. Prime Minister Howard had secured Habibie's acceptance of a substantial (250-strong) UN police contingent in a meeting with him in late April; Australia supplied the first aircraft, helicopters, and jeeps, offered extensive human resources, and began discreet planning for an extraction force.[53] Australian contributions, in kind and financial, were rapidly joined by those from other states. Portugal, Japan, and the United States, followed by the EU, were with Australia the largest contributors to the United Nations' trust fund and helped ensure that about $50 million of UNAMET's total cost of about $80 million was covered by voluntary contributions.[54]

In mid-June Marker traveled to Jakarta and Dili to assess whether security conditions would allow for the registration phase of the consultation to begin. The report that the secretary-general presented to the Security Council on his return was not encouraging. It described intimidation and violence by the prointegration militias and limited opportunities for public expression by proindependence activists. Balancing concerns by Indonesia that the United Nations not overly emphasize its security failings with very real logistical problems, Annan recommended a three-week delay in the process on both grounds.[55] The Council responded with a "Core Group–inspired" presidential statement that expressed concern at the level of violence and called for restraint, but in language that had been watered down by some Council members' wish not to criticize Indonesia unduly. Days later, a UNAMET office in Maliana came under direct attack, but as Indonesia intensified its challenge to the United Nations' impartiality, there was no realistic prospect of the Council imposing additional security requirements on Indonesia.[56]

Discussions within the Core Group and at a meeting between senior officials of Indonesia and Portugal in mid-July were blunt in their recognition that the satisfactory security conditions for the ballot to be conducted did not exist. Ian Martin, the special representative of the secretary-general (SRSG) in Dili, was inclined to recommend calling a halt to the ballot preparations on this basis. But doing so was opposed by many East Timorese, including the CNRT, as well as senior UN officials in New York. Core Group states expressed their reluctance to paint "too bleak a picture" and urged the United Nations to move forward and not lose momentum.[57] As the ballot approached, Martin and others in UNAMET, supported by CNRT and almost all their diplomatic interlocutors, came to agree that, despite fears that it might be impossible to open polling in some areas, the consultation should go ahead.[58]

In the days before the ballot was held on August 30, 1999, diplomatic pressure on the Indonesians intensified. But the militias continued to operate with impunity. Although officials publicly expressed the view that Indonesian promises to fulfill their commitments on security had not "percolated" to the ground, in private they concurred that Defense Minister General Wiranto had the power to rein in the militias if he so chose.[59] On August 24 and 26, Kieran Prendergast briefed informal meetings of the Security Council in blunt terms. On both occasions he urged the Council to send a mission to Jakarta and Dili to express the importance attached by the international community to the ballot and the announcement of its results. But the Council had not dispatched such a mission since the one that went to Western Sahara in 1995, and was little inclined to do so now. For reasons that Ambassador Peter Van Walsum of the Netherlands, who assumed the presidency of the Security Council for September, recalled as being "reportedly on account of hesitations within the Core Group," it was not until the ballot itself had taken place, and violence erupted in its aftermath, that these hesitations were put aside.[60]

Crisis and Response

The violence that erupted in the aftermath of the ballot led to the deaths of some one thousand people, the destruction of Dili and much of the infrastructure across the territory, and the displacement of hundreds of thousands of Timorese into neighboring West Timor. It also exposed fundamental flaws in the UN process. There had been plenty of indications of the risk of violence, which was thought more likely to be targeted toward disrupting the consultation than its aftermath, but worst-case scenario planning did not take place. Indonesia's inability to contemplate—and thus discuss with any seriousness—the possibility of a ballot result in favor of independence; the limitations imposed on the secretariat by the politics of the Security Council; and quite separate limitations of the secretariat itself had led planning for the period immediately following announcement of the ballot result to be restricted to the scenarios foreseen in the May 5 agreement.[61] The scorched-earth policy implemented by Indonesia in the aftermath of the ballot exceeded the expectations of even those most pessimistic about the security situation in the run-up to the ballot. But even so, it was apparent that the secretariat had been restrained by Indonesia and its supporters in the Council—including Russia and China, as well as Bahrain and Malaysia, Gambia and Gabon—from telling the Council what it needed to hear.[62]

Positions in the Core Group had not helped. Although states had at various stages encouraged the secretariat to plan for things to go wrong, they had done so somewhat abstractly and without the political support for such planning. Thus, although Penny Wensley had visited the under-secretary-general for peacekeeping as far back as February 1999 to encourage contingency planning for best- and worst-case scenarios, Australia was not itself contemplating major troop deployment until the United Nations assumed responsibility for a transitional administration, and in no circumstances would take part in peace enforcement without the consent of the

Indonesians.[63] The position of the United States was still less helpful. U.S. officials were bound to consult Congress regarding changes in the UN presence in East Timor, and in early August had told the secretariat in blunt terms that planning for the period following the consultation could only begin in detail once the outcome was known. Congress, it argued, would feel "more comfortable" if it knew exactly with what it was dealing.[64]

The crisis that developed in the days following the announcement that 78 percent of those who had voted in East Timor's popular consultation favored independence prompted a remarkable period of diplomatic activity. The Security Council mission first suggested by Prendergast as a preventive action before the ballot was finally dispatched to Indonesia and East Timor on September 6. It played an important role both as an instrument of pressure on the Indonesians and as an opportunity for Security Council members to see and report on the devastation in East Timor for themselves.[65] Pressure from all quarters mounted on Habibie to accept the deployment of a multinational force authorized by the Security Council to stabilize the situation. This was eventually achieved on September 15 when Resolution 1264 establishing the International Force for East Timor, INTERFET, was adopted. During this period the personal involvement of the secretary-general was essential. From his office in New York Annan worked the telephones incessantly as UN staff and premises in East Timor came under attack (at least twelve staff members were killed),[66] frightened and displaced Timorese sought refuge in the UN compound in Dili, and UNAMET, under Martin's lead, faced wrenching decisions about whether the United Nations could or should stay or go.

The secretary-general's "extraordinary diplomacy" in these days, as Prendergast would describe it, was greatly assisted by the existence of the Core Group, which met almost daily during this period in New York and regularly in Jakarta. The group's members were in constant contact, sharing information and coordinating their representations to others as they sought to garner the support of the Security Council and ensure the coherence of bilateral diplomacy through capitals and in the region. Throughout the crisis, Australian diplomacy was in what Wensley would describe as "overdrive." The personal engagement of Prime Minister Howard, Australia's robust military capacity, and early offer to lead and to provide a major contribution to INTERFET all contributed to the rapid approval and deployment of this force (which began arriving in East Timor on September 20). In the meantime, Australia worked in close cooperation with the United Nations to evacuate to Darwin UN staff and the Timorese who had sought refuge with them at the height of the violence.[67]

The engagement of the United States also, crucially, shifted to a new level. This was evident in the efforts of the newly appointed permanent representative to the United Nations, Richard Holbrooke, who helped focus the attention of President Clinton on the issue, and in the application of substantial pressure from Washington. A summit meeting of the Asia Pacific Economic Cooperation that began in Auckland on September 9 provided an opportune occasion for high-level discussions between leaders of Core Group states and others from the region. On his way to the meeting, Clinton called for Indonesia to accept an international force; two days later he announced that the United States was suspending military assistance. This significant, if belated, move was accompanied by credible threats from the international financial institutions that assistance to Indonesia was in jeopardy.[68]

A final push on Habibie came from an open meeting of the Security Council held on September 11. The secretary-general began the meeting by urging Indonesia to accept an international force forthwith. His appeal was echoed in many of the interventions of the more than fifty delegations that followed him. While some underlined the requirement for Indonesian consent (never in question) to the force, none challenged the need for the force itself. In the background for many members was the experience of Kosovo where, earlier in the year, an inability to secure consensus in the Council led North Atlantic Treaty Organization (NATO) countries to launch military intervention outside the United Nations altogether.[69] Speaker after speaker reinforced the urgency of the crisis in East Timor, and the central role of the United Nations in its solution. Habibie's agreement to the deployment of an international force led by Australia, but authorized by the United Nations, was secured the next day.

The United Nations Takes Charge

Both shock at the tragic events that unfolded in East Timor in early September 1999 and the extraordinary efforts taken to achieve the Security Council's authorization of INTERFET helped bind the states that made up the Core Group to the future of East Timor. A number of the individuals involved would remain deeply engaged with planning and executing the United Nations Transitional Administration in East Timor (UNTAET) and its successor, the United Nations Mission of Support in East Timor (UNMISET), and take particular satisfaction from East Timor's transition to independence in May 2002.

Planning for UNTAET began late and was conducted under significant time pressure. It has been criticized for the extent to which the mission's structure followed that of a traditional peacekeeping operation,
rather than its mandate to prepare the territory for independence; for the
lack of consultation with the Timorese; and consequently, for the mission's
poor provision for their participation in transitional structures.[70] These
deficiencies, as well as the state of near destruction in which Indonesia left
East Timor and the problems created by the enormous gap between the
responsibilities given to the United Nations in East Timor and the paucity
of its resources to fulfill them, dogged the mission from the start. However, they were, over time, at least partly outweighed by other factors.
These included the propitious environment of the effort to assist the Timorese transition and the commitment to the independence of East Timor
by UNTAET itself and by the broader international community, whose
assistance was coordinated through donor meetings organized by the
World Bank.[71]

That the process was not without problems was reflected in the measured assessment given by the SRSG, Sergio Vieira de Mello: UNTAET, he
believed, was a "relative success."[72] However, mistakes made by UN and
other actors were to have lasting consequences. Some had their origins in
failures of understanding, not least of the history of the Timorese resistance
and the complex web of political interests this had given rise to. A lack of
sensitivity to this issue lent credence to the belief that as the most divisive
issue between Timorese—whether or not they should continue to be part
of Indonesia—had been decided in the referendum of August 1999, the
United Nations' role was the relatively straightforward one of devolving
power to an identified "proindependence" group. UNTAET consequently
privileged an overly narrow choice of interlocutor. This was most obvious
in the premium placed on the relationship with Gusmão himself and contributed, for example, to the hurried creation of Timor's defense force (the
Falintil—Defense Forces of Timor-Leste (F-FDTL) in early 2001 in large
part to stanch growing discontent amongst Falintil veterans.[73] It stood in
contrast to attempts to foster conditions in which contending groups could
compete for legitimacy, as has been the case in other situations in which
the United Nations has had transitional responsibilities.

UNTAET's relationship with the Security Council benefited from the
unanimous support on which it counted. No member of the Council could
negate efforts to establish a stable and independent East Timor. However,
once it appeared that another major security crisis was unlikely—despite
the persistent threat represented by militias in West Timor and the

difficulties encountered in establishing credible Timorese security forces—the Council itself proved poorly equipped to supervise the complex process on which the United Nations embarked. Eager for good news among a daily diet of conflict and crisis from the Congo to the Middle East and beyond, many of its members looked to East Timor as a success and began to think about how to draw down the UN presence.

Representations from some Core Group states, particularly the United States, had at the beginning helped divert UNTAET from an overt commitment to the nation building that was clearly its central task.[74] However, over time, a reluctance to have the Security Council remain engaged in such activities partially receded. Negotiations within the Core Group preceded mandate renewals and UNMISET was extended until mid-2005. At that point the Council established the United Nations Office in East Timor (UNOTIL) with a one-year mandate that looked forward to a rapid transition from a political presence to sustainable development assistance.[75] Interviewed in May 2004, Karmalesh Sharma, who had represented the secretary-general in East Timor since Vieira de Mello's departure at Timor's independence, attributed this shift to a change in positions assumed by the United States.[76] Awareness of the risks inherent in potentially failing states had been driven home by the dramatic reversal of fortunes seen in Haiti earlier in 2004. However, the perception of success in East Timor contributed to an underestimation of the serious obstacles ahead.

Throughout its engagement in East Timor, the United Nations remained closely—if inconsistently—involved in issues relating to justice and accountability, providing a range of assistance as well as support to the creation of several ad hoc mechanisms. These included a serious crimes unit and special panels established inside East Timor to prosecute and try those responsible for serious human rights violations, as well as an independent Commission for Reception, Truth, and Reconciliation. But although successive Security Council resolutions set out clear principles of accountability, efforts to uphold them were hindered by problems of political will, resources and capacity, within the United Nations as well as in East Timor.[77] While popular demands for accountability remained, Timorese authorities sought to balance a principled approach to transitional justice issues with the political need for East Timor to develop a harmonious relationship with its powerful neighbor Indonesia.[78] Indonesia, meanwhile, had no inclination to cooperate in any process that might see its senior military officials prosecuted for violations, and instead agreed with the Timorese to establish a joint Commission for Truth and Friendship in March 2005. In time, a lack of accountability for the past and the weakness of the justice system overall became serious sources of grievances in themselves.

The potential for collision between the Security Council's desire to move on from East Timor and the demands of the situation on the ground became increasingly evident as the end of UNOTIL's mandate approached. Discontent within the Timorese defense force, grounded in alleged discrimination by senior officers from the east of the country with deep ties to Falintil, led to demonstrations in February and March 2006 that culminated in the dismissal of 594 soldiers (almost 40 percent of the F-FDTL), mostly from the west of the country, and a spate of violent incidents in Dili. Meanwhile, a series of letters from senior Timorese officials—Prime Minister Mari Alkatiri, Foreign Minister José Ramos Horta, and then President Gusmão himself—urged Annan and the Security Council to establish a "special political office" to provide assistance for the elections to be held in 2007 and for the justice and defense sectors. Annan in late April presented an outline of an "integrated United Nations office" without knowing what degree of support it would find in the Core Group and Council at large.[79] However, before the Council could consider his proposals, the rapid deterioration of the situation in Timor had rendered them all but obsolete, plunging the country into what he would later describe as "a political, humanitarian and security crisis of major dimensions."[80]

Core Group Dynamics

The sparse diplomatic representation in East Timor and plenipotentiary powers afforded Vieira de Mello as the United Nations' transitional administrator militated against the establishment of a Core Group in Dili. Vieira de Mello nevertheless remained in close contact with the group in New York, meeting with it on his regular visits to UN headquarters and talking directly with some of its key members when the occasion required, while also maintaining—like his successors—regular contact with diplomats, Core Group and non–Core Group alike, posted in Dili. In New York, meanwhile, the Core Group's primary interlocutor became the Department of Peacekeeping Operations (DPKO), which had taken over the backstopping of East Timor after the establishment of UNTAET. Meetings were held to prepare for action within the Security Council or when the group as a whole, or one of its members, wished to raise other issues with the secretariat.

As a forum in which differing positions of its members could be resolved before recommendations were submitted to the Council, the Core

Group functioned effectively. Although positions within the group were not fixed, the United Kingdom habitually fulfilled the role of a useful broker poised, at least until the latter stages of UNMISET, between Australia "that wanted everything," as one official put it, and the United States that tended to want "less than what was being proposed" because of concern about costs. This was a role that British diplomats handled deftly, drafting and coordinating texts for presentation to Council members with sufficient time and tact for the perception of Core Group faits accompli to be largely avoided. Portugal, which had been excluded from the group when it first was formed because it was a "party" to the tripartite talks, became a most active member from 2001 on, its inclusion changing the internal dynamics of the group by bringing with it more direct representation of the positions of the Timorese than that of other states.[81] Potential differences between Portugal and Australia—whose relationship was complicated by the two states' long and conflicting history on East Timor—would, during 2001 and 2002, be negotiated amicably by their respective ambassadors before Core Group meetings to avoid any apparent divisions between them.[82]

The Core Group helped ensure that the Security Council's management of East Timor was grounded in the knowledge of the states that were most interested in the issue, as well as East Timor's largest donors.[83] In so doing it offered those of its members that were not members of the Security Council an influence in the decision-making process that was far greater than that usually available to troop or other contributors to a mission. The composition of the Core Group—including just two permanent members of the Security Council—ensured that the full Council had to be consulted on the draft resolutions and other documents that emerged from the Core Group. Yet most decisions on policy were made within Core Group meetings. Moreover, in deference to the Core Group's non-Council members, an unusually high proportion of Security Council debates on East Timor took place in formats that allowed them full participation.

Particularly unusual was the status of Australia, whose substantive weight and, at times, overt leadership on East Timor was both acknowledged and welcomed by the United States and the United Kingdom, the two permanent members of the Security Council on the group. This deference reflected various factors: gratitude that Australia had "stepped up to the plate" in September 1999; acknowledgment that, in the end, Australia would be left with the issue of East Timor on its doorstep and if things went wrong, would likely be called on to intervene once again; and especially after 2003 and Australia's support of the United States on Iraq, a desire to accept the lead of a valued ally on an issue that mattered to it at a variety of levels. And as Robert Orr would write, the configuration of actors on East Timor, in which the United States assumed the role of "junior partner" to Australia, had its own attraction: "What U.S. policy makers really like about the East Timor 'model' is that the United States did not have to take the lead."[84]

This visible Australian lead was, however, a sensitive issue for the Timorese, who viewed their large and wealthy neighbor and its increasingly hegemonic tendencies in the region with a complex range of emotions. Gratitude for the role it had played in 1999 was among them, but it was not without suspicion that Australia somehow had designs on East Timor and its resources beyond its often-expressed concern for Timor's development and stability. These suspicions were fuelled both by the memories of Australia's past policies towards East Timor and by the hard line that Australia maintained in negotiations it conducted with the Timorese on the development of mineral resources in the Timor Sea, an issue with enormous implications for the new country's future economic welfare.[85]

Mandating Transition

Two-way discussion between the members of the Core Group and the secretariat became more marked as the UN presence in East Timor began to draw down. The Core Group gradually asserted itself as a forum that not only shaped action taken by the Security Council, but also addressed substantive differences with the secretariat over the functions to be assumed by a series of gradually diminishing field operations. Over time, the Core Group pressed for less-robust presences than those sought by the secretary-general and his representatives; some of its members made no secret of their belief that the secretariat was overestimating the threats to East Timor's stability that still remained.

A second Security Council mission had visited East Timor in late 2000, shortly after three staff of the United Nations High Commissioner for Refugees had been brutally murdered by militias in West Timor. The mission returned to New York impressed with the progress made in East Timor, but concerned that Timorese expectations were not being met and troubled by the delays in the investigation of serious crimes and the slow progress in the judicial sector more generally. The mission unanimously endorsed the secretariat view that a substantial UN presence would be required in East Timor after independence.[86]

UNMISET's mandate was drawn up after a lengthy planning process, closely monitored by the Core Group. As planning advanced, the most contentious issue became the use of assessed contributions for financing civilian technical advisers, which was actively resisted by the United States. Within the Council the United States had support from France, which had been somewhat put out to be excluded from the Core Group and favored a rapid downsizing of troops in East Timor. Its position was based on the view that East Timor had received preferential treatment by the international community at the expense of France's own priorities in Africa.[87] U.S. objections came to a head in a Core Group meeting held in early October 2001, which had been preceded by a particularly blunt bilateral exchange with the secretariat. However, despite the protestations of U.S. officials, the Core Group eventually agreed that 100 key civilian positions could be financed out of assessed contributions.

Differences between DPKO and the Core Group began to resurface in early 2003. The latter part of 2002 had seen a marked deterioration in the security situation. Riots in December had led to the death of two Timorese as well as the wounding of others as the police responded to the protests with indiscriminate violence. Seen as symptomatic of deeply rooted problems fueled by poverty and unemployment, the riots were directed at targets selected to undermine the government and had included the burning of the prime minister's private residence. They exposed disarray within UNMISET, serious deficiencies within the UN-trained police force—whose formation had been complicated from the start by the high proportion of its officials who had served within the Indonesian police force and was increasingly manipulated by the new Minister of the Interior, Rogerio Lobato—and the alarming fragility of the newly independent state.[88] In January 2003, five more people were killed in attacks on villages near the town of Atsabe by a group of twenty to thirty armed men. The United Nations dispatched a mission, led by DPKO's newly appointed inspector general, Maurice Baril, to assess the situation. The mission concluded, as one participant put it, "that downsizing had been too abrupt and rapid and, if we were not careful, we would all end up in the soup."[89]

Baril, who had been the United Nations' military adviser during the Rwandan genocide, was a strong advocate of the secretary-general's responsibility to be forthright with the Security Council. He briefed the Core Group on his findings, which were then presented to the Security Council in a special report from the secretary-general in March 2003.[90] But the Core Group, motivated by a combination of Australia's independent assessment that the secretary-general's recommendations were excessive and the United States' inclination to cut back as soon as possible, rejected some of the findings of the special report and even asked for it to

be rewritten. A solution was devised whereby a letter from Under-Secretary-General Guéhenno, reflecting a compromise hammered out in the
Core Group, was sent to the British ambassador, Sir Jeremy Greenstock,
who then circulated it to all members of the Security Council. The letter
was the basis for the resolution eventually passed in early April 2003.[91]

The episode presaged a protracted period of discussion regarding the
extension of UNMISET. Sensing the possible reluctance from the United
States to contemplate further engagement in East Timor, Australia had
embarked on its own planning process in the fall of 2003. The United
States was convinced by the "good case" made by Australia and supported
its proposals.[92] But the secretariat was somewhat irritated by Australia's
presentation of its own model for a post-UNMISET mission to the Security Council in October 2003, preempting different recommendations
from the secretary-general.[93] To the surprise of some Core Group members, resolving the difference between Australia and DPKO required extensive discussions. These at times risked splitting the group between its
most powerful members—Australia received the backing of the United
States and the United Kingdom, and the secretariat was backed by Japan,
New Zealand, and Portugal. They were concluded only when effective
lobbying by the Timorese brought about a sudden change in position by
the United States.[94] This allowed the Core Group to support inclusion of
a formed police unit that would answer Australia's concerns as well as the
military personnel judged necessary by the secretary-general within the
extension of UNMISET's mandate. This somewhat cumbersome process marked a shift in the group's internal dynamics, highlighting the leading position of Australia. It also contributed to a decision by the United
Kingdom to cede its coordinating role to Brazil, which had joined the
Security Council for 2004–05 and enthusiastically assumed a place in the
Core Group.[95]

A more assertive Core Group would again be evident in 2005 when,
facing the end of UNMISET but still concerned to maintain international
presence to help ensure long-term security and development, Annan recommended a reconfigured mission, almost half of which would be a back-
up security capacity.[96] But the independent assessments of Australia, the
United Kingdom, and the United States were that such a capacity was not
necessary. Portugal and Brazil stood by the recommendation of the secretary-general and an express request of the Timorese that the Security
Council support it. After difficult discussions in the Core Group—to
which France at this late stage had surprisingly added itself—the United
States took its preferred draft to the full Council and pushed it through,

overriding the instinctive tendencies of other states to support recommendations put forward by the secretary-general.[97]

Differences within the Core Group also contributed to the Council's decision to dodge the complex issues surrounding transitional justice raised by a Commission of Experts appointed by the secretary-general in February 2005 to assess the prosecution of serious human rights violations in 1999. The commission's report was delivered too late to be considered by the Council as it established the mandate of the new UN office, UNOTIL, which—partly as a consequence of this—made no provision for continuing the serious crimes process. The report itself, however, explicitly recommended that the process should be extended and Indonesia's efforts reviewed.[98] The secretary-general forwarded the report to the Council for its consideration. However, the strong sympathies of many member states, among them Australia and the United States, for the preference of the Timorese to prioritize reconciliation with Indonesia over justice led the Council to return it to the secretary-general in September 2005. It asked that he submit, by an unspecified date, a report on justice and reconciliation in East Timor, "with a practically feasible approach."[99]

In the end a response to this far-from-easy request was—sadly—facilitated by the harsh light thrown on the failings of justice and reconciliation in East Timor by the violence that broke out in April, May, and early June 2006. Consequently when the secretary-general presented his report to the Security Council in late July, its members accepted his recommendations for the resumption of the investigative functions of the former serious crimes unit and enhanced assistance to East Timor for both justice and restorative measures with relative ease.[100]

Crisis Again, and Beyond

The depth of the crisis that developed in East Timor in 2006 took many by surprise. Even those international actors who had considered themselves well-informed on East Timor were forced to acknowledge their "lack of appreciation," as the Security Council Report put it rather delicately, "of the depth of the country's political problems."[101] With its immediate origins in the dismissal of the "594 group" of soldiers from the F-FDTL, escalating violence in April, May, and early June exposed bitter divisions within and between Timor's defense and police force—elements of which had been transformed into a personal power base by Lobato—but also the power imbalance between the Fretilin government and its political opponents and rivalries amongst individual Timorese in positions of authority. These were rooted in personal animosities that stretched back decades.

As the number of persons killed in the violence grew to more than thirty, and riots and looting forced the displacement of approximately 150,000 (two-thirds of Dili's population), deep fissures in Timorese society emerged.[102] These included antagonism between "easterners" and "westerners" (*lorosae* and *loromonu*), exacerbated by patterns of residency in Dili established after the departure of the Indonesians, but also a stark generational divide in a context of poverty and youth unemployment in which even those not directly involved in the conflict were veterans of the experience of occupation.[103] These elements proved an incendiary mix and quite overwhelmed the young state's fragile institutions. "Governance structures and existing chains of command broke down or were bypassed"; as the report of the commission of inquiry established by the UN high commissioners for human rights to investigate the violence put it, "roles and responsibilities became blurred; solutions were sought outside the existing legal framework."[104] Before the crisis abated it had tarnished the standing of most senior political figures (including Gusmão) and forced a series of high-profile resignations, including those of Foreign Minister Ramos Horta, Lobato, the minister of defense, and finally Alkatiri himself. Most serious of the allegations were that these senior government officials—with Ramos Horta the obvious exception—had illegally distributed weapons to civilians at the height of the crisis.

The international community struggled to understand what had happened, and how. UNOTIL's SRSG, Sukehiro Hasegawa, was widely perceived to owe his appointment to head UNMISET in 2004 more to his Japanese nationality than to his qualifications for the job.[105] Criticized, like others in senior UN positions, for passivity in face of some of the serious problems that had emerged in the years since Timor's independence, he was quite out of his depth, "an uncomprehending bystander" as the International Crisis Group put it, as the crisis built in the early months of 2006.[106] However, as the gravity of the situation became clear, the United Nations and the broader international community responded promptly to appeals from the Timorese for military assistance and an independent inquiry into the violence. Australia, New Zealand, Malaysia, and Portugal readily agreed to dispatch troops to help restore stability. Kofi Annan asked Ian Martin, then heading the UN human rights office in Nepal, to return to Timor as his special envoy.[107] After briefing the Security Council on his initial findings, Martin led an assessment mission that helped craft recommendations to the Security Council for a new peacekeeping operation and a new, Timorese-led "compact" to promote a more effectively coordinated partnership between East Timor and the international community.[108]

In late April the Core Group had been divided and uncertain regarding its response to the secretary-general's suggestion of a small political presence to follow on from UNOTIL. In August, however, it spoke as one in encouraging the United Nations to field a robust presence to assist the Timorese in overcoming the many challenges—most evidently a complete overhaul of the security sector, and preparations for elections in 2007—they now faced. Core Group meetings in the run-up to an open debate in the Security Council held on August 15, and the debate itself, reflected a broad consensus on this point.[109] But they also exposed bitter disagreement on whether the Security Council should accept the secretary-general's recommendation, and a request from José Ramos Horta, newly appointed prime minister, that the Australian-led military force should be "re-hatted" into a multidimensional peacekeeping operation.[110]

Australia rejected this suggestion categorically, and found forceful backing as it did so from both the United States and the United Kingdom. This raised the possibility of vetoes by two permanent members of the Security Council of any resolution that endorsed the recommendations of the secretary-general in their entirety. Attempts by Japan, France, and New Zealand to find a compromise had little success, as Portugal and Brazil, their positions reinforced not only by Malaysia but by other regional actors such as Singapore and the Philippines, supported the recommendation for "re-hatting" no less vehemently. Such support reflected respect for the publicly expressed desires of the Timorese, but also preference for the legitimacy and impartiality of a UN operation, as well as wariness of the complex profile of Australia.[111]

In the end, Security Council Resolution 1704 authorized a large police component for the new United Nations Integrated Mission in Timor-Leste (UNMIT), but neither a military component, nor an Australian-led force. Instead it requested the secretary-general to review and report back on "the arrangements to be established between UNMIT and the security forces" before October 25, 2006.[112] By the time came, however, the issue was moot. The Timorese had indicated that they would not be revisiting the question of a UN military component with the Security Council. The secretariat was involved in a quite separate struggle to appoint a new SRSG (during the summer months Japan had launched a concerted and somewhat unseemly effort to keep Hasegawa; although he eventually departed in September, member state intervention in the process of selection of his replacement remained unusually high).[113] Meanwhile political attention in Dili was riveted on the report of the special commission of inquiry that had been released in mid-October. Blunt and hard-hitting in its assessment of the origins of and responsibilities for the crisis, few among its protagonists were spared. Individual prosecutions were recommended for the former ministers of the interior and defense and commander of the armed forces for their role in arming civilians. Once again, the spotlight in East Timor would be shone on issues of accountability, with profound implications for the country's political future and its ability to address the deep problems the crisis had exposed.

Conclusions

The international community's neglect of East Timor came to an abrupt end in 1999, a product of dramatic changes within Indonesia and the gradual realignment of the major external actors around them. The response of the United Nations to the fast-breaking developments on the ground was helped by two factors: the patient engagement of the secretariat in the preceding years, both in the facilitation of the tripartite talks with Indonesia and Portugal and in the development of ties to the Timorese themselves; and the formation of the Core Group, which proved an effective means to harness the influence and resources of interested states to the effort led by the secretary-general, greatly increasing the leverage and capacities of the United Nations.

The history of East Timor since that time illustrates, like that of Western Sahara, the hard truths of interest and realpolitik governing the potential for UN action. The satisfaction of the members of the Core Group to be finally contributing to the United Nations' ability to do the right thing by East Timor could not obliterate a history in which for many years most of those same states had quite simply looked the other way. Francesc Vendrell had rightly resisted earlier suggestions to form a group of Friends because the interests of such Friends would not have allowed them to provide actual, as opposed to rhetorical, support for Timorese self-determination. When it was formed, the membership of the group was carefully planned to ensure a mix of very interested and very benevolent actors from the region and outside. That the states on the Core Group had been meeting in different formats before the Core Group as such was constituted—in some cases as a direct result of the secretariat's cultivation of their engagement—contributed to the sense (a helpful one) that it was a self-selecting group and not an artificial construct. Meanwhile, pressure for wider member state involvement was contained by the creation of the larger Support Group that met more infrequently for briefing purposes.

A number of factors contributed to the efficacy of the Core Group in its early years. In addition to its small size (five in its earliest incarnation) and early exclusion of parties or party proxies, its members, despite evident differences between them, were by 1999 like-minded in their aspirations for a peaceful popular consultation and an orderly transition to an independent state. Core Group members were concerned about stability in Indonesia but also broadly sympathetic to the plight and aspirations of the Timorese, and evidently impressed by the leadership displayed by Gusmão. Key among the other characteristics working in the group's favor included the strong representation of regional actors, reflecting the somewhat anomalous relationship of the emerging nation of East Timor to the region itself. At the moment of its independence, East Timor was the poorest and least developed state in Asia.[114] Yet its physical location, poised between Southeast Asia and Australia, placed it at the heart of a relatively rich and developed neighborhood. Regional actors had historically been constrained in the policies they adopted toward East Timor by the importance they attached to good relations with Indonesia. However, as the UN process developed, Australia, Japan, and New Zealand became increasingly involved. The Core Group proved a valued means by which they could help shape the policy response to a security threat in their region to which they were prepared to make a sustained commitment. It also allowed them to retain a guiding hand in the Security Council's management of the Timorese transition in the ensuing years.

The Core Group's relationship to the secretariat evolved over time. During the difficult months preceding and following the August 1999 consultation, the Core Group and the informality that came to characterize its operating style made a significant difference to the secretariat's ability to move the process forward. It also helped ensure a smooth transition from a "good offices" effort led by the secretary-general to the full engagement of the Security Council. Although, as this chapter has argued, not everything possible was done to exert pressure on Indonesia regarding security, the United Nations was not left alone as it sought compliance by Indonesia with agreements it had signed but was not fully committed to implementing. Moreover, the Core Group helped marshal international pressure to secure Indonesia's acceptance of an international security force to restore order after the postballot crisis, providing essential support to the secretary-general's diplomacy. Core Group states, most notably Australia, took the leading role in the rapid deployment of INTERFET and continued to provide much-needed support to the UN missions established afterward, even if they were slow to recognize all the requirements of the transition and then too quick to consider it successfully achieved. Overall, the group's existence contributed directly to the rediscovery by the Security Council that it could indeed make a difference to policy.

During East Timor's transition, the Core Group remained effective as a forum in which the differences between the key external actors could be confidentially resolved and as an interface between the secretariat and the Security Council. But how the Core Group related to both entities shifted according to the phase of the process. Core Group states and the secretariat alike bear responsibility for the limitations of the initial mandate given to the UNTAET, and in particular the lack of attention to nation building that should have been its central task. East Timor benefited directly from the broader international environment in which its transition took place and the gradual emergence of positions within the Security Council that were more accepting of the need to remain engaged to create the basis for a stable state. Yet the level of engagement the United Nations did maintain was not achieved without quiet struggles between the secretariat and some of the members of the Core Group. And, as the events of 2006 were to demonstrate, it was not enough.

The establishment of UNTAET brought a more predictable pattern to the Core Group's activity, which centered on discussions between the secretariat and Core Group members on decisions to be taken by the Security Council. However, the composition of the Core Group, with three permanent members of the Council excluded from it, was such that further consultation was sometimes required. This process, skillfully handled through much of the Core Group's existence by the United Kingdom, was one much appreciated by other Council members (including those from Asia), not least because of the evident contrast it provided to the working practices of other groups.

Over time, however, alliances between the Core Group states, and particularly its more powerful members, contributed to the gradual increase of the group's autonomy. This would lead it to challenge recommendations made by the secretary-general to the Security Council to an extent that secretariat officials—who believed it was the secretary-general's responsibility to report and put recommendations before the Security Council—found disquieting. Differences between Australia, the United States and the United Kingdom and other members of the Core Group evident in 2005 rose to the surface in the summer of 2006 as a consequence of their open opposition to the proposed military component of UNMIT.

The latent threat of vetoes overrode the ability of the Core Group to present itself to the Security Council as a viable mechanism through which to promote consensus. The episode was overcome by a change of position on the part of the Timorese. But it illustrated the extent to which the longevity of the Core Group and its expansion from a tight-knit group of five to a much more diverse eight had effectively transformed the terms on which its members related to the secretary-general, to each other, and to the wider UN membership.

8

Groups and the Variable Geometry of UN Peacemaking

The United Nations' involvement in East Timor had many exceptional aspects. By the early 2000s situations in which the UN role in a peace process was so clearly established were few and far between and largely limited to conflicts long present on the UN agenda. Elsewhere other peacemakers had come to the fore; the United Nations was involved without a clearly established mandate, providing a fig leaf for international inaction or, across Africa in particular, working to support peacemaking efforts led by other actors. This proved to be not so much a loss of business for the United Nations as a change in the nature of the work. The many UN envoys, offices, and peace operations were in themselves testament to the central importance of the organization's contribution to the long-drawn-out efforts required to bring conflicts to a self-sustaining peace. But how the UN secretary-general and those who worked on his behalf managed their relations to the many other actors involved had never been so pressing.

Both the nature of the conflicts and the multiple external actors militated against the formation of groups of Friends similar to those seen in the past. Groups of different kinds and purposes proliferated nonetheless, with different roles in them for the United Nations. Some of these more varied structures, as in Afghanistan or Cyprus, were formed in situations in which the United Nations' long history in the conflict had left it in the lead of complex processes involving numerous bilateral and multilateral actors. In other situations such as in the Middle East, Colombia, and multiple locations in Africa, the secretary-general and his representatives cultivated international frameworks favorable to peacemaking even when the United Nations had no clear lead of the effort. The peace process for southern Sudan offered a different model in that the UN officials gradually engaged with an intricate structure supporting negotiations from which the United Nations had originally been excluded. Within a slow opening of Sudan's future to international involvement, the role played by an informal group of states—the Troika of Norway, the United Kingdom, and the United States—supporting regional mediation led by Kenya, was notable.[1] Collectively these mechanisms revealed an extraordinary degree of flexibility and creativity in how the international community sought to promote peace, but also the very real impediments, often to be found within that same "community," to its attainment.

This chapter distinguishes between situations in which the United Nations had the lead in the peace effort and those in which secretariat officials encouraged the formation of groups (working from "below," so to speak) or endeavored to support a peace process from outside, as in Sudan. With the obvious limitations of a very broad canvas, the chapter examines to what extent the wide variety of groups involved in these most challenging cases helped or hindered efforts to fulfill the goals of peace. As in the single-case chapters, it emphasizes the individual diplomatic agency behind the groups' formation, as well as their relationship to regional dynamics and the conflict parties, the strengths and weaknesses of their composition, and the phase of the particular peace process with which they were engaged. In many respects it is in the nature of the cases addressed in this chapter that they collectively present a somewhat cautionary tale. Promoting consensus among the external actors may seem an obvious means to focus attention and resources on the effort at hand—improving the leverage available to the United Nations or other mediator—but forming and sustaining a group to this end is neither easy nor necessarily the answer.

Leading from the Front

However insurmountable the obstacles to a peace process may appear, a clearly accepted lead to the good offices or mediation effort brings with it significant advantages for structuring the diplomatic initiative. By any estimation, the four cases briefly discussed below—Myanmar,[2] Afghanistan before the transformational events of September 11, 2001, and the latter stages of long-drawn-out peace processes in Angola and Cyprus—chronicle situations of daunting intractability, in regions that were, at a minimum, inhospitable, and commanding little international urgency to resolve them. Stuck on the UN agenda for lack of any better ideas and for the relative comfort with which the membership could "support the UN role," only the secretary-general's reengagement with Cyprus in late 1999 offered any real chance of success, and even in that case the possibility was slim.

Not one of the four situations presented itself as suitable for a closed group of Friends such as were seen in the earlier case chapters. However, the prior experience of several of the officials involved, most obviously Alvaro de Soto and Francesc Vendrell, led them to consider some form of group or Friends mechanism to build consensus in the international community and increase the leverage available to the secretary-general. With the exception of the very particular role played on Cyprus by the key states of the United Kingdom and United States—the closest of the Friends, never explicitly identified, supporting the secretary-general between 1999 and 2004—the mechanisms were not conceived to interact with the conflict parties. Rather, it was hoped that their support might help revive or give life to the otherwise flagging or stalemated processes.

Collectively the mechanisms had a mixed progression. The United Nations made few inroads to Myanmar's authoritarian regime and had its peacemaking in Angola and Afghanistan overtaken by outside events. The death of Jonas Savimbi, the longtime leader of the National Union for the Total Independence of Angola (UNITA), in early 2002 precipitated a rapid end to the conflict, while the attacks of September 11, 2001, tragically brought home to the West the cost of its neglect of Afghanistan and transformed the terms with which the international community engaged with the country. The Cyprus effort came tantalizingly close to a solution, helped by the exemplary support of the secretary-general by his Friends. But it also provided a salutary lesson in the limitations of even a well-managed peace process, actively backed by the coordinated support of powerful states and multilateral actors: it was able to produce a peace plan widely accepted as credible, but unable to generate the political will to accept it in one of the parties to the conflict and the population behind it.

Myanmar: No Friends, but Informal Consultation

That the United Nations had a good offices role in Myanmar at all was in many respects surprising. Sandwiched between China and India, the country is located in a region traditionally resistant to external interference and was admitted to the regional organization, the Association of Southeast Asian Nations (ASEAN), only in 1997. Moreover, the secretary-general's good offices were developed not to address the country's long-running ethnic insurgencies but the threat to democracy and human rights that many states saw in the imposition of martial law in 1988, the denial of elections won in 1990 by the National League for Democracy (NLD), and the detention under house arrest in the years that followed of the NLD's charismatic leader, Aung San Suu Kyi.

China and other states for many years vehemently protested any effort to bring the situation in Myanmar before the Security Council. It was first considered in December 2005 under "other matters" and formally accepted on the Council's agenda on September 15, 2006, as a consequence of vigorous U.S. diplomacy on the issue.[3] But from 1991 an annual resolution of the General Assembly had called on the authorities in Myanmar to improve the human rights situation, recognize the results of the elections, and release Suu Kyi and other political prisoners.[4] During 1993 Francesc Vendrell had quietly suggested to Swedish officials that they add a request for the secretary-general to "assist in the implementation of the present resolution" to the somewhat expanded General Assembly text that was adopted that December.[5] Although a specific mention of "good offices" would not appear in the resolution until 2002, secretariat officials interpreted the earlier request as a "virtual" good offices mandate and proceeded on that basis.[6]

In 1995 the occasional mantle of the secretary-general's special envoy to Myanmar was assumed by Alvaro de Soto, then assistant secretary-general for political affairs. A central issue he faced was how to engage the distinctly opposed views on Myanmar held by states in the region whose trade and other interests led them to resist moves to put pressure on Myanmar, and by those outside the region, which viewed the country largely through the lens of human rights and democratization and over the years imposed upon it an incremental series of sanctions.[7] An early idea for the formation of a group of Friends was soon dismissed. Countries from the region that should surely have been involved were well aware of the entrenched opposition to the junta in the West and were unhappy with the level of intervention they thought was suggested by this approach. Instead de Soto, with Vendrell's support, devised a more neutral sounding "informal consultation mechanism" that would bring together key Western actors (Sweden, the United Kingdom, and the United States), Australia, and selected Asian states (Japan, Malaysia, the Philippines, and Thailand) with some degree of openness to addressing the situation in Myanmar. Meetings were held in New York, but their utility remained limited: the developed countries saw the General Assembly's commitment to "democracy" as a means to promote regime change, while regional actors made their trade and other interests in the country a priority along with the principle of nonintervention in another's affairs.[8]

A more direct attempt to engage with the regional dynamics of the issue came with the appointment of Razali Ismail, a former ambassador of Malaysia and president of the General Assembly, as the secretary-general's special envoy. The idea had received a boost from a meeting of what had become known as the Informal Consultation Group on Myanmar (ICGM), hosted by the government of South Korea in Seoul in March 2000.[9] Between his appointment the following month and March 2004, Razali conducted twelve missions to Myanmar. On all of them he presented himself not just as an envoy of the secretary-general, but also as a prominent figure in ASEAN. His efforts were widely credited with helping facilitate the direct dialogue between the junta and Aung San Suu Kyi that began in October 2000 and led to her release from house arrest in May 2002. However, her rearrest in May 2003 and the ensuing crackdown on the NLD ruptured this process. The United States and the European Union introduced tightened sanctions, while ASEAN called for the release of Suu Kyi, a peaceful transition to democracy, and a visit to Yangon by a ministerial "troika."[10] The junta responded with a proposal for a seven-step "road map" to democracy promising the reconvening of the National Convention, a new constitution, and eventually, free and fair elections. No mention was made in the road map of Aung San Suu Kyi, or indeed of a role in the National Convention for the NLD.

The ICGM remained a mechanism without a formal structure or mandate but evolved into a regular forum for the exchange of information. This took place in two formats: briefings in New York by Assistant Secretary-General Danilo Türk (who had succeeded de Soto in this post), sometimes with Razali present, and more formal and policy-oriented meetings of the "expanded ICGM" that brought together representatives of foreign ministries in Geneva, New York, and Tokyo in 2001, 2002, and 2003. However, the utility of the group remained constrained by divisions within it, as well as by its unwieldy size. When first convened by Türk in 2000, thirteen states had attended, already a group too large for frank discussion. But coinciding as it did with Razali's appointment and a degree of optimism about the future ("Myanmar was suddenly fashionable," as one secretariat official would recall), many more clamored to get in, particularly from the EU. With no clear definition of what the group was for or criteria for membership, the secretariat could do little to limit it. Accordingly, the group grew to some twenty members, some of which, the secretariat found, did not have anything to offer.[11] Meanwhile, sensitive political contacts—including with China, which had greatly increased its interests and influence in Myanmar during the country's years of political deadlock and could not be persuaded to participate in the ICGM—were pursued outside the group meetings.[12]

The 2003 crackdown on the NLD and Yangon's launching of the road map process contributed to a growing realization among some in the international community that their efforts had failed to influence the crisis in Myanmar. Rigidity in an international approach centered on a narrow definition of human rights and expressed through sanctions had contributed to a situation in which the grip on power maintained by the military authorities was stronger and the influence of external actors on the internal process less than ever before.[13] Razali turned increasingly to the region, encouraging, for example, the hosting by Thailand of an international meeting on Myanmar in Bangkok in December 2003. However, the limitations of regional leverage were exposed by Myanmar's objections to a second meeting in Bangkok and ASEAN's continued reluctance to take steps to demonstrate its support of his efforts that it had pledged in June 2003. Toying with the idea of "Friends," in September 2004 Razali engineered a high-level meeting between the secretary-general himself and a more select group of states than the ICGM represented. The hope was that it might generate a sense of common purpose in assisting Myanmar to move toward a more credible democratic transition.[14] But the bleak prospects for political movement inside the country and lack of incentive for external engagement combined to create conditions in which a single high-level meeting could add little.

A further blow to the prospects for reconciliation in Myanmar came in October 2004 when the chairman of the military junta, Senior General Than Shwe, removed Prime Minister Khin Nyunt from office. Khin Nyunt had played a leading role in negotiating cease-fires with the ethnic insurgencies and had been Razali's primary interlocutor. Razali was unable to negotiate a return to the country after his departure, and resigned his position in early 2006. Under-Secretary-General Ibrahim Gambari picked up the good offices baton and visited the country in both May and November 2006, reporting back to the ICGM as well as the Security Council as he did so. The visits represented reengagement by the United Nations with Myanmar at the political level, the significance of which was amplified by the parallel progress within the Security Council. But the challenges ahead remained daunting.[15]

Groups on Afghanistan: The Struggle for Attention

Like Myanmar, Afghanistan during the 1990s was Friend-less. Indeed, the U.S.-led military action that toppled the Taliban in late 2001 was the result not of international peacemaking, but of the spectacular neglect of the shattered state that had been left behind in the aftermath of the Cold War.[16] Over the years Kofi Annan and his officials had tried to counter this situation by encouraging the formation of a wide variety of groups to create "a solid international framework" to address the external aspects of the conflict.[17] It was a strategy that had only limited success.

In 1997 Annan appointed Lakhdar Brahimi his special adviser on Afghanistan. At that point the Taliban was in control of much of the country, the opposition United Islamic Front for the Salvation of Afghanistan (or Northern Alliance) held territory only in the north, and the conflict itself extended outward across the region, fueled by the ready trade in arms and drugs and the political and military support provided to the contending parties by Afghanistan's neighbors, principally Pakistan, on the one hand, and Iran and Russia, on the other.[18] States whose post–Cold War priorities had led their attention and resources elsewhere, like the foreign backers of the Afghan parties, "enthusiastically proclaim[ed] their support to the United Nations peacemaking efforts," leaving the United Nations' role, as Annan reported to the Council, as little more than "an alibi to provide cover for the inaction—or worse—of the international community at large."[19]

Brahimi embarked on a thirteen-nation tour of Afghanistan, the region, and donor nations. He was extremely discouraged by what he found and in particular by the profound differences between Pakistan and Iran.[20] On his return, he convened a series of small, informal meetings in New York with a group of eight countries—Afghanistan's six neighbors (China, Iran, Pakistan, Tajikistan, Turkmenistan, and Uzbekistan), plus Russia and the United States. He had hoped that this group of "six plus two" would provide a forum in which the possibility of curbing arms flows into Afghanistan could be raised and regional differences discussed, as well as a means to encourage the reengagement of the United States.[21] (The meetings offered the United States an opportunity for the first contacts with Iran since diplomatic relations between the two were broken off in 1979.) However, the neighbors' support for their Afghan proxies continued unabated, and over time the gap between rhetoric and reality in the statements and actions of the "six plus two" only became more blatant. Months of careful preparation lay behind the group's "Tashkent Declaration on the Fundamental Principles for a Peaceful Settlement of the Conflict in Afghanistan" in July 1999. But the irrelevance of the diplomatic effort was harshly demonstrated just a week later when the Taliban launched a major offensive in the Shomali Plains. Brahimi resigned shortly afterward, citing his "bitter disappointment" with the "six plus two."[22] He would later recall his two-year effort as one of "shouting in the wilderness . . . almost from day one I was pleading, 'you cannot ignore this conflict, one day it will spill over, it already has with drugs and it will not stop there.' But no one was listening."[23]

The failings of the "six plus two" reflected broader problems. The secretariat's attempt to work through this group and with the support of a

Group of 21 states that met periodically in New York was increasingly overtaken by the preoccupation of the Security Council with the Taliban and the sanctuary its leaders had offered to Osama bin Laden.[24] Francesc Vendrell was appointed the secretary-general's personal representative and head of the UN Special Mission to Afghanistan in early 2000. He had few illusions as to what the "six plus two" might achieve. But in a style that was consistent with the proactive stance he had taken elsewhere, he sought to promote other mechanisms that might bring support to his efforts to per-suade the Taliban and the United Front to engage in a process of dialogue and, failing that, galvanize the international community to engage more coherently with Afghanistan. These ranged from an informal "luncheon group" of Islamabad-based ambassadors of donor states (also members of a larger Afghan Support Group that sought to coordinate external assistance to Afghanistan),[25] to "Track II" talks among former officials of the key states of Iran, Pakistan, Russia, and the United States and a series of meet-ings between the United States and the international sponsors of the three main Afghan exile initiatives (Italy, Iran, and Germany) that became known as the Geneva Initiative.[26]

Vendrell's efforts were notably creative as an attempt to build con-stituencies. They provided an avenue for the involvement of a number of states that had resented their exclusion from the "six plus two"[27] and yet could expect to be involved in any future process of reconstruction. But they could not overcome the central problem facing the United Nations during this period: a classically conceived "peace process" could gain little traction on a situation in which one party to the conflict, the Taliban, con-trolled much of the national territory yet, because of its ideology, practices (on human rights, toward women), and increasingly close ties to al-Qaeda, stood no chance of gaining international legitimacy. Meanwhile, the pow-erful states that were happy to engage in a seemingly endless number of coordination mechanisms and other groups (the "six plus two," Group of 21, Afghan Support Group, luncheon group, Geneva Initiative, and so forth) showed no inclination to commit the serious time, attention, and resources required to address the plight of Afghanistan, its long-suffering population, and the pernicious spread of its conflict across the region. Sep-tember 11, 2001, changed all that.

Lakhdar Brahimi was reappointed the secretary-general's special envoy to Afghanistan on October 3, 2001. He brought to the job several significant advantages: his diplomatic skills and experience were widely admired at the United Nations;[28] his personal history—he was a former foreign minister of Algeria, with proven credentials in representing Algeria's National Liberation Front in the 1950s—was one that commanded respect; and his efforts before 1999 ensured that he knew Afghanistan and the region intimately. Together, these attributes allowed him to play an important role in developing international consensus on the political future of Afghanistan, most notably in the diplomatic whirl of activity leading up to the Bonn agreement reached between Afghanistan's opposition forces on December 5, 2001. That this was possible reflected the transformation of the conditions in which the international community addressed Afghanistan after September 11. As the U.S.-led coalition initiated military action against the Taliban, there was, for the first time, agreement among Afghanistan's neighbors that their interests would be best served by a broad-based, representative government in Kabul, accountable to its citizens, friendly to its neighbors, and enjoying internal and external legitimacy.[29]

Both Brahimi's own preference for flexible interaction with his counterparts and conditions in Afghanistan militated against the creation of any fixed group of Friends. The states present during the Bonn negotiations included those most involved in Afghanistan: Germany, Iran, India, Italy, Pakistan, Russia, the United Kingdom, and the United States. They were called on to put pressure on the factions and individuals they had championed or backed in the past.[30] But they did so as bilateral actors moving toward a shared goal, rather than as representatives of any group mechanism. Once established as the head of the UN Assistance Mission to Afghanistan (UNAMA), Brahimi continued to promote good relations across the region and to provide quiet good offices among Afghans who came to see him, as Ashraf Ghani, Afghanistan's finance minister in this period, put it, as an "uncle of the nation."[31]

Jean Arnault served as Brahimi's deputy and then succeeded him as head of UNAMA. He would recall that suggestions to form a group of Friends came up "periodically," but were consistently resisted. Although Arnault's own experience in Guatemala might have predisposed him toward Friends, in this instance he considered that any small—and therefore effective—group would have involved costly political exclusion. It would not have been possible to have a group that did not include Iran or Pakistan; nor would it have been acceptable to exclude any major donor. Accordingly, more flexible methods of consultation, with different sounding boards and partners for different issues, were pursued, even as a variety of mechanisms were instituted by donors and the Afghan government to support the country's reconstruction.[32]

Friends of Angola: Not a Good Precedent

A very different approach was adopted on Angola, for which the secretary-general himself, most unusually, took the initiative to form a group of Friends. In 1998 the United Nations had to withdraw a small military observer mission that had succeeded a series of peacekeeping operations. Toward the end of the year, the country fell back into a full-blown war that rapidly displaced nearly 1 million people, or about 10 percent of Angola's population. The United Nations was profoundly concerned about this humanitarian crisis. However, its capacity to exercise leverage on either side in the conflict had been eroded by its uneven track record in the country and the increasingly one-sided support given to the government of Angola by states in the Troika—Portugal, Russia, and the United States—that had played a leading role in the country's checkered peace process since the early 1990s.[33] In mid-1999 the secretariat was embroiled in complex negotiations over the terms of reference for a UN political office that the government of Angola quite clearly did not want when Annan decided to form a group of Friends. He thought such a group might helpfully bring collective pressure to bear on both the government and UNITA to restart the peace process. An additional goal was to try to dilute the influence of the Troika, which was perceived to be holding UN policy on Angola hostage to positions and interests that had shifted considerably since the early 1990s.[34]

The Cold War had left Russia aligned with the government and the United States sympathetic to UNITA. Portugal, as the former colonial power, was seen to be influential with both, although its relations with the government were much stronger. However, over time the dynamics of the peace process changed. In the classic action of a spoiler, UNITA's Savimbi refused to accept the outcome of elections held in 1992, withdrew to the bush, and used the spoils of the lucrative diamond business to rearm his forces. The United States switched its allegiance and the Troika became, as one ambassador on the Security Council put it, "the real friends of Angola."[35] Oil revenues allowed the government to rebuild its army as surely as diamonds fueled UNITA. Russia remained the largest arms supplier to the Angolan government, while Portugal continued its cooperation with the Angolan armed forces. Meanwhile, the interests of the United States were increasingly aligned with the (relative) stability of the government: by 1997 Angola supplied the United States with up to 7 percent of its oil imports and in 1999 it was the second largest site for U.S. investment (most of it oil related) and its third largest trading partner in Sub-Saharan Africa.[36]

That the group of Friends was designed to balance the Troika but of necessity had to include the three states among its numbers complicated its composition. But a lack of attention to "gatekeeping" doomed it from the start. It was widely known that the Friends were being formed at the request of the secretary-general. Names of potential Friends were submitted to Annan for his approval. But this was even as an effort to protect him from being seen to choose which states were (and as important, were not) his Friends led to a request to Gabon—which was on the Security Council at the time and in the past had hosted meetings between the government of Angola and UNITA—to initiate a process of the Friends' "self-selection."[37] The group grew to at least nineteen members, met infrequently, and achieved little. Indeed, when the Angola dossier passed to the secretary-general's special adviser on Africa, Ibrahim Gambari, in early 2000, his first thought was to abolish the Friends altogether. However, Annan, as Gambari recalled, "wisely said no." Instead, Gambari obtained Annan's approval to change the format under which the group met. He cut it down to a more manageable eleven and replaced formal meetings with the secretary-general himself, necessarily truncated by the pressures on his schedule, with more informal gatherings, often over lunch or dinner in the residence of one of the ambassadors.[38]

This smaller Core Group met from mid-2000 on and represented a more helpful forum in which interested states could have their say.[39] However, its composition was not without problems: few of its members could doubt that everything said would not be immediately reported back to the government of Angola—which was unhappy with the existence of the Friends at all—while differences between some of the Friends were substantial. In addition to the Troika, the eleven consisted of five countries "of interest and influence"—Brazil, Canada (which had assumed a very active chairmanship of the Angola sanctions committee), Norway (a major donor with substantial interests in the oil sector), France, and the United Kingdom—plus three African states: Nigeria (close to the government), and Namibia and South Africa (close to UNITA). The United Kingdom, Nigeria, and South Africa consistently pushed for dialogue, while Namibia—which was increasingly affected by the spillover of the conflict across its borders—and the United States were more skeptical.

A shift toward a set of circumstances more favorable to dialogue gradually began to emerge during 2001.[40] But whether the hope for dialogue was realistic was never put to the test, as the killing of Savimbi in February 2002 rendered all such efforts moot. In one of the most dramatic transformations of a conflict landscape in recent history, a cessation of hostilities and the signature that April of a "Memorandum of Understanding" effectively brought the conflict to an end. A United Nations Mission in Angola, with Gambari at its head, was established in August, but found itself—like the group of Friends—redundant in a matter of months.[41]

Cyprus: Good and Better Friends

Cyprus has the dubious distinction of representing the most long-standing good offices assignment on the agenda of the secretary-general. Negotiations pit Greek Cypriots, who are recognized by all states except Turkey as representing the Republic of Cyprus, yet since 1974 have controlled only the southern two-thirds of the island, against Turkish Cypriots, who in 1983 declared the independence of their territory—in which a large contingent of mainland Turkish troops was stationed—as the "Turkish Republic of Northern Cyprus" (TRNC). The conflict is both communal, with its origins in a colonial struggle against British rule, and regional, determined by the relationship of each of the two communities to Greece and Turkey. But with armed hostilities forestalled by the presence since 1964 of a UN peacekeeping operation, the United Nations Force in Cyprus (UNFICYP), there are no insurgents to deal with or guerrilla organizations to bring in from the cold.

Over the decades, progress has been limited. Obstacles have included bitter divisions between the two sides, the support that each has received from their respective mother countries, and the reluctance of the United States and other powers to put pressure on either Greece or Turkey, both members of the North Atlantic Treaty Organization (NATO). This hesitation reflected a Cold War preoccupation to not risk divisions on the alliance's southern extremity and, in the post–Cold War period, a degree of resignation to the status quo in Cyprus in the face of more pressing concerns elsewhere. In the absence of credible regional and international engagement, successive secretaries-general struggled to move the process from a stalemate tolerable to the parties toward a solution that would require concessions from both sides on core issues ranging from sovereignty and political equality to territory and security.[42]

Direct talks between Glafcos Clerides (outside the framework of the UN talks recognized as the president of the Republic of Cyprus) and Rauf Denktash, the self-proclaimed president of the TRNC, were held in 1994 and again in 1997, but little was gained. However, in the summer of 1999 the confluence of a number of different elements raised hopes that more favorable conditions were developing. These included the adoption by the Security Council of Resolution 1250, providing clear parameters for negotiation,[43] an evolving rapprochement between Greece and Turkey, and the prospect of the enlargement of the EU by up to ten new members, including Cyprus. Recognizing a moment of unique opportunity, Annan appointed Alvaro de Soto his special adviser and embarked on an effort of an unprecedented scale to resolve the long-standing problem of Cyprus.[44]

De Soto's experience of Friends groups in El Salvador and elsewhere had left him keenly aware of the benefits to be gained from the leverage of key interested states, but also of the risks posed by a proliferation of would-be mediators or a too formally constituted group. Consequently, as he began work on Cyprus, he viewed the bevy of special envoys—from Australia, Canada, Finland (president of the EU at the time), Germany, Russia, Sweden, the United Kingdom, and the United States—already in place with some trepidation.[45] He chose not to recommend to the secretary-general a "group" of Friends, as to do so would have involved a large and incoherent structure or potentially damaging exclusion. Instead, he worked closely with layers of unspecified "Friends of the Secretary-General," as well as with the EU. These Friends, as Annan would later acknowledge, provided "advice as well as diplomatic and practical support . . . avoiding the temptation to duplicate or supplant my efforts."[46] First among equals were the two key external actors on Cyprus, the United Kingdom and the United States, who were specifically asked by Annan to "respect the UN's independence and impartiality and . . . accept at every stage that the UN was in the lead."[47] This they did with remarkable consistency, not least because they thought the United Nations offered the only possible chance of a success.[48]

The United Kingdom was the former colonial power and, with Greece and Turkey, one of the three "guarantors" of Cyprus's independence; it maintained sovereign military bases and extensive economic and other ties to the island. These contributed to its own deep knowledge of the issues at hand, but also to a degree of suspicion of its motivations by Greek Cypriots in particular that would surface periodically. Meanwhile, the United States' complex but close partnership with Turkey and many years of experience calming its tensions with Greece put it in a unique position to exert influence when it chose to do so. The two habitually prepared the first draft of any resolution in the Security Council and had worked through the Group of Eight (G-8) to achieve the subtle but significant changes in the framework for proposed negotiations that had been endorsed in Resolution 1250.[49] They would remain at the center of the complex architecture of international support developed around the UN process.

The negotiations themselves were conducted exclusively by the United Nations, with de Soto's efforts reinforced by the secretary-general himself at key moments. But de Soto maintained regular—and at times daily—contact with the British and U.S. envoys; the former British ambassador at the United Nations, David Hannay; and Alfred Moses and then Thomas Weston from the United States.[50] The trust that developed between them allowed the envoys to offer advice (sometimes but not always heeded) and share sensitive information. Meanwhile, their frequent briefing by de Soto helped ensure that their countries' representatives would be "singing from the same song sheet," whether in New York, Brussels, Ankara, Athens, or elsewhere. As a practical matter, the United Kingdom undertook a lot of necessary legwork within the structures of the EU (where the United Nations has relatively little experience), the United States maintained a constant channel of communication to Ankara, and both countries periodically helped fend off assaults on the United Nations' integrity launched by the parties, and Denktash and his Turkish supporters in particular.

Distinct outer layers were formed by the EU, the other permanent members of the Security Council, and countries, such as Australia, whose interest in Cyprus stemmed from the presence of significant Cypriot immigrant populations. As the process advanced, officials from the European Commission also worked with the United Nations' technical committees to ensure the legal compatibility of the approach taken by the emerging "Annan plan" for Cyprus with the requirements of the EU itself. Although de Soto took pains to brief the permanent five on a regular basis, the relationship with Russia, France, and China was somewhat strained—particularly in New York—by the three's sense of exclusion from the inner circle formed by the United Nations, the United Kingdom, and the United States. Over time, Russia's support of the Greek Cypriot position would become a substantive problem.[51] This came to a head in April 2004 with Russia's surprise veto of a resolution that had offered Security Council commitment to implementation of the Annan Plan in the days before its consideration in simultaneous referenda by the two Cypriot communities.[52]

The process that culminated in the referenda held on April 24, 2004, went through several stages. Its outcome—the rejection of the Annan Plan by a ratio of three to one of the Greek Cypriot population, even as a ratio of two to one of the Turkish Cypriot population gave it their support—owed much to events extraneous to the negotiating table. Indeed, crucial elections in both Cypriot communities and in Turkey, the ongoing

EU accession process, and at different stages, the shadow of the war in Iraq conspired to ensure that the United Nations rarely had comparable leverage on both parties.[53] Primary responsibility for the failure to secure agreement on the Annan Plan in 2002 and 2003 could be attributed to Denktash and the unconditional support he received from Turkey.[54] But by the time the process resumed in early 2004 both these factors had been overcome: Denktash had been marginalized by Turkish Cypriot opposition to his position on the talks and a new Turkish government, led by Recep Tayyip Erdogan, had thrown its weight decisively behind the Annan Plan.[55] However, the position of the Greek Cypriots had changed too. Elections held in February 2003 had brought Tassos Papadopoulos, a conservative lawyer who had run on a platform that criticized Clerides for giving too much away in the UN talks, to the presidency.

Papadopoulos told Annan the following month that he would be prepared not to reopen the UN plan and to put it to a referendum.[56] In taking the decision to resume the talks in early 2004, UN officials decided to call his bluff. They were gambling that the combined international pressure of the United Nations and its Friends would be able to exert enough pressure and encouragement for a united Cyprus to enter the EU in good standing.[57] They were underestimating Papadopoulos in a number of respects. On the basis of what diplomats involved would come to see as a hard political calculation that Greek Cypriots would be able to extract a better deal in the future, from inside the EU and while Turkey itself pursued a coveted spot in it, he set about trying to undermine the Annan Plan. He demanded that every single piece of federal legislation be in place before the referendum and arrived at critical meetings held in Bürgenstock, Switzerland, in late March in the presence of Greece, Turkey, the secretary-general, and senior envoys from the United States, the United Kingdom, the EU, and Russia with an expanded set of demands and a continued refusal to prioritize them. In the meantime, opposition to the UN effort in the always sensationalist Greek Cypriot media was mounting.[58] Under such circumstances the ability of the United Nations and its Friends to meet the public expectations of the Greek Cypriots was limited.

Peacemaking from Below

A peacemaker working without a clearly established lead in a peace process faces limitations quite distinct from the problems that may beset a lead mediator, or even good officer. Yet in widely differing circumstances in the Middle East, Colombia, and in a variety of situations in Africa, Kofi

Annan and his colleagues encouraged the formation of groups as a means to promote international coherence, increase leverage on the conflict parties, and engage the United Nations in circumstances in which it might otherwise be relegated to a process instrument.

An innovative—and quite atypical—example of this approach was represented by the Quartet, a grouping of the most powerful external actors involved on an issue, the Middle East peace process, at the very top of the international agenda. Developed by Annan and his personal representative, Terje Rød-Larsen, the Quartet became established as the central forum for the coordination of international positions on the highly volatile developments in the region. Although it was only in the aftermath of the terrorist attacks of September 2001 that the Quartet emerged as a public entity, its creation dated back to an intense diplomatic effort undertaken by Annan, with Rød-Larsen's support, to address the crisis precipitated by the outbreak of what became known as the "second intifada" in September 2000. A ten-day visit to the region culminated in a summit meeting held at Sharm el Sheikh. This was cochaired by the presidents of the United States and Egypt, although Annan himself retained a central hand in its direction.[59]

The United Nations never aspired to lead the mechanism that emerged the following year binding the Middle East's "little three," as Quartet members referred to the EU, Russia, and the United Nations, to the dominant "one" of the United States.[60] Its composition, as Rød-Larsen has described it, matched the "power of the United States, the money of the European Union, and the legitimacy of the United Nations" with a political need to respect Russia's role in the region. Meeting at the level of principals as well as at the "envoy" level, and working closely with Egypt, Jordan, and Saudi Arabia, in practice the Quartet's actions were often coordinated by Rød-Larsen and the secretariat. This allowed the United Nations a role in brokering the sometimes diverging views of the United States and the EU and the ability to maintain influence on the broader political process.[61] It also informed the year-long process of negotiation in the Quartet—most specifically, not engaging the conflict parties directly—that resulted in the launching of a road map for the Middle East peace process in April 2003.[62]

A "backroom" aspect of the Quartet—by which, for example, U.S. officials could work to bridge differences between positions emanating from the White House and what was acceptable to the United States' international partners—lent the Quartet a utility of a kind even in years following 2003 when the peace process made little progress. But the structure of the mechanism was not without considerable risks for the United Nations. These became evident as it was increasingly perceived to be beholden to policies determined by the United States. Indeed, Alvaro de Soto, who succeeded Rød-Larsen in mid-2005, would conclude as he left his post two years later that by that point the quartet was "pretty much a group of friends of the US." It may have given the United Nations "the illusion of a seat at the table," but this came at the cost of an ability to maintain even-handedness that undermined the legitimacy with which it purported to act.[63]

More closely related to earlier Friends' initiatives was the strategy adopted by the secretary-general's special adviser on Colombia, the Norwegian diplomat Jan Egeland. With his encouragement, separate groups of Friends were formed to support talks between the government and the two largest guerrilla organizations involved in the country's long-running internal conflict. However, the proliferation of mechanisms not anchored to the support of any third-party lead, the weakness of the process itself, and the continuing ambivalence of the United Nations' role in it all adversely affected their utility. Meanwhile, across Africa UN officials worked with regional mediators and other involved diplomats to encourage the formation of a wide variety of groups. This effort took on a more deliberate nature after the endorsement of Annan's encouragement of a group approach to African conflicts in the Africa Action Plan adopted by the G-8 in mid-2002. Perhaps unsurprisingly, given the complexity of the situations they engaged with, the direction of these mechanisms was mixed, and the United Nations' capacity to "steer" the processes was often limited.

Colombia's Multiple Friends

During the 1990s the United Nations neither had nor sought a role in efforts to end Colombia's conflict. Indeed, officials within the secretariat had been surprised when in 1999 President Andrés Pastrana publicly committed himself to a peace process and asked Annan to appoint an envoy to the country, albeit to a position he specified should not include a "political" role and that he hoped would help marshal international support for the U.S.-backed Plan Colombia.[64] Fund-raising for the "soft" economic and social aspect of a plan perceived as heavily weighted toward U.S. counterdrug efforts was not acceptable to the United Nations. But the request was reflected in the ambiguity of the position to which Annan appointed Egeland—special adviser for international assistance to Colombia —in December 1999.[65]

Egeland's long experience of peace processes allowed him to develop a role of "discreet facilitation." But his efforts were never able to overcome either the limitations of the process itself, which was in reality a series of dialogues and talks almost exclusively restricted to procedural questions fitfully undertaken through separate channels to the Revolutionary Armed Forces of Colombia (FARC) and the National Liberation Army (ELN), or deep-seated ambivalence among Colombian actors toward the United Nations' involvement.[66] Other international actors, meanwhile, responded to Pastrana's efforts with a mix of skepticism and encouragement. The United States, by a wide margin the preeminent external player in Colombia, was aloof and focused its resources on Plan Colombia.[67] European donors, on the other hand, committed themselves to support the peace process and targeted assistance on the social and economic causes of the conflict, an emphasis that received broad support in Latin America.[68] In part to help bridge these differences, Egeland promoted meetings outside the country of senior officials from the United States, Canada, Mexico, and several European countries in what became known as the "Informal" or "Brussels" Group.[69] In Colombia he also tried to break the historic isolation of the guerrillas in order to build confidence among the parties. One of the ways he did this was by encouraging groups of Friends.[70]

The guerrillas and the government were, for different reasons, extremely critical of the Central American peace processes and suspicious of the UN role in them.[71] However, it was with Norway's experience as a leading Friend in Guatemala in mind that Egeland prepared a "nonpaper" outlining the advantages that Friends might offer and shared it with the government and both guerrilla leaderships. The Colombian guerrillas were markedly different from those in Central America in many respects, not least in their growing dependence on income from drugs and other resources and their insistence on maintaining practices such as kidnapping and other human rights' abuses, inherently abhorrent to any international actors. However, Egeland believed that Friends might help persuade the guerrillas of the advantages that interaction with the outside world could bring, while edging them toward greater respect for humanitarian principles in their conduct of the war. The existence of a group or groups could also be helpful as a means to coordinate the interests and initiatives of individual states and strengthen the United Nations' weak hand.

In practice the initiative led to the creation of mechanisms that were unable to sustain internal coherence. They suffered from pressure placed on them by the lack of political will among the parties to the conflict, as well as contradictions in the role played by ambassadors accredited to the Colombian government yet somehow professing "friendship" of a guerrilla organization. This was complicated by the fact that very few of the ambassadors posted in Bogotá had experience with a peace process and some had only intermittent support from their respective capitals.[72] The continuing ambiguity of the United Nations' role did not help. In the absence of the clear leadership given by an accepted third-party mediator, a tendency for multiple channels of communication with the guerrilla leaderships soon developed.[73]

Egeland had emphasized the advantages to any group of a small and balanced membership. And indeed in June 2000 a group consisting of Cuba, France, Norway, Spain, and Switzerland was formed to support the talks between the ELN and the government. A degree of coherence was given by the relative openness of the ELN to the international community, Cuba's investment in the process, and the strong role played by Spain.[74] However, the panorama was complicated by the formation in early 2001 of a second group of countries (Canada, Germany, Japan, Portugal, and Sweden) interested in verifying a demilitarized "meeting zone" proposed in "pre-accords" reached between the ELN and the government. Problems in the engagement of Friends emerged even more starkly in the FARC process. An unwieldy group created in February 2001 included no fewer than twenty-five countries as well as the Vatican, the United Nations, and the EU; it was hindered from the beginning by uncertainties as to what it was supposed to do.[75] Colombians were skeptical of what they saw as a misguided attempt by Europeans and others to inoculate "their" citizens against the threat of kidnapping through the promise of "friendship." The fallacy of any such proposition was demonstrated by the FARC's kidnapping during July 2001 of three German nationals and in a separate incident, a former governor of the province of Meta, snatched from a UN vehicle in which the resident representative for the United Nations Development Programme was riding.[76] The incidents prompted overwhelming condemnation and illustrated what James LeMoyne, Egeland's deputy, would describe as the FARC's readiness to commit "diplomatic suicide."[77] With access to resources from coca production and other sources assured, FARC had little interest in any "carrot" represented by international involvement and consequently, saw no contradiction between this involvement and their usual practices.

The limitations of the FARC Friends were only partly overcome by the constitution of a smaller facilitating commission.[78] LeMoyne, who took over from Egeland in late 2001, and the ten members of the facilitating commission would be thrust into the political limelight in early 2002 as, amid persistent crises, they were asked to broker terms for the continuation of the process. This they did, and the talks limped on, even achieving agreement on a framework for a cease-fire. However, on February 20, 2002, after the FARC hijacked an airplane and kidnapped a prominent senator, the process broke down irrevocably. In the days that followed, the FARC completed its alienation of the international community by kidnapping Ingrid Betancourt, a candidate in Colombia's presidential elections, but also a French citizen. Disillusionment with the behavior of the FARC prompted a hardening of attitudes in Europe—and indeed was considered by Colombian officials as a significant benefit of the Friends venture.[79]

The collapse of the Pastrana peace process helped propel the conservative candidate, Alvaro Uribe Vélez, to a decisive victory in presidential elections held in May 2002. A dramatic increase of military pressure on the guerrillas was warmly supported by the United States. Indeed, Uribe's emphasis on the "terrorist" nature of his opponents fit well with the global war on terrorism and a shift in U.S. policy toward Colombia to the direct targeting of military assistance for counterterrorism operations.[80] Uribe had asked for the secretary-general's good offices to be continued. But a bottom-line expectation of UN support for the Colombian state in its legitimate fight against terrorists brought the government into confrontation with much of the United Nations' work on human rights and other humanitarian issues, as well as good offices undertaken on the basis that Colombia's internal conflict had political causes at its root. The result was a relationship that steadily deteriorated.[81] Negotiations were limited to a controversial process with the self-defense forces, paramilitaries, and drug lords in the United Self-Defense Forces of Colombia (AUC), with which the United Nations, at its own insistence, was not directly engaged.[82]

LeMoyne maintained channels of communication with guerrilla leaders and engaged with the multiple external actors involved, but the Friends of the past largely fragmented. Without a clear process to pursue, or the obvious desire of the conflict parties for what it could offer, the United Nations' good offices role became a lightning rod for criticism by the Colombian government and, in January 2005, the secretary-general decided that it should be for the time being brought to an end.[83] International peacemaking passed to a complex and shifting array of other actors that undertook initiatives of different kinds. The Catholic Church and Switzerland—on its own and in combination with France and Spain—conducted discreet conversations regarding a possible humanitarian exchange of prisoners with the FARC. Meanwhile Mexico and then Norway, Spain, and Switzerland facilitated discussions with the ELN. While these showed some progress in a series of meetings that took place in Cuba during 2006, persistent problems in the demobilization of the paramilitaries and the absence of a viable political process with the FARC served to illustrate how distant a goal lasting peace remained.[84]

The Challenge of Groups in Africa

Across Africa, UN officials and other international actors pursued the formation of groups on the basis of a broad consensus on what best practices might look like. This was determined, on the one hand, by the political imperative of a strong African role in the pursuit of solutions to Africa's conflicts and, on the other hand, by a perennial need for resources and capacity, at times including political leverage, from outside. In most circumstances, mechanisms that might be able to combine "regional and African ownership" (as Ibrahima Fall, a Senegalese official with a long history inside the United Nations, put it of the large group of Friends established to support the International Conference on the Great Lakes) with "the partnership of the international community" were perceived to represent an optimum form of organization of interested external actors.[85] However, creating and maintaining groups of this kind was not easy. Moreover, the very nature of the United Nations' post–Cold War engagement with African conflicts—which, with a few notable exceptions, has been characterized by the relative scarcity of UN-led peacemaking but a proliferation of forms in which the organization has supported the peacemaking of others and then been asked to establish peace operations[86]—ensured that its influence on the many different structures varied widely.

The inability of a number of groups not specifically anchored to the implementation of a peace agreement to realize the hopes that were placed in them reflected not only the complexity of African conflicts themselves, but also fundamental problems underlying the engagement of neighboring countries and external actors motivated by their own interests, or lack of them, in the outcome of a given conflict. These problems were exacerbated by a tendency for states to push for inclusion in available mechanisms even under circumstances in which they had little to offer. Neighboring states might have favored stability in the country in conflict, but in the absence of stability on their terms, they opted for increased instability rather than stability on the terms of others. Under such circumstances they threatened to fulfill roles that were more akin to "spoiler" than "friend" and were hardly welcome as partners. Meanwhile, donor and other powerful states reacted with caution to the proposition of "befriending" countries headed by widely discredited leaders and in which they had no immediate security interests.

The effort to form a Committee of Friends of Somalia in early 2002 illustrated both these points. States from the region, widely considered more "enemy" than "friend" by many Somalis, pressed for inclusion, while the big powers on the Security Council, haunted by the events of the early 1990s and unsure how to engage with a country lacking a recognized government, steered well clear of any heavy lifting.[87] Under the circumstances it was unsurprising that Somalia remained Friend-less. The secretariat fell back instead on a large Contact Group that closely mirrored an earlier group of External Actors on Somalia that had met periodically in New York, even as a smaller group of donor states was, with the secretariat's encouragement, convened by Norway.[88] (The lack of impact of any of these efforts to support the Transitional Federal Government (TFG) formed in late 2004 was evident as, in the following two years, Somalia drifted steadily back toward new conflict between the TFG and its backers in Ethiopia and the Eritrea-backed Council of Somali Islamic Courts. Re-engagement of the major western powers was marked by the creation in June 2006 of a new, capital-based, International Contact Group on Somalia, largely as an expression of an abrupt shift in U.S. policy after Islamists gained control of Mogadishu from U.S.-backed and warlord-led militias. This time around, the effort to include regional actors, except in an observer capacity, was abandoned, and the outside powers provided open support to the efforts of the TFG and its backers in Ethiopia to counter the Islamist advances.[89])

In late 2002 and early 2003 the secretary-general and his senior advisers on Africa had held meetings in New York to discuss follow-up to the Africa Action Plan's endorsement of the secretary-general's proposal that international partners should join him in establishing Contact Groups and similar mechanisms to work with African countries to resolve specific conflicts.[90] The first of these was with the permanent representatives of the members of the G-8; the second was with representatives of eighteen African states who sat on the implementation committee of the New Partnership for Africa's Development (NEPAD). The secretariat had circulated in advance a background paper on "the Concept of the Group of Friends" to all participants.[91] This provided critical analysis of groups in place across Africa, but made no reference to the use of Friends outside Africa, or indeed to the recommendations on groups that had been developed in the Security Council's Ad Hoc Working Group on Conflict Prevention and Resolution in Africa earlier that year.[92] It included some recommendations for modifications that might make the African groups more effective and also proposed the creation of new mechanisms, specifically in the

Democratic Republic of the Congo (DRC), where the complexity of regional engagement and differences between the principal external actors had complicated efforts to resolve the conflict and militated against the creation of a group.

The paper and the meetings it was designed to animate represented an unusual diplomatic exercise, but not one that could be considered a success. Secretariat officials had taken on the delicate task of highlighting some of the shortfalls of the groups to states that were both members of the groups and had been, or might be, the subject of their ministrations. However, the format of the two meetings was not well suited to give-and-take: representatives of states whose own action and inaction had determined the limits of the mechanisms' utility were largely unprepared to enter into the substance of the secretariat's paper in the presence of the secretary-general. The United Kingdom was the exception in this respect. Sir Jeremy Greenstock, the British ambassador, offered several concrete suggestions, one of which, that the Troika on Angola should be reformed (a blunter reiteration of the secretariat's more tactful call for "a new Contact Group" on Angola), prompted an immediate protest from his Russian colleague. The latter insisted that Russia would prefer to keep the Troika—and thus its own privileged influence in it—in place, a position that came as no surprise to anyone.[93]

The meeting with the African ambassadors was if anything even less productive. The ambassadors appeared wary of the request for their attention to be directed toward the question of groups. They were reluctant to see an emphasis on peace and security detract from a more holistic approach to the Africa-wide initiatives represented by NEPAD and the Africa Action Plan; the secretary-general even had to remind them that the proliferation of conflict in Africa was a major impediment to development assistance. Doubts about the utility of the group initiative itself—which, as one participant in the meeting reflected, the African ambassadors "obviously hadn't been thinking about at all"—included suspicion of the capacity of the G-8 states to act in any way other than in their own narrow interests.[94]

Perhaps understandably, no further meetings were configured in this format, nor was specific follow-up to the question of groups pursued with such a broad brush. The secretary-general's push for groups had been a timely recognition of a particular approach to African peace and security that was gaining increasing currency. It also reflected both the potential and limitations of the United Nations' own role. The secretary-general and those who represented him across Africa could from "below" propose and encourage, but not necessarily deliver, the kinds of initiatives or mechanisms they believed might advance the cause of peace in Africa. In some situations the underlying conditions of the peace process and fortuitous mix of interested states and committed individuals could help them prosper, but this was by no means always the case.

The Democratic Republic of the Congo and the Emergence of CIAT

During 2002 secretariat officials had discussed at length, including with some member states, the need for a more coordinated approach to the conflict in the Congo and the advantages that some kind of group might bring to negotiations led by South Africa but conducted with significant support from the United Nations.

Ending the war in the DRC was never going to be easy. At its simplest, the conflict involved two opposing sides competing for the resources and influence offered by the boundless territory of the Congo: the government in Kinshasa, supported by Angola, Namibia, and Zimbabwe as well as various paramilitary forces on one side, and rebels (the Congolese Rally for Democracy and the Movement for the Liberation of Congo) and their backers in Rwanda and Uganda on the other. Obstacles to a coherent response by the Security Council were presented not just by the expected reluctance of the United States and other powers to be burdened by costly UN peacekeeping, but also by profound differences determined by the history and allegiances of some of the Council's permanent members. France had pushed for a broad, internationally led Great Lakes Conference to end the war. Like Belgium, the former colonial power, it was concerned about the prospect of any partition of the country and the possible spillover of the conflict to Congo-Brazzaville and Gabon (both francophone and oil-producing allies) as well as the continued exploitation of the Congo's resources by its neighbors.[95] The United States and the United Kingdom were, in contrast to France, more sympathetic to Rwanda and Uganda. Both countries were led by presidents, Paul Kagame and Yoweri Museveni, respectively, with close ties to the anglophone West and had received considerable amount of development and, in the case of Uganda in particular, military assistance.

The secretary-general had appointed Mustapha Niasse, a former minister for foreign affairs of Senegal, as his special envoy to support an Inter-Congolese Dialogue charged with negotiating a new political dispensation and national reconciliation. In the latter part of 2002 Niasse, with the support of a highly skilled former Eritrean diplomat, Haile Menkerios, worked closely with South Africa as the latter negotiated agreements between the DRC and Rwanda and Uganda, paving the way for the withdrawal of their forces from Congolese territory.[96] The agreement with Rwanda, signed in Pretoria, had created an unusual Third-Party Verification Mechanism (TPVM), comprising both the United Nations and South Africa, which was to monitor and verify its implementation. For the secretariat, the mechanism proved something of a headache and contributed to a sense that a broader group of Friends might be helpful.[97] Meanwhile, concerns that continuing mediation among the Congolese parties would certainly be required, Congolese demands for international guarantors (dismissed by one official involved in the negotiations as "absurd" in that "nobody could guarantee it except themselves"), and a perennial desire to try to improve coordination among the main external actors on Congo all bolstered arguments to create some kind of group.[98]

In the end the "global and all-inclusive" peace agreement signed in December 2002 provided a more formal mechanism than a group of Friends, the International Commission to Accompany the Transition (CIAT), that in some sense responded to all these demands (indeed, the agreement even gave the CIAT the capacity to arbitrate among the Congolese).[99] Some involved in the negotiations had hoped to restrict the membership of the CIAT to "three plus two" viewed as the essential actors on the DRC in the UN context: France, the United Kingdom, and the United States, plus Belgium and South Africa. But it rapidly grew to include the major regional and international players and organizations.[100] Convened by the special representative of the secretary-general (SRSG) and staffed by a small UN secretariat, the CIAT gradually emerged as a central actor in the political process leading up to the elections held in late 2006, undertaking mediation tasks and publishing regular communiqués that hoped to maintain pressure on the parties to abide by their commitments. Secretariat officials remained somewhat ambivalent about its efficacy, privately regretting that the United Nations had not insisted on chairing, rather than "convening," the mechanism and criticizing the extent to which its most influential members (such as South Africa and Belgium) used the CIAT to promote national interests that had long characterized their engagement in the Congo.[101] However, over time its internal differences were tempered by the urgency of trying to maintain the DRC's fragile political transition, and even the more critical officials acknowledged that things were better than if the CIAT had not been there.[102]

International Contact Groups in West Africa: Liberia and Beyond

It was perhaps unsurprising that West Africa—since the early 1990s characterized as much by the complexity of its intertwined conflicts as by the determined efforts of the subregion's leaders and organizations, especially the Economic Community of West Africa (ECOWAS), to address them— should have seen a particularly high number of Contact and other groups. These ranged from wholly informal and temporary groupings of regional leaders, who periodically came together for short-term peacemaking and preventive diplomacy, to more formal Internaitonal Contact Groups on Sierra Leone, Liberia, and Guinea-Bissau, as well as the International Working Group established to address the conflict in Côte d'Ivoire.

The Contact Group on Sierra Leone was instituted by the United Kingdom in late 1998 and was typical of the other mechanisms in its broad ambitions to mobilize and coordinate support for the country's efforts to emerge from conflict. (Less typical was a distinct and more informal Core Group the United Kingdom created in 2000 to help ensure that its strong lead in the Security Council on Sierra Leone had the support of African and other troop contributors to the United Nations' peacekeeping operation).[103] Neighboring Liberia also had two mechanisms—both Contact Groups—created at turning points in the country's history. The first came in 1996 as, after years of failed peace initiatives by the ECOWAS and general international neglect, a more consensual approach to peacemaking gradually developed. The group, which was composed of the United Nations, the United States, and other leading donor states, as well as ECOWAS and the Organisation of African Unity (OAU), met repeatedly over the following year, generally in New York, and played a helpful role in run-up to the presidential elections in July 1997. However, after the landslide victory of Charles Taylor, it faded from the scene.

Such attention as remained on Liberia turned, too precipitately, to peacebuilding. A small UN peacebuilding office (the United Nations Peacebuilding Support Office in Liberia, UNOL) promoted national reconciliation and good governance, but Taylor's government was increasingly characterized by human rights abuses, harassment of political opponents, and the destabilization of neighboring Sierra Leone through support to the rebels in the Revolutionary United Front. UNOL was identified in the country as being overly supportive of Taylor and soon lost credibility.[104] Meanwhile, a policy of isolation of Liberia pursued by the Security Council —which imposed sanctions in March 2001—was opposed by ECOWAS's belief that resolution of the region's conflicts demanded engagement with Taylor through a combination of pressure and dialogue.

In the first half of 2002, generally positive assessments of the early groups encouraged officials within the UN secretariat to raise with individual Security Council members the possibility of creating a Contact Group to address West Africa's spiraling descent into conflict. The idea received reinforcement from a Security Council workshop on the Mano River Union held in July.[105] But the International Contact Group that finally emerged in the latter part of 2002 was focused on Liberia itself. This was not least because the United States—which retained a proprietary interest in Liberia perceived in the Security Council to parallel the interests of Britain and France in their former colonies of Sierra Leone and Côte d'Ivoire—saw Taylor's Liberia as the primary source of regional instability and therefore pushed other members to tackle the "eye of the regional storm" head on.[106] The International Contact Group on Liberia (ICGL) came to be cochaired by ECOWAS (represented by Senegal at the time) and the EU and included members from inside the region and beyond (France, Morocco, Nigeria, the United Kingdom, and the United States, in addition to the African Union and the United Nations). Its mandate was deliberately vague and focused on a desire to "assist ECOWAS and the UN in promoting lasting peace in Liberia and strengthening peace in the Mano River Union."[107] However, in the following year it played an effective role in helping overcome differences of the past to project an emerging consensus on the need to engage directly with Taylor and engineer his departure from the country.

This process was facilitated by the partnership that developed between the ICGL's cochairs, Hans Dahlgren, the state secretary of Sweden, and Nana Addo Dankwa, the foreign minister of Ghana and, during 2003 and 2004, chair of ECOWAS. Dahlgren was already the EU presidency's special representative to the region and had followed West Africa since his representation of Sweden on the Security Council from 1997 to 1998. He and Nana Addo Dankwa coordinated meetings of the ICGL in advance and conducted missions together in the region on several occasions.[108] Among these was a visit to Taylor himself in the spring of 2003 as the conflict escalated, in which they impressed upon him that the country was in no condition to undertake elections and that his own options were dwindling.[109] All parties eventually agreed to enter into talks in Accra, Ghana, under the facilitation of General Abdusalami Abubakar, the former Nigerian head of state. These began in early June and continued under intense international pressure until the signing of a Comprehensive Peace

Agreement in August and Taylor's departure from the country. The following month the Security Council authorized the UN Mission in Liberia (UNMIL), actively backed by the United States, to take over from the ECOWAS force that had been deployed in the country at the height of the crisis.[110]

The ICGL had been assigned specific tasks in the peace agreement, including membership of an Implementation Monitoring Committee established under ECOWAS's lead.[111] As UNMIL got under way, representatives of the ICGL established themselves as a group that met on a regular basis in Monrovia (indeed, more regularly than the monitoring committee itself). Although not directly affiliated with the periodic meetings of its capital-based representatives, this constituted a useful forum for coordinating international positions on the evolving priorities of the peace process. Meanwhile, the EU and the United Nations sought, once more, to push the capital-level ICGL to broaden its attention outward to the region so as to be able to address the increasingly precarious situation in Guinea. Hesitation within ECOWAS and the bitter opposition of Guinea meant that this shift was a drawn-out process. However, from March 2005 on, the group met as the International Contact Group on the Mano River Basin (ICGMRB), with its utility as an informal forum in which to promote coordination among the region's principal actors intact.[112]

Beyond the Mano River basin, West African and international actors had in the meantime become increasingly concerned by the unexpected descent of Côte d'Ivoire—long a bastion of political and economic stability within the region—into conflict in late 2002 after a failed attempt to oust President Laurent Ggagbo. The rebellion that followed divided the country in two, and neither the deployment of French and then UN peacekeepers nor a series of peace agreements brokered by France and South Africa were able to make headway toward credible national elections. Increasing engagement by ECOWAS and then the African Union led to their development of a political roadmap and both an International Working Group (IWG), composed of the principal regional and international actors engaged on Côte d'Ivoire, and a smaller Mediation Group, to help shepherd it forward. The former, which was cochaired by the African Union and the UN SRSG—the Swedish diplomat Pierre Schori—met in Abidjan on a monthly basis at a ministerial level and was in itself a significant expression of international determination to move the country's political process out of the stalemate into which it appeared to have sunk.[113]

The latter part of 2006 saw the creation of yet another mechanism to help focus attention on a persistently fragile state. The International

Contact Group on Guinea-Bissau, which met for the first time in September 2006, followed two distinct mechanisms in New York—the Friends of Guinea-Bissau and a more effective Ad Hoc Advisory Group on Guinea-Bissau in the Economic and Social Council (ECOSOC)—that had since 1999 and 2002 addressed the country within the framework of the United Nations. Their efforts had been hindered by the low strategic priority afforded Guinea-Bissau by the major powers even as the country's inability to secure sufficient financing to maintain the basic structures of the state became a growing worry to other states in the region. Accordingly, ECOWAS executive secretary Mohamed Ibn Chambas pushed for the creation of a group that would meet at capital level and combine Guinea-Bissau's principal external actors—Portugal, France and the members of the Community of Portuguese-Speaking Countries (CPLP)—with its most significant regional interlocutors, Gambia, Guinea, Senegal and ECOWAS itself.[114]

Engaging from Outside: Sudan and the Troika

By the early 2000s, conflict had raged in southern Sudan for all but eleven years since the country's independence in 1956. In the course of it both the government and the Sudanese People's Liberation Movement/Army (SPLM/A) had benefited from shifting alliances with armed ethnic militias and regional states deeply divided over the fundamental issues of religion and the self-determination of the south, as well as resources such as water, oil, and land.[115] Progress toward peace had been thwarted by the complex relationship that these alliances bore to competing regional peace initiatives: a process led by Kenya on behalf of the Intergovernmental Authority on Development (IGAD), also involving Ethiopia, Eritrea, and Uganda—all countries that had at different times provided political and military support to the SPLM/A in the south—and a joint initiative of Egypt and Libya that reflected their long-standing interest in the unity of the Sudanese state.

The government's fear of the Security Council as a tool of U.S. policy had led Sudan to reject a formal role for the United Nations in any peace process. However, from the late 1990s, humanitarian officials and other members of the international community sustained regular contacts with the conflict parties in order to implement Operation Lifeline Sudan, an extensive relief operation in southern Sudan.[116] Meanwhile, from 1998 on Kieran Prendergast took a number of steps to engage the United Nations in the political process in a quiet way. These included not only visits to the region and meetings of a cumbersome donor structure, the IGAD Partners Forum (IPF) established in 1997 to support the peace effort,[117] by either himself or the secretary-general's adviser Mohamed Sahnoun, an Algerian diplomat with a long trajectory in the region, but also discreet consultations in New York. He met regularly with Sudan's permanent representative, Elfatih Muhamed Erwa, and convened roundtable discussions with international experts to assess the prospects for peace in Sudan and a possible UN role in it. He also maintained frequent communication with Hilde Johnson, the Norwegian minister for development, whose commitment to the region underpinned Norway's active role in the process. In all these meetings, he stressed the importance of unified support for the peace process and, as time went by, encouraged that support to be put behind Lazaro Sumbeiywo, a Kenyan general he had known and respected since the early 1990s, designated the chief mediator in the talks by President Daniel arap Moi.[118]

Alan Goulty, the British special representative for the Sudan, recalled in an interview in late 2003 that the Troika—a group he described as a "behind the scenes ginger group, not formal 'Friends of'"—began to evolve in late 1999.[119] It was a product both of frustration at the lack of action in the IPF and the lengthy personal involvement of a number of individuals, including Goulty himself, with Sudan.[120] With the United Nations unable to take an active political role, representatives of Norway, the United Kingdom, and the United States increasingly began to work together. A significant development was the change in the U.S. administration in early 2000. The Clinton administration's punitive policy toward Khartoum had won friends in the south, but failed to make headway either in ending the war or influencing the conduct of the government for the better.[121] A number of factors combined to induce more direct engagement from the Bush administration. Most obvious of these was congressional pressure on issues such as slavery and the forcible imposition of Sharia law, as well as a growing conviction that U.S. interests would be served by engaging more directly with a vast country that straddled a fault line between Africa and the Middle East, had a history of promoting Islamic fundamentalism and supporting terrorists—including Osama bin Laden—and was mired in a conflict that was increasingly shaped by the country's growing production of oil. These issues would become all the more urgent after the attacks of September 2001, when the Sudanese government offered collaboration in the war on terrorism and sought to downplay its avowedly Islamic identity.

The Troika endeavored to support Sumbeiywo and to keep other potential mediators at bay. These tasks became gradually easier after agreement on the Machakos Protocol was reached in July 2002, foreseeing acceptance of a secular Sudan and the right of self-determination in return for a commitment from the Sudan People's Liberation Army (SPLA) to work toward the unity of Sudan as "the priority of the parties."[122] Together the Troika states brought expertise and resources and collectively, as one U.S. diplomat put it, "a sense of urgency and purpose that the parties did not have."[123] They were not without their differences—the United States was more overtly favorable to the south, the United Kingdom to the government, and Norway somewhere in between. But in many respects these differences also constituted strengths, facilitating an effective division of labor within the Troika and between it and other actors such as Switzerland, which participated in mediating an agreement on the Nuba Mountains. The United States brought unrivaled, if not always welcome, diplomatic pressure to bear on all parties.[124] As the former colonial power, the United Kingdom had a deep understanding of the north and a profound sense of responsibility shaped by the tragic contours of Sudan's postindependence history. Meanwhile, the Norwegians had been extensively involved in humanitarian assistance, particularly to the south. Indeed, Halvor Aschjem, Norway's special envoy, was a veteran of Norwegian Church Aid and had known many of the senior Sudanese involved in the negotiations since they were young men.[125]

Negotiations moved forward in Naivasha, Kenya, and the United Nations' involvement increased. Sahnoun and secretariat officials joined the AU, Italy, and the Troika as formal "observers" of the process and maintained regular contact with the Troika in New York.[126] As the likely outline of an agreement took shape, advice to Sumbeiywo and his team on technical issues gradually shifted into more active planning for a peacekeeping operation. In the meantime, however, the prospect of a deal for the south that would address its economic and political marginalization, but ignore similar structural problems in the rest of the country, had helped foment a quite separate crisis in Darfur, in western Sudan, where open warfare erupted in early 2003. Government-backed militias responded to rebel actions by aggressively targeting civilians. Intense international interest in making the southern process work contributed to masking the extent of the displacement, killings, rape, and looting that ensued. And when the world did wake up to the gravity of a situation that the United States recognized as genocide, the response of the Security Council was to prioritize the lead of the AU and otherwise vacillate between heated rhetoric and painstakingly slow and inadequate action. Progress on Darfur stalled, and it became increasingly clear that securing agreement on the south would be essential for peace in the country as a whole. Intense international pressure was brought to bear, and the (misnamed) Comprehensive Peace Agreement (CPA) was finally signed in early 2005.

The CPA was rightly welcomed as a "triumph for international mediation" in recognition of the effective combination of regional leadership and international heavy lifting that the engagement of the Troika had facilitated.[127] Sadly, however, the first two years of the CPA's implementation were to demonstrate how difficult similar commitment and coherence would be to maintain during the six-year transition that lay ahead. The United Nations Mission in Sudan (UNMIS) was established in March 2005 under the leadership of SRSG Jan Pronk, a former minister of development of the Netherlands with extensive experience of the Sudan. But although UNMIS was invested with a broad sweep of responsibilities, it had no direct role in the coordination of other external actors.[128] This suffered from the political and financial distraction represented by the ongoing crisis in Darfur, the untimely death of the SPLA's leader, John Garang, whose diplomatic skills and contacts had helped galvanize the international community during the long years of war and peacemaking, and an unfortunate degree of competition and even infighting among the various actors involved, who were perceived to share neither the same priorities for Sudan's future nor a common approach for achieving their goals.[129] Donors met and coordinated at senior levels—including in annual meetings of the Sudan Consortium for broad discussion of strategic priorities—and, in Sudan, both a Cease-fire Political Commission and an Assessment and Evaluation Commission (the latter chaired by Norway) met to monitor the peace process. But the limitations of these processes led in December 2005 to the formation of a new Contact Group at the initiative of the United Kingdom. This comprised Canada, France, the Netherlands, Norway, the United States, the African Union, European Union, and United Nations, in addition to the United Kingdom, and met periodically at the capital level, in Khartoum and also in New York.[130]

The efficacy of international support to the negotiations on southern Sudan would stand in marked contrast to the incoherence of the effort in Darfur. Indeed, many of those involved in the African Union–led negotiations that took place in Abuja, Nigeria, and led to the signing of the Darfur Peace Agreement (DPA) on May 5, 2006, would come to see the peacemaking effort as "a case study in how not to do it."[131] In addition to the African Union team, the negotiations were variously attended by representatives of the United Nations and European Union, Nigeria, Chad, Libya, and Eritrea (the latter three with pronounced interests of their own at stake) and a changing cast of representatives of individual states (among them the United States, the United Kingdom, Canada, France, the Netherlands, and Norway) that varied in number and level over the course of the negotiations. Competing levels of interest and commitment ensured that the conflict parties received a variety of messages from these disparate "partners" that directly encouraged their intransigence.[132]

Problems in the mediation were rooted in a lack of willingness amongst the parties to engage in substantive negotiations and a marked disparity—in negotiating capacity as much as military force—between the government of Sudan and the increasingly fragmented Darfurian rebels. But they were also exacerbated by the confusion of the international support the process received; the inability of the African Union's chief mediator, Dr. Salim Ahmed Salim, to impose any discipline upon it; and the increasingly muscular use of "deadline diplomacy" by the United States and United Kingdom in particular to force through an agreement—in the end only signed by two out of four of the parties it was intended for—that was doomed from the start. The imperfect conclusion of the DPA contributed to the escalation of violence and precipitated a lengthy struggle by the international community to force the government in Khartoum to accept UN peacekeepers in Darfur—itself something of a distraction from the need to "fix the politics first" if the peacekeeping was to follow.[133]

Conclusions

By the 2000s the ubiquity of a group response to peacemaking marked the distance traveled since the emergence of Friends in the immediate aftermath of the Cold War. Groups were formed to marshal international attention and resources, encourage the exchange of information, and further coordinate fragmented international efforts toward peace. However, the paths traced in this chapter demonstrate how far from a guarantee of success the decision to form a group might be, and how dim the prospects may be for groups formed, as one secretariat official put it, by "desperate officials who had run out of better ideas."[135] And indeed, when operational support of a complex and evolving peacemaking effort was required, mediators sometimes found a more informal and flexible form of interaction with their partners more productive than the public constitution of a group, which could be fraught with problems regarding its composition and management.

Regardless of whether their creation responded to an initiative by the United Nations, the groups collectively underlined the importance of the regional environment to the efficacy of the peacemaking of which they formed a part. But they also demonstrated the obstacles encountered by mediators wishing to persuade determined regional actors to abandon positions rooted in their perceived national interests. The limitations of the informal consultation mechanism on Myanmar, "six plus two" in Afghanistan, and difficulties in pursuing coherent efforts toward peace in diverse African contexts all illustrated that groups involving regional actors were, in and of themselves, ineffective as tools for peacemaking until—as was seen in Afghanistan, Liberia, and Sudan—other developments conspired to convince them that an end to the conflict in their neighborhood was to their benefit. Meanwhile, as the conflict in Colombia demonstrated, the significance of regional support dwindles notably when the nonstate actors have access to resources sufficient to render them self-sufficient.

Most of the groups in this chapter were conceived primarily as instruments to foster international coherence, rather than support an ongoing mediation, and thus engage directly with conflict parties. The exceptions include the anomalous case of Cyprus—where the pressures were other than armed conflict and the United Nations' primary interlocutors from both parties were experienced lawyers sustained by complex ties to their domestic and international constituencies—but also Colombia and Sudan. In Colombia the creation of Friends represented a bold attempt to engage directly with parties that had little concept of what a serious negotiation would entail, and in the case of the guerrillas, little intention of moving beyond the behavior and practices that prioritized their own survival. Despite the best efforts of the individuals involved, as a pedagogical exercise they largely failed. Many of their states were poorly prepared to engage with nonstate armed actors, while those that persisted beyond the Pastrana years found they had little traction on well-resourced guerrillas and a popular government under no obvious pressure to make concessions. The situation was quite different in southern Sudan, where many years of conflict had brought both sides to see that a military solution was beyond their reach. Members of the Troika and others on IGAD's negotiating team knew representatives of both parties well. Indeed, the long engagement of the SPLM/A with the outside world greatly facilitated its realization that the international community could be helpful and the leverage consequently available to the Troika and others.

The "variable geometry" of this chapter's title is most readily illustrated by the groups' composition. All the groups struggled with the tension between the efficacy of a small group and the legitimacy represented by more inclusive structures. A lack of attention to gatekeeping, closely related to a lack of clarity in overall strategy, allowed states to press for inclusion in mechanisms on Angola, Myanmar, Colombia, and the DRC. States clamoring to get in included both those from the immediate neighborhood—sometimes motivated by interests not consistent with a peaceable solution—and more distant actors that found it difficult to resist the lure of involvement that the formation of a group represented. Collectively, the groups highlighted the risks inherent in a process of "self-selection" and reinforced the need for a guiding hand or hands in their creation. In other circumstances secretariat officials structured the composition of groups to operate at distinct levels and with distinct ends in mind. The purposes of the "six plus two" and Vendrell's "luncheon group" in Afghanistan, for example, determined their composition: one met internationally, sometimes at the highest level, and tried in vain to foster regional cooperation, while the other, much more modest, endeavor met for the most part as an informal group of Western ambassadors in Islamabad. Cyprus, meanwhile, saw a concerted strategy to maximize the potential of the external forces at play. In this instance, the formation of a group was deliberately avoided, in part to facilitate the direct operational engagement of those Friends with most to offer the UN effort.

Experience in Liberia and Sudan demonstrated no less clearly that it is the presence or absence of leadership by someone or indeed something (not necessarily the United Nations), as well as the capacity of those exercising it, that will determine the utility of a collective effort rather than the precise role of the United Nations. Discreet encouragement on the part of secretariat officials, as well as their partners in concerned member states, had some success in encouraging the formation of the International Contact Group on Liberia. But its efficacy as an actor in the evolving Liberian process was attributable to capable leadership from its cochairs in the EU and ECOWAS. The leadership of the Kenyan mediator, General Sumbeiywo, and the role played by the Troika in ensuring that international efforts reinforced rather than undermined him were no less significant in the case of southern Sudan. As an emerging structure of support the Troika was welcomed by the United Nations from outside and indeed facilitated the United Nations' own growing role in the process. It would stand in stark contrast to the disorder that characterized the negotiations in Darfur, where the role of the AU was complicated by the presence of numerous other actors, little clarity with respect to the roles they were expected to assume, and a tendency for the Darfurian rebels to play one against the other.

The groups discussed in this chapter were formed at different phases of the process and were sustained over widely varying lengths of time. In

Afghanistan an attempt to forge an international framework conducive to a genuine peace effort altered neither the regional dynamics of the conflict nor the broader indifference of the international community. The Friends in Colombia was formed to support a publicly heralded peace process that never advanced beyond prenegotiation and was undone by the lack of will to advance to substantive talks. Experience in Cyprus and across Africa demonstrated the importance of timing. Collaboration with Friends or a different group structure worked best when other factors, internal and external to the conflict, created conditions that allowed a real job to be done. When the task at hand was clear—be it a need to address the situation in Liberia as a cause of regional destabilization, to support a peace process in Sudan that showed potential for progress, or to sustain support of a pacted transition in the DRC—a group was able to harness the otherwise varying interests of external actors to support a course of action on which they could collectively agree. But without an identifiable process to support, or with fundamental differences in a group's members, the utility of even the best-intentioned effort is necessarily constrained.

9

Conclusions

The mechanism of Friends of the Secretary-General, first seen in the negotiations on El Salvador, was particular in its conceptual design, in its purpose, and in the unwritten rules that established a disciplined support of a peace process led by the United Nations. In the fifteen years following its creation, an explosion of groups to support peacemaking, peacekeeping, and peacebuilding activities took place, mirroring the extraordinary upsurge in a range of efforts to address global security in the period between the end of the Cold War and the mid-2000s. Comparative analysis of these groups is complicated by the great diversity they represent: groups were small and large; formed by the secretary-general and by member states; operationally engaged at the heart of a peace process, or little more than talking shops for the exchange of information. They met in New York or in flexible combinations of New York, the field, and the Friends' national capitals; they provided coherent support to clearly structured processes led by the United Nations, fractured under the pressure of their own divergent interests, or muddled along somewhere in between.

The circumstances in which a small group of states analogous to the original Friends of the Secretary-General will be formed may be unlikely to repeat themselves, but informal groups of states show no signs of disappearing. Indeed, between 2003 and 2006 the possibility of forming groups of Friends to address widely varying situations in Guinea, Ethiopia-Eritrea, Myanmar, Nepal, and Darfur were all at one time or another under discussion in the UN secretariat. Friends of Guinea were considered a means of engaging international actors with a country that many saw as presenting a high risk of conflict; UN envoys to Myanmar and Ethiopia and Eritrea briefly considered forming Friends to facilitate movement in processes that otherwise offered little hope. National diplomats and nongovernmental advocates began to consider the utility of a Contact Group on Nepal, while secretariat officials had struggled to think of a means by which some configuration of Friends might bring greater coherence to the various "partners" closely following talks on Darfur led by the African Union (AU).[1] By the end of 2006, none of these mechanisms had transpired, but their very suggestion indicated the extent to which consideration of groups had become a routine occurrence. Meanwhile, groups to support implementation, particularly in Africa, continued to gain currency, even as the creation of the Peacebuilding Commission promised country groups of a different kind and UN actors gradually engaged with groups formed outside the United Nations, such as a Core Group on Northern Uganda.[2]

This book set out to explore how and in what circumstances the United Nations can work productively with groups of states in resolving conflict. In order to do so, it has considered the benefits and drawbacks that groups of Friends have brought to peacemaking in cases in which they have been ostensibly established to provide support to a UN-led effort. Case studies of groups of Friends engaged in El Salvador, Guatemala, Haiti, Georgia, Western Sahara, and East Timor, as well as the wider variety of groups discussed in chapter 8, present a mixed picture. As an auxiliary device for peacemaking, Friends cannot on their own create the conditions for peace. But they can contribute to their emergence—even help "ripen" a process, as was the case in Guatemala and southern Sudan—in a variety of ways: they bring leverage to the secretary-general or other lead mediator in his or her relationship to the parties, helping cajole, persuade, pressure, and even fund conflict parties who may be edging toward peace; they can level the playing field between the parties or act as a cushion between them and the mediator; and they provide a channel for the engagement of external actors in the conflict that may help coordinate their efforts and lessen the risk of rival mediations developing. The sustained interest and financial support that Friends may offer constitute important informal guarantees of the vigilance of the international community over a fragile peace.

But a number of the cases addressed in this book demonstrate that these benefits do not inevitably accrue from the involvement of Friends. Largely positive experiences with Friends in El Salvador, during the peacemaking phase in Guatemala, and with the Core Group in East Timor were not without moments in which the unity of the effort was threatened. Friends provided strong support to the secretary-general's efforts on Cyprus, facilitated by the absence of a group structure, but were unable to help overcome the obstacles the negotiations encountered. Elsewhere, the path taken by Friends revealed a tension between a procedural utility and problems that limited an effective contribution to conflict resolution. Most of these were attributable to a lack of compatibility between the interests of the states concerned and the overall demands of the process. The Friends in Haiti drove a UN engagement that was shaped by the domestic needs of the United States as the highest priority. Russia's role in Abkhazia or France's unwavering support of Morocco on Western Sahara were significant factors in the intractability of these two conflicts. Friends in Colombia were formed to help accompany parties embarked on an uncertain peace process, but they ended up adding little to it. Friends and other groups initiated across Africa ran into a range of problems, in some cases because of a lack of clarity in their purposes, but also as a consequence of the aspirations of neighbors and the uneven interests and engagement of outside powers.

The principal explanation of this mixed record is that ending civil wars is difficult and can be attempted only with the greatest humility. Despite the extensive literature on the subject, there is much that is not known about why, as Elisabeth Jean Wood puts it, "some enduring civil conflicts [are] resolved with essentially self-enforcing agreements . . . while others seem unamenable to negotiated resolution even with extensive third party intervention."[3] Obstacles are presented by factors intrinsic to the conflicts themselves—ethnic and other identity grievances, ideological differences, economic gain, multiple conflict parties, weak institutional capacity, regional interference, and the presence of lucrative criminal networks—but also from outside. Third parties have struggled to counter the complexity of the conflicts they seek to end with structures sophisticated enough to maximize their own potential. But they are rarely disinterested actors, and their own ambitions, capacities, and institutional cultures frequently collide.

The circumstances under which Friends may be constituted suggests that whether a group will or will not be present relates not so much to the internal characteristics of the conflict as to external actors' interests and the agency of a few key individuals. Indeed, a propensity to create or join more Friends by those with experience of the mechanism has undoubtedly had an effect on their occurrence. How effectively a group of Friends will then perform will depend on multiple factors. Among the most fundamental factors are, perhaps, to what extent individual state interests will allow Friends to be like-minded in their pursuit of the conflict's settlement and in support of an accepted lead of the peacemaking effort, and whether the timing in each case positions Friends to help maximize potential in a peace process. Mechanisms with distinct characteristics engaged in El Salvador, Guatemala, Tajikistan, East Timor, and southern Sudan had in common a shared commitment to the successful outcome of processes that gradually matured to allow for the negotiation of core grievances. Friends in Georgia and Western Sahara, on the other hand, replicated to a differing extent the "winner-take-all" positions assumed by the parties and prioritized other issues rather than made an effort to move beyond them.

Conditions for Success

Comparative analysis of Friends' groups, as was noted at the outset of this study, is complicated by the self-selecting basis on which they have occurred, their extraordinary diversity, and the difficulty of establishing a clear relationship between the performance of a group of Friends and the outcome of a peace process. However, consideration of the five core factors or variables upon which the case studies have concentrated —*the regional environment* within which the conflict takes place; the *conflict parties'* demands, practices, and interaction with the United Nations; a group's *composition* and the resources it may bring with it; questions of *leadership*; and *timing* or *the phase of the process* in which the Friends are engaged—provides the basis for broad conclusions regarding conditions under which groups of Friends might be helpfully involved, and recommendations derived from them.

Table 1 summarizes the variables in the six core cases. It indicates whether the regional environment in which a group was established was supportive, and whether the conflict parties sought the engagement of the Friends. The composition of a group is described in terms of its size (core members; the number before the colon in the table), the numbers of Friends from the region, and the number that were permanent members of the Security Council (SC). The leading actor(s) within the group's engagement and phase of the process with which it was involved—peacemaking (Pm on table), peacekeeping (Pk), and/or peacebuilding (Pb)—are also indicated, as is whether the group contributed to a "desired outcome" within the time frame under review. This goal stands in contrast to the criteria for success adopted by Downs and Stedman and cited in the introduction—stopping large-scale violence in the short term and ending the war on a self-sustaining basis—and reflects the broad universe of cases and varied phases of an individual process in which groups of Friends have been involved. Under the different circumstances addressed by the case studies, such an outcome included negotiation and/or implementation of a peace agreement, self-determination, or the restoration and consolidation of democracy (as in Haiti).

The table should be read with an obvious caveat regarding questions of causality. It also has limitations regarding information that it cannot convey. Not reflected in it are, for example, the vicissitudes of the long and complex history of some of the groups or, more fundamental, issues relating

Table 1: Variables and the Core Case Studies

Case Studies	Group	Supportive Region	Engaged Parties	Size/ Composition	Lead	Phase	Desired Outcome
El Salvador	Friends of the Secretary-General	X	X	4: 3 regional	UN	Pm/Pb	X
Guatemala	Friends of the Guatemalan Peace Process	X	X	6: 3 regional, 1 SC	UN	Pm/Pb	X
Haiti	Friends of the Secretary-General	X	Mixed	4: 1 regional, 2 SC	UN/U.S.	Pm/Pb	0
Georgia/ Abkhazia	Friends of the Secretary-General	0	Mixed	5: 1 regional, 4 SC	UN/Russia	Pm/Pk	0
Western Sahara	Friends of Western Sahara	0	X	5: 0 regional, 4 SC	UN/states	Pm/Pk	0
East Timor	Core Group	X	Mixed	5: 3 regional, 2 SC	UN	Pm/Pb	X

to the diplomatic agency of the individuals involved, the specific interests of Friends in a given conflict, or the extent to which Friends were able to serve a useful purpose as an instrument of process even in cases in which conditions on the ground remained inauspicious. However, it shows some broad conclusions on which to base further analysis.

The correlation suggested between desired outcomes in El Salvador, Guatemala, and East Timor and their supportive regional environment is a clear one. Other conditions for success that the three cases point toward include parties that (with the exception of Indonesia) engaged directly with the Friends, the small size common to all six groups, a strong representation of regional actors within their membership, and clarity in leadership of the effort by the UN secretary-general. Conversely, the two groups that made the least headway toward their stated goals (Georgia and Western Sahara) are distinguished by the hostile regional environment, preponderance of permanent members of the Security Council among their numbers, poor representation of regional actors (related, of course, to the regional environment), and a leadership of the effort that was, while nominally under the secretary-general, in practice disputed by the strongly held positions of states among the Friends.

Table 2 attempts a similar exercise for other groups formed to support peacemaking considered in this study, largely but not exclusively in chapter 8 (as a mechanism primarily created to support implementation, the International Commisson to Accompany the Transition [CIAT] in the Democratic Republic of the Congo [DRC] is not included, while the Friends of Tajikistan, briefly considered in chapter 5, are).

With the exception of the anomalous case of Angola, where the desired outcome (settlement of the conflict) could be directly attributable to the death of Jonas Savimbi, positive outcomes, in the short term at least, were achieved only in Liberia, southern Sudan, and Tajikistan. These were all situations in which, with the ripeness of time, the peacemaking effort and the various mechanisms employed to reinforce it came to count on a supportive regional environment and the direct involvement of regional actors in either mediation or a group mechanism to support it. (At the time of writing it is too soon to judge whether the conflict in southern Sudan has ended on a self-sustaining basis, but the Troika did help reach the peace agreement at Naivasha.) In the very different contexts of southern Sudan and Tajikistan, conflict parties engaged directly with members of the Friends and Troika from whom they could evidently wrest advantage. The lack of this engagement in the case of Liberia, in contrast, reflects a mechanism—the International Contact Group on Liberia (ICGL)—that

Table 2: Other Cases

Case Studies	Group	Supportive Region	Engaged Parties	Size/ Composition	Lead	Phase	Desired Outcome
Afghanistan	Six plus Two	O	O	8: 6 regional, 2 SC	UN	Pm	O
Angola	Friends of Angola, Core Group	Mixed	Mixed	Approx. 20, Core Group: 11: 4 SC, 3 regional	UN	Pm	X
Cyprus	Informal Friends	Mixed	Mixed	2 plus: 2 SC plus	UN	Pm/Pk	O
Colombia	Various Friends	O	Mixed	National Liberation Army (ELN): 5:1 SC, 1 regional Revolutionary Armed Forces of Colombia (FARC): 10: 1 SC, 3 regional	O	Pm	O
Liberia	International Contact Group on Liberia (ICGL)	X	O	5: 3 SC, 2 reg, AU, EU, UN, Economic Community of West African States (ECOWAS)	ECOWAS/ EU	Pm/Pb	X
Myanmar	Informal Consultation Group	O	O	Up to 20: SC, reg, donors	UN	Pm	O
Southern Sudan	Troika	X	X	3: 2 SC	Intergovernmental Authority on Development (IGAD)	Pm/Pb	X
Tajikistan	Friends of Tajikistan	X	X	13: 10 regional, 2 SC	UN/Russia	Pm	X

had the ousting of Charles Taylor, one of the conflict parties, from Liberia's presidency clearly in mind as an essential step to be taken toward peace in Liberia and security in the wider region.

But beyond the similarity in these results, table 2 highlights the differ-ences between the mechanisms it considers and those examined in the earlier case studies, most notably regarding the size of the groups and the greater variety they represent with respect to affiliation with the conflict parties and with the United Nations. These factors both complicate com-parison between them and highlight the importance of a variable approach to peacemaking by the United Nations. The following sections conse-quently outline conclusions derived from the somewhat limited universe of the selected cases in table 1, supplemented where appropriate by insights drawn from experience of the more diverse mechanisms of table 2.

Region and Regional Environment

Finding: The external context of which any group of Friends will form a part will be central to its efficacy, with a supportive regional environ-ment more important a factor than either the region where the process is located or the kind of conflict to be addressed. Regionally entwined con-flicts or conflicts that take place under the shadow of neighbors with strong interests in their outcome may not be well suited to the formation of a closed group of Friends, as the question of what to do about the neighbors will consistently arise.

The formation of the Friends of the Secretary-General in El Salvador was directly related to the regional peace efforts that had preceded the United Nations' engagement. The group proved an effective means by which the commitment by Mexico, Colombia, and Venezuela to resolve the conflicts in Central America could be channeled into support for a UN-led peace process. Its success, as well as the very visible role of Venezuela in the Friends of Haiti in the early 1990s, held great importance for Latin Amer-ican diplomacy. It enhanced confidence in regional responsibility for peace and security and regional action to preserve it, contributed directly to the creation of the Friends of the Guatemalan Peace Process, and encouraged participation in the less successful Friend efforts seen in Colombia and Venezuela in the early 2000s, as well as the leading role taken by Latin American states when the United Nations returned to Haiti in 2004.

But the potential utility of a group relates more specifically to the regional environment than it does to the region itself. From tiny East Timor, with a "solution" to its conflict eventually determined by the results of its popular consultation, to Sudan, which reached agreements in the south only after many years of diplomatic travails, many of them directly attributable to divisions within the region, support from the region has been an essential prerequisite for resolving internal conflicts. In its absence, and particularly when regional actors have been actively engaged in fueling a conflict, as in Afghanistan or the DRC, peacemaking stands little hope. Indeed, across Africa the regionally entwined nature of its conflicts and the resulting deep suspicion of the neighbors has been one of the factors impeding both peacemaking and the creation of groups of Friends similar to those seen elsewhere. In Asia, the United Nations' low level of engagement in peacemaking contributed directly to the paucity of group mechanisms with which it was involved. But in circumstances in which a group was formed, in Myanmar for example, efforts to achieve a coherent international approach were jeopardized by resistance in the region to the idea of external intervention, as well as by trade and other issues that were bigger priorities for neighboring large states.

A different set of conditions is encountered in efforts to end conflicts in the shadow of a regional power. This power is likely to play a central role in solving any conflict in its orbit, even in those cases in which the conflict itself is largely internal (as was demonstrated, for example, by the positive role played by India in moving the various parties in Nepal towards the agreement signed in November 2006). The presence of this power—the United States in Latin America and the Caribbean, Russia in Georgia and Tajikistan—in a group of Friends will have an overriding influence on what that group may be able to achieve. Its involvement may be benign, like the United States during implementation of the agreements in El Salvador and throughout the peace process in Guatemala, and Russia in Tajikistan, or more complex, as the varied history of the United States in Haiti, or the more aggressively ambiguous role played by Russia in the Georgian-Abkhaz peace process, demonstrated. In all cases the powers concerned derived considerable benefits from their participation in a multilateral process under the lead of the United Nations. But this was not least because progress, or not, toward a lasting settlement was determined by their own interests.

The cases suggest that whether Friends offer a suitable means through which to engage a regional power will vary. The United States was too close to being a party to the conflict to be engaged in the Salvadoran Friends at the outset of the process, but for different reasons found it preferable to work in groups of Friends in both Haiti and Guatemala, sharing the burden of the resulting interventions with other members of the United Nations. Peace processes that take place in the shadow of powers such as Indonesia or India, on the other hand, contend with a traditional caution against international intervention in their affairs, particularly by the United Nations. This caution was one of the factors that explained Indonesia's acceptance of first, the Centre for Humanitarian Dialogue, and second, the former president of Finland, Martti Ahtisaari, as a mediator in Aceh; or India's readiness to work with Norway as a facilitator in Sri Lanka. In that instance Norway consciously decided against forming a group of Friends, considering that its delicate but all-important relationship with India would be best served by prioritizing bilateral contacts while involving other major external actors as "cochairs" of a Sri Lankan donor group.[4]

Conflict Parties

> Finding: Groups of Friends that seek to engage with conflict parties to support peacemaking can be distinguished from mechanisms primarily formed as a means to encourage coherence among international actors. Friends, as representatives of states, engage with a natural pro-state bias that complicates interaction with nonstate armed actors. The circumstances under which this may be overcome are not determined by the conflict's typology—whether it is, for example, over territory or ideology —but by the practices and strategies pursued by the conflict parties, as well as Friends' broader interests in the conflict arena.

The initial impetus to form a group of Friends came from an insurgent organization, the Farabundo Martí National Liberation Front (FMLN), in El Salvador. The FMLN's lead negotiators were wary of the influence of the United States in the Security Council and sought a means by which to counter it. In this they had common cause with the UN secretary-general, whose own capacity for independent action in the backyard of the United States was limited by the Cold War politics of the Security Council. The Friends were able to overcome the initial reluctance of the Salvadoran government and, in addition to the leverage they lent to the secretary-general, came to fill a helpful role as a "cushion" between the various actors involved in the negotiations.

The doubts of the Salvadoran government reflected a widespread structural problem. A state in conflict, under threat from one or more insurgencies or secessionist movements, is likely to see itself as an upstanding member of the United Nations, besieged by actors it holds as delinquent, criminal, or terrorist. This fact in itself will, in most circumstances, complicate the engagement of a group of Friends in support of a peace process. A government may grudgingly come to accept the need for the secretary-general to exercise impartiality between the conflict parties. But the implicit recognition of the legitimacy of nonstate actors by states that the government may automatically expect to be *its* Friends may be still more problematic. The president of Guatemala originally sought Friends for himself, only to have the Friends themselves insist on a more balanced involvement. Officials in Tbilisi welcomed the involvement of Western Friends whose clear rejection of the aspirations of Abkhazia's secessionist forces undermined any prospect of impartiality. In the absence of a third-party mediator, the Colombian government never ceased to see the ambassadors involved in the Friends mechanism as agents of its own interests.

The particular dilemma of Friends relates to the broader challenge presented by the asymmetries of peacemaking in an international system that is overwhelming state-centric. As Liz Philipson has suggested, "systemic state bias" manifests itself in different ways in conflict resolution.[5] In addition to legitimacy, state actors tend to have more familiarity with diplomatic norms and the rules of the system, and inevitably have greater access to the United Nations than do their nonstate counterparts. They also will view the specific dynamics of a conflict in the context of their own relationship with other states. As the histories of East Timor before 1999 and Western Sahara illustrated, international acceptance of the rightness of the cause and internationally palatable or even sympathetic nonstate actors counted for little in the face of the realpolitik with which the major powers maintained their relationships with Indonesia and Morocco. Moreover, in the changed international environment following the attacks of September 11, 2001, an increased propensity to label—or threaten to label—nonstate armed actors as "terrorist" exacerbated existing asymmetries and, in many cases, complicated or inhibited engagement by state actors.[6] In this respect it is not coincidental that the two states in continental Europe that have played the most prominent roles in conflict resolution—Norway and Switzerland—are not members of the EU, and therefore have been able to operate outside boundaries set by EU positions on terrorists and terrorism when they felt it necessary.

Successful examples of the engagement of Friends, whether in Central America, East Timor, or southern Sudan, have all involved well-established nonstate armed actors with effective leadership, control of territory, or a defined political agenda. They are also consistent in the extent to which underlying characteristics of the conflict or strategies adopted by the nonstate actors contributed to counter any inherent bias against them. These included core demands, whether for reform of the state or self-determination, broadly acceptable to the international community, as secession itself was not. They were legitimized by practices—such as flouting of the rule of law and violations of human rights—adopted by the state actors involved (not that the nonstate actors were blameless in this area). But they also reflected a history of engagement with external actors that helped sensitize nonstate and international actors to each other's expectations. This in turn contributed to the nonstate actors' development of sophisticated strategies for diplomatic involvement, including liaison with the United Nations.[7] The point was put succinctly by Joaquín Villalobos, who moved on from a position as the most prominent military leader of the FMLN to a life as an Oxford academic. He described how the FMLN had maintained contacts with a broad spectrum of non-Marxist countries, forces, and political leaders "for reasons of legitimacy, choice, and self-interest." Such contacts had been possible because "there was enough tolerance of the insurgency and belief in its potential transformation and the viability of negotiations."[8] That in many cases the rebel or resistance forces were represented by highly articulate individuals able to hold their own (or more) with their official counterparts was, of course, another factor that helped reinforce the impression they made on their international counterparts.

Groups of Friends, in contrast, have struggled to engage effectively in circumstances in which their members are less genuinely "friendly" to the conflict parties or in which armed groups blur with criminal organizations, informal militias, and paramilitary structures. The authorities in Sukhumi, it should be recalled, were described as representing a "repellent secessionist regime" by one so-called Friend in New York whose own exposure to the Abkhaz was minimal. More complex still were situations such as Angola and Colombia, where well-resourced nonstate actors involved in an active conflict showed little inclination to engage with the outside world and still less to modify human rights or other practices easy to dismiss as criminal to suit the demands of self-styled "Friends." Experience in Colombia, particularly with the FARC, brought home to many involved in the country's uncertain peace process the risks of what one Swiss diplomat would describe as "a group that did not know what it was doing, interacting with conflict parties who did not know what they were doing either."[9]

Composition Is Key

Finding: The composition of a group of Friends will determine the group's relationship to the secretary-general; to the Security Council; to the conflict, country, or region in question; and to the likelihood of it fulfilling a constructive role in a peace process. Effective groups have been small in size (four or five) and consisted of states like-minded in holding the settlement of the conflict as their highest goal. Most have involved some mixture of Security Council members (including the permanent five), interested regional actors, and midsized donor states with experience in the conflict.

The inverse relationship between the number of participants in a multiparty mediation and the likelihood of developing and sustaining a coordinated strategy is borne out by experience of groups of Friends formed to support a single mediating effort.[10] In interviews for this study, mediators and representatives of states alike consistently stressed the importance of small size for the efficacy of Friends, even as they recognized the tension—ever present at the United Nations—between the efficacy represented by a small group and the greater legitimacy a larger structure could offer.[11] The deliberate institution of "tiers"—seen in the Core and Support Groups in East Timor or, more informally, in the layers of Friends in Cyprus—helpfully addressed this problem in a number of instances, but in other circumstances the political conditions or adroit diplomacy required to pull this off were lacking.

Laxity with respect to gatekeeping, as experiences in Angola, Colombia, Somalia, and elsewhere demonstrated, allowed states to press for inclusion in a Friends mechanism whether or not they had much to offer it. This led to larger structures too unwieldy for flexible and collaborative engagement in a complex process. The prospect of an outcome that might benefit both domestic and foreign policy agendas alike was obviously attractive. But a desire to become a Friend also reflected the curious fact that, in the public sphere at least, states had little to lose, as the appearance of making a contribution to even an ineffective group was almost as relevant as actually doing so. (Jamaica's polite rejection of an invitation to join the Friends of Haiti represented a rare example of a state saying "no" to the possibility of becoming a Friend.)

More fundamental even than size is the extent to which groups of Friends reflect a commonality of interests among their members and an acceptable balance between big powers likely to mirror their national and global priorities within the narrow confines of a group, regional actors, and well-intentioned "helpful fixer" states with less at stake and also less real leverage over the conflict parties. The interests may be diverse—regional actors such as Mexico in Central America, Australia in East Timor, or Ghana in West Africa had interests at stake that might be quite distinct from those of distant powers—but the cases demonstrate that, in order to be successful, Friends should hold in common an overriding interest in a peaceful settlement of conflict and a shared sense of what that might look like. In situations in which individual Friends had a greater interest in the stability or continuing existence of one or other parties to the conflict—as was the obvious case in Georgia and Western Sahara—the utility of the Friends as a means to move toward a settlement suffered.

Four categories of states can be identified as constituting Friends, each with different contributions to make:

1. With the notable exception of El Salvador, the *United States* has been a member of almost all groups of Friends.[12] Indeed, given its preeminent power in the post–Cold War period and influence within the United Nations, an effective group of Friends on an issue on the agenda of the Security Council that did not count the United States among its members is not conceivable. (Conflicts that have not or will not reach the agenda of the Council may be a different matter.) Friends provided the United States with opportunities to work multilaterally within the relative security of a small group on issues that were of significance to it, but far from the top of its policy agenda. In some circumstances, such as Haiti, Friends allowed the United States to give a multilateral veneer to a domestically contentious policy, while in others—Georgia most notably—groups served a helpful role in downplaying expectations of the U.S. contribution.

2. *Other members of the Security Council's permanent five*, with the exception of China, have routinely been members of Friends. Like the United States they brought with them the promise of heavy lifting in the Security Council and significant resources. The United Kingdom—with its mastery of Security Council procedure and bridging role between the United States and other states—was particularly effective in managing relations between groups of Friends and the Council as a whole. It consequently benefited from its membership in groups even in circumstances, such as East Timor, in which it had no direct interests at stake. However, as Georgia and Western Sahara demonstrated, a dominance of permanent members among the Friends could limit the opportunities presented to the secretariat in a peace process, while also contributing to groups' resentment by other member states, perhaps especially elected members of the Council, as "subgroups" of the Security Council.

3. *Regional actors* with much to gain from the peaceful settlement of a conflict played leading roles in groups of Friends (Mexico in Central America; Canada in Haiti; Australia, New Zealand, and Japan in East Timor; Nigeria, South Africa, and other states in a variety of African

mechanisms). However, in regionally entwined conflicts the engagement of neighboring countries has been more problematic. Neighbors
might have favored stability in the country in conflict, but in the
absence of stability on their terms opted for increased instability rather
than stability on the terms of others. Under such circumstances it was
feared that they would be more "spoiler" than "friend" and consequently ill-suited to be partners in the quest for peace.

4. *Helpful fixers* played effective roles in groups of Friends, not least because their freedom from interests associated with other actors well
placed them to represent "honest brokers." Norway was most successful in this regard, with the role it played as a Friend in Guatemala or
Troika member in Sudan complementary to the peacemaking it undertook bilaterally elsewhere. Switzerland was an active member of the
groups formed in Colombia (and worked in parallel with the Troika in
Sudan). Such involvement, however, has contributed to an increasingly competitive field among these and other states interested in
making their mark on peacemaking (including Canada, the Netherlands, and Sweden, for example). Competition among these traditionally benign international actors may complicate the formation of
Friends in the future.

Leadership

Finding: Leadership of a group of Friends plays a crucial role in the development and maintenance of coordinated support for the peacemaking
effort. In cases in which the United Nations has the leading role, its
maintenance will be a delicate art and depend on a willingness of the
Friends to forego unilateral policy objectives or initiatives out of conviction that a process led by the secretary-general is one that offers the best
possible prospects for success. Representatives of the secretary-general
have relied on informality, flexibility, and discretion to bind Friends to
them, in addition to the personal respect that their own conduct of the
mediation effort may garner.

As the cases examined in chapter 8 suggested, it is the fact of an accepted
and capable lead, not whether that leading role is taken by the United
Nations, that may make a difference to peacemaking. But where the UN
secretary-general *was* charged with a leading role, the value of clear but
responsive leadership was evident. This was never automatically achieved.
Indeed, it is a peculiarity of the secretary-general's fragile authority, and the
fact that much of the legwork in an ongoing peace effort is undertaken not
by the secretary-general himself but by those charged to act on his behalf,

that in each instance respect for the United Nations had to be won and maintained by the capacity and diligence of the individuals involved. Only significant time invested by the mediators in cultivating partnerships among Friends and other actors allowed the development of the trust, respect, and even a degree of complicity (sometimes employed with respect to each official's parent bureaucracy) required to sustain support and forestall the appearance of rival initiatives. Although the establishment of a peace operation under the authority of a special representative of the secretary-general (SRSG) in theory introduced a degree of clarity to the situation, SRSGs themselves commanded widely varying levels of influence according to the different political contexts, mandates, and personalities involved.[13]

That some officials emerged as better endowed than others with the patience and skills required to manage the multiple actors was not surprising, particularly given the United Nations' notoriously haphazard means of appointing its senior officials.[14] However, the ability to maintain clear and effective leadership did not come down to individual qualities alone. In many cases the conditions that allowed the development of a role akin to a UN impresario, as pioneered by de Soto in his relationship to the Friends in El Salvador or Aldo Ajello with his Core Group in Mozambique, were simply not present, and other means of engagement with the Friends had to be pursued. Unsurprisingly, circumstances in which a permanent member of the Security Council believed its interests were directly at stake were particularly complex. In Haiti, Georgia, or Western Sahara, for example, the strong grip on the diplomatic process maintained by the United States, Russia, and France ensured that the bottom line was not subject to "leadership" from the secretariat. In each, the Friends and the process as a whole departed markedly at different times from one "led" by the secretary-general.

A justifiable suspicion of the secretariat's ability to "manage" member states (not to mention member states' willingness to subject themselves to such management) has contributed to a division of opinions in the secretariat as to whether a group of Friends should be essentially self-selecting or identified by the secretary-general.[15] Wariness of the latter course of action (seen in Angola, for example) also reflected a reluctance to involve the secretary-general himself in making a distinction between those states that are "Friends" on a particular issue and those that—by implication—are not. However, those with most direct experience of the United Nations' peacemaking consider a strong—but necessarily discreet—hand in a group's formation to be essential. In both El Salvador and East Timor, for example, groups of states that had the appearance of emerging organically were carefully nurtured by the officials involved. A cautious approach ("precooking") ensured that they knew their interlocutors well before either group took shape. As the processes advanced the respective secretaries-general (Pérez de Cuéllar and Annan) engaged with Friend and Core Group actors both in New York and at a capital level, with their involvement greatly enhanced by the quality of the diplomacy on which it was built.

A particular benefit offered by groups of Friends is the potential they represent for interaction with counterparts in New York, in the field, and in the Friends' various capitals. Multiple incarnations of a group of Friends have been a product of the seriousness with which a process moves forward even as maintaining coherence among them sometimes became a challenge (Friends in San Salvador and Guatemala City took shape as the negotiations in each process advanced; groups were formed in Port-au-Prince and Tbilisi when peacekeeping operations were deployed to Haiti and Georgia, respectively; meanwhile, Friends in Colombia remained limited to Bogotá and those for Western Sahara to New York.) Different locations of a single group of Friends developed different characteristics, with Friends accredited as ambassadors to a state that was also a conflict party (as in Georgia or Colombia) in a particularly vulnerable position. However, their existence also greatly facilitated efforts to attain coherence among those engaged in a particular peace effort, both in the field and in the positions transmitted to the Security Council. A related benefit, noted by one secretariat official who interacted frequently with the Troika on southern Sudan, was the extent to which the existence of a group mechanism encouraged each member to develop its own internal coherence on the issues at stake—something that peacemakers engaging with multiple departments and agencies of a large state take for granted at their peril.[16]

The informality and flexibility that underlined the utility of these complex relationships could both be undermined by the gradual "institutionalization" of some of the more long-lasting Friends. Diplomats engaged in groups formed to address the negotiating efforts in Central America, the crisis in Haiti in the early 1990s, or the dramatic developments in East Timor during 1999 brought with them or gained considerable expertise on the issue at hand. Moreover, the ready identification of a clear goal—the negotiation of a settlement, return of an exiled president to power, or conduct of a popular consultation—lent their efforts a degree of urgency that helped bind them to each other and to the UN officials leading the process. Over time, however, diplomats change, and structures that depended on the caliber and continuity of the individuals involved became less useful.

Where the urgency of the political moment also decreased, this represented a natural development, but in other more persistent—and resistant—processes, such as Haiti or East Timor, a degree of "Friend fatigue," or the tendency for Friends to go their own way, was more damaging. Such experiences contributed to the instinctive aversion to the creation of an established group by a number of highly skilled diplomats. Valuing the informality of their contacts above the benefits of instituting a group, they preferred instead to interact with a range of different actors for different purposes, whether identified as Friends of the Secretary-General (as in the Cyprus case) or not (as in Afghanistan after 2001).

Timing or Phase of the Process

Finding: Friends and other groups fulfilled distinct but interrelated roles during peacemaking, in implementation of a subsequent agreement, and in support of peacebuilding. Although what such groups offered varied at different stages of the process, they were most productively engaged when they had a process to support or a clearly assigned job to do. Donor coordination—both before and after an agreement is reached—extends beyond the confines of a small group of states. Groups formed specifically to support implementation have consequently been more inclusive than the small groups of Friends engaged in peacemaking.

Cases that span a range of phases in a process (El Salvador, Guatemala, Haiti, East Timor) and others in which it proved possible only to introduce a group mechanism to support implementation (as in the DRC) illustrate that different moments in a peace process have different needs to which groups of different kinds have variously tried to respond.

Under certain circumstances external actors were able to play a role in moving parties toward substantive negotiations. Knowledge of the parties involved and a profound commitment to an eventual peace could, for example, be seen in the efforts of Spain, Mexico, and Norway to nurture Guatemala's fragile peace process from its earliest days. This was facilitated by the disposition of their Guatemalan counterparts to move out of conflict as well as the evolution of developments outside the country. However, the accompaniment provided by international actors, acting independently and then configured as Friends once the process took hold, provided essential continuity to the process. The limits of such accompaniment—"prenegotiation"—were in contrast, demonstrated by efforts to engage the FARC in Colombia. Friends and facilitators of a fragile peace process were unable to overcome the internal dynamics of the conflict and the lack of political will among the conflict parties to engage in the substance of a peace process. The experience suggested the extent to which Friends' utility to peacemaking may be related to the inherent potential of a peace process. Friends were usefully engaged to bring extra leverage, resources, and encouragement to processes that demonstrated, for the first time in many years and for reasons related to both internal and external factors, a readiness to move toward resolution. But they could not by themselves push through a peaceful settlement.

Once a settlement has been reached, however, the value of a mechanism to coordinate the key states involved is clearer, not least because they will have a defined task ahead of them. Writing on the strategic coordination of peace implementation, for example, Bruce D. Jones noted the use of a Friends group or other deliberate process to bring together key governments as "one of the striking commonalities among cases of successful implementation."[17] Friends or related mechanisms did indeed contribute positively to the performance of peace operations in Central America, Cambodia, Mozambique, Haiti, East Timor, and even Georgia—where the Tbilisi-based Friends provided consistent support of the United Nations' peacekeeping operation alongside a more complex interaction with the political process—as well as in the DRC, Liberia, Sudan, and Côte d'Ivoire. The various groups represented a degree of continuity that maximized the potential to coordinate bilateral strategies. Although the very great differences in the implementation environment inhibit direct comparisons, the impact of the Friends appears particularly favorable in the light of the unwieldy coordination mechanisms in the Balkans, where the competing organizational cultures of the United Nations, the Organization for Security Cooperation in Europe (OSCE), the North Atlantic Treaty Organization (NATO), and the European Union complicated international efforts already confused by differences among the key bilateral actors.[18]

In the more successful cases, the Friends were able to reinforce and multiply the limited influence of an SRSG heading a peace operation, thereby increasing the international credibility of the United Nations' effort to sustain peace. Exactly how Friends helped individual SRSGs varied from case to case and according to the individual dispositions of the officials involved (some SRSGs worked harder to "cultivate the Friends" than others). But they fulfilled a number of functions. These included exerting political influence on the parties to the conflict, sharing information regarding local developments and thinking in their capitals and in New York, acting as a sounding board for new ideas and initiatives, and helping build and maintain consensus in the Security Council. However, as the course taken by the Friends in Central America revealed (and in particular the emergence of the Dialogue Group in Guatemala), the requirements of implementation extend beyond a small group of states formed to support a negotiation effort. This is not least because, as peacebuilding becomes the focus of the international effort, the leverage of international actors will be increasingly related to the power they wield as donors. And since donor priorities and tensions between the political and economic demands made by the international community render their coordination extraordinarily difficult, different strategies and mechanisms will need to be employed.[19]

The variety of groups established to channel the efforts of external actors toward implementation of agreements reached in Africa—although not created as donor coordination mechanisms—represented one approach to the problem. These mechanisms were not Friends, being more formally constituted, with their composition and functions often provided for in the peace agreement itself. However, in a case such as the DRC, where peacemaking had long been hindered by the active participation in the conflict by states of the region as well as competing allegiances in the Security Council, a larger group, such as the CIAT, had its own logic and purpose. The limitations of such a large group—also evident in the Core Group created for Haiti in 2004, or the Burundi Partners' Forum created in late 2005—included those natural to its size, as well as government sensitivity regarding the "intervention" it represented. Groups of more than a dozen members were forums ill suited to address the substantive differences held by their members on the complex process in which they were engaged. But these did not undermine the potential they represented for building consensus among the key members of the international community and, on the basis of that consensus, encouraging forward momentum in the complex transitions under way. Nor did they—quite obviously—prevent the development of alternative, more informal, channels for consultation with key partners.

Friends engaged with situations of political stalemate have raised different issues. These derive from an inherent contradiction between the existence of a degree of external interest sufficient to sustain the group at all and a level of comfort with the status quo reflected in the groups' very longevity. In neither the Georgian-Abkhaz nor Western Sahara conflict, for example, did the existing conditions—of cease-fire, refugees, and political acrimony between the parties in contention—directly impinge upon the economic or security interests of the members of the group of Friends. Consequently, they were content to prevent a deterioration of the situation into open hostilities while making little headway in moving it forward.

Their involvement and the support they gave through the Security Council to the UN operations in place represented a set of informal guarantees that neither side would be able to transgress beyond certain established limits. But although the Friends represented a useful means by which the principal external actors could manage their relations with each other and, in the case of Georgia, work to reinforce the United Nations' peacemaking effort, their actual contribution to the resolution of the conflict was more questionable.

A related factor is the self-evident difficulty in bringing a group of Friends to an end—a problem not limited to Friends and other structures, but common to multilateral bodies of all kinds, which are constitutionally averse to their own demise. Groups of Friends, as in the case of El Salvador or Guatemala, or indeed Angola or Colombia, have dwindled naturally with the fading urgency of a peace process, while other mechanisms—such as the Core Group in Mozambique, or the CIAT in the DRC—have been more specifically linked to the requirements of a particular transition. There are, however, several examples (Haiti at different moments, Georgia in 2006, Western Sahara during the Baker period, and East Timor in 2005 and 2006) of groups that had as a central purpose the forging of consensus within the Security Council that have nevertheless fractured under the pressure of their political differences, at least for a period of time. Ending the Friends has in none of these cases been suggested as a possibility. This indestructibility of Friends' groups is a characteristic that should introduce a note of caution into those who seek to create them.

Recommendations

These brief conclusions, as the case studies from which they are drawn, present a complex panorama. But the comparative analysis on which they are based does provide a basis for some modest but practical recommendations for policymakers in the United Nations and its member states that may contemplate the creation of, or involvement in, such groups in the future.

1. A group of Friends or a related mechanism should be *at the service of strategy for international engagement in a peace process*, and not a substitute for one. Due consideration should be paid to the decision to create or join such a group in the first place, with particular regard to the readiness and suitability of the conflict for the involvement of such a mechanism and, especially, the presence or absence of a supportive regional environment. In reaching such a decision, UN mediators or

other lead actors in a process should recall that a group of Friends—like mediation itself—is not a panacea and that a group formed without a clear strategic function may complicate efforts to move the process forward.

2. *Form should follow function:* what a group is expected to do is an essential element of its formation. In circumstances in which the mediator has direct control or more discreet influence over the formation of a group, efforts should be made to ensure that its membership is results oriented. This involves an awareness of who brings what to the table, as well as a commitment from the member states involved to support the lead actor, sustain their diplomatic engagement, and invest resources of other kinds in the outcome of a peace process. It also suggests that it may be necessary to distinguish between a group formed to support negotiations and one specifically created to encourage coordinated support of implementation.

3. Groups intended to provide operational support to peacemaking *have been most successful when they remain small* and represent a natural grouping of like-minded states that has the appearance of being self-selecting (diplomatic "precooking" of the membership is recommended when possible). In cases where a large number of states press for inclusion in Friends or Support Groups, a Core Group of states has been a helpful device by which to balance the competing demands for efficiency and legitimacy. Large groups of states may serve their own purposes: bringing attention to forgotten conflicts, sharing information on external actors' actions and priorities, and encouraging the provision of resources to a peace process.

4. Although a peacemaker may choose his or her Friends with a view to their potential utility as *partners in implementation*, a lack of financial or material resources should not preclude the involvement of regional or other actors with political leverage over one or more parties to the conflict. Nor should membership of the Security Council, whether permanent or temporary, be taken as a determining criterion in membership of a group. However, the inclusion of states with an overriding strategic interest in the outcome of a particular conflict, or proxy relationship to one of the parties, has inevitable consequence for the engagement of a Friends' group and should generally be avoided. States or other actors with a lack of direct interest in the outcome of a conflict may offer certain advantages, not least the perception of representing an "honest broker." Personal experience and capacities can be critical to the efficacy of a group of Friends.

5. There may be occasions when the formation of a closed group of Friends will bring little benefit (and indeed could create problems of its own). Consideration of a strategy involving Friends may need to include more informal coalitions or time spent testing potential Friends in separate and noncommittal meetings before a group is constituted. In either case the *support that can be offered by "friendship" in a peace effort* is the priority, and should prevail over a desire to create a group for a group's sake.

The Way Ahead

By the mid-2000s the extraordinary profusion of groups engaged in conflict resolution was a significant feature of a slowly (and somewhat painfully) emerging system of post–Cold War global security governance. While the dominance of the United States within this system remained unquestioned, a propensity to form groups demonstrated the extent to which this dominance was diffused by the emergence of regional and other actors— such as the European and Nordic states—with distinct interests at stake and policies by which to pursue them. Far from informal groups representing a discreet "variant" of collective security, this book has suggested that a group approach to conflict management cuts across a variety of different types of intervention by external actors, complicating its analysis.

The groups had very different relationships to the United Nations— and as we have seen, very different impacts on the conflicts themselves —but in many respects they served it well. Their flexibility allowed for different interactions between the secretary-general and member states with a particular interest in a given conflict. They facilitated the work of the Security Council (if on occasion undermining its authority in the process) even as their characteristic mix of permanent members and other states provided an effective means by which the deliberations and decisions of the Council could be more inclusive than its outmoded membership generally allowed. Engagement by the secretary-general and other officials with groups formed outside the United Nations at times also proved a means to slide into the margins of a peace process and help prepare all parties to establish a UN peace operation to help oversee implementation of a settlement.

Yet benefits to the United Nations and the peace and security it pursued were not assured. The rise in the numbers of groups reflected a more complex field of conflict resolution than had been seen in the immediate aftermath of the Cold War when Friends of the Secretary-General first emerged. No longer were Cold War powers using the United Nations as leverage over former clients and proxies embarked on peace processes. Instead, the broader surge in conflict prevention, conflict management, and post-conflict peacebuilding activities of which the rise in groups formed a part reflected a significant shift in attitudes toward conflicts in far-flung places. This responded both to normative changes with respect to violence and the abuse of human rights and to an expanded sense of the security and other interests of the developed world at stake. But the growth of the groups also suggested an increasingly competitive environment in which state and nonstate actors seeking peace struggled to maintain their own prominence. Conflicts were addressed by unique configurations of international actors in what Martin Griffiths has described as each peace process's own "peculiar cocktail."[20] In this cocktail the United Nations itself could appear as one among many other actors—regional organizations, states, and private mediators—vying for a role. And the diversity of the contributions made by states engaged as Friends left the question posed in this book's title—*Friends Indeed?*—an open one.

The balancing act between the independence of the secretary-general and the interests and involvement of member states, a constant since the organization's creation in 1945, remained vividly present as a new secretary-general, Ban Ki-Moon of South Korea, took office in January 2007. Groups of Friends openly committed to the greater good of peace had prioritized their own concerns within a given conflict and would continue to do so in the future. In their actions they starkly illustrated the tension between international norms and national interests that has always lain behind states' engagement with the United Nations. The experience of Ban's more immediate predecessors—secretaries-general Javier Pérez de Cuéllar, Boutros Boutros-Ghali, and Kofi Annan—suggested that the great skill required to navigate between the two, norms and interests—enlisting the latter at the service of the former whenever possible—was one of the more valuable attributes required to live up to the full potential of this most demanding of jobs. Under the right circumstances an informal group of states represented an attractive means by which to pursue this goal.

Looking forward, the one certainty is that groups of Friends and related mechanisms will continue to proliferate. This book has suggested that the lessons to be learned from the use of Friends in the past are relevant to their formation and engagement in the future. Although a direct correlation between a group of Friends and a successful outcome of a peace process cannot be established, conditions that might allow for Friends to contribute to a well-crafted diplomatic engagement can be identified.

There will be many circumstances in which Friends are not the answer, but when they might be able to help, their "worth and choice," as Ben Jonson put it, remain essential.

Appendix

The United Nations' Groups of Friends and Other Mechanisms

NOTE: The groups contained in the following table reflect a broad understanding of Friends as ad hoc, issue-specific minicoalitions of states and intergovernmental organizations that become involved in and provide support for the resolution of conflicts and the implementation of peace agreements. They correspond to the four categories of groups engaged in some respect with the United Nations outlined in the introduction (pages 9–11), but do not include groups or ad hoc coalitions formed without UN involvement (the Organization for Security and Cooperation in Europe's Minsk Group, for example, or the Six-Party mechanism engaged in talks on North Korea in the mid-2000s). Exceptions are those groups formed without UN involvement but in situations (Rwanda, Georgia) where the United Nations played a role in the broader political process. An attempt has been made to update the list until December 31, 2006. Such a list cannot hope to be exhaustive and is bound to contain numerous inaccuracies, as in some cases the composition of groups has been fluid. The author takes full responsibility for errors and omissions that the list may contain and will gratefully accept corrections.

Conflict	Group/Core Members	Initiative	Phase of Process
AFRICA			
Angola	**Troika:** Portugal, Russia, United States. 1990–2002	States	Peacemaking, peacekeeping
	Joint Commission: Parties, Portugal, Russia, United States, and United Nations (chair). 1994–2002	Agreement	Peacemaking
	Friends of Angola: At least nineteen states, reduced to a **Core Group** of eleven, including Brazil, Canada, France, Namibia, Nigeria, Norway, Portugal, Russia, South Africa, United Kingdom, and United States. 1999–2002	Secretary-General (SG)	Peacemaking
Burundi	**NGO Friends of Burundi:** 1994–1995	Special Representative to the Secretary-General (SRSG)	Peacemaking, peacekeeping, peacebuilding
	Economic and Social Council Ad Hoc Advisory Group on Burundi: Belgium, Burundi, Ethiopia, France, Japan, and South Africa (chair), plus president of ECOSOC and chair of **Security Council Working Group on Conflict Prevention and Resolution in Africa.** 2003–present	Burundi and ECOSOC	Peacekeeping, peacebuilding
	Implementation Monitoring Committee: Parties, government, Burundians, Regional Peace Initiative, African Union (AU), European Union (EU), United Nations, donors. 2000–2005	Agreement	Peacebuilding
	Burundi Partners Forum: Regional Peace Initiative, donors, AU, and United Nations (chair). 2005–present	SG/SRSG	Peacebuilding
Central African Republic	**Friends of Central African Republic (CAR):** Canada, Colombia, Côte d'Ivoire, Egypt, France (chair), Gabon, Germany, Japan, and Kenya. 1998–2002	France	Peacekeeping, peacebuilding

Congo	**Congo Advisory Committee:** Eighteen states (troop contributors). 1960–1963	SG	Peacekeeping
Democratic Republic of the Congo	**International Commission to Accompany the Transition (CIAT):** Permanent five (P-5), Angola, Belgium, Canada, Gabon, South Africa, and Zambia, plus the AU and the EU and European Commission (EC), and UN (convener). 2002–2006	Agreement Dec. 2002	Peacekeeping, peacebuilding
	Three plus Two: France, United Kingdom, and United States; Belgium and South Africa. 2004–present	States	
Côte d'Ivoire	**Economic Community of West African States (ECOWAS) Contact Group:** Ghana, Guinea-Bissau, Mali, Nigeria, Niger, Togo (lead), and AU. 2002–2003	States	Peacemaking
	Comité de Suivi (Follow-up Committee): United Nations, AU, ECOWAS, European Commission, Francophonie, Bretton Woods institutions, G-8 military reps. of troop contributors, and France. 2003–2006	Agreement	Peacekeeping
	UN-AU-ECOWAS Monitoring Group: 2004–present	Agreement	
	International Working Group (IWG): Benin, France, Ghana, Guinea, Niger, Nigeria, South Africa, United Kingdom, United States, AU (cochair), ECOWAS, EU, Francophonie, International Monetary Fund (IMF), UN (cochair), and World Bank. **Mediation Group:** South Africa (chair), AU, ECOWAS, Francophonie, UN (SRSG and High Rep. for Elections). 2005–present	AU	Peacemaking, peacekeeping
	Committee of Representatives (Co Rep): both a revival of the Comité de Suivi, and a grouping of local representatives of the IWG, plus Canada, Japan, and Norway. 2006–present.		

Conflict	Group/Core Members	Initiative	Phase of Process
Ethiopia-Eritrea	**Friends of the United Nations Mission in Ethiopia and Eritrea:** Algeria, Canada, Denmark, India, Italy, Jordan, Kenya, the Netherlands, Norway, and the United States were initial members; but membership expanded, and varies in different locations. 2000–present	Netherlands	Peacekeeping
Great Lakes Region	**Friends of the Great Lakes Conference:** Cochaired by Canada and the Netherlands. Twenty-eight states and ten multilaterals attended first meeting. 2003–present	UN initiative states	Peacebuilding
Guinea-Bissau	**Friends of Guinea-Bissau:** Brazil, Canada, France, Gambia (chair), Germany, Guinea, Italy, the Netherlands, Nigeria, Portugal, Senegal, Sweden, Togo, and United States. 1999–present	Gambia	Peacebuilding
	ECOSOC Ad Hoc Advisory Group: Brazil, Guinea-Bissau, the Netherlands, Portugal, and South Africa (chair); also attended by ECOSOC president, Gambia (as chair of Friends), and chair of **Security Council's Working Group on Conflict Prevention and Resolution in Africa.** 2002–present	Guinea-Bissau and ECOSOC	Peacebuilding
	International Contact Group on Guinea-Bissau: Angola, Brazil, Cape Verde, France, Senegal, Gambia, Guinea, Niger, Portugal (cochair), the Community of Portuguese-Speaking Countries (CPLP, cochair), ECOWAS (cochair), and the United Nations. 2006–present	ECOWAS	Peacebuilding
Liberia	**International Contact Group on Liberia:** Belgium, Canada, Denmark, France, Germany, Italy, Japan, Netherlands, Norway, Sweden, Switzerland, United Kingdom, United	United Nations/ United States	Peacekeeping

Country	Description	Facilitator	Type
	States, ECOWAS, EC, Organisation of African Unity (OAU), and United Nations (in lead). 1996–1997	States with United Nations	Peacemaking, peacekeeping, peacebuilding
	International Contact Group on Liberia (ICGL): France, Morocco, Nigeria, United Kingdom, United States, AU, ECOWAS (cochair), EU (cochair), United Nations. 2002–2005. In 2005 the group was renamed the **International Contact Group on the Mano River Basin,** with a membership that included Ghana, Germany, Nigeria, Niger, United Kingdom, United States, ECOWAS, EU, AU, United Nations, and World Bank. 2005–present		
	Implementation Monitoring Committee: Chaired by ECOWAS; also includes United Nations, AU, EU and ICGL (a **Joint Monitoring Committee,** also including the parties, was established in connection with the cease-fire). 2003–2006	Agreement	Peacekeeping
Mozambique	**Core Group:** France, Germany, Italy, Portugal, United Kingdom, and United States. 1992–1994	SRSG	Peacekeeping
Namibia	**Western Contact Group:** Canada, France, Germany, United Kingdom, United States, 1977–1990	States	Peacemaking
	Joint Monitoring Commission: Chaired by SRSG, included parties and Angola, Cuba, and South Africa, with Russia and United States as observers. 1988–1990	Agreement	Peacekeeping
Rwanda	**Five Musketeers:** France, Belgium, United States, Germany, papal nunciature (lead). 1992–1994	States	Peacemaking
Sierra Leone	**International Contact Group on Sierra Leone:** Belgium, Canada, China, Egypt, France, Germany, Italy, Japan, the Netherlands, New Zealand, Nigeria, Norway, Sierra Leone, Sweden, United Kingdom (in lead), United States, the Commonwealth Secretariat, ECOWAS, European Commission, UN and World Bank. 1998–1999	United Kingdom	Peacekeeping

Conflict	Group/Core Members	Initiative	Phase of Process
	Core Group (Friends of Sierra Leone): Bangladesh, Guinea, Mali, Nigeria, Pakistan, United Kingdom (lead), and United States. 2000–2002	United Kingdom	Peacekeeping
Somalia	Core Group/Committee of Friends: Arab League, OAU, Organization of Islamic Conferences (OIC), and United Nations. 1993	Members	Peacemaking
	Contact Group: Large membership reflecting previous, (1998–2000) Meetings of External Actors on Somalia: 2002–present	SG	Peacemaking
	Friends of the Somali National Reconciliation Conference: Members included China, Germany, Italy, Norway (chair), Switzerland, Sweden, United Kingdom, United States, and EU. 2002–2006	Norway (with UN support)	Peacemaking
	International Contact Group on Somalia: Italy, Norway (chair), Sweden, Tanzania, United Kingdom, United States, EU, with AU, Intergovernmental Authority on Development (IGAD), League of Arab States, and United Nations as observers. 2006–present	United States	Peacemaking
Sudan	Friends of Intergovernmental Authority on Development (IGAD): Canada, Italy, Japan, Russia, Netherlands, Norway, Switzerland, United Kingdom, United States, and EU. 1995–1997	States	Peacemaking
	IGAD Partners' Forum (IPF) Core Group: Canada, Italy, Netherlands, Norway, United Kingdom, United States, and United Nations. 1997–present	States	
	Troika: Norway, United Kingdom, and United States. 1999–2004	States	Peacemaking
	Assessment and Evaluation Commission: Parties, Ethiopia, Kenya, Norway (chair), United Kingdom, with AU, EU, United Nations, and Arab League as observers. 2005–present	Agreement	Peacekeeping

	Contact Group on Sudan: Canada, France, Netherlands, Norway, United Kingdom (chair), United States, AU, EU/EC, and United Nations. 2005–present	United Kingdom	Peacekeeping, peacemaking
Western Sahara	**Friends of Western Sahara:** France, Russia, Spain, United Kingdom, United States. In its early years, other states, including Argentina, Cape Verde, Egypt, Kenya, Gambia, and Venezuela, also served as members of the group as they rotated through the Council. 1993–present	United States	Peacemaking, peacekeeping

AMERICAS

Colombia	**Friends of the Government of Colombia and National Liberation Army (ELN):** Cuba, France, Norway, Spain, and Switzerland. 2000–2004	Special Adviser to the SG/parties	Peacemaking
	Group of Verifiers of the Government of Colombia and ELN: Canada, Germany, Japan, Portugal, and Sweden. 2001	States	
	Friends of Talks between the Government of Colombia and the Revolutionary Armed Forces of Colombia (FARC): A large group of twenty-five-plus states, the European Union, United Nations, and the Vatican, of which Canada, Cuba, France, Italy, Mexico, Norway, Spain, Sweden, Switzerland, and Venezuela formed a **Facilitating Commission.** 2001–2002	SASG/parties	
	Informal group/Brussels group: Canada, Mexico, United States, United Nations, and European countries. 2000–present	SASG/states	
El Salvador	**Friends of the Secretary-General for El Salvador:** Colombia, Mexico, Spain, Venezuela, plus the United States, in implementation. 1990–1997	SG	Peacemaking, peacekeeping, peacebuilding
Guatemala	**Friends of the Guatemalan Peace Process:** Colombia, Mexico, Norway, Spain, United States, and Venezuela. 1993–2004	Parties	Peacemaking, peacebuilding
	Grupo de Diálogo (Dialogue Group): Canada, Germany, Japan, the Netherlands, Norway, Spain, Sweden, United States, EU, Inter-American Development Bank (IDB), and the	States	Peacebuilding

Conflict	Group/Core Members	Initiative	Phase of Process
	World Bank, with the United Nations Development Programme (UNDP) and United Nations' Verification Mission (MINUGUA) as observers. 2000–present		
Haiti	**Friends of the Secretary-General for Haiti:** Canada, France, United States, Venezuela (then Argentina from 1994 and Chile from 1996; in 1999–2000 Spain and Germany joined in Haiti). 1992–2001	SG	Peacemaking, intervention, peacebuilding
	Group of Friends of OAS (Organization of American States) **Secretary-General:** Established in October 2001 as Argentina, Bahamas, Belize, Canada, Chile, Dominican Republic, Guatemala, Mexico, United States, and Venezuela, with France, Germany, Norway, and Spain as permanent observers, but its membership was not closed. 2001–2004.	OAS	
	Friends of Haiti: Brazil, Canada, Chile, France, United States (Argentina from 2005, Peru from 2006). 2004–present	States	
	Core Group: Argentina, Brazil, Canada, Chile, France, Germany, Mexico, Spain, United States, EC/EU, IDB, IMF, World Bank, OAS, Caribbean Community (CARICOM), and United Nations (chair). 2004–present	SG/Security Council Resolution (SCR) 1542	Peacekeeping, peacebuilding
	ECOSOC Ad Hoc Advisory Group on Haiti: Benin, Brazil, Canada (chair), Chile, Haiti, Spain, and Trinidad and Tobago, with participation of ECOSOC president and SRSG. 2004–present	Haiti/states ECOSOC	
Venezuela	**Friends of Venezuela:** Brazil, Chile, Mexico, Portugal, Spain, United States, with the OAS and United Nations as observers in its earliest days. Gradually evolved into	States	Internal dispute

Group of Friends of the OAS Secretary-General on Venezuela, with which the United Nations was not involved. 2003–2004

ASIA

Afghanistan	**Six plus Two:** China, Iran, Pakistan, Tajikistan, Turkmenistan, Uzbekistan, Russia, and United States . 1997–2001	SG/Special Envoy	Peacemaking
	Group of 21: Member states "with interest" in Afghanistan. 1997–2001	SG	
	Geneva Initiative: Germany, Iran, Italy, and United States, convened by United Nations. 2000–2001	Personal representative (PR) of SG PRSG	
	Luncheon Group: France, Germany, Italy, Japan, Sweden, Norway, and United Kingdom. 2000–2001		
Cambodia	**P-5:** China, France, United Kingdom, United States, and USSR. 1988–1991	States	Peacemaking
	Extended P-5 (in Phnom Penh) and **Core Group** (in New York): P-5 plus fluid membership of leading troop contributors, including Australia, France, Indonesia, Japan, Malaysia, Thailand, and United States. 1992–1993	SRSG	Peacekeeping
East Timor	**Core Group:** Australia, Japan, New Zealand, United Kingdom, and United States (plus Portugal from 2001, Brazil from 2004, and France from 2005). 1999–present	SG	Peacemaking, intervention, peacebuilding
	Support Group: Including Australia, Austria, Brazil, Canada, France, Germany, Japan, Malaysia, Netherlands, New Zealand, Norway, Singapore, Thailand, United Kingdom, and United States. 1999–2000	SG	

Conflict	Group/Core Members	Initiative	Phase of Process
Myanmar	**Informal Consultation Mechanism/Group:** Australia, Japan, Malaysia, Philippines, Thailand, Sweden, United Kingdom, United States (grew to include Korea, Norway, EU, France, India, and more). 1995–present	SG	Peacemaking
EUROPE and the Former USSR			
Cyprus	United Kingdom and United States, but also other interested states. 1999–2004	SG	Peacemaking
Kosovo	**Friends of Kosovo:** Including Austria, Belgium, Canada, China, Denmark, Finland, France, Germany, Greece, Italy, Japan, Netherlands, Russia, Spain, Sweden, Turkey, United Kingdom, United States, EU, OIC, and OSCE. 1999	SG	International intervention
	Contact Group: France, Germany, Italy, Russia, United Kingdom, and United States. 1994–present (**Quint**—the Contact Group without Russia—from 1999)	States	Peacebuilding, peacemaking
	Coordination and Drafting Group (CDG): France, Germany, Italy, Russia, United Kingdom, United States, Western members of the SC. 1994–present	States	
Former Yugoslavia	**Contact Group:** (as above) France, Germany, Russia, United Kingdom, United States. 1994–present	States	Peacemaking, peacekeeping, peacebuilding
	Coordination and Drafting Group (CDG): (as above) France, Germany, Russia, United Kingdom, United States, plus Western members of the Security Council (SC). 1994–present	States	
Georgia	**Friends of Georgia/of the Secretary-General for Georgia** (after 1997): France, Germany, Russia, United Kingdom, United States, and (temporarily and only in New York) Ukraine (2000–2001), Bulgaria (2002–2003), and Slovakia (2006–2007). 1993–present	States	Peacemaking, peacekeeping

	New Friends of Georgia: Bulgaria, Estonia, Latvia, Lithuania, Poland, and Romania. 2005–present	Georgia	Peacemaking
Tajikistan	**Friends of Tajikistan:** Afghanistan, Iran, Kazakhstan, Kyrgyzstan, Pakistan, Russia, Saudi Arabia, Turkey, Turkmenistan, Uzbekistan, United States, OSCE, and OIC. 1995–1997	SG	Peacemaking
	Contact Group: Afghanistan, Iran, Kazakhstan, Kyrgyzstan, Pakistan, Russia, Turkmenistan, and Uzbekistan (guarantor states), UN, OSCE, and OIC. 1997–2000	Agreement	Peacekeeping, peacebuilding

MIDDLE EAST

Egypt	**United Nations Emergency Forces (UNEF) Advisory Committee:** Brazil, Canada, Ceylon, Colombia, India, Norway, and Pakistan. 1956–1959 (a single meeting was held in 1967, with the addition of Yugoslavia)	SG	Peacekeeping
Iraq	**Friends of Iraq:** More than forty-five states. 2003–2004	SG	Intervention
Lebanon	**Consultative Group on United Nations Observation Group in Lebanon (UNOGIL):** Brazil, Canada, Ceylon, Colombia, India, Norway, and Pakistan. 1958	SG	Peacekeeping
	Core Group: Egypt, France, Italy, Lebanon, Russia, Saudi Arabia, United Kingdom, United States, European Union/European Commission, United Nations, and World Bank. 2005–present	United States	Peacebuilding
Middle East	**Quartet:** EU, Russia, United Nations, and United States. 2001–present	SG	Peacemaking

Notes

Introduction

1. Javier Pérez de Cuéllar, *Pilgrimage for Peace: A Secretary-General's Memoir* (New York: St. Martin's Press, 1997), opposite 215.

2. Alvaro de Soto, "Ending Violent Conflict in El Salvador," in *Herding Cats: Multiparty Mediation in a Complex World*, ed. Chester A. Crocker, Fen Osler Hampson, and Pamela Aall (Washington, DC: United States Institute of Peace Press, 1999), 368.

3. *Report of the Secretary-General, The Situation in Central America*, A/57/384/Add.1, December 17, 2002.

4. In this context civil wars are understood as violent armed conflicts involving more than 1,000 battle deaths. Human Security Centre, *Human Security Report 2005: War and Peace in the 21st Century* (New York and Oxford: Oxford University Press, 2005), 153.

5. Michael W. Doyle, Ian Johnstone, Robert C. Orr, eds., *Keeping the Peace: Multidimensional UN Operations in Cambodia and El Salvador* (Cambridge, UK, New York and Melbourne: Cambridge University Press, 1997); see also Michael W. Doyle, "War Making, Peace Making and the United Nations," in *Turbulent Peace*, ed. Chester A. Crocker, Fen Osler Hampson, and Pamela Aall (Washington, DC: United States Institute of Peace Press, 2001), 541.

6. Annex to the letter dated August 29, 2002, from the Permanent Representative of Mauritius to the President of the Security Council, S/2002/979, August 30, 2002.

7. Crocker et al., eds., *Herding Cats*. This volume did not explicitly address the role of Friends in a comparative context, although it contains much useful material on their uses within the case studies.

8. Doyle et al., eds., *Keeping the Peace*; Doyle, "War Making, Peace Making and the United Nations"; De Soto, "Ending Violent Conflict in El Salvador"; Diego Arria, "Bringing Leverage to the Peace Process in El Salvador and Central America," in *Leveraging for Success in UN Peace Operations*, ed. Jean Krasno, Bradd C. Hayes, Donald C.F. Daniel (Westport, CT: Praeger Publishers, 2003), 55–80. Chester A. Crocker, *High Noon in Southern Africa: Making Peace in a Rough Neighborhood* (New York: W. W. Norton, 1992) and "Peacemaking in Southern Africa: The Namibia-Angola Settlement of 1988," in *Herding Cats*, ed. Crocker et al., 211–14. See also analysis of the role played by the Friends in Haiti in David M. Malone, *Decision-Making in the Security Council: The Case of Haiti* (Oxford: Clarendon Press, 1998).

9. Krasno's early work was more fully developed in Jean Krasno, "The Friends of the Secretary-General: A Useful Leveraging Tool," in *Leveraging for Success*, ed. Krasno et al., 235–47 and in Jean Krasno and Jochen Prantl, "Informal Groups of Member States," in *The United Nations: Confronting the Challenges of a Global Society*, ed. Jean E. Krasno (Boulder, CO: Lynne Rienner Publishers, 2004), 311–58.

10. Jochen Prantl, *The UN Security Council and Informal Groups of States: Complementing or Competing for Governance?* (Oxford and New York: Oxford University Press, 2006).

11. Ibid., 37–44. Prantl is citing Adam Roberts, "The United Nations: Variants in Collective Security" in *Explaining International Relations since 1945*, ed. Ngaire Woods (Oxford: Oxford University Press, 1996), 309–36.

12. A Lessons Learned Unit established within the Department of Peacekeeping Operation had little influence on the work of the department until it was reinvented as the Peacekeeping Best Practices Unit in 2001–02; the Department of Political Affairs, which backstopped most of the UN's peacemaking, had no equivalent capacity. However, in 2006 it established a small Mediation Support Unit and a Web site, UN Peacemaker (www.peacemaker.unlb.org), that sought to capture lessons learned from peacemaking experience for use by international peacemaking professionals.

13. Security Council Resolution 1645 (2005), December 20, 2005.

14. Stephen John Stedman, introduction to *Ending Civil Wars: the Implementation of Peace Agreements*, ed. Stephen John Stedman, Donald Rothchild, and Elizabeth M. Cousens (Boulder, CO: Lynne Rienner Publishers, 2002), 16.

15. A Burundi Partners Forum was created in September 2005. Discussion of the creation of a "Committee of Friends" of Somalia in the early 2000s fell prey to Somali complaints that some of the states considered for the group were more enemy than Friend. A larger Contact Group was formed instead, but it had so little impact that when a new International Contact Group on Somalia was formed in 2006, it was without reference to its prior existence. See chapter 8, 244.

16. The significant differences in the incidence of peacekeeping operations are with respect to Europe and the Middle East, where Friends groups have not been much in evidence in reflection of a preference of the major Western powers to address conflicts bilaterally. Michael Gilligan and Stephen John Stedman, "Where Do the Peacekeepers Go?" *International Studies Review* 5, no. 4 (2003): 37–54.

17. William Zartman has warned that "writers about interests in international politics have always found it hard to make statements that are both significant and generalizable." I. William Zartman, "Systems of World Order and Regional Conflict Resolution," in *Cooperative Security: Reducing Third World Wars*, ed. I. William Zartman and Victor A. Kremenyuk (Syracuse, NY: Syracuse University Press, 1995), 11–15.

18. Joseph S. Nye Jr., "Redefining the National Interest," *Foreign Affairs* 78, no. 4 (July–August 1999): 22–35.

19. Citing the work of John Mueller, *The Remnants of War* (Ithaca, NY: Cornell University Press, 2004) in *Human Security Report*, 149.

20. Robert Cooper, *The Breaking of Nations: Order and Chaos in the Twenty-First Century* (New York: Atlantic Monthly Press, 2003), 111.

21. Chester A. Crocker, Fen Osler Hampson, and Pamela Aall, *Taming Intractable Conflicts: Mediation in the Hardest Cases* (Washington, DC: United States Institute of Peace Press, 2004), 21–43. See also Bruce W. Jentleson's description of power, peace, prosperity, and principles as the four core goals of U.S. foreign policy, *American Foreign Policy: The Dynamics of Choice in the 21st Century*, 2nd ed. (New York: W. W. Norton and Company, 2004), and Saadia Touval and I.William Zartman, "International Mediation in the Post–Cold War Era," in *Turbulent Peace*, ed. Crocker et al., 427–43.

22. The example of Norway is telling in this respect. Its small size, geographic position, and oil wealth determine that its own strategic or economic interests in distant conflicts are limited; however, a track record as a peacemaker has assured it a place on the world stage that it had otherwise lost with the demise of the Cold War, during which its border with Russia and membership in NATO had assured an Atlantic focus to its foreign policy.

23. I am grateful to Barnett R. Rubin for pointing me in Wittgenstein's direction. Rubin cites Wittgenstein's *Philosophical Investigations*, translated by G.E.M. Anscombe (Oxford: Blackwell, 1967), in *Blood on the Doorstep, The Politics of Preventive Action* (New York: Century Foundation Press, 2002), 10.

24. See *Report of an Assessment of the Ad Hoc Advisory Groups of the Economic and Social Council on African Countries Emerging from Conflict*, E/2004/86, June 25, 2004, for an account of the groups on Burundi and Guinea-Bissau.

25. Since the 1960s, a system of five regional groups has developed at the United Nations (Group of African States, Group of Asian States, Group of Eastern European States, Group of Latin America and the Caribbean States, and Western European and Others Group). Seats on UN bodies are allocated to the groups and each group nominates countries from among its members for its seats. The groups also coordinate policy and present unified negotiating positions.

26. These groups have presented useful meeting grounds for states likeminded in their concern for action on the part of the United Nations, but their impact in the organization has been relatively modest.

27. In addition to an undefined number of the committee's thirty-one members, country-specific meetings of the commission would be attended by the country under consideration, regional countries engaged in the post-conflict process, and other countries involved in relief efforts and political dialogue, as well as regional and subregional organizations; the major financial, troop, and civilian police contributors involved in the recovery effort; UN officials; and other relevant regional and international representatives. SC Resolution 1645, op. para 7. The first country-specific meetings of the commission, on Burundi and Sierra Leone respectively, were held in October 2006.

28. George Downs and Stephen John Stedman, "Evaluation Issues in Peace Implementation," in *Ending Civil Wars*, ed. Stedman et al., 43–69.

29. Michael W. Doyle and Nicolas Sambanis, in the most serious quantitative study of international peacebuilding to date, develop a simpler but compatible set of factors that contribute to "sustainable peace": the degree of hostility of the warring factions, the extent of local capacities remaining after the war, and the amount of international assistance provided. *Making War and Building Peace: United Nations Peace Operations* (Princeton and Oxford: Princeton University Press, 2006), 4.

30. No group of Friends was formed on the DRC during the active years of the conflict; on Somalia, see note 15, above. Meanwhile, Norway, the facilitator of talks between the government of Sri Lanka and the Tamil Tiger rebels, considered and then rejected the creation of a Friends group on the grounds that it might compromise a sensitive bilateral relationship with India that was central to Norway's engagement in Sri Lanka. Interview, Norwegian official, March 2, 2004.

31. See Robert Ricgliano, ed., *Choosing to Engage: Armed Groups and Peace Processes*, Accord Issue 16 (London: Conciliation Resources, 2005).

32. This point is made by Martin Griffiths, "Talking Peace in a Time of Terror: United Nations, Mediation and Collective Security" (Geneva: Centre for Humanitarian Dialogue, 2005), 6. As director of the Centre for Humanitarian Dialogue, Griffiths writes as one of the most prominent of the "new mediators" working outside the United Nations.

1. At Cold War's End

1. See Simon Chesterman, ed., *Secretary or General? The UN Secretary-General in World Politics* (Cambridge, UK, and New York: Cambridge University Press, 2007) for an exploration of these distinct roles.

2. James Traub, "Kofi Annan's Next Test," *New York Times*, March 29, 1998. Traub's full account of Annan's tenure as secretary-general is contained in James Traub, *The Best Intentions: Kofi Annan and the UN in the Era of American World Power* (New York: Farrar, Straus and Giroux, 2006). Stanley Meisler's biography of Annan, *Kofi Annan: A Man of Peace in a World of War* (Hoboken, NJ: John Wiley and Sons, 2007), was published a few months later.

3. Bailey and Daws relate that Trygve Lie recalled that he had invoked article 99 when war broke out in Korea, but warn that his memory was "unreliable." In bringing the Congo crisis to the Council in 1960, Dag Hammarskjöld—like Secretaries-General U Thant and Kurt Waldheim after him, with respect to the situation in 1971 in "East Pakistan vis-à-vis the adjoining states" and the

1979 hostage crisis in Iran—"used the language of Article 99 without expressly citing it." Sydney D. Bailey and Sam Daws, *The Procedure of the UN Security Council*, 3rd ed. (Oxford: Clarendon Press, 1998), 111–13. See also A. Walter Dorn, "Early and Late Warnings by the UN Secretary-General of Threats to the Peace: Article 99 Revisited," in *Conflict Prevention from Rhetoric to Reality, Volume II: Opportunities and Innovations*, ed. Albrecht Schnable and David Carment (Lanham, MD: Lexington Books, 2004), 305–44.

4. For a discussion of the legal basis of the secretary-general's independent role, see Ian Johnstone, "The Role of the UN Secretary-General: The Power of Persuasion Based on Law," *Global Governance* 9 (2003): 441–58.

5. Brian Urquhart, *Hammarskjöld* (New York and London: W.W. Norton, 1994), 105.

6. The Hague Convention on the Pacific Settlement of International disputes (1907) states, "Powers [that are] strangers to a dispute have the right to offer good offices or mediation even during the course of hostilities. The exercise of this right can never be regarded by either of the parties in dispute as an unfriendly act." The Hague Convention I, Article 3, *United States Treaty Series*, 36 stat. 2199, no. 536. See also the *Handbook on Peaceful Resolution of Disputes*, 60–68, attached as an annex to *Report of the Special Committee on the Charter of the UN and on the Strengthening of the Role of the Organization*, A/46/33, September 15, 1991.

7. See Thomas M. Franck and Greg Nolte, "The Good Offices Function of the UN Secretary-General," in *United Nations, Divided World: The UN's Roles in International Relations*, 2nd ed., ed. Adam Roberts and Benedict Kingsbury (Oxford and New York: Oxford University Press, 1996), 143–82.

8. Dag Hammarskjöld, "The International Civil Servant in Law and in Fact," Lecture delivered in congregation at Oxford University, May 30, 1961, in *Public Papers of the Secretaries-General of the United Nations, Volume V, Dag Hammarskjöld, 1960–1961*, ed. Andrew W. Cordier and Wilder Foote (New York and London: Columbia University Press, 1975), 471–89.

9. Kofi A. Annan, Address to the Council on Foreign Relations, New York, January 19, 1999. UN Press Release, SG/SM/6865, January 19, 1999.

10. See Alvaro de Soto's response to Saadia Touval's analysis of "Why the U.N. Fails," in *Foreign Affairs* 73, no. 5: 44–57; De Soto's response was published under the title, "The U.N. Responds," *Foreign Affairs* 74, no. 1: 186–87.

11. Under article 100 (2), each member state "undertakes to respect the exclusively international character of the responsibilities of the Secretary-General and the staff and not to seek to influence them in the discharge of their responsibilities."

12. Hammarskjöld, "The International Civil Servant in Law and Fact," 487–88. These committees built on Hammarskjöld's successful experience with an advisory committee established to help guide the preparations for the Atoms for Peace Conference held in Paris in August 1955 (the Advisory Committee on

the Peaceful Uses of Atomic Energy). See Prantl and Krasno, "Informal Groups of Member States," 320–27; and Prantl, *The UN Security Council and Informal Groups of States*, 47–69, for detailed accounts of the advisory committees.

13. In this respect they differed from the more informal advisory committee on Lebanon—in reality the UNEF committee meeting under another name—Hammarskjöld put in place in mid-1958 when the Security Council deadlocked over whether to expand the United Nations Observation Group in Lebanon (UNOGIL) established earlier that year to deter Syrian infiltration across Lebanon's borders. Ibid., 60–61.

14. General Assembly resloution A/1001 of November 7, 1956.

15. Although in the case of the UNEF committee, not all the troop contributors, as Prantl points out, in reflection of Hammarskjöld's efforts to keep the committee small. Prantl, *The UN Security Council and Informal Groups of States*, 51.

16. Hammarskjöld, "The Element of Privacy in Peacemaking," UN Press Release SG/656.

17. *Report of the Secretary-General, Summary Study of the Experience Derived from the Establishment and Operation of the Force*, A/3943, October 9, 1958, para. 181.

18. These "earlier cases" of good offices are discussed in Franck and Nolte, "The Good Offices Function of the UN Secretary-General," 144–8; and Thomas M. Franck, "The Secretary-General's Role in Conflict Resolution: Past, Present, and Pure Conjecture," *European Journal of International Law* 6, no. 3 (1995): 360–87. See also Kjell Skjelsbaek, "The UN Secretary-General and the Mediation of International Disputes," *Journal of Peace Research* 28, no. 19 (1991): 99–115.

19. Pérez de Cuéllar, *Pilgrimage for Peace*, 14.

20. "Report of the Secretary-General on the Work of the Organization, 1997," in Javier Pérez de Cuéllar, *Anarchy or Order: Annual Reports 1982–1991* (New York: United Nations, 1991), 135–36.

21. Pérez de Cuéllar, *Pilgrimage for Peace*, 178. The P-5 had been meeting together to discuss the Iran-Iraq war since late 1986, following an initiative taken by the British Permanent Representative, Sir John Thompson, to invite the five ambassadors to an informal meeting at his residence. David M. Malone, Introduction, *The UN Security Council: From the Cold War to the 21st Century*, ed. David M. Malone (Boulder, CO:, Lynne Rienner Publishers, 2004), 4.

22. UN press release, SG/SM/3956, January 13, 1987.

23. Cameron R. Hume, *The United Nations, Iran and Iraq: How Peacemaking Changed* (Bloomington, IN: Indiana University Press, 1994), 89.

24. Brian Urquhart, "The UN and International Security after the Cold War," *United Nations: Divided World*, ed. Roberts and Kingsbury, 81.

25. Between 1946 and 1989, some 270 vetoes were cast. As of March 2003, only 14 vetoes had been cast in public meetings since January 1990. See

Susan C. Hulton, "Evolving Council Working Methods," in *The UN Security Council*, ed. Malone, 238–39.

26. This change is evident in a review of the "Annual Joint Statements of Permanent Members," reproduced in Hume, *The United Nations, Iran and Iraq*, 231–35.

27. See Vivienne Jabri, *Mediating Conflict: Decision-Making and Western Intervention in Namibia* (Manchester, UK: Manchester University Press, 1990); and Heribert Weiland and Mathew Braham, eds., *The Namibian Peace Process: Implications and Lessons for the Future* (Freiburg: Arnold-Bergstraesser-Institut, 1994) for accounts of the Namibian peace process; and Crocker, *High Noon in Southern Africa: "Peacemaking in Southern Africa"*; Prantl, *The UN Security Council and Informal Groups of States*, 95–157; and Thomas Olson and Stephen John Stedman, *The New Is Not Yet Born: Conflict Resolution in Southern Africa* (Washington, DC: Brookings Institution, 1994) for southern Africa more generally.

28. Olson and Stedman, *The New Is Not Yet Born*, 93–94.

29. Crocker, *High Noon in Southern Africa*, 36.

30. Marrack Goulding describes a "multifunctional peacekeeping operation" as one "established to help the parties implement a negotiated settlement to their conflict; the peacekeepers are deployed after the peacemakers have done their job. This task requires a larger, more complicated and costlier operation than traditional peacekeeping because the functions performed extend far beyond the traditional supervision of cease-fires and buffer zones." *Peacemonger* (London: John Murray Publishers, 2002), 15.

31. Richard H. Solomon, "Bringing Peace to Cambodia," in *Herding Cats*, ed. Crocker et al., 282. See also Solomon's volume, *Exiting Indochina* (Washington, DC: United States Institute of Peace Press, 2000), and Jin Song, "The Political Dynamics of the Peacemaking Process in Cambodia," in *Keeping the Peace*, ed. Doyle et al., 53–81, for accounts of this many-layered process. A detailed account of the UN engagement in Cambodia is contained in the UN Blue Book on *The United Nations and Cambodia, 1991–1995* (New York: United Nations Department of Public Information, 1995).

32. See documents 1 and 2 in the Blue Book on Cambodia, 87–92, S/21087 of January 18, 1990, and A/45/472–S/21689 of August 31, 1990.

33. Document 19 in the Blue Book on Cambodia, 132–48. Letter dated October 30, 1991, transmitting full texts of agreement signed in Paris, October 23, 1991, A/46/608 –S/23177.

34. Doyle, "War Making, Peace Making and the United Nations," in *Turbulent Peace*, ed. Crocker et al., 540– 41; and Doyle et al., "Strategies for Peace: Conclusions and Lessons," in *Keeping the Peace*, 376–78.

35. China's ability to communicate with the Khmer Rouge and Russia's with Hun Sen were particularly valuable. Interview, former UNTAC official, March 26, 2004.

36. Cameron Hume, *Ending Mozambique's War: The Role of Mediation and Good Offices* (Washington, DC: United States Institute of Peace Press, 1994).

37. Ajello also met regularly with key African states: Botswana, Malawi, Kenya, Zimbabwe, and South Africa. Aldo Ajello, "Mozambique: Implementation of the 1992 Peace Agreement," in *Herding Cats*, ed. Crocker et al., 628; and Richard Synge, *Mozambique: UN Peacekeeping in Action, 1992–1994* (Washington, DC: United States Institute of Peace Press, 1997).

38. Statement by the President of the Security Council, January 31, 1992. S/23500.

39. Post-conflict peacebuilding was defined as "action to identify and support structures which will tend to strengthen and solidify peace in order to avoid a relapse into conflict." Boutros Boutros-Ghali, *An Agenda for Peace*, Report of the Secretary-General pursuant to the statement adopted by the Summit Meeting of the Security Council on January 31, 1992, A47/277–S/24111, June 17, 1992, para. 21.

40. Ibid., para. 62.

41. Figures from *Supplement to the Agenda for Peace*, Position Paper of the Secretary-General on the Occasion of the Fiftieth Anniversary of the United Nations, A/50/60–S/1995/1, January 3, 1995.

42. Doyle, "War Making, Peace Making and the United Nations," 531.

43. Goulding, *Peacemonger*, 260.

44. Only the Haiti group was constituted as Friends "of the Secretary-General" from the outset. The "Friends of Georgia" became the "Friends of the Secretary-General for Georgia" in 1997.

45. Richard Holbrooke, *To End a War* (New York: Random House, 1998).

46. On the distinction between "criminal" and "disciplined" warfare, see Mueller, *The Remnants of War*, 8–23.

47. See, for example, Mary Kaldor, *New and Old Wars: Organized Violence in a Global Era* (Stanford, CA: Stanford University Press, 1999); the Research Note by Stathis N. Kalyvas, "'New' and 'Old' Civil Wars: A Valid Distinction?" *World Politics* 54 (October 2001): 99–118; and Mueller, *The Remnants of War*, 86.

48. The literature on intervention is extensive. See International Commission on Intervention and State Sovereignty, *The Responsibility to Protect: Report of the International Commission on Intervention and State Sovereignty*, December 2001; Simon Chesterman, *Just War or Just Peace? Humanitarian Intervention and International Law* (Oxford: Oxford University Press, 2001); Mark R. Duffield, *Global Governance and the New Wars: The Merging of Development and Security* (London: Palgrave MacMillan, 2001); Martha Finnemore, *The Purpose of Intervention: Changing Beliefs about the Use of Force* (Cornell, NY: Cornell University Press, 2003); J.L. Holzgrefe and Robert O. Keohane, eds., *Humanitarian Intervention* (Cambridge, UK: Cambridge University Press, 2003); Nicholas J.

Wheeler, *Saving Strangers: Humanitarian Intervention in International Society* (Oxford: Oxford University Press, 2003).

49. See William Shawcross, *Deliver Us From Evil: Peacekeepers, Warlords and a World of Endless Conflict* (New York: Simon and Schuster, 2000), 118–23.

50. These included a pledge to consult Congress before voting to create a UN peacekeeping operation and the prohibition of U.S. troops serving under a UN command. See White House, Office of the Press Secretary, Statement by the Press Secretary, "President Clinton Signs New Peacekeeping Policy," May 5, 1994.

51. See Adekeye Adebajo and Chadra Lekha Sriram, *Managing Armed Conflicts in the 21ˢᵗ Century* (London: Frank Cass Publishers, 2001); Mats Berdal, *Whither UN Peacekeeping?* Adelphi Paper no. 281 (London: International Institute for Strategic Studies, 1993); William J. Durch, ed., *UN Peacekeeping, American Policy, and the Uncivil Wars of the 1990s* (New York: St. Martin's Press, 1996); and Bruce Jones with Feryal Cherif, "Evolving Models of Peacekeeping: Policy Implications and Responses," paper prepared for DPKO's Peacekeeping Best Practices Unit, 9/2003, available on www.un.org/depts/dpko/lessons.

52. Guatemala receives not a single mention in Boutros Boutros-Ghali's memoir, *Unvanquished: A U.S.–U.N. Saga* (New York: Random House, 1999).

53. Interview, Marrack Goulding, January 25, 2005.

54. *Supplement to An Agenda for Peace*, paras. 83–84.

55. Marrack Goulding, "The UN Secretary-General and the Security Council," in *The UN Security Council*, ed., Malone, 267–80.

56. Marrack Goulding, Internal report to the secretary-general on "Enhancing the United Nations' Effectiveness in Peace and Security," June 1997.

57. Kofi A. Annan, "Walking the International Tightrope," *New York Times*, January 19, 1999. The op-ed piece reproduced remarks Annan had delivered at the Council on Foreign Relations the same day. UN press release, SG/SM/6865, January 19, 1999.

58. *Report of the Panel on United Nations Peace Operations*, A/55/305–S/2000/809, August 21, 2000. The panel was headed by Brahimi; its report is currently referred to within the United Nations as the "Brahimi report."

59. For the sake of consistency, this book refers to Timor-Leste by its earlier name of East Timor, both before and after its independence.

60. Interview, Kieran Prendergast, July 14, 2004.

61. Madeleine Albright's remark was taken from an interview with her on NBC-TV, *The Today Show* with Matt Lauer, February 19, 1998. The use of the phrase "permanent one" by John R. Bolton, U.S. ambassador to the United Nations from August 2005 until December 2006, was cited in a *New York Times* editorial of March 9, 2005, "The World According to Bolton."

62. See David Malone, "Goodbye UNSCOM: A Sorry Tale in U.S.-UN Relations," *Security Dialogue* 30, no. 4 (December 1999): 393–411; David M.

Malone, *The International Struggle Over Iraq: Politics in the UN Security Council 1980–2005* (Oxford and New York: Oxford University Press, 2006); and Traub, *The Best Intentions*, for accounts of the complex evolution of this relationship.

63. "So serious" was the violation of the charter considered by the international legal scholar Thomas M. Franck that it put in question "the very concept and function of the entire post-war international system." Thomas M. Franck, "La charte des nations unies est-elle devenue un chiffon de papier?" *Le monde*, April 2, 2003. The assessment of Annan's High-Level Panel on Threats, Challenges and Change was understandably more nuanced: "That all states should seek Security Council authorization to use force is not a time-honoured principle; if this were the case, our faith in it would be much stronger. Our analysis suggests quite the opposite—that what is at stake is a relatively new emerging norm, one that is precious but not yet deep-rooted." Report of the High-Level Panel on Threats, Challenges and Change, *A More Secure World: Our Shared Responsibility* (New York: United Nations, December 2004), para. 82.

64. UN press release SG/SM/8643 of March 19, 2003; see also Kofi A. Annan, "Address at the College of William and Mary," Williamsburg, Virginia, February 8, 2003, SG/SM/8600, February 10, 2003; and Kofi Annan, "Keep the U.N. United," *Wall Street Journal*, March 11, 2003.

65. The Abu –Hafs al-Masri Brigade, a group affiliated with al-Qaeda, issued a statement claiming the United Nations is "a branch of the US State Department," cited in Quds Press (London), "Text of Al-Qaida Statement on Baghdad UN Headquarters Bombing," August 25, 2003. Richard Holbrooke, the former U.S. ambassador to the United Nations, wrote that the attack was not just an attack on the United Nations, but the United States as well, because the United Nations was "fulfilling an essential part of America's policy objectives." "Give the UN a Self-Protection Force in Iraq," *International Herald Tribune*, August 26, 2003.

66. The statement was made in an interview with BBC World Service. See "Excerpts, Annan interview," *BBC News*, September 16, 2004. www.news .bbc.co.uk.

67. Brian Urquhart, "The UN Oil-for-Food Program: Who Is Guilty?" *New York Review of Books*, February 9, 2006. Urquhart's summary of the differences between the North and South is a useful one: "The leading interests of the South are development; reducing poverty; reducing obstacles to free trade like farm subsidies in the U.S. and Europe; and preserving state sovereignty in an unequal world, by using the South's majority vote as leverage in the UN General Assembly. The North sees the UN as a forum for putting forward its political views; is more prepared to take action against errant states; champions human rights, peace and security and UN peacekeeping (ironically now carried out largely by soldiers from the South); favors more development by the private sector; and wishes to give more administrative

power to the secretary-general to counter micromanagement from the General Assembly."

68. David Malone describes how "with NATO offering only limited support, and the Coalition slowly unraveling, the United States was increasingly reliant on symbolic support from the UN to underpin its efforts in Iraq." *The International Struggle over Iraq*, 232. Lakhdar Brahimi was dispatched to Iraq in early 2004 as an envoy of the secretary-general charged with exploring ways forward toward representative government; the United Nations provided assistance in advance of the elections in Iraq held in early 2005.

69. UN Peacekeeping Operations, background note, October 31, 2006, www.un.org/depts/dpko.

70. General Assembly A/Res/60/1, agreed on September 15, 2005, World Summit Outcome, published on October 24, 2005.

71. UN press release, "Transcript of Press Conference by Secretary-General Kofi Annan at United Nations Headquarters," SG/SM/10809, December 19, 2006.

72. The Core Group met for the first time in September 2005 in New York. Its original members included Egypt, France, Italy, Lebanon, Russia, Saudi Arabia, the United Kingdom, the United States, the European Union/European Commission, the United Nations, and the World Bank. See Colum Lynch and Robin Wright, "U.S., U.N. Organize Support for Lebanon," *Washington Post*, September 20, 2005.

73. Alvaro de Soto was the envoy; his end of misssion report was sharply critical of both decisions. Alvaro de Soto, United Nations Special Coordinator for the Middle East Peace Process, "End of Mission Report," May 2007, www .guardian.co.uk.

74. *Report of the Secretary-General on the Work of the Organization*, A/57/1, September 2002, para. 25.

75. Suman Pradhan, "Long and Winding Road to UN mediation," *South Asia Intelligence Review* 4, no. 2 (July 25, 2005).

76. International Crisis Group, "Nepal's Crisis: Mobilising International Influence," *Asia Briefing* no. 49, April 19, 2006.

77. UN News Centre, "Praising Peace Deal in Nepal, Annan Calls on All Sides to 'Maintain the Momentum,'" November 8, 2006; *Report of the Secretary-General on the Request of Nepal for United Nations Assistance in Support of Its Peace Process*, S/2007/7, January 9, 2007; Tilak P. Pokharel, "Annan, Catalyst of Nepal Peace, Adieu!" *Kathmandu Post*, December 30, 2006.

78. See the *Human Security Report*; and Mikael Eriksson and Peter Wallensteen, "Armed Conflict, 1989–2003," *Journal of Peace Research* 41, no. 5 (2004); 625–36; Havard Hegre, "The Duration and Termination of Civil War,"

Journal of Peace Research 41, no. 3 (2004); 244; and Monty G. Marshall and Ted Robert Gurr, *Peace and Conflict 2003: A Global Survey of Armed Conflicts, Self-Determination Movements and Democracy* (College Park, MD: University of Maryland Center for International Development and Conflict Management, 2003).

79. High-Level Panel, *A More Secure World*, paras. 85–6; Paul Collier et al., *Breaking the Conflict Trap: Civil War and Development Policy* (Washington, DC: World Bank and Oxford University Press, 2003), 7.

80. On the OAU's efforts, see Margaret Vogt and Monde Muyangwa, "An Assessment of the OAU Mechanism for Conflict Prevention, Management, and Resolution, 1993–2000" (New York: International Peace Academy, 2000); see also Funmi Olonisakin, "African Peacekeeping at the Crossroads: An Assessment of the Continent's Evolving Peace and Security Architecture," paper prepared for the Best Practices Unit of the United Nations' Department of Peacekeeping Operations, September 2004, available on www.un.org/depts/peace/lessons.

81. See Adekeye Adebajo and Ismail Rashid, eds., *West Africa's Security Challenges: Building Peace in a Troubled Region* (Boulder, CO, and London: Lynne Rienner Publishers, 2004); Monica Juma and Aida Mengistu, *The Infrastructure of Peace in Africa: Assessing the Peacebuilding Capacity of African Institutions* (New York: International Peace Academy for the Ford Foundation, 2002); and Funmi Olonisakin and Comfort Ero, "Africa and the Regionalization of Peace Operations," in *The United Nations and Regional Security: Europe and Beyond*, ed. Michael Pugh and Waheguru Pal Singh Sidhu (Boulder, CO: Lynne Rienner Publishers, 2003), 233–51.

82. See, for example, Crocker et al., "Why Powerful States Mediate," *Taming Intractable Conflicts*, 21–43.

83. Interviews, Norwegian officials, January 29–30, 2004. On Norway's role in peace processes, see Vidar Helgesen, "Peace, Mediation and Reconciliation: The Norwegian Experience," speech by the State Secretary of Foreign Affairs of Norway, Brussels, May 21, 2003.

84. Switzerland was actively engaged in efforts toward peace in Colombia for many years, while Swiss mediators worked with the United States to facilitate an agreement on the Nuba Mountains in Sudan that was signed in Burgenstock, Switzerland, in January 2002; they also supported civil society involvement in the Middle East process that culminated in signing of the "Geneva Initiative" in December 2003 as well peacemaking efforts in Nepal and Uganda in 2005–06.

85. Griffiths, "Talking Peace in a Time of Terror," 6. For an indication of the range of activity conducted by the private peacemakers, see Crisis Management initiative, "Private Diplomacy Network: Mapping of Member Organisations," Fall 2006, www.cmi.fi.

86. Ahtisaari facilitated peace talks between the government of Indonesia and the Free Aceh Movement as chairman of the Crisis Management Initiative, the NGO he founded in 2000. His standing in Europe helped secure support of

the process by powerful allies and the prompt establishment of a monitoring operation jointly undertaken by the European Union and regional states in the latter part of 2005. See "The Method of Sant'Egidio," available on the Web site of the Community of Sant'Egidio, www.santegidio.org. The limits of private mediators are suggested by Konrad Huber in *The HDC in Aceh: Promises and Pitfalls of NGO Mediation and Implementation*, Policy Studies, no. 9 (Washington, DC: East-West Center, 2004).

87. Teresa Whitfield, "A Crowded Field: Groups of Friends, the United Nations and the Resolution of Conflict," an occasional paper of the Center on International Cooperation: Studies in Security Cooperation (Volume I), New York University, June 2005.

88. Chester A. Crocker, Fen Osler Hampson, and Pamela Aall, in *Herding Cats*, ed. Crocker et al., 40.

89. See James Fearon, "Why Do Some Civil Wars Last So Much Longer Than Others?" *Journal of Peace Research* 41, no. 3 (May 2004); 275–30; and Roy Licklider, "Comparative Studies of Long Wars," in *Grasping the Nettle*, ed. Crocker et al., 33–46.

90. As Madeleine Albright had observed, "for every crisis, it seemed the international community formed a group." See *Madam Secretary: A Memoir* (New York: Miramax Books, 2003), 322. In the aftermath of the tsunami of December 26, 2004, the United States announced the creation of a Core Group consisting of itself, Australia, India, and Japan. Its formation prompted immediate resistance among other donors and humanitarian actors, including within the UN secretariat, and it was disbanded on January 6, 2005. See Traub, *The Best Intentions*, 277–80.

91. Christopher Schewgmann, "Modern Concert Diplomacy: The Contact Group and the G7/8 in Crisis Management," in *Guiding Global Order, G8 Governance in the Twenty-First Century*, ed. John J. Kirton, Joseph P. Daniels, and Andreas Freytag (Aldershot, UK: Ashgate, 2001); Prantl, *The UN Security Council and Informal Groups*, 209–48.

92. The origin of the Quint was the staunch opposition by Russia to the positions taken by the Western members of the Contact Group on the Kosovo crisis, notably the authorization of NATO's military action in the spring of 1999.

93. See Luigi R. Einaudi, "The Ecuador-Peru Peace Process," in *Herding Cats*, ed. Crocker et al., 405–29.

94. The formation of the Friends reflected mounting international concern during the national strike launched by Venezuela's opposition in December 2002. Chávez would claim that the idea to form a group of Friends—which he had hoped would include both Russia and Cuba—had been his, and that its eventual composition (Brazil, as coordinator, plus Chile, Mexico, Portugal, Spain, and the United States)—was the result of the initiative's hijacking by Brazil and the United States. Annan had been directly involved in the messy

process that led to the group's formation and toyed with the idea of appointing former Spanish President Felipe González as his special envoy, in part because the United Nations doubted at the time that Gaviria's efforts to resolve the crisis would bear fruit. The crisis was defused by agreement on a recall referendum, which Chávez won with 58 percent of the vote in August 2004. Interviews, UN officials, March 26, 2003; September 2, 2004. "Chávez lanzó advertencia a cancilleres del Grupo de Amigos," El Nacional (Caracas), January 23, 2003.

95. The Wise Men were former statesmen from a variety of countries acting in their personal capacities, while the Tokyo Group was composed of the European Union, Japan, the United States, and the World Bank. Interview, Martin Griffiths, September 20, 2004.

96. By the early 2000s, many issues within the Council were "staffed" by identifiable groups under the coordination of a lead nation, whether explicitly acknowledged as such. See Pascal Teixeira, "Le Conseil de sécurité à l'aube du XXIème siècle," UNIDIR/2002/7, 12–15.

97. Interview, January 9, 2003.

98. See, for example, the remarks of Ireland, Jamaica, and Singapore in the wrap-up discussion on June 2001, S/PV.4343; Singapore in the wrap-up on November 2001, S/PV.4432.

99. The Africa Action Plan specifically endorsed Annan's proposal to establish "contact groups and other similar mechanisms to work with African countries to resolve specific African conflicts." Africa Action Plan, www.g7.utoronto.ca. In 1998, in an influential report on African conflict, Annan had noted, "The establishment of contact groups of interested countries, whether in the form of groups of 'Friends' or a special conference as in the case of Liberia, can be effective in mobilizing international support for peace efforts." Report of the Secretary-General, The Causes of Conflict and the Promotion of Durable Peace and Sustainable Development in Africa, S/1998/318, April 13, 1998.

100. Ould-Abdallah had thought that the NGOs could helpfully lobby for him with parliaments and through the media, but the group, as he would recall it, ended up having "unintended consequences"—the NGOs had "their own agenda related to questions of visibility and fundraising," and consequently would exaggerate Burundi's problems with a destabilizing effect on his own work. Interview, September 17, 2003.

101. The Netherlands had been so traumatized by the experience of its peacekeepers as powerless bystanders to the atrocities perpetrated in Srebrenica in 1995 that it had withheld contributing troops to any UN operation since that time. The decision to take part in UNMEE, taken alongside a number of northern states that rarely sent peacekeepers to Africa, was made on the basis that "UNMEE looked safe." But, even in an environment of relative safety, the Netherlands was concerned that it would never again be caught up in a peace-

keeping operation in which it had no control. It therefore led the effort to create the Friends of UNMEE. Interview, December 12, 2001.

102. Guinea-Bissau was one of three countries in Africa where the United Nations established a small peacebuilding office (the others being Liberia and the Central African Republic). The Friends of Guinea-Bissau was formed on the initiative of Gambia in early 1998 and was originally conceived as a means to help mobilize resources for peacebuilding and development. The secretariat suggested that the group should also articulate its support for the secretary-general in his efforts to consolidate peace within the country. Interviews, October 7, 2002, and March 26, 2003. See also *Report of the Secretary-General Pursuant to Security Council Resolution 1216 (1998) relative to the situation in Guinea-Bissau*, March 17, 1999, S/1999/294. The International Contact Group on Guinea-Bissau met for the first time in New York in September 2006; it was formed on the initiative of ECOWAS, with the support of the Community of Portuguese-Speaking Countries (CPLP) in an attempt to maintain international attention on Guinea-Bissau and its development. See *Report of the Secretary-General on developments in Guinea-Bissau and the activities of the United Nations Peace-building Support Office in that country*, S/2006/783, September 29, 2006, para. 5 and chap. 8, 250–51.

103. See *Special Report of the Secretary-General on the United Nations Operation in Burundi*, S/2005/586, September 14, 2005, paras. 40–43.

104. Groups of Friends were among the issues discussed at an Open Meeting of the Security Council on the Ad Hoc Working Group on Conflict Resolution and Prevention in Africa on May 22, 2002. See S/PV.4538 of May 22, 2002.

105. Annex to the letter dated August 29, 2002, from the permanent representative of Mauritius to the president of the Security Council, S/2002/979, of August 30, 2002.

2. The First Friends

1. Jeanne Kirkpatrick, U.S. Ambassador to the United Nations, 1981, cited in Walter LaFeber, *Inevitable Revolutions: The United States and Central America*, 2nd ed. (New York: W. W. Norton, 1993), 5. Some of the material in this chapter was developed in Teresa Whitfield, "The Role of the United Nations in El Salvador and Guatemala: A Preliminary Comparison," in *Comparative Peace Processes in Latin America*, ed. Cynthia J. Arnson (Stanford and Washington, DC: Stanford University Press and Woodrow Wilson Center Press, 1999), 257–90.

2. In assessing the outcome of the peace processes, it is important to consider what they actually aimed to achieve: the Salvadoran accords did not, for example, address economic and social issues in any depth; if implemented, the relatively modest reforms proposed in the Guatemalan agreements would have helped raise economic and social indicators in Guatemala, but not introduced a radical transformation. For the challenges of evaluating the implementation of peace agreements, see Downs and Stedman, "Evaluation Issues in Implementation."

3. See James Dunkerley, *The Pacification of Central America: Political Change in the Isthmus, 1987–1993* (London: Verso, 1994).

4. The two major political-military organizations, the Popular Liberation Forces (FPL) and the People's Revolutionary Army (ERP), were formed in 1970 and 1972. In 1980 they would join with the National Resistance (RN), the Salvadoran Communist Party (PCS) and its Armed Forces of National Liberation (FALN), and the Central American Revolutionary Workers' Party (PRTC) to form the FMLN.

5. The Revolutionary Democratic Front (FDR) had arisen out of the moderate Social Democrat and Christian Democrat movements of the 1970s. It would remain a wholly political organization even when allied with the politico-military organizations in the FMLN.

6. See Robert Armstrong and Janet Shenk, *El Salvador: The Face of Revolution* (Boston: South End Press, 1982); and Raymond Bonner, *Weakness and Deceite: U.S. Policy and El Salvador* (New York: Times Books, 1984) for compelling histories of this period.

7. See James K. Boyce, ed., *Economic Policy for Building Peace: The Lessons of El Salvador* (Boulder, CO: Lynne Rienner Publishers, 1996), especially chapters by Alexander Segovia; and Alvaro de Soto and Graciana del Castillo, "Obstacles to Peacebuilding," *Foreign Policy* 94 (Spring 1994): 69–83, for discussion of the tension between the structural adjustment and the peace process.

8. *Report of the Secretary-General on the United Nations Observer Mission to El Salvador (ONUSAL)*, S/25006, December 23, 1992, Annex II, Document 60 in the UN Blue Book, *The United Nations and El Salvador, 1990–1995* (New York: United Nations Department of Public Information, 1995), 281.

9. Elisabeth Jean Wood, *Forging Democracy From Below: Insurgent Transitions in South Africa and El Salvador* (Cambridge, UK, and New York: Cambridge University Press, 2000).

10. See Joaquín Tacsan, "Searching for OAS/UN Task Sharing Opportunities," in *Beyond Subcontracting: Task Sharing with Regional Security Arrangements and Service Providing NGOs*, ed. Thomas G. Weiss (New York: St. Martin's Press, 1998), 91–114.

11. For a detailed account of the actions of Contadora and the development of the Esquipulas Process, see Jack Child, *The Central American Peace Process, 1983–1991* (Boulder, CO: Lynne Rienner Publishers, 1992).

12. De Soto, "Ending Violent Conflict in El Salvador," 353.

13. S/Res/5300 of May 19, 1983, had somewhat timidly "commended" the efforts of Contadora.

14. Pérez de Cuéllar, *Pilgrimage for Peace*, 398–402.

15. The International Verification and Follow-up Commission (CIVS) consisted of the foreign ministers of the Contadora and Support Group countries as well as their Central American counterparts and the secretaries-general of the United Nations and OAS.

16. Marrack Goulding describes how the United Nations' "real objective" with ONUCA had two purposes: "to raise the political price that would be paid by any of [the Central American countries] that reneged on Esquipulas II; and to win for the UN a role in mediating settlements of the conflicts in Nicaragua, El Salvador, and Guatemala." *Peacemonger*, 218.

17. See Deborah Barry and Rodolfo Castro, "Negotiations, The War and Esquipulas II," in *A Decade of War: El Salvador Confronts Its Future*, ed. Andjali Sundaram and George Gelber (London and New York: Catholic Institute for International Relations and Monthly Review Press, 1991), 102–27; and Teresa Whitfield, *Paying the Price: Ignacio Ellacuría and the Murdered Jesuits of El Salvador* (Philadelphia: Temple University Press, 1994), 291–320, for discussion of earlier efforts at dialogue and negotiation.

18. The classic account of this process is Ignacio Ellacuría, "Una nueva fase en el proceso salvadoreño," *Veinte años de historia salvadoreña (1969–1989)*, *Tomo III, Escritos Políticos* (San Salvador: UCA Editores, 1991), 1855–97; for the viewpoint of the FMLN (or part of it; Salvador Samayoa was the FPL's representative on the Political-Diplomatic Commission during this period), see chapter on "El escenario de la pacificación imposible," in Salvador Samayoa, *La Reforma Pactada* (San Salvador: UCA Editores, 2002), 33–100.

19. I. William Zartman, "Ripening Conflict, Ripe Moment, Formula and Mediation," in *Perspectives on Negotiation: Four Case Studies and Interpretation*, ed. Diane B. Bendahmane and John W. McDonald Jr. (Washington, DC: Foreign Service Institute, U.S. Department of State, 1986), 205–07.

20. Joaquín Villalobos, "The Salvadoran Insurgency: Why Choose Peace?" in *Choosing to Engage*, ed. Ricigliano, 38.

21. The Franco-Mexican Declaration of August 1981 is reprinted in Robert S. Leiken and Barry Rubin, *The Central American Crisis Reader* (New York: Summit Books, 1987), 628–29.

22. Samayoa summarized the FMLN's fundamental problem with the Central American peace process as follows: "The regional agenda did not in any way touch upon the political and military reality of the war in El Salvador. On the contrary, it supposed that by deactivating a determined number of external factors, the Salvadoran crisis would automatically be overcome." *La Reforma Pactada*, 61 [author's translation].

23. Goulding, *Peacemonger*, 153–54. The FMLN raised the issue at a meeting with Vendrell in the margins of a nonaligned meeting in Harare; they had been fired up by President Mugabe, who warned them of the extent to which the United Nations would be manipulated. Interview, Francesc Vendrell, November 16, 2003.

24. Arms still flowed from elsewhere, including Cuba, which was much more ambivalent about the prospect of negotiation. Soviet Foreign Minister Eduard Shevardnadze had told the United States that Cuba still felt bound by "moral obligations" to support the FMLN, parallel, he suggested, to "the U.S. commitment to UNITA." National Security Archive, Washington, DC, declassified State Department cable, October 10, 1989.

25. Interview, Schafik Handal, December 3, 2002.

26. Letter from Schafik Handal, on behalf of the FMLN General Command, to the Secretary-General, December 18, 1989. Some aspects of these ideas had been discussed earlier with Vendrell.

27. Alvaro de Soto, interviewed by Jean Krasno, April 9, 1996, Yale/UN Oral History Project.

28. "Declaration of San Isidro, Coronado," annex to A/44/872–S/21019, Document 6 in *The United Nations and El Salvador*, 105–07. The summit meeting was described by Anders Kompass, a Swedish diplomat who attended it as Oscar Arias's adviser, as "terrible" and Cristiani as "visibly shaken" by the pressure upon him. Kompass and two other Swedish diplomats, Lars Franklin and Michael Frühling, had previously lobbied Arias, Guatemalan President Vinicio Cerezo, and Daniel Ortega, respectively, on the need to involve the United Nations in El Salvador. Interviews, Anders Kompass, February 5, 2003, and de Soto, June 12, 2003.

29. FMLN notes, Meeting with the United Nations, January 11, 1990.

30. Interviewed for the Yale/UN Oral History Project, Vendrell related the formation of the group of Friends to the "kind of support group of countries" with which the United Nations was working on ONUCA. These countries were West Germany, Canada, and Spain. Vendrell, interviewed by Jean Krasno, April 18, 1886, Yale/UN Oral History Project.

31. Text of the Geneva Agreement, Annex I, A/45/706–S/21931, November 8, 1990. Document 11 in *The United Nations and El Salvador*, 116.

32. Interview, Alfredo Cristiani, December 2, 2002.

33. Interview, David Escobar Galindo, December 3, 2002.

34. Cited in Whitfield, "The Role of the United Nations," 258.

35. Cristiani drew a parallel between this pressure and that put on the FMLN by the fall of the USSR. Interview.

36. Sweden, for example, financed a consultation with human rights experts in Geneva in May 1990, the conclusions of which would be reflected directly in the human rights agreement reached in June 1990.

37. Interview, Juan Antonio Yañéz-Barnuevo, December 19, 2004.

38. Interviews in El Salvador, Guatemala, and Mexico, December 2002 and February 2003.

39. Interview, Escobar Galindo.

40. Interview, Jorge Montaño, February 4, 2003.

41. See Diego Arria, "Bringing Leverage to the Peace Process in El Salvador and Central America," in *Leveraging for Success in UN Peace Operations*, ed. Jean Krasno, Bradd C. Hayes, and Donald C. F. Daniel (Westport, CT: Praeger, 2003), 56–7.

42. Interview, Salvador Samayoa, December 2, 2002.

43. Yañéz-Barnuevo had served as foreign policy adviser to Felipe González before his posting to New York; in that capacity he had been very involved in Central America since the end of 1982. Manuel Montobbio, who served in Spanish embassies in San Salvador, Mexico, and Guatemala City during the Central American peace processes, described a "Spanish-Mexican understanding" by which Spanish policy toward Latin America during the González period was constructed on the basis of prior agreement with Mexico. Interview, May 27, 2004.

44. Ties between the region and Europe were institutionalized from 1984 in the annual meetings of the San José Forum, consisting of the foreign ministers of the EU, the Contadora, and Central American countries. Interview, Montobbio. See also Manuel Montobbio, *La metamorfosis de pulgarcito: Transición política y proceso de paz en El Salvador* (Barcelona: Icaria Editorial, 1999), 180.

45. Interview, Fernando Cepeda, March 8, 2004.

46. Interview, Samayoa.

47. Yale/UN Oral History interview, de Soto.

48. A communiqué issued by the Friends and the United States on December 15, 1992, the day of the ceremony marking the cessation of the armed conflict in El Salvador, refers to the October 1990 start date. See Letter to the Secretary-General dated December 17, 1992, A/47/842–S/25007, December 23, 1992, annex, document 59 in *The United Nations and El Salvador*, 298. Details of the negotiations and the secretary-general's meetings described in this paragraph are drawn from the Javier Pérez de Cuéllar Papers, Manuscripts, and Archives, Yale University Library, especially strictly confidential notes to the secretary-general of September 21, 24, and October 1, 1990, and notes of the secretary-general's meetings with the FMLN, and the presidents of El Salvador, Spain, Mexico, and Venezuela on September 20, 29, and October 1. Detailed versions of these events are also contained in Prantl, *The UN Security Council*, 180–87.

49. Pérez de Cuéllar Papers, Nota confidencial sobre la reunión de Secretario General con los Representantes Permanentes de Colombia, España, Mexico, and Venezuela, December 12, 1990.

50. De Soto, "Ending Violent Conflict," 368–69.

51. Interview, Handal.

52. See Samayoa's account of this incident, *La Reforma Pactada*, 439–41.

53. A declassified memorandum from the State Department to Brent Scowcroft in the White House, dated July 9, 1991, noted that "President [Carlos Andrés] Pérez (CAP) has taken a very active role in pushing a global negotiation package favored by Salvadoran President Cristiani with the FMLN. Neither CAP nor the Mexicans have brought us into this effort, although Cristiani has kept us informed." The memo suggested that President Bush call President Salinas and ask him to support the Venezuelan initiative: "Frankly, I do not think the UN negotiator alone can bring the parties together this way. . . . If you, Carlos Andrés Pérez, and the other Friends of the Secretary-General could play a more direct role in establishing such a negotiation and pressing the FMLN to reach a ceasefire, I think it could be successful." National Security Archive, Washington, DC.

54. Interview, Yañéz-Barnuevo.

55. On November 17, 1989, Assistant Secretary of State Bernard Aronson had told Congress that the only fitting memorial to the Jesuits murdered in El Salvador the day before would be a "renewed commitment" to a negotiated solution in El Salvador. Cited in Whitfield, *Paying the Price*, 162.

56. See Clifford Krauss, "UN Aide Assailed in Salvadoran Talks," *New York Times*, February 1, 1991; Pérez de Cuellar, *Pilgrimage for Peace*, 426–30; de Soto, "Ending Violent Conflict in El Salvador," 371–75. In interviews with the author conducted during 1991–92, U.S. officials were quite outspoken in expressing these views.

57. The FMLN sent a steady stream of "nonpapers" to the State Department to explain its position on different aspects of the negotiations, but did not have contact with State Department officials until the very end of the process when, in July and August 1991, U.S. Ambassador William Walker visited an FMLN camp in El Salvador, the first time in the company of Representative Joe Moakley. Subsequently, as is mentioned below, discreet meetings between the FMLN and U.S. officials were arranged in New York.

58. This episode is described in detail by Samayoa, *La Reforma Pactada*, 550.

59. See de Soto, "Ending Violent Conflict in El Salvador," 371, and Pérez de Cuéllar Papers, Strictly confidential note to the file, October 1, 1990.

60. Pérez de Cuéllar, Papers, strictly confidential note of the secretary-general's meeting with the president of the United States, May 9, 1991.

61. Jorge Montaño would recall, "We always considered the United States a partner in the enterprise. They were the only ones who had leverage with the military. We could talk to the government, we could talk to the guerrillas, but the military would not pay any attention to us." Interview, February 4, 2003.

62. Joint letter dated August 1,1991, from the Secretary of State of the United States of America and the Minister of Foreign Affairs of the Union of Soviet Socialist Republics (USSR), transmitted to the Security Council in

S/22947 of August 15, 1991. Document 20 in *The United Nations and El Salvador*, 142–43.

63. In an e-mail to the author, de Soto would comment that "by convening a meeting at UNHQ [UN headquarters] of the full FMLN high command and Cristiani himself [Pérez de Cuéllar was] in effect daring the United States to deny visas to the comandantes (some of whom were extremely blacklisted) and daring Cristiani to refuse to turn up." February 20, 2004.

64. The Friends were all involved in discussion of the mechanisms by which former members of the FMLN would participate within a new national civilian police. The New York meetings concluded in agreements that provided for the creation of the National Commission for the Consolidation of Peace to oversee implementation of the political agreements, and for purification of the armed forces and the establishment of the national civil police. A related agreement on "the compressed negotiations" established that all substantive agreements would be negotiated and agreed before a cease-fire. See A/46/502/Add.1–S/23082/Add.1, annex.

65. Pérez de Cuéllar Papers, note to the secretary-general, December 7, 1991.

66. Interview, Yañéz-Barnuevo.

67. Interviews, Arria, Montaño, and Yañéz-Barnuevo.

68. Arria, "Bringing Leverage to the Peace Process in El Salvador and Central America," 72–76.

69. At this juncture Montaño recalled being handed a note by Bernard Aronson, offering to call the Federal Air Authority and stop the secretary-general's plane. His own interpretation of the secretary-general's position was that "he may just have been pushing the parties." Interview.

70. Barbara F. Walter identified three characteristics of a "credible" third-party guarantee: self-interest in upholding the guarantee; willingness to use force; and an ability to signal resolve. "The Critical Barrier to Civil War Settlement," *International Organization* 51, 3 (Summer 1997): 335–64.

71. Colombia, Spain, and Venezuela were among the countries contributing military observers to ONUSAL's military division, which was under the command of Spanish Brigadier General Victor Suanzes Pardo. Chile, Spain, and Mexico also contributed police observers. S/23999, May 26, 1992, document 41, *The United Nations and El Salvador*, 238–46. Mexico's decision to contribute police observers responded to a request made by Felipe González to Salinas to send military observers. Highway police were sent instead—the "least bad option" according to the then Mexican ambassador in El Salvador, who recalled the little confidence he had held in the other branches of Mexico's security forces. Interview, Hermilo López-Bassols, February 4, 2003.

72. ONUSAL was brought to an end in April 1995, but was succeeded by smaller political missions mandated by the General Assembly, the Mission of the

United Nations in El Salvador (MINUSAL) from May 1995 to April 1996, and United Nations Verification Office (ONUV) from May to December 1996. Verification duties were transferred to the United Nations Development Programme (UNDP) and were formally closed in December 2002.

73. See de Soto and del Castillo, "Obstacles to Peacebuilding," and James K. Boyce, ed., *Economic Policy for Building Peace: The Lessons of El Salvador* (Boulder, CO: Lynne Rienner Publishers, 1996).

74. On implementation of the peace agreements in El Salvador, see Boyce, ed., *Economic Policy for Peacebuilding*, especially Elisabeth J. Wood, "The Peace Accords and Postwar Reconstruction," 73–105; Charles C. Call, "Assessing El Salvador's Transition from War to Peace," in *Ending Civil Wars*, ed. Stedman et al.; Doyle et al., *Keeping the Peace*; de Soto and del Castillo, "Obstacles to Peacebuilding"; David Holiday and William Stanley, "Under the Best of Circumstances: ONUSAL and Challenge of Verification and Institution Building," in *Peacemaking and Democratization in the Western Hemisphere*, ed. Tommie Sue Montgomery (Boulder, CO: Lynne Rienner Publishers, 1999), 37–65; Roland Paris, *At War's End: Building Peace after Civil Conflict* (Cambridge, UK: Cambridge University Press, 2004); Jack Spence et al., *Chapúltepec: Five Years Later, El Salvador's Political Reality and Uncertain Future* (Cambridge, MA: Hemisphere Initiatives, 1997); Margarita S. Studemeister, ed., *El Salvador: Implementation of the Peace Accords*, Peaceworks No. 38 (Washington, DC: United States Institute of Peace, January 2001).

75. See *Report of the Secretary-General on the monitoring of agreements by ONUSAL*, S/23402, January 13, 2002, and S/Res/729, January 14, 1992, documents 34 and 35 in the *United Nations and El Salvador*, 187–93.

76. Samayoa, *La Reforma Pactada*, 552; interviews, Cristiani and Santamaría.

77. See Blanca Antonini, "El Salvador," in *The UN Security Council*, ed. Malone, 423–36.

78. A notable example was the renegotiation of the land transfer program in October 1992. See Goulding, *Peacemonger*, 241–44, and Graciana del Castillo, "The Arms-for-Land Deal in El Salvador," in *Keeping the Peace*, ed. Doyle et al., 346–51.

79. To suggest, as has Manuel Montobbio, that the Friends represented a direct counterpart to ONUSAL as a "double institutionalization of international participation in the process" is an exaggeration of the weight they carried. Manuel Montobbio, "Coherencia de políticas y construcción de la paz," in *Financiación del desarrollo y coherencia en las políticas de los donantes*, ed. José Antonio Alonso and Valpy FitzGerald (Madrid: Catarata, 2003), 273.

80. The overwhelming weight of the United States among external actors in El Salvador is illustrated by contributions to external assistance. UNDP reported that of $698.9 million in official external assistance contributed to El Salvador between 1992 and 1995 by bilateral actors, $535.9 million had come from the

United States. Cited in James K. Boyce, "External Resource Mobilization," in *Economic Policy for Building Peace: The Lessons of El Salvador*, ed. Boyce, 131.

81. Interview, Iqbal Riza, June 17, 2003.

82. Interview, Enrique ter Horst, January 24, 2002.

83. See Teresa Whitfield, "Staying the Course in El Salvador," *Honoring Human Rights: From Peace to Justice*, ed. Alice H. Henkin (Washington, DC: Aspen Institute, 1998), 184.

84. See Report of the Secretary-General, *Assessment of the Peace Process in El Salvador*, July 1, 1997, A/51/917.

85. Interview, February 4, 2003.

86. After the final demobilization in December 1992 (as was referred to on page 72), major hurdles in implementation were presented by the Salvadoran government's continuing failure to dismiss military officers in accordance with the recommendations of the ad hoc commission, the publication of the findings of El Salvador's Truth Commission, in March 1993, and the explosion of a secret cache of FMLN weapons in Managua, Nicaragua, in May 1993.

3. Friends and the "Ripening" of Peace in Guatemala

1. See UN news release, "In final report, Annan hails UN mission in Guatemala as model of success," April 14, 2005.

2. This process is described by Susanne Jonas, *Of Centaurs and Doves: Guatemala's Peace Process* (Boulder, CO: Westview Press, 2000), 21–30.

3. See James Dunkerly, *Power in the Isthmus* (London: Verso, 1988); Susanne Jonas, *The Battle for Guatemala* (Boulder, CO: Westview Press, 1991); Jennifer Schirmer, *The Guatemalan Military Project: A Violence Called Democracy* (Philadelphia: University of Pennsylvania, 1998).

4. See Annex II, S/1997/432, of June 4, 1997. The four organizations that made up the URNG were the Revolutionary Organization of the People in Arms (ORPA), the Rebel Armed Forces (FAR), the Guatemalan Workers' Party (PGT), and the Guerrilla Army of the Poor (EGP).

5. In an interview, former URNG commander Rodrigo Asturias cited much weaker ties between the URNG and the Soviet bloc, and even Cuba, than had been enjoyed by the FMLN. December 7, 2002. A senior official of the Cuban Communist party explained the difference in Cuban support as follows: "The main difference was a different military prowess and yield. There was also a politically different presence of the FMLN in El Salvador from that of the URNG in Guatemala." Interview cited by Jorge G. Castañeda, *Utopia Unarmed: The Latin American Left after the Cold War* (New York: Alfred A. Knopf, 1993), 95.

6. During 1982–83 nearly 80 percent of the male population in indigenous rural areas were militarized into the PACs. Susan C. Peacock and Adriana

Beltrán, *Hidden Powers in Post-Conflict Guatemala* (Washington, DC: Washington Office on Latin America, December 2003), 25.

7. Cristiani created an interparty commission composed of representatives of the nine political parties in the legislative assembly to interact with the parties to the negotiations. It was largely peripheral to the negotiations, but played an essential role in securing legislative support for their outcome. Tricia Juhn, *Negotiating Peace in El Salvador: Civil-Military Relations and the Conspiracy to End the War* (London and New York: Macmillan and St. Martin's Press, 1998), 58.

8. See William D. Stanley, "Justice and Public Security Reform in Post-War Guatemala," in Charles T. Call, ed., *Constructing Justice and Security after War* (Washington, DC: United States Institute of Peace Press, 2006), 113–55.

9. Jean Arnault, "Reflections," *Comparative Peace Processes*, ed. Arnson, 293.

10. United Nations, *The Guatemala Peace Agreements* (New York: Department of Public Information, 1997).

11. Dinorah Azpuru, "Peace and Democratization in Guatemala," in *Comparative Peace Processes*, ed. Arnson, 97–125.

12. An unsuccessful meeting with the URNG was convened by the Spanish government and held in Madrid in October 1987. A comprehensive account of the Guatemalan peace process is given in Jonas, *Of Centaurs and Doves*. See also Enrique Alvarez, "The Grand National Dialogue and the Oslo Consultations: Creating a Peace Agenda" (London: Conciliation Resources, 2003); and David Holiday, "Guatemala's Long Road to Peace," *Current History* 96, no. 606 (February 1997): 68–74.

13. The Oslo Agreement, Annex III to A/45/706–S/21931, of November 8, 1990, Document 11 in *The United Nations and El Salvador*, 118–19.

14. Héctor Rosada-Granados, *El Lado Oculto de las Negociaciones de Paz* (Guatemala: Fundación Friedrich Ebert, 1998).

15. Interview, General Julio Balconi, December 6, 2002.

16. A government proposal to replace Vendrell with a retired president was vigorously opposed by the URNG, which was understandably concerned about the institutional allegiances of presidents.

17. The research institute Fafo, under the leadership of Terje Rød-Larsen, developed the Oslo channel in the Middle East Peace Process; Norwegian Church Aid helped land a role for Norway in the Sudan, while individual contacts made outside the Foreign Ministry led to Norway's involvement in Sri Lanka.

18. Interviews, Rolf Berg, December 5, 2002, and Jan Egeland, January 15, 2004.

19. Senior military officers were brought to Oslo on several occasions and treated "like officers and gentlemen" while the benefits of peace were explained to them. Interview, Arne Aasheim, January 30, 2004.

20. Jean Arnault, e-mail to the author, February 6, 2003. Susanne Jonas relates how in 1993, when formal negotiations were stalled, Norway, which she describes as the "honest broker" among the Friends, prepared for a secret "second track" that was to also involve Israel because of its ties to the army. Even then, this initiative was designed to pave the way for the resumption of negotiations, under a UN lead. Jonas, *Of Centaurs and Doves*, 43.

21. Proposal for the immediate signing of the agreement of the agreement on a firm and lasting peace in Guatemala, annex to A/47/873–S/25134, January 21, 1993.

22. E-mail from Alvaro de Soto, who recalled several accounts of this meeting, April 10, 2005. Marilyn McAfee, "The Search for Peace in Guatemala: Ending a 36-Year Conflict," March 1997, mimeo, 6. (McAfee served as U.S. ambassador to Guatemala from 1993 to 1996.) Serrano also met in this period with President Cristiani of El Salvador and, having been reassured of the Friends' utility, confirmed that he needed some Friends too. Interview, Oscar Santamaria, December 3, 2002.

23. Rosario Green also asked President Salinas to call Serrano to underline the points that had been made to him in their meeting in Guatemala. Telephone interview, Rosario Green, June 19, 2003. Also interviews with Arria; Rodrigo Asturias, December 7, 2002; and Manuel Tello, February 5, 2003.

24. Pérez even arranged a secret meeting between Serrano and the URNG in this period.

25. Rodrigo Asturias explained, "It was also a strategic decision on our part —we thought that the involvement of the United States would strengthen our hand with respect to the private sector and the army." At one point the government suggested the inclusion of Chile; the URNG countered with Costa Rica, confident that army-less Costa Rica would be anathema to the armed forces and that both ideas would be dropped forthwith, which they were. Interview. Rolf Berg, then Norwegian ambassador to Mexico, remembered "arguing Norway's way on to the group" with Serrano by insisting that Norway had an objective commitment to the cause of peace. Interview, December 4, 2002.

26. As a member of an international support group, also composed of Canada, France, and Sweden, Mexico facilitated the negotiation of agreements by the United Nations High Commissioner for Refugees reached in October 1992 that provided for the refugees' return to Guatemala in advance of the formal end to the conflict.

27. Telephone interview, Green.

28. In the aftermath of Serrano's *autogolpe*, the OAS secretary-general, João Baena Soares, held meetings with both the government and the URNG to discuss a role in the peace process. The URNG had suggested to Arnault the possibility of joint mediation by the two organizations, but had been told that a joint effort was unlikely to prosper.

29. Interview, Egeland.

30. "The Framework Agreement for the Resumption of the Negotiating Process between the Government of Guatemala and the Unidad Revolucionaria Nacional Guatemalteca," in *The Guatemala Peace Agreements*, 9–14.

31. Four of these consultations were held, in Washington, Costa Rica, Guatemala, and Oslo. This section draws on discussions with Jean Arnault, as well as an interview conducted by Connie Peck as part of the United Nations Institute for Training and Research (UNITAR) Programme for Briefing and Debriefing Special and Personal Representatives and Envoys of the UN Secretary-General. Consulted with the permission of Jean Arnault.

32. Interview, Gert Rosenthal, February 11, 2003.

33. UNITAR interview, Arnault.

34. E-mail, Arnault.

35. During the negotiations de Soto had made the point on several occasions that U.S. officials would benefit from direct interaction with the FMLN.

36. Telephone interview, John Hamilton, June 18, 2003; McAfee, "The Search for Peace in Guatemala," 14.

37. See Susanne Jonas, "Dangerous Liaisons: The U.S. in Guatemala," *Foreign Policy* 103 (Summer 1996): 144–60; and *Of Centaurs and Doves*, 119–66. Pressure on the administration intensified after revelations in March 1995 that a Guatemalan officer on the payroll of the Central Intelligence Agency had been involved in the murders of a guerrilla commander, Efraín Bamaca, the partner of a U.S. lawyer, Jennifer Harbury; and a U.S. citizen, Michael DeVine.

38. Interview, Montobbio.

39. E-mail, Arnault.

40. The report of the Commission on the Truth was attached as an annex to S/25500, April 1, 2003.

41. Interviews, Asturias, Berg, and Egeland. The direct pressure of Norway on the URNG would also be exerted in October 1994, when Egeland encouraged Asturias to accept an early resumption of the stalled talks. That Sweden was not a Friend of Guatemala (although URNG officials would later muse in interviews that "it easily could have been"), while Norway was, had been a blow to it: Sweden—unlike Norway—had a large embassy in Guatemala and had been deeply involved in promotion of peace in Central America throughout the 1980s.

42. Despite its weak mandate, the Guatemalan commission produced a hard-hitting report that considerably exceeded expectations. It attributed 93 percent of violations documented to the military or state-backed paramilitary forces and held the state responsible for acts of genocide against Mayan commities. See Priscilla B. Hayner, *Unspeakable Truths: Confronting State Terror and Atrocity* (New York and London: Routledge, 1991), 45–49.

43. Whitfield, "The Role of the United Nations," 272–73.

44. Arnault's views, which are discussed in note 58 below, were somewhat different.

45. Operations mandated by the Security Council are financed by assessed contributions to the peacekeeping budget, which place a greater burden on the United States.

46. In the end only a small military component of MINUGUA would be authorized by the Security Council to oversee the demobilization of URNG combatants, while the bulk of the mission remained under the authority of the General Assembly.

47. See de Soto and del Castillo, "Obstacles to Peacebuilding," and Boyce, ed., *Economic Policy for Building Peace: The Lessons of El Salvador.*

48. Interview, Jean Arnault, February 2, 1997. World Bank, *aide memoire* of the informal meeting on Guatemala held on June 15, 1994, Paris.

49. Arzú dismissed a number of senior officers associated with abuses of the past from the army, introduced a revision to the military code to allow military officials to be prosecuted for common crimes in civilian courts, and announced that the infamous civilian defense patrols (the PACs) would be demobilized by November 15. This section draws on interviews with Arnault, Asturias, Balconi, Ricardo Stein, and Raquel Zelaya, the latter both conducted on December 6, 2002. See also comments of Julio Balconi in *Comparative Peace Processes*, ed. Arnson, 127–28.

50. Interview, Stein.

51. David Holiday and William Stanley make a similar point, "Broad Participation, Diffuse Responsibility: Peace Implementation in Guatemala," in *Ending Civil Wars*, ed. Stedman et al., 437.

52. The other Friends had been perturbed by Spain's call for a meeting in Madrid on the financial needs of the peace process, to coincide with the signing of the agreement on reintegration. This was in the end limited to issues relating to reintegration.

53. John Hamilton recalled receiving a telephone call from Arnault asking him to travel to Mexico that day to talk to the URNG and convince Asturias to sit out the final rounds of negotiations. He would describe doing so as "really the only identifiable thing I did as a Friend, and in a sense payback for all the time invested in building relationships beforehand." Telephone interview. That Asturias was the guerrilla commander with the closest relationship to the Friends made the incident especially painful.

54. Particularly damaging for the United Nations were allegations that Arnault was implicated in the cover-up of the disappearance of a member of the URNG captured during the operation to rescue the kidnapped woman. Although no evidence emerged to substantiate the accusations against Arnault, the scandal served to weaken MINUGUA, of which he had just assumed leadership, at a critical moment in the peace process, and the precise details of the episode remained deeply contested by many of the UN officials involved. See

Jack Spence et al., *Promise and Reality: Implementation of the Guatemalan Peace Accords* (Cambridge, MA: Hemisphere Initiatives, August 1998), 59–62.

55. Interview, Montobbio; "Agreement on a Firm and Lasting Peace," in *The Guatemalan Peace Agreements*, 252.

56. On implementation of the peace agreements in Guatemala, see Jean Arnault, "Good agreement? Bad agreement? An implementation perspective," Center on International Studies, Princeton University, 2003, www.peacemaker .unlb.org/; Stanley and Holiday, "Broad Participation, Diffuse Responsibility," in *Ending Civil Wars*, ed. Stedman et al.; Jonas, *Of Centaurs and Doves*; Paris, *At War's End*; Hilde Salvesen, *Guatemala: Five Years after the Peace Accords: The Challenges of Implementing Peace*, a report for the Norwegian Ministry of Affairs (Oslo: PRIO, March 2002); Jack Spence et al., *Promise and Reality*; Jack Spence et al., *Who Governs? Guatemala Five Years After the Peace Accords* (Cambridge, MA: Hemisphere Initiatives, January 2002); and A Report by the Bureau for Crisis Prevention and Recovery (BCPR) of UNDP, "Guatemala: The Long Struggle for Peace," January 2002, mimeo.

57. Report of the Secretary-General, *United Nations Verification Mission in Guatemala*, A/59/307, August 30, 2004, paras. 60-71.

58. How much difference the lack of Security Council oversight made to the course of implementation in Guatemala is difficult to assess. Arnault, who had not shared Goulding's conviction in 1994 that the Security Council was necessarily the best way to go, remained agnostic on the issue. He had always believed that the Security Council's "notorious uninterest" in nonsecurity issues, such as the socioeconomic, indigenous, and institutional reforms at the center of the Guatemalan process, did not suggest that it would have played an effective role. But he also accepted that a lack of access to the Security Council made more difference than he had expected when MINUGUA was established under the General Assembly, not least because of the disappointing performance of the Friends. UNITAR and author interviews. Tom Koenigs, the special representative of the secretary-general during MINUGUA's final two years, considered that it made no difference to his work. Interview, October 13, 2004. As noted below (note 87) other officials working on Guatemala in this period thought the Security Council might have been helpful on CICIACS. However, it is worth recalling that even if MINUGUA had been initiated under a Council mandate, it would in all likelihood have been moved to the General Assembly by this time.

59. Involving the deployment of military observers, this was the single aspect of implementation that came under the authority of the Security Council. See *Report of the Secretary-General on the Military Observers Attached to MIUGUA*, S/1997/432, June 4, 1997.

60. This point was made by several former officials of the Arzú government interviewed in December 2002. See also BCPR report, "Guatemala: The Long Struggle for Peace," 10.

61. The "hidden" or "parallel" powers (*poderes paralelos*) represented a particularly alarming impediment to progress in Guatemala. Peacock and Beltran described them as an "informal amorphous network of powerful individuals in Guatemala who use their positions and contacts in the public and private sectors both to enrich themselves from illegal activities and to protect themselves from prosecution from the crimes they commit." *Hidden Powers in Post-Conflict Guatemala*, 5.

62. Most of these visits were by Kieran Prendergast, under-secretary-general for political affairs throughout the period of implementation of Guatemala's peace agreements.

63. As Arnault described it, "For the first time in the country's electoral history, the population was split with ominous clarity along ethnic lines: the reform agenda won in areas populated by an majority of indigenous population; it lost elsewhere." "Good Agreement? Bad Agreement?" note 6, 5. The Guatemalan constitution requires that reforms to it be approved by a two-thirds vote in Congress, followed by a popular referendum. A strength of the Salvadoran process was the constitution's provision for the relatively expeditious approval of legislative and constitutional reform.

64. Arnault, UNITAR interview. A Norwegian official with long experience of the Guatemalan process expressed his personal view that "it was a monumental blunder to dump in their lap some of history's most complex accords when they were no way equipped to implement them. The international community wanted it all at once and the capacity was just not there." Interview, December 5, 2002.

65. This was significant because the Friends' status during peacemaking had—in contrast to the group in El Salvador—been established by the Framework Agreement.

66. E-mail, Arnault.

67. Montobbio, "Coherencia de políticas y construcción de la paz," 267–94. Spain was particularly sensitive to the substitution of Latin American actors by rich donor states from the global North, in part because it affected Spain's own influence as a bridge between Latin America and Europe.

68. Gino Costa, "The United Nations and Reform of the Police in El Salvador," *International Peacekeeping*. 2, no. 3 (Autumn 1995): 365–90; Stanley, "Justice and Public Security Reform," 133; Whitfield, "Staying the Course in El Salvador," 169–70.

69. In August 2004 the secretary-general described the Guatemalan police force as being in "a deplorable condition." A/59/307. Donor competition within the security and justice sectors was typified by but not limited to Spain and the United States which became increasingly preoccupied by issues relating to drug trafficking and organized crime. Stanley comments: "The disunity of international donors has amplified, rather than dampened, the parochialism of Guatemalan state institutions." "Justice and Public Security Reform," 139.

70. Interview, MINUGUA official, December 4, 2002; telephone interview, Gerd Merrem, February 14, 2005.

71. James K. Boyce, "External Assistance and Peace Building," in Shepard Forman and Stewart Patrick, eds., *Good Intentions: Pledges of Aid for Post-Conflict Recovery* (Boulder, CO: Lynne Rienner Publishers, 2000), 367–82.

72. Figure cited in Report of the Secretary-General, *United Nations Mission for the Verification of Human Rights and of Compliance with the Commitments of the Comprehensive Agreement on Human Rights in Guatemala*, A/51/828, para. 5.

73. The second post-peace Consultative Group, held in October 1998 in Brussels, was delayed from June by EU concerns that the Guatemalans had not lived up to their commitments. See Montobbio, "Coherencia de políticas y construcción de la paz," 280; and Jonas, *Of Centaurs and Doves*, 177–80, for discussions of the mixed trajectory of peace conditionality in Guatemala.

74. Interview, Stein, December 6, 2002.

75. Jonas, *Of Centaurs and Doves*, 177.

76. The IMF did not maintain representation within Guatemala. Although a cooperative partner during the early years of implementation, it proved less so from 2000 on. In 2001 it approved a standby loan on the basis of a tax revenue of 10.7 percent of GDP (not the stated goal of 12 percent), thereby undermining peace implementation in the eyes of some UN officials. Interview, MINUGUA official, December 4, 2002.

77. The Dialogue Groups emerged from a donor meeting held in Stockholm in May 1999. Sweden's prominence in Guatemala was helped by the presence of a former Swedish diplomat, Lars Franklin, as resident representative of UNDP until 2001. Interview, Kompass.

78. The Dialogue Group consisted of Canada, Germany, Japan, the Netherlands, Norway, Spain, Sweden, the United States, the EU, the IDB, and the World Bank, with the UNDP and MINUGUA as observers.

79. Interview, Maria Leissner, December 4, 2002.

80. On October 10, 2002, Otto Reich, the assistant secretary of state for Western Hemispheric Affairs, denounced extensive corruption and drug trafficking among government officials and their associates. See "Corruption and other threats to democratic stability in the Dominican Republic and Guatemala," House International Relations Subcommittee on the Western Hemisphere. Guatemala was subsequently "decertified" by the United States as a country that had "failed demonstrably" to meet its international counternarcotics requirements. Statement by Paul E. Simons, acting assistant secretary of state for international counternarcotics and law enforcement affairs, "Briefing on the President's FYI 2003

Narcotics Certification Determinations," Washington DC, January 31, 2003. Statements on www.state.gov.

81. Telephone interview, Merrem.

82. The 2002 Consultative Group meeting had concluded with the government's assumption of nine commitments to advance the peace process; MINUGUA's report to the 2003 meeting chronicled that little progress had been made in their implementation. Interview, Juan Pablo Corlazolli, December 6, 2002.

83. In 2003, for example, consensus within the Dialogue Group on the need for a strong statement to be issued at the conclusion of the Consultative Group meeting eroded in the face of appeals from the Guatemalan government to the IDB for gentler treatment. Interview, Tom Koenigs, May 24, 2004.

84. Interview, Rosenthal. Rosenthal had been executive director of the United Nations' Economic Commission on Latin America and the Caribbean and then served as a civil society "notable" within the Follow-up Commission established to oversee implementation of Guatemala's accords. He was greatly respected in New York, where he was seen to represent the wider interests of his country rather than the Portillo administration.

85. An agreement to form the Commission of Investigation of Illegal Groups and Clandestine Security Forces (CICIACS) was signed on January 7, 2004. This was a civil society initiative vocally supported by Guatemalan human rights groups, international NGOs and governments concerned by the rising tide of attacks and threats against human rights defenders, justice officials, lawyers, journalists, union leaders, academics, and others. Guatemala's Constitutional Court issued a nonbinding advisory opinion against CICIACS on August 6, 2004, and the commission was never formed.

86. Report of the Secretary-General, *United Nations Verification Mission in Guatemala,* A/59/746, March 18, 2005, paras. 47–58.

87. One official involved in the CICIACS effort would contrast the United Nations' experience in trying to get the commission off the ground, with the support of the Friends and General Assembly, with the formation of the Joint Group for the Investigation of Politically Motivated Illegal Armed Groups in El Salvador. This was done at an earlier stage of the implementation process (late 1993), and with the full support of the Security Council. E-mail communication with the author, April 18, 2006.

88. UN press release, "Guatemala and UN Sign Deal for Independent Body to Probe Illegal Armed Groups," December 12, 2006. Although CICIG had a weaker mandate than that of CICIACS, its agreement was warmly welcomed by human rights groups, who had followed the travails of CICIACS with concern.

89. See, for example, the chapters by Diego Arria and Jean Krasno in Krasno et al., *Leveraging for Success.*

90. Spain's ambassador to the United Nations underlined the significance of the fact that meetings of the Friends in New York took place in English,
not Spanish, to accommodate Norwegian and U.S. diplomats. Interview, Yañez-
Barnuevo.

91. Telephone interview, Hamilton.

4. Principal Friend

1. See chapter 5, 145.

2. On this point see, for example, Paul Farmer, "Who Removed Aris-
tide?" *London Review of Books* 26, no. 8 (April 15, 2004). For background to
Haiti's history, see Robert Debs Heinl Jr. and Nancy Fordon Heinl, *Written in
Blood: The Story of the Haitian People, 1492–1971* (Boston: Houghton Mifflin,
1978); Robert Fatton Jr., *Haiti's Predatory Republic: The Unending Transition to
Democracy* (Boulder, CO: Lynne Rienner Publishers, 2002); and Michel-Rolph
Trouillot, *Haiti, State against Nation: The Origins and Legacy of Duvalierism* (New
York: Monthly Review Press, 1990).

3. This point is made by Sebastian Einseidel and David Malone, "Haiti,"
in *The UN Security Council*, ed. Malone, 467.

4. Georges A. Fauriol, "U.S. Policy and the Ouster of Duvalier," *Haitian
Frustrations: Dilemmas for U.S. Policy*, ed. Georges A. Fauriol (Washington, DC:
Center for Strategic and International Studies, 1995), 50.

5. See Robert Maguire et al., *Haiti Held Hostage: International Responses to
the Quest for Nationhood, 1986–1996* Occasional Paper no. 23, (Providence, RI:
Thomas J. Watson Jr. Institute for International Studies, 1996), 13–28.

6. This history of the United Nations' engagement in Haiti between
1990 and 1996 is documented in the UN Blue Book, *Les Nations Unies et Haïti,
1990–1996* (New York: United Nations Department of Public Information,
1996). David Malone, *Decision-Making in the UN Security Council: The Case of
Haiti* (Oxford: Clarendon Press, 1998) is an invaluable resource on the United
Nations' engagement in Haiti between 1990 and 1997.

7. See Lawyers Committee for Human Rights, *Paper Laws, Steel Bayo-
nets: Breakdown of the Rule of Law in Haiti* (New York, 1990) for an account of the
military in this period.

8. See Lawyers Committee for Human Rights, *Haiti: A Human Rights
Nightmare* (New York, 1992); Americas Watch/National Coalition for Haitian
Refugees, *Silencing a People: The Destruction of Civil Society in Haiti* (New York,
1993); and Human Rights Watch/Jesuit Refugee Service/National Coalition for
Haitian Refugees, *Fugitives from Injustice: The Crisis of Internal Displacement in
Haiti* (New York, 1994).

9. The Coast Guard reported the interdiction of 9,941 Haitians in 1991,
31,401 in 1992, 2,329 in 1993, and 24,850 in 1994. Cited by Andrew S. Faiola,
"Refugee Policy: The 1994 Crisis," in *Haitian Frustrations*, ed. Fauriol, 88.

10. *Report of the Secretary-General to the General Assembly*, A/55/618, November 9, 2000.

11. Robert Maguire, "U.S. Policy Toward Haiti: Engagement or Estrangement?" *Haiti Papers*, no. 8 (Washington DC: Trinity College, 2003).

12. Ambassador Timothy Carney, remarks at the Opening of the Haiti Democracy Project, Washington, DC, November 19, 2002.

13. These arguments are put forward by Ernest H. Preeg and Elliot Abrams in "What Are the Real U.S. Interests in Haiti?" and "Haiti: Playing out the Options," in *Haitian Frustrations*, ed. Fauriol, 7–12 and 69–74. See also Maguire, "U.S. Policy Toward Haiti."

14. U.S. Department of Justice, Drug Enforcement Administration, "Testimony of Donnie R. Marshall before the Senate Caucus on International Narcotics Control," May 15, 2001.

15. OAS–AG/Res 1080 (XXI-0/91) of June 5, enabling the "Santiago Commitment to Democracy and Development and the Renewal of the Inter-American System."

16. James A. Baker III (with Thomas M. DeFranck), *The Politics of Diplomacy: Revolution, War and Peace, 1989–1992* (New York: Putnam, 1995), 601–2.

17. See statement of Madeleine Albright in S/PV.3413 of July 31, 1994.

18. Brian Knowlton, "Powell Sees 'No Enthusiasm' for Sending Peacekeepers to Haiti," *International Herald Tribune*, February 17, 2004.

19. James Dobbins et al., *America's Role in Nation-Building: From Germany to Iraq* (Santa Monica, CA: RAND Corporation, 2003), 82.

20. Maguire, "U.S. Policy Toward Haiti," 4–6; interview, Luigi Einaudi, April 6, 2004. See also Walt Bogdanich and Jenny Nordberg, "Mixed U.S. Signals Helped Tilt Haiti Toward Chaos," *New York Times*, January 29, 2006.

21. Christopher R. Marquis, "Aristide Flees After a Shove from the U.S.," *New York Times*, March 1, 2004. See also James Dobbins, "A Fresh Start for Haiti?" Testimony Presented to the Senate Committee on Foreign Relations, Subcommittee on Western Hemisphere, Peace Corps, and Narcotics Affairs, March 10, 2004.

22. A detail drawn to my attention by Robert Maguire. Interview, May 13, 2003.

23. Interview, Diego Arria, September 30, 1992; and Diego Arria, "Diplomacy and the Four Friends of Haiti," *Haitian Frustrations*, ed. Fauriol, 90.

24. Pérez de Cuéllar, *Pilgrimage of Peace*, 440.

25. Goulding, *Peacemonger*, 270.

26. Letter from Mme. Ertha Pascal-Trouillot to the Secretary-General of June 23, 1990, annex to A/44/965 of July 17, 1990. Document 1, *Les Nations Unies et Haïti*, 127–28.

27. Arria, "Diplomacy and the Four Friends of Haiti," 92.

28. See Maguire et al., *Haiti Held Hostage*, 32–33; David Cortright and George A. Lopez, eds., *The Sanctions Decade: Assessing UN Strategies in the 1990s* (Boulder, CO: Lynne Rienner Publishers, 2000), 91.

29. Malone, *Decision-Making in the UN Security Council*, 74.

30. Boutros-Ghali, *Unvanquished*, 60–63, and *Les Nations Unies et Haïti*, 25–26. Diego Arria attributed Latin American indifference to Haiti's fate in part to racism. Interview.

31. A/Res/47/20, Document 36 in *Les Nations Unies et Haiti*, 247–48.

32. In December 2004 the Canadian development agency, CIDA, identified five key factors contributing to Canada's sustained engagement in Haiti: the significance of Haitian demographics in the Caribbean (at 8.3 million Haiti's population was the largest in the region); the "perceived neutrality, established trust, and non-colonial history" of Canadian cooperation in the Caribbean; Canada's large Haitian diaspora; its trade interests in the Free Trade Area of the Americas; and its commitment to the Francophonie. Canadian International Development Agency, "Canadian Cooperation With Haiti: Reflecting on a Decade of 'Difficult Partnership,'" December 2004.

33. Interview, Francesc Vendrell, November 16, 2003.

34. Interview, Hervé Ladsous, October 11, 2004.

35. Interviews, Arria, Malone.

36. Telephone interview, Edward Walker, August 2, 2004.

37. Warren Christopher, opening remarks at a news conference attended by Dante Caputo and Ambassador Lawrence Pezzullo, Washington DC, July 19, 1993, in *U.S. Department of State Dispatch* 4, no. 30 (July 26, 1993).

38. MICIVIH would twice be forced out of Haiti in the following years, but it has been widely recognized as one of the most successful aspects of international engagement in Haiti. See Lawyers Committee for Human Rights, *Haiti: Learning the Hard Way, the UN/OAS Human Rights Monitoring Operation in Haiti, 1993–1994* (New York: Lawyers Committee for Human Rights, 1995), and Colin Granderson, "Institutionalizing Peace," in *Honoring Human Rights: From Peace to Justice*, ed. Henkin, 227–56.

39. The White House, Office of the Press Secretary, "Remarks of the President and President Aristide of Haiti," March 16, 1993.

40. Those Friends and secretariat officials who criticized Caputo alleged that there were times when Caputo seemed like Pezzullo's "deputy" or even "puppet."

41. Aristide had accepted the prospect of an amnesty for political crimes (the coup), in accordance with the Haitian constitution since the Washington agreement. But under pressure, he was now willing to agree not to oppose the broader amnesty that lay within the powers of the Haitian parliament. See letter dated April 14, 1993, from Caputo to Cédras, *Les Nations Unies et Haiti*, doc. 14, 152–53. On the amnesty issues more broadly, see Ian Martin, "Haiti: Inter-

national Force or National Compromise?" *Journal of Latin American Studies* 31 (October 1999): 711–34.

42. Document 64, *Les Nations Unies et Haiti*, 303.

43. Report of the Secretary-General, *The Situation of Democracy and Human Rights in Haiti*, A/47/975–S/26063, July 12, 1993.

44. How great was the slight to the second-tier Friends varies according to the account cited. Arria would recall in an interview that Governors Island was "terrible . . . the United States owned the negotiations and Pezzullo rode roughshod over the other Friends. We went home because it was agreed that no one was talking to us." The more diplomatic Malone recalled of the Friends that "not all of [them] were equal at Governors Island." Malone, *Decision-Making in the UN Security Council*, 86.

45. Accounts by Malone, *Decision-Making in the UN Security Council*, 86–88, and James Morrell, "The Governors Island Accord on Haiti," *International Policy Report* (Washington, DC: Center on International Policy, 1993). Boutros-Ghali was quoted in the *Miami Herald* of July 3, 1993, as saying, "Don't think, Mr. President, just sign it."

46. See A/47/975–S/26063.

47. Most vocal in opposing what had happened at Governors Island was Francesc Vendrell, who withdrew from Caputo's team shortly thereafter. William O'Neill, who was serving with MICIVIH at the time, noted, "It was as though the army was [sic] saying to the people, 'Watch out, Aristide may be coming back, but we are in charge.'" E-mail communication to the author, March 28, 2006. The deterioration in human rights culminated in the September assassination of a prominent Aristide supporter, Antoine Izmery, and the October execution of the justice minister Guy Malary.

48. George Stephanopoulos, *All Too Human* (Boston, New York, and London: Little, Brown and Company, 1999), 217.

49. Confidential interview.

50. Security Council resolutions 873 and 875 of October 13 and 16, 1993.

51. Published as an annex to A/48/766–S/26881 of December 15, 1993.

52. Confidential interview.

53. Emanuel Constant, for example, the feared leader of the FRAPH militia (who the United Nations was informed by an exasperated Pezzullo was on the payroll of the Central Intelligence Agency), was king of Port-au-Prince's black market. On the sanctions regime, see Elizabeth D. Gibbons, *Sanctions in Haiti: Human Rights and Democracy under Assault* (Washington, DC: Center for Strategic and International Studies Press, 1999), and Cortright and Lopez, eds., *The Sanctions Decade*, 87–106.

54. The extent to which this policy overrode action by the Friends was illustrated by the fact that the U.S. draft resolution to introduce the new sanctions, which was adopted on May 6, was circulated to Council members the same day as a different draft prepared by the French. Malone, *Decision-Making in the UN Security Council*, 105.

55. Confidential interview.

56. "UN View of Haiti Intervention," *Wall Street Journal*, June 16, 1994.

57. Malone reports a "sour" meeting of GRULAC on July 29, at which Argentina's was the only voice raised in the resolution's favor. *Decision-Making in the UN Security-Council*, 109.

58. Caputo resigned following the United States' resort to former President Jimmy Carter, rather than the United Nations, for last-minute negotiations to secure a peaceful, and not forced, intervention in Haiti.

59. UNMIH's mandate was spelled out in S/RES/940.

60. UNMIH was replaced by the United Nations Support Mission in Haiti (UNSMIH) in June 1996; the United Nations Transition Mission in Haiti (UNTMIH) in July 1997; the United Nations Civilian Police Mission in Haiti (MIPONUH) from November 1997 until March 2000; and the Civilian Support Mission in Haiti (MICAH) from March 2000 to March 2001.

61. Interview, Lakhdar Brahimi, October 1, 2004. Dobbins et al., *America's Role in Nation-Building*.

62. Dobbins et al., *America's Role in Nation-Building*, 78.

63. Anthony Lake, U.S. national security adviser at the time, recalled U.S. officials' urging Aristide to announce that he would serve out only the remainder of his term, "although a legal argument could have been made to extend it." Anthony Lake, *Six Nightmares: Real Threats in a Dangerous World and How America Can Meet Them* (Boston, New York, and London: Little, Brown and Company, 2000), 135.

64. Brahimi was appointed in October 1994; ter Horst succeeded him in March 1996 and served until December 1997; Harston served from December 1997 to September 1999; and Cabral from September 1999 until the closure of MICAH at the end of March 2001.

65. The United States maintained a small military Support Group in Haiti as a trip wire until late 1999, when it lost congressional backing and was pulled out. Jim Garamone, "U.S. Support of Haiti Continues, Despite Changes," *American Forces Press Services*, September 1999.

66. The Argentine contribution was provided in the context of Argentina's broad political rapprochement with the United States. Malone, *Decision-Making in the UN Security Council*, 154.

67. A reluctance or inability to follow through on positions the Friends had assumed was evident as early as the flawed local and parliamentary elections held in June 1995. Colin Granderson remembered in particular an incident in which the United Nations had tried to galvanize the Friends to speak strongly to the chairman of the electoral authority regarding a list of political parties that had been drawn up with obvious and unacceptable omissions. But what was conceived of as a dressing down became a "most sociable chat" in the margins of a function at the U.S. ambassador's residence. Interview, December 3, 2003. The International Crisis Group cited the "dangerous precedent" set by acceptance of the 1995 elections, which happened in part because it would have been "too embarrassing for those who supported Aristide and the elections, especially the U.S. government, to do otherwise." "A New Chance for Haiti?" International Crisis Group, *Latin America/Caribbean Report*, no. 10, November 18, 2004, 5.

68. See *Report of the Secretary-General of the United Nations Transition Mission in Haiti*, S/1997/832 of October 31, 1997.

69. Interview, William Swing, October 13, 2004. Swing would go on to serve the United Nations as SRSG in Western Sahara and the Democratic Republic of the Congo.

70. Ter Horst, interview, and "La verificación del cumplimiento del Acuerdo de Paz de El Salvador y algunas observacionis comparativas sobre la operación de paz de la ONU in Haiti," 2002, mimeo, 9. James Dobbins et al. cite the speed with which U.S. troops departed Haiti as a factor that undermined the efficacy of the United States' nation-building efforts. *America's Role in Nation-building*, 164. On the challenges faced by institution building in Haiti, see Colin Granderson, "Institutionalizing Peace: The Haiti Experience," in *Honoring Human Rights: From Peace to Justice*, ed. Henkin, 227–56; International Peace Academy, "Lessons Learned: Peacebuilding in Haiti," IPA Seminar Report on meeting of January 23–24, 2002, New York; Chetan Kumar, "Haiti," in *Peacebuilding as Politics: Cultivating Peace in Fragile Societies*, ed. Elizabeth M. Cousens and Chetan Kumar (Boulder, CO: Lynne Rienner Publishers, 2001), 21–52; and James R. Morrell, Rachel Neild, and Hugh Byrne, "Haiti and the Limits to Nation-Building," *Current History*, March 1999.

71. See Janice M. Stromsen and Joseph Trincellito, "Building the National Police: A Retrospective and Prospective View," *Haiti Papers*, no. 6 (Washington, DC: Trinity College, 2003), 8–9.

72. See Sandra Beidas, Colin Granderson, and Rachel Neild, "Justice and Security Reform afer Intervention: Haiti," in *Constructing Security and Justice after War*, ed. Call, 169–112; Charles T. Call and William Stanley, "Civilian Security," in *Ending Civil War*, ed. Stedman et al., 303–25; Stromsen and Trincellito, "Building the Haitian National Police."

73. Fatton, *Haiti's Predatory Republic*, 88.

74. See Stromsen and Trincellito, "Building the Haitian National Police"; International Crisis Group, "A New Chance for Haiti?"; and *Report of the Secretary-General on Haiti*, S/2004/300, April 16, 2004.

75. Lama Khouri-Padova, "Haiti: Lessons Learned," Discussion Paper, United Nations Peacekeeping Best Practices Unit, March 2004, 7, www.un.org/

depts/dpho/lessons/. See also Permanent Mission of the Netherlands to the United Nations, "No Exit without Strategy," background paper prepared for consideration by the Security Council, October 2000.

76. The initiative was in the context of discussions in the United Nations regarding the reactivation of Article 65 of the UN Charter (which provides for ECOSOC to "assist the Security Council upon its request") and contemplated using Haiti as a "test case" for ECOSOC in postconflict situations.

77. The idea of including Jamaica was Francesc Vendrell's, acting assistant secretary-general for political affairs at the time.

78. A related factor was a funding crisis that had developed in MICIVIH following the revelation that the OAS was in arrears regarding payments for its half of the mission (which were owed to the United Nations). Consequently, it was decided to shut down MICIVIH, rolling some of its staff and functions into the new mission, MICAH.

79. See *Report on a needs assessment mission to Haiti 11 to 15 October 1999,* attached as an annex to letter dated 22 November 1999 from the Secretary-General Addressed to the President of the General Assembly, A/54/629, November 22, 1999.

80. Confidential interview. It had been agreed that the mission would be funded jointly from the UN regular budget ($9.2 million) and from voluntary contributions ($14.7 million), most of which was expected to come from the United States.

81. Lopes Cabral's appointment was widely considered within the secretariat to reflect a political debt owed him for his support of Kofi Annan's candidacy for secretary-general on the Security Council, of which Guinea-Bissau was a member from 1996 to 1997.

82. Press release issued by the Permanent Mission of the United States to the United Nations on the meeting of the Friends of the UN Secretary-General for Haiti on September 13, 2000.

83. Confidential interview. Japan, which was a major donor to Haiti, complained that Germany and Spain had been asked to join the group but Japan had not.

84. The group was formally established in October 2001, with the membership of Argentina, Bahamas, Belize, Canada, Chile, Dominican Republic, Guatemala, Mexico, the United States, and Venezuela, with France, Germany, Norway, and Spain as permanent observers. See OAS Press Release, "Establishment of the OAS Secretary-General's Group of Friends on Haiti," October 2, 2001.

85. Interview, Juan Gabriel Valdés, October 13, 2004.

86. Interview, U.S. official, September 7, 2004. In July 2003 Valdés was moved from New York to become ambassador to Argentina. Maggie Farley and Richard Boudreaux, "Mexico's Envoy to UN Leaves with Defiance," *Los Angeles Times,* November 22, 2003.

87. Walt Bogdanich and Jenny Nordberg, "Mixed U.S. Signals Helped Tilt Haiti Toward Chaos," *New York Times*, January 29, 2006.

88. Aristide's use of informal gangs as a means to secure his own hold on power was a long-standing practice. Some of these gangs, with ties to former police and military, now turned on him, contributing to a highly fluid and anarchic security situation. See Permanent Council of the OAS, "Report on OAS Activities Involving Haiti from November 11, 2003, to March 10, 2004," CP/doc.3849/04 corr. 1, March 17, 2004.

89. See S/2004/300.

90. UN press release, SG/A/867, February 26, 2004; UN news report, "CARICOM, Haiti appeal to Security Council for Help as Haitian Security Worsens," February 26, 2004; Statement by the President of the Security Council, S/PRST/2004/4, February 26, 2004. As one UN official working on Haiti at the time put it, "[U.S. ambassador] Negroponte and France made sure in advance that nothing would happen because they wanted Aristide to fall." E-mail communication with the author, October 5, 2005.

91. Declaration by Foreign Minister Dominique de Villepin on the situation in Haiti, February 25, 2004. Interview, U.S. official, September 7, 2004. See also Christopher Marquis, "Powell, Too, Hints Haitian Should Leave," *New York Times*, February 27, 2004. A second statement issued by de Villepin upped the pressure, stressing that "each hour counts"; it also underlined that the United States, Canada, and France shared the same views on Haiti. Reuters, "France Makes New Call for Aristide to Quit," February 27, 2004.

92. See International Crisis Group, "A New Chance for Haiti?" 9–13; and Daniel P. Erikson, "Haiti after Aristide: Still on the Brink," *Current History*, February 2005.

93. Interviews, U.S. official, September 7, 2004; UN official, November 16, 2004.

94. On the OAS appeal, see OAS press release, "OAS Urges UN efforts on Haiti Crisis," February 26, 2004, E-028/04.

95. Kofi A. Annan, "Haiti: This Time We Must Get It Right," *Wall Street Journal*, March 16, 2004.

96. In November 2004 a report jointly released by UNDP and the government of Haiti found that in twenty-five years Haiti had not known a single period of lasting economic growth; in 2002, GDP represented barely 61 percent of its value in 1980. "Millennium Development Goals look out of reach for increasingly impoverished Haiti," UNDP press release, November 17, 2004.

97. International Crisis Group, "A New Chance for Haiti?"

98. Note from the Secretary-General of the OAS to the Secretary-General of the United Nations to ensure the coordination and complementarity of the roles of the two organizations in Haiti, OEA/Ser.G, GP/INF.4964/04, March 31, 2004.

99. S/2004/300, para. 81.

100. Interview, UN official, November 16, 2004.

101. In addition to Canada, the advisory group's members were Benin, Brazil, Chile, Spain, Trinidad and Tobago, and Haiti itself. France and the United States had resisted its formation out of fears that it would confuse the work of the Core Group; they also feared the role it might provide Caribbean nations (such as Jamaica) they saw as aligned with Aristide and potential spoilers of the UN effort. Interview, French official, January 5, 2005.

102. As of February 15, 2005, for example, Brazil was providing 1,212 and Latin America 2,697 out of a total of 6,013 troops deployed (a proportion that had actually decreased as the mission built up its force). France, Canada, and the United States, which had a total of nine officers in the UN mission between them, had, together with Chile, contributed troops to the multinational force, but they were quickly withdrawn. *Report of the Secretary-General on the United Nations Stabilization Mission in Haiti*, February 25, 2005, S/2005/124.

103. Juan Gabriel Tokatlian, "Intervención en Haití, misión frustrada. Una crítica de América Latina", Fundación para las Relaciones Internacionales y el Diálogo Exterior (FRIDE), Madrid, www.fride.org (author's translation).

104. See *Security and Defense Studies Review*, Special Edition, Peacekeeping Operation Haiti 2004 no. 1 (Spring 2005), especially John T. Fishel and Andrés Saenz, "Lessons of Peacekeeping Capacity Building: What We Have Learned from the Case of Haiti," www.ndu.edu/chds/Journal/. Debate over the engagement of Brazil was particularly fierce and intensified after the apparent suicide of the Brazilian force commander in January 2006. See Amélie Gauthier and Sara-Lea John, "Brazil in Haiti: Debate over the Peacekeeping Mission," Fundación para las Relaciones Internacionales y el Diálogo Exterior (FRIDE), Madrid, www.fride.org/; Andrew Hay "Brazil Looks for Way Out of Haiti Mission," *Reuters*, January 12, 2006; Mario Osava, "Haiti: General's Death Revives Debate on Brazil's Peacekeeping Role," Inter Press Service January 12, 2006; and Emir Sader, "What Is Brazil Doing in Haiti?" Americas Program, Interhemispheric Resource Center, July 6, 2004.

105. Interview, Valdés.

106. At the working level, regular consultations among the United Nations, Canada, France, and the United States, sometimes attended by Brazil and the OAS, were instituted. Interview, MINUSTAH official, April 26, 2005.

107. S/2005/124; Erikson, "Haiti after Aristide"; Haiti Democracy Project, "Findings and Recommendations from Fact-Finding Delegation to Haiti, February 17–23, 2005," www.haitipolicy.org; International Crisis Group, "Haiti's Transition," *Latin America/Caribbean Briefings*, no. 7, February 8, 2005, and Memorandum to Members of the United Nations Security Council Mission to Haiti, "Update on Haiti," April 8, 2005.

108. Cited by Ginger Thompson, "Fear and Death Ensnare UN's Soldiers in Haiti," *New York Times*, January 24, 2006.

109. *Report of the Secretary-General on the United Nations Stabilization Mission in Haiti*, S/2006/60, February 2, 2006, para. 18.

110. Particularly damaging to MINUSTAH's reputation had been a large-scale operation conducted on July 6, 2005, in Cité Soleil with the support of the Haitian National Police. The operation aimed to capture a prominent gang leader, but escalated when MINUSTAH came under heavy gunfire and responded in kind. Civilians were killed in the crossfire, but the details of what exactly transpired remained obscure.

111. Interviews, UN official, January 23, 2006; Juan Gabriel Valdés, June 27, 2006.

112. Interview, UN official, November 7, 2006.

113. *Report of the Secretary-General on the United Nations Stabilization Mission in Haiti*, S.2006/592, July 28, 2006, para. 89.

114. Fatton, *Haiti's Predatory Republic*, 12.

115. Boutros-Ghali, *Unvanquished*, 250.

5. The Georgian-Abkhaz Conflict

1. See Charles King, "The Benefits of Ethnic War: Understanding Eurasia's Unrecognized States," *World Politics* 53 (July 2001), 524–52, and "The Uses of Deadlock: Intractability in Eurasia," in *Grasping the Nettle*, ed. Crocker et al., 267–94; Dov Lynch, *Engaging Eurasia's Separatist States: Unresolved Conflicts and De Facto States* (Washington, DC: United States Institute of Peace Press, 2004); and Ghia Nodia, "Dimensions of Insecurity," in *Statehood and Security: Georgia after the Rose Revolution*, ed. Bruno Coppieters and Robert Legvold (Cambridge, MA, and London: MIT Press, 2005), 39–82.

2. In a press conference on January 31, 2006, Putin posed the rhetorical question: "If someone believes that Kosovo should be granted full independence as a state, then why should we deny it to the Abkhaz and the South Ossetians?" Radio Free Europe/Radio Liberty, "Russia: Putin Calls For 'Universal Principles' to Settle Frozen Conflicts," February 1, 2006. See also Thomas de Waal, "Abkhaz Leader Presses Independence Claim," Institute for War and Peace Reporting (IWPR), *Caucasus Reporting Service*, no. 329, March 2, 2006.

3. See Svante E. Cornell, "Security Threats and Challenges in the Caucasus after 9/11," in *Eurasia in Balance: The U.S. and Regional Power Shift*, ed. Ariel Cohen (Aldershot, UK: Ashgate, 2005); and Peter Forster, "The Paradox of Policy: American Interests in the Post-9/11 Caucasus," in *Security Sector Governance in the Southern Caucasus*, ed. Anja H. Ebnöther and Gustav. E. Gustenau, (Geneva: Centre for the Democratic Control of Armed Forces, 2004), 12–33.

4. Georgia's ambassador to the United Nations would cite this phrase as one repeatedly used by Eduard Shevardnadze. Interview, Revaz Adamia, June 4, 2003.

5. Information on Abkhazia, clearly reflecting an Abkhaz version of history, can be obtained at www.abkhazia.org. For general introductions to the conflict in Abkhazia, see Jonathan Cohen, ed., *A Question of Sovereignty: The Georgia-Abkhazia Peace Process*, Accord Issue 7 (London: Conciliation Resources, 1999); Bruno Coppieters, *Contested Borders in the Caucasus* (Brussels: VUB University Press, 1996); Bruno Coppieters, David Darchiashvili, and Natella Akaba, *Federal Practice: Exploring Alternatives for Georgia and Abkhazia* (Brussels: VUB University Press, 1999); Catherine Dale, "The Case of Abkhazia (Georgia)," in *Peacekeeping and the Role of Russia in Eurasia*, ed. Lena Jonson and Clive Archer (Boulder, CO: Westview Press, 1996); Lynch, *Engaging Eurasia's Separatist States;* and International Crisis Group, "Abkhazia Today," *Europe Report*, no. 176 (Tbilisi/ Brussels: International Crisis Group, September 15, 2006)

6. In contrast to Abkhazia, South Ossetia had been included in the Georgian Republic of 1922 as an Autonomous Region; in November 1989 the Supreme Soviet voted to upgrade its status to Autonomous Republic, but this was never accepted by the authorities in Tbilisi. Lynch, *Engaging Eurasia's Separatist States*, 30–31.

7. Reports to the UN Security Council of this period refer openly to Georgian allegations of the presence of "illegal north Caucasian elements," which Shevardnadze claimed numbered "about 3,000" as well the collusion of Russian troops with the Abkhaz forces. See S/24794 of November 11, 1992, and S/25188 of January 28, 1993.

8. Dmitri Trenin, "Russia's Security Interests and Policies in the Caucasus Region," in *Contested Borders in the Caucasus*, ed. Coppieters, chapter 3.

9. King, "The Benefits of Ethnic War," 525. See Lynch, *Engaging Eurasia's Separatist States* for a comparative assessment of these four de facto states. Sir Brian Fall suggests that rather than "frozen conflicts," it would be better to think of the conflicts as "frozen rivers": "the surface ice may be thick and apparently immobile, but underneath it, currents continue to run." "Conflict in the South Caucasus," *Asian Affairs*, vol. XXXVII, no. 11 (July 2006): 201–2.

10. In the early 2000s UNOMIG was probably the biggest employer in Abkhazia after the government, with the United Kingdom's Halo Trust not far behind. In 2001 King described humanitarian agencies as "injecting as much as four to five million dollars into the economy each year through rents, services, and payment of local staff." *The Benefits of Ethnic War*, 549.

11. The European Union aspired to be the largest donor in Abkhazia by mid-2006, implementing projects worth €25 million. These included 10 million earmarked for rehabilitating the Enguri hydropower plant and a new €4 million three-year program that promised to support rehabilitation and recon-

struction in the conflict zone and adjoining areas in order to create conditions for the return and reintegration of IDPs and refugees. See International Crisis Group, "Conflict Resolution in the South Caucasus: The EU's Role," *Europe Report*, no. 173 (Tbilisi/Brussels: International Crisis Group, March 20, 2006), 17.

12. Nodia, "Dimensions of Insecurity," 52.

13. This point is made by Dmitri Trenin, "Russia's Security Interests and Policies in the Caucasus Region."

14. Cited by Lena Jonson and Clive Archer, "Russia and Peacekeeping in Eurasia," in *Peacekeeping and the Role of Russia in Eurasia*, ed. Jonson and Archer, 4.

15. Robert H. Donaldson and Joseph L. Nogee, *The Foreign Policy of Russia* (Armonk, NY: M.E. Sharpe, 2002), 130–1; Dov Lynch, *Russian Peacekeeping Strategies in the CIS: The Cases of Moldova, Georgia, and Tajikistan* (London: Royal Institute of International Affairs, 1999).

16. Interview, Boris Pastukhov, July 18, 2003.

17. Russia's complex interests and involvement in Abkhazia are analyzed by Oksana Antonenko, "Frozen Uncertainty: Russia and the Conflict over Abkhazia," in *Statehood and Security*, ed. Coppieters and Legvold, 205–69.

18. The New Friends of Georgia consisted of Bulgaria, Estonia, Latvia, Lithuania, Poland, and Romania. The group met in Tbilisi for the first time on February 4, 2005. Press Release, Ministry of Foreign Affairs of Georgia, February 7, 2005.

19. The Georgia "Train and Equip" Program (GTEP) was launched on April 29, 2002, and came to an end two years later, having trained four light infantry and one mechanized armor company. Information from the U.S. embassy to Georgia, www.georgia.usembassy.gov. In April 2005 U.S. support to the Georgian armed forces was renewed through the Sustainment and Stability Operations Program (SSOP), which was designed to train Georgians for deployment to Iraq. See International Crisis Group, "Abkhazia Today," 21.

20. Alan Parastayev, "U.S. Deployment in Georgia Angers South Ossetia," IWPR, *Caucasus Reporting Service*, no. 121, March 22, 2002.

21. Text of the speech by President George W. Bush, May 10, 2005, www.georgia.usembassy.gov.

22. In early 2005 both the Parliamentary Assembly of the Council of Europe (PACE) and Human Rights Watch issued reports critical of Saakashvili's government. Meanwhile, within the country its popularity began to slip as a result of resistance to education reform, a police scandal, clear inequities in his anticorruption drive, and criticism from national and international human rights groups. See Joel Myers, "Saakashvili on the Ropes?" *Central Asia-Caucasus Analyst*, May 4, 2005.

23. Before the trip Foreign Minister Sergei Lavrov took the unusual step of writing to Secretary of State Condoleezza Rice to complain of an itinerary that had

President Bush's visit to Moscow to attend a commemoration of the end of World War II sandwiched between visits to Latvia and Georgia. Peter Baker and Jim VandeHei, "Georgian Crowd Embraces Bush," *Washington Post*, May 11, 2005.

24. Saakashvili's statement to the General Assembly on September 15, 2005, is cited in *Report of the Secretary-General on the Situation in Abkhazia, Georgia*, S/2005/657, October 19, 2005, para. 13.

25. Georgia's spending on defense rose more than that of any other country in the world in 2005. Stockholm International Peace Research Institute (SIPRI), *Yearbook 2006: Armaments, Disarmament and International Security*, 231–32; Ariel Cohen, "Washington Challenged by Georgian-Russian Crisis," A *EurasiaNet Commentary*, October 18, 2006.

26. Interviews, UN official, December 3, 2001; Edouard Brunner, March 27, 2003. Brunner had known Ambassador Fassier, who had previously served in Bern, from before.

27. Note by the President of the Security Council, September 10, 1992, S/24542.

28. Letter dated November 10, 1992, from the Secretary-General to the President of the Security Council, S/24794, November 11, 1992.

29. Joint letter dated December 7, 1993, from the Minister for Foreign Affairs of the Russian Federation and the Minister of Foreign Affairs of Georgia, S/26478.

30. This section is derived from interviews conducted in 2001 and 2002 with UN officials who took part in the early meetings with the Friends.

31. See S. Neil Macfarlane, "On the Front Lines in the Near Abroad: The CIS and the OSCE in Georgia's Civil Wars," in *Beyond UN Subcontracting: Task-Sharing with Regional Security Arrangements and Service Providers*, ed. Thomas G. Weiss (New York: St. Martin's Press, 1998), 115–36; and Olivier Paye and Eric Remacle, "UN and CSCE policies in Transcaucasia," in *Contested Borders in the Caucasus*, ed. Coppieters.

32. The cochairs of the Minsk Group—France, Russia, and the United States—would assume a primary role for operational purposes.

33. Interview, Sergei Shamba, July 9, 2003.

34. Bruno Coppieters, "Western Security Policies and the Georgian-Abkhaz Conflict," in *Federal Practice*, ed. Coppieters et al., 21–68.

35. Dov Lynch, ed., "The South Caucasus: A Challenge for the EU," *Chaillot Papers*, no. 65 (Paris: Institute for Security Studies, December 2003); and International Crisis Group, "Conflict Resolution in the South Caucasus: The EU's Role."

36. *Declaration on the Granting of Independence to Colonial Countries and Peoples*, UN General Assembly Resolution 1514, December 14, 1960. See Lynch,

Engaging Eurasia's Separatist States, 16–19, for a discussion of the tension between de facto states and the principle and practice of self-determination.

37. "The members of the Council, stressing the urgent necessity for a political settlement of the conflict by peaceful means, through negotiations, reaffirm the inadmissibility of any encroachment upon the principle of territorial integrity and upon Georgia's internationally recognized borders." S/24542, September 10, 1992.

38. The Quadripartite Agreement on the Return of Refugees and Displaced Persons, signed on April 4, 1994, is attached as Annex II to S/1994/397. As the International Crisis Group notes, demography remains "a highly political issue" and Abkhazia's population uncertain. In January 2005 the electoral roll comprised 129,127 individuals "suggesting an overall population between 157,000 and 190,000." Although the Abkhaz claim to represent the majority of this population, Georgians estimate that ethnic Armenians may outnumber them. International Crisis Group, "Abkhazia Today," 9.

39. S. Neil Macfarlane points out that the "statist nature" of the United Nations also revealed itself in the exclusion of areas under Abkhaz control from needs assessment and delivery of services by the United Nations' humanitarian agencies in the early years of UN involvement. "The Role of the UN," in *A Question of Sovereignty*, ed. Cohen, 38.

40. Interview, Astamur Tania, July 11, 2003. Abkhaz war crimes were identified as "ethnic cleansing" in the final document of the CSCE Summit in Budapest in 1994. Reproduced in S/1994/1435. In an interview on July 8, 2003, a Western Friend ambassador in Tbilisi strongly expressed the view that the United Nations should also have identified the Abkhaz's expulsion of the Georgians from Gali as ethnic cleansing.

41. Another Friend commented, "I stand between a recognized government and a separatist movement that does not begin to accept the need to talk about a solution. I do not see both on the same level." Interviews, May 13, 2003; November 18, 2002.

42. Interview, UN official, October 2, 2002. Matters were not helped by the Abkhaz's insistence that they issue visas to visitors to Abkhazia.

43. The United Nations Observer Mission in Liberia (UNOMIL) had been authorized by the Security Council in September 1993 to deploy alongside the Nigerian-led Economic Community of West Africa States (ECOWAS) Monitoring Group (ECOMOG).

44. Macfarlane, "On the Frontlines in the Near Abroad," 130–31; and Dmitri Danilov, "Russia's Role," in *A Question of Sovereignty*, ed. Cohen, 42–49. Discussions at the United Nations foresaw the deployment of forces from elsewhere in the former Soviet Union in the CIS force, but no troops other than Russians ever materialized.

45. S/PV.3407, July 21, 1994.

46. "Moscow's Ambassador, Yuli Vorontsov, presented me with a series of questions about our mission, hinting that Russia's backing on Haiti would depend on U.S. support for Russian proposals on Georgia." Madeleine Albright, *Madam Secretary* (New York: Miramax Books, 2003), 158. A Russian official supporting these talks recalled, "There were parallels between Georgia and Haiti. No one would tell you that support of one in the Council was contingent on the other, but the linkage was there." Interview, April 2, 2003.

47. Editorial, "A U.N. License to Invade Haiti," *New York Times*, August 2, 1994.

48. See *Report of the Secretary-General Concerning the Situation in Abkhazia, Georgia*, S/1999/497, June 10, 1998, paras. 2–8, for the events in Gali. The Georgians expelled from Gali were returned refugees from previous expulsions during the fighting in 1992–93. The destruction in Gali led to the loss of several million dollars' worth of foreign aid and increased the reluctance of international donors to engage in Abkhazia. Damien Helly and Giorgi Gogia, "Georgian Security and the Role of the West," in *Statehood and Security*, ed. Coppieters and Legvold, 286–87.

49. In 2005 an official of the Russian Ministry of Defense reported that ninety-nine Russian servicemen had been killed in Abkhazia since 1994. "Georgia Seeks to Oust Russian Peacekeepers from Breakaway Regions," *MosNews*, October 29, 2005.

50. Ambassador Adamia described Shevardnadze as having had "one hand going towards the West, and the other still in Russia"; the ambiguity of his position had "partly worked, but partly led to irritation on the part of Russian officials who thought he was trying to trick them." Interview, January 14, 2004.

51. "The Russians were always calling the Abkhaz behind our backs and telling them to hang tough," another official recalled. Interviews, December 3, 2001, and October 2, and 18, 2002.

52. Interview, Pastukhov, July 17, 2003, Lev Mironov, who assumed the role of Russian special envoy after Pasktukhov, recalled the Friends' appearing in 1997–98.

53. Interview, December 3, 2001.

54. *Report of the Secretary-General Concerning the Situation in Abkhazia, Georgia*, S/1997/827, October 28, 1997.

55. International Crisis Group, "Tajikistan: An Uncertain Peace," *Asia Report*, no. 30 (Oslo/Brussels: International Crisis Group, December 24, 2001), 2.

56. Catherine Barnes and Kamoludin Abdullaev referred to the external actors as "secondary parties" to the conflict. Introduction, *The Politics of Compromise: The Tajikistan Peace Process*, Accord Issue 10, ed. Kamoludin Abdullaev and Catherine Barnes (London: Conciliation Resources, 2001), 8–13.

57. Vladimir Goryayev, "Architecture of International Involvement in the Tajik Peace Process," in *The Politics of Compromise*, 32–37.

58. Elena Rigacci Hay, "Methodology of the Inter-Tajik Negotiation Process," in *The Politics of Compromise*, 38–43.

59. Interview, Vladimir Goryayev, December 20, 2001.

60. Olivier Roy, "Iranian Foreign Policy toward Central Asia," and Barnett R. Rubin, "Introduction to the Tajikistan Peace Agreement" (New York: Open Society Institute, 1998), www.eurasianet.org.

61. Telephone interview, Gerd Merrem, February 14, 2005.

62. Interview, October 2, 2002.

63. See *Report of the Secretary-General Concerning the Situation in Abkhazia, Georgia*, S/1998/51, January 19, 1998, para. 3.

64. The Concluding Statement of the resumed Geneva meeting held November 17–19, 1997, can be found in Cohen, ed., *A Question of Sovereignty*, 72–73.

65. The UN Needs Assessment mission was conducted by representatives of UN agencies, the World Bank, and bilateral representatives of Germany, the Netherlands, and the United States, www.abkhazia.org. See Macfarlane, "The Role of the UN," 40.

66. Interview, UNOMIG official, July 12, 2003.

67. *Report of the Secretary-General Concerning the Situation in Abkhazia, Georgia*, S/2001/1008, October 24, 2001. UNOMIG suspended patrols in the Kodori Valley after these incidents; they were only resumed after Georgia's special operation in the upper Kodori Valley in July 2006.

68. *Report of the Secretary-General Concerning the Situation in Abkhazia, Georgia*, S/2002/88 January 18, 2002, para. 24.

69. Tania, Interview. Interviewees in Abkhazia distinguished between their personal assessments of Dieter Boden and the paper attached to his name. "Poor Boden," commented Liana Kvartchelia, a leading representative of Abkhaz civil society. "He tried so hard. It's such a pity he has to be remembered for the Boden paper." Interview, July 10, 2003. See also Antonenko's analysis of the "The Boden Initiative," in *Frozen Uncertainty*, 238–45.

70. Interviews, UN officials, July 12, 2003, and September 17, 2003.

71. Interview, July 7, 2003. Kakabadze expressed greater appreciation for what the Friends had been able to offer Georgia bilaterally—citing their support of democratic rule, the training of border guards, the GTEP program, the BTC pipeline, and U.S. assistance in general—than their contribution to the peace process. "The Boden paper and the Geneva process [2003] are good, but not enough for me."

72. Interviews, April 17, 2003; May 14, 2003; July 16, 2003.

73. Interview, Tania, July 11, 2003.

74. Interview, Shamba, July 9, 2003.

75. Interview, May 16, 2003. Individual ambassadors would make occasional visits to Abkhazia on their own accord, not in representation of the Friends.

76. UN officials noted that the United Kingdom and even the United States developed a more balanced approach, while France and Germany adhered more tightly to the Georgian positions. But differences between the group's members varied according to the individuals involved as well as national priorities.

77. One senior UN official commented, "Georgia is a little country and the movers and shakers of foreign policy of these big countries just do not get sent there." Interview, June 27, 2003.

78. In 2003 the ambassador of Germany, who had just taken over as coordinator of the group from France, began one meeting by thanking his Russian hosts with the line, "We are pleased that you can meet with the Western Friends." Interview, July 16, 2003. Vasily Kolotusha, the Friends' primary interlocutor at the expert level, complained about the "unbalanced" position of Germany but otherwise commented, "Generally we have warm relations with our international friends. Information is exchanged here, because the Friends have problems in obtaining objective information on how things are." Interview, July 17, 2003.

79. Ukraine was closely aligned with Georgia and deemed unlikely to affect the underlying dynamics of the group, but the prospect of enlarging the group risked opening the door to other contenders for membership, which included both Turkey—a neighboring state with a complex agenda in the Caucasus—and Greece.

80. Recalling the irritation of a meeting in which the Friends discussed a draft of the Boden paper that was not made available to other members of the Council, a representative of Colombia commented, "Really, there is no need to have the political discussion of Georgia on the agenda of [the] Security Council at all, because it doesn't take place in the Council." Interview, November 12, 2002.

81. Interview, Andrey Granovsky, June 26, 2003.

82. Interview, November 18, 2002; see *Reports of the Secretary-General on the Situation in Abkhazia, Georgia,* S/2002/742 of July 10, 2002, and S/2002/1141 of October 14, 2002.

83. See Resolution 1393 (2002) of January 31, 2002, and Resolution 1427 (2002) of July 29, 2002.

84. Interview, Adamia, June 4, 2003.

85. In mid-September Putin sent a letter to Annan invoking article 51 of the charter to threaten Russia's adoption of "adequate measures" if the Georgian leadership did not take "concrete actions to destroy the terrorists." Robin Shep-

herd, "Russia Plans to Attack Rebels Based in Georgia," *Timesonline*, September 14, 2002.

86. The Abkhaz were concerned that Georgia would use its U.S.-trained forces against them. Although this was explicitly not the U.S. intention, drill songs sung by Georgians undergoing GTEP training included the refrain "Back to Abkhazia! Back to Abkhazia!" Interview, Georgian working with GTEP, July 13, 2003.

87. Interview, Richard Miles, July 14, 2003. The zero-sum reading of U.S. and Russian interests was shared by a Pentagon official, who argued that "the diplomats are working with the Russians as if they are dealing in good faith—and they are not. U.S.-Russian interests in the South Caucasus are diametrically opposed to one another." Interview, May 14, 2003.

88. Cited by Antonenko, *Frozen Uncertainty*, 255.

89. These doubts did not undervalue the Boden paper for the negotiations' "endgame," but reflected, as one British official put it, the view that "if we keep pushing Boden we are less likely to move forward on solving the conflict." The doubts were shared by some experts in countries that were still publicly insistent on prioritizing the Boden paper within the process. Interviews. May–July 2003.

90. Interview, June 26, 2003.

91. Jean-Marie Guéhenno, statement for the press, Geneva, February 20, 2003.

92. Interview, Mironov.

93. Interview, July 12, 2003.

94. "Final Statement of the Meeting of the Russian Federation, Mr. V. Putin, and the President of Georgia, Mr. E. Shevardnadze," www.georgiaemb.org.

95. Interview, April 17, 2003.

96. In an interview with the author, Antadze restrained himself to the comment, "Naturally it is very difficult to argue with the president of Russia during a summit meeting." July 14, 2003.

97. Interview, Jean-Marie Guéhenno, June 27, 2003.

98. International Crisis Group, "Saakashvili's Ajara Success: Repeatable Elsewhere in Georgia?" *Europe Briefing*, no. 34 (Tbilisi/Brussels: International Crisis Group, August 18, 2004).

99. Jean-Christophe Peuch, "Georgia: South Ossetian Leaders Hold Direct Talks with Government Amid Unabated Tensions," *Eurasia Insight*, November 5, 2004.

100. *Report of the Secretary-General on the Situation in Abkhazia, Georgia*, October 18, 2004, S/2004/822.

101. See Inal Kashig, "Abkhazia Rivals Strike Deal," IWPR, *Caucasus Reporting Service*, No. 265, December 8, 2004; and "Timeline of the Abkhaz Crisis," *Civil Georgia*, January 12, 2005.

102. Interview, April 28, 2005.

103. *Report of the Secretary-General on the Situation in Abkhazia, Georgia,* S/2005/269, April 25, 2005.

104. "U.S. Diplomats Visit Abkhazia in the Wake of Geneva Talks," *Civil Georgia,* April 10, 2005.

105. Press conference of January 31, 2006.

106. Cited in "Update on Georgia," *Security Council Report,* February 2, 2006.

107. Security Council Resolution 1656 (2006), January 31, 2006.

108. UNOMIG Press Release, "High-Level Meeting of the Group of Friends of the Secretary-General, Geneva, February 2–3, 2006," February 3, 2006.

109. Security Council Resolution 1666, March 31, 2006.

110. See *Report of the Secretary-General on the Situation in Abkhazia, Georgia,* S/2006/435, June 26, 2006, paras. 4–7, and also "Tbilisi Tries to Revitalize Abkhaz Peace Process," *Civil Georgia,* March 22, 2006; Liz Fuller, "Georgia: Abkhaz Leader Unveils New Peace Plan," *Radio Free Europe/Radio Liberty,* May 10, 2006; and "Group of Friends of UN Secretary-General Visits Tbilisi, Sukhumi," *Civil Georgia,* May 25, 2006.

111. Reporting on this episode to the Security Council, the secretary-general noted that UNOMIG had issued thirteen violation reports of the cease-fire agreement to the Georgian side, and two to the Abkhaz. *Report of the Secretary-General on the Situation in Abkhazia, Georgia,* S/2006/771, September 28, 2006, para. 7.

112. Interview, UN official, October 5, 2006. One European member of the Friends described a "difference of perspective" on the events in Kodori. The European states were never going to "condemn" the operation, as they saw Georgia as exercising its sovereign right to restore order within its territory; however, they were worried that that Georgia might overestimate the "strategic support" it had from the West and that its "brinkmanship" with Russia could result in a miscalculation. Interview, November 21, 2006.

113. Security Council Resolution 1716 (2006), October 13, 2006.

114. One German official explained that Germany's membership on the Security Council from 2003 to 2004 made little difference to its influence on the Georgia file due to its membership in the Friends. Interview, May 16, 2003. After Germany left the Council, arrangements were made to allow it to participate in closed sessions of the Council at which Georgia was discussed.

115. In May 2005 President George W. Bush offered U.S. support to Saakashvili's plan for autonomy in South Ossetia and Abkhazia, but with clear limits: "The United States cannot impose a solution nor would you want us to . . . what we can do is to work with international bodies. We can work with the UN, for example." "Bush Praises Georgian Democracy," *BBC News,* May 5, 2005.

116. Interview, September 17, 2003.

6. Self-Determination and Realpolitik

1. See note 59, below.

2. Tony Hodges, *Western Sahara: The Roots of a Desert War* (Westport, CT: Lawrence Hill and Company, 1983), vii.

3. In addition to Hodges, see also John James Damis, *Conflict in Northwest Africa: The Western Sahara Dispute* (Stanford, CA: Hoover Institution Press, 1983), and I. William Zartman, *Ripe for Resolution: Conflict and Intervention in Africa* (New York and Oxford: Oxford University Press, 1985), 19–81. For more recent accounts, see Erik Jensen, *Western Sahara: Anatomy of a Stalemate*, International Peace Academy Occasional Paper Series (Boulder, CO, and London: Lynne Rienner Publishers, 2005); Toby Shelley, *Endgame in the Western Sahara: What Future for Africa's Last Colony?* (London: Zed Press, 2004); and Anna Theophilopoulou, "The United Nations and Western Sahara: A Never-ending Affair," United States Institute of Peace Special Report 166, July 2006.

4. For the historical role of Spain and France in Western Sahara, see Philip C. Naylor, "Spain, France, and the Western Sahara: A Historical Narrative and Study of National Transformation," in *International Dimensions of the Western Sahara Conflict*, ed. Yahia H. Zoubir and Daniel Volman (Westport, CT: Praeger, 1993), 17–51, as well as Hodges, *Western Sahara*.

5. General Assembly Resolution 229, 1966.

6. International Court of Justice, *Western Sahara: Advisory Opinion of 16 October 1975* (The Hague: International Court of Justice, 1975).

7. These events are described in *Repertoire of the Practice of the Security Council, Supplement 1975–1980* (New York: United Nations, 1987), 243–48.

8. Kissinger's remark that "the United States will not allow another Angola on the east flank of the Atlantic Ocean" was cited by Leo Kamil, *Fueling the Fire: U.S. Policy and the Western Sahara Conflict* (Trenton, NJ: Red Sea Press, 1987), 44.

9. Richard Gillespie, *Spain and the Mediterranean* (London: MacMillan Press, 2000), 43.

10. Zartman writes of three overlapping conflicts: "A Moroccan-Algerian rivalry of growing powers across a long inexistent border, a Moroccan struggle for national independence and integrity, and Mauritanian and Saharan efforts to find political forms for a desert society that the decolonization of the Spanish Sahara has brought about." *Ripe for Resolution*, 25.

11. The Organisation of African Unity had determined in Resolution 16 (1) of July 1964 that the boundaries of Africa's new states should be based on former colonial boundaries.

12. See Daniel Volman, "The Role of Foreign Military Assistance," in *International Dimensions of the Western Sahara Conflict*, ed. Zoubir and Volman, 151–61.

13. Estimates of Moroccan expenditure vary, but John Damis assessed that in the years before 1987, when the "berm" was completed, Morocco was spending $1 billion a year on expansion into Western Sahara. "Morocco and Western Sahara," *Current History* 89, no. 546 (April 1990): 166. Jarat Chopra cites an occupying force of 120,000, armed with "comparatively high technology from fourteen countries," that was estimated to have cost $2 million a day. "A Chance for Peace in Western Sahara," *Survival* 39, no. 3 (Autumn 1997): 53.

14. Shelley, *Endgame in the Western Sahara*, 48.

15. Cited in Hodges, *Western Sahara*, 312.

16. Erik Jensen, who worked in Western Sahara for five years as head of the Identification Commission and then chief of the UN mission, MINURSO, provides the most comprehensive account of the problems encountered in identifying the Saharan electorate in *Western Sahara: Anatomy of a Stalemate*.

17. Hodges, *Western Sahara*, 308.

18. See Pérez de Cuéllar, "The Western Sahara," *Pilgrimage for Peace*, 333–52, and Goulding, "Western Sahara," *Peacemonger*, 199–214.

19. Goulding, *Peacemonger*, 201.

20. "My sense was, and remains, that Hassan II was sincere in his support of a referendum, but only under circumstances in which a majority vote for some form of association with Morocco would be assured. He stated this position quite clearly at the beginning of the conflict." Pérez de Cuéllar, *Pilgrimage for Peace*, 336.

21. The implementation plan provided for the referendum to be held twenty-four weeks after the introduction of a cease-fire. The settlement proposals and implementation plan are contained in *The Situation Concerning Western Sahara: Report of the Secretary-General*, S/21360, June 18, 1990.

22. Morocco's movement of 170,000 "Sahrawis" into the Western Sahara was reported to the Security Council in deceptively bland terms: "As is well known, a number of persons who are claimed to belong to Western Sahara have been moved into the Territory." *Report of the Secretary-General on the Situation Concerning Western Sahara*, S/23299, December 19, 1991.

23. John Bolton, "Resolving the Western Sahara Conflict," address to 1998 Congressional Defense and Foreign Policy Forum, Defense Forum Foundation, March 27, 1998.

24. Resolution 725 (1991) of December 31, 1991, asked the secretary-general (the new one) to report back to the Council on Western Sahara "as soon as possible, but in any event within two months."

25. See Ahmed Boukhari (representative of Polisario to the United Nations), "Las dimensiones internacionales del conflicto del Sahara occidental y sus repercusiones para una alternativa marroquí" (Madrid: Real Instituto Elcano De Estudios Internacionales y Estratégicos, April 19, 2004).

26. Polisario had previously objected to Boutros-Ghali's suggestion of General Vernon Walters, also a friend of King Hassan. Interview, Ahmed Boukhari, April 14, 2004; and "Las dimensiones internacionales del conflicto."

27. Interviews, former UN official, November 18, 2002; former U.S. official, April 19, 2004; telephone interview, Walker.

28. On the international context and interests in Western Sahara, see Shelley, *Endgame in the Western Sahara*, 6–25; Jordi Vaqueri Fanés, "The European Union and Western Sahara," *European Foreign Affairs Review* 9 (2004): 93–113; and Yahia H. Zoubir, "The Geopolitics of the Western Sahara Conflict," in *North Africa in Transition*, ed. Yahia H. Zoubir (Gainesville, FL: University Press of Florida, 1999), 195–211.

29. See Stephen Zunes, "Morocco and Western Sahara." *Foreign Policy in Focus* 3, no. 42 (December 1998).

30. Shelley reports that France accounts for 30 percent of all overseas investments in Morocco, 40 percent of industrial investments, and in 2000, 33.6 percent of exports and 24.3 percent of imports. (Spain, Morocco's second trading partner, had 12.7 percent of exports and 9.8 percent of imports.) Between 1991 and 2000 France supplied Morocco with some $250 million in weapons, the highest figure for any country in Africa and almost five times the quantity delivered to Algeria. Shelley, *Endgame in the Western Sahara*, 18–20.

31. Polisario protested Morocco's agreement to those contracts to the Security Council. In January 2002 the United Nations' Legal Counsel ruled that "if further exploration and exploitation activities were to proceed in disregard of the interests and wishes of the people of Western Sahara," they would be illegal. See letter dated January 29, 2002, from the Under-Secretary-General for Legal Affairs, the Legal Counsel, addressed to the President of the Security Council, S/2002/161, February 12, 2002.

32. Report by David Bamford for the BBC, December 3, 2001, www.bbc .co.uk; Vaquer i Fanés, "The European Union and Western Sahara," 98–99. For French perspectives on Western Sahara, see T. de Saint Maurice, *Sahara Occidental 1991–1999: L'enjeu du referendum d'autodetermination* (Paris: l'Harmattan, 2000).

33. Interview, Mohammed Bennouna, June 6, 2004.

34. Interview, June 2, 2005.

35. Ties with Spain have been built up by Polisario's practice of sending children from its camps in Tindouf to spend summers with Spanish families.

36. Perejil was occupied by Moroccan police and troops on July 11, 2002. After vehement Spanish protests, including to the United Nations, they were evicted without bloodshed by Spanish naval forces. On July 20, 2002, Spain agreed to withdraw its troops from the island. See Richard Gillespie, "Spain and Morocco: A Case of Crisis in Euro-Mediterranean Relations," paper presented at the Second Pan-European Conference of the Standing Group on EU Politics, Bologna, June 24–26, 2004, www.jhubc.it/ecpr-bologna.

37. Interviews, Spanish officials, May 11 and 27, 2004. See also Gillespie, *Spain and the Mediterranean*, 44; and Naylor, "Spain, France, and the Western Sahara," 17–51; for a history of Spain and Western Sahara, see J. R. Diego Aguirre, *Guerra en el Sáhara* (Madrid: Istmo, 1991).

38. The instruments regulating sovereignty over natural resources in nonselfgoverning territories were reviewed in the letter addressed by the UN Legal Counsel to the President of the Security Council in January 2002, S/2002/161. See also Fish Elsewhere, "Briefing: EU-Morocco Fisheries Partnership Agreement: Why Western Sahara should be excluded," February 2006, www.fishelsewhere.org.

39. Other members included Argentina, Egypt, Kenya, and Gambia, which served on the Council from 1998 to 1999 and was the last of these temporary Friends. Russia's initial interest was described by UN and Russian officials as responding primarily to the active role taken by its expert in that period.

40. Interview, Russian official, June 26, 2003.

41. Interview, November 18, 2002.

42. Telephone interview, Walker.

43. Algeria and Mauritania were officially "observers" of the process led by Baker. Mauritania has assumed a position of caution with respect to the UN process, a reflection of its need to balance rapprochement with Morocco with not antagonizing Polisario, whose members circulate freely in the north of the country.

44. Jensen was succeeded by Charles Dunbar (1998–99), William Eagleton (1999–2001), and William Lacy Swing (2001–03), all former U.S. officials. Polisario found considerable support from Democrats and Republicans alike in the U.S. Congress. It had trusted the United States in the early 1990s, and valued highly a U.S. initiative to encourage direct talks between Morocco and Polisario in 1993, but saw it as overtly favoring Morocco during 1994–96. Interviews with Boukari and Mouloud Said, Polisario representative in Washington, April 5, 2004.

45. In an interview, the British ambassador in this period, Sir David Hannay, had no recollection at all of the existence of the Friends of Western Sahara. November 20, 2003.

46. *Report of the Security Council Mission to Western Sahara from 3 to 9 June 1995*, S/1995/498, June 21, 1995.

47. This point was contained in an early draft of Theophilopoulou, "The United Nations and Western Sahara," kindly shared by the author. Security Council Resolution 1017 was approved on September 22, 1995, without the amendments.

48. Telephone interview, April 26, 2004.

49. Interview, October 11, 2004.

50. Interview, November 18, 2002. Namibia abstained from the vote on Resolution 1282 of December 14, 1999; it then voted against Resolution 1301 of June 1, 2000, while Jamaica and Mali abstained.

51. Interview, James A. Baker III, June 7, 2004.

52. The phrase was first used in *Report of the Secretary-General on the Situation Concerning Western Sahara*, S/2000/1029, para. 30, October 25, 2000. UN officials would maintain that it was not the same as "administering Power," the standard expression used to refer to to non-self-governing territories, but the semantic quibble only mollified Polisario and Algeria to a certain extent.

53. Charges that Morocco had "pressured the United Nations into making concessions in its favor and deliberately obstructed the process" were presented in a report by Human Rights Watch, *Western Sahara: Keeping It Secret: The United Nations Operation in the Western Sahara* (New York: Human Rights Watch, October 1995), 5. The report followed widely publicized allegations by former U.S. official Frank S. Ruddy, who had served in MINURSO as deputy chairman of the Identification Commission, that "the UN had lost control of the mission" and that it had "become an instrument of the Moroccan government." See Chris Hedges, "Morocco, Defending Claim in the Desert, Exerts a Hand on Neighbor's Vote," *New York Times*, March 5, 1995.

54. See accounts of problems in identification given by two former SRSGs: Jensen, *Western Sahara*, especially chapter 5, and Charles Dunbar, "Saharan Stasis: Status and Prospects in the Western Sahara," *The Middle East Journal* 54, no. 4 (Autumn 2000).

55. Interview, April 19, 2004.

56. See Chopra, "A Chance for Peace in Western Sahara," 58–61.

57. See Gilonne d'Origny, "Western Sahara's Difficult Path," *Washington Times*, July 3, 1997. Chopra on several occasions raised the idea in testimony before the UN General Assembly's Fourth Committee.

58. S/1995/913, November 5, 1996.

59. Interview, Baker. Goulding's recollection was only that he had encouraged Baker to "try to negotiate a deal based on enhanced autonomy for Western Sahara within the Kingdom of Morocco." Goulding, *Peacemonger*, 214. Kofi Annan's letter of appointment to Baker is reproduced, in part, on the Web site of the James A. Baker III Institute for Public Policy, Rice University, Houston. It describes a threefold mission: "to assess, in consultation with the parties, the implementability of the [Settlement] Plan in its current form; to examine whether there are adjustments, acceptable to the parties, which would significantly improve the chances of implementing it in the near future; and, if not, to advise me on other possible ways of resolving the conflict." These "other possible ways" included a "deal" negotiated through direct talks or shuttle diplomacy that might consist of Morocco giving Western Sahara "a greater deal of autonomy than the country's other regions, together with a special status for the Polisario leadership, in return for which Polisario would agree to the Territory being part of Morocco." Letter from Kofi A. Annan to James Baker, March 3, 1997; Virtual Museum, James A. Baker III Institute for Public Policy of Rice University, www. bakerinstitute.org.

60. Pérez de Cuéllar had told Hassan that he was "all the happier to hear his idea, since I had found that the King's Maghreb colleagues supported a political compromise as constituting the ideal solution for the Western Sahara." *Pilgrimage for Peace*, 350.

61. Goulding, *Peacemonger*, 212; Theophilopolou, "The United Nations and Western Sahara," 5.

62. *Report of the Secretary-General on the Situation Concerning Western Sahara*, S/1997/166 of February 27, 1997.

63. Detailed accounts of the unfolding of the process are given in *Reports of the Secretary-General on the Situation Concerning Western Sahara*, S/2000/131 and S/2001/613, of February 17, 2000, and June 20, 2001, respectively. The Houston Accords are attached as Annex III to *Report of the Secretary-General on the Situation Concerning Western Sahara*, S/1997/742, September 24, 1997.

64. Interview, December 12, 2001.

65. Shelley, *Endgame in the Western Sahara*, 145.

66. Interview, January 7, 2003.

67. Confidential interview.

68. S/2000/131.

69. "We don't have a policy on Western Sahara," one State Department official explained in April 2004. "We just support Baker." Interview, April 6, 2004.

70. Interview, Baker.

71. S/2001/613, June 20, 2001.

72. The draft framework agreement was attached as Annex I to S/2001/613.

73. Resolution 1359 was adopted on June 29, 2001. Specific complaints against the working practices of the Friends were made by both Singapore and Ireland in the "wrap-up" discussion on the work of the Council for the month of June held that afternoon. Both delegations asked for fuller discussion in the Council in order to ensure, as the Irish ambassador put it, "that we all come to the resolution with the same sense of…having an input into the resolution." See S/PV.4343 of June 29, 2001.

74. These options were outlined in *Report of the Secretary-General on the Situation Concerning Western Sahara*, S/2002/178, February 19, 2001.

75. Interview, Baker.

76. Interview, November 11, 2003.

77. Interview, January 7, 2003. An Irish diplomat would describe this draft as "utterly one-sided in its approach; it was a violation of international legal principles, and had already been rejected by one party to the dispute." Cited in Ian Williams and Stephen Zunes, "Self-Determination Struggle in the Western Sahara Continues to Challenge the UN," *Foreign Policy in Focus*, September 2003.

78. An official from Singapore reported that Western Sahara was the only issue before the Council on which his foreign ministry was lobbied at a high level.

Interview, January 7, 2003. Ireland was also lobbied, but Morocco's efforts did little to sway its cross-party support of Polisario. Interview, January 7, 2003.

79. Resolution 1429, July 30, 2002. Kieran Prendergast would describe this tortuous process as the Security Council "at its worst" and a demonstration of its "very large 'too difficult' tray." Interview.

80. *Report of the Secretary-General on the Situation Concerning Western Sahara*, S/2003/565, May 10, 2003. The peace plan is attached as Annex II.

81. Abdelaziz was reportedly summoned by three leading Algerian officials at the end of June 2003 in an attempt to pressure him to change Polisario's stance. Algerian press report, cited by Toby Shelley, "Behind the Baker Plan for Western Sahara," *Middle East Report Online*, August 1, 2003.

82. Interview, Boukhari, April 14, 2004. Polisario saw the plan as offering it an opportunity to demonstrate its commitment to fair and democratic government and in the process, woo the votes of Moroccan settlers in the referendum. See Jacob A. Mundy, "Stubborn Stalemate in Western Sahara," *Middle East Report Online*, June 26, 2004.

83. Confidential interview.

84. Interview, November 18, 2003.

85. Attached as an annex to *Report of the Secretary-General on the Situation Concerning Western Sahara*, S/2004/325, April 23, 2004.

86. Resolution 1541 of April 29, 2004.

87. The letter, which also noted that Polisario had been unwilling to negotiate on the basis of the framework agreement, continued: "And this rejection of the Peace Plan comes after Morocco's refusal to continue under the Settlement Plan, which it publicly supported for over 10 years, and to even discuss a division of the territory, notwithstanding having actually negotiated and implemented a division thereof with Mauritania in 1976." Letter from James A. Baker III to the Secretary-General, June 1, 2004.

88. "Baker Resigns as UN Envoy on W. Sahara," *Middle East Online*, June 14, 2004.

89. Interview, Boukhari, April 14, 2004. Secretariat officials interviewed between 2002 and 2006 confirmed that Annan and officials from the Department of Peacekeeping Operations in particular had been sensitive to lobbying from France and Morocco, often conducted at the highest level, on the Western Sahara file.

90. Letter dated June 11, 2004, from the Secretary-General to the President of the Security Council, S/2004/492, June 15, 2004.

91. Interview, Boukhari, September 2, 2004. Algeria's objections were made known to senior secretariat officials. Interview, UN official, October 14, 2004.

92. Interview, October 11, 2004.

93. Hurried visits to both Morocco and France had followed quickly upon Prime Minister Zapatero's assumption of office as part of an effort to improve relations with both. Zapatero had declared in Paris that the issue of Western Sahara could be worked out in six months; Spain had also supported a proposal for a four-way summit among France, Spain, Algeria, and Morocco to address Western Sahara outside the UN framework (an idea quickly shot down by Algeria). However, as the months passed, Spain began to move back toward its earlier position of neutrality. Interviews, Spanish officials, May 11 and 27, 2004; interview, Boukhari, September 2, 2004; "Insecurity over Spanish Position in Sahara Conflict," *Afrol News*, May 3, 2004; "Spain, Algeria Back Baker Plan for Western Sahara," *Middle East Online*, October 27, 2004.

94. Interview, Abdallah Baali, May 24, 2004.

95. Lisa Abend and Geoff Pingree, "Prisoner Release Gives Hope for W. Sahara Peace," *Christian Science Monitor*, August 22, 2005.

96. Bastagli left MINURSO at the end of September 2006. A team from the Office of the UN High Commissioner for Human Rights visited Western Sahara in May and June 2006 and found the human rights situation to be "of serious concern"; however, its report was never released to the public. "U.N. expresses 'serious concern' over alleged rights abuses in Western Sahara," *Associated Press*, October 9, 2006.

97. Cited in Irwin Arieff, "More Talks Ahead in Western Sahara Impasse —UN Envoy," *Reuters*, January 18, 2006.

98. Van Walsum's briefing to the Security Council of January 18, 2006, is described in *Report of the Secretary-General on the Situation Concerning Western Sahara*, S/2006/249, April 19, 2006, paras. 31–39.

99. Direct comparisons of East Timor and Western Sahara are made by Francois Rigaux, "East Timor and Western Sahara: A Comparative View," in Catholic Institute for International Relations and International Platform of Jurists for East Timor, *East Timor, International Law and the Question of East Timor* (London: CIIR/IPJET, 1995), 166–73; and Pedro Pinto Leite, "East Timor and Western Sahara: A Comparative Perspective," in *The East Timor Question*, ed. Paul Hainsworth and Stephen McCloskey (London and New York: I.B. Tauris & Co., 2000), 167–84.

7. East Timor and the Core Group

1. In the United Nations, East Timor became Timor-Leste at the moment of its independence, although in casual conversations references to East Timor remained common. For the sake of consistency, this chapter refers to East Timor throughout, with the exception of the current reference.

2. A/57/PV.20, September 27, 2002.

3. The Commission on Truth, Reception, and Reconciliation (CAVR) found that "the minimum figure" for conflict-related deaths between 1975 and 1999 was 102,800. Executive Summary, "Report of the Commission on Truth, Reception and Reconciliation," 2006, 44. The CAVR report was presented to the secretary-general of the United Nations in January 2006, www.cavr-timor-leste.org. Twenty-five hundred pages long, the report represents an extraordinary resource on the history of East Timor.

4. Antony Parsons, *From Cold War to Hot Peace: UN Interventions 1947–1994* (London: Michael Joseph, Ltd., 1995), 183.

5. East Timor is about 265 kilometers from east to west, but it also includes the enclave of Ocussi Ambeno, situated in West Timor about 120 kilometers from the East Timor/West Timor border, as well as the islands of Atauro and Jaco.

6. On Australia's role during the war, see Final Report of the Senate Foreign Affairs, Defence and Trade References Committee, *East Timor* (Canberra: Parliament of the Commonwealth of Australia, December 2000), 6.2–6.13. For histories of East Timor, see Jill Joliffe, *East Timor: Nationalism and Colonialism* (Queensland: University of Queensland Press, 1978), and Barbedo de Magalhaes, *East Timor: Land of Hope* (Oporto: President's Office, Oporto University, 1990).

7. Security Council Resolution 384 and Security Council Resolution 389 of December 22, 1975, and April 22, 1976, respectively. See *Repertoire of Practice, 1975–1980*, 243–53.

8. In a cable dated August 1975 discussing the likely annexation of East Timor, the Australian ambassador, Richard Woolcott, recommended to his superiors "a pragmatic rather than a principled stand, but that is what national interest and foreign policy is all about." Cited in Jim Aubrey, "Canberra: Jakarta's Trojan Horse in East Timor," in *The East Timor Question*, ed. Paul Hainsworth and Stephen McCloskey (London and New York: I.B. Tauris & Co., 2000), 136.

9. Kissinger had stressed that Indonesian action should "succeed quickly" and asked that Suharto hold off on initiating it until the Americans were back in Washington. Declassified Embassy Jakarta Telegram 1579 to Secretary of State, December 6, 1975, in *Ford, Kissinger and the Indonesian Invasion, 1975–1976*, National Security Archive Electronic Briefing Book, no. 62, doc. 4, ed. William Burr and Michael L. Evans (Washington, DC: National Security Archive, December 6, 2001).

10. For detailed accounts of these events see chapters 3 and 5 of the CAVR report and Edward Rees, "Under Pressure: Falintil—Forças de Defesa de Timor Leste, Three Decades of Defence Force Development in Timor Leste 1975–2004," *Working Paper*, no. 139, Geneva Centre for the Democratic Control of Armed Forces, April 2004, 37–44. See also International Crisis Group, "Resolving Timor-Leste's Crisis," *Asia Report*, no. 120 (Dili/Brussels: International Crisis Group, October 10, 2006), 2–5.

11. Gusmão had chosen to initiate dialogue—through proxies—with the Indonesians and, in the interests of national unity, to reach out to the Catholic Church and other political parties and abandon the Marxism to which Fretilin was committed. CAVR report, chapter 5, paras. 116–18, and Rees, "Under Pressure," 41.

12. Rees, "Under Pressure," 44–54. See also *Report of the United Nations Independent Special Commission of Inquiry for Timor-Leste*, Geneva, October 2, 2006, para. 25, www.ohchr.org.

13. The Australian Senate indicated that Indonesia spent $A18.8 million on infrastructure over a period of seventeen years up until 1992, "a paltry sum." Final Report of the Senate Foreign Affairs Committee, 2: 30.

14. CAVR report, chapter 3.18, para. 484.

15. General Assembly Resolution 37/32 of November 23, 1982.

16. Interview, March 23, 2004.

17. Interview, José Luis Guterres, March 19, 2004. Guterres was appointed foreign minister in July 2006.

18. Ian Martin, *Self-Determination in East Timor: The United Nations, the Ballot and International Intervention* (Boulder, CO: Lynne Rienner Publishers, 2001), 17–18; interview, UN official, March 23, 2004.

19. The United States voted in favor of Security Council Resolution 384 of December 22, 1975, and abstained from Security Council Resolution 389 of April 22, 1976. The General Assembly resolution passed in 1976, but the United States then voted against all General Assembly resolutions from 1977 to 1982; Australia voted in favor of the General Assembly resolutions in 1976 and 1977, abstained in 1978, and voted against resolutions from 1979 to 1982.

20. See Department of Foreign Affairs and Trade, *East Timor in Transition 1998–2000: An Australian Foreign Policy Challenge* (Canberra: Department of Foreign Affairs and Trade, 2000), 11–13.

21. See Roger S. Clark, "Timor Gap," in *East Timor at the Crossroads*, ed. Peter Carey and G. Carter Bentley (Honolulu: University of Hawaii Press, 1996), 73–94.

22. The involvement of the United Nations had been intended to facilitate the decolonization of Dutch West New Guinea through the realization of its population's right to self-determination. But the UN role, which John Saltford has described as being "assigned to [it] by Washington in 1962," became instead "to ensure that the territory became a recognized part of Indonesia with the minimum of controversy and disruption." The Act of Free Choice involved just more than one thousand people, "representative" of the broader population but handpicked by Indonesia after open intimidation by its security forces. Unsurprisingly, the vote was unanimously in support of integration with Indonesia. See John Saltford, *The United Nations and the Indonesian Takeover of West Papua, 1962–1969: The Anatomy of Betrayal* (London: Routledge Curzon, 2003), especially 178–84.

23. UN press release, "Secretary-General reiterates intention to assist in solution to East Timor question and to monitor human rights situation there," SG/SM/5095, September 17, 1993.

24. Ambassador Marker chronicled the history of his efforts in Jamsheed Marker, *East Timor: A Memoir of the Negotiations for Independence* (Jefferson, NC: McFarland and Company, Inc., 2003).

25. Ibid., 79.

26. Don Greenlees and Robert Garran, *Deliverance: The Inside Story of East Timor's Fight for Freedom* (Crows Nest, N.S.W.: Allen and Unwin, 2002), 24.

27. The autonomy plan, which would be the subject of negotiations until January 1999, is described by Marker, *East Timor*, 101–02.

28. Tamrat Samuel describes how "[t]he military was eager not to be seen as the perpetrator of atrocities, and sought to portray itself as the force of law and order in the midst of a chaotic conflict involving two opposing East Timorese sides." "East Timor: The Path to Self-Determination," in *From Promise to Practice: Strengthening UN Capacities for the Prevention of Conflict*, ed. Chandra Lekha Sriram and Karin Wermester (Boulder, CO: Lynne Rienner Publishers, 2003), 203.

29. The Howard letter is cited in the Final Report of the Senate Foreign Affairs Committee, *East Timor*, 7:87. For a full account of circumstances surrounding the letter and its impact, see Greenlees and Garran, *Deliverance*, 81–95.

30. Citations from Greenlees and Garran, *Deliverance*, 88 and 93.

31. The May 5, 1999, agreements are attached as annexes to A/53/951–S/1999/513 of May 5, 1999.

32. The *Washington Post* cited an internal memorandum written by a senior UN official just before the signing: "I cannot hide my apprehension regarding the course on which we are about to embark," he wrote. A diplomat familiar with the negotiations was reported to have commented that "Alatas took Portugal to the cleaners." Steven Mufson and Colum Lynch, "East Timor Failure Puts UN on Spot: Interventionist Ability in Doubt," *Washington Post*, September 26, 1999.

33. Edmund McWilliams, political counselor in the U.S. embassy in Jakarta until July 1999, would question the extent to which U.S., Australian, and UN officials all "bought in" to the analysis of Alatas, a skilled diplomat who had developed a reputation as a "senior professional voice" more trustworthy than the erratic Habibie. Interview, April 5, 2004.

34. Prendergast would note that the high-handedness of Indonesia's response showed that it "had a degree of protection" from Australia and the United States. Interview. For further discussion of the May 5 agreements and security, see Marker, *East Timor*, 144–60; Martin, *Self-Determination in East Timor*, 29–34; and Samuel, "East Timor," 211–15.

35. Interview, Vendrell. Inclusion of states sympathetic to the Timorese, such as Ireland and Norway, would not have been credible.

36. Interview, Stewart Eldon, November 14, 2002. The advantage of this process was that formation of the group felt, as Eldon put it, like "spontaneous combustion."

37. It was always understood that UNAMET would be funded from "voluntary contributions" from member states rather than from assessed contributions to the United Nations' regular or peacekeeping budget. This greatly facilitated the relative speed with which the mission was launched. An early suggestion that Brazil should be included as a member of the Core Group was abandoned, a consequence of concern that it would either act as, or be perceived to act as, a proxy of Portugal, one of the parties to the May 5 agreements.

38. Interview, March 2, 2004.

39. Penny Wensley, ambassador and permanent representative of Australia to the United Nations, "East Timor and the United Nations," delivered in Sydney on February 23, 2000, mimeo.

40. On the evolution of U.S. policy toward Indonesia, see Charles Scheiner, "The United States: From Complicity to Ambiguity," in *The East Timor Question,* ed. Hainsworthy and McCloskey, 117–32.

41. The importance of Suharto as a cooperative economic partner should not be underestimated. David E. Sanger, "Real Politics: Why Suharto Is In and Castro Is Out," *New York Times,* October 31, 1995.

42. McWilliams had submitted a cable to Washington through the dissent channel in July 1998 suggesting a shift in U.S. policy to support autonomy with the proviso that, "within a fixed period, East Timorese be permitted an opportunity to express themselves regarding their political status." McWilliams discussed the cable with Roth in October 1998, who dismissed the proposition on the grounds of East Timor's lack of economic viability. Declassified cable dated July 22, 1998, "Proposed Revision of U.S. Policy on East Timor." Interview, McWilliams, April 5, 2004.

43. Confidential interview.

44. Interview, Japanese official, March 26, 2004. The civilian police were contributed to UNAMET and seven hundred engineers—Japan's largest contribution to a peacekeeping operation at the time and the first to an operation mandated under chapter VII of the charter—to UNTAET and UNMISET from March 2002 on. Hasegawa was the first Japanese national to head a peacekeeping operation since Yasushi Akashi served in Cambodia and the former Yugoslavia in the early and mid-1990s, a point of some sensitivity to Japan given the country's extensive financial contributions to the United Nations.

45. Interview, New Zealand official, May 7, 2004.

46. Stewart Eldon, "East Timor," in *The UN Security Council: From the Cold War to the 21ˢᵗ Century,* ed. Malone 551–56.

47. See, for example, Press Release from the Indonesian Mission, "UNAMET Suspected of Taking the Side in Favor of Pro-Independence," June 4, 1999.

48. Eldon, "East Timor," 552. UN officials directly engaged in the process agree with this assessment. See Martin, *Self-Determination in East Timor*, 33, and Samuel, "East Timor," 225.

49. Interview, UN official, September 19, 2002.

50. Interview, McWilliams. On the withholding of Australian intelligence, see "A Suicide in Alexandria," *Counterpunch*, June 1–15, 2001, and Patrick Walters, John Kerin, and Greg Roberts, "Officer's List of Spy Failures," *The Australian*, April 14, 2004.

51. Both U.S. ambassador to Jakarta Stapleton Roy and Secretary of State Madeleine Albright met with representatives of militia groups in Jakarta, reinforcing the Indonesian position that the militia groups reflected legitimate opposition actors. Interview, McWilliams. See also Allan Nairn, "U.S. Complicity in Timor," *The Nation*, September 27, 1999.

52. See, for example, the letter dated May 27, 1999, from Makarim Wibisono, Permanent Representative of Indonesia, addressed to the President of the Security Council, Ambassador M. Denis Danque Rewaka.

53. Interview, UN official, December 20, 2001.

54. Martin, *Self-Determination in East Timor*, 39.

55. S/1999/705 of June 22, 1999.

56. Eldon, "East Timor," 554; the Presidential Statement was PRST/1999/20, June 19, 1999; and the attack on Maliana on June 29.

57. Interview, UN official, September 19, 2002.

58. Martin, "Self-Determination in East Timor," 84.

59. Samuel cites a meeting between Wiranto and Gusmão and Ramos-Horta in June in which Wiranto had told them he would disarm and dissolve the militia in forty-eight hours if Falintil also disarmed. "East Timor," 214.

60. Prendergast would recall that he suggested the mission to the Security Council three times—"I felt like Saint Peter," as he put it—but had found that the United Kingdom was almost as reluctant as the Russians (the main obstacle in the Security Council) to take up his idea. (Others attributed hesitation in the Core Group to Japan.) Van Walsum was informed by the United Kingdom and the United States that the Core Group "might not be opposed to the dispatch of a Security Council mission" on September 5. Peter van Walsum, "The Security Council Mission to East Timor," Paper presented to the Seminar on the Occasion of the Carnegie Foundation Centenary, Peace Palace, The Hague, June 6–7, 2004, mimeo.

61. Planning on East Timor, both for the immediate postballot period and for the transitional administration to independence that all recognized as the

most likely scenario, was seriously marred by turf battles between the Department of Political Affairs (which had responsibility for UNAMET and the ballot) and the Department of Peacekeeping Operations (which would assume responsibility for the INTERFET and UNTAET periods).

62. One secretariat official had told the Core Group in mid-July that "only the two best-case scenarios" could be presented to the Security Council—not a third scenario of postballot chaos, which was the one that indeed transpired. Confidential interview.

63. Confidential interview. See also discussion of the Australian position in Conflict Security and Development Group, King's College, London University, "A Review of Peace Operations: A Case for Change, East Timor Study," 1.15.

64. Confidential interview.

65. See *Report of the Security Council Mission to Jakarta and Dili, September 8–12, 1999*, S/1999/976, September 14, 1999; see also Eldon's account of the mission, "East Timor," 557–58, and van Walsum, "The Security Council Mission to East Timor."

66. Ian Martin, e-mail to the author, August 6, 2005. The deaths of five local staff members were confirmed at the time; other deaths or disappearances were reported after the United Nations' return. Martin, *Self-Determination in East Timor*, 102.

67. Wensley, "East Timor and the United Nations."

68. The International Monetary Fund suspended discussions with Indonesia regarding the review of its ongoing $12.3 billion economic bailout following the Asian financial crisis; the World Bank linked its earlier suspension of a loan to Indonesia to the situation in East Timor, while the United Kingdom—like the United States, which took action late in the day—suspended the sale of Hawk fighters to Jakarta on September 11. See discussion of these developments by Samuel, "East Timor," 216.

69. This was of particular importance for Russia. The position of China, which might also have been expected to be wary of intervention in Indonesia, was helped by China's less-than-cordial relations with Jakarta, stemming in part from Indonesia's treatment of its ethnic Chinese population. See Peter van Walsum, "The East Timor Crisis and the Doctrine of Humanitarian Intervention," presentation given at Asialink seminar, Melbourne, February 7, 2002, mimeo.

70. The planning process was also plagued by personal and bureaucratic differences within the United Nations, as note 61 suggests. See Simon Chesterman, "East Timor in Transition: Self-Determination, State-Building and the United Nations," *International Peacekeeping* 9, no. 1 (Spring 2002): 45–76; Conflict, Security and Development Group, *East Timor*, 222–8; Ian Martin, "East Timor: A Field Perspective," in *The UN Security Council*, ed. Malone; Astri Suhrke, "Peace-keepers as Nation-Builders: Dilemmas of the UN in East Timor," *International Peacekeeping* 8, no. 4 (Winter 2001): 1–20.

71. Thirteen such meetings were held between September 1999 and April 2006; after East Timor's independence they became known as "Timor-Leste and Development Partners Meetings," www.worldbank.org/tl.

72. Assessments of UNTAET, many by former staff members, have varied widely. Anthony Goldstone, team leader for the King's College study, and a former UN staff member in East Timor (who cites Vieira de Mello's comment), gives a balanced account in "UNTAET with Hindsight: The Peculiarities of Politics in an Incomplete State," *Global Governance* 10 (2004): 83–98. Speaking in the Security Council on June 27, 2000, Vieira de Mello had drawn attention to the need "to review both our thinking and our administrative mechanisms" if the United Nations were to undertake similar operations in the future. S/PV.4165.

73. Rees notes that UNTAET "was manipulated and made mistakes" in the creation of F-FDTL. "Under Pressure," 45–48.

74. In this they were helped by positions taken by the secretariat. Goldstone writes that the time frame of East Timor's transition to independence "was largely UN driven, determined by what the secretariat judged major country contributors' budgets and by what the Security Council's limited patience with nation building would bear." "UNTAET with Hindsight," 87.

75. Security Council Resolution 1599, April 28, 2005.

76. Interview, Karmalesh Sharma, May 10, 2004.

77. See *Report of the Secretary-General on Justice and Reconciliation for Timor-Leste*, S/2006.580, July 26, 2006, for a succinct overview. Critical assessments are given in David Cohen, *Indifference and Accountability: The United Nations and the Politics of International Justice in East Timor* Special Report, No. 9, (Honolulu: East-West Center June 2006); and Megan Hirst and Howard Varney, *Justice Abandoned: An Assessment of the Serious Crimes Process in East Timor* (New York: International Center on Transitional Justice, June 2005).

78. See, for example, the statement made by Gusmão to the Security Council in January 2006, days after his presentation of the CAVR report to the secretary-general. Seeking to distance himself from some of the recommendations made by the CAVR, Gusmão hailed as "true justice" for the East Timorese "the recognition by the international community of the right of people of Timor-Leste to self-determination and independence." S/PV.5351, January 23, 2006.

79. *End of Mandate Report of the Secretary-General on the United Nations Office in Timor-Leste*, S/2006/251, April 20, 2006. Security Council Report's *Monthly Forecast* for May 2006 noted that "the Council is divided on whether there should be a continuing UN political presence in Timor-Leste." See www.securitycouncilreport.org.

80. *Report of the Secretary-General on Timor-Leste pursuant to Security Council resolution 1690 (2006)*, S/2006/628, August 8, 2006, para. 2.

81. The inclusion of Portugal was initially resisted by Japan. Japan's suggestion that Indonesia also be included did not prosper. Interview, January 7, 2003.

82. Interview, March 25, 2004.

83. Although Core Group states were the largest donors, and as such would take part in the meetings organized by the World Bank, the group as it was constituted in New York did not stray in its discussions beyond the political and security issues that were before the Security Council.

84. Robert C. Orr, "Making East Timor Work: The United States as Junior Partner," *National Security Studies Quarterly* 7, no. 3 (Summer 2001): 133.

85. In May 2002, the newly independent East Timor had signed the Timor Sea Treaty, negotiated with the assistance of UNTAET, with Australia, giving it a 90/10 split of oil and gas revenues within a specified area. The treaty was signed "without prejudice" to the delimitation of East Timor's maritime boundary, which would determine the fate of the substantial deposits that lay under the Timor Sea, but outside the areas covered by the treaty, between Australia and East Timor. However, Australia stalled on negotiations on establishing a permanent boundary, including by withdrawing from the international legal mechanisms—the International Court of Justice and the International Tribunal for the Law of the Sea—established to resolve boundary issues that cannot be settled by negotiation. See press release issued by East Timor Action Network, April 14, 2004.

86. *Report of the Security Council Mission to East Timor and Indonesia,* S/2000/1105, November 21, 2000.

87. Interviews, November 6 and 14, 2002. See also comments by France within the Security Council meetings of December 22, 1999; June 27, 2000; and October 31, 2001, in S/PV.4085, S/PV.4165, and S/PV.4404, respectively. At different points Russia also required intense persuasion by Core Group members of East Timor's ongoing need. Interview, Core Group official May 7, 2004.

88. Shepard Forman, "UN Haste Puts East Timor at Risk," *International Herald Tribune*, February 2, 2003; Sonny Inbaraj, "Riots Show Fragility of World's Newest Nation," Inter Press Service, December 13, 2005; John Ward and Peter Symonds, "UN and East Timor Government Push for Tougher Police Measures," World Socialist Web site, December 20, 2002, www.wsws.org.

89. Interview, UN official, March 2, 2004.

90. *Special Report of the Secretary-General on the United Nations Mission of Support to East Timor,* S/2003/243, March 3, 2003.

91. Interview, March 2, 2004. The letter, circulated as an annex to S/2003/379 on April 3, 2003, spelled out "a more gradual downsizing to 1,750 military peacekeepers in December 2003 than had been foreseen, although not full retention of 3,870 up to that period as was reflected in the annex to the Secretary-General's report." Resolution 1473 was adopted on April 4, 2003.

92. "We were going to be adamant about ending UNMISET," as one U.S. official put it, "but Australia really wanted it." Interview, April 6, 2004.

93. See statement by Ambassador John Dauth to the Security Council on October 15, 2003, S/PV.4843. Australia favored a formed police unit; the secretary-general would recommend 310 military personnel to provide protection for military liaison officers, maintain a "reassuring presence" in the border regions, and be capable of quick reaction if required. *Special Report of the Secretary-General on the United Nations Mission of Support to East Timor*, S/2004/117, February 13, 2004.

94. Foreign Minister José Ramos Horta's suggestion to the Bush White House that it did not want to risk instability in East Timor in an election year was judged to have done the trick—a petition helped by the fact that East Timor had supported U.S. action in Iraq. Interview, U.S. official, April 6, 2004.

95. Like the United States, the United Kingdom had originally believed that neither the formed police unit nor the peacekeepers were strictly necessary, but ended up supporting both. Interview, U.K. official, March 11, 2004. Brazil had cultural ties to the lusophone Timorese and a long-standing interest in their fate; it also had offered to provide the manpower for the new response unit.

96. *Progress Report of the Secretary-General on the United Nations Mission of Support in East Timor*, S/2005/99, February 18, 2005.

97. Interview, Core Group member, June 2, 2005. East Timor's prime minister had written to the secretary-general in February to request a continued UN presence. See annex to letter dated February 23, 2005, from the Permanent Representative of Timor-Leste to the United Nations addressed to the Secretary-General, S/2005/103.

98. The report is attached as an annex to letter dated June 24, 2005, from the Secretary-General addressed to the Presdent of the Security Council, S/2005/458.

99. Letter dated September 28, 2005, from the President of the Security Council addressed to the Secretary-General, S/2005/613.

100. The secretary-general's recommendations are contained in S/2006/580, para. 32, and were endorsed by Security Council Resolution 1704, August 25, 2006, op. para. 4.

101. Security Council Report, *Monthly Forecast*, August 2006, www.securitycouncilreport.org. Several secretariat officials expressed their surprise, in conversations during June and July 2006, at the depth of the problems exposed in the security forces.

102. *Report of the United Nations Independent Special Commission of Inquiry*, paras. 100–01.

103. Timor was beginning to benefit from petroleum production, but it was "still among the world's poorest countries." Non-petroleum GDP per captia fell from some US$450 in 2001 to an estimated $360 in 2005. Meanwhile, youth unemployment in urban areas was estimated at 43 percent. World Bank, "Timor Leste Country Brief," www.worldbank.org.

104. *Report of the United Nations Independent Special Commission of Inquiry*, Summary.

105. Hasegawa had been a long-standing staff member of UNDP. Before becoming SRSG of UNMISET he had served as one of the deputies to Sharma. His performance in that capacity led several of his UN colleagues to question his suitability for an appointment to SRSG that was perceived a consequence of pressure on the secretary-general from Japan. Interviews, UN officials, December 13, 2005; November 7, 2006.

106. International Crisis Group, "Resolving Timor-Leste's Crisis," 18. Hasegawa was also criticized for being too close to Gusmão—as other UN representatives before him—and thus both blinded to some of the complexities of the situation and alienated from the government.

107. Martin sensibly insisted that he be accompanied by Tamrat Samuel, the single individual in the secretariat with the deepest knowledge of the Timorese and their history. Interview, June 12, 2006.

108. S/3006/628. See also Ian Martin's remarks to the Security Council, S/PV.5512, August 15, 2006.

109. S/PV.5512. See also Security Council Report, *Monthly Forecast,* August 2006.

110. José Ramos Horta's request was contained in a letter addressed to the President of the Security Council on August 4, 2006, annexed to S/2006/620, August 7, 2006.

111. As the International Crisis Group points out, Timor's relationship with Australia was more complicated in 2006 than 1999 for a number of different reasons: Australian officials had been openly critical of Alkatiri; animosity towards Australia had been fuelled by two years of difficult negotiations over oil in the Timor Sea (although these had culminated in a treaty in January 2006, differences over where the gas would be processed, and suspicions regarding Australia's intentions, remained); Australian troops in Dili in 2006 had, in contrast, to 1999, been unable to prevent new violence because of the greater complexity of its origins. "Resolving Timor-Leste's Crisis," 17–19. On the Core Group positions, see Security Council Report, *Update Report,* no. 3, August 17, 2006, www.securitycouncilreport.org, and S/PV.5512.

112. Security Council Resolution 1704, op. para. 2.

113. A strong candidate from Cape Verde was rejected after the secretariat came under pressure from Australia and the United States; the confirmation of the successful candidate—Atul Khare of India—was then held up for weeks by Japanese objections raised within the Fifth Committee of the General Assembly. Interviews, UN officials, November 7 and 9, 2006.

114. East Timor ranked 158 out of 177 countries on the United Nations Development Programme's Human Development Index for 2002. Only African countries ranked below it.

8. Groups and the Variable Geometry of UN Peacemaking

1. J. Stephen Morrison and Alex de Waal, "Can Sudan Escape Its Intractability?" in *Grasping the Nettle*, ed. Crocker et al., 161–82.

2. As this chapter addresses the role of the United Nations in the UN member state recognized as the Union of Myanmar, the name Myanmar, not Burma, is adopted.

3. See S/PV.5526 and S/Agenda/55226, September 15, 2006.

4. The first resolution on Myanmar was A/RES/46/132 of December 17, 1991.

5. Interview, Vendrell. A/RES/48/150, *Situation of Human Rights in Myanmar*, adopted by the General Assembly on December 20, 1993.

6. A/RES/57/231, *Situation of Human Rights in Myanmar*, adopted by the General Assembly on December 18, 2002, requested the secretary-general "to continue to provide his good offices and to pursue his discussions on the situation of human rights and the restoration of democracy with the government and people of Myanmar."

7. See International Crisis Group, "Myanmar: Sanctions, Engagement or Another Way Forward?" *Asia Report*, no. 78 (Yangon/Brussels: International Crisis Group, April 26, 2004).

8. De Soto continued to meet representatives of key states individually and when in Yangon, finding it most productive to hold separate meetings with the Western countries and Asian states in order to fine-tune his message to each. Interview, June 12, 2003.

9. Interview, UN official, September 16, 2004.

10. International Crisis Group, "Myanmar: Sanctions, Engagement or Another Way Forward?" 3; Seth Mydans, "Neighbors Join Critics of Burmese," *New York Times*, June 17, 2003.

11. Interview, UN official, September 16, 2004.

12. India, China's strategic rival in Myanmar, did take part in the ICGM, but "measured its participation carefully." Interview, UN official, September 2, 2004.

13. See John H. Badgley, ed., "Reconciling Burma/Myanmar: Essays on U.S. Relations with Burma," National Bureau of Asian Research, *NBR Analysis* 15, no. 1 (March 2004).

14. The possibility of forming a group of Friends was discussed within the secretariat before this meeting. States attending what was in the end described as a "high-level informal consultation" included Australia, France, Indonesia, Japan, Malaysia, the Netherlands, Norway, Singapore, Thailand, the United Kingdom, the United States, and Vietnam. China had been invited but, under instructions from Beijing, declined. United Nations, "Statement attributable to the Spokesman of the Secretary-General on Myanmar," September 29, 2004.

15. Gambari briefed the Security Council after his second visit to Myanmar on November 27, 2006, as the United States was preparing a draft resolution demanding that Myanmar's authorities release Suu Kyi, and curb refugee flows, drug trafficking, and policies permitting the transmission of infectious diseases outside the country. But with the Council divided and China adamantly opposed to the resolution, it could not prosper. Security Council Report, *Update Report*, November 2006, no. 3, November 22, 2006, and Warren Hoge, "World Briefing: Asia: U.S. Wants U.N. Action Against Junta," *New York Times*, November 28, 2006.

16. See Barnett R. Rubin, Ashraf Ghani, William Maley, Ahmed Rashid, and Olivier Roy, "Afghanistan: Reconstruction and Peacebuilding in a Regional Framework," *KOFF Peacebuilding Reports*, 1/2001 (Center for Peacebuilding, KOFF, and Swiss Peace Foundation, [SPF], 2001). A comprehensive introduction to Afghanistan is provided by Barnett R. Rubin, *The Fragmentation of Afghanistan: State Formation and Collapse in the International System*, 2nd ed. (New Haven and London: Yale University Press, 2002).

17. Report of the Secretary-General, *The Situation in Afghanistan and Its Implications for International Peace and Security*, S/1997/894, November 14, 1987, para. 45.

18. See Human Rights Watch, *Afghanistan: Crisis of Impunity, The Role of Pakistan, Russia, and Iran in Fueling the Civil War*, vol. 13, no. 3 (C), (New York: Human Rights Watch, July 2001); Ahmed Rashid, *Taliban: Militant Islam, Oil and Fundamentalism in Central Asia* (New Haven, CT: Yale Nota Bene, 2001), 183–206; Rubin et al., "Afghanistan: Reconstruction and Peacebuilding in a Regional Framework"; and Peter Tomsen, "Geopolitics of an Afghan Settlement," *Perceptions, Journal of International Affairs* 5, no. 4 (December 2000–February 2001).

19. S/1997/894, November 14, 1987, paras. 42 and 55.

20. Interview, Brahimi.

21. The importance of Pakistan and Iran to the future of Afghanistan was such that Brahimi would recall that the "six plus two" was in many respects "really two."

22. UN press briefing by Special Envoy to Afghanistan, October 20, 1999.

23. Interview, Brahimi.

24. The first meeting of the Group of 21, also described as a group of "states with influence" over Afghanistan, had been held in November 1996. Under the chairmanship of Kieran Prendergast, the group consisted of China, Egypt, France, Germany, India, Iran, Italy, Japan, Kazakhstan, Kyrgyzstan, the Netherlands, Pakistan, Russia, Saudi Arabia, Sweden, Tajikistan, Turkey, Turkmenistan, the United Kingdom, the United States, and Uzbekistan. The Organization of the Islamic Conference (OIC) also participated in its meetings.

25. The members of the "luncheon group"—France, Germany, Italy, Japan, Sweden, Norway, and the United Kingdom—were selected because they did not have a vested interest in the conflict, yet had similar views on it. Interview, Vendrell.

26. Italy, Iran, and Germany were backers of the "Rome process," the "Cyprus process," and the earlier "Bonn process," respectively. Iran and the United States found the group (and opportunities to engage on its sidelines) a more effective means than the "six plus two" through which to have bilateral discussions on a range of issues. Interview, UN official, December 15, 2004.

27. Pakistan did not want additional states admitted to the group to increase the pressure on it regarding relations with the Taliban; Russia enjoyed the exclusivity that left it as the counterpart to the United States.

28. His role in the preparation of the "Brahimi report" on peace operations, published in August 2000, had only enhanced his reputation.

29. See UN press report, "'Six plus Two' group stresses need for broad-based Afghan government," New York, November 12, 2001.

30. Pakistan had a low-level presence at Bonn and was visibly "quite unwelcome." Russia was initially unhelpful, but gradually came to support the UN-led effort and put pressure on members of the Northern Alliance to accept the agreement. Interview, Barnett Rubin, October 15, 2004.

31. Ghani's remark was made at a meeting attended by the author in February 2006 and is cited with his permission. Dobbins et al. describe international coordination in Afghanistan as "much more ad hoc and dependent on personal relationships" than in the Balkans, for example. *America's Role in Nation-Building*, 142.

32. Interview, Jean Arnault, January 6, 2005. The reconstruction mechanisms included an Afghan Reconstruction Group, which met under the cochairmanship of the United States, the EU, Japan, and Saudi Arabia, and then an Afghanistan Development Forum instituted by the Afghan government. Meanwhile, a smaller group of states, assigned lead roles in different aspects of security reform on the initiative of the Group of Eight (G-8), met in Kabul as well as more infrequently outside the country. Interview, UN official, December 15, 2004; e-mail, Barnett Rubin, July 27, 2005.

33. For firsthand accounts of earlier phases of the peace process in Angola, see Margaret Joan Anstee, *Orphan of the Cold War: The Inside Story of the Collapse of the Angolan Peace Process, 1992–93* (London: Palgrave Macmillan, 1996), and Paul Hare, *Angola's Last Best Chance for Peace: An Insider's Account of the Peace Process* (Washington, DC: United States Institute of Peace Press, 1998). A Security Council embargo on arms and oil had been in place since 1993 and both the government and UNITA had agreed to halt new arms acquisitions. But the embargo against UNITA was not enforced and Troika members subsequently announced that they were lifting their national prohibitions on military sales to the government. In 1995 the United States and the United Kingdom attempted to push for a new total ban on weapons imports but found that Russia opposed it in the Security Council. Human Rights Watch, *Angola Unravels: The Rise and Fall of the Lusaka Peace Process* (New York: Human Rights Watch, 1999).

34. Interview, UN official, December 20, 2001.

35. Interview, November 20, 2002.

36. See Tony Hodges, *Angola: From Afro-Stalinism to Petro-Diamond Capitalism* (Bloomington and Indianapolis: Indiana University Press, 2001); Human Rights Watch, *Some Transparency, No Accountability: The Use of Oil Revenue in Angola and Its Impact on Human Rights* (New York: Human Rights Watch, 2004).

37. Confidential interview.

38. Interview, Ibrahim Gambari, March 31, 2003.

39. Gambari would also recall the utility to him of individual Friend ambassadors in Luanda, particularly those of the Troika states, Brazil, and Namibia. Interview.

40. See *Report of the Secretary-General on the United Nations Office in Angola* (UNOA), October 10, 2001, S/2001/956.

41. See *Interim Report of the Secretary-General on the United Nations Mission in Angola*, December 12, 2002, S/2002/1353.

42. Fen Osler Hampson, "Cyprus," in *Nurturing Peace*, 27–51; Brian S. Mandell, "The Cyprus Conflict: Explaining Resistance to Resolution," in *Cyprus: A Regional Conflict and Its Resolution*, ed. Normal Salem (New York: St. Martin's Press, 1992), 201–26.

43. Resolution 1250, adopted on June 29, 1999, called on the two Cypriot leaders to give their full support to a comprehensive negotiation, conducted under the auspices of the secretary-general, and to commit themselves to four principles: no preconditions; all issues on the table; continuation of negotiations until a settlement is reached; and full consideration of relevant UN resolutions and treaties.

44. These circumstances are described in *Report of the Secretary-General on his mission of good offices in Cyprus*, S/2003/398, April 1, 2003, paras. 4–7.

45. Interview, Alvaro de Soto, June 12, 2003.

46. *Report of the Secretary-General on his mission of good offices in Cyprus*, S/2003/398, April 1, 2003, para. 149.

47. David Hannay, *Cyprus: The Search for a Solution* (London: I.B. Taurus, 2005), 119.

48. Interview, Thomas Weston, January 19, 2005.

49. Most significant had been the resolution's commitment to "full consideration of relevant United Nations resolutions and treaties." This represented what de Soto described as a "slight but meaningful nod" to the Turkish side, as Greek Cypriots had always maintained that a solution to the Cyprus problem had to be "on the basis of" existing resolutions, which favored their positions. Interviews, de Soto, June 12, 2003, and David Hannay, November 20, 2003.

50. Hannay would recall that he and his first U.S. counterpart, Alfred Moses, "shadowed" the proximity talks that took place in Geneva and New York to an extent that was "at the edge of being unacceptable." They had found this necessary because neither the United Kingdom nor the United States had high-ranking diplomats in either place with a detailed knowledge of the issues. Once direct talks got under way in Cyprus the physical presence of the U.K. and U.S. envoys (Weston at this point) was less necessary because each maintained large and knowledgeable embassies in Nicosia. They were also asked by Turkey to keep their distance on the theory that Denktash would be more flexible if they weren't "breathing down his neck." However, they maintained close contact with de Soto by (secure) telephone. Interview and *Cyprus: The Search for Solution*.

51. Russia's support of the Greek Cypriot position dates back to the Cold War period. It reflects cultural ties related to the Orthodox faith and, more fundamentally, Russia's strategic concern with Turkey and lack of enthusiasm for its membership in the EU. Russia has long sold arms to Cyprus and may also, as one official suggested, have seen utility in Cyprus's accession to the EU (without the Turkish Cypriots). Interviews, May 6, 2004; December 20, 2004.

52. Interviews, Russian, U.K., and UN officials, May 6, 2004; November 17, 2003; June 5, 2003; May 11, 2004. One UN official had been told that the Russian veto was made "at the request" of the Greek Cypriots.

53. See *Reports of the Secretary-General on his mission of good offices in Cyprus*, S/2003/398 and S/2004/437, published on April 1, 2003, and May 28, 2004. Although general elections were held in Greece in March 2004, the secretary-general noted in his May 2004 report that the Cyprus issue did not become a subject of party politics; indeed, he commented that he had "always been able to count on Greece's support for my efforts." S/2004/437, para. 77.

54. The secretary-general was blunt on this point in his report of April 1, 2003, S/2003/398.

55. See Jan Asmussen, "Cyprus after the Failure of the Annan Plan," brief no. 11, (Flensburg, Germany: European Centre for Minority Issues, July 2004) for an account of these events.

56. See S/2003/398, para. 56, and S/2004/437, para. 4.

57. International support for the Annan Plan was widespread. Martti Ahtisaari and Gareth Evans admitted that there was much in it that both sides would find "problematic," but they concluded that there was "no better alternative that can be reached by negotiation, now or in the foreseeable future." "Three Advantages of the Annan Peace Plan," *International Herald Tribune*, April 19, 2004. See also Robert I. Rotberg's description of the Annan Plan as "a carefully developed, fully integrated basis for the island's reunification." *Cyprus After Annan: Next*

Steps Towards a Solution, WPF Report no. 17, (Cambridge, MA: World Peace Foundation, 2003), 1.

58. The high (or low) point of this campaign was an incendiary speech by Papadopoulos himself, broadcast on Cypriot television on April 7, 2004, in which he called on the people to reject the plan with "a resounding No." After watching it on television de Soto recalled that he knew "the game was up." Transcript, April 7, 2004 speech; interview, May 11, 2004.

59. Kieran Prendergast recalled that Annan had originally wanted Russia to join "a sort of four plus two," with the two being Egypt and Jordan, but the United States had stalled on whether to involve Russia at this stage until it was too late. Saudi Arabia was later added as a third Arab state engaged at one remove from the Quartet itself. Kieran Prendergast, telephone conversation, December 14, 2005.

60. Interview, UN official, September 2, 2004.

61. See *Policy or Process? The Politics of International Peace Implementation,* Report of the Peace Implementation Network (PIN) forum on International Cooperation in Peace Implementation: The Polices and Practices of Peacemaking and Peacebuilding (Oslo: Fafo Institute for Applied International Studies, 2004). The forum, for which the author served as rapporteur, was held in the Holmenkollen Park Hotel, Oslo, January 29–30, 2004.

62. The road map was presented as "A Performance-Based Roadmap to a Permanent Two-State Solution to the Israeli-Palestinian Conflict" in April 2003 and is available on the Web sites of the U.S. Department of State and United Nations. An original impetus for the road map had been the speech on the Middle East made by President George W. Bush on June 24, 2001. Although UN officials did not have a high opinion of this speech, they decided to work with the elements with which they did agree—specifically the acknowledgment that the process would conclude with a Palestinian state—and then try to establish a road map to get there. Interview, Kieran Prendergast, July 14, 2004.

63. De Soto, "End of Mission Report," 23–34. De Soto was particularly critical of developments within the Quartet since late 2005, and notably so since the Palestinian elections of January 2006. These developments, he claimed, "led the UN onto thin ice" in that UN personnel in the field were in the uncomfortable position of trying to alleviate the effects of an economic "siege" introduced by the international community in the wake of Hamas' electoral victory and by all appearances condoned by the United Nations. Chris Patten, the former European Commissioner for External Relations, describes how, after 2003, "some of our moderate Arab friends understandably began to refer to the 'Quartet, *sans trois.*'" *Not Quite the Diplomat* (London: Penguin Books Ltd., 2005), 111.

64. This was a multiyear proposal to counter drug production; foster economic development, human rights, and democratic governance; and support the peace process. In January 2000 the Clinton administration submitted an aid request

for $1.6 billion to support the plan, some 80 percent of which was allocated to military and police assistance related to drug eradication and interdiction.

65. Egeland's mandate was "to serve as the focal point for the United Nations system in its efforts to mobilize international assistance for social, humanitarian, human rights, drug control (alternative development projects), and peace-building activities in Colombia." UN press release, SG/A/715, December 9, 1999.

66. This analysis draws on Cynthia J. Arnson and Teresa Whitfield, "Third Parties and Intractable Conflicts: The Case of Colombia," in *Grasping the Nettle*, ed. Crocker et al. See also Marc Chernick, "Negotiating Peace amid Multiple Forms of Violence: The Protracted Search for Settlement to the Armed Conflicts in Colombia," in *Comparative Peace Processes in Latin America*, ed. Arnson, 159–95; and "Colombia: International Involvement in Protracted Peacemaking," in *From Promise to Practice*, ed. Lekha Sriram and Wermester, 233–66.

67. The Clinton administration had welcomed Pastrana's commitment to peace and even authorized State Department officials to meet with the FARC in Costa Rica in December 1998. However, such direct involvement was curtailed by the murder by the FARC in March 1999 of three U.S. advocates for indigenous rights and a barrage of criticism of the administration for meeting with "terrorists."

68. On the EU and Plan Colombia, see Joaquín Roy, "Europe: Neither Plan Colombia nor Peace Process—From Good Intentions to High Frustration," *Working Paper Series*, no. 11, (Miami: Dante B. Fascell North-South Center, January 2003).

69. Representatives of the European countries involved in this group asked that they not be identified, as their participation was not sanctioned by the EU.

70. Another was through the organization of a "Euro tour" for senior FARC leaders and Colombian government officials, who together visited France, Italy, Norway, Spain, Sweden, and Switzerland in February 2000. Interview, Egeland, January 15, 2004.

71. The FARC, in particular, was highly critical of the model followed in El Salvador and Guatemala, by which guerrillas disarmed in exchange for promises of reform. The government remained wary of a UN role that was perceived as intrusive in these two cases. Interviews, James LeMoyne, December 6, 2001; Fernando Cepeda, March 8, 2004.

72. Yago Pico de Coaña, who played an influential role as Spain's ambassador from 1996 to 2002, was the obvious exception in terms of experience. As director general for IberoAmerica within Spain's Foreign Ministry, he had been deeply involved in the Central American peace process.

73. This paragraph derives from interviews with international diplomats, many of them ambassadors who had taken part in the groups of Friends, jointly conducted in Bogotá in March 2002 by the author and Cynthia J. Arnson.

74. Interview, James LeMoyne, December 6, 2001. The United Nations worked well with the Cubans, but always suspected it was not kept fully informed of what they were up to.

75. An agreement between the FARC and the Colombian government in February 2001 was for "a group of friendly countries and international bodies, to inform them about the state and evolution of the process and motivate their collaboration." Comunicado Conjunto del Gobierno Nacional y las FARC, "Acuerdo de los Pozos," Los Pozos, Caquetá, February 9, 2001.

76. One Mexican diplomat recalled a conversation with the FARC's leader, Manuel Marulanda, on the subject. He had "spared no effort in telling the FARC that they could not have their cake and eat it. We had to be conscious of public opinion at home." Marulanda answered, "Do you think I ask for passports?" Interview, February 6, 2003.

77. Interview, LeMoyne.

78. The larger group included Austria, Belgium, Brazil, Canada, Chile, Costa Rica, Cuba, Denmark, Ecuador, Finland, France, Germany, Italy, Japan, Mexico, the Netherlands, Norway, Panama, Peru, Portugal, Spain, Sweden, Switzerland, the United Kingdom, Venezuela, the Vatican, the EU, and the United Nations. The facilitating commission consisted of Canada, Cuba, France, Italy, Mexico, Norway, Spain, Sweden, Switzerland, and Venezuela. Its means of selection was somewhat arbitrary. Egeland recalled in October 2004 that France was selected because of the FARC's preference for a "socialist country." His protestations that President Jacques Chirac could by no means be described as a socialist were overruled by the FARC's insistence on the point, so France remained in.

79. One Colombian diplomat accredited to the United Nations noted with appreciation that "even the Swedes" had had to shift their opinion of the FARC. Interview, November 12, 2002. The FARC—but not the ELN—joined the paramilitaries on the EU's list of terrorist organizations in June 2002, after an effort led by the Spanish government of José María Aznar. See Roy, "Europe: Neither Plan Colombia, nor Peace Process," 5–6.

80. Cynthia J. Arnson, "The Peace Process in Colombia and U.S. Policy," in *Peace, Democracy and Human Rights in Colombia*, ed. Christopher Welna and Gustavo Gallón (South Bend, IN: University of Notre Dame Press, 2004).

81. The occasional outspoken interview by LeMoyne—who led members of the government to accuse him of justifying guerrilla violence by stating that "it was a mistake to think that the FARC members are only drug-traffickers and terrorists"—did not help. See Andrew Selsky, "Debate Surrounds UN Envoy Colombia Quip," Associated Press, May 21, 2003; Agence France Press, "Bogotá rechaza los comentarios del delegado especial de la ONU," *El Nuevo Herald*, May 21, 2003; and Rodrigo Pardo García-Peña, "La ONU Lejana: Multilateralismo y

Conflicto Armado en Colombia," documento de trabajo, Centro de Investigación para la Paz, Madrid, June 14, 2004, www.euro-colombia.org.

82. The United Nations saw no obvious need for its facilitation, as the government had established channels of communication with the paramilitary leadership with ease; it was also reluctant to give the paramilitaries the recognition as a political actor that its participation would imply. Agence France Press, "Descartar la ONU mediar con los 'paras,'" *El Nuevo Herald*, May 19, 2003; Associated Press, "UN May Stay Out of Colombia Talks," May 20, 2003.

83. UN press release SG/SM/9688, "Senior UN Officials Meet with High-Level Delegation from Colombia," January 26, 2005.

84. "Diplomatic Efforts with the Insurgents" in International Crisis Group, "Colombia: Presidential Politics and Peace Prospects," *Latin America Report*, no. 14 (Bogotá/Brussels: International Crisis Group, June 16, 2005), 24–8; Ambassador Andrés Valencia Benavides, "The Peace Process in Colombia with the ELN: The Role of Mexico," *Latin America Program Special Report*, ed. Cynthia J. Arnson (Washington, DC: Woodrow Wilson Center for International Scholars, March 2006); and Cynthia J Arnson et al. "Colombia's Peace Processes: Multiple Negotiations, Multiple Actors," *Latin America Program Special Report*. (Washington, DC: Woodrow Wilson Center for International Scholars, December 2006.)

85. Interview, Ibrahima Fall, May 25, 2004. The Group of Friends of the Great Lakes Region was established in December 2003. In its initial incarnation it included twenty-eight states and ten multilateral organizations and institutions. See *Report of the Secretary-General on preparations for an international conference on the Great Lakes region*, S/2003/1099, November 23, 2003.

86. In 1998 Marrack Goulding identified just three instances since 1988 in which the United Nations had had a clear lead in mediating negotiated peace agreements in Africa: Western Sahara, the Lusaka Protocol of 1994 in Angola, and Sierra Leone in the mid-1990s. In 1999–2006 there were no further examples, although UN officials heading peace operations were engaged in peacemaking of one kind or another on an almost constant basis. Marrack Goulding, "The United Nations and Conflict in Africa since the Cold War," *African Affairs* 98 (1999): 155–66.

87. The proposal that the secretary-general create a "Committee of Friends" "for the exchange of information and the coordination of efforts among external actors" was contained in the *Report of the Secretary-General on the Situation in Somalia*, S/2001/963, of October 11, 2001. Ireland and Norway were among the states encouraging this initiative.

88. The Contact Group, like the group of External Actors that had preceded it, met under the chairmanship of Kieran Prendergast, the under-secretary-general for political affairs. Members of the "Friends of the Somali National Reconciliation Conference" led by Norway included China, Germany, Italy,

Switzerland, and Sweden (both from mid-2004), United Kingdom, United States and the European Union. Interviews, UN official, May 11, 2004; Norwegian official, May 20, 2004.

89. The formation of the International Contact Group on Somalia was announced by the U.S. State Department on June 9; when it met for the first time in New York a few days later it included the European Union, Italy, Norway, Sweden, Tanzania, and the United States, and agreed that the AU, IGAD, League of Arab States, and United Nations should have observer status. Karen de Young, "U.S. to Hold International Meeting on Somalia," *Washington Post*, June 10, 2006; Permanent Mission of Norway to the United Nations, Communiqué, International Somalia Contact Group, June 15, 2006, www.norway-un.org.

90. See chapter 1, note 99, 310.

91. "Background Paper on the Concept of the Group of Friends," distributed to G-8 states in December 2002 and to African states in February 2003.

92. See introduction, note 6, and chapter 1, 47–8.

93. Confidential interview, March 27, 2003.

94. Interview, senior UN official, March 31, 2003.

95. See International Crisis Group, "Scramble for the Congo: Anatomy of an Ugly War," *Africa Report*, no. 26 (Nairobi/Brussels: International Crisis Group, December 20, 2000) for a breakdown of the respective armed actors and their interests in the Congo.

96. See Emeric Rogier, "The Inter-Congolese Dialogue: A Critical Overview," in *The Challenge of Peace Implementation: The UN Mission in the Democratic Republic of the Congo*, ed. Mark Malan and João Gomes Porto (Cape Town: Institute for Security Studies, 2004), 25–42.

97. South Africa deployed into the DRC without informing the UN Mission (MONUC) and needed constant reminding that the mission had a mandate for which it was answerable to the Security Council. Under the guise of the TPVM, South Africa brought "all sorts of dodgy people, including intelligence agents" into the east of the DRC. Interview, UN official, May 10, 2004.

98. Interview, UN official, August 4, 2005.

99. The creation of the CIAT is provided for in Annex IV of the Global and All-Inclusive Agreement on a Transition for the Democratic Republic of the Congo, signed in Pretoria on December 16, 2002, www.monuc.org.

100. The five permanent members of the Security Council, who had long been active in Kinshasa, Angola, Belgium, Canada, Gabon, South Africa, Zambia, the African Union, and the European Union and Commission, in addition to the United Nations.

101. Interview, August 4, 2005.

102. Ibid. An account of the work of the CIAT is given by Ugo Solinas, "Le comité international d'accompagnement de la transition: Son rôle y ses activités," www.monuc.org.

103. The group met in New York and allowed the United Kingdom to pre-empt sensitivities arising from the fact that it had sent troops to Sierra Leone under its own authority and not as part of the United Nations Mission in Sierra Leone (UNAMSIL). Interviews, UK officials, November 14 and 30, 2002.

104. In an internal UN review of its peacebuilding offices prepared in July 2001, UNOL was considered by all those consulted in Monrovia to be "too close to the Government." Department of Political Affairs and United Nations Development Programme, "Report of the Joint Review Mission on the United Nations Post-Conflict Peacebuilding Support Offices," July 20, 2001, 14, mimeo.

105. "Summary of Key Themes prepared by the Presidency," Security Council workshop on the Mano River Union, July 18, 2002, www.ukun.org.

106. International Crisis Group, "Tackling Liberia: The Eye of the Regional Storm," *Africa Report*, no. 62, (Freetown/Brussels: International Crisis Group, April 30, 2003). Interview, UN official, May 12, 2004.

107. ECOWAS, "Proposed International Contact Group on Liberia (ICGL): Draft Concept Paper," circulated at First Working Session of the International Contact Group on Liberia, Dakar, December 19, 2002, mimeo.

108. Interviews, June 29, 2004, and July 2, 2004.

109. Interview, Hans Dahlgren, September 16, 2004. See also International Contact Group on Liberia, Statement to the Press, Brussels, May 19, 2003.

110. Resolution 1509 (2003), establishing the United Nations Mission in Liberia (UNMIL), was adopted by the Security Council on September 19, 2003. It provided for the deployment of up to 15,000 military personnel and up to 1,115 civilian police, making UNMIL the largest peacekeeping operation at the time.

111. "Comprehensive Peace Agreement between the Government of Liberia (GOL), the Liberians United for Reconciliation and Democracy (LURD), the Movement for Democracy in Liberia (MODEL), and the Political Parties," Accra, Ghana, August 18, 2003, Peace Agreements digital collection, United States Institute for Peace, www.usip.org.

112. International Contact Group on the Mano River Basin, Statement to the Press, Stockholm, March 21, 2005. Interview, EU official, June 23, 2005.

113. The first meeting of the International Working Group on November 8, 2005, was cochaired by the Nigerian foreign minister, who represented the president of the African Union, and Schori, and was attended by representatives of ECOWAS, Benin, Ghana, Guinea, Niger, South Africa, the United Kingdom, the United States, the EU, the Francophonie, and the World Bank and IMF. Members of the Mediation Group included the United Nations (SRSG and High Representative for Elections), the African Union, ECOWAS, the Francophonie, and South Africa. Somewhat frustrated by the limited composition of this group, Schori in 2006 revived the earlier "Comité de Suivi" that had been established within the Linas Marcoussis agreement brokered by France in 2003 to create a third mechanism, which he dubbed the "CoRep" (Committee of Representatives). This was composed of local representatives of the IWG, plus the key donors of Japan, Canada, and Norway. Interview, Pierre Schori, February 28, 2007.

114. Telephone interview, João Honwana, December 22, 2006. See also chapter 1, note 102, 311.

115. For a succinct account of the efforts to end Sudan's civil war, see Morrison and De Waal, "Can Sudan Escape Its Intractability?" An accessible "mapping" of the issues and actors involved is given in International Crisis Group, *God, Oil and Country: Changing the Logic of War in Sudan* (Brussels: International Crisis Group Press, 2001).

116. In addition to the presence of the United Nations' relief agencies, the secretary-general was represented by a special envoy for humanitarian affairs in the Sudan, a position held from 1998 to 2004 by Ambassador Tom Vraalsen of Norway. On the relationship of Operation Lifeline Sudan to the peace process, see Lam Akol, "Operation Lifeline Sudan: War, Peace and Relief in Southern Sudan," in Ricigliano, ed., *Choosing to Engage*, 52–5.

117. Somewhat confusingly, the IPF developed from an earlier and more informal mechanism known as the "Friends of IGAD." IGAD Secretariat, "The Criteria for Membership and Modalities of Partnership for the IGAD Partners Forum," Djibouti, February 15, 1999, mimeo.

118. Prendergast had served as British High Commissioner in Kenya from 1992 to 1995. Interview, July 16, 2004.

119. Interview, Alan Goulty, November 18, 2003.

120. This involvement, which in the case of Goulty, as that of the Norwegian special envoy Halvor Aschjem, stretched back to the early 1970s, led one Norwegian diplomat to describe the Troika as composed of "Sudan addicts." Interview, May 20, 2004. By the late 1990s the IPF had grown to about twenty members, with a Core Group consisting of Canada, Italy, the Netherlands, Norway, the United Kingdom, the United States, and the United Nations. However, doubts had emerged among some of the group's members regarding the objectivity of Italy, which was seen to prioritize good relations in the Mediterranean (including with Egypt and Libya) over anything else. These doubts were confirmed when Italy, as IPF cochair, let Egypt into the IPF as an observer even as the latter's initiative with Libya was seen as a spoiler to the IGAD effort. Meanwhile, Canada's relations with Khartoum deteriorated and the Netherlands ceded its role as the other cochair of IPF to Norway.

121. Center for Strategic and International Studies, "Report of the CSIS Task Force on U.S.-Sudan Policy" (Washington, DC: Center for Strategic and International Studies, February 1, 2001).

122. Machakos Protocol, July 20, 2002, Peace Agreements digital collection, United States Institute for Peace, www.usip.org.

123. Interview, April 7, 2004.

124. Overt linking of such pressure from domestic U.S. political events, such as the state of the union address given by President George W. Bush in January 2004 or the presidential elections of November of the same year, led to foot-dragging on the part of the Sudanese. Interview, General Lazaro Sumbeiywo, June 28, 2005.

125. Interview, Halvor Aschjem, January 29, 2004.

126. One UN official would describe the coordination the Troika facilitated as "beautiful." Interview, January 10, 2006.

127. Alex de Waal, "Peace Deal Is Only the Start," *Financial Times*, January 13, 2005.

128. Security Council Resolution 1590, March 24, 2005.

129. International Crisis Group, "Sudan's Comprehensive Peace Agreement: The Long Road Ahead," *Africa Report*, no. 106 (Khartoum/Brussels, International Crisis Group, March 31, 2006), 25–9; Karen von Hippel with Sinead Hunt, "Consolidating Peace in Sudan" (Washington, DC: Center for Strategic and International Studies, March 2006).

130. UNMIS official, e-mail, May 25, 2006. The African Union was invited to participate in Contact Group meetings, but rarely attended.

131. Interview, November 21, 2006. See also accounts of the Abuja talks written by two individuals involved as advisers to the AU's mediation team: Laurie Nathan, "No Ownership, No Peace: The Darfur Peace Agreement," *Crisis States Working Paper*, no. 5, (London: Crisis States Research Centre, London School of Economics, September 2006); and Alex de Waal, "I Will Not Sign," *London Review of Books*, vol. 28, no. 23, (November 30, 2006).

132. The rebels were consistently encouraged to believe that the support they received from the West, and the United States in particular, would strengthen their hand. Meanwhile, public and private criticism of the AU-led effort, including by representatives of the United Nations, created an impression that the UN was undermining the process as a whole (in this the UN was not helped by the lack of a dedicated senior envoy on Darfur, or the poor relations between Pronk and Salim) and fed speculation on the part of some of the rebels that they would fare better if the Abuja mediation collapsed and was replaced by a United Nations–led process. Interviews, advisers to the AU process, July 24, 2006; UN official, November 21, 2006.

133. De Waal, "I Will Not Sign."

134. E-mail correspondence, July 22, 2004.

9. Conclusions

1. The group on Guinea never materialized because of uncertainty about its membership (what to do about the neighbors?) and the extreme sensitivity of Guinea to international involvement in its affairs. Groups on Myanmar and

Ethiopia-Eritrea were briefly considered by the secretary-general's envoys in each instance (Razali Ismail and Lloyd Axworthy) in mid-2004 and early 2005, largely because in the face of stonewalling by Myanmar's military authorities and Eritrea's president, Isaias Afworki, they could not think what else to do. A Contact Group on Nepal bringing together the key external actors—India, the United Kingdom, the United States, and the United Nations—did not materialize in 2006, partly because of sensitivities with regard to India and partly because of the likely pressure for involvement by donors and other interested states. The possibility of a group of Friends of Darfur was discussed by senior UN officials in January 2006 in the context of the AU-led mediation at Abuja; obstacles included the complexities of the relationship between the United Nations Mission in Sudan (UNMIS) and the AU and the mixed messages transmitted by key member states to the parties. Interviews, UN officials, September 17, 2003; July 1, 2004; September 16, 2004; March 23, 2005; January 11, 2006; U.K. official, June 2, 2005. International Crisis Group, "Nepal's Crisis: Mobilising International Influence."

2. This was an informal group composed of the Netherlands, Norway, the United Kingdom, and the United States that took shape in 2004 to support the efforts of mediator Betty Bigombe to bring peace to Northern Uganda.

3. Elisabeth Jean Wood, "Civil Wars: What We Don't Know," *Global Governance* 9, no. 2 (April–June 2003): 247–60.

4. Members of the Sri Lanka Donor Cochairs Group, formed in June 2003 to monitor reconstruction assistance to Sri Lanka and the peace process, were the EU, Japan, Norway, and the United States. Interview, Norwegian official, March 2, 2004.

5. Liz Philipson, "Engaging Armed Groups: The Challenges of Asymmetries," in *Choosing to Engage: Armed Groups and Peace Processes*, 68–71.

6. Philipson describes, for example, how holding two international conferences on Sri Lanka in 2003 without the participation of the Liberation Tigers of Tamil Eelam (LTTE) (the first because it was held in Washington, which the LTTE could not attend because of U.S. antiterrorist legislation, and the second in Tokyo, which the LTTE boycotted) contributed to the deadlock in the peace process. The conferences, as she put it, "were as much to do with the aspirations of the host nations as the peace process in Sri Lanka." Ibid., 70.

7. The author recalls walking into UN headquarters in the late 1990s with Rafael Moreno, who had for many years represented the FMLN internationally on human rights issues. A UN security guard greeted him with the welcome, "Good to see you again, Ambassador."

8. Joaquín Villalobos, "The Salvadoran Insurgency: Why Choose Peace," in *Choosing to Engage: Armed Groups and Peace Processes*, 38.

9. Interview, October 18, 2002.

10. See chapter 1, 43.

11. Perhaps unsurprisingly, those states that most adamantly defended the importance of small groups were those—such as the United Kingdom and United States—most frequently included as Friends. States from the developing world, and notably Africa, pressed instead for more inclusive structures, including, for example, in the recommendations of the Ad Hoc Working Group on Conflict Prevention and Resolution in Africa cited in chapter 1, 47–48.

12. The United States was not a member of the Friends of the Central African Republic. Although not a member of the groups formed in Colombia, the United States took part in meetings of the distinct "Informal group," sometimes referred to as the "Brussels group," referred to in chapter 8, 240.

13. See Peace Implementation Network/Programme for International Co-operation and Conflict Resolution, *Command from the Saddle: Managing United Nations Peace-Building Missions* (Oslo: Fafo Institute for Applied Social Science, 1999).

14. Ibid. As any observer of the United Nations will acknowledge, the quality of those called on to represent the secretary-general varies greatly, with profound implications for the United Nations' efficacy.

15. In an interview, Iqbal Riza, at the time the secretary-general's chief of staff, expressed the view that it was "generally better" if groups were "self-generating." June 17, 2003. Officials within the Department of Political Affairs tended to prefer a model by which groups are in some way "precooked" in the secretariat.

16. Interview, January 10, 2006.

17. Bruce D. Jones, "The Challenges of Strategic Coordination," in *Ending Civil Wars*, ed. Stedman et al., 99.

18. Elizabeth M. Cousens, "From Missed Opportunities to Overcompensation: Implementing the Dayton Agreement on Bosnia," in *Ending Civil Wars*, ed. Stedman et al., 531–66.

19. See Shepard Forman and Stewart Patrick, eds., *Good Intentions: Pledges of Aid for Post-Conflict Recovery* (Boulder, CO: Lynne Rienner Publishers, 2001); Joanna Macrae, *Aiding Recovery: The Crisis of Aid in Chronic Political Emergencies* (New York: Zed Books, 2001); and Susan L. Woodward, "Economic Priorities for Successful Peace Implementation," in *Ending Civil Wars*, ed. Stedman et al., 183–214.

20. Griffiths, "Talking Peace in a Time of War," 6.

Index

Aall, Pamela
  Taming Intractable Conflicts, 8
Abdelaziz, Mohamed
  Framework Agreement on the
    Status of Western Sahara and,
    181
Abdullaev, Kamoludin
  regional actors in the Tajikistan
    peace process, 342 n56
Abkhazia. *See also* Georgian-Abkhaz
    conflict
  Boden paper and, 150–154, 162
  CIS economic blockade of, 138,
    150
  concern that Georgia would use
    its U.S.-trained forces against
    them, 345 n86
  declaration of independence in
    1999, 138
  election issues, 158
  emigration of young people from,
    162–163
  energy resources, 136, 138,
    143–144, 338 n11
  Enguri hydropower plant, 138,
    338 n11
  ethnic conflict in, 136–139, 144
  Friends of Georgia's view of as a
    secessionist regime, 144, 341
    n41
  Geneva process (1997) and,
    149–150, 154
  Geneva process and, 156–157
  historical background, 136–137
  lack of diplomatic representation
    in the United Nations, 144

Quadripartite Agreement on the
    Return of Refugees and Dis-
    placed Persons and, 341 n38
  request for secession from Georgia,
    137, 338 n6
  strategic importance of, 136
  UN Military Observer Mission in
    Georgia and, 135
  UN Needs Assessment mission,
    150, 343 n65
  vacation destination for Russians,
    140
Abubakar, Gen. Abdusalami
  International Contact Group on
    Liberia role, 249
Ad Hoc Advisory Group on
    Guinea-Bissau
  establishment and activities of,
    251
Ad Hoc Advisory Group on Haiti
  formation and responsibilities,
    122, 128
  membership, 336 n101
Ad Hoc Working Group on Conflict
    Prevention and Resolution
    in Africa
  groups of Friends and, 311 n104
  recommendations of, 47–48, 244
Advisory committees
  on the Peaceful Uses of
    Atomic Energy, 301 n12
  UN Emergency Force, 23–24,
    302 n15
  UN Observation Group in
    Lebanon, 302 n.13
  UN Operation in the Congo, 23

381

Afghanistan
    Bonn agreement and, 34, 231
    Group of 21 and, 229–230, 366
        n24
    informal "luncheon group" and,
        230, 257, 366 n25
    regional environment and, 267
    "six plus two" group and, 229–
        231, 256
    Soviet Union invasion of, 21
    Taliban and, 228, 229, 231
    Tashkent Declaration on the
        Fundamental Principles for a
        Peaceful Settlement of the
        Conflict in Afghanistan, 229
    Track II talks and, 230, 367 n26
    UN Assistance Mission to
        Afghanistan and, 231
    UN Good Offices Mission in
        Afghanistan and Pakistan
        and, 21
    United Nations involvement,
        223, 225, 228–231
    United States' role, 228, 229–231
    withdrawal of Soviet troops from,
        26, 56
Africa. *See also specific countries and
    regions*
    Ad Hoc Working Group on
        Conflict Prevention and Res-
        olution in Africa, 47–48, 244,
        311 n104
    challenges of Groups in,
        243–246, 373 n86
Africa Action Plan, 46, 239,
    244–245, 310 n99
African Union
    Peace and Security Council, 41
    regional conflicts and, 41
    role in Sudan, 253, 257, 260,
        378 n2
An Agenda for Peace (Boutros-
    Ghali), 29, 31–32

Ahmed, Rafeeuddin
    Cambodian peace process and, 27
Ahtisaari, Martti
    Annan Plan and, 369 n57
    efforts in Kosovo, 35
    peacemaking efforts in Aceh, 43,
        268, 308 n86
AIETD. *See* All-Inclusive Intra-East
    Timorese Dialogue
Aimé, Jean-Claude
    assessment of the need for UN
        assistance to Haiti, 111
Ajello, Aldo
    Mozambique peace process and,
        28–29, 46, 274, 304 n37
Akashi, Yasushi
    Cambodian peace process and,
        28
Alasania, Irakli
    appointment of, 160
Alatas, Prime Minister Ali (Indo-
    nesia)
    tripartite agreement and, 199,
        357 n33
Albright, Madeleine
    contradictory messages on the
        Indonesian militias, 359 n51
    Friends of Georgia and, 145, 342
        n46
    Friends of the Secretary-General
        for Haiti and, 123
    U.S. involvement in Haiti and,
        109, 113
    views on the emergence of
        groups, 309 n90
    views on the United Nations, 36,
        305 n61
Alexandre, President Boniface
    (Haiti)
    assumption of the presidency, 125
Algeria
    rivalry with Morocco, 168, 169,
        347 n10, 347 n11

Algeria *(cont.)*
    role in UN process on Western
        Sahara, 175–190, 350 n43
    support for Polisario, 168
    Western Sahara's self-
        determination and, 165,
        166–190
Alkatiri, Prime Minister Mari
        (East Timor)
    Fretilin leadership, 194
    letters to Annan and the Security
        Council, 211
    resignation of, 217
All-Inclusive Intra-East Timorese
        Dialogue
    role of, 196
Angola. *See also* Core Group on
        Angola; Friends of Angola
    diamonds and, 232
    Lusaka Protocol and, 46
    Memorandum of Understanding,
        234
    National Union for the Total
        Independence of Angola and,
        225, 232–234
    nonstate actors and, 270
    oil resources and, 232
    role in the Democratic Republic
        of the Congo, 246
    Troika on Angola, 232, 233–234,
        245
    UN Mission in Angola, 234
    United Nations role, 225,
        232–234, 257
    withdrawal of Cuban troops from,
        27, 56
Annan, Secretary-General Kofi
    Africa Action Plan and, 46, 239,
        244–245, 310 n99
    Boden paper and, 151
    defense of the impartiality of the
        secretary-general, 21–22
    Geneva process and, 150

Guatemalan peace process and, 94
    negotiations with Saddam Hus-
        sein, 20
    personality of, 34
    Quartet and, 38–39, 238–239
    relationship with the U.S., 36–40
    role in Afghanistan, 228–231
    role in Angola, 232–234
    role in Colombia, 239–243
    role in Cyprus, 224, 234–237,
        369 n54, 369 n57
    role in East Timor, 194–195, 197,
        199, 200, 205, 207, 211, 215,
        217–218, 363 n97
    role in El Salvador, 2
    role in Middle East, 34, 38–39,
        238–239
    role in Somalia, 244
    role in the Democratic Republic
        of the Congo, 246–247
    role in the Western Saharan
        conflict, 165, 178–182,
        184–185, 186, 187
    tripartite talks on East Timor and,
        194–195, 197, 198–199
    UN involvement in Haiti and,
        126, 130
    UN peacekeeping efforts and,
        34–40
    UN reform and, 34, 37–38
    U.S. invasion of Iraq and, 36–40,
        306 n63, 306 n65
Antadze, Merab
    meeting with Putin and Shevard-
        nadze at Sochi, 157
Antonenko, Oksana
    Georgian-Abkhaz conflict and,
        155
Arbenz, Jacobo
    overthrow of, 80
Ardzinba, "President" Vladislav
        (Abkhazia)
    elections of 2004 and, 158

Ardzinba, "President" Vladislav
(Abkhazia) (cont.)
meeting with Yeltsin, 147
relationship with Russia, 146
relationship with the United
Nations, 144
ARENA. See Nationalist Republican
Alliance
Argentina
Friends of the Secretary-General
for Haiti role, 118
Western Saharan conflict and,
176, 350 n39
Arias, Oscar
Esquipulas agreement and, 55
Aristide, President Jean-Bertrand
(Haiti)
amnesty for political crimes and,
114, 330 n41
biographical information, 107
coup against, 107, 111, 132
election of, 107, 132
exile of, 106, 125, 126
Governors Island Agreement
and, 114–115
Lavalas movement and, 107, 123
meeting with Cédras, 116
personal attributes of, 1–6, 105,
110, 116
promotion of those loyal to, 121
resignation of, 110, 125, 126,
131–132
return to the presidency, 106,
114–115, 118, 119, 124, 131
UN efforts to restore to power,
108
use of informal gangs, 335 n88
Armed Forces for the National
Liberation of East Timor
meeting with the Indonesian
army, 193
severing of connections with
Fretilin, 193–194

Armed Forces of National Liberation
role, 312 n4
Armenia
Georgian-Abkhaz conflict and,
140
Arnault, Jean
Friends of the Guatemalan Peace
Process role, 82, 84–98, 102,
322 n31, 324 n58
MINUGUA leadership, 96
personality of, 90
role in Afghanistan, 231
Arria, Diego
Friends of the Secretary-General
for El Salvador and, 71
Friends of the Secretary-General
for Haiti and, 113
Haitian elections and, 111
Arzú, President Alvaro (Guatemala)
military reforms, 93, 101, 323 n49
political challenge from the
Guatemalan Republican
Front, 95
role in the Guatemalan peace pro-
cess, 82–83, 91–93, 95, 97–98
ASC. See Assembly of Civil Society
Aschjem, Halvor
role in Sudan, 253
ASEAN. See Association of South-
east Asian Nations
Asia Pacific Economic Cooperation
East Timor and, 208
Assembly of Civil Society
role in Guatemala, 82, 87–88, 92
Association of Southeast Asian
Nations
Myanmar and, 225, 227, 228
support for Indonesia, 195
Asturias, Rodrigo
Guatemalan peace process and,
93, 101, 321 n25, 323 n53
Atoms for Peace Conference,
advisory committee for, 301 n12

AU. *See* African Union
AUC. *See* United Self-Defense
   Forces of Colombia
Australia
   contributions to the UN Mission
      in East Timor, 204
   relationship with Portugal, 212
   role in Cyprus, 236
   role in East Timor, 191, 192, 193,
      195, 198, 200, 201, 204, 206–
      207, 212–213, 214–216, 217,
      218, 220–221, 355 n6, 355 n8,
      356 n13, 356 n19
   support for the United States on
      Iraq, 212
   treaty with Indonesia concerning
      the Timor Gap region, 195
   UN Mission of Support in East
      Timor and, 215, 362 n92
   withholding of intelligence on
      Indonesian militias, 204
Aznar, President José María (Spain)
   Guatemalan peace process and,
      97
   Spain's relations with Morocco
      and, 173

Baena Soares, João
   Contadora group and, 55
   Guatemalan peace process and,
      321 n28
Bagapsh, Sergei
   election of, 158
   letter to the Security Council,
      159
Bailey, Sydney D.
   Trygve Lie's invocation of article
      99, 300 n3
Baker, James A., III
   Framework Agreement on the
      Status of Western Sahara and,
      181–183, 352 n73, 352 n77,
      352 n78, 353 n79

Peace Plan for Self-Determination
      for the People of Western
      Sahara, 183–185, 353 n81,
      353 n82, 353 n87
   resignation of, 185
   role in the Western Saharan
      conflict, 35, 165–166, 172,
      178–186, 187, 351 n59, 352
      n69
   view of Aristide, 109
Balconi, Gen. Julio
   Guatemalan peace process and,
      92–93
Balkan states. *See also specific coun-*
      tries; Contact Group on the
      former Yugoslavia
   United Nations role, 7, 31, 36,
      208, 277
Baril, Maurice
   special report on East Timor,
      214–215
Barnes, Catherine
   regional actors in the Tajikistan
      peace process, 342 n56
Bastagli, Francesco
   UN Mission for the Referendum
      in Western Sahara and, 187,
      188, 354 n96
Belgium
   role in the Democratic Republic
      of the Congo, 246
Belo, Bishop Carlos Filipe Ximenes
   Nobel Peace Prize award, 194
Berger, President Oscar
      (Guatemala)
   government of, 99
Betancourt, Ingrid
   kidnapping of, 242
Bigombe, Betty
   Core Group on Northern
      Uganda and, 377 n1
bin Laden, Osama
   Taliban and, 230

Boden, Dieter
    Friends of the Secretary-General
        for Georgia role, 150–161, 164
Boden paper
    Abkhaz views on, 151–152
    controversial "status" paragraph
        on Abkhazia and, 151
    doubts about utility of, 155–156,
        345 n89
    Friends of the Secretary-General
        for Georgia and, 150–161,
        164, 343 n71
    impasse created by, 154–157
    limited life span of, 154
    Security Council and, 153, 154,
        344 n80
Bonn agreement on Afghanistan,
    34, 231
Bosnia
    massacres in the safe area of
        Srebrenica, 32
Bota, Liviu
    Geneva process (1997) and, 149
Boukhari, Ahmed
    Peace Plan for Self-Determination
        for the People of Western
        Sahara and, 184, 353 n82
Bouteflika, President Abdelaziz
    (Algeria)
    Framework Agreement on the
        Status of Western Sahara
        and, 182
    referendum on Western Sahara
        and, 180
Boutros-Ghali, Secretary-General
    Boutros
    An Agenda for Peace, 29, 31–32
    Friends of the Secretary-General
        for El Salvador and, 29
    Georgian-Abkhaz conflict and,
        142, 147
    Governors Island Agreement
        and, 114–115

    Guatemalan peace process and,
        84
    ONUSAL expansion and, 73
    personality of, 33
    post-conflict peacebuilding and,
        29, 31–33, 304 n39
    reelection battle, 32
    role in East Timor, 196
    role in the Western Saharan
        conflict, 170–171, 175, 177,
        179, 188, 348 n24
    Supplement to the Agenda for
        Peace, 33
    Tajikistan peace process and,
        147
    UN involvement in Haiti and,
        111–112, 117–118, 133
Brahimi, Lakhdar
    personal history and attributes,
        230–231, 367 n28
    relationship with Friends of the
        Secretary-General for Haiti,
        119–120
    report on UN peace operations,
        34
    role in Afghanistan, 228,
        230–231, 366 n21, 367 n28
    UN Mission in Haiti and,
        118–119, 332 n64
    view of Aristide, 119
Brazil
    Friends of Haiti and, 126
    quest for a permanent seat on the
        Security Council, 128
    role in Angola, 233
    role in East Timor, 218
    role in Haiti, 128–129
    troop contribution to Haiti, 128,
        336 n102
Brunner, Edouard
    Friends of Georgia role, 142,
        146–147
Burma. See Myanmar

Burundi
  NGOs as Friends of, 46, 310 n100
Burundi Partners Forum
  formation of, 278, 298 n15
  relationship with the Security
    Council, 47
Bush, President George H.W.
  meeting with Pérez de Cuéllar,
    68–69
  meeting with Salinas, 63
  U.S. involvement in Haiti and,
    109, 110
Bush, President George W.
  Middle East peace process and,
    370 n62
  support for Saakashvili's plan for
    autonomy in Abkhazia, 346
    n115
  trade talks with Morocco, 172
  visit to Georgia, 141, 339 n23
Bush administration. See also
    United States
  role in Sudan, 252, 377 n124

Cambodia
  Core Group in, 28, 277
  secretary-general's good offices
    and, 27–28, 35
  UN Transitional Authority in
    Cambodia, 28
  Vietnam's invasion of, 27
Canada
  Friends of the Secretary-General
    for Haiti role, 105, 110–134,
    330 n32
  role in Angola, 233
  role in Colombia, 240, 371 n69
Cape Verde
  Friends of Western Sahara and,
    174
Caputo, Dante
  criticism of, 330 n40
  departure from Haiti, 116

  deployment of the International
    Civilian Mission in Haiti and,
    113
  Friends of the Secretary-General
    for Haiti and, 112, 113,
    114–116
  Governors Island Agreement
    and, 115
  relationship with the United
    States, 114
  resignation of, 332 n58
Caribbean Community
  accusation that the United
    States had failed to respect the
    Inter-American Democratic
    Charter, 127
  Core Group and, 128
  Group of Six, 125
  role in Haiti, 124–125, 126,
    132
CARICOM. See Caribbean
    Community
Carter, President Jimmy
  U.S. involvement in Haiti and,
    332 n58
CAVR. See Commission on
    Truth, Reception, and
    Reconciliation
Cédras, Gen. Raul
  demand for amnesty, 114
  Governors Island Agreement
    and, 114–115
  meeting with Aristide, 116
  refusal to meet with Caputo, 116
Central America. See also specific
    countries
  conflicts of the 1980s, 52
  Esquipulas agreement, 55
  Hurricane Mitch damage, 98
  San José Forum, 315 n44
Central American Revolutionary
    Workers' Party
  role, 312 n4

Central Intelligence Agency
involvement in Guatemala's civil
war, 89
Centre for Humanitarian Dialogue
nongovernmental peacemaking
and, 42
peacemaking in Aceh and,
42–43, 268
Tokyo Group of donors, 44
Wise Men group of donors, 44,
310 n95
Cepeda, Fernando
Friends of the Secretary-General
for El Salvador role, 64
Cerezo, President Vinicio
(Guatemala)
Esquipulas II agreements and, 83
Chambas, Mohamed Ibn
role in Guinea-Bissau, 251
Chávez, President Hugo
(Venezuela)
Friends of the OAS Secretary-
General César Gaviria and,
44, 309 n94
Chile
Friends of the Secretary-General
for Haiti role, 122, 124, 126,
128, 130
opposition to the U.S. invasion
of Iraq, 124
China
Cambodian peace process and,
28, 303 n35
criticism of the Friends of the
Secretary-General for Haiti,
122
Hammarksjöld's "Peking formula"
for negotiations with, 20–21
normalization of relations with
Vietnam, 28
relations with Indonesia, 360 n69
role in Myanmar, 225–226, 227,
366 n15

Chirac, President Jacques (France)
friendship with Kings Hassan II
and Mohammed VI, 173
Peace Plan for Self-Determination
for the People of Western
Sahara and, 184
Western Saharan conflict and,
173
Chopra, Jarat
Joint Monitoring Committee for
the Western Sahara and, 178
Chou En-Lai, Premier (China)
Hammarksjöld's "Peking formula"
for negotiations with, 20–21
Christopher, Ambassador Robin
role in East Timor, 203
Christopher, Secretary of State
Warren
Governors Island Agreement
and, 115
CIAT. See International Commission
to Accompany the Transition
in the DRC
CICIACS. See Commission of Inves-
tigation of Illegal Groups and
Clandestine Security Forces
CIS. See Commonwealth of Inde-
pendent States
Clerides, President Glafcos (Cyprus)
talks with Denktash, 234
Clinton, President Bill
appointment of Lawrence Pezzullo
as his special advisor for Haiti,
114
commitment to the restoration of
Aristide to power, 114
East Timor and, 208
Clinton administration. See also
United States
Friends of the Guatemalan Peace
Process and, 89
Friends of Western Sahara and,
171

Clinton administration (*cont.*)
Plan Colombia and, 239, 370 n64
role in Sudan, 252
U.S. involvement in Haiti and,
108, 109, 117, 119, 329 n13
U.S.S. *Harlan County* incident
and, 115
CNRM. *See* National Council of
Maubere Resistance
CNRT. *See* National Council of
Timorese Resistance
Cold War. *See also* Post–Cold War
period
Cyprus and, 234
peacemaking efforts during, 24
Shevardnadze's role in ending, 143
Colombia
"Brussels" Group, 240, 371 n69,
379 n12
Contadora group and, 54
contribution to ONUSAL's
military division, 317 n71
drug trafficking and, 239, 242,
370 n64
"Euro tour" for FARC and
government officials, 371 n70
experience of ambassadors with
the peace process and, 240–241
facilitating commission,
241–242, 372 n78
"friendly countries" group, 241,
258, 372 n75
Friends of the Guatemalan Peace
Process role, 79, 85, 91, 101
Friends of the Secretary-General
for El Salvador role, 60, 64, 76
National Liberation Army and,
240–243
nonstate actors and, 270
paramilitary groups and,
242–243, 373 n82
Revolutionary Armed Forces of
Colombia and, 240–243

significance of regional support
for, 256
United Nations involvement, 35,
223, 257
United Nations role, 223,
239–243
United Self-Defense Forces of
Colombia, 242
Commission of Investigation of
Illegal Groups and Clandestine Security Forces
efforts to establish in Guatemala,
99, 100, 327 n85, 327 n87
Commission on Truth, Reception,
and Reconciliation
estimate of conflict-related
deaths in East Timor, 355 n3
human rights violations and, 210
Commonwealth of Independent
States
economic blockade of Abkhazia,
138, 150
peacekeeping operations and,
135, 145
Community of Sant'Egidio
Guatemalan peace process and, 92
Mozambique peace process and,
29
nongovernmental peacemaking
and, 43
Comprehensive Peace Agreement
provisions, 254, 377 n129
Conference on Security and Cooperation in Europe
Nagorno-Karabakh experience
and, 143
Southern Caucasus role, 143
Congo. *See also* Democratic Republic
of the Congo
UN Operation in the Congo, 23
Congressional Black Caucus
protests against U.S. activities in
Haiti, 117

Constant, Emanuel
  Haitian black market and, 331
    n53
Consultative Group
  Guatemalan peace process and,
    95, 96–98, 99, 326 n73, 327
    n82
Contact Group on Namibia
  description, 26–27
  formation of, 46
Contact Group on Nepal
  consideration of forming, 259,
    378 n2
Contact Group on Sierra Leone
  establishment and activities, 248
Contact Group on the former
    Yugoslavia
  Balkan conflict and, 7, 44, 309
    n91
  Quint and, 44, 309 n92
  Security Council and, 45–46
Contadora group
  formation of, 54
  proposals for achieving progress,
    54
  secretary-general's role, 54–55
  Support Group for, 54
Cooper, Robert
  peace as a foreign policy goal, 8
Core Group on Angola. See also
    Friends of Angola
  composition and activities of, 233
Core Group on Cambodia
  contributions, 28, 277
Core Group on East Timor
  Australia's role, 191, 200, 201,
    204, 206–207, 212–213,
    214–216, 218
  compared to the Friends of West-
    ern Sahara, 191
  composition of, 191–192, 200,
    212, 219, 221
  conditions for success, 264

confidentiality of meetings, 200
consultation process, 203–206
contributions of, 191–192, 219,
  277
differences among members of,
  221
as donors to East Timor, 212,
  362 n83
downsizing of troops in East Timor
  and, 214
dynamics of, 211–213
effectiveness of, 211–212,
  220–221
elections of 1999 and, 203–208,
  359 n61, 360 n62
formation of, 16, 200, 219
formed police unit and, 215, 363
  n95
France's role, 218
International Force for East
  Timor and, 207, 208, 220
Japan's role, 191, 202, 204, 218
New Zealand's role, 191, 202, 218
non-Council members of, 212
positive experience of, 260
reconfigured mission for,
  215–216, 363 n97
regional environment and, 266
relationship with the secretary-
  general, 192, 213, 221
UN Integrated Mission in Timor-
  Leste and, 218, 221
UN Mission in East Timor and,
  201, 203–206
UN Mission of Support in East
  Timor and, 208, 213–214, 215
UN Office in East Timor and,
  218
UN Transitional Administration
  in East Timor and, 208,
  210–211
United Kingdom's role, 191, 201,
  202–203, 212

Core Group on East Timor (cont.)
United States' role, 191,
201–202, 204, 207, 208,
212–213, 214–216
Core Group on Haiti
composition of, 127–128
differences in political priorities
within, 128
establishment of, 127
formality of consultations, 129,
130, 336 n106
size issue, 134
troop contributors, 128
Valdés' view of, 129
visit to Haiti for meeting
with presidential candidates,
130
Core Group on Lebanon
composition of, 307, n72
establishment of 38, 307, n72
Core Group on Mozambique
contributions, 28–29, 46, 277
Core Group on Northern Uganda
composition of, 377 n1
formation of, 259
Côte d'Ivoire
conflict in, 250–251
International Working Group,
250, 375 n113
CPA. See Comprehensive Peace
Agreement
Cristiani, President Alfredo (El
Salvador)
election of, 56
Friends of the Secretary-General
for El Salvador and, 60, 76
interparty commission to interact
with peace process negotiators, 320 n7
meeting with Pérez de Cuéllar in
New York, 69
United Nations involvement
and, 60

view of Friends of the Secretary-
General for El Salvador, 73
Crocker, Chester
Contact Group on Namibia
and, 5
Namibia settlement and, 27
Taming Intractable Conflicts, 8
CSCE. See Conference on Security
and Cooperation in Europe
Cuba
Farabundo Martí Liberation
Front and, 52, 314 n24
Guatemalan National Revolu-
tionary Unity and, 319 n5
relations with Mexico, 62
role in Colombian peace process,
241, 242, 372, n74
role in El Salvador peace process,
58, 59, 61, 66
withdrawal of troops from Angola,
27, 56
Cyprus
Annan Plan, 235–237, 260,
369 n57
election issues, 236–237
external actors and, 257
Security Council role, 234–235,
236, 368 n43, 368 n49
Turkish Republic of Northern
Cyprus and, 234
UN Force in Cyprus and, 234
United Kingdom's role, 235,
236
United Nations role, 35, 223,
224, 225, 234–237, 260
United States' role, 235, 236

Dahlgren, Hans
International Contact Group
on Liberia role, 249
Dankwa, Nana Addo
International Contact Group on
Liberia role, 249

Darfur Peace Agreement
negotiations for, 254–255
Daws, Sam
Trygve Lie's invocation of article
99, 300 n3
Dayton accords
negotiation of, 31
de Soto, Alvaro
Contadora group role, 54–55
firsthand accounts of Friends
group activities, 5
Friends of the Secretary-General
for El Salvador and, 59–69,
73, 76, 274, 322 n35
Guatemalan peace process and,
84, 321 n22
meetings with FMLN in Montreal,
57, 58–59
Middle East and, 187, 238–239,
307 n73, 370 n63
personality of, 65, 90
photograph of with Pérez de
Cuéllar, 1–2
role in Cyprus, 235–236
role in Myanmar, 225, 226, 365
n8
Western Saharan conflict and,
186–187
Democratic Republic of the Congo
complexity of the conflict in,
244–245, 246
Great Lakes Conference and,
246
Inter-Congolese Dialogue, 246
International Commission to
Accompany the Transition,
47, 247, 374 n99
regional environment and, 267,
278
Third-Party Verification Mechanism, 247, 374 n97
United Nations role, 34,
246–247, 257, 374 n100

Democratic Revolutionary Front
joint FMLN-FDR Political-
Diplomatic Commission,
57, 76
role, 53
Denktash, Rauf
talks with Clerides, 234
Turkey's support for, 237
Denmark
Friends of the Secretary-General
for El Salvador and, 74–75
Diallo, Issa
Western Saharan conflict and,
169–170
Dialogue Group of donor states
Guatemalan peace process and,
80, 95, 96–100, 103, 326 n77,
326 n78
limits of, 99, 327 n83
membership, 326 n78
Dobbins, James
RAND Corporation study on
nation building, 119
Downs, George
Ending Civil Wars: The Implemen-
tation of Peace Agreements,
12–13
Doyle, Michael
factors contributing to "sustain-
able peace", 300 n29
functional benefits of Friends
groups, 4
multilateralism and the United
Nations, 30
DPA. See Darfur Peace Agreement
DPA. See UN Department of Political Affairs
DPKO. See UN Department of
Peacekeeping Operations
DRC. See Democratic Republic of
the Congo
Dumas, John Reginald
appointment of, 126

Dunbar, Charles
    role in the Western Saharan con-
        flict, 350 n44
Duvalier, President François "Papa
    Doc" (Haiti)
    tontons macoutes and, 107
Duvalier, President Jean-Claude
    "Baby Doc" (Haiti)
    government of, 107

Eagleton, William
    role in the Western Saharan
        conflict, 350 n44
East Timor. See also Core Group on
    East Timor
    accountability issues, 210–211
    All-Inclusive Intra-East Timorese
        Dialogue and, 196
    Commission for Truth and
        Friendship, 210–211
    compared with Western Sahara,
        165, 188–189, 354 n99
    creation of Falintil—Defense
        Forces of Timor-Leste, 209
    decolonization, 191, 192–194
    elections of 1999, 203–206,
        359 n61
    estimate of conflict-related
        deaths in, 191, 355 n3
    fissures in Timorese society, 217
    geographic description, 192, 220,
        355 n5
    high-profile resignations of
        officials, 217
    historical background, 191–194,
        219
    independence of, 34, 208
    Indonesia's annexation of, 194,
        355 n9
    participation in the Indonesian
        elections of 1987, 195
    political imbalances and,
        216–217

poverty of, 217, 220, 363 n103
reconciliation with Indonesia,
    216
regional actors, 220
renewed violence in, 216–219
Support Group, 200, 220
Timor Sea Treaty, 213, 362 n85
tripartite talks on, 194–195, 197,
    198–199, 219
UN role pre-1999, 191, 194–196
World Bank organization of
    donor meetings for, 209, 361
    n71, 362 n83
Economic and Social Council
    Ad Hoc Advisory Group on
        Guinea-Bissau, 251
    Ad Hoc Advisory Group on
        Haiti, 122, 128, 336 n101
    Haiti and, 122, 334 n76
Economic Community of West
    Africa
    conflict mediation and resolution
        role, 41, 248
    Implementation Monitoring
        Committee in Liberia and,
        250, 375 n111
    International Contact Group on
        Liberia and, 249, 257
    Monitoring Group in Liberia,
        341 n43
    role in Côte d'Ivoire, 250
    role in Guinea-Bissau, 251
    role in Liberia, 248–249
    role in Sierra Leone, 248
ECOSOC. See Economic and
    Social Council
ECOWAS. See Economic Com-
    munity of West Africa
Ecuador
    border dispute with Peru, 44
Egeland, Jan
    Guatemalan peace process and,
        87

Egeland, Jan (*cont.*)
    role in Colombia, 239–241, 371
        n65
Egypt
    role in Middle East peace process,
        238
El Salvador. *See also* Friends of
    the Secretary-General for
    El Salvador; Mission of the
    United Nations in El Sal-
    vador; UN Observer Mission
    in El Salvador
    background of the conflict in,
        52–53
    Contadora group, 54–55
    formal signing of the peace
        agreement, 72
    International Monetary Fund
        and, 92
    land transfer program, 72, 318 n78
    peace agreements ending the
        civil war, 1, 53, 64
    peace process compared with
        Guatemala's, 81–82
    peace process outcomes, 311 n2
    political-military organizations,
        52, 312 n4
    Reagan administration and, 56
    request for help from the United
        Nations, 57
    Truth Commission, 90, 319 n86,
        322 n40
Eldon, Stewart
    East Timor and, 200
ELN. *See* National Liberation Army
Emergence of groups. *See also*
    Friends groups; *specific groups
    and countries*
    individual states as peacemakers,
        41–42
    Kofi Annan's role, 34–40
    nongovernmental organizations,
        42–43

post–Cold War period, 19,
    24–33, 48
proliferation of groups, 43–48,
    309 n90
regional organizations, 40–41
secretary-general's good offices,
    20–24, 27–28, 34, 35, 302 n18
subregional organizations, 40–41
*Ending Civil Wars: The Implementation
    of Peace Agreements* (Downs
    and Stedman), 12–13
Erdogan, Recep Tayyip
    Annan Plan for Cyprus and, 237
Eritrea
    consideration of Friends of
        Ethiopia-Eritrea, 259, 378 n2
    Friends of the UN Mission in
        Ethiopia and Eritrea, 47, 310
        n101
    UN peacekeeping operation in,
        34, 47, 310, n101
ERP. *See* People's Revolutionary
    Army
Erwa, Elfatih Muhamed
    meetings with Prendergast, 252
Escobar Galindo, David
    "cushion" role of the Friends of
        the Secretary-General for El
        Salvador, 60, 69
    purpose of the Friends of the
        Secretary-General for El
        Salvador, 60
Esquipulas agreements
    impact on Guatemala, 83
    provisions, 55
    verification mechanism, 55,
        312 n15
Ethiopia
    consideration of Friends of
        Ethiopia-Eritrea, 259, 378 n2
    Friends of the UN Mission in
        Ethiopia and Eritrea, 47, 310,
        n101

Ethiopia (*cont.*)
    UN peacekeeping operation in,
        34, 47, 310 n101
European Commission
    role in Cyprus, 236
European Union
    assistance to Abkhazia, 338 n11
    contributions to the UN Mission
        in East Timor, 204
    fisheries agreement with
        Morocco, 174
    Georgia's request for membership
        in, 141
    International Contact Group on
        Liberia role, 250
    Middle East peace process and,
        238
    regional security and, 41
    role in Cyprus, 235, 236, 237
    role in Liberia, 257
    role in Sri Lanka, 378 n4
    Spain's standing within, 64, 102
Evans, Gareth
    Annan Plan and, 369 n57

F-FDTL. *See* Falintil—Defense
        Forces of Timor-Leste
Fafo
    Middle East Peace Process and,
        320 n17
Falintil. *See* Armed Forces for
        the National Liberation of
        East Timor
Falintil—Defense Forces of Timor-
        Leste
    creation of, 209
    dismissal of 40 percent of the
        soldiers in, 211, 216
Fall, Sir Brian
    Boden paper and, 156, 345 n89
    Geneva process (2003) and, 156
FALN. *See* Armed Forces of
        National Liberation

Farabundo Martí Liberation Front
    alliance of the Democratic Revo-
        lutionary Front with, 53
    contacts with non-Marxist
        countries, 270
    demands for dissolution of the
        Salvadoran army, 65
    demobilization of, 71–73, 319
        n86
    formation of, 312 n4
    Friends of the Secretary-General
        for El Salvador and, 65–78
    joint FMLN-FDR Political-
        Diplomatic Commission, 57,
        76
    meetings with de Soto in Mon-
        treal, 57, 58–59
    meetings with the Nationalist
        Republican Alliance, 56
    military offensive of 1989, 56, 60,
        66, 67
    Miraflores declaration and, 67
    "nonpapers" sent to the U.S.
        State Department, 316 n57
    post–Cold War shift in inter-
        national relations and, 58,
        76
    secret arms caches in Nicaragua,
        72, 319 n86
    UN recognition of, 57
FARC. *See* Revolutionary Armed
        Forces of Colombia
Fassier, Bernard
    Friends of Georgia role, 142
Fatton, Robert, Jr.
    "predatory democracy" in Haiti,
        132
FDR. *See* Democratic Revolutionary
        Front
FMLN. *See* Farabundo Martí Libera-
        tion Front
Ford, President Gerald
    meeting with Suharto, 193

Former Yugoslavia. *See* Contact
Group on the former
Yugoslavia
FPL. *See* Popular Liberation Forces
France
contributions to police assistance
in Haiti, 120
early rule of Haiti, 106
Friends of Georgia role, 142
Friends of the Secretary-General
for Haiti role, 105, 110–134
Friends of Western Sahara role,
166, 171, 172–173, 184
peace process in Cambodia and,
28
relationship with Morocco,
172–173, 349 n30
role in Angola, 233
role in Colombia, 241, 372 n78
role in Côte d'Ivoire, 250
role in East Timor, 214, 218
role in the Democratic Republic
of the Congo, 246
Franco, Gen. Francisco
Western Sahara and, 166
Franco-Mexican Declaration
provisions, 57, 62, 313 n21
Fréchette, Louise
Friends of the Secretary-General
for Haiti and, 113
Fretilin. *See* Revolutionary Front for
an Independent East Timor
FRG. *See* Guatemalan Republican
Front
Friends groups. *See also* Emergence
of groups; *specific Friends
groups and countries*
benefits of small size of, 280
benefits to the United Nations,
281–282
case selection and book organization, 15–17
categories of, 9–11

categories of states for, 272–273
commonality of interests among
members and, 271–272
composition of, 6, 14, 262,
270–273
conceptual design of, 259
conditions for success, 262–279
conflict parties and, 6, 13–14,
262, 268–270
Contact Groups, 10–11
contributions of, 4, 260
coordination of key states and,
277
core factors or variables, 2–7,
262–279
country-specific meetings, 11,
299 n27
creation of, 30–31, 33
decline in the number of civil
wars and, 4, 297 n4
different locations and characteristics of a single group and, 275
diversity of, 259, 262, 282
ending participation of, 279
external actors and, 261,
276–278
factors in performance of,
261–262
flexibility of, 5, 275, 281
formation and function of, 280
"Friend fatigue" and, 276
Friends of a country, 10
Friends of the Secretary-General,
9–10, 16
functional benefits of, 4
future of, 281–283
gatekeeping issues, 271
geographic tendencies, 7–8, 298
n16
Goulding's recommendations on
the future of, 33
growth in the number of, 3–4,
259

Friends groups (*cont.*)
  "helpful fixers" and, 271, 273
  as honest brokers, 280
  implementation and monitoring
    groups, 11
  informal groups of states and,
    259–260, 264–266, 379 n11
  interests of individual state
    members and, 8–9, 298 n17
  international engagement in a
    peace process and, 279–280
  lack of documentation of the
    work of, 6
  leadership issues, 6, 14–15, 262,
    264, 273–276
  lessons to be learned from,
    282–283
  members, initiatives, and
    phases of processes (table),
    285–294
  mixed record of, 4–7, 260–261
  nonstate actors and, 269, 379
    n11
  number of groups of friends and
    other mechanisms, 1946-2006
    (figure), 3
  peacekeeping efforts of the
    United Nations and, 16–17
  political stalemate situations and,
    278–279
  purpose of, 259
  recommendations for, 17,
    279–281
  regional environment and, 6, 13,
    262, 264, 266–268, 272, 300
    n30
  regional groups, 11, 299 n25
  Security Council and, 5–6
  self-selection of members, 7–9,
    262, 274, 379 n15
  special representatives of the
    secretary-general and, 274,
    277–278
  standards for success of, 11–15,
    300 n29
  support in peace efforts, 281
  "systemic state bias" and, 269
  thematic groups, 11, 299 n26
  timing or phase of the process
    and, 6, 15, 262, 276–279
  variables and the core case studies
    (tables), 263, 265
Friends of Albania
  peacemaking efforts, 44
Friends of Angola
  composition of, 233
  formation of, 233
Friends of Ethiopia-Eritrea
  consideration of forming, 259,
    378 n2
Friends of Georgia. *See also* Friends
    of the Secretary-General for
    Georgia
  bias of the Western members and,
    135–136, 144–145, 341 n39
  composition of, 135, 142
  contradictory interests of the
    Western members, 143–144
  creation of, 135, 142, 162
  energy resources of the region
    and, 143–144
  passivity of internal actors and,
    136
  resistance to calling itself Friends
    of the Secretary-General for
    Georgia, 143
  Russia's role as peacekeeper and,
    145–147
  strategic importance of Georgia
    and, 135
Friends of Guinea
  consideration of forming, 259,
    378 n2
Friends of Guinea-Bissau
  establishment and activities of,
    251, 311 n102

Friends of the Guatemalan Peace Process. *See also specific countries*
  Assembly of Civil Society and, 82, 87–88
  briefings and meetings in Mexico, 89–90
  compared with Friends of the Secretary-General for El Salvador, 79, 91–92, 100–101, 264
  conditions for success, 264
  contributions, 100
  criticism of, 90–91, 322 n42
  displacement of, 94–96
  factors in the disappearance of, 96–97, 325 n65
  Framework Agreement, 87–91, 325 n65
  Guatemalan National Revolutionary Unity and, 79, 82–95, 101
  "hidden" or "parallel" powers and, 95, 325 n61
  implementation phase, 94–96
  levels of involvement, 89
  Madrid meeting, 93, 323 n52
  membership, 79–80, 101, 102
  positive experience of, 260
  "post-peace" role, 93–94
  primary function of, 88
  regional environment and, 266
  roles of the Friends, 88
  signing tour, 93–94
  success of, 30, 32, 305 n52
  United Nations role, 79–80, 83–103
  United States' role, 88–96, 102
Friends of Myanmar
  consideration of forming, 226, 228, 259, 365 n14, 378 n2
Friends of the Secretary-General for El Salvador. *See also specific countries*
  choice of states, 61–64, 75, 77

  compared with Friends of the Guatemalan Peace Process, 79, 91–92, 100–101, 264
  conditions for success, 264
  contributions of, 1–2, 16, 29, 73–74, 77–78, 318 n79
  credibility of the United Nations and, 2
  "cushion" role, 60, 69
  donor states and, 74–75
  El Salvador Peace Accord and, 1, 72
  Farabundo Martí Liberation Front and, 1–2, 65–78, 268
  formation of, 61–67, 76, 268, 315 n48
  Iberoamerican Summit and, 67
  implementation issues, 71–75, 317 n71, 318 n74
  origins of, 57–60
  positive experience of, 260
  regional environment and, 266
  relations with the United Nations, 1–2, 65–67, 76
  Security Council and, 2, 73, 75, 77, 268
  success of, 51–52
  United States' role, 67–71, 268
Friends of the Secretary-General for Georgia. *See also* Friends of Georgia *and specific countries*
  addition of Ukraine and, 153–154, 344 n79
  autonomy of, 153
  Boden paper and, 151–161, 164, 344 n76, 344 n77, 344 n78
  composition of, 163, 346 n114
  creation of, 135, 162
  definition of the status of, 149
  designation of, 30, 304 n43
  differences in perspective of the Western members, 153, 344 n76, 346 n112

Friends of the Secretary-General for
   Georgia (cont.)
Geneva process and, 149–150,
   154–161, 162, 164
Kosovo precedent and, 159
presidential statement of the
   Security Council and, 161
reconstitution of the Friends of
   Georgia as, 149
reconvening of after the December 2004 meeting, 158–159
Security Council authorization
   of, 149
success of, 16, 30, 33, 277
UNOMIG mandate renewal and,
   159, 160, 161
Western Friends as an entity,
   152-153, 344 n77, 344 n78
Friends of the Secretary-General for
   Haiti. See also specific countries
composition of, 105, 126, 131, 133
contributions of, 132, 277
designation of, 30, 304 n44
donor coordination and, 121
elections and, 120, 121, 124,
   332 n67
formation of, 110–113
Governors Island Agreement
   and, 113, 114–116, 131
International Civilian Support
   Mission in Haiti and, 123–124
long-term influence of, 122–124
political process and, 113–116
reactivation of, 125–126, 131
regional environment and, 266
resignation of Aristide and, 132
resilience of, 133–134
UN peacekeeping missions and,
   119–121
United Nations role, 110–134,
   328 n6
United States' role, 30, 105–106,
   110–134, 260–261

U.S.S. Harlan County incident
   and, 116–118
Friends of Tajikistan
formation and role of, 148
success of, 30
Friends of the Secretary-General of
   the Organization of American
   States (Haiti)
Core Group and, 128
differences with the Friends of
   the Secretary-General for
   Haiti, 128–129
establishment of, 124, 131
membership of, 334 n84
Friends of the Secretary-General of
   the Organization of American
   States (Venezuela)
formation and crisis resolution
   efforts, 44, 309 n94
Friends of the UN Mission in
   Ethiopia and Eritrea
peacekeeping efforts, 47, 310 n101
Friends of Venezuela
formation, 44, 309 n.94
Friends of Western Sahara
compared to the Core Group on
   East Timor, 191
divisions among members,
   182–183, 188
exclusion of regional actors and,
   189
flawed mechanism of, 188
formation of, 30,165–166, 171,
   188, 189
France's role, 166, 172–173
limited utility of, 165, 166,
   189–190
low-profile adopted by, 176–178,
   350 n45
Peace Plan for Self-Determination for the People of Western
   Sahara and, 183–186
procedural contributions, 190

Friends of Western Sahara (*cont.*)
  relationship with the secretary-
    general, 189–190
  release of prisoners of war and,
    177–178, 187
  Russia's role, 166, 174, 187
  Security Council and, 174, 175–
    176, 189
  shift in membership, 174
  Spain's role, 166, 173–174, 187
  status quo and, 175–178, 350 n45
  temporary members, 350 n39
  United Kingdom's role, 166
  United States' role, 166,
    171–172, 175, 181, 187

G-8. *See* Group of 8
Gagulia, Gennady
  meeting with Putin, 156
Gama, Jaime
  role in East Timor, 199
Gambari, Ibrahim
  role in Angola, 233, 234, 368
    n39
  role in Myanmar, 228, 366 n15
Gambia
  role in forming Friends of
    Guinea-Bissau, 309 n101
Gamsakhurdia, President Zviad
    (Georgia)
  nationalist policies and coup
    against, 137
Garang, John
  Sudan peace process and, 254
Geneva agreement
  provisions, 60, 68
Geneva process (1997)
  frustration with progress of, 150
  launching of, 149
Geneva process (2003)
  launching of, 156
  reaction of Russia to, 156
  meetings under, 156, 157, 159

recommendation for the estab-
    lishment of task forces, 156
  Western Friends of the Secretary-
    General for Georgia and,
    156–157
Georgia. *See also* Friends of Georgia;
    Friends of the Secretary-
    General for Georgia; Georgian-
    Abkhaz conflict; UN Military
    Observer Mission in Georgia
  arrest of Russian military intelli-
    gence officers on espionage
    charges, 160–161
  Baku-Supsa pipeline and, 141
  Boden paper and, 151
  energy resources, 141, 143
  increase in defense spending,
    141, 340 n25
  independence of, 137
  New Friends of Georgia, 141, 339
    n18
  relationship with Russia, 138,
    140, 141, 154–155, 159, 339
    n23, 344 n85
  request for membership in
    NATO, 141, 155
  request for membership in the
    European Union, 141
  strategic importance of, 135,
    139
  Sustainment and Stability Oper-
    ations Program, 339 n19
  U.S. support for, 141
Georgia Train and Equip Program,
    141, 339 n19, 345 n86
Georgian-Abkhaz conflict
  Boden paper and, 150–161, 164
  Chechnya and, 137, 155, 338
    n7
  displacement of Georgians and,
    137, 156, 160, 341 n38
  distrust between the parties and,
    138

Georgian-Abkhaz conflict (cont.)
  dual characterization of, 161
  ethnic conflict in Abkhazia,
    136–139
  Friends of Georgia role, 135,
    142–147, 149, 161–162
  Friends of the Secretary-General
    for Georgia role, 135, 149–
    161, 162, 163–164
  Geneva process (1997) and,
    149–150
  Geneva process (2003) and,
    154–161, 164
  Georgia's suspension of peace-
    keeping operations in Abk-
    hazia, 160
  lack of tangible results, 164
  Moscow Agreement on a
    Cease-fire and Separation of
    Forces, 137
  Quadripartite Agreement on
    the Return of Refugees and
    Displaced Persons, 341 n38
  Russia's role, 135, 137–138,
    139–141, 145–147, 150–163
Germany
  Friends of Georgia role, 142, 146
    n114
  role in Afghanistan, 230, 231,
    367 n26
  role in Haiti, 123–124
  Western Saharan conflict and,
    176
Ggagbo, President Laurent (Côte
  d'Ivoire)
  failed attempt to oust, 250
Ghani, Ashraf
  view of Brahimi's leadership, 231,
    367 n31
Goldstone, Anthony
  assessment of the UN Transi-
    tional Administration in East
    Timor, 361 n72

González, Prime Minister Felipe
  (Spain)
  Friends of the Secretary-General
    for El Salvador role, 63, 315
    n44
  Guatemalan peace process and, 97
Good offices concept
  confidentiality and, 22
  description, 20–21
  impartiality of the secretary-
    general and, 21–22
  peacemaking efforts and, 22–24,
    34, 35, 302 n18
Goulding, Marrack
  Friends of Georgia and, 142
  Governors Island Agreement
    and, 115
  Guatemalan peace process and,
    84, 87, 91, 324 n58
  phased demobilization of the
    FMLN, 71–72
  purposes of the UN Observer
    Group in Central America,
    313 n17
  recommendations on the future
    of Friends groups, 33
  success of UN peacekeeping
    missions, 30
  UN Observer Mission in El
    Salvador and, 73
  UN peacemaking in Africa, 373
    n86
  United States' insistence on
    deadlines for the El Salvador
    peace process and, 68
  Western Saharan conflict and,
    170, 176, 179, 351 n59
Goulty, Alan
  role in Sudan, 252, 376 n120
Governors Island Agreement
  collapse of, 113, 115, 116, 131
  human rights violations and,
    115

Governors Island Agreement (*cont.*)
  importance of the U.S. role, 115,
    331 n44
  negotiations for, 114–115
  provisions, 115, 331 n47
  signing of, 113
Granderson, Colin
  U.S. role in Haiti, 120–121, 332
    n67
Gray, William
  appointment of, 117
Greece
  Cyprus and, 234, 237
Green, Rosario
  Friends of the Guatemalan
    Peace Process and, 85–86,
    321 n23
Greenstock, Sir Jeremy
  Core Group on East Timor and,
    215
  Framework Agreement on the
    Status of Western Sahara
    and, 183
  reform of the Troika on Angola
    and, 245
Griffiths, Martin
  peace processes' "peculiar cock-
    tail" and, 282, 379, n20
Group of 8
  formation of, 44
Group of Latin American and
    Caribbean States
  UN involvement in Haiti and,
    111, 332 n57
GRULAC. *See* Group of Latin
    American and Caribbean
    States
GTEP. *See* Georgia Train and Equip
    Program
Guatemala. *See also* Friends of the
    Guatemalan Peace Process;
    UN Verification Mission in
    Guatemala

Arzú's military reforms, 93, 101,
    323 n49
  background of the conflict in,
    80–81, 100
  Civil Guard, 97, 325 n69
  Commission of Investigation of
    Illegal Groups and Clandestine
    Security Forces, 99, 100, 327
    n85, 327 n87
  Consultative Group and, 95,
    96–98, 99, 326 n73, 327 n82
  Dialogue Group of donor states,
    80, 95, 96–100, 103, 326 n77,
    326 n78, 327 n83
  economic issues, 79, 92
  ethnic issues, 80, 325 n63
  paramilitary "civilian self-defense
    patrols," 81, 319 n6, 323 n49
  peace process compared with El
    Salvador's, 81–82
  peace process outcomes, 311 n2
  rejection of constitutional
    reforms, 96, 325 n63
  rejection of U.S. military assis-
    tance, 81
Guatemalan Friends. *See* Friends
    of the Guatemalan Peace
    Process
Guatemalan National Revolutionary
    Unity
  demobilization of, 81, 323 n46
  kidnapping involvement, 93–94,
    323 n54
  meeting with Serrano, 83
  political strength of, 82
  relationship with the Soviet bloc
    and Cuba, 319 n5
  relationships with Mexico,
    Venezuela, and Spain, 86
  role in the peace process, 79,
    82–95, 101
  Spain's attempted meeting with,
    320 n12

Guatemalan National Revolutionary
Unity (cont.)
unification of the guerrilla move-
ment in, 81
Guatemalan Republican Front
challenge to Arzú, 95
Guéhenno, Jean-Marie
Boden paper and, 156, 157
Core Group on East Timor and,
215
Geneva process and, 159–160
Guinea
consideration of Friends of
Guinea, 259, 378 n2
International Contact Group on
Mano River Basin and, 250
Guinea-Bissau
Friends of Guinea-Bissau, 47, 251
International Contact Group,
250–251
UN peacebuilding, 47, 311 n101
Gusmão, President Xanana (East
Timor)
address to the UN General
Assembly, 191
establishment of the National
Council of Maubere Resis-
tance, 193
initiation of dialogue with
Indonesia, 356 n11
letters to Annan and the Security
Council, 211
meeting with Gen. Wiranto and
Ramos-Horta, 359 n59
meeting with Vendrell, 196
release from prison, 203
severing of Falintil's connections
with Fretilin, 193–194
UN Transitional Administration
in East Timor and, 209
Gutteres, José Luis
comparison of the Western
Sahara with East Timor, 195

Gyanendra, King (Nepal), 39

Habibie, President B.J. (Indonesia)
deployment of a multinational
force and, 207, 208
East Timor's autonomy and,
197–198, 199, 200, 201
Hague Convention for the Pacific
Settlement of International
Disputes
good offices concept, 21, 301 n6
Haiti. See also Core Group on Haiti;
Friends of the Secretary-
General for Haiti; International Civilian Mission in
Haiti; International Civilian
Support Mission in Haiti;
Operation Uphold Democracy;
UN Mission in Haiti, UN
Stabilization Mission in Haiti
background of the conflict in,
106–108
Council of Wise Men transitional
government, 126–127
degeneration into "mob rule,"
125, 335 n88
deployment of a multinational
force to, 125
deterioration of the Haitian
National Police, 108
Economic and Social Council
and, 122, 334 n76
economic issues, 116–117, 127,
129, 335 n96
election issues, 120, 121, 124,
129, 130, 332 n67
factors in the failure to stabilize,
127
floods in, 127
fragility of the transitional government, 129
illegal drug trafficking, 108–109,
121, 329 n13, 329 n14

Haiti (*cont.*)
  kidnappings in, 129
  security situation in, 129
  strategic importance of, 106
  UN naval blockade of, 116
  UN sanctions against, 105, 108,
    114, 116–117, 331 n54
  U.S. interests and, 108–110, 329
    n13
Halo Trust
  role as employer in Abkhazia,
    338 n10
Hamilton, John
  Friends of the Guatemalan Peace
    Process and, 89, 232 n53
Hammarksjöld, Secretary-General
  Dag
  advisory committees and, 23–24,
    302 n12, 302 n13
  article 99 and, 300 n3
  defense of the impartiality of the
    secretary-general, 21
  forms of interaction with states,
    22–23
  "Peking formula" for negotiations
    with China, 20–21
  Thailand-Cambodia border dis-
    pute and, 24
Hampson, Fen Osler
  Taming Intractable Conflicts, 8
Handal, Schafik
  letters to Mikhail Gorbachev, 58
Hannay, David
  Friends of Western Sahara and,
    350 n45
  role in Cyprus, 236, 369 n50
Harston, Julian
  relationship with Friends of the
    Secretary-General for Haiti, 120
  UN Mission in Haiti and, 332 n64
Hasegawa, Sukehiro
  role in East Timor, 202, 217, 218,
    364 n105, 364 n106

Hassan II, King (Morocco)
  Baker's initial meeting with, 179
  bid to reclaim the Western
    Sahara, 166–167, 169
  commitment to grant autonomy
    to Western Sahara, 179, 352
    n60
  friendship with Chirac, 173
  "Green March" and, 167
  OAU's guidelines on the Western
    Saharan conflict and, 169,
    170, 348 n20
Holbrooke, Richard
  August 2003 attack on UN in
    Iraq, 306 n.65
  role in East Timor, 208
Holiday, David
  speed of the Guatemalan Peace
    Process, 323 n51
Houston Accords
  Western Saharan conflict and, 179
Howard, Prime Minister John
  (Australia)
  letter to Pres. Habibie, 198, 357
    n29
  role in East Timor, 207
Human Rights Watch
  criticism of Saakashvili, 339 n22
Hume, Cameron
  Iran-Iraq war and, 25
Hun Sen regime in Cambodia, 27
Hurricane Mitch
  damage to Central America, 98

Iberoamerican Summit, 67
ICGL. *See* International Contact
  Group on Liberia
ICGM. *See* Informal Consultation
  Group on Myanmar
ICGMRB. *See* International Contact
  Group on the Mano River
  Basin
ICJ. *See* International Court of Justice

IDB. *See* Inter-American Development Bank
IGAD. *See* Intergovernmental Authority on Development
IGAD Partners Forum
    activities of, 251, 376 n117
IMF. *See* International Monetary Fund
India
    role in Afghanistan, 231
    role in Myanmar, 365 n12
    role in Nepal, 39, 267
    role in Sri Lanka, 268, 378 n4
Indonesia
    accountability issues, 210–211
    Act of Free Choice, 196, 356 n22
    All-Inclusive Intra-East Timorese Dialogue and, 196
    annexation of East Timor, 194, 355 n9
    Commission for Truth and Friendship, 210–211
    elections of 1999, 203–206, 359 n61
    human rights violations, 194, 210
    Jakarta Informal Meetings on Cambodia, 27–28
    peace agreement in Aceh and, 42–43, 308 n86
    Peoples' Consultative Assembly, 199
    role in East Timor, 191, 193, 194, 198–199, 203–204, 205–206, 210–211, 219
    treaty with Australia concerning the Timor Gap, 195
Informal Consultation Group on Myanmar
    composition of, 226, 227
    formats for, 227
    utility of, 227

Inter-American Democratic Charter
    accusation by CARICOM that the United States had failed to respect the charter, 127
Inter-American Development Bank
    Core Group and, 128
    Guatemalan peace process and, 92, 98, 99
INTERFET. *See* International Force for East Timor
Intergovernmental Authority on Development
    conflict mediation and resolution role, 41
    role in Sudan, 251–252
International Civilian Mission in Haiti
    deployment of, 113
    evacuations of, 116, 117
    funding issues, 334 n78
    human rights monitoring and institution building responsibilities, 118, 119
    success of, 330 n38
International Civilian Support Mission in Haiti
    closure of, 124
    extension of the mandate for, 123
    Friends of the Secretary-General for Haiti role, 123
    funding issues, 122, 123
    replacement of MIPONUH, 332 n60
International Commission to Accompany the Transition in the DRC
    establishment and activities of, 247, 374 n99
    relationship with the Security Council, 47
International Contact Group on Guinea-Bissau
    establishment and activities of, 250–251

International Contact Group on
    Liberia
  establishment and activities of,
    248, 249–251, 257, 264, 266
  leadership of, 46–47
International Contact Group on the
    Mano River Basin
  establishment and activities of,
    250
International Contact Group on
    Somalia
  composition of, 374 n89
  formation of, 244, 373 n88, 374
    n89
International Court of Justice
  self-determination of Western
    Sahara, 165, 167
International Force for East Timor
  Australian contribution to, 207
  authorization for, 207, 208
  Core Group on East Timor role,
    220
International Monetary Fund
  economic bailout of Indonesia
    and, 360 n68
  economic condition of Haiti
    and, 129
  El Salvador's commitments to,
    92
  Guatemalan peace process and,
    92, 98, 326 n76
IPF. See IGAD Partners Forum
Iran
  role in Afghanistan, 229, 230,
    231, 366 n21, 367 n26
Iran-Iraq war
  Security Council and, 25, 26,
    303 n26
Iraq
  attack on UN staff, 37, 306 n65
  invasion of Kuwait, 25
  U.S. invasion of, 36–38, 306 n63,
    306 n65, 307 n68

Ireland
  Framework Agreement on the
    Status of Western Sahara
    and, 183
  Friends of Western Sahara and,
    352 n73, 352 n77
Ismail, Razali
  role in Myanmar, 226–228
Italy
  role in Afghanistan, 230, 231,
    367 n26

Jamaica
  invitation to join the Friends of
    the Secretary-General for
    Haiti, 122, 271, 334 n77
Japan
  contributions to the UN Mission
    in East Timor, 204, 358 n44
  financial assistance to Indonesia,
    202
  peacekeeping operations and,
    202
  role in East Timor, 191, 202, 204,
    215, 218, 220, 364 n113
  role in Sri Lanka, 378 n4
Jensen, Eric
  role in the Western Saharan
    conflict, 175, 350 n44
Johnson, Hilde
  role in Sudan, 252
Jones, Bruce D.
  coordination of peace implemen-
    tation, 277
Jordan
  role in Middle East peace process,
    238

Kagame, President Paul (Rwanda)
  support for the Democratic
    Republic of the Congo, 246
Kakabadze, Malkhaz
  Boden paper and, 151, 343 n71

Kenya
    role in Sudan, 224, 252
Kerr-McGee
    contract with Morocco to explore
        the waters off Western Sahara,
        172–173, 349 n31
Khajimba, Raul
    Abkhazia elections and, 158
Khare, Atul
    appointment of, 218, 364 n113
Ki-Moon, Secretary-General Ban
    takes office, 282
King, Charles
    nature of the Georgian-Abkhaz
        conflict, 138
Kissinger, Henry
    Indonesian annexation of East
        Timor and, 355 n9
    meeting with Suharto, 193
Kosovo
    Contact Group on the former
        Yugoslavia and, 44, 309 n92
    NATO role, 36, 208
    Quint and, 44, 309 n92
    UN role, 34, 35–36
Kozyrev, Foreign Minister Andrei
    (Russia)
    Georgian-Abkhaz conflict and,
        139, 147
Krasno, Jean
    Carnegie Commission on Pre-
        venting Deadly Conflict
        and, 5
Kuwait
    Iraq's invasion of, 25
    U.S. involvement in, 172

Ladsous, Hervé
    Friends of the Secretary-General
        for Haiti and, 112, 113
Laheurte, Louise
    Western Saharan conflict and,
        176

Latortue, Prime Minister Gérard
    (Haiti)
    meeting with the Core Group, 130
Lavrov, Sergei
    Bush's visit to Georgia and, 339
        n23
Lebanon
    Core Group on Lebanon, 38, 307
        n72
    UN role, 38–39, 307 n72
    U.S. role, 38–39, 307 n72
Leissner, Maria
    Dialogue Group of donor states
        role, 98
LeMoyne, James
    role in Colombia, 241–243, 372
        n81
León de Carpio, President Ramiro
    (Guatemala)
    caretaker government of, 82, 87
Liberation Tigers of Tamil Eelam
    international conferences on
        Sri Lanka and, 378 n6
Liberia
    Comprehensive Peace Agree-
        ment, 249–250, 375 n111
    Economic Community of West
        Africa Monitoring Group in
        Liberia, 341 n43
    International Contact Group on
        Liberia, 248, 249–251, 257
    sanctions against, 248
    UN Mission in Liberia, 250
    UN Observer Mission in Liberia,
        341 n43
    UN Peacebuilding Support
        Office in Liberia, 248–249,
        375 n104
    UN peacekeeping operation in, 34
Libya
    military assistance to Polisario, 168
    responsibility for the Lockerbie
        bombing, 35

Lie, Secretary-General Trygve
  Berlin Crisis and, 24
  invocation of article 99, 300 n3
Lobato, Rogerio
  East Timor police force and, 214,
    216
  resignation of, 217
Longchamp, Fritz
  lobbying by Haiti for support from
    the Security Council and, 114
Lopes Cabral, Alfredo
  International Civilian Support
    Mission in Haiti and, 123,
    334 n81
  relationship with Friends of the
    Secretary-General for Haiti,
    120
  UN Mission in Haiti and, 332 n64
Loshchinin, Valery
  meetings on the Boden paper
    and, 156
LTTE. See Liberation Tigers of Tamil
  Eelam
Lusaka Protocol, 46
Lutheran World Federation
  Guatemalan peace process and,
    84, 85, 321 n20
Lynch, Dov
  nature of the Georgian-Abkhaz
    conflict, 138

Macfarlane, S. Neil
  "statist" nature of the United
    Nations effect on aid to
    Abkhazia, 341 n39
Machakos Protocol
  provisions, 253
Madrid Accords
  provisions, 167
Major, Prime Minister John (Great
  Britain)
  UN role in peace and security
    and, 29

Malaysia
  role in East Timor, 217, 218
Malone, David
  Friends of the Secretary-General
    for Haiti and, 113, 332 n57
Malval, Prime Minister Robert
  (Haiti)
  appointment of, 116
Mansur, Omar
  Polisario and, 171
Marker, Jamsheed
  role in East Timor, 197, 199, 200,
    201, 205, 357 n24, 357 n27
Martin, Ian
  role in Nepal, 39, 217
  role in East Timor, 205, 207,
    217–218, 364 n107
Mauritania
  decolonization of Western
    Sahara and, 165, 166
  Madrid Accords and, 167
  Western Saharan conflict and,
    350 n39, 350 n43
McWilliams, Edmund
  Alatas and the tripartite agree-
    ment, 357 n33
  shift in U.S. policy on Indonesia,
    358 n42
Menkerios, Haile
  role in the Democratic Republic
    of the Congo, 246–247
Mérimée, Jean-Bertrand
  Friends of Georgia and, 142
Merrem, Gerd
  MINUGUA leadership, 98
Mexico
  Contadora group and, 54, 62
  contribution to ONUSAL's
    military division, 317 n71
  Dialogue Group and, 99
  facilitation of the return of
    refugees to Guatemala, 321
    n26

Friends of the Guatemalan Peace
Process role, 79, 85–87,
89–96, 101, 102
Friends of the Secretary-General
for El Salvador role, 60,
62–63, 76, 77
relations with the United States,
62
role in Colombia, 240, 242, 371
n69, 372 n76
URNG's relationship with, 86
Western Saharan conflict and,
183
MICAH. See International Civilian
Support Mission in Haiti
MICIVIH. See International Civil-
ian Mission in Haiti
Middle East peace process
Quartet role, 7, 38-39, 238–239,
370 n63
road map, 238–239, 370 n62
Miles, Richard
U.S. role in the Georgian-Abkhaz
conflict, 155
Minsk Group
composition of, 340 n32
establishment of, 143
peacemaking efforts, 44
MINUGUA. See UN Verification
Mission in Guatemala
MINURSO. See UN Mission for
the Referendum in Western
Sahara
MINUSAL. See Mission of the
United Nations in El Salvador
MINUSTAH. See UN Stabilization
Mission in Haiti
MIPONUH. See UN Civilian Police
Mission in Haiti
Miraflores declaration, 66–67
Mission of the United Nations in
El Salvador
formation of, 317 n72

Mitterand, President François
(France)
meeting with Pres. Pérez of
Venezuela on Haiti, 110
Mohammed VI, King (Morocco)
economic and political reforms,
172
friendship with Chirac, 173
referendum on Western Sahara
and, 180
Moi, President Daniel arap (Sudan)
role in Sudan, 252
Monroe Doctrine
U.S. involvement in Haiti and,
108
Montaño, Jorge
confidential meetings between
the United States and the
FMLN, 70
meeting between Salinas and
Bush, 63
Pérez de Cuéllar and, 71, 317 n69
personality of de Soto, 65
United States' role in the Friends
of the Secretary-General for
El Salvador, 316 n61
Venezuela's rivalry with Mexico,
63
Montobbio, Manuel
contribution of the Friends of
the Secretary-General for El
Salvador, 318 n79
Morocco
as "administrative power" in
Western Sahara, 177, 351 n52
decolonization of Western
Sahara and, 165, 166–167
expenditures in Western Sahara,
168, 348 n13
fisheries agreement with the
European Union, 167, 174,
350 n38
Madrid Accords and, 167

Morocco (cont.)
  occupation of the island of Perejil,
    173, 349 n36
  Peace Plan for Self-Determination
    for the People of Western
    Sahara and, 185–186
  relationship with Spain, 173–174
  rivalry with Algeria, 168, 347
    n10, 347 n11
  support for the U.S. involvement
    in Kuwait, 172
  trade talks with the United States,
    172
  Treaty of Friendship, Good
    Neighborliness, and Coopera-
    tion with Spain, 173
  United States support for, 168, 172
  Western Sahara's self-determina-
    tion and, 165, 166–190
Moses, Alfred
  role in Cyprus, 236, 369 n50
Mozambique
  Core Group on, 28–29, 46, 277
  Supervision and Monitoring
    Commission, 29
Mulroney, Prime Minister (Canada)
  Pérez's request for support for
    Haiti and, 110
Museveni, President Yoweri
    (Uganda)
  support for the Democratic
    Republic of the Congo, 246
Myanmar
  ASEAN membership, 225
  China's role, 225–226
  geographic location, 225
  Informal Consultation Group on
    Myanmar, 226–228
  National League for Democracy
    and, 225
  possibility of creating a group of
    Friends for, 226, 228, 259, 365
    n14, 378 n2

  "roadmap to democracy," 227
  sanctions against, 228
  United Nations role, 225–228,
    256, 257

Namibia. See also Contact Group
    on Namibia; UN Transition
    Assistance Group
  role in Angola, 233
  role in the Democratic Republic
    of the Congo, 246
  self-determination of, 26–27
National Council of Maubere
    Resistance
  establishment of, 193
National Council of Timorese
    Resistance
  opposition to elections, 205
  proindependence movement and,
    198, 199
National League for Democracy
  Myanmar elections and, 225
  rearrest of Suu Kyi and, 227
National Liberation Army
  demobilization of paramilitary
    groups and, 242–243
  talks with the government, 241
  UN role in Colombia and, 240
National Reconciliation Com-
    mission
  creation and leadership of, 83
  secret talks in Oslo with
    Guatemalan National Revo-
    lutionary Unity, 83, 320 n13
National Resistance
  role in El Salvador, 312 n4
National Resistance of Mozambique
  peace process and, 29
National Union for the Total Inde-
    pendence of Angola
  diamonds as a funding source for,
    232
  Savimbi's death and, 225

National Vanguard Party
role in the Guatemalan peace
process, 82, 95
Nationalist Republican Alliance
election of Cristiani and, 56,
72
macroeconomic policy, 91
meetings with FMLN, 56, 95
NATO. See North Atlantic Treaty
Organization
Negroponte, John
reactivation of the Friends of the
Secretary-General for Haiti
and, 125–126
NEPAD. See New Partnership for
Africa's Development
Nepal
consideration of formation of
Contact Group on, 259–260,
378 n2
UN role in, 39–40
The Netherlands
Core Group on Northern
Uganda and, 377 n1
East Timor and, 192
Friends of the Secretary-
General for El Salvador
and, 74–75
Friends of the UN Mission in
Ethiopia and Eritrea and, 47,
310 n101
New Friends of Georgia
composition of, 339 n18
creation of, 141
New Partnership for Africa's
Development
Africa Action Plan and, 245
Friends groups and, 244
New Zealand
role in East Timor, 191, 202, 215,
217, 218, 220
NGOs. See Nongovernmental
organizations

Niasse, Mustapha
role in the Democratic Republic
of the Congo, 246–247
Nicaragua
explosion of FMLN arms' caches
in, 72, 319 n86
victory of the Sandinista Front
for National Liberation over
the Somoza dynasty, 52
Nigeria
role in Angola, 233
Nikken, Pedro
Miraflores declaration and, 67
NLD. See National League for
Democracy
Nodia, Ghia
Georgian-Abkhaz conflict and,
138
Nongovernmental organizations.
See also specific organizations
as Friends of Burundi, 46, 310
n100
mediation and conflict resolution,
42–43
North Atlantic Treaty Organization
Cyprus and, 234
Georgia's request for membership
in, 141
peacekeeping efforts, 277
role in Kosovo, 36, 208
Norway
Core Group on Northern
Uganda and, 377 n1
Friends of the Guatemalan Peace
Process and, 79, 83, 84–96,
101, 320 n13, 321 n20
Friends of the Secretary-General
for El Salvador and, 74–75
peacemaking efforts, 42, 84, 299
n22, 320 n17, 320 n19, 321
n20
role in Angola, 233
role in Colombia, 240, 241, 242

Norway (cont.)
  role in Middle East, 42
  role in Somalia, 244, 373 n88
  role in Sri Lanka, 268, 378 n4
  role in Sudan, 223–224, 251–255
  Troika role in Sudan, 223–224
Norwegian Church Aid
  Guatemalan peace process and,
    84–85, 320 n19
  Sudan and, 320 n17
Nuccio, Richard
  Friends of the Guatemalan Peace
    Process and, 89
Nyunt, Prime Minister Khin
  (Myanmar)
  removal from office, 228

OAS. See Organization of American
  States
OAU. See Organisation of African
  Unity
Oil-for-food program, 37
ONUC. See UN Operation in the
  Congo
ONUCA. See UN Observer Group
  in Central America
ONUSAL. See UN Observer Mission
  in El Salvador
ONUV. See UN Verification Office
Operation Lifeline Sudan
  implementation of, 251, 376
    n116
Operation Uphold Democracy
  return of Aristide to power, 118
Organisation of African Unity. See
  also African Union
  respect for state sovereignty, 41
  role in Liberia, 248
  Western Sahara's self-
    determination and, 165,
    168–169, 170–171, 347 n11
Organization for Security and Coop-
  eration in Europe

High Commissioner for National
  Minorities, 40
  peacekeeping efforts, 40, 277
  Russian military bases in Georgia
    and, 141
  Tajikistan peace process and, 148
Organization of American States.
  See also Friends of the Secretary-
    General of the Organization
    of American States
  agreement between the Lavalas
    movement and opposition
    parties and, 124
  Core Group and, 128
  Esquipulas agreement and, 55,
    312 n15
  Guatemalan peace process and,
    87, 321 n28
  regional conflicts and, 41
  role in Haiti, 106, 107, 111,
    112, 124, 125, 126, 127,
    130–131, 132
  role in Venezuela, 44
  Santiago Declaration and, 109
  U.S. domination of, 53–54
Orr, Robert
  Core Group on East Timor com-
    position, 213
OSCE. See Organization for Security
  and Cooperation in Europe
Ould-Abdallah, Ahmedou
  NGO Friends of Burundi and, 46,
    310 n100

PACE. See Parliamentary Assembly
  of the Council of Europe
Pakistan
  role in Afghanistan, 229–231,
    366 n21, 367 n27, 367 n30
  UN Good Offices Mission in
    Afghanistan and Pakistan
    and, 21
PAN. See National Vanguard Party

Panama
  Contadora group and, 54
Papadopoulos, President Tassos
    (Cyprus)
  Annan Plan for Cyprus and, 237,
    370 n58
Paris Peace Conference
  peace process for Cambodia,
    28
Parliamentary Assembly of the
    Council of Europe
  criticism of Saakashvili, 339
    n22
Pastrana, President Andrés
    (Colombia)
  peace process and, 239, 242,
    256
Pastukhov, Boris
  Georgian-Abkhaz conflict and,
    140
Patten, Chris
  Quartet and, 370 n63
PCS. *See* Salvadoran Communist
    Party
People's Revolutionary Army
  role, 312 n4
Pérez, President Carlos Andrés
    (Venezuela)
  Friends of the Guatemalan Peace
    Process and, 85, 321 n24
  meeting with Pres. Mitterand of
    France on Haiti, 110
  Miraflores declaration and,
    66–67, 316 n53
  request to the OAS for support
    for Haiti, 111
  Salvadoran peace process and,
    63, 66–67, 316 n53
  support for UN intervention in
    Haiti, 110, 111
Pérez de Cuéllar, Secretary-General
    Javier
  Contadora group role, 54–55

  effectiveness of, 51
  end of the term of, 71
  Friends of the Secretary-General
    for El Salvador role, 66–67,
    69–71, 317 n63
  Iran-Iraq war and, 25
  meeting with President Bush,
    68–69
  nonpaper soliciting views on
    mechanism to support dia-
    logue on El Salvador, 59
  peacemaking efforts and,
    24–25
  personality of, 33
  photograph of, 1–2
  Pilgrimage for Peace, 1
  UN assistance to Haiti and,
    110–111
  Western Sahara's self-
    determination and, 165,
    169–170, 171, 190, 352 n60
Perina, Rudolph
  meetings on the Boden paper
    and, 156
Peru
  Rio de Janeiro Protocol and, 44
Pezzullo, Lawrence
  appointment of, 114
  Governors Island Agreement
    and, 115
  resignation of, 117
Philipson, Liz
  international conferences on Sri
    Lanka, 378 n6
  "systemic state bias" and conflict
    resolution, 269
Pickering, Ambassador Thomas
  Friends of the Secretary-General
    for El Salvador role, 70
Pico de Coaña, Ambassador Yago
  role in Colombia, 371 n72
Pilgrimage for Peace (Pérez de
    Cuéllar), 1

Polisario
   compared with the Revolutionary
      Front for an Independent East
      Timor, 195
   declaration of Western Sahara's
      independence, 167
   guerrilla actions, 166, 168
   incursions into Western Sahara,
      168
   military assistance to, 168
   antagonism to Boutros-Ghali,
      170–171, 349 n26
   opposition to de Soto, 186
   relationship with Baker, 186
   support from the United States,
      350 n44
   ties with Spain, 173, 349 n35
   Western Saharan self-
      determination and, 168–172,
      176–179, 181–182, 184,
      186–188, 189, 353 n81, 353
      n82, 353 n87
Popular Front for the Liberation of
      Saguia el Hamra and Rio de
      Oro. See Polisario
Popular Liberation Forces
   role, 312 n4
Porras, Gustavo
   Guatemalan peace process and, 92
Portillo, President Alfonso
      (Guatemala)
   government of, 98, 99, 326 n80
   Guatemalan peace process and,
      95, 98
Portugal
   contributions to the UN Mission
      in East Timor, 204
   role in Angola, 232, 233–234
   role in East Timor, 192, 194, 195,
      198, 199, 204, 205, 212, 215,
      217, 218, 219, 361 n81
Post–Cold War period. See also
   Cold War

Cyprus and, 234
   emergence of groups and, 3, 19,
      24–33, 48, 281
   transformation of the United
      Nations and, 19
Powell, Colin
   views on U.S. involvement in
      Haiti, 109–110
Powles, Michael
   role in East Timor, 202
Prantl, Jochen
   The UN Security Council and
      Informal Groups of States,
      5–6
Prendergast, Kieran
   Guatemalan peace process and,
      96, 324 n62
   Quartet and, 370 n59
   role on Afghanistan, 366 n24
   role on East Timor, 200, 205–206,
      207, 357 n34, 359 n60
   role on Sudan, 251–252, 376
      n118
   UN role in Kosovo, 36
Préval, President René (Haiti)
   Aristide's influence over, 119
   Brahimi's meetings with, 120
   election of, 130
   popular support for, 130
   relationship with the United
      Nations, 120, 129
Primakov, Yevgeny (Russia)
   Russian role in Georgia and,
      139, 147
PRTC. See Central American Revo-
      lutionary Workers' Party
Putin, President Vladimir (Russia)
   meeting with Shevardnadze at
      Sochi, 156, 157
   Geneva process and, 156, 157
   relationship with Georgia, 159
   role in the Georgian-Abkhaz
      conflict, 136, 337 n2

Quadripartite Agreement on the
    Return of Refugees and Dis-
    placed Persons
    provisions, 341 n38
Quartet
    composition of, 7, 238, 370 n59
    creation of, 238
    de Soto views of, 238–239, 370
        n63
    dynamics within, 239, 370 n63
    functions of, 7, 238–239
    road map on the Middle East and,
        238–239, 370 n62
    Rød-Larsen and, 238-239
    role in the Middle East peace
        process, 38–39, 238–239, 370
        n62, 370 n63
Quezada Toruño, Bishop Rodolfo
    Assembly of Civil Society and, 87
    Friends of the Guatemalan Peace
        Process and, 86
    National Reconciliation Com-
        mission leadership, 83
Quint
    formation of, 44, 309, n92

Ramírez Ocampo, Augusto
    UN Observer Mission in El
        Salvador and, 74
Ramos Horta, José
    letters to Annan and the Security
        Council, 211
    meeting with Gen. Wiranto and
        Gusmão, 359 n59
    Nobel Peace Prize award, 194
    request for military aid from
        Australia, 218, 364 n110
    resignation as Foreign Minister,
        217
    United States' position shift on
        East Timor and, 363 n94
RAND Corporation
    study of nation building, 118–119

Reagan administration
    relations with Mexico and, 62
    role in El Salvador, 56
Regional organizations. See also
    specific organizations
    peacekeeping efforts, 39–40
Revolutionary Armed Forces of
    Colombia
    agreement with the Colombian
        government on a "friendly
        countries" group, 372 n75
    demobilization of paramilitary
        groups and, 242–243
    "Euro tour" for, 371 n70
    international opinion of, 372 n79
    kidnappings by, 241, 242, 372
        n76
    United Nations role in Colombia
        and, 240, 371 n71
Revolutionary Front for an Indepen-
    dent East Timor
    compared with Polisario, 195
    control of the territory, 192
    political imbalances and, 216
    severing of connections with
        Falintil, 193–194
Rio de Janeiro Protocol, 44
Riza, Iqbal
    UN Observer Mission in El Sal-
        vador and, 66, 74
    self-generating nature of Friends
        groups, 379 n15
RN. See National Resistance
Robinson, Randall
    hunger strike protesting U.S.
        activities in Haiti, 117
Rød-Larsen, Terje
    Middle East peace process and,
        238–239, 320 n17
    Quartet role, 238–239
Roman Catholic Church
    Assembly of Civil Society, 82
    Guatemalan peace process and, 81

Roman Catholic Church (*cont.*)
 meetings between the Nationalist Republican Alliance and
 FMLN, 56
 opposition to "Baby Doc" Duvalier, 107
 role in Colombia, 242
Romero, Archbishop Oscar
 assassination of, 53
Rosenthal, Gert
 MINUGUA role and, 99, 327 n84
Roth, Stanley
 role in East Timor, 201
Roy, Stapleton
 contradictory messages on the
 Indonesian militias, 359 n51
Russia. *See also* Soviet Union
 criticism of the Friends of the
 Secretary-General for Haiti,
 122
 Friends of Georgia role, 142,
 145–147, 161–162, 342 n51
 Friends of Western Sahara role,
 16, 166, 174, 183, 184, 187,
 350 n39
 Georgian-Abkhaz conflict role,
 135, 137–138, 139–141,
 145–147, 150–163, 267, 342
 n46, 342 n49, 342 n51
 Georgia's arrest of Russian military intelligence officers on
 espionage charges and,
 160–161
 Middle East peace process and,
 238
 multinational force for Indonesia
 and, 360 n69
 relationship with Georgia, 138,
 140, 141, 154–155, 159, 267,
 339 n23, 344 n85
 role in Afghanistan, 229–231,
 267 n30
 role in Angola, 232, 233–234

role in Cyprus, 236, 237, 369 n51
 role in Tajikistan, 267
Rwanda
 role in the Democratic Republic
 of the Congo, 246
 United Nations role, 32

Saakashvili, President Mikheil
 (Georgia)
 accusation that Russia had blown
 up Georgia's gas pipeline, 159
 appeal to the United Nations, 141
 Bush's comments on, 141
 commitment to Georgia's territorial integrity, 139, 158
 criticisms of, 141, 339 n22
 leadership of, 138–139
 relationship with Western leaders,
 140–141
SADC. *See* Southern African
 Development Community
Saddam Hussein
 Annan's negotiations with, 20
SADR. *See* Saharan Arab Demo-
 cratic Republic
Saharan Arab Democratic Republic
 admission to the OAU, 169
 Boutros-Ghali's opposition to
 entrance of SADR to the
 OAU, 170–171
 as the independent state of
 Western Sahara, 167
Sahnoun, Mohamed
 role in Sudan, 252, 253
Salinas de Gortari, President Carlos
 (Mexico)
 Friends of the Secretary-General
 for El Salvador and, 62–63
 Guatemalan peace process and, 86
 meeting with George H.W. Bush,
 63
Saltford, John
 UN role in West Papua, 356 n22

Salvadoran Communist Party
    role, 312 n4
Samayoa, Salvador
    on the FMLN's problem with
        the Central American peace
        process, 313 n22
    views of Friends of the Secretary-
        General for El Salvador, 65
Sambanis, Nicolas
    factors contributing to "sustain-
        able peace," 300 n29
Samuel, Tamrat
    role in East Timor, 195–196, 197,
        357 n28, 364 n107
    role in Nepal, 39
San José Forum
    ties between Central America
        and Europe and, 315
        n44
Sandinista Front for National
        Liberation
    victory over the Somoza govern-
        ment in Nicaragua, 52
    view of the OAS, 53–54
Santamaria, Oscar
    view of Friends of the Secretary-
        General for El Salvador, 73
Santiago Declaration
    provisions, 109
Saudi Arabia
    role in Middle East peace process,
        238
Savimbi, Jonas
    death of, 225, 233, 264
    elections of 1992 and, 232
Schori, Pierre
    role in Côte d'Ivoire, 250, 375
        n113
Secretary-general of the United
        Nations. See also Friends of
        the Secretary-General for
        specific countries; specific
        secretaries-general

article 99 of the UN charter and,
        20, 300 n3
article 100 (2) of the UN charter
        and, 301 n11
creation of Friends groups, 30–31,
        33
envoys' roles, 35
good offices concept, 20–24,
        27–28, 34, 35, 61, 302 n18
impartiality of, 21–22
peacemaking efforts during the
        Cold War, 24
role of, 20–24
"tools" for, 22–23
Security Council
    Ad Hoc Working Group on
        Conflict Prevention and
        Resolution in Africa, 47–48,
        244–245, 311 n104
    Contadora group and, 55
    Economic and Social Council,
        122, 334 n76
    Extended P-5 group in Cambodia,
        28
    Friends groups and, 45–46
    Friends of the Guatemalan
        Peace Process and, 91, 95, 324
        n58
    Friends of the Secretary-General
        for El Salvador and, 73, 75,
        77
    Friends of the Secretary-General
        for Georgia and, 149, 153,
        154, 161, 344 n80
    Friends of the Secretary-
        General for Haiti and, 106,
        111, 114, 116, 117–118,
        122, 125, 127, 133, 332
        n57
    funding for operations, 323 n45
    Georgian-Abkhaz conflict
        and, 135–136, 142, 145,
        150, 153,

Security Council (cont.)
  154, 338 n7, 341 n37, 341 n38,
  341 n39
  growth in the number of resolu-
    tions passed by, 30
  Iran-Iraq war and, 25, 26, 303
    n25
  Note by the President of the
    Council on groups of Friends,
    45–46
  ONUSAL expansion and, 73
  peacekeeping operation in
    Lebanon, 39
  perceived bias of, 36, 144
  "permanent five" members, 25–
    26, 45
  post–Cold War transformation
    of, 19
  role in Afghanistan, 230
  role in Cyprus, 234–235, 236,
    368 n43, 368 n49
  role in East Timor, 191–192, 192,
    203–207, 208–211, 213–219,
    220, 221–222, 359 n60
  role in Myanmar, 225–226, 366
    n15
  role in Sierra Leone, 248
  role in Somalia, 244
  role in the Democratic Republic
    of the Congo, 246
  role in the Western Saharan
    conflict, 165–166, 167, 170,
    174–186, 187, 188, 189
  sanctions against Liberia, 248
  transparency issues, 45
  two-tiered structure of, 45
  UN Observer Group in Central
    America and, 55
  vetoes by permanent members,
    25, 302 n25
  workshop on the Mano River
    Union, 249
September 11 terrorist attacks

changes in the international
  environment after, 225, 269
Sudan's collaboration on the war
  on terrorism, 252
Serrano Elías, President Jorge
  (Guatemala)
  autogolpe of, 82, 87, 321 n28
  meeting with Guatemalan
    National Revolutionary
    Unity, 83
  peace process and, 83, 84–87
Sharma, Karmalesh
  role in East Timor, 210
Shelley, Toby
  voter identification in Morocco
    and, 180
Shevardnadze, President Eduard
  (Georgia)
  becomes president of Georgia, 137
  Cuba's support for FMLN,
    314 n24
  meeting with Annan, 150
  meeting with Putin at
    Sochi,156–157
  meeting with Yeltsin, 147
  ouster of, 138
  proposed meeting with the
    FMLN, 58
  relationship with Western
    leaders, 140–141
  role in ending the Cold War, 143
  role in the Georgian-Abkhaz
    conflict, 136, 137, 140, 142,
    146, 342 n50
Shwe, Gen. Than
  removal of Prime Minister Khin
    Nyunt from office and, 228
Sierra Leone
  Contact Group on, 248
  Core Group on, 248, 375 n103
  UN peacekeeping operation in,
    34
Sihanouk, Prince (Cambodia), 27

Singapore
  Friends of Western Sahara and,
    352 n73, 352 n78
Skauen, Peter
  Guatemalan peace process and,
    84–85
Soderberg, Nancy
  role in East Timor, 202
Solomon, Richard
  Cambodian peace process and,
    27
Somalia
  Committee of Friends of , 244,
    373 n87
  Council of Somali Islamic
    Courts, 244
  death of U.S. Army Rangers in,
    32, 115
  Meetings of External Actors on ,
    244, 373 n88
  International Contact Group on,
    244, 373 n88, 374 n89
  Transitional Federal Government,
    244
Somoza, Anastacio
  Sandinista Front for National
    Liberation and, 52
South Africa
  Namibia and, 26–27, 57–58
  role in Angola, 233
  role in Côte d'Ivoire, 250
  role in the Democratic Republic
    of the Congo, 246, 247, 374
    n97
South Korea
  role in Myanmar, 227
Southern African Development
  Community
  conflict mediation and resolution
    role, 41
Soviet Union. See also Common-
  wealth of Independent States;
  Russia; specific republics

Cambodian peace process and,
  28, 303 n35
  dissolution of, 70–71
  Farabundo Martí Liberation
    Front and, 58
  Guatemalan National Revolu-
    tionary Unity and, 319 n5
  invasion of Afghanistan and, 21,
    26, 56
  Namibia and, 26–27
  post–Cold War relationship with
    the United States, 19
  support for Vietnam, 27
Spain
  attempted meeting with the
    Guatemalan National Revo-
    lutionary Unity, 320 n12
  contribution to ONUCA, 64
  contribution to ONUSAL's
    military division, 317 n71
  decolonization of Western
    Sahara, 165, 166–167, 173,
    188
  Dialogue Group in Guatemala
    and, 99
  fishing agreement with Morocco,
    167, 174
  Friends of the Guatemalan Peace
    Process role, 79, 89–96, 97,
    102, 323 n52, 325 n69, 328
    n90
  Friends of the Secretary-General
    for El Salvador role, 60, 61,
    63–64, 70, 77, 102
  Friends of Western Sahara role,
    166, 171, 173–174, 183, 187
  Madrid Accords and, 167
  relationship with Morocco,
    173–174
  role in Colombia, 241, 242, 371
    n72
  role in Haiti, 123–124
  ties with Polisario, 173, 349 n35

Spain (cont.)
  Treaty of Friendship, Good
    Neighborliness, and Cooper-
    ation with Morocco, 173
  URNG's relationship with, 86
SPLA. See Sudan People's Liberation
  Army
SPLM/A. See Sudanese People's
  Liberation Movement/Army
Sri Lanka
  Norway's role in, 320 n17
Sri Lanka Donor Cochairs Group
  composition of, 268, 378 n4
Stålsett, Gunnar
  Oslo meeting on Guatemala role,
    85, 320 n19
Stanley, William
  speed of the Guatemalan Peace
    Process, 323 n51
Stedman, Stephen John
  Ending Civil Wars: The Implementa-
    tion of Peace Agreements, 12–13
Stein, Eduardo
  Friends of the Guatemalan Peace
    Process and, 93
Stein, Ricardo
  donor coordination in
    Guatemala views, 97–98
Stephanopoulos, George
  U.S.S. Harlan County incident
    and, 115
Suanzes Pardo, Brig. Gen. Victor
  contribution to ONUSAL's
    military division, 317 n71
Subregional organizations. See also
    specific organizations
  Conflict management and,
    39–40, 41
Sudan
  Assessment and Evaluation
    Commission, 254
  Cease-fire Political Commission,
    254

  competing levels of interest and
    commitment from the inter-
    national community and, 255,
    377 n132
  Comprehensive Peace Agree-
    ment, 254, 377 n129
  consideration of forming Friends
    of Darfur, 259, 378 n2
  Contact Group on, 254
  Darfur crisis, 253–255
  Darfur Peace Agreement,
    254–255
  IGAD Partners Forum, 251
  Intergovernmental Authority on
    Development, 251–252, 256
  Islamic fundamentalism and, 252
  Machakos Protocol, 253
  Operation Lifeline Sudan, 251
  regional environment and,
    266–267
  Sudan People's Liberation Army,
    253, 254
  Sudanese People's Liberation
    Movement/Army and, 251,
    256
  Troika role, 223–224, 251–255,
    256, 264
  UN Mission in Sudan, 254, 378
    n2
  United Nations role, 223, 251–255
Sudan People's Liberation
    Army/Movement
  peace process and, 251, 253, 254
Suharto, President
  fall of, 197
  Indonesia's annexation of East
    Timor and, 194
  meeting with Pres. Ford and
    Kissinger, 193
  "New Order" regime, 193
  relationship with the United
    States, 358 n41
  rise to power, 193

Sukarnoputri, Megawati
    rivalry with Habibie, 199
Sumbeiywo, Gen. Lazaro
    role in Sudan, 252, 253, 257
Supplement to the Agenda for Peace
    (Boutros-Ghali), 33
Support Groups
    Contadora group, 54
    East Timor and, 200, 220
    U.S. military Support Group in
        Haiti, 332 n65
Sustainment and Stability Opera-
    tions Program
    Georgia and, 141
Suu Kyi, Aung San
    detention of, 225
    rearrest of, 227
    release of, 227, 366 n15
Sweden
    Dialogue Group of donor states
        and, 98, 326 n77, 326 n78
    Friends of the Guatemalan Peace
        Process and, 90, 322 n41
    Friends of the Secretary-General
        for El Salvador and, 74–75
    opinion of the FARC, 372 n79
    support for United Nations
        efforts in Central America, 61,
        314 n36
Swing, William
    role in the Western Saharan
        conflict, 350 n44
    U.S. role in Haiti and, 121
Switzerland
    conflict resolution efforts, 42,
        308 n85
    role in Colombia, 241, 242
    role in Sudan, 253

Tagliavini, Heidi
    Boden paper and, 151, 153, 154
    Geneva process (2003) and,
        157

Tajikistan. *See also* UN Mission of
        Observers in Tajikistan
    informal group of Friends of , 30,
        48–149
    Inter-Tajik negotiations, 148
    regional actors and, 147, 267,
        342 n56
    United Nations involvement in
        the peace process, 32, 147–149
Takasu, Yukio
    interest in East Timor, 202
Taming Intractable Conflicts (Crocker,
        Hampson, and Aall), 8
Taylor, President Charles (Liberia)
    departure of, 249, 250, 264, 266
    election of, 248
    peace process and, 249
ter Horst, Enrique
    Friends of the Secretary-General
        for El Salvador role, 74
    relationship with Friends of the
        Secretary-General for Haiti,
        119–120, 121
    UN Mission in Haiti and, 332
        n64
    UN Observer Mission in El
        Salvador and, 74
Thailand
    role in Myanmar, 228
Thant, Secretary-General U
    article 99 and, 300 n3
    Cuban missile crisis and, 24
Theofilopoulou, Anna
    Western Saharan conflict and,
        176
Third-Party Verification Mechanism
    Democratic Republic of the
        Congo and, 247
Timor-Leste. *See* East Timor
Timor Sea Treaty
    signing of, 213, 362 n85
Tokatlian, Gabriel
    troop contributors to Haiti, 128

TotalFinaElf
    contract with Morocco to
        explore the waters off West-
        ern Sahara, 172–173, 349
        n31
TPVM. *See* Third-Party Verification
    Mechanism
Traub, James
    role of the UN secretary-general,
    20
TRNC. *See* Turkish Republic of
    Northern Cyprus
Türk, Danilo
    role in Myanmar, 227
Turkey
    Cyprus and, 234, 237
    Georgian-Abkhaz conflict and,
        140, 163
    relationship with the United
        States, 235
Turkish Republic of Northern
    Cyprus
    declaration of independence
        for, 234

Uganda
    Core Group on Northern
        Uganda, 259, 377 n1
    role in the Democratic Republic
        of the Congo, 246
Ukraine
    Friends of the Secretary-General
        for Georgia and, 153–154, 163,
        344 n79
UN Assistance Mission to
    Afghanistan
    Brahimi's leadership, 231
UN Civilian Police Mission in
    Haiti
    Argentina's rapid reaction force
        and, 120, 332 n66
    replacement of UNTMIH, 332
        n60

UN Department of Peacekeeping
    Operations
    Core Group on East Timor and,
        211, 214
    East Timor elections of 1999 and,
        359 n61
    Lessons Learned Unit, 298 n12
    mandates for operations in
        Haiti, 122
UN Department of Political Affairs
    Core Group on East Timor and,
        200
    East Timor elections of 1999 and,
        359 n61
    Mediation Support Unit, 298 n12
    role in East Timor, 196
    role in Nepal, 39
UN Development Programme
    Guatemalan peace process and,
        98–99
    Needs Assessment mission in
        Abkhazia, 150, 343 n65
UN Emergency Force
    establishment of, 23,
    advisory committee for, 23–24,
        302 n15
UN Force in Cyprus
    long-term presence of, 234
UN Good Offices Mission in
    Afghanistan and Pakistan, 21
UN High Commissioner for Refugees
    murder of staff members in West
        Timor, 213
UN Integrated Mission in Timor-
    Leste
    police component, 218, 221
UN Legal Counsel
    January 2002 letter to the Security
        Council on Western Sahara,
        174, 349 n31, 350 n38
UN Military Observer Mission in
    Georgia
    role of, 135

UN Mission for the Referendum in
    Western Sahara
  establishment, 165, 190
  extension of the mandate for,
    183
  Friends of Western Sahara and,
    175
  Identification Commission, 177,
    351 n53
  isolated location of, 175
  limitations imposed on, 188
  Moroccan control of, 171
  proposed termination of, 185
  proposed withdrawal of, 182
  unanimous votes taken by the
    Security Council and, 176
UN Mission in Angola
  establishment and leadership
    of, 234
UN Mission in East Timor
  attack on, 205
  Australian contributions, 204
  Core Group on East Timor and,
    201
  detailed plans for, 203
  funding for, 203, 204–205, 358
    n37
  Timorese refugees and, 207
UN Mission in Ethiopia and Eritrea
  Friends of, 47, 310 n101
UN Mission in Haiti
  Canada's role, 120
  mandate for, 118, 332 n59
  replacement by subsequent UN
    missions, 332 n60
UN Mission in Liberia
  establishment and activities of,
    250, 375 n110
UN Mission in Sudan
  responsibilities of, 254
UN Mission of Observers in
    Tajikistan
  monitoring role, 148, 149

UN Mission of Support in East
    Timor
  commitment to the independence
    of East Timor, 209
  Core Group on East Timor and,
    208
  extension of, 215
  mandate for, 213–214
UN Observer Group in Central
    America
  Esquipulas agreement and, 55,
    313 n16
  Security Council authorization
    for, 55
  Spain's contribution to, 64
UN Observer Mission in El Salvador
  Colombia, Venezuela, and
    Spain's contribution to, 64,
    317 n71
  end of, 317 n72
  expansion of, 73
  mediation role, 73
UN Observer Mission in Georgia
  authorization of, 142
  mandate renewals for, 154, 159,
    160, 161
  monitoring of the cease-fire with
    Abkhazia, 135, 138, 346 n111
  role as employer in Abkhazia,
    338 n10
UN Observer Mission in Liberia
  authorization of, 341 n43
UN Office in East Timor
  establishment of, 210
  mandate for, 216
  support for, 211
UN Operation in the Congo
  Hammarksjöld's creation of, 23
UN Peacebuilding Commission
  creation of, 6, 38, 259
  Organizational Committee's
    country-specific meetings, 11,
    299 n27

UN Peacebuilding Support Office in
    Liberia
    establishment and activities of,
    248–249, 375 n104
*The UN Security Council and Informal
    Groups of States* (Prantl), 5–6
UN Stabilization Mission in Haiti
    coordination and liaison mecha-
    nisms, 127–128
    Core Group, 127–131
    criticism of, 129
    damage to the reputation of,
    129–130, 337 n110
    establishment of, 127
    funding issues, 130
    resistance of Haiti to recommen-
    dations by, 129
    troop contributors, 128, 130, 336
    n102
    working relationships with inter-
    national partners, 130
UN Support Mission in Haiti
    replacement of UNMIH, 332
    n60
UN Transition Assistance Group
    Namibia settlement and, 27
UN Transition Mission in Haiti
    replacement of UNSMIH, 332
    n60
UN Transitional Administration in
    East Timor
    assessments of, 361 n72
    Core Group on East Timor and,
    208, 210–211, 221
    extension of mandate for, 210
    planning for, 208, 209, 360 n70
    relationship with Gusmão and,
    209
    relationship with the Security
    Council, 209–210
    timeframe for East Timor's inde-
    pendence and, 210, 361 n74
    Timorese resistance to, 209

UN Transitional Authority in Cam-
    bodia, 28
UN Verification Mission in
    Guatemala
    demobilization of the URNG,
    323 n46
    mandate for, 94, 102–103
    peace process role, 95–96,
    98–100, 102–103
    successful deployment of, 92
UN Verification Office
    El Salvador role, 317 n72
UNAMA. *See* UN Assistance
    Mission to Afghanistan
UNAMET. *See* UN Mission in East
    Timor
UNDP. *See* UN Development
    Programme
UNEF. *See* UN Emergency Force
UNFICYP. *See* UN Force in Cyprus
UNITA. *See* National Union for
    the Total Independence of
    Angola
United Kingdom
    Core Group on Northern
    Uganda and, 377 n1
    Friends of Georgia role, 142, 155,
    156, 345, n89
    Friends of Western Sahara role,
    166, 182–183
    role in Afghanistan, 231
    role in Angola, 233
    role in Cyprus, 225, 235, 236, 237
    role in East Timor, 191, 201,
    202–203, 212, 215, 355 n8,
    363 n95
    role in Sierra Leone, 248
    role in Sudan, 223–224, 251–255
    role in the Democratic Republic
    of the Congo, 246
    suspension of the sale of Hawk
    fighters to Indonesia, 360 n68
    Troika role in Sudan, 223–224

United Nations. *See also* Secretary-
General of the United
Nations; Peacebuilding Commission, Security Council;
*specific agencies, countries, de-
partments, offices, and operations*
achievements of the 1990s, 51
Africa Action Plan, 46, 239,
244–245, 310 n98
challenges of Groups in Africa,
243–246, 373 n86
Contact Groups, 44, 45, 310 n98
expansion of peacekeeping operations, 29–30, 38
multilateralism and, 30
oil-for-food program, 37, 306
n67
peacekeeping budget, 30
post–Cold War conflicts in weak,
new states and, 31–33
post–Cold War transformation
of, 19
reform efforts, 37–38
United Nations charter
article 99, 20, 300 n3
article 100 (2), 22, 301 n11
Chapter VII provisions, 31
United Self-Defense Forces of
Colombia
drug trafficking and, 242
United States. *See also specific leaders
and administrations*
accusation by CARICOM of
failure to respect the Inter-
American Democratic
Charter, 127
Congressional Black Caucus
protests against U.S. policy in
Haiti, 117
contributions to the UN Mission
in East Timor, 204
Core Group on Northern
Uganda and, 377 n1

death of U.S. Army Rangers in
Somalia, 32, 115
Farabundo Martí Liberation
Front and, 89, 322 n35
Friends of Georgia role, 142
Friends of the Guatemalan Peace
Process role, 79, 88–96, 102
Friends of the Secretary-General
for El Salvador role, 67–71,
74, 318 n80
Friends of the Secretary-General
for Haiti role, 105–106,
110–134
Friends of Western Sahara role,
166, 170, 171–172, 175, 179,
181, 187, 347 n8, 352 n69
Georgia Train and Equip Program,
141, 339 n19, 345 n86
invasion of Iraq, 36–38, 306 n63,
306 n65, 307 n67
involvement in regional peace
processes, 267
Miraflores declaration and, 67,
316 n53
Plan Colombia, 239, 240, 370 n64
post–Cold War relationship with
the Soviet Union, 19
preemptive action doctrine, 37,
306 n63
Presidential Decision Directive
25, 32, 305 n50
relationship with de Soto, 68–69
relationship with Indonesia,
201–202, 204, 358 n41
relationship with Turkey, 235
role in Afghanistan, 228,
229–231
role in Angola, 232–234
role in Colombia, 240, 371 n69,
379 n12
role in Cyprus, 225, 235, 236, 237
role in the Democratic Republic
of the Congo, 246

United States (*cont.*)
  role in East Timor, 191, 193, 195,
    199, 201–202, 204, 207,
    212–213, 214–216, 221, 355
    n9, 356 n19, 357 n32, 357
    n33, 363 n95
  role in El Salvador, 2, 53, 67–71,
    267, 268, 318 n80
  role in Georgia, 141, 155, 161,
    339 n18, 345 n86
  role in Guatemala, 81, 267
  role in Haiti, 16, 105–134,
    260–261, 267
  role in Middle East, 38-39, 238-
    239, 370 n62
  role in Myanmar, 226, 227, 366
    n15
  role in Somalia, 244, 374 n89
  role in Sri Lanka, 378 n4
  role in Sudan, 223–224, 251–
    255, 377 n132
  support for Morocco, 168, 172
  support for peace negotiations in
    El Salvador, 67, 316 n55
  Support Group in Haiti, 332 n65
  trade talks with Morocco, 172
  Troika role in Sudan, 223–224
  UN Mission of Support in East
    Timor and, 215, 362 n92
UNMEE. *See* UN Mission in
    Ethiopia and Eritrea
UNMIH. *See* UN Mission in Haiti
UNMIL. *See* UN Mission in Liberia
UNMISET. *See* UN Mission of
    Support in East Timor
UNMIT. *See* UN Integrated Mission
    in Timor-Leste
UNMOT. *See* UN Mission of
    Observers in Tajikistan
UNOL. *See* UN Peacebuilding
    Support Office in Liberia
UNOMIG. *See* UN Observer
    Mission in Georgia

UNOMIL. *See* UN Observer Mission
    in Liberia
UNOTIL. *See* UN Office in East
    Timor
UNSMIH. *See* UN Support Mission
    in Haiti
UNTAC. *See* UN Transitional
    Authority in Cambodia
UNTAET. *See* UN Transitional
    Administration in East Timor
UNTMIH. *See* UN Transition
    Mission in Haiti
Uribe Vélez, President Alvaro
    (Colombia)
  election of, 242
  request for UN assistance, 242
URNG. *See* Guatemalan National
    Revolutionary Unity
Urquhart, Brian
  functioning of the Security
    Council, 25
  UN oil-for-food program and,
    37, 306 n67
U.S. Coast Guard
  interception of Haitian refugees,
    107–108, 328 n9
U.S. Department of State
  contradictory messages on the
    Indonesian militias, 204,
    359 n51
U.S. Navy
  interception of Haitian refugees,
    107–108, 328 n9
U.S.S. *Harlan County*
  Haitian protests against the
    landing of troops on, 115

Valdés, Juan Gabriel
  role in Haiti, 124, 129, 130
Van Walsum, Peter
  role in East Timor, 206, 359 n60
  Western Saharan conflict role,
    187–188

Vendrell, Francesc
    Friends of the Secretary-General
        for Haiti and, 112
    Guatemalan peace process and,
        83–84, 320 n16
    idea for including Jamaica in
        the Friends of the Secretary-
        General for Haiti, 334 n77
    opposition to the Governors
        Island Agreement, 331, n47
    role in Afghanistan, 230, 257
    role in Central America, 55
    role in East Timor, 196, 197, 200,
        202, 203, 219
    role in Myanmar, 225, 226
Venezuela
    Contadora group and, 54
    contribution to ONUSAL's
        military division, 317 n71
    Friends of the Guatemalan Peace
        Process role, 80, 85, 101
    Friends of the Secretary-General
        for El Salvador role, 60, 63, 76
    Friends of the Secretary-General
        for Haiti role, 105, 110–116,
        132
    Friends of Western Sahara and,
        174
    URNG's relationship with, 86
Vieira de Mello, Sergio
    assessment of the UN Transitional
        Administration in East Timor,
        361 n72
    death of, 37
    role in East Timor, 209, 211
Vietnam
    invasion of Cambodia, 27
    normalization of relations with
        China, 28
Villalobos, Joaquín
    contacts between FMLN and
        non-Marxist countries, 270
    FMLN's use of force and, 57

Vraalsen, Tom
    role in Sudan, 376 n116

Walker, Ambassador Edward
    description of U.S. involvement
        in Haiti, 112
    Friends of the Secretary-General
        for Haiti and, 113
    Friends of Western Sahara and,
        171
Walter, Barbara F.
    characteristics of "credible"
        security guarantees, 317 n70
Walters, Gen. Vernon
    Polisario's opposition to, 349
        n26
Wensley, Penny
    role in East Timor, 201, 206, 207
West Africa
    Economic Community of West
        Africa role, 248, 249–251
    International Contact Group on
        the Mano River Basin, 250
    International Contact Groups,
        248–251
    Security Council workshop on
        the Mano River Union, 249
Western Saharan conflict
    Algeria's role, 165, 166–190
    background of, 166–168
    compared with East Timor, 165,
        188–189, 354 n99
    Framework Agreement on the
        Status of Western Sahara,
        181–183, 352 n73, 352 n77,
        352 n78, 353 n79
    Friends of the Western Sahara,
        165–166, 171–175, 189–190
    Houston Accords and, 179
    identification of the electorate,
        169, 170, 171, 177, 179–180,
        183–184, 348 n16, 348 n22,
        351 n53

Western Saharan conflict *(cont.)*
  Joint Monitoring Committee
    and, 178
  Morocco's role, 165, 166–190
  Peace Plan for Self-Determination
    for the People of Western
    Sahara, 183–185, 353 n81,
    353 n82, 353 n87
  phosphate deposits and, 168
  Polisario's role, 168–172,
    176–179, 181–182, 184,
    186–188, 189
  pursuit of a "third way" to resolve,
    179, 190
  referendum after the cease-fire,
    170, 348 n21
  Spain's decolonization and, 165,
    188
  UN Mission for the Referendum
    in Western Sahara, 165, 170,
    175, 176, 177, 179–180, 183,
    185, 187–188, 190
Weston, Thomas
  role in Cyprus, 236, 369 n50
Wiranto, General
  control over Indonesian militias,
    205
  meeting with Gusmão and
    Ramos-Horta, 359 n59
Wood, Elisabeth Jean
  political mobilization in El
    Salvador, 53
  ending civil conflicts, 261
Woolcott, Richard
  annexation of East Timor and,
    355 n8

World Bank
  Core Group and, 128
  Guatemalan peace process and,
    92, 98
  loan to Indonesia suspended over
    East Timor, 360 n68
  donor meetings for East Timor,
    209, 361 n71, 362 n83

Yañéz-Barnuevo, Juan Antonio
  Friends of the Secretary-General
    for El Salvador role, 63, 315
    n43
  Iberoamerican Summit and, 67
Yaqub-Khan, Sahabzada
  role in the Western Saharan
    conflict, 171, 175
Yeltsin, President Boris (Russia)
  meeting with Shevardnadze and
    Ardzinba, 147

Zapatero, Prime Minister José Luis
    Rodríguez (Spain)
  Spain's relations with Morocco
    and, 173–174, 354 n93
Zartman, William
  interests of individual states,
    298 n17
  "ripeness" concept, 56–57
Zhirinovsky, Vladimir
  Georgian-Abkhaz conflict and,
    155
Zimbabwe
  role in the Democratic Republic
    of the Congo, 246

About the Author

Teresa Whitfield is director of the Conflict Prevention and Peace Forum, a program of the Social Science Research Council that specializes in providing UN decision makers with country and regional analyses of the conflicts with which they are engaged. A filmmaker in her early career, her publications include *Paying the Price: Ignacio Ellacuría and the Murdered Jesuits of El Salvador* (Temple University Press, 1994). She served as an official within the United Nations' Department of Political Affairs from 1995 to 2000 and conducted much of her research for *Friends Indeed?* while she was a visiting fellow at New York University's Center on International Cooperation from 2003 to 2005.

United States Institute of Peace

The United States Institute of Peace is an independent, nonpartisan institution established and funded by Congress. Its goals are to help prevent and resolve violent conflicts, promote post-conflict peacebuilding, and increase conflict-management tools, capacity, and intellectual capital worldwide. The Institute does this by empowering others with knowledge, skills, and resources, as well as by its direct involvement in conflict zones around the globe.

Chairman of the Board: J. Robinson West
Vice Chairman: María Otero
President: Richard H. Solomon
Executive Vice President: Patricia Powers Thomson
Vice President: Charles E. Nelson

Friends Indeed?

This book is set in Goudy. Jeff Urbancic designed the book's cover; Katharine Moore designed the interior. Helene Y. Redmond made up the pages. The text was edited and proofread by EEI Communications, Inc. The index was prepared by EEI.